American Politics and Government

Structure, Processes, Institutions, and Policies

American Politics and Government

Structure, Processes,
Institutions, and Policies

Barbara Hinckley
New York University

Sheldon Goldman
University of Massachusetts

SCOTT, FORESMAN/LITTLE, BROWN HIGHER EDUCATION
A Division of Scott, Foresman and Company
Glenview, Illinois   London, England

Acknowledgments

Unless otherwise acknowledged, all photos are the property of Scott, Foresman and Company. Page positions are as follows: (T) top, (C) center, (B) bottom, (L) left, (R) right, (INS) inset.

5 New York Public Library, Astor, Lenox and Tilden Foundations   **29** Library of Congress   **36** William Franklin McMahon   **51** U. S. Bureau of Printing and Engraving   **55** UPI/Bettmann Newsphotos   **60** Bill Fitz-Patrick   **69** Owen Franken/Stock Boston   **88L** Paul Conklin   **88R** AP/Wide World   **92** Universal Press Syndicate. Reprinted with permission. All Rights Reserved.   **110ALL** Kobal Collection/Superstock   **112** AP/Wide World   **145** New York Public Library, Astor, Lenox and Tilden Foundations   **150** UPI/Bettmann Newsphotos   **153** AP/Wide World   **160L** Courtesy Roger Butterfield   **160R** AP/Wide World   **170** R. Maiman/Sygma   **189** AP/Wide World   **198** © Robert Mizono   **217** AP/Wide World   **232** Paul Conklin   **245** Paul Conklin   **252(ALL)** Courtesy Howard E. McCurdy, "An Insider's Guide to the Capitol," Washington, D.C.: The American University, 1977. Art by Susan Lee.   **256** © Terry Ashe/Time Inc.   **267** George Tames   **283** Meyer/San Francisco Chronicle   **288** © Wally McNammee/Newsweek Magazine   **297** Diana Walker   **306** Michael Evans/The White House   **328** AP/Wide World   **333L** AP/Wide World   **333R** UPI/Bettmann Newsphotos   **339** UPI/Bettmann Newsphotos   **345** Milt & Joan Mann/Cameramann International, Ltd.   **354** Courtesy Congressional Quarterly   **374** Harley Schwadron, The National Law Journal   **401** Supreme Court Historical Society   **404** Joseph J. Scherschel and Arlan R. Wiker. Copyright, National Geographic Society. Photo: Supreme Court Historical Society.   **424** Doug Menuez/Picture Group   **432** AP/Wide World   **440** AP/Wide World   **455** AP/Wide World   **467** AP/Wide World   **472** 1971/NYT Pictures   **480** Reprinted by permission: Tribune Media Services   **486** UPI/Bettmann Newsphotos   **490** Florida Department of Correction   **497** Library of Congress   **506** June, 1867, Frank Leslie's Illustrated Newspaper   **511** Elliott Erwitt/Magnum Photos   **516** UPI/Bettmann Newsphotos   **518** UPI/Bettmann Newsphotos   **525** EBONY Magazine/Johnson Publishing   **539** © 1986 The National Law Journal and Joseph Farris   **540** UPI/Bettmann Newsphotos   **548** Cathleen Curtis/Washington Times   **552** UPI/Bettmann Newsphotos   **570** Randy Taylor/Sygma   **575** UPI/Bettmann Newsphotos   **582** AP/Wide World

Literary permissions for the copyrighted materials not credited on the page where they appear are listed in the "Acknowledgments" section beginning on page 636. This section is to be considered an extension of the copyright page.

Library of Congress Cataloging-in-Publication Data.

Hinckley, Barbara
        American politics and government: structure, processes,
    institutions, and policies / Barbara Hinckley. Sheldon Goldman.
            p.   cm.
        Includes bibliographical references.
        ISBN 0–673–39813–7
        1. United States—Politics and government.   I. Goldman, Sheldon.
    II. Title.
    JK274.H545   1990   89-10843
    320.973—dc20   CIP

1 2 3 4 5 6-VHJ-94 93 92 91 90 89

Of the many events marking the five-year bicentennial celebration begun in 1987, one of the most fitting is the publication of an American Government text. Such a text gives concrete evidence that the basic design of the government—the Constitution—still works two hundred years later. Americans often think of their country as new, but it has the oldest continuous democratic government. Features of its original design—such as a strong legislature and independent judiciary—also characterize the present government. Many original sources of controversy remain important issues today: the question of how far presidential power should extend or how responsibility should be divided between the national government and the states. Even more recent problems—questions of privacy, of the role of science in government, of covert operations and undeclared wars—can be examined more clearly by returning to the constitutional base. The Constitution was an "experiment in government," Thomas Jefferson and John Adams agreed in their correspondence. The modern American government continues the experiment.

This text reflects the bicentennial spirit in another way as well, by combining traditional and contemporary approaches. Students will learn more about the legal and constitutional issues of government than they would from most texts, but they will also learn about the use and importance of polling techniques, the politics of the budget process, and ways to predict election results. This balance of traditional and contemporary approaches is reflected in a special feature—Materials of Political Science—found in all the chapters. Materials include case studies and Supreme Court decisions, primary results and congressional voting scores, as well as reports by observers of and participants in the political scene. By illustrating and expanding on points made in the chapter, these materials should give students a sense of the breadth and diversity of political science and stimulate their interest in such materials. The text and exhibits continue this balance and emphasis.

Our objective in writing *American Politics and Government* is to provide a comprehensive and readable mainstream introductory text of moderate length. Because this is a relatively inexpensive paperback that concentrates on essential material, instructors are free to supplement the text with other materials of their own choosing. While this text has fewer colors, cartoons, and special features than the hardcover texts, it does not sacrifice substance. All the major institutions and processes of government are covered in depth in separate chapters. Some chapters, in fact, reflecting the authors' expertise and interests, provide more material than would be found in the larger texts. Standard tables and footnotes drawing on contemporary scholarship add depth and provide resources for instructors and students.

Part One consists of two chapters that set forth the constitutional framework of American government. The text then turns, like the Constitution itself, to the people, examining in Part Two how the American public forms opinions and selects representatives. Following an organization many instructors find useful, the text then moves to the institutions of government in Part Three and the policies they produce in Part Four. All the chapters are self-contained and so can be rearranged to suit different course organizations. The chapter on civil liberties, for example, could be assigned with the first two constitutional chapters, and the chapter on the presidency could precede the chapter on Congress.

Two supplements to accompany this text have been written by Larry Elowitz of Georgia College. The *Instructor's Manual* includes, for each chapter, a set of learning objectives; a lecture outline; key chapter terms and concepts; suggested lecture themes, classroom activities, and research projects; additional learning resources, such as excerpts, abstracts, or data from current scholarly works; and, when appropriate, audiovisual sources. A test bank with at least fifty questions per chapter rounds out the *Instructor's Manual,* and includes multiple-choice, true-false, completion, matching, and short-answer questions, along with a final comprehensive examination. The *Study Guide* includes learning objectives and chapter outlines similar to those in the *Instructor's Manual;* preview questions; matching questions to reinforce key terms; chapter check-ups with suggested answers for essay questions and true-false questions that require students to correct false statements; and sections that require students to think more deeply about a chapter-related concept or problem.

Books of this kind require the work and skills of many people, and we would like to thank those who so carefully read and made suggestions on the chapters, particularly:

Danny M. Adkison	*Oklahoma State University*
John F. Bibby	*University of Wisconsin at Milwaukee*
Jon Bond	*Texas A&M University*
Keith O. Boyum	*California State University, Fullerton*
John P. Burke	*University of Vermont*
Pamela Johnston Conover	*University of North Carolina, Chapel Hill*
George Edwards	*Texas A&M University*
Robert Harmel	*Texas A&M University*
Christine Harrington	*New York University*
Thomas Keating	*Arizona State University*
Burdett A. Loomis	*University of Kansas*
Michael Margolis	*University of Pittsburgh*
Lynn Mather	*Dartmouth College*
Andrew Milnor	*State University of New York, Binghamton*
Alan D. Monroe	*Illinois State University*
Karen O'Connor	*Emory University*
Richard B. Riley	*Baylor University*

Barbara Sinclair	*University of California, Riverside*
Cynthia Slaughter	*Southwest Texas State University*
Walter J. Stone	*University of Colorado at Boulder*
Martin Wattenberg	*University of California, Irvine*
Jerry L. Yeric	*North Texas State University*

We would also like to thank those who brought the book to its present form, particularly Diane Culhane, the Development Editor, and Mark Grimes, the Project Editor. We are especially indebted to John Covell, who never lost faith in the project, and to Bruce Nichols, whose enthusiasm and hard work were indispensable to its completion. Finally, we would like to mention our debt of gratitude to the late Susan Friedman, whose ideas are reflected in the final version of the text and who worked so hard to make it a success.

Contents

Exhibits

PART ONE

The Structure of American Government

CHAPTER ONE

The Constitution

A s Americans in September 1987 celebrated the 200th anniversary of the Constitution and embarked upon a five year bicentennial celebration that would conclude with the 200th anniversary of the Bill of Rights in 1991, there was an understandable nationwide feeling of pride and accomplishment. The United States of America, after numerous wars (including a traumatic Civil War, two World Wars, a war in Korea, and a war in Vietnam) and many economic crises (including the Great Depression of the 1930s) had, nevertheless, come through 200 years governed according to a document originally drafted by several dozen eighteenth-century gentlemen. Ours is the longest operating written constitution in the history of the world. The structure of our governmental institutions today, and, indeed, much of the fabric of our daily lives, is dictated by this document.

The Constitution, by the process of amendment, but most importantly by political and judicial interpretation, is a vital document adaptable to political, social, and economic change. It continues to work in an advanced industrial, highly technological mass society now containing over 250 million people, a society that could not have been envisioned by the founders. The adaptability of the Constitution has been its greatest strength, not only in its ability to respond to changing economic conditions but also to changing political and social forces. American government has been transformed by laws and even constitutional amendments from a country in which only white men of property participated in the affairs of state to one in which both sexes, all races and ethnic groups, and those at every income level have the opportunity to participate and to have their rights and interests protected.

This chapter first examines the origins of the Constitution and the political ideas that most influenced the framers. Then it considers the Constitutional Convention itself, the delegates to it, the different plans before it, and how major political concepts were worked into the document. The controversy over ratification is discussed and then the ways in which the Constitution has been extended, amended, and otherwise adapted to new times and conditions.

ORIGINS OF THE CONSTITUTION

An understanding of the origins of the Constitution requires an understanding of how written constitutions came about, of the historical developments that directly led to the Constitutional Convention of 1787, and of the political ideas that guided the framers of the Constitution.

The Concept of a Written Constitution

Written constitutions embodying the fundamental law of a nation date back to the ancient world. For example, the Ten Commandments and the Old Testament served, in effect, as a written constitution for ancient Israel. In the western world, the first example of the acceptance of the concept of a higher written law limiting the exercise of sovereignty is the Magna Carta. The Magna Carta resulted from a historic meeting in Runnymede in the year 1215 between the English King John and the barons who successfully sought certain written guarantees of rights. Despite this precedent, the English have never adopted *one* written document to serve as a constitution, as we have in the United States. Instead they have developed, over the centuries, what they consider to be an unwritten constitution. That is, various historic documents, laws, customs, traditions, or practices are considered to embody the English Constitution.

Americans, however, began a tradition of written documents to serve as the basis of law and civil government quite early in our colonial history. The Mayflower Compact of 1620 was the first document written and was followed by others, including compacts in Rhode Island, New Haven, and the elaborate Fundamental Orders of Connecticut (1639). The corporate charters issued by the King of England to found certain colonies also utilized the concept of a written document providing the structure of government and the exercise of governmental power. Interestingly, the royal charters suggested the most important feature of a written constitution, that is, that it is not merely ordinary law defining the institutions and powers of government but rather that it is higher law superior to ordinary law to which ordinary law must conform.

The distinction between higher law and ordinary law, along with the corollary that ordinary law must be consistent with higher law or be declared void, was also familiar to the colonists by the provisions for review of colonial legislation. Colonial laws were subject to review by the Privy Council in England which had the power to "disallow" them as inconsistent with superior English law. In practice, close to six percent of all laws submitted for approval were disallowed.[1] Once independence was declared and war began, most of the former colonies scrapped their colonial charters and wrote and adopted new constitutions that established *their* higher law.[2] Thus, by the time of the revolutionary period, Americans were beginning to conceptualize a written constitution not only as the establishment of a framework for government but also as providing the higher law for the political system.[3]

From the Revolution to the Constitution

The events leading to the colonies' break from England and the Revolutionary War are many, varied, and highly dramatic. There was a clash of wills between the colonial legislatures and the English Parliament and deep resentment among the colonists over direct taxation by England and over the imposition by the English of their economic policy on the colonies. But there also was the underlying perception of Americans that they were betrayed by the mother country, that is, that their *rights* as Englishmen were being flagrantly denied. The English government proved inconsistent in its

Americans throwing English tea into Boston Harbor on December 16, 1773.

approach toward the American colonies, alternating between conciliatory gestures and stubborn intransigence. Matters worsened toward the mid-1770s.

The First Continental Congress convened in Philadelphia in September of 1774 to deal with the worsening crisis. One of the first decisions of the Congress was to give each colony one vote. This principle of equality was to become the hallmark of the **Articles of Confederation** and was to become the principal source of controversy and the object of eventual compromise in the framing of the Constitution. The Continental Congress issued The Declaration and Resolves, in which it asserted in the name of the colonies exclusive legislative power over taxation and internal affairs, the rights of life, liberty, and property, as well as "all the rights, liberties, and immunities of free and natural-born subjects within the realm of England."[4] It also asserted the right to peaceably assemble and to petition the crown. The English government, however, turned a deaf ear and proceeded with a tax on tea. The protest over the tax on tea led to the famous "Boston Tea Party."

Parliament enacted legislation to punish Massachusetts for the destruction of tea and an attempt was made at enforcement by the sending of British troops to Lexington and Concord in April of 1775. The result, as they say, is history. The British met armed resistance and this event was a major milestone on the road to revolution. Skirmishes with British soldiers also

[1]Richard B. Morris, *Studies in the History of American Law,* 2nd ed., p. 63, as cited in Lawrence A. Friedman, *A History of American Law* (New York: Simon and Schuster, 1973), p. 44.

[2]Friedman, *op. cit.,* p. 101.

[3]See Bernard Bailyn, *The Ideological Origins of the American Revolution* (Cambridge, Mass.: Harvard University Press, 1967), pp. 175–98.

[4]As quoted in Alfred H. Kelly, Winfred A. Harbison, and Herman Belz, *The American Constitution: Its Origins and Development,* 6th ed. (New York: Norton, 1983), p. 60.

occurred elsewhere. In May of 1775, the Second Continental Congress was convened and organized an army to continue resistance until Parliament ceased what the colonists considered illegal actions in America.

At this moment in history an extraordinary publication appeared which dared to put into print radical, even treasonous, ideas. Thomas Paine, in his pamphlet **Common Sense,** in crisp, frank language, denounced the English monarchy and the English system of government. He urged the establishment of an independent American **republic**, where the people, not a monarch, would be the source of power. Paine outlined the reasons why colonial ties to the crown were ruinous for Americans and offered the alternative principle of **popular sovereignty** whereby the people and not royalty would govern. Were there a best seller list in early 1776, this pamphlet would have ranked in first place. In its first three months after publication in January 1776, it sold 120,000 copies. It has been estimated that over a six-month period, most colonists had either read *Common Sense*, had it read to them, or heard about it in some detail.[5] Paine's pamphlet encouraged American sentiment for independence.

The Declaration of Independence.   Events pushed towards independence during the spring of 1776 and the Virginia Assembly took the lead by instructing its delegate to the Continental Congress, Richard Henry Lee, to introduce a resolution for independence. On June 7, Lee arose to move "[T]hat these United Colonies are, and of right ought to be, free and independent States, and that they are absolved from all allegiance to the British Crown, and that all connection between them and the State of Great Britain is, and ought to be, totally dissolved." This resolution triggered heated debate, for, indeed, the stakes were enormously high. This was an act of treason against the King. Six of the colonial legislatures had specifically instructed their delegates to oppose independence. Four days later, debate was suspended to enable delegates to return to their legislatures for new instructions. At the same time, a committee was formed to draft a declaration of independence in the event there was sufficient sentiment for a complete break with England. Members of the committee included John Adams, Benjamin Franklin, Thomas Jefferson (designated as chairman), Robert Livingston, and Roger Sherman. Jefferson took the responsibility for drafting the document. Congress reconvened and on July 2 Lee's resolution was enacted and on July 4 **the Declaration of Independence** was approved. The revolutionary war was on.

The Declaration of Independence (see the Appendix at the end of this book for the complete text) offered the reasons for the break with England, but it is, of course, famous for its justification of the right of revolution and

---

[5]Carl J. Friedrich and Robert G. McCloskey, *From the Declaration of Independence to the Constitution: The Roots of American Constitutionalism* (New York: The Liberal Arts Press, 1954), p. XXXV.

its philosophy of the purposes of government. Jefferson's brilliant rhetoric drew principally upon the political ideas of seventeenth and eighteenth-century political thinkers, particularly those of the great English philosopher John Locke.

The Declaration asserts in both ringing and concise language: "We hold these truths to be self-evident, that all men are created equal, that they are endowed by their Creator with certain unalienable Rights, that among these are Life, Liberty, and the pursuit of Happiness." For Jefferson, this meant that all persons were born morally or spiritually equal in the eyes of God and that they ought to be politically equal with no legal or political privileges accruing to an individual merely because of the accident of birth. All people have certain basic natural rights, argued Jefferson, including the pursuit of happiness, which apparently was Jefferson's graceful way of saying that one is entitled to pursue both material happiness, through the lawful acquisition of property, and non-material happiness. Jefferson's statement of natural law and natural rights is deeply ingrained in American thinking and constitutes the ideals to which we continually aspire. However, Jefferson accepted the sad reality that at that time blacks and women were not treated as equal, that his colleagues did not consider them to be equal, and that this was implicitly understood by the signers of the Declaration.[6]

The Declaration, once it establishes these fundamental human rights, notes that "[T]o secure these rights, Governments are instituted among Men, deriving their just powers from the consent of the governed. That whenever any Form of Government becomes destructive of these ends, it is the Right of the People to alter or to abolish it, and to institute new Government. . . ." The purpose of government, then, is to protect the unalienable rights of all people. Government comes into being when *men* (Jefferson regarded women as not equipped to participate in public affairs) agree, by social compact, to establish it in order to secure those rights. In government by popular consent, the consent granted can be withdrawn whenever government fails to secure or protect unalienable rights or to accord all of the governed equality in law and in the exercise of their rights. The people, thus, always retain the right of revolution. These were radical ideas.

The Articles of Confederation.

Once the Declaration of Independence was issued, it remained for the Continental Congress to construct a new form of government. The Congress debated and drafted a structure for a new confederation of now independent states. The Articles of Confederation, America's first constitution, was approved by the Continental Congress in November 1777 and sent to the states for ratification. Maryland was the last state to ratify, in March 1781, at which time the Articles legally took effect. Even before ratification, however, beginning in mid-1776, the Conti-

[6]Ralph Lerner, *The Thinking Revolutionary: Principle and Practice in the New Republic* (Ithaca, New York: Cornell University Press, 1987), pp. 63–69; Donald L. Robinson, *Slavery in the Structure of American Politics 1765–1820* (New York: Harcourt, Brace Jovanovich, 1971), pp. 82–83.

nental Congress had operated upon the principles embodied in the Articles of Confederation. Under the Articles, as in the Continental Congress itself, each state had one vote in a one-house Congress. The states retained their sovereignty in most matters. Congress had limited authority in others. Sovereignty was based in the states except when they voluntarily surrendered it to Congress. In some ways, the government established by the Articles of Confederation was like a compact among independent nations.

Under the Articles of Confederation, not only did Congress consist of one house in which each state delegation had one vote, but the president was simply the presiding officer of Congress. Executive authority was based in committees and, later, departments created by Congress. The judiciary consisted of tribunals that Congress was authorized to establish to deal with interstate boundary disputes, as well as those arising from matters concerning rivers, harbors, navigation, waterways, and the high seas. Affairs of state, when Congress was in recess, were to be conducted by a Committee of the States consisting of one delegate from each state. The consent of nine states was needed for the Committee to act. Likewise, nine states had to consent for action to be taken on the most important matters when Congress was in session.

Congress was responsible for national defense (waging war, regulating land and naval forces) and foreign relations (including entering into treaties or alliances). Congress made requests to the states for funds with which to conduct the revolutionary war and the operations of government, and Congress itself raised money, but it did not directly tax or regulate state or interstate domestic activities. The Articles authorized Congress to coin money and regulate its value, to regulate the trade with and manage the affairs of the Indians, and to establish and run the post office. In Article XI, Canada was invited to join the United States. Amendments to the Articles could only be added if *every* state legislature approved, an exceptionally rigid requirement.

Congress could exercise various powers, but nowhere in the Articles was it actually stated that Congress made *laws*.[7] In the language of the Articles, Congress could "requisition," regulate, or make determinations, but it could not make *laws* carried out by a national government and subject to adjudication by a national judiciary. The framers of the Articles saw the states as the ultimate repository of the sovereign power of lawmaking, and the states, including the state judiciaries, had the responsibility of voluntarily abiding by Congress's determinations.

It is clear that Congress had relatively little power. This does not necessarily mean that the Articles were doomed to fail. Indeed, Congress under the Articles successfully concluded the War of Independence and conducted foreign affairs. It established national policy for the settlement, government, and eventual admission to the Union of the territories when it enacted the Northwest Ordinance of 1787. It is also possible that the concept

---

[7]This point is made by Kelly, Harbison, and Belz, *op. cit.*, p. 83.

of executive authority stemming from congressional committees and the concept of the president being a member of a one-house Congress as its presiding officer could have evolved into a parliamentary-cabinet form of government similar to the government of England. Under such a form of government the executive and legislative branches are intertwined and members of the cabinet and the chief executive are also members of the legislature and accountable to it on a daily basis. But this was not to be.

The Articles of Confederation provided for a weak national government and cries for reform of the Articles gained momentum in the mid-1780s because the new nation was beset by severe economic problems. It faced inflation, a massive debt, and near anarchy in the realm of interstate commerce. In western Massachusetts, angry debt-ridden farmers could not pay their mortgages or taxes and were losing their farms. Starting in the summer of 1786, unruly crowds managed to disrupt the state courthouses that were conducting foreclosures and tax delinquency proceedings. In the winter of 1786, approximately 2,500 farmers, led by Revolutionary War Captain Daniel Shays, marched on the Springfield Arsenal.[8] The state militia eventually put down Shays' Rebellion, but the threat of economic breakdown and anarchy was real.

In September of 1786, a convention was held at Annapolis to discuss commercial problems among the states. Although only five states sent representatives, Alexander Hamilton and James Madison used the opportunity to review the defects of the Articles of Confederation that went beyond matters of commerce. Their words had a particular urgency in light of events that constituted Shays' Rebellion. They issued a call for a convention, to be held in May 1787 in Philadelphia, for the purpose of correcting the defects of the Articles of Confederation. On February 21, 1787, Congress approved the proposed Philadelphia convention that was to scrap the Articles of Confederation and write a new Constitution.

Political Ideas that Shaped the Constitution

The ideas of constitutionalism, a written constitution, and a constitution as higher law superior to ordinary law were familiar to the founders. The ideas were, in part, derived from those emerging from England's turbulent seventeenth century as well as from such English philosophers as John Locke in his *Second Treatise of Government* (1690) and James Harrington in *The Commonwealth of Oceana* (1656). Harrington created his hypothetical commonwealth based on certain principles that he deduced as fundamental to a well-ordered and just society. A basic principle for Harrington, which provides the intellectual foundation for constitutionalism, is that government should be a "government of laws and not of men," a concept that was as

---

[8]Richard D. Brown, "Shays' Rebellion and the Ratification of the Federal Constitution in Massachusetts," in Richard Beeman, Stephen Botein, and Edward C. Carter II, eds., *Beyond Confederation: Origins of the Constitution and American National Identity* (Chapel Hill: University of North Carolina Press, 1987), pp. 115–16, note 5.

appealing to American students of law and government in 1787 as it is today.

Those assembled in Philadelphia during the spring and summer of 1787 were also familiar with the idea of **separation of powers**, which is related to the concept of a mixed form of government that has roots in the thought of Plato and Aristotle. For Locke, it was important to divide the parliamentary legislative power rather than strictly separate the executive and legislature (the judiciary did not figure much in Locke's thought). Locke was concerned that the legislative power not be abused and he considered a sharing of legislative power by king, lords, and commons as a means by which each would provide checks and balances on the other. In contrast, the French philosopher Montesquieu, in his famous work *Spirit of the Laws* (which was well–known to the framers of the Constitution), conceptualized an independent life-tenured judiciary, a separate executive power with responsibility for both domestic and foreign affairs, and an autonomous legislative power.

Underlying the concepts of separation of powers and checks and balances was the fear that government, unless properly restrained, was inherently oppressive. In his revolutionary pamphlet, *Common Sense*, Thomas Paine had articulated this fear: "Society in every state is a blessing, but government, even in its best state, is but a necessary evil, in its worst state an intolerable one...."[9] Separation of powers with checks and balances, both within the legislative power and among the legislative, executive, and judiciary, seemed to the framers the sensible way to minimize the potential abuses of governmental power.

The idea of **natural rights** was important not only for the Declaration of Independence but also for the adoption of the Constitution. It was not until a pledge was made to add a Bill of Rights to the Constitution that the Constitution was ratified. But failure of the framers to include a Bill of Rights does not mean that they were insensitive to the concept of natural rights. Rather, they assumed that it was unnecessary to add a Bill of Rights because the state constitutions protected basic freedoms. The framers understood and appreciated the idea of natural rights that inhere in each individual.

The framers were also committed to the idea of **federalism** or divided sovereignty. The concept of federalism had been embodied in the Articles

---

[9]As quoted in Friedrich and McCloskey, *op. cit.*, p. XVII. Note that this section on "Political Ideas that Shaped the Constitution" relies heavily on the Friedrich-McCloskey analysis. Also see Bailyn, *op. cit.*; Lerner, *op. cit.*; Forrest McDonald, *Novus Ordo Seclorum: The Intellectual Origins of the Constitution* (Lawrence, Kansas: University Press of Kansas, 1985). For a brief overview of the literature of modern historians see Richard Beeman, "Introduction," in Beeman, et. al., *op. cit.*, pp. 3–19.

of Confederation, whereby certain powers were reserved for the confederation government and other powers were retained by the states. But the marked tilt towards state sovereignty crippled the exercise of national sovereignty. The theoretical foundation of federalism owes much to the framers of the Constitution. The framers, to be sure, did not explicitly develop a theory of federalism but rather made certain political compromises and were willing to experiment in dividing power between the nation and the constituent states. Federalism stands as a major American contribution to the art of government.

Somewhat more problematic as an idea that shaped the Constitution is the concept of **democracy**. The theory of popular sovereignty, that sovereignty is reposed within the people and not a monarch, provided the rationale for the Declaration of Independence and defines a republic. But many of the framers, including Alexander Hamilton, feared pure democracy and had visions of wild, uncontrollable mobs running riot, such as, in his view, had occurred during Shays' Rebellion. A number of the framers had been educated in the English aristocratic tradition and when they referred to "the people" their frame of reference was not "the common man" but the educated man of property, such as those represented in the English House of Commons. Other framers, including Benjamin Franklin, were more genuinely committed to democracy. For them, government by the consent of the governed meant *all* the people or at least all white males, and not just the "better" classes. But even for these democrats there was a concern that popular sovereignty could lead to the suppression of those not with the political majority.

The framers' ideas of democracy were shaped not only by their own education as Englishmen with their exposure to English history and English political philosophers, but also by their experience as Americans in towns, villages, on the frontier, and in colonial government. In fact, the theory of popular sovereignty and the Lockean principles of natural rights which impelled towards democracy, as suggested by the Declaration of Independence, clashed with the realities of significant portions of American life. Women played little part in political life. Most blacks were slaves and were considered by many whites to be subhuman property. Native American Indians were regarded as savages; it was inconceivable that they could or would be "Americanized." All colonies and, later, states had some form of property qualification in order for men to vote, although the qualifications varied. Thousands of white residents were indentured servants, and until their terms of service were completed, they had few legal rights and in some respects were not that much better-off than slaves, although nothing could be as pernicious as the institution of slavery itself. This ambivalence towards democracy in practice was also part of the intellectual baggage that the framers of the Constitution brought with them to Philadelphia as they embarked upon their historic mission.

◼◼◼ THE CONSTITUTIONAL CONVENTION

Powerful ideas were at work in America and many events helped to shape them at the time the delegates met in Philadelphia in May of 1787. This section looks at the men who attended the Constitutional Convention and who wrote the Constitution. This is of special concern because certain scholars have argued that the economic interests with which the framers were identified motivated them to write a Constitution for the protection of those interests. The unfolding of the Convention is also examined, including the two major plans that came before it and the compromises that were reached. This section ends by examining how the major ideas of the framers were transformed into concrete constitutional provisions.

The Delegates

Fifty-five delegates actually went to Philadelphia and participated in the writing of the Constitution. Some nineteen more had been selected by their state legislatures but for various reasons did not attend. Only the state of Rhode Island refused to participate. Of the fifty-five participants, all were white men and about one-sixth were foreign born. Almost all had played some part in the Revolution. Their average age was between forty-two and forty-three. About three out of four had served in Congress under the Articles of Confederation and about all were well-known in their states and had held important public offices.[10] About half of them had graduated from college, an accomplishment that was certainly unrepresentative of the general population, and it is fair to characterize the assemblage as an educated elite. But was it also an economic elite that single-mindedly sought to protect its interests?

Charles A. Beard challenged the motivations of the framers in his classic work, *An Economic Interpretation of the Constitution of the United States*, published in 1913. Beard analyzed the economic holdings of the delegates and saw the Constitution as "an economic document drawn with superb skill by men whose property interests were immediately at stake; and as such it appealed directly and unerringly to identical interests in the country at large."[11] Beard emphasized that a majority of delegates were lawyers, most of whom came from heavily populated areas where wealth was concentrated, and that small farmers and tradesmen were unrepresented. Beard concluded that "The overwhelming majority of members [of the Convention], at least five-sixths, were immediately, directly, and personally interested in the outcome of their labors at Philadelphia, and were to a

[10]Max Farrand, *The Framing of the Constitution of the United States* (New Haven: Yale University Press, 1913), p. 39.

[11]Charles A. Beard, *An Economic Interpretation of the Constitution* (New York: Macmillan, 1960 reprint), p. 188.

greater or less extent economic beneficiaries from the adoption of the Constitution."[12]

Does this description of the delegates and their motives, which is certainly at odds with the traditional image of the framers as unselfish patriots fashioning a structure of government meant to endure for generations, withstand scrutiny? Later scholars examining the same evidence as that considered by Beard as well as new evidence have challenged Beard's conclusions.

Historian Forrest McDonald assembled a wealth of data about the delegates and closely analyzed their votes in Philadelphia. He found that, with few exceptions, delegates came from the major geographical areas and were drawn from the major political factions in the twelve states. By McDonald's count, thirty-one out of thirty-four political factions were represented in the Convention. Half the delegates who had served in their state legislatures (thirteen) had voting records in their respective states supporting debtor-relief measures. In all, concluded McDonald, "the delegations constituted an almost complete cross section of the geographical areas and shades of political opinion existing in the United States in 1787."[13]

As for the economic interests of the delegates, McDonald found them varied. Twenty delegates were identified with farming, thirteen with mercantile-commercial interests, two of the lawyers derived their incomes from both agriculture and legal practice with commercial clients, twelve earned most of their incomes from their salaries as public officials, two were physicians, three were well-to-do retirees, and three were in difficult economic circumstances who managed financially, in part, by family loans or gifts (James Madison, one of the key framers, was one of these three). Thirty-four were lawyers, but, as McDonald's research suggests, most lawyers, with the exception of public officials, did not earn their living exclusively from the practice of law.[14] Unlike Beard, McDonald concluded that the members of the Convention were *not* an unrepresentative economic elite with common economic interests.[15]

McDonald's analysis of voting at the Convention showed no voting split between commercial and agricultural interests.[16] Even concerning two of the guarantees of the Constitution that safeguard creditors or property owners (the restriction on states from issuing paper money and the contract clause preventing states from interfering with the carrying out of lawful contracts), at least thirty-three delegates (of the forty-one whose attitudes could be determined) voted against one or both of these safeguards.[17]

---

[12]*Ibid.*, p. 149.

[13]Forrest McDonald, *We the People: The Economic Origins of the Constitution* (Chicago: University of Chicago Press, 1958), p. 37.

[14]*Ibid.*, pp. 86–88.

[15]*Ibid.*, p. 92.

[16]*Ibid.*, p. 94.

[17]*Ibid.*, p. 108.

This suggests that motivations aside from the strictly economic were relevant for many of the framers. McDonald's conclusion, after studying each delegate and his voting behavior, was that: "Some delegates, a dozen at the outside, clearly acted according to the dictates of their personal economic interests, and about as many more according to their philosophical convictions, even when these conflicted with their economic interests. But the conduct of most of the delegates, while partly a reflection of one or both of these personal considerations, was to a much greater extent a reflection of the interests and outlooks of the states and local areas they represented."[18]

During the approximately four months of almost continuous sessions, the average daily attendance was thirty delegates.[19] Some of the leading participants included George Washington, then fifty-five years old, who was the head of the Virginia delegation. Washington, popular and revered, was elected presiding officer of the Convention. According to all accounts, he presided in an orderly, impartial, and dignified fashion and spoke little during debate. However, he apparently was active in the informal discussion. His fellow Virginian, James Madison, was a gifted student of public affairs. He, perhaps more than any other delegate, had a vision of what American government should be. He was well versed in political philosophy and history and participated intensely in each debate. Madison, who was thirty-six years old at the time of the Convention, is sometimes called the "Father of the Constitution" because he drafted a plan that ultimately provided the accepted framework for government. It is Madison, too, who provided the details of the Convention, for his notes are the most complete record of the proceedings which were closed to the public.

Although Virginians played leading roles, several noted Virginians did not attend. Thomas Jefferson was in Paris on diplomatic business for the country. Richard Henry Lee declined to serve, as did Patrick Henry, who later opposed the Constitution. In 1788, when Henry was asked his reasons for not having participated in the creation of the Constitution that he then denounced, he reportedly responded, "I smelt a Rat."[20] Such a comment no doubt gave encouragement more than a century later to scholars, including Beard, to explore the economic motivations and interests of the framers. However, the more common view at the time of the Convention was that of Jefferson who, when he learned who would be attending from Virginia and from other states, observed, "[I]t really is an assembly of demi-gods" by which he meant extraordinary individuals.[21]

Other state delegations included well-known public figures, some of whom were important contributors to the writing of the Constitution. For

[18]*Ibid.*, pp. 415–16. Also see, Gordon S. Wood, "Interests and Disinterestedness in the Making of the Constitution," in Beeman, et. al., *op. cit.*, pp. 69–109, and Calvin C. Jillson and Cecil L. Eubanks, "The Political Structure of Constitution Making: The Federal Convention of 1787," *American Journal of Political Science*, 28 (1984), pp. 435–58.

[19]Farrand, *op. cit.*, p. 61.

[20]Farrand, *op. cit.*, p. 15.

[21]As quoted in Farrand, *op. cit.*, p. 39.

example, Pennsylvania's delegation included Benjamin Franklin, who at eighty-one years of age was the oldest delegate, and his reputation as a public figure was second only to Washington's. It also contained James Wilson, a brilliant lawyer and law professor (later a justice on the United States Supreme Court) who played a major role in writing the first draft of the Constitution, and Gouverneur Morris, who is credited with writing the final draft of the Constitution.[22] Delaware's delegation included John Dickinson, who had helped write the Articles of Confederation.

The New York delegation included Alexander Hamilton, who, at thirty years of age, was well-known nationally and had played an active role in the Revolution, in state legislative affairs, and in convening the Constitutional Convention. Although his participation during the proceedings was spotty (he even left Philadelphia for a time after being continually outvoted by the other two delegates from New York), he was an influential member of the committee that produced the final draft of the Constitution. Connecticut's Roger Sherman, the mayor of New Haven, was especially active and was responsible for the compromise that led to the resolution of the struggle over representation in Congress.

Max Farrand, a leading historian of the Constitutional Convention, offered a composite portrait of the delegates when he wrote in 1913:

> "Great men there were, it is true, but the convention as a whole was composed of men such as would be appointed to a similar gathering at the present time: professional men, business men, and gentlemen of leisure; patriotic statesmen and clever, scheming politicians; some trained by experience and study for the task before them, and others utterly unfit."[23]

It should be evident that this assemblage did, in large part, represent the political and economic elite of the nation and the document that emerged from their labors reflected the political and economic thinking of the men who framed it.

The Work of the Convention: Proceedings, Plans, and Compromises

Although the Convention was scheduled to begin on Monday, May 14, it was not until Friday, May 25, that seven states were represented and the decision was made to begin to organize. At that meeting, the group decided that each state would be entitled to one vote, that the presence of seven states would constitute a quorum, that voting would be by state and not by individual, that the sessions were to be closed to the press and public, and that secrecy should prevail to ensure full and uninhibited debate. George Washington was elected presiding officer. The next meeting was scheduled for

[22]Farrand, *op. cit.*, pp. 181–84.
[23]Farrand, *op. cit.*, p. 40.

the following Tuesday, May 29, to allow time for more delegates to arrive. On the 29th the main business began with ten states represented by a total of forty delegates in attendance. From May 29 until September 17, the Convention was in continuous session with the exception of Sundays, a two-day July 4th holiday, and a break from July 26 to August 6 to permit the Committee on Detail to construct a draft of the Constitution. Formal sessions were generally from 10:00 in the morning to about 3:00 in the afternoon. But after hours, there was much informal discussion and caucusing.

Congress's official call for the Convention stipulated that it was "for the sole and express purpose of revising the Articles of Confederation."[24] But on the second full day of the Convention, May 30, the Convention adopted a resolution "that a *national* government ought to be established consisting of a *supreme* Legislative, Executive and Judiciary."[25] This clearly set the Convention on the course of creating an entirely new government and governing charter for the nation and not simply revising the Articles of Confederation. This resolution, in fact, was a substitute for the first resolution offered in the Virginia Plan, which had been introduced the day before.

The Virginia Plan.   **The Virginia Plan** consisted of fifteen resolutions and embraced the concept of a central government with three branches. It proposed a two-house (*bicameral*) legislature, with the lower house chosen directly by the people and the upper house chosen by the lower house. The plan specified a national executive but did not spell out the duties of the office. The executive, which theoretically could have consisted of one or several people, was to be elected by the legislature.

The Virginia Plan, like the Articles of Confederation within its limited sphere, made the legislative branch supreme over the other branches (although it gave the judiciary a measure of independence by providing for lifetime appointment). The Virginia Plan, like the Articles of Confederation, had conceptual links with English parliamentary government. The Virginia Plan envisioned a truly national government and as such made no provision for equality among the states.

Another feature of the Virginia Plan, equally disturbing to delegations from some smaller states as well as those for whom state sovereignty was of prime importance, was the proposal for a *Council of Revision.* The council, to be composed of the executive and a member of the national judiciary, was to have veto power over acts of Congress *and* of state legislatures. That veto was to hold unless overridden by an unspecified proportion of each branch of the legislature whose acts were at issue. In addition, Congress was to have the absolute power "to negative all laws passed by the several states, contravening in the opinion of the national legislature, the articles of Union."[26] This was, in effect, the power we know today as judicial review

---

[24]As quoted in Farrand, *op. cit.*, p. 28.
[25]As quoted in Farrand, *op. cit.*, p. 73.
[26]As quoted in Farrand, *op. cit.*, p. 226.

but instead of the courts it would have been exercised by Congress. This provision of the plan, too, was intolerable for the proponents of states' rights.

The New Jersey Plan.   After more than two weeks of debating and voting on various provisions of the Virginia Plan, the New Jersey delegation, in the person of William Paterson, introduced nine resolutions that historians call **the New Jersey Plan** but at the Convention were referred to as the Paterson Resolutions. These resolutions were supported by delegates from Connecticut, Delaware, Maryland, and New York.

The New Jersey Plan resolutions were specifically offered to revise, correct, and enlarge the Articles of Confederation rather than replace them as the resolution to establish a new national government adopted on May 30 had proposed. This was clearly a call for the Convention to do an about–face. The New Jersey Plan would have given Congress greater powers than under the Articles, particularly concerning taxation and commerce. It retained, however, the principle from the Articles of each state having one vote. The plan also provided for a federal executive and a federal judiciary to be appointed for life by the executive. As in the Virginia Plan, the executive could have consisted of more than one person. But unlike the Virginia Plan, which allowed Congress to strike down state laws in conflict with the Constitution and the Council of Revision's veto power over state laws, the New Jersey Plan simply declared that all acts of Congress and all treaties "shall be the supreme law of the respective States" to be enforced by the *state* judiciaries. It is indeed ironic that the supremacy clause of the Constitution that has been used by the federal courts to exercise federal control over the states had its genesis in a provision designed to prevent such national control.

On June 19, the Convention voted on which plan to use as the basis for their resolutions and deliberations. Seven states voted to continue with the already amended Virginia Plan. New York, New Jersey, and Delaware voted for the New Jersey Plan and the Maryland delegation was evenly divided and thus cast no vote.

Compromises.   Once the New Jersey Plan was out of the way, the Convention proceeded in the spirit of compromise. It made some changes in the language of resolutions and some in their substance. But, given the centrality of Congress's power under the Virginia Plan, the issue of Congress's make-up and the basis for representation—whether population or simply one state, one vote—soon threatened to break up the Convention. Looking back, Gouverneur Morris observed that "the fate of America was suspended by a hair."[27]

The resolution to this crisis emerged from a committee elected by the Convention to search for a compromise. **The Great Compromise** (some-

[27]As quoted in Farrand, *op. cit.,* p. 94.

times called the Connecticut Compromise because it was formally offered by Connecticut delegate Roger Sherman) consisted of two propositions that were to be adopted as a package: (1) The first branch of Congress would be apportioned according to population. Apportionment would be based on the free inhabitants of each state plus three-fifths of the slaves. All bills concerning the spending of money were to originate in this branch. (2) The second branch would give equal representation to each state.

Interestingly, the three-fifths formula, that is, counting five slaves as the equivalent of three free persons, was not a new formula. It had been used by Congress in 1783 in a revenue measure and was essentially agreed to by the delegates as a pragmatic solution to the consideration of slaves for certain legislative purposes. The institution of slavery, however, as reprehensible and inconsistent with the ideas of natural rights as it is, was for the most part not the subject of debate. At one point in the Convention, the delegates debated whether to abolish the importation of slaves into the country. Several northern delegates and a southern delegate, George Mason of Virginia, passionately attacked the slave trade. Mason called slavery an "infernal traffic" and warned that it would bring on "the judgment of Heaven." He continued: "As nations cannot be rewarded or punished in the next world, they must be in this. By an inevitable chain of causes and effects, Providence punishes national sins by national calamities."[28] The Civil War was certainly such a calamity and a century or more of racial struggle also proved Mason correct. However, several southern delegates made it clear that their states would not join the nation if either slavery or the slave trade were abolished. The final compromise was to permit the slave trade to continue for another twenty years until 1808 but not to otherwise undermine slavery. The term slavery itself was not used in the Constitution. Slaves were referred to as "other persons" or "such persons."

The Convention also voted on major resolutions concerning the powers of Congress and the shape of the executive branch. The delegates rejected the Council of Revision and any power of the national legislature to invalidate state laws in conflict with national law. Instead, as proposed by Luther Martin of Maryland, an advocate of the New Jersey Plan, the Convention approved what would eventually be called the **supremacy clause.** It stated "that the legislative acts of the United States. . .shall be the supreme law of the respective states,"[29] and that the state judiciaries would be bound by national law.

Drafting the Constitution. By the third week in July, the Convention had increased the fifteen original Virginia Plan resolutions to twenty-three and had made many major changes from the original. It still needed to work out many of the details of the resolutions and elected a five-man Committee

---

[28]As quoted in Arthur Taylor Prescott, *Drafting the Federal Constitution: A Rearrangement of Madison's Notes* (New York: Greenwood, 1968), pp. 698–99.
[29]As quoted in Farrand, *op. cit.,* p. 120.

on Detail to do so. The delegates decided to adjourn the Convention from July 26 until August 6. When the Convention reassembled on August 6, the committee presented its draft. From then until September 10, the Convention was in continuous session, debating, amending, or approving the draft worked out by the committee. On September 8, a Committee on Style was appointed "to revise the style of and arrange the articles" agreed to by the Convention. Among its members were Alexander Hamilton of New York, James Madison of Virginia, and Gouverneur Morris of Pennsylvania. Morris was responsible for much of the elegant language of the final draft of the Constitution, in particular the Preamble, which eloquently stated the purposes of the new government:

> "We the People of the United States, in Order to form a more perfect Union, establish Justice, insure domestic Tranquility, provide for the common defence, promote the general Welfare, and secure the Blessings of liberty to ourselves and our Posterity, do ordain and establish this Constitution for the United States of America."

The Committee on Style also made substantive changes. One of the most important was to prohibit state laws from impairing the obligations that people or businesses accepted when they became parties to contracts. This is known as the contract clause. The Convention had previously voted down the same provision but now in the closing days it was accepted.

On its last full workday, Saturday, September 15, at about six P.M., the Convention approved the new Constitution. The last formal session was on September 17 when the Constitution was signed by thirty-nine delegates from twelve states, and a cover letter and resolution to Congress transmitting and recommending the new Constitution was approved. The Convention adjourned for the last time at four P.M. The following day's edition of the newspaper the *Pennsylvania Packet and Daily Advertiser* was devoted entirely to a printing of the new Constitution. (The text of the Constitution appears in the Appendix at the end of this book.)

In evaluating the process of constitution-making, it is common to describe it as one in which the spirit of compromise prevailed. The Constitution itself is often described as a bundle of compromises. In one way, of course, this description is true because various delegates held different opinions on specific provisions on which they ultimately compromised. But this description obscures the fact that there was widespread consensus among the delegates on a number of basic ideas. First of all, they agreed on the need for a written constitution. Second, they agreed that the country should remain a republic (as opposed to a monarchy) with sovereignty residing with the people. Third, they agreed that within the national government there should be separation of powers and **checks and balances.** Fourth, there was a consensus that sovereignty should be divided between the national government and the individual states. Finally, they were in agreement that, in its sphere, the national government was to be the supreme law of the land.

To consider the Convention as having been split into factions from large states versus small states is also misleading. Size of population in and of itself did not then and has not since been a significant factor in shaping politics. Part of the reason is that the differences in population between the "large" and "small" states were not great. If the heavily populated state of Virginia is excluded, the average population of the "large" states was 307,000. If the sparsely populated Delaware is excluded from the "small" states, the average population of the small states was 278,000.[30] Clearly, the large-state-versus-small-state explanation of conflict in the Convention is an inadequate one. Rather, regional economic interests were the most significant source of difference of views. The industrial-mercantile North (with both large and small states) had different economic needs from the southern, agrarian, slave-holding (large and small) states. Here there were compromises that were necessary to meet the needs of these two major regions of the country.

The second principal but also cross-cutting source of disagreement among large and small state delegations was over how powerful the new central government was to be, or to put it another way, how much sovereignty the states were to surrender. The protection of states' rights and powers was paramount among the supporters of the New Jersey Plan. It can be argued that the controversy over representation resolved by the Great Compromise was more a sectional controversy and one about states' rights versus a strong central government than it was a power struggle between large and small states.[31]

Translating Theory into Specifics

Turning to the Constitution itself shows the concrete application of the abstract ideas or theories of government that were discussed earlier.

Separation of powers is built into the Constitution, though there is no explicit reference to it. The Constitution gives each of the three major branches of government—legislative, executive, and judiciary—separate and distinct functions. Article I describes the legislative branch, Article II the executive branch, and Article III the judiciary. The Constitution prohibits anyone from being a member of two branches of government at the same time with the exception of the vice-president who presides over the Senate and votes in the event of a tie. The prohibition of any person serving in both the legislative and executive branches at the same time was a rejection of parliamentary government. Although, in practice, there has been

[30]Kelly, Harbison, and Belz, *op. cit.,* p. 97.
[31]See Gerald M. Pomper, "Conflict and Coalitions at the Constitutional Convention," in Sven Groennings, E.W. Kelley, and Michael Leiserson, eds., *The Study of Coalition Behavior* (New York: Holt, Rinehart and Winston, 1970), pp. 209–25; Calvin C. Jillson, "Constitution-Making: Alignment and Realignment in the Federal Convention of 1787," *American Political Science Review,* 75 (1981), pp. 598–612.

some blurring of the line separating the legislative from the executive, particularly with the rise of numerous federal agencies and commissions that
issue detailed regulations that have the force of law, it is nevertheless recognized that Congress has the responsibility and authority to set public policy and sketch in at least the framework within which the federal bureaucracy formulates its regulations.

Separation of powers is also reflected in the Constitution's provisions
for the terms of office in the three branches of government. The judiciary
was given lifetime tenure ("during good behavior") and the Constitution
specifically prohibited any reduction in judges' salaries. The president and
vice-president were to be elected every four years by an electoral scheme
divorced from Congress unless no one received a majority of the electoral
college vote. Members of the House of Representatives were to serve two-
year terms and members of the Senate were to serve six-year terms.

The Constitution applies *checks and balances* to the interrelationships
among the branches of government and to the workings within the legislative branch. For example, both the House and the Senate are needed to
enact legislation. Both branches of Congress thereby check and balance
each other. The president must sign an enactment before it becomes law, or
the president may veto legislation, which in turn can become law only if it
is passed again, but this time by a minimum of two-thirds of each house of
Congress. The president's power of executive and judicial appointment is
checked by the constitutional provision that nominees must be approved
by the Senate (that is, the Senate must give its advice and consent). Although the president has the responsibility for the conduct of foreign policy, Congress has the legal power to declare war, to spend money for diplomatic missions and for other aspects of foreign policy, and the Senate has
the power to ratify treaties (by giving or withholding its advice and consent). The kinds of cases that may be appealed to the Supreme Court are
determined by Congress and Congress has the power to create lower federal courts. But federal judges with guarantees of lifetime appointment and no
reduction in salary are free to rule, if need be, against the interests of members of Congress or executive branch officials including the president. The
Constitution allows judges to interpret federal law as they see fit. Implicit
(but *not* explicit) in the Constitution is the idea that the judges also may
refuse to enforce a law that they believe violates the Constitution. In effect,
the president can name supporters of his policies to the Supreme Court and
to lower federal courts, but an independent judiciary is not beholden to the
president or the Senate for continued employment. Thus, by the so-called
system of checks and balances the framers hoped to prevent the unre-
strained exercise of oppressive power by any one branch of government.

The idea of *federalism* was a relatively novel one but one that was central to the Constitution. The Constitution embodies the principle that the
same geographical area and its inhabitants are subject to two separate sovereign powers, a national government and a state government. The national
government was given specific powers by the Constitution and the

supremacy clause of Article VI, Section 2, made it clear that national law supercedes conflicting state law. In practice, state legislation and state judicial proceedings that touch on federal law are subject to review by the federal courts. The Constitution also spells out the powers of the national government and specific matters in which states cannot act (see Article I, Section 10). Implicit in the Constitution is that all other governmental functions not specifically delegated to the national government are retained by the states. Eventually the Tenth Amendment made explicit this understanding of federalism.

Not only did the Constitution spell out the relationship between the national government and the states, it also spelled out aspects of the relationship among the states. In this matter, the framers borrowed from the Articles of Confederation. Article IV, sections 1 and 2 of the Constitution, include provisions that require each state to give "full faith and credit" to "the public acts, records, and judicial proceedings of every other state," and to accord "the citizens of each state . . . all privileges and immunities of citizens in the several states." Article III, Section 2, extends federal court supervision to disputes between or among states, between a state and a citizen of another state, between citizens of different states, or between a state and a foreign government or individual.

The *natural rights* ideas of the framers had only limited impact in the document that emerged from Philadelphia. Article I, sections 9 and 10, contains certain guarantees of individual rights. Section 9 restricts the national government, unless required for the public safety during rebellion or invasion, from suspending the **writ of habeas corpus** (the guarantee that no one will be jailed without judicial proceedings to determine the legal basis for detention). It also prevents the national government from enacting **bills of attainder** (statutes aimed at specific individuals) or **ex post facto laws** (retroactively applying a new law—for example, punishing someone for an action that was not illegal when it was performed).[32] Section 10 imposes these restrictions on the states and, in addition, contains the contract clause prohibiting the states from impairing the obligation of contracts. This latter guarantee was used by the federal courts during the first half of the nineteenth century to protect property rights, which, of course, were considered by the framers to be important natural rights. Article III, Section 2 also committed the national government to trial by jury of all ordinary crimes with the guarantee that the trial "shall be held in the state where the said crimes shall have been committed." Article VI guarantees that no religious test shall ever be required for someone to hold public office. It was not until the adoption of the Bill of Rights in 1791, however, that broad fundamental protection of individual rights was guaranteed from encroachment by the national government.

---

[32]By judicial interpretation, the ex post facto clause applies only to criminal law. See *Calder* v. *Bull* (1798).

The framers' ideas about *popular sovereignty* and *democracy* were translated into the Constitution in several ways. First, the government was to continue to be a republic, with the people and not a monarch as sovereign. But the framers were divided over the extent to which direct democracy should prevail in the institutions of government. There was fear that a temporary majority could trample upon minority rights. There was suspicion that an ill-informed electorate might fall prey to a demagogue. The institutions devised by the framers, particularly checks and balances, were intended to inhibit misuse of power. The provisions for the election of senators by state legislatures and the president by the electoral college were also designed to prevent ill-advised electoral decisions. Democratic principles were, of course, maintained by direct voting for members of the House of Representatives. The electorate also voted for their state legislators who, in turn, elected senators. (This method for choosing senators prevailed until 1913, when the Seventeenth Amendment took effect, providing for direct election of senators.) The electoral college for choosing the president and vice-president was also, in the minds of the framers, consistent with the theory of popular sovereignty and democracy but guarded against the excesses of democracy. The framers, it should be noted, generally left to the states the establishment of voting qualifications of the electorate.

What Is Not in the Constitution of 1787

Today major gaps are apparent in the Constitution of 1787. The framers did not protect the rights of women, African-Americans, or native Americans. Slavery, although discussed during the Convention in terms of the slave trade, emerged untouched. The qualifications of voters were left to each state to determine. The framers failed to include a Bill of Rights to protect citizens from the power of the central government, although they included some criminal procedural guarantees within the body of the Constitution. The full scope and the powers of the presidency and judiciary were implied rather than made explicit, and even some explicit grants of power to Congress were couched in general phrases. (For example, just what did "the commerce power" mean?) The Constitution made no mention of how candidates for office were to be selected and did not consider political parties, an institution that had yet to develop. Nothing in the Constitution mentions the president's cabinet, administrative agencies, or the federal bureaucracy that Americans know today.

The Constitution that emerged from the Philadelphia Convention had gaps and some imperfections but it is a remarkable document that has long endured. It represented the best efforts of a special group of men who were not a cross section of the general population but nevertheless reflected the political and economic thinking of their time. The genius of the Constitution is that it is adaptable and provides for change. Almost immediately after the text of the Constitution was transmitted to Congress and the states, people recognized that the absence of a Bill of Rights was a serious flaw. Most framers had thought that the state Bills of Rights sufficiently protected citizens, but, in the face of opposition, they supported amending the Constitution to include a federal Bill of Rights. Other gaps in the Constitution have been filled in by formal amendment, legislation, judicial interpretation, and extra-constitutional practices and institutions (to be discussed later in this chapter).

The Constitution was written and submitted to Congress, however it had yet to be ratified. The following section details how the Constitution came to be adopted and the politics and debate surrounding ratification.

■ RATIFICATION OF THE CONSTITUTION

The framers of the Constitution created a new governing charter for the nation rather than offering amendments to the Articles of Confederation. Had the Constitution been offered as amendments, they would have required the consent of all thirteen states, an unlikely occurrence. Article VII of the Constitution required that it be approved by the conventions of only nine states. The framers also recommended to Congress that the ratifying conventions be popularly elected. In making this recommendation, the framers hoped to avoid relying on the approval of state legislatures, where, they feared, vested political and economic interests opposed to a central government might prevail. If state legislatures ratified the Constitution, ratification would have the status of state law and might be open to repeal in the future. Having the people elect delegates to ratifying conventions was in accord with the republican theory of sovereignty residing in the people. Once the people were to speak by approving the Constitution, no act by a state legislature would be able to repeal it.[33]

This section takes a closer look at the politics of ratification and at the most important work of political theory to emerge from the ratification controversy, *The Federalist Papers.* This section also looks at those who opposed ratification.

The Politics of Ratification

On September 27, 1787, Congress under the Articles of Confederation submitted the new Constitution to the states and charged them to hold ratifying conventions, with delegates chosen by the electorate. On April 30, 1789, George Washington was inaugurated as the nation's first president. The nineteen months between these momentous events were a time of intense debate and political activity.

The signers and supporters of the Constitution vigorously promoted the cause of ratification. They called themselves **federalists.** This was a clever semantic trick because until that time a federalist was someone who fa-

---

[33]McDonald, *op. cit.,* p. 114, note 2, makes this point.

vored a confederation of sovereign states, such as provided for in the Articles of Confederation. The supporters of ratification, however, were nationalists in favor of a strong central government to be built on powers surrendered by the states to the national government. By calling themselves federalists, they made it harder for their opponents to brand them as enemies of state sovereignty. On top of that, the supporters of ratification called their opponents **anti-federalists**, another shrewd move that emphasized the negative character of the opposition. The federalist terminology has survived in that we call our national government the *federal* government.

Of the nine states that were needed to ratify the Constitution, five smaller states, incapable of functioning as sovereign nations and clearly standing to benefit from the Constitution, quickly and decisively voted for ratification. In these states (Connecticut, Delaware, Georgia, Maryland, and New Jersey), there was little, if any, opposition to ratification, and a relatively broad consensus cut across class and economic lines.[34] Only in Maryland was there vigorous debate over ratification, but the Constitution was approved by a 63 to 11 vote of the ratifying convention.

The federalists considered four other states likely to vote for ratification only after a hard fight. They were Pennsylvania, Massachusetts, South Carolina, and New Hampshire. But Pennsylvania surprised the federalists when on December 15, 1787, it became the second state to ratify the Constitution (by a vote of 46 to 23 and just eight days after Delaware). Pennsylvania's story of ratification contained at least one dramatic episode, recounted in the box on page 26.

Massachusetts ratified the Constitution on February 6, 1788, by a vote of 187 to 168. The delegates had been selected by town meetings and most had not been given instructions on how to vote. Massachusetts federalists waged a shrewd campaign and obtained Governor John Hancock's support reportedly after he was promised that they would promote him for the vice-presidency or even the presidency if George Washington were not available.[35] They won considerable support among farmers, artisans, and mechanics (a fact that undermines a strictly economic interpretation of the ratification controversy). Significantly, the federalists supported nine recommendations of the Massachusetts Convention that were made along with ratification, some of which were eventually incorporated in the Bill of Rights.[36]

South Carolina was the eighth state to ratify and did so by a vote of 149 to 73. South Carolina's ratification, like Massachusetts', came with recommendations including one that eventually became, in somewhat different

[34]Discussion of ratification relies heavily on McDonald, *op. cit. passim.* Also see the essays in Leonard W. Levy and Dennis J. Mahoney, eds., *The Framing and Ratification of the Constitution* (New York: Macmillan, 1987).

[35]McDonald, *op. cit.,* p. 185.

[36]These resolutions are reprinted in Arthur E. Sutherland, *Constitutionalism in America* (New York: Blaisdell, 1965), pp. 179–80.

Pennsylvania Ratifies the Constitution

Pennsylvania politics had been dominated by two factions. One faction, led by Robert Morris (a framer of the Constitution), favored ratification and controlled the state assembly. The opposing faction did not favor ratification and hoped that their ranks would increase in legislative elections scheduled for October. The Assembly was scheduled to adjourn on September 29. But the day before, by special courier, it received the formal resolution of Congress calling for popularly elected ratifying conventions. Morris and his federalist allies in the Assembly immediately introduced legislation to provide for an election of delegates to a convention to be held on November 21. But the opposition walked out. According to one account, members of the Morris party forcibly brought back two opponents to be physically present in order for there to be a quorum and then passed the law providing for the convention. In the campaign for popular support that followed, Morris and the federalists were well-organized and, in the words of a leading scholar of this period, used "a powerful and carefully planned propaganda campaign."[1] The federalists wooed and won most of Philadelphia's artisans, mechanics, tradesmen, and the small farmers in the county. The federalists won decisively in the election of delegates, but debate in the convention was vigorous. In the end, of course, the Constitution was ratified.

[1]Forrest McDonald, *We the People: The Economic Origins of the Constitution* (Chicago: Univ. of Chicago Press, 1958), p. 164.

form, the Tenth Amendment. New Hampshire was the ninth state to ratify, on June 21, 1788, by a vote of 57 to 47 after months of vigorous campaigning by federalists who also agreed to support recommendations for a Bill of Rights. The new Constitution was now legally adopted.

Four days after New Hampshire ratified, Virginia did the same, but only after a lengthy battle. Virginia was extremely important to the federalists not only because of its size and wealth but also because without Virginia in the Union, George Washington would not be eligible to become president. Governor Edmund Randolph, who had played an important role at the Constitutional Convention but had not signed the Constitution, was won over to ratification apparently after Virginia federalists promised him the position of attorney general of the new United States government, a post to which he indeed was appointed.[37] The vote of the Virginia Convention to ratify was 89 to 79. Virginia federalists also supported a recommendation for a Bill of Rights.

In New York, the politics of ratification became quite dramatic. The federalists knew that they had a formidable uphill battle. The Governor of New York, George Clinton, was a staunch opponent of the Constitution. He believed that New York had the ability and resources to function as an inde-

[37]Forrest McDonald, "The Anti-Federalists, 1781–1789," *Wisconsin Magazine of History,* XLVI (Spring, 1963), p. 212.

pendent country if need be. Clinton envisioned New York as the Empire State, and saw economic disadvantages from joining the new government.[38] Public opinion, insofar as it can be discerned, was opposed to the new Constitution. But opinion was different in New York City, which had suffered from British occupation during the Revolutionary War. There, sentiments for a strong national government and for the Constitution prevailed. Outside New York City, a large majority of anti-federalists were elected to the state ratifying convention and they, under the leadership of Governor Clinton, had firm control. But then came word that New Hampshire and Virginia had ratified. The pressure was on the anti-federalists by such federalists as Alexander Hamilton. Since support of the Constitution was largely based in New York City, Hamilton and other federalists strongly hinted to Clinton that New York City would secede from the state and join the new United States government.[39] Clinton took this seriously and in a caucus with his followers they agreed that a few would switch sides and vote for ratification. On July 26, New York ratified the Constitution by a vote of 30 to 27 and also voted a resolution urging, in effect, the adoption of a Bill of Rights.

After the necessary nine ratifications, Congress, still functioning under the Articles of Confederation, appointed a committee to recommend legislation for starting up the new government under the Constitution. On September 13, 1788, Congress adopted a timetable for the election of the president and the convening of the new Congress. In February, Washington was chosen by the presidential electors to be president and John Adams to be vice-president. On April 30, 1789, Washington was inaugurated and the new government was launched. But two states still had not ratified the Constitution.

North Carolina's convention rejected the Constitution by a vote of 184 to 84 in early August of 1788, and this was after proposing a series of amendments akin to the Bill of Rights. Federalist forces regrouped, and another election was held for a new ratifying convention to convene in November 1789. In the interim, North Carolina saw the new national government take shape with Washington as president. They saw the first Congress introduce and pass the proposed amendments that would constitute a Bill of Rights. When the votes were counted, federalists were overwhelmingly elected and on November 21, 1789, by a vote of 194 to 77, North Carolina ratified the Constitution and became part of the United States of America.

The last of the former colonies to enter the Union was Rhode Island and then only by a narrow vote of 34 to 32 in the ratifying convention held on May 28, 1790. Evidently it was the town of Providence's secession from the state with the promise not to return unless the Constitution were unconditionally ratified that turned the tide. Exhibit 1.1 lists the dates when all fifty states joined the Union.

---

[38]*Ibid.*, pp. 209–12.
[39]See the account in McDonald, *We the People, op. cit.,* pp. 287–88.

| EXHIBIT 1.1 | Dates of Ratification of the Constitution and Entry into the Union of the Fifty States |

1.	Delaware *December 7, 1787*	18.	Louisiana *April 30, 1812*	35.	West Virginia *June 20, 1863*
2.	Pennsylvania *December 12, 1787*	19.	Indiana *December 11, 1816*	36.	Nevada *October 31, 1864*
3.	New Jersey *December 18, 1787*	20.	Mississippi *December 10, 1817*	37.	Nebraska *March 1, 1867*
4.	Georgia *January 2, 1788*	21.	Illinois *December 3, 1818*	38.	Colorado *August 1, 1876*
5.	Connecticut *January 9, 1788*	22.	Alabama *December 14, 1819*	39.	North Dakota *November 2, 1889*
6.	Massachusetts *February 6, 1788*	23.	Maine *March 15, 1820*	40.	South Dakota *November 2, 1889*
7.	Maryland *April 28, 1788*	24.	Missouri *August 10, 1821*	41.	Montana *November 8, 1889*
8.	South Carolina *May 23, 1788*	25.	Arkansas *June 15, 1836*	42.	Washington *November 11, 1889*
9.	New Hampshire *June 21, 1788*	26.	Michigan *January 26, 1837*	43.	Idaho *July 3, 1890*
10.	Virginia *June 25, 1788*	27.	Florida *March 3, 1845*	44.	Wyoming *July 10, 1890*
11.	New York *July 26, 1788*	28.	Texas *December 29, 1845*	45.	Utah *January 4, 1896*
12.	North Carolina *November 21, 1789*	29.	Iowa *December 28, 1846*	46.	Oklahoma *November 16, 1907*
13.	Rhode Island *May 29, 1790*	30.	Wisconsin *May 29, 1848*	47.	New Mexico *January 6, 1912*
14.	Vermont *March 4, 1791*	31.	California *September 9, 1850*	48.	Arizona *February 14, 1912*
15.	Kentucky *June 1, 1792*	32.	Minnesota *May 11, 1858*	49.	Alaska *January 3, 1959*
16.	Tennessee *June 1, 1796*	33.	Oregon *February 14, 1859*	50.	Hawaii *August 21, 1959*
17.	Ohio *March 1, 1803*	34.	Kansas *January 29, 1861*		

Source: Commission on the Bicentennial of the United States Constitution

Each state had its own mixture of political and economic forces. Generalizations about the supporters and opponents of the Constitution are apt to be misleading if not wrong. But in each state, some of the best minds in the country entered the debate over ratification. From this debate about the nature of government, a set of remarkable newspaper articles emerged. **The Federalist Papers**, more commonly referred to as *The Federalist*, explained and favored the Constitution. These essays have become an essential historical document.

The Federalist Papers

The *Federalist Papers* were authored by James Madison, Alexander Hamilton, and John Jay, but were published under the pen name "Publius." They consisted of eighty-five essays designed to win ratification in the state of New York and appeared regularly in several New York newspapers between October 1787 and July 1788. The articles were published as a book and were also used as part of the federalist campaign in Virginia and North Carolina. Although historians believe that these essays had little or no influence except in New York City, they remain the most cogent and elaborate statement of federalist theory and one of the most authoritative commentaries on the Constitution.[40] Their ideas and themes were common ground for federalist debates throughout the country.

The authors of *The Federalist* had several goals. They sought to explain each branch of government and its delegated powers as conceptualized in the Constitution. They hoped to quiet fears that the new Constitution would bring about a centralized tyranny. They emphasized the separation of powers and checks and balances. They aimed to persuade their readers that the states could neither go it alone nor continue under the weak Articles of Confederation. *The Federalist* emphasized that sovereignty lay with the people and the doctrine of popular sovereignty meant that the people could delegate sovereignty to the national government *and* to the states. Furthermore, the people would always retain the power to alter the national government, to diminish or enhance its authority.

Alexander Hamilton led the fight in New York for ratification of the Constitution and coauthored the Federalist Papers.

The papers also elaborated upon the theory of federalism especially in numbers 32, 39, 45, 46, and 51. They constituted a skillful answer to antifederalists, who argued that the new Constitution provided for a central government so strong that it threatened the states and individual liberty.[41] The authors argued that the Constitution created a new government with characteristics of both a nation and confederation. In its source of power, the new government was a confederation. First, the people, acting within the sovereign states in state conventions, conferred powers on the national government by ratification of the Constitution. Second, it was a confederation also in the structure of the Senate, to which each state legislature elected two senators. Third, the delegation of specific powers to the central government with everything else retained by the states was the mark of a confederation. Yet, in the structure of the House of Representatives whose members were chosen directly by the people, and in the supreme enumerated powers of Congress, the Constitution provided for a national form of government. The supremacy of the Constitution within its sphere of designated powers over the states was also the mark of a national government.

[40]McDonald, *op. cit.,* p. 284.

[41]See Jacob E. Cooke, ed., *The Federalist* (Cleveland: World Publishing, 1961). Also see, David F. Epstein, *The Political Theory of The Federalist* (Chicago: University of Chicago Press, 1984) and Morton White, *Philosophy, The Federalist, and the Constitution* (New York: Oxford, 1987).

To those suspicious of the Constitution's ability to protect individual rights and liberties, Madison addressed their concerns in one of the best known of the Federalist essays. In No. 10, he argued that a national legislature ultimately would protect individual rights and interests better than state legislatures. Madison recognized that it is a fact of political life that a variety of interests or factions play an active role in governmental affairs. The legislative process, with its requirement of majority rule, can be expected to balance competing interests, except when a faction is so large as to constitute the majority. Then, the danger lies in the neglect of the general welfare and of minority rights and interests. (This already, suggested Madison, had occurred in some states.) But, Madison wrote, in an expanded arena of politics as in a national legislature, minority interests are protected because no one faction can dominate a national legislature drawn from the entire country with its multiplicity of interests. Madison saw the United States as a pluralistic society in which the struggle of competing interests and factions can usually produce the general good.

The Anti-Federalists

Like the federalists, the anti-federalists accepted certain political ideas such as separation of powers, checks and balances, and natural rights. But they found the Constitution to be deficient in each of these realms.[42] The president and the Senate shared too many powers (appointments, ratification of treaties) to the exclusion of the democratically elected House. Not only did this, in their view, create the potential for misuse of power, but it also violated the principle of separation of powers. Because House approval was not required, there was no check or balance. Furthermore, they believed that the extensive list of enumerated powers given to Congress along with the supremacy clause raised the specter of despotism by the legislature. Finally, the absence of a Bill of Rights from the Constitution clinched the anti-federalists' suspicion that the federalists were more interested in grabbing power than in protecting individual liberties.

True, some opponents of ratification, like some supporters, may have been motivated by economic interests. But they cast their debate in political and ideological terms, and the evidence suggests that ideology rather than economics was at the heart of their differences.

The anti-federalists believed that sovereignty was indivisible. To them, the alternative was either unitary government or a confederation of sovereign states as under the Articles of Confederation. Few of them opposed the idea that the Articles of Confederation should be strengthened, and few advocated that their states become independent entities. But they genuinely feared that a central government would displace the states, a fear based on their skepticism of the new federalist conception of sovereignty. The anti-

---

[42]See Herbert J. Storing, *The Anti-Federalist: Writings by Opponents of the Constitution* (Chicago: University of Chicago Press, 1985).

federalists saw the Constitution creating a unitary government in the powers it delegated to the central government and in the explicit provision that in the exercise of these powers, the Constitution was superior to conflicting state laws *and* state constitutions. Rather prophetically, the anti-federalists predicted that if the Constitution were adopted, power would eventually flow to the central government, the states would be weakened, and republicanism, in the sense of the people's direct control of government, would be undermined.

In political terms, the federalists outmaneuvered, and, to some extent, outdebated the anti-federalists. But perhaps even more importantly, a majority of the country recognized that government under the Articles of Confederation was not workable and that even an imperfect Constitution was preferable to the Articles. Once the Constitution was approved and the new government took form, those who had been in the forefront of the campaign against ratification for the most part embraced the new Constitution. Criticism of the Constitution virtually stopped and new political lines were drawn.

Under the new government, two distinct political factions developed that formed the core of emerging political parties. One faction consisted of most of the former supporters of the Constitution. They supported a strong central government and, like Secretary of the Treasury Alexander Hamilton, favored an expansive reading of Congress's enumerated powers. This faction coalesced into the Federalist Party. The opposing faction was led by Thomas Jefferson and among its supporters were important former federalists, including James Madison and many former anti-federalists. This faction became known as the Democratic-Republican Party. It stood for a more limited reading of the central government's power, a greater concern for states' rights, and a particular sensitivity to popular sovereignty. Jefferson's party had its greatest support in the agrarian areas of the South and the West, whereas the political base of the Federalist Party was in the Northeast. The Federalist Party was particularly sensitive to the economic needs of the mercantile eastern seaboard. Thus, although the composition of the emerging political parties differed from that of the opposing camps during the ratification controversy, the major outlines of American political conflict for the next seventy years took shape during ratification. The Civil War would settle the disagreements over the nature of the Union by force of arms.

EXTENDING THE CONSTITUTION

The document that was ratified in 1788 as the Constitution of the United States was an unfinished one. It provided a framework for government, guaranteed certain rights, contained certain prohibitions on the actions of government, and left room for altering its provisions to meet new needs. In reality, the Constitution has been altered by the difficult process of amendment, by acts of Congress, by judicial interpretation, by the practices of the president, Congress, and the Supreme Court, and by such institutions as political parties and organized interest groups which the Constitution nowhere mentions. The Constitution has endured, in part, because it has proven flexible enough to permit each new generation of Americans to adapt it to their compelling problems. But it also has been rigid enough to make fundamental change difficult, if not impossible, without an overwhelming national consensus.

The following sections look at some of the Amendments adopted since 1788 and how Congress has elaborated on the Constitution. They also look at how judicial interpretation has changed the Constitution and at major practices and customs that have emerged over the last 200 years to become part of our living Constitution.

Amending the Constitution

The Constitution offers a process for change to the document itself. In Article V, the Constitution states that amendments may be proposed by a two-thirds vote of both houses or through a national convention called by Congress at the request of two-thirds of the state legislatures. The convention approach to amend the Constitution thus far has not been used. Once proposed, an amendment must be ratified by three-fourths of the states either by their legislatures or by special ratifying conventions.

Only twenty-six amendments have been ratified and the first ten were approved in 1791. In the following 200 years, only sixteen amendments have become part of the Constitution, a tribute to the difficulty of the process. Of these sixteen amendments, one negates another (the Eighteenth Amendment outlawing alcoholic beverages was repealed fourteen years later by the Twenty-First).

The Bill of Rights, as the first ten amendments are known, had its genesis during the ratification controversy. The federalists responded to fears that a strong national government would too easily threaten individual rights by promising to add basic guarantees to the Constitution. Along with the Eleventh and Twelfth Amendments, the Bill of Rights was designed to perfect the Constitution. The remaining three amendments adopted during the nineteenth century were the result of the Civil War and were aimed at securing the rights of black people.

As originally drafted by James Madison, a member of the House of Representatives of the first Congress, the Bill of Rights applied to both federal and state governments. But as modified and approved by the Senate, the Bill of Rights applies only to the federal government. Among the most important of the guarantees are those contained in the First, Fourth, Fifth, Sixth, and Eighth Amendments (see the box on pages 34–35 on Key Amendments to the Constitution; the entire Constitution is reprinted in the Appendix at the end of this book).

The Bill of Rights limits the powers of the federal government. Only after the Fourteenth Amendment was adopted in 1868 were the states gradually held to account for the protection of similar individual rights. Indeed, as shown in Chapters Twelve (on civil liberties) and Thirteen (on minorities, women, and equality), the road to incorporating the basic protections of the Bill of Rights under the Fourteenth Amendment's definitions of liberty, due process, and equal protection of the laws was a tortuous one, taking close to a century to be near completed.

The Eleventh Amendment was a direct response to an early Supreme Court decision and was designed to overturn the Court's ruling that it had the authority to hear suits brought by a citizen of one state against another state's government.[43] The Twelfth Amendment became necessary because a crisis occurred in the election of 1800 when there was a tie vote in the electoral college. The Twelfth provides for separate voting by presidential electors for president and vice-president.

Not until the Civil War era did the need emerge for adding to the Constitution. The guarantees of the Fourteenth Amendment, in particular, were written in broad terms: that no state shall "abridge the privileges or immunities of citizens" nor "deprive any person of life, liberty, or property, without due process of law; nor deny to any person within its jurisdiction the equal protection of the laws." Eventually, as shown in Chapter Twelve, this due process clause was interpreted by the Supreme Court as prohibiting the states from abridging most of the guarantees in the Bill of Rights. Likewise, as shown in Chapter Thirteen, the Fifteenth Amendment guaranteeing the vote to African-Americans did not stop southern states from denying the vote to most black people by means of unfair literacy tests, poll taxes, and other subterfuges. Only in the last quarter-century has the intent of the Fifteenth Amendment gradually become realized with the enactment of voting rights laws and their enforcement in the South.

Another long period of time followed until the ratification of the next amendment, the Sixteenth, in 1913. An interesting facet of the Eighteenth Amendment (1919), which brought on the prohibition of alcoholic beverages, was that it came about as a result of a movement primarily led by women. Women also assumed the leadership in another long crusade that resulted, in 1920, in the Nineteenth Amendment, which gave women the right to vote.

In 1961, the Twenty-third Amendment was ratified and it gave the vote in presidential elections to the residents of the District of Columbia. Indeed, by 1961, the District had a larger population than several states. The adoption of this amendment was a victory for democratic principles. However, the District still lacks voting representation in Congress. In 1978, Congress sent to the states for ratification a proposed constitutional amendment that would have provided full congressional representation for the District, but it failed to win enough support and died in 1985. Congress could grant the District (which votes heavily Democratic in presidential elections) statehood by ordinary legislation.[44] Were the District to become a state, it would be entitled to two senators in the United States Senate and one representa-

[43]*Chisholm* v. *Georgia* (1793).
[44]See, "The 'Battle of the Last Colony,' " *New York Times,* May 18, 1985, p. 9.

Materials of Political Science: CONSTITUTIONAL PROVISIONS

Key Amendments to the Constitution

The First Amendment guarantees freedom of religion and that Congress shall not establish a religion. It also provides for freedom of speech, press, assembly, and the right to petition government.

The Fourth Amendment protects against warrantless searches and seizures of people, homes, papers, and other personal property, and guarantees that search warrants can only be issued on probable cause with a specific description of the place to be searched and the person or things to be seized.

The Fifth Amendment is a compendium of guarantees including the requirement of a grand jury indictment before proceeding with a federal trial, the guarantee against being tried twice for the same crime after an acquittal (double jeopardy), the right not to be forced to be a witness against oneself (the guarantee against self-incrimination), and the guarantee that private property not be taken for public use without just compensation. In addition to these specific guarantees, the Fifth Amendment also contains a broadly phrased guarantee of criminal and civil procedure, that no one "be deprived of life, liberty, or property, without due process of law."

The Sixth Amendment also is a bundle of criminal procedural guarantees including the right to a speedy and public trial by an impartial jury, the right to be informed of the charges, the right to confront adverse witnesses, the right to compel the appearance of witnesses favorable to the accused, and, most prominent of all, the right to the assistance of a lawyer.

The Eighth Amendment forbids excessive bail and fines and prohibits "cruel and unusual" punishment.

The Tenth Amendment explicitly leaves to the states or to the people that which is not delegated to the United States government. This amendment has been utilized by advocates of states' rights as justification for the exercise of power by the states.

The Thirteenth Amendment abolished slavery and prohibited involuntary servitude except as punishment for a crime.

The Fourteenth Amendment was intended by its framers to provide basic civil rights and liberties for African–Americans, but the language that they used is racially neutral and therefore applies to all Americans. The Fourteenth Amendment also specifically prohibits the states from violating basic freedoms and warns them that the federal government has the authority to intervene and protect individuals from the unconstitutional actions of a state or local government.

The Fifteenth Amendment, the last of the Civil War amendments to be ratified, barred both the federal and state governments from denying citizens the right to vote because of "race, color, or previous condition of servitude" (that is, because one was a slave).

tive in the House of Representatives (based on its current population). Since the majority of the District's population is black, it is likely that its members of Congress would be black.

Starting with the Twenty-third Amendment in 1961, a total of four constitutional amendments were ratifbed over a ten year period, a record equaled only in the 1913–1920 Progressive Era period and only once before that with the ratification of the Bill of Rights in 1791. It is a matter of speculation whether this was merely coincidence or reflective of the activist politics of the 1960s.

The Twenty-sixth Amendment deserves special mention. It was proposed and ratified in record time in 1971 and came about after the Supreme

The Sixteenth Amendment, in 1913, overturned a constitutional law ruling of the Supreme Court of some eighteen years earlier and now allowed Congress to enact a graduated income tax. This tax has become the principal source of revenue for the federal government.

The Seventeenth Amendment (1913) was one of the major achievements of the progressive movement in American politics to make our system of government more democratic. This amendment provides that United States Senators shall be directly elected by the electorate.

The Nineteenth Amendment guaranteed women the right to vote. This amendment was a striking success in correcting the fundamental injustice to women that had reduced them to second-class citizenship. Although a number of states had already enfranchised women, the amendment extended female suffrage nationwide.

The Twenty-second Amendment (1951) limited the number of presidential terms of office to two. This amendment was a response to President Franklin D. Roosevelt having sought and won third and fourth terms, thus violating the two-term tradition that had been established by George Washington.

The Twenty-fourth Amendment (1964) clearly grew out of the civil rights struggle. It abolished the poll tax as a prerequisite for voting in federal elections or primaries. The poll tax had been used and was in force by five states to prevent the poor, primarily blacks but also whites, from voting.

The Twenty-fifth Amendment (1967) provides for presidential succession in the event of death or disabling illness of the president. It was spurred by the illnesses of President Eisenhower and the assassination of President Kennedy. In addition, when there is a vacancy, the amendment directs the president to nominate a vice-president subject to confirmation by majority vote of both houses of Congress. Within eight years of the adoption of this amendment it was used three times: when vice-president Spiro Agnew resigned prior to his criminal conviction for income tax evasion, President Nixon named Gerald Ford to be vice-president; when Nixon himself was forced to resign because he faced impeachment for criminal acts related to the Watergate scandal, Gerald Ford became president and then named New York Governor Nelson A. Rockefeller to be vice-president. The Twenty-fifth Amendment thus allowed the country to have for the first time in its history an unelected president and vice-president.

The Twenty-sixth Amendment prevents denial of the right to vote on account of age to citizens eighteen years of age and older.

Court had struck down part of the Voting Rights Act of 1970 which had given the vote to eighteen to twenty-one–year–old citizens in both state and federal elections. The Court upheld the legislation only for federal elections which meant that the states faced administrative chaos unless they changed their laws.[45] A constitutional amendment was the quickest and most efficient solution, hence its rapid approval.

One year after the Twenty-sixth Amendment was ratified, Congress approved and sent to the states the proposed Equal Rights Amendment. This

[45]*Oregon* v. *Mitchell* (1970).

Supporters of the Equal Rights Amendment.

was a major effort to extend the rights of women and to explicitly establish sexual equality within the Constitution. The amendment stated: "Equality of rights under the law shall not be denied or abridged by the United States or by any State on account of sex." It was primarily intended to overturn discrimination against women in education, employment, the business world, access to housing, distribution of public benefits, and domestic relations law. It was also meant to signal the nation's commitment to sexual equality and associate that value with the expression of the nation's highest constitutional ideals. The proposed amendment came close to, but did not achieve, the ratification of thirty-eight states and its failure was seen by civil libertarians as a setback. However, amendments are not the only way to change the Constitution. A more frequent method of constitutional change is by legislation and by judicial interpretation. As shown in Chapter Thirteen, legislation and judicial interpretation have made sexual equality in large measure a part of the Constitution despite the failure of the Equal Rights Amendment.

Legislative Elaboration

The Constitution is specific concerning the structure of Congress but not concerning the executive and judicial branches. Legislation was therefore necessary to fill in the gaps. The first Congress proceeded to enact legislation and in so doing created institutions that have acquired a permanence like that enjoyed by provisions of the Constitution itself.

For the executive branch, Congress established three departments, State, Treasury, and War, that became prototypes of future departments. In the twentieth century, Congress created independent regulatory agencies that stood apart from the agencies and departments of the executive branch of government in their accountability, fixed terms of office for key personnel, and level of political independence. This, too, must be seen as an extension of the Constitution. Another twentieth-century development was the introduction of the **legislative veto** whereby executive branch agencies were authorized to fill in the gaps of legislation or to take other actions that would stand unless one or both houses of Congress objected within a specified time. This veto was incorporated in legislation for well over a half century until the Supreme Court in 1983 struck it down as unconstitutional.[46] In revised form, however, the legislative veto continues to be used.[47]

For the judicial branch, Congress enacted the **Judiciary Act of 1789** that created a federal court structure including federal trial courts and the Supreme Court consisting of five associate justices and a chief justice. It specified the powers of the Supreme Court and the kinds of cases it was authorized to hear on appeal. The Supreme Court was given power to review decisions of state courts that denied a federal claim based on federal law, the federal Constitution, or a federal treaty. Legislation in the nineteenth and twentieth centuries has expanded and changed the lower courts. The Circuit Court of Appeals Act of 1891 created the modern courts of appeals. The Judiciary Acts of 1925 and 1988 gave the Supreme Court virtual control over its workload.

Over the early years of the nation, different statutes varied the number of justices on the Supreme Court. But in 1869, the number was fixed at eight associate justices and one chief justice. This number has since acquired a quasi-constitutional status. In fact, in 1937 when President Franklin D. Roosevelt sought to increase the number of justices so that the Supreme Court would contain a majority favorable to his administration's New Deal policies, some of the opposition came from New Dealers themselves who disliked the attempt to tamper with the independence of the judiciary. Roosevelt's failure to change the size of the Court virtually assured that the number of justices will endure as if it were fixed by the Constitution.

Through congressional legislation at the behest of the president and as approved by the Supreme Court, the powers of Congress have been transformed to address the problems of the modern industrial state. The commerce clause giving Congress the power "to regulate commerce. . .among the several states" has been the source of much of the power of the federal government today over the nation's economic life. The social welfare state has been derived primarily from the commerce clause and from Congress's

---

[46]*I.N.S.* v. *Chadha* (1983).
[47]Louis Fisher, *Constitutional Dialogues* (Princeton: Princeton University Press, 1988), pp. 224–29.

taxing and spending powers. The Constitution, thus, has been transformed, extended, enlarged, indeed built upon by acts of Congress, but in no way is this inconsistent with the basic document itself. The Constitution states as one of its purposes promoting "the general welfare" and gives Congress the power "to make all laws which shall be necessary and proper." Thus the Constitution, an eighteenth-century document, can be seen as assuring the flexibility essential for running a modern government.

Judicial Interpretation

The Constitution has been adapted to new problems and issues by the rulings of the United States Supreme Court. The Court, early in its history, staked its claim as the authoritative interpreter of the Constitution, the institution of government that has the final say as to what the Constitution means. Only if a later Court reverses a Supreme Court decision *or* a constitutional amendment is adopted can a Supreme Court ruling on constitutionality be overturned.

The theory behind the Court's supremacy in interpreting the Constitution comes from the great Chief Justice John Marshall, in the landmark case from 1803, **Marbury v. Madison.** That case arose out of President Thomas Jefferson's refusal to have his secretary of state, James Madison, deliver commissions to certain men who had been approved as judges by the outgoing administration of John Adams. Marshall addressed the question whether the Court had the legal authority to hear the case and to order Madison to deliver the commissions. In ruling that part of the act of Congress that conferred such authority violated the Constitution (Article III, Section 2), Marshall offered the justification for the Supreme Court exercising final constitutional interpretation by way of judicial review. The key to his argument was that "It is, emphatically, the province and duty of the judicial department, to say what the law is." Because it is the duty of the Supreme Court when adjudicating disputes to say what the law is (why else have a judiciary?), because the Constitution is superior to all other law, federal or state, and because judges have sworn to support the Constitution, the justices of the Supreme Court are obliged to strike down any law in conflict with the Constitution.

The power of the Supreme Court grew over the years, and within a century of its existence the Supreme Court was firmly established as having the power to definitively interpret the Constitution, and in so doing, either to uphold or strike down any conflicting law or any action of any government official from the president on down. Although at times the Court has used this power to hamper progress and social justice, at other times the Court has accommodated fundamental political, economic, and social changes by a generous interpretation of the Constitution, and the Constitution has been transformed into a governing charter suitable for a modern industrial state. In many chapters of this book, there are references to Supreme Court decisions in which the Constitution is interpreted. That they are here is testimony to the vital role of the Court in the processes of constitutional change.

The Constitution, however, is not infinitely flexible. To be sure, were the Constitution more narrowly written, had it taken the shape of a more detailed code of law, were it without its broad phrases, judges (or, for that matter, legislators or presidents) probably would not have been able to adapt the Constitution to new conditions. There are limits to the adaptability of the Constitution, however, because fundamental institutions and checks and balances remain constant. The diffusion of power within the federal government makes it difficult to move swiftly, decisively, and comprehensively in many policy areas. Some observers question whether the structure of government dictated by an eighteenth-century document will be adequate for the twenty-first century.

Extra-constitutional Practices, Customs, and Institutions

The American system of government has developed certain extra-constitutional practices, customs, and even institutions that have helped make the system work. These practices, customs, and institutions were not in the minds of the framers and cannot be found in the document they wrote.

Perhaps foremost of these extra-constitutional institutions are political parties. They quickly changed the electoral college into a mere formality and democratized the election of the president. Although on November 8, 1988, Americans thought they were voting for George Bush or Michael Dukakis for president, they actually were voting for presidential electors designated by each party to vote for the party's candidate for president and vice-president in the electoral college. Electors are not legally bound to vote for the party's choice but almost always have done so (one West Virginia Democratic elector in 1988 voted for Lloyd Bentsen for president and Michael Dukakis for vice-president).

Not only do political parties with their national conventions, party platforms, and choice of a national ticket organize the selection process for the presidency, but they also help to organize and run Congress. Political party affiliation is also of prime importance for presidential appointments in the executive branch, independent regulatory agencies, and to the federal courts. At the state level as well, political parties organize and shape politics and the running of government. They conduct party primaries to select candidates to run on the party label. Only at the local level of government, particularly in smaller cities and towns, are political parties sometimes less pervasive in their influence.

The presidency has grown from the broad provisions of Article II into one of the world's most powerful offices. Presidential power has increased during periods of national crisis, of war, or massive economic distress. The bold powers assumed by President Lincoln during the Civil War, the unprecedented actions by Woodrow Wilson during World War I in assuming control of the economy, the programs of President Franklin Roosevelt during the Great Depression and World War II, and then the actions of American presidents during the nuclear age all have transformed both the presidency and the role and scope of the national government.

The institution of the president's cabinet is not mentioned in the Constitution nor did the framers envision the vast federal bureaucracy over which the cabinet officers now preside. The vast and unwieldy military bureaucracy, led by the secretary of defense, would have been inconceivable to the founders. The customs of regular presidential press conferences and radio or television addresses to the nation were unimagined by the framers. The practice of executive privilege invoked by modern presidents to withhold certain information from Congress was not considered by the founders. The Korean and Vietnam wars were waged at the president's initiative and Congress's acquiescence but without a congressional declaration of war as required by the Constitution.

Congressional practices and customs also have altered the framers' vision as set down in Article I. They never imagined the powers of the Speaker of the House and the Senate Majority Leader, the powers of committee chairs, the custom of seniority, all of which emerged over the years and are now enveloped in an aura of quasi-constitutionality.

Turning to the judiciary, the exercise of judicial review over the acts and actions of government officials is a major extra-constitutional power that has assumed constitutional status. This is a practice, indeed an institution, that was carefully nurtured by the Supreme Court during the nineteenth century.

The next chapter takes a closer look at the federalism which underlies our system of government. The burden of this and subsequent chapters is to flesh out the institutions and processes of American government and politics. By the end of this book it will be apparent that while the shape and practice of government and politics is far different than that conceptualized by the framers, there is a common denominator that remains (including separation of powers, checks and balances, commitment to individual liberty, skepticism of government power and fear of its concentration, and high ideals for the collective good as suggested by the Constitution's preamble) that would probably be recognizable today by the framers. Although it is important not to be complacent and insensitive to the variety of social ills and problems that remain, it is appropriate for the nation to feel pride in the accomplishment of coming through over two centuries as well as it has with a sense of idealism and purpose.

CHECKLIST FOR REVIEW

1. The concept of a written constitution has deep historical roots and, at the time of the American revolution, was widely accepted along with the concept of higher law to which ordinary law must conform. The framers

were familiar with a variety of important political ideas that had their roots primarily in English but also in continental political philosophy. The ideas of separation of powers, checks and balances, natural rights, federalism, and democracy were to have great influence in the writing of the Constitution.

2. The work of the Constitutional Convention was not driven, as historian Charles Beard suggested, by the economic self-interest of the framers. The evidence reveals a more complex portrait of the framers. The framers however, were not a cross section of the American population; they were the political and economic elite of the nation.

3. The Convention considered two major proposals. The Virginia Plan would have established a strong national government with Congress being the repository of power; the New Jersey Plan revised the Articles of Confederation and retained much more state power than under the Virginia Plan. The question of representation in Congress was settled by The Great Compromise, which specified that representation in the House of Representatives be based on population while representation in the Senate be based on equal representation for each state. The divisions in the Convention had little to do with state size and more to do with conflicting regional economic interests (North versus South) and philosophy (states' rights proponents versus the supporters of a strong national government).

4. The politics of the ratification of the Constitution involved a battle between the federalists who supported ratification and the anti-federalists who opposed it. Support for and opposition to the Constitution cut across economic class lines. The promise that a Bill of Rights would be added to the Constitution was important for ratification. The lines of argument used by the federalists were spelled out in one of the major documents to emerge from the ratification controversy, *The Federalist Papers*. While the anti-federalists came around to supporting the Constitution once it was ratified, their states' rights position held enormous appeal and has profoundly influenced American politics.

5. The Constitution has been extended and changed by a variety of ways. The first is by formal constitutional amendment. The second method is by the actions of Congress which have been instrumental in filling in the details and bringing to life the structures created by the Constitution. Congressional legislation has adapted the Constitution so that it remains a vital, relevant governing charter. Third, judicial interpretation has been a vehicle for adapting the Constitution to new eras and new national needs. Lastly, a variety of extra-constitutional practices, customs, and institutions have arisen that were not envisioned by the framers—however, they were not forbidden, and they have also performed important functions in the governing of the nation.

KEY TERMS	

Articles of Confederation

Common Sense

republic

popular sovereignty

The Declaration of Independence

separation of powers

natural rights

federalism

democracy

The Virginia Plan

The New Jersey Plan

The Great Compromise

supremacy clause

checks and balances

writ of habeas corpus

bill of attainder

ex post facto law

federalists

anti-federalists

The Federalist Papers

The Bill of Rights

legislative veto

Judiciary Act of 1789

Marbury v. *Madison*

Federalism and the States

- You are a student attending a state university in a neighboring state but your tuition is more than three times as much as in-state students pay. Is that fair? You are classified as "out-of-state" and pay more What is going on here? You are a United States citizen. This is one country, isn't it?

- You are a physician having just completed your residency in New Mexico and you have successfully passed the licensing exam entitling you to practice medicine there. Within a short period of time professional colleagues of yours in Dallas, Texas, persuade you to join their lucrative practice. But you have to take a licensing exam all over again forcing you to expend time, energy, and money. Does this make sense? Why doesn't Texas accept the New Mexico license? This is one country, isn't it?

- Your parents own and run a business. They are subject to numerous federal regulations *and* state regulations. They must file numerous federal forms *and* state forms. They must withhold federal *and* state taxes from their employees' wages. They must deal with federal agencies in Washington, D.C. *and* state agencies in the state capital. Your parents, their lawyers, and their accountants spend countless hours filling out forms, many of them requiring the same or slightly different information and the expense to your parents is considerable. Is this an efficient use of their time and resources? Is this a productive use of the nation's resources? This is one country, isn't it?

- An acquaintance from childhood has grown up to be a lawbreaker who masterminded an interstate stolen car operation that was based in Alabama and did business in both Alabama and Georgia. He was caught in Atlanta and was indicted by both Georgia and Alabama grand juries and faced two trials and two separate sentences. Is this fair to be penalized twice for the same crime? This is one country, isn't it?

- You are driving on Interstate 91 in Vermont heading towards Massachusetts, cruising along at Vermont's speed limit of 65 miles per hour, when you cross the Massachusetts border where the speed limit is 55. You maintain your speed and soon see flashing lights, a state trooper, and a speeding ticket deposited in your trembling hands. What is going on here? This is an *interstate* highway. This is one country, isn't it?

The answer to all these questions is yes, we *are* one country, but we operate under a unique system of government—a *federal* system. As shown in the previous chapter on the Constitution and its genesis, *federalism* has distinct historical roots as the central idea in the framing of the Constitution and our becoming one nation. These roots and the values that accompany them are so deep that this nation has, for the most part, tolerated what seem like the anomalies, inconsistencies, and inefficiencies described in the examples just given. The American system of government is complex, confusing, cumbersome, even inefficient, but it provides its citizens more choices than a **unitary system** of government, where the source of all power is in the central government and all other governmental units are subordinate to it. This chapter explores the reasons for federalism and its persistence, varieties, characteristics, and roots in politics. This chapter also examines the historical development of federalism, considers some examples of federalism, and offers a brief overview of state government.

WHY FEDERALISM?

If we were designing a form of government for the United States today, would a federal system make any sense? Why should *one* country have fifty different sets of laws covering a wide variety of day-to-day activities and occupational pursuits, to say nothing of state activities that duplicate or overlap federal activities in such matters as taxation, law enforcement, the court and prison systems, welfare, health, and education? Why should there be so many different standards for certifying teachers, doctors, lawyers, and automobile drivers? Why should there be different laws covering marriage, divorce, child custody, and qualifications to vote? Why should there be different building, safety, and health standards? Why should there be different amounts of unemployment compensation, welfare benefits, and state scholarships? Why should there be different criminal sentences for the same offenses in different parts of the country? To answer these questions, it is necessary to recognize that federalism is deeply embedded in our history and politics. These points deserve further exploration.

The Historical and Constitutional Bases of Federalism

America is a nation of states. The original states were colonies of Great Britain that were governed under individual colonial charters and were administered separately. All, however, were under the ultimate authority of Parliament and the King of England. Once the colonies were settled and developed, there was little reason for Great Britain to consolidate them into one large colony with one colonial government. First, in geographic terms, the distances that separated the colonies made consolidation impractical for administrative purposes. Then, in political terms, there was little to be gained from consolidation. All of the colonies operated under the laws of England, and the colonists had the rights of Englishmen (except for representation in Parliament). But in the absence of consolidation, Americans identified with and felt loyalty to their own colonies. One was a Virginian or North Carolinian or New Yorker, rather than an American.

The colonists' experience with England stimulated a distrust of centralized government and an appreciation of direct democracy. But the American Revolution required the colonists to cooperate in the conduct of the war, and, afterwards, in establishing a limited form of national government, the Articles of Confederation. As shown in Chapter One, the Articles did not adequately deal with nationwide problems, and the Constitutional Convention was called to remedy the defects of the Articles. The states were jealous of their sovereign powers but willing to surrender some sovereignty to the new national government. The states were not willing to abandon all of their sovereignty, however, and be transformed into administrative units under a unitary government. Indeed, they would have considered such a notion ludicrous.

The framers of the Constitution readily accepted the fundamental tenet of federalism—that the same geographical area may be subject to the sovereign power of more than one government. This was politically necessary for creating a constitution that would remedy the defects of the Articles of Confederation and for the ratification of that constitution. It also fit the deeply held political beliefs of the framers. They not only shared their fellow Americans' distrust of centralized government at a time when the bitter taste of the experience with England remained, but they believed that the best form of government was one of separation of powers with checks and balances. They transformed their ideas into the structures of the new national government and, to some extent, the relationship of the federal government to the states. The states retained separate and distinct sovereign powers. In 1791, this understanding was made explicit with the adoption of the Tenth Amendment. The Constitution provided for the states to check the federal government politically through the Senate, if not the House of Representatives. The federal government could check the states either by legislation, new constitutional amendments, or by the decisions of the Supreme Court.

Are the historical events that gave rise to a distrust of centralized government and the concepts of checks and balances and separation of powers still relevant today? Most scholars of American government believe they are even now, over 200 years since the United States Constitution came into operation. Although the balance between the states and the nation has shifted, with power tending to move to Washington, federalism remains a part of American government. The states retain their sovereignty and independence in many spheres of activity.

Varieties of Federalism and Their Political Bases

American federalism takes three essential forms. One form is that of *separate and independent functions:* both the federal and state governments independently perform certain functions. The federal government, for example, conducts foreign affairs and has embassies and diplomatic missions around the world. If you are a native of Texas and plan a trip to France, you apply for a United States passport. There is no such thing as a Texas passport. The states, on the other hand, have their own exclusive functions such as marriage, divorce, administering estates, and the licensing of certain professionals. If you intend to marry, you do not apply to the federal government for a marriage license.

Many functions that the states perform independently are also performed by the federal government. An example of this is the administration
of justice. Each state, like the federal government, has its own constitution,
its own criminal laws, its own law enforcement personnel and bureaucracy,
and its own judges, courthouses, and prisons. To be sure, local governments (which are legal creations of the state) have responsibility for day-to-
day law and order, including enforcement of traffic law. But certain types of
offenses are violations of both state and federal law. These include drug
trafficking, bank robbery, and kidnapping.

In practice, there is informal cooperation between the federal and state
or local authorities. Ordinarily, when criminal law is involved, the federal
government tries the suspect first and state authorities decide whether to
proceed on their own. In other instances, as when a state or local government official is charged with murder, violations of state criminal law and
federal civil law (depriving the deceased of civil rights) are involved. In
these instances, the criminal law violation is tried first. If there is an acquittal in state court, federal authorities can bring a suit in federal court. Still
another example of the first type of federalism is taxation. The state and
federal governments have independent taxation agencies and enforcement
machinery (although just as with the administration of justice, there may be
informal cooperation and sharing of information between federal and state
agencies).

Federalism takes a second form: *formally shared functions.* That is, the
federal and state governments assume responsibility for performing the
same function and they formally and legally share the administration of that
function. For example, the federal government helps finance Medicaid, a
program of medical and hospital benefits for the poor. The federal government also provides regulations, standards, and general administrative oversight. The states actually administer and implement the program. In administering the program, state and federal agencies are in routine contact.

A third form of federalism is *separate but cooperative.* The cooperation
is formalized, usually by virtue of financial strings attached by the federal
government in the distribution of federal grants. An example is aid to elementary and secondary education. Federal agencies ordinarily do not directly oversee or administer the programs, but they cooperate with state
and local agencies in determining needs, eligibility, and the standards attached to the programs.

In practice, the relationship of the federal government to the states has
been characterized by a major scholar of federalism, Morton Grodzins, as a
marble cake.[1] American federalism, suggested Grodzins, is not a layer cake,
with the federal government neatly overlaying state government. Instead,

---

[1]Morton Grodzins, "The Federal System," in *Goals for Americans: Report of the President's
Commission on National Goals* (Englewood Cliffs, N.J.: Prentice-Hall, Spectrum, 1960), pp. 265–
82. See the discussion in Deil S. Wright, *Understanding Intergovernmental Relations* (North
Scituate, Mass.: Duxbury, 1978), pp. 46–48. In general, see Daniel J. Elazar, *Exploring Federalism*
(Tuscaloosa: University of Alabama Press, 1987).

federal and state officials interact and cooperate whether or not they are formally required to do so. In a wide variety of activities there is no clear separation of functions.

American federalism is inextricably a part of the American political system. Federalism flavors many of our political institutions. For example, American politics is locally organized, and Americans elect members of the House of Representatives from **single-member constituencies.** That is, people who reside in one designated geographical area are entitled to elect one member of the House. The localism of congressional elections means that members of Congress are beholden to local interests and have political ties to state and local governments. They have a stake in the perpetuation of federalism. This would still be true if representatives, like senators, were elected statewide. But things would be dramatically different if we had a system of proportional representation whereby the voters nationwide would cast their ballots for a political party and each party would receive the proportion of seats in the House in accord with the proportion of votes it received. Such an electoral scheme would encourage a multi-party system, radically change American federalism and politics, and perhaps result in the election of those with political views ranging from the extreme left to the extreme right.

Not only are congressional districts single-member constituencies, but most state and local elective offices are locally based. Party politics is built on state and local organizations. There are fifty Democratic parties and fifty Republican parties and the state party organizations are not controlled by the national party organization. The American political tradition has nurtured the states' sensitivity toward their powers and prerogatives. Common political rhetoric of governors and state legislators revolves around the need for less meddling by the federal bureaucracy and the importance of preserving state sovereignty.

The president is elected through the electoral college based in the states. A president must win a majority of electoral college votes apportioned among the states and won on a winner-take-all system per state. This, too, reinforces federalism and ties the highest national office holders politically to the continuation of federalism.

The states, while jealous of their powers, are also eager recipients of federal largess. Members of the House and Senate try to make sure that their states and districts receive their share of federal government grants, projects, contracts, and other forms of aid. Because seniority generally determines congressional committee assignments, including committee chairmanships, members of Congress with high seniority placed in committees that distribute federal funds are in the best position to get federal money for their constituents. Because certain committees appropriate or supervise how federal agencies spend their budgets, senior members of Congress can influence federal bureaucrats to decide matters that affect particular districts or states such as the awarding of defense contracts. Presidents, too, are sensitive to the political realities facing members of the president's party in Congress up for reelection, and they also recognize that they can cement the political support of members of Congress by supporting, at critical times, grants for certain projects, contracts, or aid. Presidents and key members of Congress can use federal grants or contracts to reward political friends and punish enemies. For example, Massachusetts was unfriendly ground for Richard Nixon in 1968 and 1972 (he lost there to his Democratic party opponents). During the Nixon presidency, Massachusetts' proportion of federal contracts and aid declined.[2]

States and local governments actively lobby Congress and federal government agencies for funds. The governors of the fifty states meet annually, as do the mayors of the major American cities (U.S. Conference of Mayors). Among their principal concerns is the relationship of the federal government to the states and localities. Typically, they pass resolutions asking for more federal aid to meet new or continuing problems.

In summary, history, the Constitution, and politics have all conspired to perpetuate federalism and our federal form of government even though in many respects, as suggested in the beginning of this chapter, it doesn't make sense. American federalism has gone through several stages, with major political consequences for American government. These stages are important to understand and are discussed in the next section.

FEDERALISM OVER TIME

To examine federalism over the history of the United States requires looking at both political and judicial developments. This means a review of national crises and Supreme Court decisions that have affected the balance of power between the states and the federal government. To examine federalism in this way shows one overarching trend: the balance of power has shifted markedly from the states during the first half century of the nation's existence to the national government during the twentieth century. Some have argued that the Constitution has, in effect, been transformed. They say that despite vestiges of state sovereignty, for most purposes, Washington, D.C. does the decision-making for important areas of public life and policy.

The First Seventy Years

Until the Civil War resolved it, the nation's overriding political issue was the relationship of the states to the federal government. On one side were those who favored a strong central government with powers that were liberally construed and supreme over the states. On the other side were supporters of states' rights, who thought that federal power should be limited and narrowly construed. They argued that the states were the repository of sover-

---

[2]Richard P. Nathan, Fred C. Doolittle, and Associates, *Reagan and the States* (Princeton: Princeton University Press, 1987), p. 139.

eignty and that the states created the federal government. Sovereignty, they insisted, flows from the states and the national government depends on the states. The supporters of a strong national government argued that the people, not the states, are the repository of sovereignty and that the people (gathered for convenience in ratifying conventions organized by states) created the national government.

To be sure, the states held the upper hand as the national government struggled to become established during the early years of the republic. One of the earliest and most significant debates within the new government concerned the interpretation of Congress's powers under Article One of the Constitution. The argument focused particularly on the eighteenth clause of Section Eight, the "necessary and proper" clause.

Article One, Section Eight, enumerates the powers of Congress and concludes that Congress shall have power "to make all Laws which shall be necessary and proper for carrying into Execution the foregoing Powers, and all other Powers vested by this Constitution in the Government of the United States, or in any Department or Officer thereof." The debate over the interpretation of this clause was centered on Secretary of the Treasury Alexander Hamilton's economic program during the first administration of President George Washington. Among his other economic measures, Hamilton proposed the creation of a national bank. His position was that the necessary and proper clause must be read as permitting Congress to select any convenient or appropriate means to carry out an enumerated power as long as there was no violation of a specific prohibition of the Constitution. Hamilton believed that the creation of a national bank was necessary and proper in carrying out Congress's monetary powers under Article One, Section Eight, clauses two and five.

Thomas Jefferson, also a member of President Washington's first cabinet, disagreed. He argued that there were no **implied powers** and that Hamilton's liberal construction of "necessary and proper" was wrong. The Constitution, Jefferson insisted, is explicit in its grant of enumerated powers to Congress. The word "necessary" means absolutely indispensable. The necessary and proper clause must be narrowly construed, or the federal government will encroach upon state sovereignty. A broad construction of the Constitution along with the supremacy clause could destroy the federal system.

Hamilton's views prevailed, and the first Bank of the United States was chartered for a twenty-year period in 1791. By the end of that period the bank was no longer controversial and few questioned Congress's power to have chartered it. Indeed, in 1816, a Jeffersonian Republican Congress and president (James Madison) rechartered the bank for another twenty years. However, the second Bank of the United States was soon plagued by charges of mismanagement and even corruption, and it was thought to have contributed to major economic problems throughout the country. The bank had a branch in Maryland where the state legislature enacted a law that in effect taxed the bank. The bank challenged the tax, a law suit was brought,

Chief Justice John Marshall wrote several landmark decisions affecting American federalism.

and the case eventually came to the Supreme Court. Could a state levy a tax on a national bank? In his landmark opinion in **McCulloch v. Maryland,** Chief Justice John Marshall said no, and in the process ruled on an important issue at the heart of federalism: national sovereignty was superior to state sovereignty. (See the box on page 52.)

In reality, however, the national government was still in an inferior position as compared to the states, and its powers were not fully exercised. This was particularly apparent with the regulation of commerce.

In another landmark decision of the Marshall Court, **Gibbons v. Ogden**, the Court in 1824 broadly interpreted Congress's commerce power. It held that Congress had power over the buying, selling, *and* transportation of goods, including navigation on interstate waterways.[3] But the Court did not confront a major issue of the time concerning Congress's power, an issue that had major implications for federalism. The issue was whether Congress's enumerated power over commerce was an *exclusive power*, which only Congress could exercise, or a *concurrent power*, which the states could also exercise. If it were an exclusive power, any area of commerce that Congress did not enter—because it either lacked a political consensus to enact regulatory legislation or lacked funds to finance a federal bureaucracy to do the regulating—would remain unregulated. The states would be barred by the Constitution from acting at all. But if the commerce power were a concurrent power, then the states *could* act in the absence of congressional regulation. Those who favored a strong federal government feared that under a concurrent powers doctrine, the states would entrench themselves in the regulatory sphere and make it politically difficult for Congress to assert its authority and supremacy. They also feared that allowing the states to regulate interstate or foreign commerce could lead to the same sort of state rivalries that culminated in the *Gibbons* v. *Ogden* litigation.

To deal with this question, the Supreme Court adopted a case-by-case approach. Finally, in an 1852 decision, the Court hit upon a compromise that retained the principle of congressional supremacy and at the same time recognized the real-world problems in commerce.[4] This particular case concerned the regulation of harbors and harbor pilots. Congress in 1789 had explicitly permitted the states to regulate harbors and harbor pilots until such time as Congress decided to impose its own regulatory scheme. The case before the Supreme Court revolved around regulations governing pilots at the port of Philadelphia. The port operated under Pennsylvania law as authorized by the act of Congress. The Court ruled that *both* state and federal laws were constitutional. The new rule for regulating commerce was *selected exclusivity*. In other words, those areas of commerce that require national uniform regulation are to be regulated exclusively by

[3]See the discussion in Robert G. McCloskey, *The American Supreme Court* (Chicago: University of Chicago Press, 1960), pp. 69–71.
[4]*Cooley* v. *Board of Wardens*.

Marshall Decides *McCulloch* v. *Maryland*

McCulloch v. *Maryland,* decided in 1819, is considered a great constitutional law landmark that established the principle of a broad construction of the powers of the national government and a restrictive view of what the states may do when Congress has exercised its powers. The Maryland state law at issue taxed a branch of the Second Bank of the United States chartered by Congress.

Lawyers for Maryland argued two main points. First, that the state tax was constitutional because the power to tax is held concurrently by the nation and the states. The states, argued Maryland's attorneys, are coequal in sovereign power with the national government and both have the same powers to tax. Second, the Bank of the United States itself was unconstitutional, because it exceeds any of the enumerated powers in Article One, Section Eight. The necessary and proper clause at the end of Article One, Section Eight, should not be broadly construed as containing implied powers of Congress. The Second Bank of the United States is not absolutely necessary for carrying out an enumerated power of Congress. The Supreme Court, therefore, not only should uphold Maryland's sovereign power to tax but should find that the object of the tax itself violates the Constitution.

Chief Justice John Marshall and his colleagues unanimously upheld the constitutionality of the bank and struck down the state tax on it. Marshall's elaborately reasoned opinion justified federal supremacy over the states and a broad rather than narrow construction of the powers of the federal government. Marshall's perspective on the nature of the American union was similar to Alexander Hamilton's. In this view, the national government is not a compact or confederation created by sovereign and independent states. Instead, the people, who are the source of sovereignty, adopted the Constitution which provides for a national government. Within its sphere, the national government is supreme. The powers of a sovereign nation must be broadly construed, and it is entirely appropriate to interpret the necessary and proper clause broadly. Marshall also noted that the structure of the Constitution itself shows that the framers intended the necessary and proper clause to be an addition to the powers of Congress and not a restraint on them. The necessary and proper clause ends the section that lists Congress's powers. The next section (Section Nine) lists the restraints on Congress. Had the framers considered the necessary and proper clause as a limit on Congress, they would have placed it with the other limitations. But they did not. They placed it with Congress's powers, and so it should be considered an addition to Congress's powers and justification for an implied powers of Congress doctrine. It justifies the doctrine that Congress may use any appropriate means to carry out the powers given to it in the Constitution, and the use of such a means is implied in its original grant along with the necessary and proper clause.

Was the Second Bank of the United States an appropriate means for implementing one of Congress's enumerated powers? Marshall reasoned that it was. He found a plausible connection with the Bank and Congress's enumerated monetary powers. Once Marshall established that the Bank was constitutional, he went on to assess the powers of a state over the bank. Marshall emphasized that within the exercise of its power, Congress is supreme over the states. The states may not retard, impede, or in any way burden the operation of constitutional laws enacted by Congress. In this case, Maryland had punitively exercised its power to tax in an attempt to retard, impede, and burden the Bank, a valid federal instrumentality. The Maryland tax, therefore, was unconstitutional and void.

Congress. But those areas of commerce that do not require national uniformity may be regulated by the states if there is no congressional regulation or, as in this instance, at the express invitation of Congress. For example, conditions at each harbor and port are different, and local conditions are diverse. Of course, when Congress *does* exercise its commerce power, it is supreme over state law.

During the first half of the nineteenth century, the Supreme Court, in a series of decisions, established supremacy over the state courts when the state courts decided disputes in which a federal claim was raised (a federal claim concerns the federal Constitution, federal law, or a federal treaty). The big issues concerning states' rights and federal supremacy, however, could not be resolved by Court decisions.

Tensions between the South and the North had been rising for years. Deep disagreements over slavery, economic policy, and the principle of federal supremacy erupted in 1861 in the Civil War. On the battlefields were fought out the deepest issues of nation versus states. The nation emerged supreme over the states, the Union victorious over the Confederacy after the bloodiest war in United States history. During the war, President Lincoln exercised power in ways never before exercised. One act of Congress after another strengthened and enhanced federal power. The Civil War and the constitutional amendments that emerged from that period dramatically changed the constitutional nature of American federalism. The Fourteenth Amendment, which became a part of the Constitution in 1868, made the federal government responsible for preventing the states from depriving people of their basic civil rights and liberties. The issue of federal supremacy and whether the United States consisted of sovereign states that were free to leave the Union was resolved. The Union was indissoluble. The national government was supreme within its sphere.

From the Civil War to the Great Depression

After the upheavals of the Civil War, the United States entered an age of rapid industrialization. Economic growth was massive, and so was social change. The federal government's proportion of all domestic governmental spending about doubled between 1840 and 1890. By 1890, close to one-third of all domestic spending in the United States was attributed to the federal government.[5] Between 1860 and 1900, the nation's railroad tracks grew approximately sevenfold, the proportion of people living in cities more than tripled, the number of industrial workers more than quadrupled, and the value of manufactured goods produced in the country more than quintupled. By the start of the twentieth century, the United States had become the greatest industrial nation in the world.

[5]William H. Riker, *The Development of American Federalism* (Boston: Kluwer Academic Publishers, 1987), p. 103.

The overriding questions of public policy during the latter part of the nineteenth century and into the twentieth centered around the relationship of government and business. In what ways and to what extent should government regulate private enterprise? Powerful political forces in the country aimed to minimize government interference with a free-market economy. They took a dim view of government regulation and social legislation. At first, the Supreme Court upheld state regulation of business. But by the last fifteen years of the nineteenth century, the Court changed its tune and formulated a series of doctrines designed to limit state regulatory power. One major doctrine was "freedom of contract," which was based on an interpretation of the Fourteenth Amendment due process clause. It prevented the states from interfering with otherwise lawful contracts freely entered into by private parties. The federal government entered the regulatory sphere in a limited manner and met with mixed success before the Supreme Court.

Once again, wartime broadened the powers of the national government. World War I required national mobilization of men and resources, and so the federal government assumed new powers. For example, it nationalized the railroads. Although it returned the railroads to their private owners at the end of the war, the government stayed on as the railroads' regulator and financial supervisor. It also took half the excess railroad profits to subsidize weaker lines. During the first two decades of the century, the federal government was expected to take responsibility for coping with nationwide problems: conducting the war, regulating nationwide monopolies, and protecting the health and safety of Americans from adulterated foods and dangerous drugs.

The federal government's powers of economic regulation were limited by several doctrines of the Supreme Court. These restrictive doctrines assumed a special significance during the early years of the Great Depression, the most severe economic crisis ever experienced in the United States. During the Depression, it was clear that no one state could adequately deal with massive and nationwide social and economic problems. President Franklin D. Roosevelt devised the New Deal, a group of programs for meeting the economic emergency and based it on Congress's powers of commerce and taxation in Article One, Section Eight. But a conservative Supreme Court used its restrictive doctrines to strike down several major measures of the New Deal.

The Court used the Tenth Amendment ostensibly to protect American federalism. The Tenth Amendment reserves to the states that which has not been delegated to the national government or expressly prohibited. The Court used this to prevent the federal government from regulating in areas of the economy that the Court considered sufficiently local so as to fall within the powers of the states reserved to them under the Tenth Amendment. For example, the nation's farmers were ruined by the Great Depression. In 1933, Roosevelt proposed and Congress passed the Agricultural Adjustment Act to get farmers back on their feet. The act provided for a tax on

President Franklin D. Roosevelt's administration radically transformed American federalism.

the food processors of basic agricultural commodities. The tax money was to be placed in a special fund to be used to compensate farmers who reduced their acreage. The idea was to cut down the supply of agricultural commodities and thereby raise farm prices, but the Court struck down the law on the grounds that agriculture is a local activity:

> The act invades the reserved rights of the states. It is a statutory plan to regulate and control agricultural production, a matter beyond the powers delegated to the federal government.[6]

It mattered not that the problem was nationwide and could not be effectively handled by any one state.

The Supreme Court used similar logic to invalidate federal law that mandated minimum wages and maximum hours. But then the Court struck down New York State's wages and hours legislation as a violation of freedom of contract.[7] With this decision, the Court showed its fidelity not to federalism but to the position that a capitalistic economy should have as little government interference as possible.

In 1935 and 1936, the Supreme Court struck down several key pieces of New Deal legislation. It faced a confrontation with a president reelected by

[6]*U.S.* v. *Butler* (1936).
[7]*Morehead* v. *New York ex rel Tipaldo* (1936).

a landslide and a strongly New Deal Congress. President Roosevelt proposed a court reform package: as many as six new justices could be appointed to the Supreme Court, thus the number of justices could increase to fifteen. The proposal, however, was controversial and Roosevelt was accused of trying to "pack the Court." Even supporters of the New Deal feared the consequences of tampering with the Court. Eventually, the proposal died in Congress. But apparently it had an effect on at least one Supreme Court justice because at the end of March, 1937, the Court, with no change in membership, suddenly began handing down decisions that upheld government economic regulation and social legislation. (Most of these decisions were by a vote of five to four). Major New Deal legislation was upheld. In fact *no* federal economic regulatory legislation was struck down after that confrontation. The Court upheld regulatory legislation and renounced the negative doctrines, including those based on the Tenth Amendment and freedom of contract under the Fourteenth Amendment.

From the Great Depression to the New Federalism of the 1980s

The Great Depression of the 1930s was followed by America's entering World War II. This meant that for some thirteen years, the federal government assumed responsibility for the welfare and safety of the nation, and as a consequence, the machinery of government vastly expanded. By the end of World War II, the federal government had assumed full control over the nation's economy and the social welfare of its citizens. This added up to a constitutional revolution not only in the Supreme Court's interpretation of the Constitution but also in the relationship of the states to the federal government. The Korean War, the Great Society programs of the 1960s, and the Vietnam War all reinforced the primacy and domination of the federal government.

Today most Americans look to Washington to solve critical problems. The federal government has the money to sponsor major programs from food stamps, medical assistance, job training, and other aid for the poor to subsidies to farmers, to disaster relief, to programs for the elderly, to aid to education, and so on. By enacting these major programs, some of which require state participation and cooperation, the federal government sets social welfare policy. By broadly interpreting its commerce and fiscal powers, the federal government regulates the money supply and the banking industry, builds and maintains interstate highways, regulates private enterprise (in such matters as working conditions for employees, air and water pollution control, and control of hazardous wastes), and, in general, sets economic policy for the nation. By the use of its powers and its purse strings the federal government has brought the states into a position of dependency. The states are coerced or induced to follow the bottom line set in Washington. For example, Congress passed a law that tied federal highway aid to raising the drinking age to twenty-one. Federal money is such a powerful inducement that every state that had a lower drinking age raised it.

Before the Civil War, the balance between the federal government and the states tilted toward the states. After the Civil War, it tilted toward the federal government. Today it tilts so dramatically toward the federal government that by the late 1970s some observers considered the state governments to be merely administrative mechanisms for the national government in the areas of economic policy and social welfare. This may be an exaggerated view for it does not acknowledge innovative policies at the state level such as universal health insurance enacted in Massachusetts in 1988.

The balance of federalism not only shifted in matters of economic and social welfare policy, it also shifted in the realm of civil liberties and civil rights (see Chapters Twelve and Thirteen). This shift was precipitated by Supreme Court decisions in the 1950s and 1960s under the leadership of Chief Justice Earl Warren. During this period, the Supreme Court ruled, with only few exceptions, that the civil liberties guaranteed by the first eight amendments to the Constitution against violation by the federal government must also be honored by the states because that is what is mandated by the Fourteenth Amendment.[8] The Warren Court ruled that state sponsored and enforced racial segregation violated the Constitution. By its decisions, the Supreme Court firmly placed the states' treatment of the rights and liberties of their citizens under the supervision of the federal courts and the federal government. In the 1960s and 1970s, Congress followed with several major laws asserting the federal government's protection of people's right not to be discriminated against on account of race, sex, religion, national origin, or age. These decisions and laws reinforced federal domination and put limits on the exercise of state sovereignty.

This profound push towards centralized government and national uniformity at the expense of state sovereignty has not occurred in silence. But many of the voices in favor of states' rights and renewed state sovereignty have often been seen as politically conservative. However, it does not follow that a desire to change the balance of federalism to make the states less dependent on the federal government and to restore some of their sovereign powers must necessarily be tied to a conservative ideology.

The Supreme Court in recent years has flirted with the dilemma that to revitalize federalism by restoring state sovereignty flies in the face of the reality that the federal government has firmly established its responsibility for dealing with the national economy. An example of such flirting occurred in 1976 with the decision in *National League of Cities* v. *Usery*. In defiance of Court precedent, a five to four majority struck down a provision of the Fair Labor Standards Act. In so doing, the Court ruled, for the first time since the mid-1930s, that Congress had exceeded its commerce powers and had invaded the powers of the states reserved to them under the Tenth Amendment (see the box on page 58 for the details).

---

[8]Note that in earlier years some rights in the Bill of Rights had been nationalized. Chapter Twelve discusses these developments.

The Supreme Court Attempts to Salvage State Sovereignty in the National League of Cities Case

The Supreme Court in the 1976 decision of *National League of Cities* v. *Usery* struck down an act of Congress that extended the statutory protection of the Fair Labor Standards Act to state and local government employees performing traditional governmental functions. In particular, these employees were to be subject to federal standards of minimum wages including overtime and maximum hours of employment. Those now covered included fire fighters, law enforcement personnel, sanitation workers, and those employed in public health, recreation, and other state and local activities. But the Court majority ruled that such state and local government workers perform the bottom-line functions of state and local government and this goes to the heart of state sovereignty. We cannot have a federal system of government, argued the majority, if Congress ties the hands of the states as to the wages and hours of those performing these essential jobs. The majority sought to rescue some semblance of state sovereignty so as to prevent Congress from dictating to the states how to make essential decisions with major financial implications.

The dissenters pointed out that there is long-standing precedent in interpreting Congress's commerce power broadly. They also pointed out that it has been forty years since the Court utilized the Tenth Amendment to prevent Congress from exercising national economic and social welfare regulation. Justice Stevens, in a separate dissent, pointed up the wide range of activities of state employees subject to federal regulation and the obvious anomaly of the majority's view. Stevens noted that with the majority's ruling the Court forbade the federal government from interfering "with a sovereign State's inherent right to pay a substandard wage to the janitor at the state capital." Yet under current federal law: "The Federal Government may . . . require the State to act impartially when it hires or fires the janitor, to withhold taxes from his paycheck, to observe safety regulations when he is performing his job, to forbid him from burning too much soft coal in the capital furnace, from dumping untreated refuse in an adjacent waterway, from overloading a state-owned garbage truck, or from driving either the truck or the Governor's limousine over fifty-five miles an hour."

The *National League of Cities* decision created quite a stir in the legal world. The Court majority seemed to be actively interested in protecting state sovereignty, at least at a certain level, but the question really became one of whether the Court was now going to use the Tenth Amendment the same way the pre-1937 Court used it—to restrict the scope of federal economic regulation. In a series of subsequent decisions, the Court, however, made it clear that federal economic regulation under the commerce clause was not threatened by the Court. In one such case, a unanimous Court upheld federal legislation regulating strip mining so as to protect the environment and explicitly noted: "nothing in *National League of Cities* suggests that the Tenth Amendment shields the States from preemptive federal regulation of *private* activities affecting interstate commerce."[1] The Court emphasized that the actions of private business affecting interstate commerce may be regulated solely by the federal government or by a cooperative program between the federal government and the states utilizing federal minimum standards. Nine years after the decision in *National League of Cities,* the Court overturned it by a vote of five to four.

[1] *Hodel* v. *Virginia Surface Mining and Reclamation Association, Inc.,* 452 U.S. 264 at 290–291 (1981).

The Court did not follow through the *National League of Cities* decision with subsequent similar rulings.[9] Finally, in 1985, the Court, again by a five to four vote, overturned *National League of Cities.* The case was *Garcia* v. *San Antonio Metropolitan Transit Authority.*[10] The Court now stressed that Congress's commerce power could not be checked by ambiguous, open-ended conceptions of state sovereignty such as "traditional governmental functions." Rather, it is up to the national political process to determine the limits of Congress's commerce power. The judiciary should not step in and create limitations on federal power.

The Court's decision in *Garcia,* subjecting 13 million state and local government employees to federal wage and hour standards, made it clear that the majority would continue the tradition since 1937 that the Court would not substitute its views for those of Congress in setting economic and social policy for the nation. The balance (or as some suggested, the imbalance) between the federal government and the states was restored. The federal government was told once again that there were virtually no constitutional limits on the exercise of Congress's commerce powers. Many governors, mayors, and other local officials reacted bitterly to the Court's decision and saw it as another nail in the coffin of federalism.[11] The general counsel of the National Governor's Association was quoted as saying "This decision can only lead to a greater exercise of Federal authority and unitary, centralized government."[12] The decision also had practical monetary consequences in that state and local governments would now have to meet federal standards for overtime pay and would be forced to spend more than one billion dollars each year. The *Garcia* majority's instincts were correct, however. The national political process *was* able to successfully deal with this problem. States and localities exerted pressure on Congress and within nine months of the *Garcia* decision Congress enacted a major modification of the law. States and localities no longer have to pay overtime wages. They can substitute time-and-a-half compensatory time-off.[13]

The Reagan administration, like the Nixon administration over a decade earlier, wanted to change the balance of federalism and return responsibility for certain problems to the states and their local subdivisions (cities and towns). This was called, by both Nixon and Reagan, the **New Federalism.** The New Federalism was based on the premise that the founders did not intend to create one national community serviced by a unitary central-

---

[9]See the discussion in Dean Alfange, Jr., "Congressional Regulation of the 'States *Qua* States': From *National League of Cities* to *EEOC* v. *Wyoming,*" in *1983 Supreme Court Review* (Chicago: University of Chicago Press, 1984), pp. 215–81.

[10]See Martha A. Field, *"Garcia* v. *San Antonio Metropolitan Transit Authority:* The Demise of a Misguided Doctrine," *Harvard Law Review,* 99 (1985), pp. 84–118.

[11]See, *New York Times,* Feb. 21, 1985, p. 1.

[12]*New York Times,* Feb. 21, 1985, p. B–8.

[13]See the discussion in *Congressional Quarterly,* November 16, 1985, pp. 2379–80.

President Ronald Reagan revived the issue of federalism in his State of the Union addresses.

ized government. Rather, the essence of the United States is a nation of diverse, smaller communities not only at the state level but the local level as well. This is a pluralistic country of many ethnic and religious backgrounds and political views. The states and localities should be free to formulate their own approaches to many of the problems for which the federal government has assumed responsibility. The people at the grass roots level should be able to make choices about the nature and extent of government services and programs, the extent to which the private sector should be involved in providing services to the public, and the level of taxation to support these programs and services.

Supporters of the New Federalism recognize that national crises such as war and depression require national action. They generally agree that social insurance programs such as Social Security and Medicare require the financial resources of the entire nation and, therefore, are a federal government responsibility (as are national defense and the conduct of foreign policy). But in most other spheres of domestic activity, the New Federalism conceptualizes the United States not as one extended family but as a pluralistic nation of diverse communities, with different needs, different priorities, and capable of devising satisfactory alternative solutions to problems.

A second major premise of the New Federalism is that the federal government, with its centralized, overgrown Washington bureaucracy, is at worst wasteful, inefficient, cumbersome, expensive, intrusive, rigid, uncaring, and insensitive to local needs and interests. This bureaucracy, argue supporters of the New Federalism, has alienated people from government and drawn them to politicians who campaign against the Washington bureaucracy and promise to cut back and better manage the federal government.

There are three main facets to the New Federalism. First is simply the goal of relinquishing federal government responsibility in a wide variety of areas by phasing out or immediately discontinuing federal programs. States would receive some federal money, but it would not be earmarked for particular programs. The states would make their own spending choices. This aspect of the New Federalism has not been successful. Federal programs have champions who come to their rescue. Also, most state and local officials are not enthusiastic about the demise of federal programs that pump federal funds into their states and localities because they see a net loss in federal funds resulting from the New Federalism.

A second facet of the New Federalism is to cut federal spending on most domestic programs. Although the cuts made in the 1980s were a response to the record-breaking federal deficits, the cuts were also consistent with the New Federalism philosophy of diminishing the federal government's responsibility. During the Reagan administration, the proportion of state and local revenue accounted for by federal aid actually did drop. In 1979, about twenty-three percent came from the federal government, but by 1987 federal aid had fallen to about sixteen percent. In the New Federalism, the states regain their sovereign powers because they, not the federal government, make decisions about taxing and spending.[14]

A third facet of the New Federalism is deregulation, that is, a move toward ending federal regulation over industry. There are two reasons behind deregulation. The end of regulation in some industries is thought to inspire competition and result in more efficiency, better service, and lower prices for consumers. This view was behind the deregulation of the airlines which actually began before the Reagan administration. Deregulation also aims to transfer power to the states. In some industries, deregulation means that there is no regulation by any level of government. The states cannot regulate oil industry prices and air fares, for example. But in other industries, federal deregulation can transfer authority to the states. In late 1985, for example, the Reagan administration abolished the Minimum Property Standards, the housing construction code of the Federal Housing Administration. In place of federal construction standards, state and local construction codes took effect. State and local governments assumed responsibility for the health, safety, livability, and durability of housing construction. This change did not occur without controversy or without worries about whether federal housing inspectors with responsibility for feder-

[14]See Richard P. Nathan and Martha Derthick, "Reagan's Legacy: A New Liberalism Among the States," *New York Times,* December 18, 1987, p. A–39.

ally assisted housing projects would be capable of mastering the thousands of local construction codes.[15]

In the areas of economic and social welfare, advocates of the New Federalism want less federal and more state responsibility. But most states while responding to some extent to federal spending cuts have not moved in the direction of greater responsiveness on economic and social welfare issues.[16] Critics argue that the New Federalism is nothing more than a semantic camouflage for highly conservative policy-making.

The New Federalism also took aim at the federal courts in the realm of civil rights and civil liberties. The Reagan administration advocated a reduced role for the federal courts in the supervision of civil rights and civil liberties in the states. Attorney General Edwin Meese went so far as to suggest that Court decisions going back more than half a century were wrong in interpreting the Fourteenth Amendment as incorporating certain specific guarantees of the Bill of Rights and therefore wrong in requiring the states to respect those rights.[17] The New Federalism presumably respects the right of states to legislate or of their highest courts to interpret state constitutions in ways that give their citizens more rights than under the federal constitution. However, the New Federalism of the Reagan administration became identified with weakened civil rights and civil liberties under the federal constitution. As a result, in the early 1980s, civil liberties groups began looking to the state supreme courts to interpret state constitutions in ways protecting if not expanding civil rights and civil liberties.[18]

Supporters of the New Federalism are not known to favor liberal civil libertarian policies at the state level. For example, they are opposed to abortion. Were the United States Supreme Court to overturn its abortion ruling from 1973, the decision whether to legalize abortion would be left to each state. It is clear that New Federalism advocates would oppose permissive state laws. The same can be said for such policies as affirmative action for women and minorities at the workplace and in educational institutions, the outlawing of prayer in the public schools, busing for the purpose of desegregating the public schools, and excluding illegally obtained evidence from a trial.

To some, then, the New Federalism is a sincere effort to revitalize the federal system and infuse new responsibilities in the states and localities. To others, it is a cover for a conservative political ideology and social agenda. Federalism is far from an abstract topic of government. It goes to the heart of American politics.

---

[15]*New York Times,* August 18, 1985, p. 1.

[16]*New York Times,* May 19, 1985, p. 1. Also see Richard P. Nathan, Fred C. Doolittle, and Associates, *Reagan and the States* (Princeton: Princeton University Press, 1987).

[17]*New York Times,* August 3, 1985, p. 7. See Edwin Meese III, "Toward a Jurisprudence of Original Intention," *Public Administration Review,* 45 (1985), pp. 701–4.

[18]Susan P. Fino, *The Role of State Supreme Courts in the New Judicial Federalism* (Westport, Conn.: Greenwood, 1987).

FEDERALISM IN PRACTICE

Having seen how federalism has grown and changed over the course of American history, this chapter now examines its workings in somewhat greater detail, such as federal-state and interstate relations, the Supreme Court's role as arbiter in the American federal system, and state-local relationships.

Federal-State Relations

As shown earlier in this chapter, the long-range trend in American history has been for power to flow to the federal government and for the federal government to assume responsibility for problems considered nationwide in scope. But at the same time, the states and local governments have increased the scope of *their* endeavors as they have worked with the federal government in new areas of activity. For example, the federal government and the states cooperate in providing health care for the poor (the Medicaid program). During this century, *all* levels of government have spent more and more money and engaged in more and more activities. To be sure, governments at all levels have increased their activity in response to public demands.

The foundation of federal-state relations, which was set in earnest during the New Deal and was reinforced and expanded under the Great Society programs of the 1960s, is called **fiscal federalism.** This is federalism fueled by money distributed by the federal government to state and local governments in typically complex ways. Fiscal federalism also describes state transfer of funds to local governments. The amount of revenue involved is many billions of dollars and involves a myriad of programs.

A distinguishing feature of fiscal federalism has been the growing dependency of the states and localities on federal money. The proportion of state and local revenue contributed by the federal government was about one percent in 1929. By 1979, that had multiplied more than seventeen-fold.[19] As shown in Exhibit 2.1, under the New Federalism in the 1980s, that percentage decreased. Even so, in absolute dollars, many billions are involved. The states and localities are still dependent on the federal government for over sixteen percent of their revenues (in 1987 this amounted to close to $104 billion). In 1929, the federal government spent $6 for every man, woman, and child in the United States in aid to the states and localities. By 1939, the per capita expenditure reached $60 and by 1964 it was $165. The 1964 figure more than doubled in only ten years. As shown in

---

[19]See Russell L. Hanson, "The Intergovernmental Setting of State Politics," in Virginia Gray, Herbert Jacob, and Kenneth N. Vines, eds., *Politics in the American States,* 4th ed., (Boston: Little, Brown and Co., 1983), pp. 27–56, and Thomas J. Anton, *American Federalism and Public Policy* (New York: Random House, 1989), chap. 6.

EXHIBIT 2.1	Federal Aid Per Capita and as Percent of All State and Local Receipts After Federal Aid, Selected Years, 1929–1987

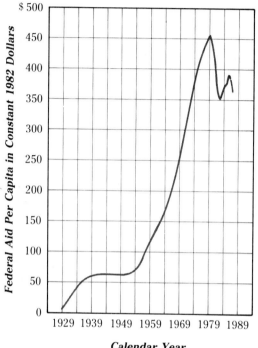

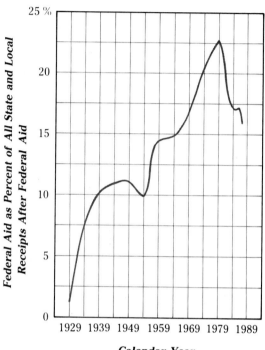

Calendar Year

Calendar Year

Calendar Year	Federal Aid Per Capita in Constant 1982 Dollars	Federal Aid as Percent of All State and Local Receipts After Federal Aid
1929	$ 6	1.3%
1939	60	10.4
1949	63	11.3
1954	68	10.0
1959	126	14.6
1964	165	14.9
1969	252	16.8
1974	380	20.6
1979	455	22.7
1981	406	20.7
1982	361	18.7
1983	353	17.7
1984	367	17.3
1985	375	17.2
1986	388	17.3
1987	362	16.1

Source: Advisory Commission on Intergovernmental Relations, *Significant Features of Fiscal Federalism, 1988 Edition,* Vol. 1 (Washington, D.C.: U.S. Government Printing Office, 1987), pp. 6, 7.

Exhibit 2.1, the per capita expenditure reached a peak of $455 in 1979. Under the Reagan administration, the per capita expenditure decreased, but the 1987 per capita expenditure of $362 was nevertheless (taking inflation into account) over six times that of which was spent during the Great Depression of the 1930s!

There have been three major types of federal financial assistance to the states and localities: categorical grants, block grants, and general revenue sharing.

Categorical grants are the traditional form of federal grants. They are targeted for specific programs and must be spent according to federal agency specifications. Historically, one of the most famous examples of categorical grants is the Morrill Land Grant Act of 1862, which granted federal land to the states for the establishment of public colleges that would teach agriculture, the mechanical arts, and military science. Today well over three out of four dollars given to the states are in the form of categorical grants for specific programs. States, localities, and in some instances private agencies are eligible to compete for funds. A special kind of categorical grant is the categorical formula grant awarded to all those eligible according to a formula. Typically, the state or local government has to contribute financially, have its plans approved in advance, and be subject to federal inspection and supervision. Elementary and secondary education programs, for example, have been categorical formula grant programs.

Categorical grants have fostered special types of intergovernmental relationships and have caused major policy problems. Problems have arisen because Congress has enacted a multitude of grant programs (in 1987 there were 422), each meant to address a specific problem. To begin with, policy is fragmented at the federal level. The grant programs are administered by a variety of federal agencies and bureaus. There is little policy coordination among the federal agencies, and each grant program is administered separately. Aid for the poor is an example. The Food Stamp program is administered by the Department of Agriculture but various other programs are administered by different governmental agencies.

The special project grant is awarded by a particular federal agency to a state or local governmental agency. The state or local agency works closely with the federal agency and is so financially tied that its frame of political reference becomes the federal agency (its patron). Those that benefit from the program lobby for continued federal governmental support and a perpetuation of the state and federal relationship. The state or local agency has little incentive to cooperate with the governor or mayor in setting broad policy. The result is a lack of policy coordination as each state or local agency develops its own symbiotic relationship with a federal agency administering a categorical grant program. This has been dubbed **picket-fence federalism.**[20] That is, the grant program ties a state or local agency

[20]See Deil S. Wright, *Understanding Intergovernmental Relations: Public Policy and Participants' Perspectives in Local, State, and National Governments* (North Scituate, Mass.: Duxbury Press, 1978), pp. 61–63.

to a federal agency, and together they exercise power and responsibility in a particular policy area. Thus, public policy in state and local government is dominated to a significant extent not by elected government officials but by fiscal pickets, each based on a different grant program and each involving a different coalition of state or local agencies, federal agencies, and vested interests who benefit from the grants.

The Nixon administration began to emphasize alternative federal aid programs, block grants, and general revenue sharing to solve the policy problems of categorical grants. Also, conservatives in the states opposed some of the liberal federal programs that had program policy dictated from Washington. The idea behind these alternatives was to move away from narrow categories of projects to financing that gave states more discretion and responsibility for expenditures, and, in the process, gave state and local governments more influence as well.

Block grants were (and are) designed for a broad policy sphere. Ordinarily, governments interested in block grants have to construct a proposal of how the money will be spent. Some block grants go directly to the states and much of the money is then funneled to the cities, towns, or counties where the various projects or programs are to be carried out. The Reagan administration preferred block grants to other federal aid programs in part because they eliminate some paperwork, undermine picket-fence federalism, and give the states more authority and discretion. The Reagan administration also used the block grant approach to consolidate a variety of separate grant programs. Block grants have been common in the health, social services, and law-enforcement areas.

General revenue sharing was a popular program for providing funds directly to local governments with no strings attached. The program originated during the Nixon administration in 1972 and originally also included the states. In 1980, the states were excluded and the money was earmarked exclusively for local governments. Major cities received most of the funds. But the Reagan administration, in its effort to reduce the federal budget deficit, eliminated general revenue sharing that had sent some $4.6 billion back to the localities each year. In 1986, the last year of general revenue sharing, some $4 billion was distributed to 39,000 local governments.

Federal-state and federal-local governmental relationships remain complex. The federal government has assumed responsibility for a wide variety of domestic economic and social concerns. It is active in regulating and financing a wide array of programs in the states and localities, meeting with some degree of success.[21]

---

[21]See Paul E. Peterson, Barry G. Rabe, and Kenneth K. Wong, *When Federalism Works* (Washington: Brookings, 1986).

Interstate Relations

Federalism includes not only the relationships between the federal government and the states but also the relationships *between* the states. Article Four of the Constitution, along with certain provisions in Articles One and Three, states the minimum constitutional requirements of interstate relationships. The most important constitutional requirement is that "Full faith and credit shall be given in each State to the public acts, records, and judicial proceedings of every other State." Congress is authorized to implement this and in fact did so for public records and judicial proceedings by legislation enacted in 1790. Supreme Court decisions undermined this guarantee, however.

In 1839, the Supreme Court ruled that the full faith and credit guarantee of Article Four, Section One, was not intended to turn one state into an automatic enforcer of another state's civil law. There was no intent to "materially . . . interfere with the essential attributes" of the law of the forum states upon whom the full faith and credit claim is being pressed.[22] Rather, when the judgment of a court of one state is being pursued in a second state, there must be a new case brought under and governed by the laws of the second state. The second state must have jurisdiction over the litigant, otherwise there may be a violation of due process.[23] The full faith and credit clause therefore does not mean automatic enforcement of one state's laws and court judgments in another state particularly if the other state's law conflicts with the first state's. Good faith rather than *full* faith is expected in the treatment of other state's laws and court judgments.

Divorce and child custody law have raised special problems in the relations among states. Consider this example, a true account.[24] Mark was living in his home state of Ohio when he met Taciana, a young woman originally from Brazil. They fell in love, were married, moved to New York City, and had a son, Christian. When the boy was about six months old, in January, 1987, Mark and Taciana separated and a New York court gave Taciana custody of Christian. The court's decision greatly disturbed Mark and he soon took Christian and left for his native Ohio where Mark's family still lived.

Mark instituted divorce proceedings in an Ohio court, a divorce was granted, and Mark was given custody of Christian. Taciana had visiting rights and during one visit she took her son and returned to New York. Mark sent private investigators to New York who threatened Taciana with arrest unless she surrendered Christian. Taciana fled New York for Northampton,

---

[22]*McElmoyle* v. *Cohen,* 13 Peters 312 at 326 as cited in *Edward S. Corwin's The Constitution and What it Means Today,* revised by Harold W. Chase and Craig R. Ducat (Princeton, New Jersey: Princeton University Press, 1973), p. 200.

[23]*McGee* v. *International Life Insurance Co.* (1957) as cited in *Corwin's The Constitution,* p. 202.

[24]This account is drawn from the *Daily Hampshire Gazette,* July 15, 1988, pp. 1, 20, and February 4, 1989, p. 3.

Massachusetts in October, 1987. The private investigators located her in November and Mark came to Northampton, confronted her at a downtown store, and roughed her up in the process. Mark called the F.B.I. and an agent arrested Taciana for taking Christian from Ohio. That charge was soon dropped when Taciana produced the earlier New York court ruling giving *her* custody. Taciana, in return, brought assault charges against Mark, he was found guilty by a Massachusetts court, and Mark was ordered to stay away from Taciana and Christian. The judge gave Taciana temporary custody of Christian and he ordered her not to leave Massachusetts until he made a final decision as to custody.

Mark was desperate to see his son and Taciana relented, agreeing to visits under the supervision of a visitation service. During one of these visits, on July 9, 1988, Mark took Christian, intending to take him back to Ohio. Instead he was arrested at the airport in Connecticut on kidnapping charges. Mark was returned to Massachusetts and in February 1989 entered a plea of guilty to reduced charges and was sentenced to ten days in jail and fined $1,250.

In the past, the United States Supreme Court had difficulty with such issues.[25] In 1948, the Court ruled that a divorce granted in one state (for example, to Mark in Ohio) in which one of the parties (Taciana) lives outside that state is nevertheless a valid divorce to be recognized by all states provided that the out-of-state party was given notice and an opportunity to appear in court. However, matters of alimony and child custody can only be decided when the spouse and the child reside within the geographic boundaries of the court.[26] Taciana had received notice and an opportunity to appear in the Ohio court. But New York's ruling on child custody carried little weight in Ohio because Christian was living in Ohio and not New York. This case became more complicated when Taciana took Christian to Massachusetts. The Massachusetts, New York, and Ohio court decisions were in conflict.

Congress has the power under Article Four, Section One, to prevent such clashes between state laws and state courts, but Congress has yet to use it. Congress could declare that a state law that provides certain standards for granting a divorce, the awarding of alimony, the division of property, and child custody shall be given full faith and credit in all states and be recognized and enforced in all state courts. In fact, Congress probably could correct many of the anomalies of federalism like the examples given at the beginning of this chapter and Mark and Taciana's plight simply by using its power to enforce the full faith and credit guarantee of the Constitution. That Congress has not even considered so acting can be explained by the persistence of federalism and notions of state sovereignty.

The Constitution requires (Article Four, Section Two) that persons who are charged with a crime in one state and flee to another state be returned

---

[25]See the discussion in *Corwin's The Constitution,* pp. 202–4.
[26]*Estin* v. *Estin* (1948) as cited in *Corwin's The Constitution,* p. 204.

The George
Washington Bridge
links New York and
New Jersey, and its
administration is an
example of
interstate
cooperation.

to the state where they committed the crime when the governor of that state so requests it. Congress, in 1793, enacted a law implementing this provision. The Supreme Court later ruled, however, that the governor of the state to which the accused fled had a legal duty to return (or **extradite**) the person but was not legally compelled to do so.[27] In practice, however, the states either through formal (written) or informal agreement with one another cooperate in this matter and it is unusual for a governor to refuse a request for extradition. In the example of Mark and Taciana, Mark was arrested in Connecticut for kidnapping but the charges were dropped and he was returned to Massachusetts to let the Massachusetts justice system deal with him.

The Constitution in two other articles specifies other aspects of interstate relations. In Article Three, Section Two, disputes between or among

[27]*Kentucky* v. *Dennison* (1861) as cited in *Corwin's The Constitution,* p. 211.

states are to be resolved by the United States Supreme Court. The most common dispute is over boundaries. Article One, Section Ten, specifies that no state shall enter into any agreement or compact with another state without the consent of Congress.

Over the past half century, interstate compacts or agreements have been frequent, though some agreements date from the 1800s. For example, New York and New Jersey began a series of compacts in 1834 concerning use of the waters between both states. In 1921, these states created the Port of New York Authority, which has served as a model of interstate cooperation. The Port Authority runs the harbors and airports as well as the bridges, tunnels, and a commuter railroad line between the two states. In recent years, states have entered into compacts covering such concerns as pollution control, protection of the environment and natural resources, energy resources, interstate navigation and other means of transportation, and law enforcement. Some compacts involve an entire region. Yet what makes interstate compacts significant is their relative lack of federal government involvement and, in some instances, the fact that the states took the initiative before the federal government was moved to act. In recent years, this has given a boost to federalism.

The states also cooperate and communicate through nationwide organizations of various state and local officials such as the National Governor's Association, the National League of Cities, and the United States Conference of Mayors. These national organizations facilitate the sharing of information among state and local officials and they also lobby on behalf of the states in the nation's capital.

Supreme Court as Arbiter

The Supreme Court is the ultimate umpire of the federal system. It decides disputes between the national government and the states and among the states themselves. In the spheres of government regulation of the economy and social welfare, Supreme Court decisions since 1937 have upheld national government regulation as well as federal supremacy over state activity in the regulatory sphere. The Court upholds the national interest by finding a state statute or activity in conflict with federal law. Where no federal law is directly involved, the Court may find that the state activity adversely affects a federal power or a national interest that is within the federal government's power to protect. This has happened primarily in the state economic regulatory sphere.

In general, it has been state commerce regulation that has produced the most litigation before the Supreme Court. Where the state's regulation resulted in a gain for the state or in-state businesses at the expense of other states or out-of-state businesses, or if the regulation was clearly a burden on interstate commerce, the Court has taken a dim view of such state legislation. But if the state regulation was primarily an inspection or safety law not in conflict with an act of Congress, the Court has been more generous.

An example of the latter instance is a case decided soon after the Court's turnabout in 1937 when the Court was demonstrating its newfound sympathy for state regulation. The state of South Carolina passed a law prohibiting the use of state highways to trucks wider than 90 inches and weighing more than 20,000 pounds. The South Carolina legislature considered the law essential for highway safety (keep in mind that this was before the era of the superhighway and interstate road network). The federal district court found that the statute unreasonably burdened interstate commerce. The Supreme Court disagreed, however—that is, it reversed the lower court's decision. The Court said that the law applied to all trucking and was a reasonable regulation made in the interest of highway safety that was enacted in the absence of congressional regulation.[28]

Most state commerce regulations, however, have been struck down when they could substantially interfere with interstate commerce. For example, in a 1945 decision, the Court invalidated the Arizona Train Limit Law of 1912. This law limited the size of railroad trains operating within Arizona to fourteen passenger or seventy freight cars.[29] The state had originally passed the law as a safety measure, but the Supreme Court saw it as unduly burdening interstate commerce. To be sure, there may be valid safety considerations in the length of passenger and freight trains, but, the Court noted, train length limits need to be uniform throughout the country and therefore must be set by the federal government.

A more recent example concerning state commerce regulation is a 1978 decision which involved a New Jersey health and environmental safety measure that, with few exceptions, prohibited the importation of garbage into the state. That is, privately owned garbage dumps could not continue their profitable business of receiving out-of-state garbage. New Jersey officials argued that out-of-state garbage including chemical waste created environmental hazards on New Jersey roads. They were also concerned with the decreased amount of landfill available for native garbage that could pose a health problem. The state's officials argued that garbage was not commerce and had no value. The Supreme Court, however, gave a broad reading to Congress's powers under the commerce clause. It ruled that the commerce clause applied to the interstate transportation of garbage. It also ruled that in the absence of congressional regulation, New Jersey could not discriminate against articles of commerce, including garbage, that came from outside the state unless there was some legitimate reason, apart from origin, for different treatment. This was protectionist legislation forbidden by the commerce clause.[30]

The Supreme Court also acts as arbiter when states are involved in boundary or resource (for example, water or oil) disputes with each other

[28]*South Carolina State Highway Dept.* v. *Barnwell Bros.* (1938).
[29]*Southern Pacific Railroad* v. *Arizona.*
[30]*City of Philadelphia* v. *New Jersey* (1978).

or with the federal government. Usually, the Court appoints a **special master,** someone who is given legal authority to conduct hearings, gather expert testimony, consider the claims of all parties, and make a report to the Court with recommendations for the resolution of the dispute. The special master's report is usually adopted by the Court.

With regard to civil rights and civil liberties, the Court has tended to be expansive since 1937. It has imposed restraints on the actions of both the national government and the states; for example, those arrested for suspected criminal activity must be read their rights. Although the Burger and Rehnquist Courts scaled back several areas of civil liberties including the rights of those accused of crime (this is considered in Chapter Twelve), the common thread since 1937, with few exceptions, has been to have uniform bottom-line standards of rights and liberties applicable nationwide.

Obscenity law is one area of civil liberties in which the Supreme Court recognized the value of federalism. It is difficult to define obscenity with precision. After several earlier rulings, the Court in 1973 ruled that each locality could decide for itself what it determined to be legally obscene so long as its definition did not stretch beyond reason to censor clearly non-obscene matter.[31]

The recent Court has also, on occasion, been sympathetic to the states in some other areas in which they have been challenged on civil rights or civil liberties grounds. For example, the Court rejected a challenge to the method of state financing of public education by use of property taxes.[32] This meant that poor school districts would continue to have far less money to spend on their school systems than wealthier districts. This inequality did not violate the Constitution. On the other side of the coin, the Court has continued the **adequate state ground doctrine.** According to this doctrine, state court decisions based solely on state law (statutory or constitutional) which grants more rights than under federal law and which does not conflict with federal law will not be struck down by the Supreme Court.[33] For some state supreme courts, the adequate state ground doctrine has motivated them to breathe new life into their state constitutions and to revitalize federalism.[34]

---

[31]See *Miller* v. *California* (1973), *Paris Adult Theatre* v. *Slaton* (1973), and *Jenkins* v. *Georgia* (1974).

[32]*San Antonio Independent School District* v. *Rodriguez* (1973).

[33]See *PruneYard Shopping Center* v. *Robins* (1980).

[34]See *The National Law Journal,* March 12, 1984, pp. 25–32; *New York Times,* May 4, 1986, p. 1; Fino, *op. cit..* But cf., Barry Latzer, "Limits of the New Federalism: State Court Responses," *Search and Seizure Law Report,* 14 (1987), pp. 89–95 and his *The New Judicial Federalism and Criminal Justice* (Westport, Conn.: Greenwood Press, 1989). In general, see G. Alan Tarr and Mary C. Porter, *State Supreme Courts in State and Nation* (New Haven: Yale University Press, 1988) and Stanley Friedelbaum, ed., *Human Rights in the States* (Westport, Conn.: Greenwood Press, 1988).

State-Local Relationships

One aspect of federalism was not considered in the federal constitution but plays a part in federalism: the state-local relationship. In one sense it can be argued that this is not federalism at all because counties, cities, and towns are the legal creations of the state, subject to absolute control by the states. The state grants local government its local lawmaking powers including its powers of taxation. Local government units are not, have not claimed to be, and in theory have not been deemed to be sovereign. The state-local relationship is that of a unitary centralized government, not a constitutionally based federal system, but the political reality is that local governments are more than mere administrative mechanisms for state control.

The state-local political relationship has analogies to the federal-state political relationship. Elections to the state legislature are by district and this fact increases the political clout of the localities, particularly the large cities. Governors must run for election and must build their coalitions from the localities. Interest groups may be locally based and promote local interests. Furthermore, some localities, particularly the major cities in the states, have direct relationships with agencies or bureaus of the federal government that may pump millions of dollars into those localities. This financial tie with the federal government, perhaps supplemented by close relationships with members of congress representing the metropolitan area, may give the locality a measure of political independence. Furthermore, state politicians with ambitions to national office try not to alienate local interests. Finally, the American tradition of local self-government and the ethic of grass-roots democracy are powerful symbols in the state-local relationship. Thus although legally the state-local relationship is unitary, politically and functionally it is closer to the federalism model.

STATE GOVERNMENT

So far, this chapter has examined the relationship of the federal government to the states in our system of federalism. But what about state government? All fifty states have state governments that resemble, in varying degrees, the institutions of government at the national level. The executive, legislative, and judicial branches of state government are separate and distinct, and the concepts of separation of powers and checks and balances are built into state government in the fifty state constitutions.

The Executive

The chief executive officer in each of the fifty states is the governor. Like the president, the governor can be a dominant political force. Like the presidency, the governorship has gained in stature and powers over the years. Governors now are elected by the people, although when the federal constitution was adopted, they were selected by the legislature and in ten of the original thirteen states for terms of only one year. Within forty years after 1788, selection of the governor was shifted to popular elections, and over the years the term of office has increased. Today, forty-seven states have four-year terms of office; the rest have two-year terms. Another similarity with the presidency is that once a two-term limit became part of the federal constitution in 1951, the states began restricting governors to two terms as well. By 1987, some twenty-five states had a two-term limit. Four other states do not permit consecutive reelection. This points up the fact that the American federal system is constructed of components with institutional similarities.

The executive branch at the state level also has faced administrative growth like that on the national level. With new problems arising at the state level, state boards, agencies, and commissions have been created sometimes independent of the governor. The governor must govern—that is, create and coordinate policy, manage the affairs of state, and chart a course that brings the state the greatest economic benefits from the federal government.

In some formal powers, governors have greater flexibility than a president; in others, less. They have less flexibility in that in most states, key executive branch officers such as the lieutenant governor, attorney general, treasurer, and state secretary of state are independently elected to office. This makes coordinated policy-making more difficult. So does the practice of picket-fence federalism, as described earlier in this chapter. But governors have more flexibility than the president in being able to **line item veto** specific parts of state laws such as particular items in a budget bill. When the governor exercises the line item veto, that particular item is vetoed but not the rest of the legislation (forty-three states allow this). To override the line item veto, twenty-nine states require a minimum three-fifths vote of the legislature and the remainder require a majority.

Scholars of the office of governor have analyzed different states' allocation of powers to the governor in terms of appointments to state office, control over the budget, ability to organize or reorganize within the executive branch, formal veto power, and maximum tenure in office allowed under state law. To be sure, there are some major differences on these dimensions across the fifty states. According to one scholar, Thad L. Beyle, and as seen in Exhibit 2.2, eight states have governors with very strong formal powers, fifteen can be classified as having strong governors' offices, twenty-one have moderate powers, and six have weak powers.[35] The strongest governorships tend to be those in the larger, wealthier, urbanized states in which there is active party competition.

The nation's governors formed the National Governor's Association which actively lobbies on Capitol Hill on behalf of the states. Over half the

[35]Thad L. Beyle, "Governors," in Virginia Gray, Herbert Jacob, and Kenneth N. Vines, eds., *Politics in the American States,* Fourth Edition (Boston: Little, Brown and Company, 1983), p. 202.

EXHIBIT 2.2	VERY STRONG GOVERNORS (8)	STRONG GOVERNORS (15)	MODERATE POWER GOVERNORS (21)	WEAK GOVERNORS (6)

States with Governors Whose Formal Powers Range from Very Strong to Weak	1. New Jersey
	   Pennsylvania
	   Utah
	2. Hawaii
	   Maryland
	   Massachusetts
	   Minnesota
	3. New York
		1. Alaska
		   Maine
		   Montana
		   Tennessee
		2. Arizona
		   Colorado
		   Delaware
		   Idaho
		   Iowa
		3. California
		   Connecticut
		   Illinois
		   Michigan
		   South Dakota
		   Wyoming
			1. Indiana
			   Oregon
			   Rhode Island
			   Vermont
			2. Alabama
			   Arkansas
			   New Mexico
			   Oklahoma
			   Washington
			3. Florida
			   Georgia
			   Kansas
			   Kentucky
			   Louisiana
			   North Dakota
			   West Virginia
			4. Missouri
			   Nebraska
			   Ohio
			   Virginia
			   Wisconsin
				Mississippi
				Texas
				South Carolina
				New Hampshire
				North Carolina
				Nevada

Source: These classifications are those of Thad L. Beyle and are based on an analysis of the formal powers of governors he conducted in "Governors," in Virginia Gray, Herbert Jacob, and Kenneth N. Vines, eds., *Politics in the American States,* Fourth Edition (Boston: Little, Brown and Company, 1983), pp. 202, 454–59. Beyle considered the appointive powers of the governors in a maximum of forty-six functions and offices in each state, the governors' budget-making and organizational powers, and each governor's veto powers. The states are listed in order of the governor's powers from the governors with the most formal powers to the governors with the least power. Within each ranking of states, the states are listed in alphabetical order. For example, the first ranking states under the *Very Strong* category are New Jersey, Pennsylvania, and Utah, which means that the governors of these states all have similar very strong formal powers.

states have individual offices in Washington to assist in lobbying Congress and in pursuing federal money. Governors are typically involved in these activities which reflect the balance (or, perhaps, imbalance) in American federalism.

The Legislatures

The legislatures of the fifty states, much like the states themselves, are in many ways similar and in many ways dissimilar. Their dissimilarities stem from their geography, natural resources and industrial development, ethnic makeup of the citizenry, and their political traditions. Except for Nebraska, the state legislatures have two houses (Nebraska has one). Over ninety percent of the elections to the legislatures are from single member districts. In thirty states, *all* lower house representatives are elected from single member districts. Thirty-eight states elect *all* their senate members this way.[36] Because the electoral system works on a winner takes all basis, the majority party's representation in the state legislature is larger than its statewide vote totals. That is, the party that wins by a margin of 51 percent of the votes in a single member district wins 100 percent of the seat. Of course, the votes of the statewide majority and minority parties differ by district, a reflection of local bases of electoral strength. But, in general, the party that gathers 55 to 60 percent of the votes statewide reaps 65 to 70 percent of the seats in the legislature.

In recent years, the federal courts have profoundly influenced state legislatures because of the Supreme Court's reapportionment policy. In 1962, the Supreme Court ruled in **Baker v. Carr** that malapportioned state legislative districts raised a constitutional issue that could be litigated in the federal courts. Malapportioned districts are those in which there is disparity in the number of voters within different legislative districts. For example, district A contains 25,000 people and elects one representative while district B has 50,000 people in it and also elects one representative. The vote in district A is worth twice that of the vote in district B. Two years after the *Baker* ruling, the Court in **Reynolds v. Sims** announced its reapportionment policy, that of one-person-one-vote, and applied it to both houses of state legislatures. Population, said the Court, must be the basis for legislative representation, and no longer could the sparsely populated rural districts of a state dominate the legislature. Electoral districts must be equally apportioned on the basis of population as determined by the latest available census. These rulings produced a flurry of activity in state and federal courts. By 1967, all states had been reapportioned on the basis of the 1960 census. After the 1970 and 1980 census, the states again reapportioned on the basis of population.

Reapportionment changed the state legislatures.[37] Almost immediately there was a dramatic increase in the number of representatives from urban and suburban areas. New members tended to be younger, better-educated, and from more diverse ethnic backgrounds than old members. More blacks and women became legislators as redistricting opened up new opportunities during a period when blacks and women were demanding equality. As more legislators came from urban and suburban areas, state legislatures became more responsive to metropolitan area problems. In the North, reapportionment tended to favor the Democratic party; in the South, it favored the Republican party. Reapportionment also tended to increase party competition, at least in the elections immediately following redistricting.

---

[36]See Samuel C. Patterson, "Legislators and Legislatures in the American States," in Virginia Gray, Herbert Jacob, and Kenneth N. Vines, *Politics in the American States* (Boston: Little, Brown and Company, 1983), pp. 140–41.

[37]Timothy G. O'Rourke, *The Impact of Reapportionment* (New Brunswick, N.J.: Transaction Books, 1980). Also see, Roger A. Hanson and Robert E. Crew, Jr., "The Policy Impact of Reapportionment," *Law and Society Review,* 8 (Fall, 1973), pp. 69–94.

State legislatures also draw congressional district lines, and congressional districts must also be apportioned under the one-person-one-vote standard. After each census, states may gain or lose representatives if they have gained or lost population compared to the rest of the country. After the 1980 census, trends that had begun earlier were dramatically demonstrated. The Northeast lost while the Sun Belt states of the South and West made impressive gains. These changes affected congressional and state legislative redistricting. Redistricting had to reflect both population increases or decreases and population shifts within the state (for example, from city to suburb).

Turning attention to legislative elections themselves, it is apparent that incumbents have the edge in legislative elections and, since the mid-1960s, more incumbents have run.[38] At the same time, there has been a decline in competition in legislative primaries; most primaries are uncontested.[39] When incumbents run for reelection, and most do, the odds are overwhelmingly in their favor—about nine out of ten incumbents are returned to office.[40]

In general, highly politically competitive state legislative elections occur in only a relatively small proportion of elections. One study of the 1970s revealed that in thirty-two states the winners won by more than sixty percent of the vote in a majority of legislative districts.[41] Most legislative districts are "safe" for either the Democratic or Republican parties. At the state legislative level itself, in most states the party in control of the legislature controls by more than fifty-five percent of the seats. This does not, however, mean that state governments are necessarily politically homogeneous. In fact, divided government with the governor of one party and the legislature of the opposing party has occurred with some frequency. In 1989, for example, thirty-one governors had legislatures in which the opposing party controlled at least one of the houses.[42]

All the state legislatures, with the exception of Nebraska (whose legislature is legally nonpartisan), are organized by either the Democratic or Republican party. Exhibit 2.3 lists for 1989 the twenty-eight states in which the Democrats controlled both houses of the state legislature, the eight states in which Republicans controlled both houses, and the thirteen states in which there was divided partisan control of the legislatures. The level of partisanship differs among the states as do the powers of the speaker of the house and the senate president. In some states, the speakership is an im-

[38]Patterson, *op. cit.,* p. 152.

[39]Patterson, *op. cit.,* p. 149.

[40]Malcolm E. Jewell, *Representation in State Legislatures* (Lexington, Kentucky: University Press of Kentucky, 1982), pp. 27, 43, 45, 46.

[41]Craig H. Grau, "The Neglected World of State Legislative Elections." Paper presented at the Annual Meeting of the Midwest Political Science Association, Cincinnati, Ohio, 1981, pp. 9–11 as cited in Patterson, *op. cit.,* p. 149.

[42]*Congressional Quarterly,* November 19, 1988, p. 3372.

EXHIBIT 2.3   Partisan Control of State Legislatures in 1989

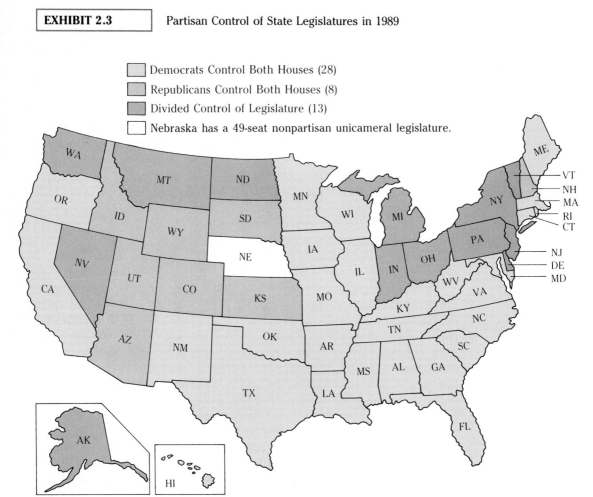

Democrats Control Both Houses (28)
Republicans Control Both Houses (8)
Divided Control of Legislature (13)
Nebraska has a 49-seat nonpartisan unicameral legislature.

Source: Election returns as reported in *Congressional Quarterly,* November 19, 1988, pp. 3372–73.

mensely powerful position, as it is in California and Massachusetts. In others it is less so, in part, because of a tradition of rotation in office (as it is, for example, in Florida and North Dakota). The speaker of the house is the presiding officer and may have the power to name committee chairs, committee members, and subordinate leadership positions. The speaker may control the movement of legislation through the house because the key chairpersons are allies of and beholden to the speaker.

In the state senates, the presiding officer is the senate president (the one exception is Tennessee where this officer is called the speaker). The lieutenant governor fills this position in twenty-eight states. In the remaining states, the senate president is drawn from the state senate itself and is analogous to the speakership of the lower house. Most state senates with the lieutenant governor as senate president are not in fact run by him or her. The role of senate president is akin to the vice-president's role of presiding over the United States Senate. It is primarily a ceremonial role. Real party leadership in the state senates is by the majority leader or an elected "temporary" president. However, there are a few state senates, such as Texas, in which the lieutenant governor does in fact have legislative clout.

The work of the legislatures consists of enacting laws and providing a check and balance on the exercise of executive power. A leading scholar of legislatures, Samuel Patterson, found that in the 1977–1978 sessions of the nation's legislatures, 198,824 bills were considered, of which 44,319 eventually were enacted.[43] As can be expected, there were variations among the states, ranging from 2,718 laws produced by the California legislature to under 300 enacted by the Wyoming and West Virginia legislatures.

There are a variety of influences on state legislative behavior. They vary in mix and intensity among the states. They include: (1) the party leadership, particularly the speaker and the senate president or majority leader; (2) the legislator's perceptions of constituency interests, needs, and desires; (3) the governor; (4) lobbyists for both private interests such as the Chamber of Commerce or a manufacturer's association and public interests such as the state universities and colleges or a particular city or group of towns; (5) the work of legislative committees; (6) the work of the legislative staff, particularly in terms of the information flow they control to the legislators and the expertise they have in drafting highly complex legislation.[44]

The Judiciary

All states have their own judicial systems that consist of trial courts and a high appellate court, usually called the supreme court. Thirty-two states also have an intermediate level of appellate courts. The state courts are concerned with disputes between people who are physically located in the state (that is, they either live in the state, are visiting the state, or passing through) or businesses that operate within the state. People or businesses that are not present in and have no ties to the state are not subject to that state's courts. A dispute brought to a state court may concern only state law or both state and federal law. Criminal cases are brought by the state authorities and involve violations of state law.

There are typically a variety of trial courts, most of which operate independently of one another. Only seven states have consolidated their trial courts so that they are administered and run as one structure. Thirty-two states have intermediate appellate level courts that provide the right to an appeal from a trial court decision, but just as with the federal court system,

---

[43]Patterson, *op. cit.,* p. 165.
[44]This list is derived from Patterson, *op. cit.,* p. 168.

appeal from an appeals court decision to the highest court is not a right. In most instances, it is at the discretion of the high court. Unlike trial courts in which only one judge hears and decides (sometimes with a jury), the intermediate appeals courts and the highest appellate courts (usually the state supreme courts) are *collegial courts* consisting of groups of judges hearing and deciding the appeals. At the appellate level, there are no juries, no witnesses, no expert testimony on the stand—only the briefs of the lawyers for the opposing sides and, for some cases, oral argument by which the lawyers summarize their legal position and answer questions asked by the judges.

State supreme courts are typically located in the state capitals and contain from three to nine justices. These courts are the ultimate authority in the interpretation of their state's constitution and can set legal policy for the state as long as it does not conflict with federal legal policy.

In numbers of courts and numbers of cases, state court systems considerably overshadow the federal court system. In 1980, the total number of state and local courts was 18,252.[45] In 1982, more than 25 million civil and criminal cases (excluding juvenile and traffic charges) were filed. By contrast, in that same year only 206,000 civil and criminal cases were begun in the federal district courts.[46] In number of judges, the state judiciaries again overshadow the federal judiciary. In New York State alone, there are over 100 more full-time state judges than in the entire federal judiciary. State courts affect the everyday lives of citizens much more than the federal courts do. State courts handle a citizen's small claims dispute with a local business, or that person's divorce, or speeding ticket, or sorting out the distribution of a deceased relative's estate when no will can be found. The courts of each state are independent of the courts of other states.

State judges are selected by one or more of five methods that include: election by the legislature (three states); appointment by the governor with the approval of either the state senate, the governor's council, or a commission (six states); partisan elections (ten states); nonpartisan elections (thirteen states); and merit selection (eighteen states). Exhibit 2.4 reports which states use what methods.

The **partisan election** method has voters elect judges who run for office under a political party label that has been designated by the party primary or convention. In a **non-partisan election,** judges do not have any party designation on the election ballot.

Merit selection is the method favored by the organized bar and judicial reformers. Under merit selection, a nominating commission submits to the governor a list of names to fill a specific judicial position. The governor is legally required to choose the appointee from that list. The nominating

---

[45]State Court Organization 1980 (Washington, D.C.: U.S. Department of Justice, Bureau of Justice Statistics, May, 1982), pp. 6–7, 10–11, 54–56.

[46]Annual Report of the Director, Administrative Office of the United States Courts, 1982. Figures for the states from Bureau of Justice Statistics, Special Report, February 1983, Table 1, p. 2.

EXHIBIT 2.4	PARTISAN ELECTION	NONPARTISAN ELECTION	LEGISLATIVE ELECTION	GUBERNATORIAL APPOINTMENT	MERIT PLAN
Principal Methods of Judicial Selection in the States	Alabama[a]	Georgia[a]	Rhode Island[b,c]	California[b]	Alaska
	Arkansas	Idaho[a]	South Carolina[a]	Delaware	Arizona[a]
	Illinois[a]	Kentucky	Virginia	Maine[a]	Colorado[a]
	Mississippi[a]	Louisiana[a]		Massachusetts	Connecticut[a]
	New Mexico	Michigan[a]		New Hampshire	Florida[c]
	North Carolina[c]	Minnesota		New Jersey[a]	Hawaii
	Pennsylvania[a]	Montana			Indiana[b]
	Tennessee[a,c]	Nevada			Iowa
	Texas[a]	North Dakota			Kansas
	West Virginia	Ohio[a]			Maryland
		Oregon[a]			Missouri[a]
		Washington			Nebraska
		Wisconsin			New York[a,b,c]
					Oklahoma[a,c]
					South Dakota[a,b,c]
					Utah
					Vermont
					Wyoming[a]

[a]Minor court judges chosen by other methods.
[b]Appellate judges only. Other judges selected by different methods.
[c]Most but not all major judicial positions selected this way.

Source: *The Book of the States 1986–1987* (Lexington, Ky.: The Council of State Governments, 1986). pp. 161–163; *Sourcebook of Criminal Justice Statistics 1985* (Washington, D.C.: Bureau of Justice Statistics, 1986). pp. 76–79; Marvin Comisky and Philip C. Patterson, *The Judiciary-Selection, Compensation, Ethics, and Discipline* (New York: Quorum, 1987); and *Judicature.* Reprinted from Sheldon Goldman and Austin Sarat, *American Court Systems,* Second Edition (New York: Longman, 1989), p. 281.

commission is charged with evaluating candidates strictly on the basis of their professional credentials. Commissions are not supposed to consider the candidates' party affiliation, political or ideological views, their social, religious, or economic backgrounds, or their political backing or lack of it. Commissions generally consist of lawyers selected by the bar, non-lawyer gubernatorial appointees, and one or more members of the judiciary. In some states (Delaware, Maryland, and Massachusetts in particular) and in some localities, executive orders issued by governors and mayors have established nominating commissions similar to the merit plan, but these orders do not have the force or permanency of constitutional or statutory law and are therefore not binding on their successors in office and the orginators can even dissolve the commission or reject its nominees.

Judicial selection in the states is complex and is often confusing to students. In the large majority of states, there are different selection methods for different court levels. For example, in New York State, the highest state court's membership is selected by a variation of the merit plan. Other New York state judges are chosen by partisan election or gubernatorial appointment (with confirmation by the state senate). In the city of New York, the mayor appoints judges of the city criminal and family courts, but Mayor Edward Koch has voluntarily used a merit-type selection process.

Common to all judicial selection methods is a political process. Not all methods, however, have the same form or mix of politics. Party organizational politics heavily influence electoral methods, including both partisan and nonpartisan elections. Party considerations play an important part in the legislative and gubernatorial methods. There is a long tradition in American politics of rewarding the party faithful who have been active on behalf of the party. Appointments can also be seen as "rewarding" certain party constituency groups including ethnic minorities. Even with merit selection, the governor is responsible for the appointment of some or all members of the nominating commission, and at least some of the governor's appointees are minimally sensitive to the political needs of the governor (for example, the need to appoint members of the governor's party to most judicial positions). Bar associations may heavily favor those who have been active in their associations and influence the deliberations of merit selection commissions. Bar groups typically pick some of the membership of the commissions.

The policy orientation of the candidates is considered to some degree in all selection methods. During electoral campaigns, the views of the candidates may become an issue. The governor may consider the policy outlook of judicial candidates particularly when groups from within the governor's party take an active interest in such views. The selection commission under the merit system may be influenced in its evaluation of judicial candidates by their judicial philosophies or perhaps even in a more subtle fashion by whether the political views of the candidates fall within the mainstream of American politics. For example, there is no known example of a commission recommending an individual who was a socialist or philosophical anarchist. Of course it is unlikely that many (or perhaps any) such individuals presented themselves to commissions in the first place.

In practice, judicial elections tend to be largely ignored by the electorate resulting in low voter interest and low turnout at the polls. Another significant aspect of the electoral method is that the majority of judges are initially selected by the governor to fill vacancies that occur between elections. When elected judges resign, retire, or die, the governor is authorized to make interim appointments which means that at the next election those appointed are able to run as incumbents with all the advantages of incumbency such as name recognition and whatever mystique surrounds the occupants of judicial office. With partisan elections, the party label is the most significant factor in the voter's choice, although most judicial elections are uncontested.

The state judiciaries today have a better mix of judges in terms of their race and gender than they had as recently as the mid-1970s. Almost every southern state supreme court has one black justice as well as black trial court judges. Women serve on several state supreme courts, occupy lower court positions, and have served as chief justice. The state judiciary also serves as a recruitment ground for the federal bench. For example, during President Reagan's presidency, close to half his appointees to the federal district courts had experience as a judge in a state judicial system and over one-third were actually serving on the state bench at the time Reagan selected them. The same was true for President Carter's federal district court appointees. This provides a link between the state judiciaries and the federal judicial system.

CHECKLIST FOR REVIEW

1. Although divided sovereignty and divided powers between the federal and state governments may seem illogical and even inefficient, our form of government has deep historical roots and has persisted. The framers had a deep-seated distrust of a unitary form of government and they believed that separation of powers and checks and balances offered the best hope of preventing tyranny.

2. The balance of power between the states and the federal government has shifted over the course of American history. During the first seventy years of the nation's existence, the states were quite powerful and the national government struggled to establish itself. After the Civil War, however, the Fourteenth Amendment changed the relationship between the states and the federal government. The balance of power had now shifted towards the federal government.

    The second major shift occurred during the Great Depression. Federalism underwent another metamorphosis that the Supreme Court at first opposed but finally ratified beginning in 1937. The federal government assumed full responsibility for the national economy and for the welfare of the American people. World War II saw an expansion of the federal government, as did the Great Society programs of the 1960s. Today Americans expect the federal government to solve our problems, create jobs, support education, sponsor health programs and health care, provide funds for care of those in need (the poor, the elderly, disabled veterans), support farmers, protect our civil rights, and so on.

3. In practice, fiscal federalism characterizes the relationship between the federal government and the states. The federal government has money and the states depend on it in the form of categorical grants, block grants, and, until 1987, general revenue sharing. State or local government agencies develop ties with federal grant dispensing agencies and do so independent of other state or local programs and agencies. Observers call this picket-fence federalism.

4. Another facet of federalism is the relationship among the states. The Constitution requires that "Full faith and credit shall be given in each State to the public acts, records, and judicial proceedings of every other State." But state laws differ on a variety of subjects such as domestic relations law and sometimes different state courts issue conflicting rulings concerning the same individuals. Criminal matters are handled differently. States generally cooperate with each other and extradite persons accused of crimes to the states in which the alleged crimes occurred.

5. The Supreme Court is the final arbiter of the federal system. Since 1937, the Court has not been hostile to state regulation but has struck it down if the state gained an economic advantage at the expense of other states, if there was a burden on interstate commerce, or if the federal government already was regulating. In matters of civil rights and liberties, the Supreme Court has made it clear that the states could give more rights under their own laws and constitutions than under the federal Constitution as long as there is no conflict with federal law.

6. Each state has executive, legislative, and judicial branches and these branches within their respective states resemble in varying degrees the federal government. Most states elect their governors for four years. Most state legislators are elected from single-member constituencies. However, state judiciaries are chosen by several methods including partisan or nonpartisan elections, merit selection, or gubernatorial appointment with the approval of another body (the state senate, the governor's council, or a commission).

KEY TERMS		
unitary system	general revenue sharing
single-member constituency	extradite
implied powers	special master
McCulloch v. *Maryland*	adequate state ground doctrine
Gibbons v. *Ogden*	line item veto
New Federalism	*Baker* v. *Carr*
fiscal federalism	*Reynolds* v. *Sims*
categorical grants	partisan election
picket-fence federalism	non-partisan election
block grants	merit selection

PART TWO

The Processes of American Politics

Public Opinion, Socialization, and the Media

$\mathbf{A}$ good way to approach the study of American government is to trace public opinion and interest. How can the power of the president be explained? One key source lies in public support for the individual in office. How can election results be analyzed? Voting is shaped by the stable party loyalties that people develop. How can the different kinds of foreign policy-making be outlined? Foreign policy is often conducted within a context of low public interest in foreign affairs. These issues, and others discussed in this chapter, will appear throughout this book—for the dynamics of public opinion and interest affect the kind of candidates selected and the processes of policy-making.

Public opinion is important not only in its presence, but in its absence. The lack of opinion on an issue affects government as much as majorities and minorities with different points of view. "We the people," the Constitution begins, will establish a government. But some people have more interest in and information about government than others. Some want to take an active part, some want specific things from government, and some want to be left alone. Furthermore, some people will get more of what they want than others. The role of these "people" in government and their opinions, activities, and differences form an appropriate beginning point for studying American government.

DEFINING AND MEASURING PUBLIC OPINION

Presidents speak in the name of the American people. Newscasters describe public reaction to an event. The polls tell us how people feel about particular candidates or issues. But what exactly is this public opinion so often invoked and reported? **Public opinion** is a term for the distribution of the public's views on politics and government. It includes ideas and deeply held values, perceptions about what is going on in the world, and attitudes about particular people and issues. Public opinion is studied to tell us about support for government, levels of information among citizens, and the popularity of candidates and issues. This opinion is of importance to all governments. It outlines the boundaries for the kind of policies that will or will not be permitted. It supports—or at times merely tolerates—a particular form of government and the kind of leaders selected. Public opinion is of fundamental importance in democracies where the people are said to form the government. Hence, government and its policies can claim to be legitimate only insofar as they claim public support. Representatives come to office, and stay there, only if they can correctly measure public opinion.

The term *public opinion* is misleading, however, in one important way. It is used in the singular, but there is not *one* public or *one* opinion. The *public* includes rich and poor, black and white, executives and unemployed, Republicans and Democrats—all with very different opinions. It is said that

Demonstrators against abortion pass the Supreme Court building on January 22 and pro-choice marchers attend a rally on the Capitol grounds on April 9 before the Supreme Court meets to reconsider the landmark *Roe* v. *Wade* decision in 1989.

public opinion opposed aid to the rebels in Nicaragua during the Reagan administration, when actually about fifty-three percent opposed that aid. Many other people supported it. Presidents elected by landslide margins receive only a small part of active support. If sixty percent of the eligible voters cast a ballot, and sixty-five percent of them vote for one candidate, the candidate has received less than forty percent of the public's support.

Recent advances in polling have begun to identify many publics, each with very different political interests and levels of interest.[1] One public relations firm, concerned with pinpointing supporters and opponents of issues with great precision, uses forty clusters, or publics, based on the kind of neighborhoods people live in. One cluster, for example, is defined as "urban/suburban, older, upper-middle class with a substantial Jewish segment." Another is "middle-aged, Southern, farm, with a large Spanish migrant element."[2] Another group of researchers targets eleven publics, each holding very different political beliefs. Consider the statement that "books containing dangerous ideas should be banned from public school libraries." Whereas eighty-two percent of one of the publics agrees that books should be banned, only ten percent of another group agrees.[3] There is not one public opinion, but many opinions on any given question.

[1]H.L. Nieburg, *Public Opinion: Tracking and Targeting* (New York: Praeger, 1984).
[2]*Ibid.*, p. 47.
[3]Norman J. Ornstein et al., *The People, The Press, and Politics* (Reading, Mass.: Addison-Wesley, 1988), see p. 36.

The notion of public opinion is misleading in another way too, in suggesting that all of the public have opinions. Even the most hotly debated issues of the day will show a substantial portion of the public who say they "do not know" or "have not thought much" about the question. Often this group is larger than any of the groups that do have opinions! At the height of the Reagan administration's "Budget Revolution," an attempt to cut spending by reducing government services, the issue of government spending was widely debated. Public opinion in the 1984 election year was divided on the issues, as shown in the top graph of Exhibit 3.1. The largest segment of the public took a moderate position, halfway between the two extremes. The second largest segment admitted that they did not know or hadn't thought much about the issue. Scholars point out that the moderate position is often used by people unsure of their own position.[4] Therefore the results probably exaggerate the people who did have positions on the issue.

Another controversial issue of the Reagan years was U.S. involvement, both political and military, in Central America, with the administration criticized by many for being too actively involved. When people were asked in 1984 to place themselves on a seven point scale from "more" to "less" involvement, the responses divided as shown in the lower portion of Exhibit 3.1. The largest segment of the public polled did not have a position on the issue; the second largest segment took the moderate position.

These results reveal certain things about public opinion. On the spending issue, opinions were fairly evenly divided. There was certainly no ground swell of support among the general public that argued for fewer services or additional budget cuts. (It would be necessary to look further to see which of the many publics referred to earlier supported or opposed the cuts.) On the Central America issue, a majority of those who had opinions opposed further involvement. Nevertheless, interpretation also must take into account the many who did not have opinions. Public opinion, in short, is a term referring to many publics and many people with no opinion.

Knowledge of public opinion is a highly prized commodity. Surveys of opinion are conducted for products, corporations, candidates, and groups. Newspapers and television networks conduct their own polls and then tell the public what the public is thinking. Polls, or public opinion surveys, can be conducted in person or by telephone; they can include short answer questions or in-depth interviews. Some polls are conducted more carefully and objectively than others, but the polls themselves seem here to stay. The student of politics needs some basic understanding of how polls are conducted and how they can be interpreted. If public opinion is important to government, the measurement of this opinion is also important.

---

[4]See Herbert Asher, *Polling and the Public: What Every Citizen Should Know* (Washington, D.C.: CQ Press, 1988), pp. 30–33.

GOVERNMENT SERVICES AND SPENDING

Public Opinion on
Two Controversial
Issues

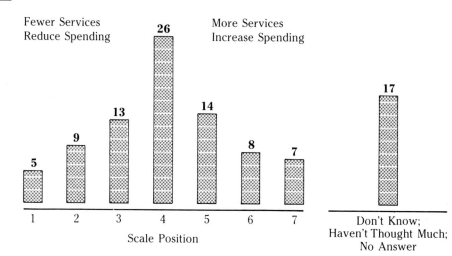

U.S. INVOLVEMENT IN CENTRAL AMERICA

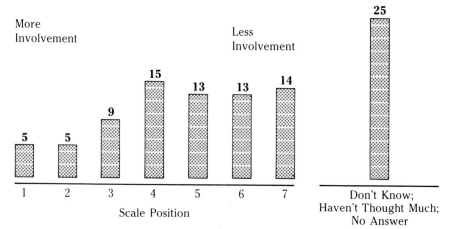

A sample of 2257 respondents were asked to place themselves on a seven-point scale for these issues.

Source: 1984 American National Election Study, Center for Political Studies, University of Michigan. The data utilized were made available by the Inter-University Consortium for Political and Social Research. Neither the original source or collectors of the data nor the Consortium bear any responsibility for the analyses or interpretations presented here.

| | POLL | ELECTION RESULT | |
YEAR	RESULT	AND WINNER	DIFFERENCE
1960	51.0	50.1 Kennedy	0.9
1964	64.0	61.3 Johnson	2.7
1968	43.0	43.5 Nixon	0.5
1972	62.0	61.8 Nixon	0.2
1976	48.0	50.0 Carter	2.0
1980	47.0	50.8 Reagan	3.8
1984	59.0	59.1 Reagan	0.1
1988	53.0	53.4 Bush	0.4

EXHIBIT 3.2

Poll Predictions and Election Results[a]

[a]The table compares the final Gallup poll taken before the election with the actual election result. Notice that almost all of the results are within the 3 percentage point sample error reported for these samples.

Source: *Gallup Report*, December, 1984, p. 31; *Congressional Quarterly Weekly Report*, November 12, 1988, p. 3244, and May 6, 1989, p. 1063.

The accuracy of modern polling techniques is derived from the **statistical theory of sampling.** The theory states that a sample of individuals selected randomly from a population can be "representative" of that population, within a specified degree of accuracy. In other words, the traits of people in the sample—their opinions or sociological characteristics—will reflect the traits of the whole population. Thus the Gallup polling organization might construct a sample of 1500 Americans to discover what the larger American population is thinking about certain issues. (The accuracy of Gallup's predictions of presidential election results since 1960 are shown in Exhibit 3.2. The table compares the prediction with the actual election result.)

Polls sample the opinions of only a small group of people and yet they predict the opinions of everyone. How can this be so? *If the sample is drawn correctly,* everyone in the larger population has the same chance of being included in the sample; hence one can state how accurate the poll should be in reflecting the larger population. To ensure this even chance, the sample should be drawn randomly. A **random sample** does not mean merely by whim, as in standing on a street corner and interviewing whoever happens to pass by. Random means that the sample has been drawn in some predetermined fashion so that everyone in the population has an equal chance of being selected for the sample. One might take a list of names (the population) and drawing a number—say fifteen—from a hat, interview every fifteenth person on the list. One has constructed a very simple random sample.

Other factors also affect the accuracy of a sample. The amount of variation in a population increases the chance that one random sample will differ from another and so decreases the accuracy of the prediction to the population. A community where everyone is very much alike, in occupation

BLOOM COUNTY   **by Berke Breathed**

© 1984, Washington Post Writers Group, reprinted with permission.

and income, would be easier to sample than one where people were diverse. The size of the sample can also affect accuracy, especially for relatively small populations. When the population is very large, as in national opinion polling, changes in sample size have very little effect. A carefully constructed poll will take these factors of variation and size into account. A poll might say, for example, that it has a 90 percent chance or better of reflecting the population within 3 percentage points. This means that a 55 percent figure reported for the sample would be anywhere from 52 to 58 percent of the population, nine times out of ten. The 3 percent figure is referred to as the **sample error.** The sample error is a statistical term that describes the limits within which the sample may deviate from the population. If 53 percent of the sample supported one candidate, and 47 percent another, we could not say which candidate is leading. The difference is so small that it is within the sample error.

Like any other kind of information, polls must be interpreted carefully. The wording of questions and their placement in the survey should be looked at carefully to see that they have not led the respondent in any way. A survey about political interests could get higher response rates than a survey about general interests, because the respondent is led to think that politics is important. Key words in a question can unintentionally lead the respondent to answer in certain ways. When people were asked what parts of the budget could be cut if funds were short, only three percent checked "aid to the needy." When the term was changed to "public welfare programs," thirty-nine percent agreed with the cuts.[5] Also worth considering is the bias implicit in an interview situation. In this social setting, with the interviewer on the telephone or at the doorstep, people might not be willing to admit prejudices or other unpopular attitudes that they hold. For example, surveys consistently show higher turnout rates than the election results show. Since voting is thought to be a good thing to do, more people say

[5]*Ibid.*, p. 42.

"Bring me my pipe, my bowl, my fiddlers three, and my pollster."

they voted than actually did vote. Even the race of the interviewer, studies show, can affect the responses given by respondents.[6]

Readers will see more survey results in this and the following chapters. Interpreted carefully, they provide many insights as to what "We the People" think about politics and government.

A MAPPING OF PUBLIC OPINION

This section examines the levels of information people have about politics and the distribution of opinions. As previously noted, opinions are best interpreted after the basic patterns of information are seen.

Differences in Interest and Information

The first fact to understand about public interest and information in government is that it is low. Take voting, for example. One has to think and do little except turn out once every two years for a national election (or in between for special elections) and push a lever or mark a ballot in a voting booth. Yet in twentieth-century presidential elections, only 50 to 60 percent

[6]See Asher, pp. 74–75, for a good review of the cautions to observe in interpreting polls.

of the voting-age population has turned out to vote for president. In congressional elections held in the "off years" (those between a presidential contest), turnout drops down into the 40 percent range or below. For special elections or primaries the figure is lower still. The first primaries in a presidential election year are often decisive in selecting the presidential nominee—approximately 10 to 20 percent of the eligible voters turn out to make these decisions in the states holding primaries.

In other kinds of activity, the percentage of people sufficiently interested to act drops even further. About one-fourth of Americans surveyed claim to have ever worked for a candidate or party in an election campaign, and about the same number say they have written to a public official to express an opinion. Fewer than ten percent say they have done one of the following: given money to a candidate or party, attended a political rally or meeting, or joined or worked with others to do something about a national problem.[7] These figures are probably somewhat overstated. Since political activity is considered a citizen's duty and a good thing to do, the actual rates of participation tend to be lower than the reported rates.

The picture changes even more dramatically when we separate presidential interest from all the rest. Most people know something about the president and presidential candidates. If they follow the news at all, they can rate the "job" the president is doing in the White House and they can say yes to a poll that asks if they have talked to anyone about the election campaigns. They have talked to people about the presidential election. However, the American national government has *two* elected branches. Both the president and members of Congress participate in national policy-making, and both are elected, in different ways, by the voters of the United States. Thus to claim a democratic basis for national government activity, one must look to the public's interest and information in both branches.

In a classic study, people were asked if they had "read or heard something" about the congressional candidates for the election in their district. Approximately one-half of those voting in the contest said they had read or heard something about one of the candidates and about one-fourth had read or heard something about both candidates.[8] Having read or heard something (no matter what and no matter whether or not it is correct) is not demanding very much by way of information. And these are the voters only—those interested enough to vote in an off-year election. So, if one asks that voters make a meaningful choice in elections, and that citizens vote after weighing information about the candidates, only one-fourth of those voting would qualify by this minimum criterion.

---

[7]See, for example, the *1984 American National Election Study*, postelection survey, Center for Political Studies, Ann Arbor, Michigan, 1984. The results are found consistently across years.
[8]Warren E. Miller and Donald E. Stokes, "Constituency Influence in Congress," *American Political Science Review*, 57(1963), pp. 45–57.

Studies show the same pattern persisting through the 1970s to the present.[9] People could place where they stood on major issues of the day and they could say where the presidential candidates and the parties stood, but they could not place where the House candidates stood, even when the representative's position was available from the record and the party of the candidate was supplied. While most people could say what they liked or disliked about the presidential candidates, only about half could do so for Senate candidates. Again, any answer, no matter how vague or incorrect, was counted. People could like Democrats because they thought they were Republicans or say they liked a candidate because of his or her "record." So again, if one asks as a minimum that a citizen weigh two facts about two candidates, barely half would qualify in Senate voting.

The second fact, then, to appreciate about the public's information in government is the sharp difference between presidential and other information. While the overall level is low, it is far lower when one hazards beyond the spotlight on the White House. So, when people say they know the issues, they mean the presidential issues; when they give money to candidates, they mean the presidential candidates. For many, political information means knowing something about the president and the issues debated at the White House level only.

The public is not alone in this differential attention. The news media, too, give disproportionate coverage to presidential elections and report national news by providing the White House story.[10] During a presidential race, it would be hard for people not to have "read or heard something" about the candidates—they are virtually bombarded with this information. In contrast, it is difficult even to find out who the candidates are in some congressional contests. Yet, the media is simply providing stories to appeal to readers' interest. Interest and information reinforce each other, producing more interest and more information.

Congress, too, has not seemed anxious to counter the presidential advantage in exposure. Although individual members supply news releases to their local media, Congress as an institution has been more reluctant to seek publicity. Television came to the American public in the 1950s; thirty years later it was still struggling for acceptance in the halls of Congress. Finally, by 1986, both the House and the Senate began television coverage of their proceedings. Congress runs its own television systems, supplying live feed to the networks, cable systems, and individual stations. Full coverage is relayed through C-span to 900 cable television systems. We may expect this coverage to increase the public's awareness of Congress, but the basic

[9]For a summary of these studies, see Barbara Hinckley, *Congressional Elections* (Washington, D.C.: CQ Press, 1981), chapter 2.

[10]See Edie Goldenberg and Michael Traugott, *Campaigning for Congress* (Washington, D.C.: CQ Press, 1984).

situation, of low public interest and information, may change only marginally. As one writer remarked, BOGSAT (a bunch of guys sitting around a table) is not particularly visual.[11] While some members will seek, and receive, more exposure, Congress itself will probably not do that well in the ratings.[12]

A third fact of importance is that interest and information vary with the social and economic status of citizens. Whether one looks at voting turnout or at other measures, one finds that the higher the education, income, and occupational status of people, the more likely they are to be politically active and informed. College-educated people tend to score higher on these measures than high school graduates, who in turn score higher than grade school graduates. Members of professions score higher than white-collar workers, who in turn score higher than skilled or semiskilled workers. Voters, campaign workers, and those who join interest groups or write letters to the editor are disproportionately middle-aged, highly educated, middle-class or upper-class citizens.[13]

The implications of these facts are obvious and important. Those groups who have already benefited in the society by social and economic circumstances are in a position to be most politically active and influential—and thus most likely to receive more benefits. Those groups already receiving less are less in a position to make their needs politically known.

This vicious circle has some subcircles as well. Political interest, say a number of studies, is a product of personal self-esteem and a sense of **political efficacy**—that is, the feeling that one can have an impact or exert influence on political affairs.[14] A migrant worker or an unemployed eighteen-year-old—perhaps not very well-stocked with personal self-esteem at the moment—might well not score high on political efficacy. If the migrant workers were asked the questions designed to measure their sense of efficacy (whether they felt they could "make a difference" or whether "people in government listened to them"), negative answers seem the only realistic and correct response. Status in society, political interest, a sense of political efficacy, and self-esteem are all closely linked to each other and to political influence. A diagram of these effects is shown in Exhibit 3.3.

There may be ways out of the circle shown in Exhibit 3.3. although they are not easy ones. Groups of low-status people can mobilize—overriding low individual self-esteem and efficacy by a sense of group strength. Work-

[11]Larry Warren, "The Other Side of the Camera," *PS*, 19(1986), p. 45.

[12]In a first study of the subject, Timothy Cook finds that the greatest television exposure tends to be found with those occupying formal leadership positions. See "House Members as Newsmakers: The Effects of Televising Congress," *Legislative Studies Quarterly,* May, 1986, pp. 203–26.

[13]Herbert Asher, *Presidential Elections and American Politics*, 3rd ed. (Homewood, Ill.: Dorsey, 1984), p. 43.

[14]For a good overview of the concept, see Paul R. Abramson, *Political Attitudes in America* (San Francisco: Freeman, 1983), chapter 8.

EXHIBIT 3.3   Citizen Interest and Socioeconomic Status: Some Links
in the Circle

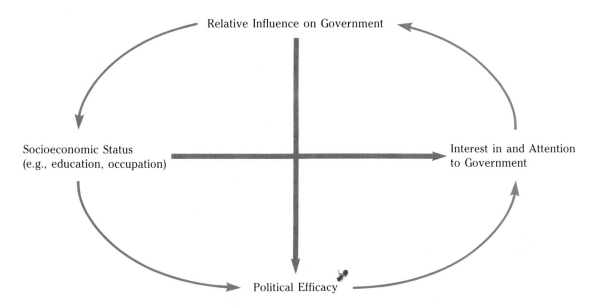

ers in labor unions, blacks in the 1960s, and women in the 1970s are cases
in point. Once the circle has been broken, interest can lead to influence: for
example, minimum wage legislation, a civil rights act, and laws about sexual
harrassment. Nevertheless, such mobilization is neither an easy nor automatic solution. The people least likely to become politically active are also
least likely to join groups and become involved in group activity. Groups
themselves vary in political influence, depending on their numbers, organizational capacity, and the social status of members. Even in groups, people
might feel that officials in government do not listen to them.

Three Levels of Interest

There is not one level of public interest, then, but at least three.[15] For a
large majority of the population, perhaps seventy-five percent, politics is
very much a part-time, low interest activity. They are marginally attentive
to national news and can discuss the presidency, presidential campaigns,
and whatever else happens to be the top issues of the day. They usually
vote. They may occasionally give money to a campaign or become involved
in some other activity. However, their main work, their hobbies, and their
recreational interests are not political. This is the broad middle group of
American public opinion, sometimes called the *voting public.*

[15]See W. Russell Neuman, *The Paradox of Mass Politics* (Cambridge: Harvard University Press,
1986), pp. 170–71. Neuman gives the estimates of the size of these three different publics.

Another large portion, perhaps twenty percent, can be called the *apoliticals.* They are not interested in politics and are willing to say so in surveys. They do not follow the national news and they do not vote. The opinions they do have, however, suggest that their behavior is quite understandable. Many do not feel they can make a difference in what happens in politics, and they do not feel that the government is concerned with helping them. A large proportion of the apoliticals are poor, often unemployed, with low education and poor English language skills. They include single women raising families, men trying to hold together their family farms, people working two jobs, and people that are looking for any job. Probably, they do not share the *rest* of the voting public's recreational activities either. They do not belong to the same clubs or take the family on the same vacations or order from the same catalogues.

The third and smallest portion, perhaps five percent, are the *activists*, sometimes called the "sophisticated" citizens or voters. They vote regularly and make it their business to know about the candidates. They are active in other ways as well, attending rallies, contributing time or money to campaigns, and reading and talking about politics with others. They are well versed in those issues given attention in the national news. They can place candidates on issue scales in relation to their own position. These are the fans. For these people, politics is a major recreational activity—or more. While the majority of the public might go to one game a year and watch the World Series (that is, the presidential election), the activists get the season tickets, know the players, and keep score.

The relative size of these three publics can be seen in Exhibit 3.4. The percentages are approximate averages of the results of many studies.[16] One can see at a glance the broad voting public, the substantial number of apoliticals, and the small group of active citizens.

In thinking about these publics, it is important to resist the bias, found in many political science books, that one is better or smarter than another. Political scientists understandably think that politics is something people should be interested in and often imply an intellectual defect when people are not. They speak of the voting public's "lack of a rich vocabulary" or say that apoliticals do not have the "cognitive ability" to answer survey questions. The activists are complimented with the term "sophisticated" voters. Certainly, education and intellect do make a difference in one's ability to read newspapers or answer surveys. But many other factors can make more of a difference. Thinking of politics as only one of many part-time activities Americans pursue helps keep public opinion in perspective. Theoretical physicists and prize-winning novelists might not be interested in politics either, but they do not have problems with their vocabularies or cognitive abilities. They simply do not like the game, or have as much time for it, as some others do.

---

[16]*Ibid.*

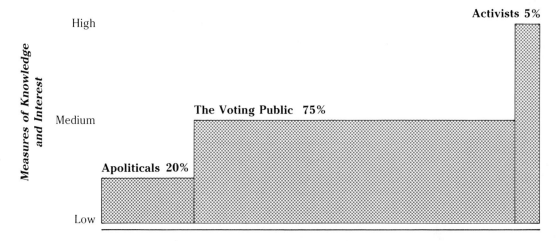

EXHIBIT 3.4   The Three Publics

The Range of Opinions

A mapping of public opinion needs to show the kind of opinions Americans hold and their range and diversity across the nation, including areas of widespread agreement, or **consensus**, on some issues and areas of disagreement and conflict on others.

Areas of Consensus.   Observers have long noted a basic consensus in American political opinion. People agree on the form of government, the form of the economy within the government, and broad democratic and constitutional principles. The protection of individual freedoms, representative government, and regular elections are broadly accepted rules of the game. People debate about whose free speech should be protected and under what conditions, but the great majority support the general principle of free speech. People might not vote, but they think that elections are necessary in a democracy. Political debate thus occurs within a *limited range of alternatives*. People debate particular policies or broad policy directives, but not the repeal of the First Amendment, the advantages of anarchy, or the blessings of benevolent dictatorships.

There is an "American Ethos," then, of support for principles of democracy, equality, and private enterprise. This means that individuals or parties attacking these principles do not make headway in American politics: the consensus screens out extremist parties and fringe groups from actively competing for power. Nevertheless, some of these principles can be in conflict with others. Asking government to ensure job equality conflicts with principles of private enterprise. Studies show that those scoring highest in support for democracy do not score highest in support for private enterprise, and vice versa.[17] Surveys also show that while people support general statements of the American ethos, they disagree sharply on specific applications. While most Americans support the principle of free speech, only about half would extend that right to Communists or extreme religious groups.[18]

The area of consensus should not be overestimated. While it is important in shaping political debate, it does not keep real and sharp differences from being heard.

Areas of Diversity.   The United States, considered large and diverse at its founding, has expanded greatly in geography, climate, life style, national origin, social setting, and means of livelihood. Political attitudes vary along with these differences and have profound effects on the kind of representatives elected and the policy-making that results.

One can see this diversity across regions and states on a number of important issues. Take the question of whether the nation is spending too much, too little, or the right amount for defense and military purposes. In 1987, 44 percent of the nationwide sample answered too much, 36 percent said about the right amount, and 14 percent said too little. But the national figure masked considerable regional variation from a high of 52 percent in the West who said too much to a low of 39 percent in the South.[19] In the same way, states vary greatly on capital punishment, aid to parochial schools, gun control, and laws about abortion. (Regional and state variation will be important in later chapters.)

National parties are formed from the diverse politics of the states. Presidents are elected through the electoral college by winning pluralities in the states. Congress is composed of senators representing those states and representatives from districts within the states. Congress on the one hand must represent those diverse constituencies, and on the other hand it must make national policy. It has to vote on the defense budget, write an education bill, and decide an abortion issue.

Other areas of diversity also exist—by education, occupation, race, and religion. The same defense spending question already cited was answered "too much" by 51 percent of college-educated people and by 39 percent of

[17]Herbert McClosky and John R. Zaller, *The American Ethos* (Cambridge: Harvard University Press, 1985).

[18]See for example James Prothro and C.W. Grigg, "Fundamental Principles of Democracy: Bases of Agreement and Disagreement," *Journal of Politics*, 22(1960), pp. 276–94; James Davis, "Communism, Conformity, Cohorts, and Categories," *American Journal of Sociology*, 81 (1975), pp. 491–513; John L. Sullivan, James Piereson, and George E. Marcus, *Political Tolerance and American Democracy* (Chicago: University of Chicago Press, 1982).

[19]*Gallup Report*, May, 1987, p. 3.

those with high school education or less. Sixty percent of the blacks answering the question said "too much," compared to 42 percent of the whites and 40 percent of the Hispanics. To take another example, Ronald Reagan was reelected in 1984 with 59 percent of the vote nationwide. But he received only 11 percent of the black vote, 32 percent of the Jewish vote, and 48 percent of the vote in union households. His share of the vote increased with income, from 45 percent in families earning below $10,000 a year to 68 percent in families earning over $40,000 a year. In 1988, the vote for George Bush increased with each income level: low-income voters favored Michael Dukakis, middle-income voters voted narrowly for Bush, and high-income voters supported Bush heavily. The effect of these differences on voting will be shown in a later chapter. Here, it is only important to see the diversity of opinion that exists. Presidents once elected become presidents of "all the people," yet they have come to office on the votes of selected groups of people.

Differences in Ideology.   People's attitudes about politics tend to be interrelated and internally consistent. When these attitudes are sufficiently developed, they are called an **ideology**. An ideology is a belief system or a set of basic beliefs about politics and government that are related in a coherent fashion. An ideology structures people's thinking and allows them to develop new opinions to fit in with their earlier views. People may have an ideology, in fact, without knowing that they do—it has been developed over time from what they have thought and heard from others.

The terms liberal and conservative are widely used in American politics to describe basic ideologies. Liberals stress the equality side of the American ethos. They look to government to cure injustices and bring social reform. Conservatives stress the private enterprise side. While they ask government to be strong enough to protect against foreign foes and to keep law and order at home, they oppose the role of the federal government in many areas of social and business life.

The graphs in Exhibit 3.5 show the ideological differences of Americans on a liberal-to-conservative scale. People were asked to place themselves on the seven-point scale from "extremely liberal" to "extremely conservative," or to indicate if they "hadn't thought much" about the question. The top graph shows the full distribution of opinion, including those who had no answer to the question, and the bottom graph shows the distribution for the smaller number who had positions.

Behind these fairly simple snapshots of opinion, several facts can be discerned. First, notice the extent of consensus. Few people place themselves at the extremes of the spectrum, and even many of these are not really extreme—most respondents would probably support the basic idea of democratic government, regular elections, and other constitutional principles. Second, even within this fairly narrow range of opinion (with few anarchists or supporters of benevolent dictatorships), further consensus is

| **EXHIBIT 3.5** | Liberals and Conservatives in American Public Opinion |

All People Asked the Question:

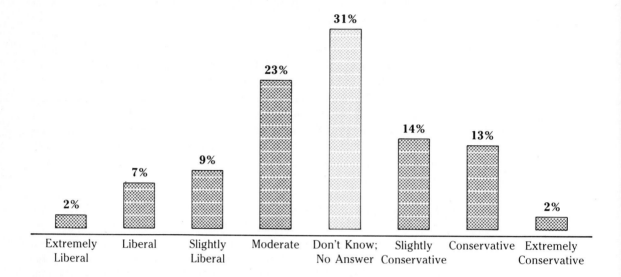

Those People Having Positions on the Question:

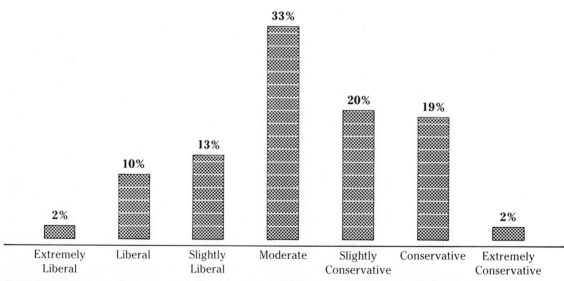

The question asked people to place themselves on a seven-point scale, ranging from extremely liberal to extremely conservative.

Source: 1984 American National Election Study, Center for Political Studies, University of Michigan. The data utilized were made available by the Inter-University Consortium for Political and Social Research. Neither the original source or collectors of the data nor the Consortium bear any responsibility for the analyses or interpretations presented here.

evident. By far the largest number of people who have positions on the question see themselves as "moderate," with the next largest groups leaning only slightly to the liberal or conservative sides. The range of attitudes, narrow to start with, narrows still further toward the middle three points of the seven-point scale.

The top graph also shows the sizable lack of opinion or interest. Almost one-third of the sample agreed they "hadn't thought much" about the question or did not know or could not state their position. However, a final point is important. Despite the consensus and the lack of opinion, a great deal of diversity remains. Even within the full sample, (top graph) there are a sizable number of "liberals" who see themselves as opposed to a sizable number of "conservatives." Of those having opinions (bottom graph), the distribution divides roughly into thirds: somewhat more than a third are conservative; one third are in the middle; and somewhat less than a third are on the liberal side.

These same points could be shown for other years and for many other political attitude questions. Their importance will become clearer in subsequent chapters. The political parties are often criticized for presenting "no real choice" to the voters. But party strategists reading the same graphs can see where the votes are and note the dangers of venturing too far from that middle range. Given the lack of interest shown by many people, factors other than the issues are crucial in explaining the vote. Yet, the diversity that exists will also be reflected at many points along the way. The parties will represent different tendencies around the broad middle ground and different positions will be taken by members of Congress, depending on the opinion found in their own states and districts.

Beyond Liberal and Conservative.   Recently, writers have pointed out that there are really four underlying ideologies at work in American politics rather than merely the liberal and conservative ones. People differ in their ideas about personal freedoms and particular democratic values and they differ about the government's role in the economy and capitalist values.[20] People high on one scale are not necessarily high on the other.[21] Combining these differences, it is possible to come up with the four-part ideological portrait shown in Exhibit 3.6. Liberals, scoring in the top left corner of the figure, would support issues of personal freedom but allow government intervention in the economy, often on the grounds of equality and fairness. Libertarians, in the upper right corner, would support free speech and oppose economic intervention. For these people, governments are best that leave everyone alone. In contrast, Populists, in the lower left corner, look to government to cure many social ills. Individual freedoms may need to be limited in the name of community or national values, while

[20]See the study by William S. Maddox and Stuart A. Lilie, *Beyond Liberal and Conservative* (Washington, D.C.: Cato Institute, 1984). See also McClosky and Zaller, *op. cit.*
[21]McClosky and Zaller, *op. cit.*

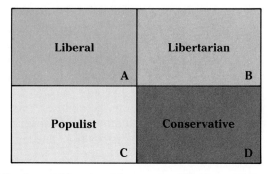

EXHIBIT 3.6

Issue Differences
and Ideological
Categories

*Support for Personal
Freedoms and Democratic
Values*

*Support for Free Enterprise and
Capitalist Values*

Source: Adapted from Maddox and Lilie, *Beyond Liberal and Conservative* (Washington, D.C.: Cato Institute, 1984), p. 5.

government help with the economy can make life better for all. Finally, the Conservatives, in the lower right hand corner, also find that individual freedoms may need to be limited in the name of larger values, but they seek to keep the economic sector free from government control. The names given in the figure do not matter: one could call the squares A, B, C, and D. The point is that these different ideologies do exist among the American public. The groups would agree with each other on some issues and disagree on others.

It is apparent now how consensus and diversity of opinion fit together. Few people are challenging the principle of personal freedom or the private enterprise system. These are part of the consensus values. Controversies arise as to where the lines should be drawn and which principles are most important. Thus, consensus values underlie ideologies and give them much of their power. All of the groups believe in *their* interpretation of freedom, equality, enterprise, and the American way of life.

Americans were found to be fairly evenly divided among these positions in the 1980s, with the lower left (Populist) category leading only slightly.[22] Since most domestic issues fit within these dimensions, the controversies can be sharp and continuing. The ideologies are strong enough to include new issues as they emerge, and so the conflict continues.

The box on pages 106–7 should allow readers to determine their own ideological position and compare it with those of others.

[22]Maddox and Lilie, *op. cit.*, p. 68.

THE SHAPING OF OPINION

Opinions, of course, do not develop in a vacuum. Issues and their interpretations do not appear spontaneously. How were consensus and diversity developed in the first place? How are they maintained? Why do some issues gain public attention and others do not? Why do people care very much about some political questions and not think much about others? To gain a sense of the shape and impact of public opinion, it is necessary to respond to more basic questions.

Political Socialization

Socialization means learning in a social context those rules and ways of thinking deemed most important for the success and survival of the individual and society—it is socially adaptive learning. Individuals are socialized in the family, in the sandbox, in college, and on the job. One learns, for a particular group context, what is bad or good, what will bring social support or approval, and what will bring ostracism or other penalties. Note the importance of the particular group context one identifies with—what is called one's group identification or **reference group**. If a child decides after some time in the sandbox that he or she would rather play catch with the bigger kids, then that child has developed a new reference group. People aren't supposed to throw shovels at each other, but they are supposed to throw balls at each other. Political socialization is merely a particular kind of this broader social learning. An individual learns (often by semiconscious, less than explicit, imitative processes) what is approved and disapproved by a particular reference group and who are the heroes and villains of the group's political universe.

The primary influences on political learning, often called **agents of socialization,** can be listed as follows:

1. family
2. schools
3. churches
4. community
5. peers
6. instruments of mass culture (films, books, television, political figures)

As in all learning, the early experiences are the most important. Scholars speak of two principles: What is learned first is learned best (called the **primacy principle**), and what is learned first structures later learning (called the **structuring principle**).[23] Thus the child's family is often the

[23]Jerry L. Yeric and John R. Todd, *Public Opinion: The Visible Politics* (Itasca, Ill.: Peacock, 1983), p. 39.

Materials of Political Science: THE QUESTIONNAIRE

Test Your Ideology

The following questions are designed to test people's basic ideologies: in particular, whether they are liberals, populists, libertarians, or conservatives. People can have ideologies without knowing that they do. Therefore, it can be interesting to see where you would place on the ideological scale in Exhibit 3.6, and how your opinions differ from other people's.

The questions are selected from a longer questionnaire that tests support for Democratic Values and Capitalist Values. While these values are broadly supported as part of the American ethos, people disagree as to how far they should be carried and which

are most important. These questions, in fact, elicit very different answers from people and show how much diversity of opinion exists.

Notice that the questions ask you to check the answer that "most nearly accords with your own." It thus discourages "neither" or "don't know" responses. Try to choose one of the two answers, even if it seems somewhat far from your own position.

A scoring key follows the questionnaire.

In the following questions, check the answer that most nearly accords with your own opinion.

PART ONE *SUPPORT FOR DEMOCRATIC VALUES*

1. Employment of radicals by newspapers and TV
   a. is their right as Americans.
   b. should be forbidden.
2. For children to be properly educated,
   a. they should be protected against ideas the community considers wrong or dangerous.
   b. they should be free to discuss all ideas and subjects, no matter what.
3. The use of federal agents to spy on radical organizations
   a. is necessary for national security.
   b. violates their right to political freedom.
4. Should a community allow the American Nazi Party to use its town hall to hold a public meeting?
   a. yes   b. no
5. Our laws should aim to
   a. enforce the community's standards of right and wrong.
   b. protect the citizens' rights to live by any moral standards they choose.
6. Tapping telephones of people suspected of planning crimes
   a. is necessary to reduce crime.
   b. should be prohibited as an invasion of privacy.
7. The freedom of atheists to make fun of God and religion
   a. should not be allowed.
   b. is a legally protected right.
8. Laws protecting people accused of crime from testifying against themselves should be

   a. strengthened.
   b. weakened or abolished.
9. For government to keep a list of people who take part in protest demonstrations is
   a. a good idea.
   b. a bad idea.
10. Complete equality for homosexuals in teaching and other public service jobs
    a. may sound fair, but is not really a good idea.
    b. should be protected by law.
11. In dealing with crime, the most important consideration is to
    a. protect the rights of the accused.
    b. stop crime even if we have to violate the rights of the accused.
12. When the country is at war, people suspected of disloyalty
    a. should be watched closely or kept in custody.
    b. should be fully protected in their constitutional rights.
13. Efforts to make everyone as equal as possible should be
    a. increased.
    b. decreased.
14. The laws guaranteeing equal job opportunities for blacks and other minorities
    a. should be made even stronger.
    b. sometimes go too far.
15. Government efforts to bring about racial integration have been
    a. too fast.   b. too slow.

PART TWO *SUPPORT FOR CAPITALIST VALUES*

1. The profit system
   a. teaches people the value of hard work and success.
   b. brings out the worst in human nature.

2. A lumber company that spends millions for a piece of forest land
   a. should, nevertheless, be limited by law to the number of trees it can cut.
   b. has the right to cut down enough trees to protect its investment.

3. The poor are poor because
   a. they don't try hard enough to get ahead.
   b. the wealthy and powerful keep them poor.

4. Workers and management
   a. have conflicting interests and are natural enemies.
   b. share the same interests in the long run.

5. Getting ahead in the world is mostly a matter of
   a. ability and hard work.
   b. getting the breaks.

6. Trade unions
   a. have too much power for the good of the country.
   b. need the power they have to protect the interests of working people.

7. Public ownership of large industry would be
   a. a good idea.
   b. a bad idea.

8. Most businessmen
   a. receive more income than they deserve.
   b. do important work and deserve high salaries.

9. The use of strikes to improve wages and working conditions
   a. is almost never justified.
   b. is often necessary.

10. Men like Henry Ford, Andrew Carnegie, and John D. Rockefeller should be held up to young people
    a. as selfish and ambitious men who would do anything to get ahead.
    b. as models to be admired and imitated.

11. When businesses are allowed to make as much money as they can,
    a. everyone profits in the long run.
    b. workers and the poor are bound to get less.

12. Government regulation of business
    a. usually does more harm than good.
    b. is necessary to keep industry from becoming too powerful.

13. Working people in this country
    a. do not get a fair share of what they produce.
    b. usually earn about what they deserve.

14. When it comes to taxes, corporations and wealthy people
    a. don't pay their fair share.
    b. pay their fair share and more.

15. Competition, whether in school, work, or business,
    a. is often wasteful and destructive.
    b. leads to a better performance and a desire for excellence.

Source: McClosky and Zaller, pp. 309–316. Selected questions.
Scoring Key provided by the authors.

SCORING KEY

Score one point for each answer.

Part One: 1a, 2b, 3b, 4a, 5b, 6b, 7b, 8a, 9b, 10b, 11a, 12b, 13a, 14a, 15b.

Scores from 0 to 7 place you in squares C or D in Exhibit 3.6. The larger the number, the closer you are to the middle horizontal line in the figure. You are either a Populist or a Conservative depending on your answers to Part Two.

Scores from 8 to 15 place you in squares A or B in Exhibit 3.6. The larger the number, the closer you are to the top horizontal line in the figure. You are either a Liberal or a Libertarian depending on your answers to Part Two.

Part Two: 1a, 2b, 3a, 4b, 5a, 6a, 7b, 8b, 9a, 10b, 11a, 12a, 13b, 14b, 15b.

Scores from 0 to 7 place you in squares A or C in Exhibit 3.6. The larger the number, the closer you are to the middle vertical line in the figure. You are either a Liberal or a Populist depending on your answers to Part One.

Scores from 8 to 15 place you in squares B or D in Exhibit 3.6. The larger the number, the closer you are to the right-hand vertical line in the figure. You are either a Libertarian or a Conservative depending on your answers to Part One.

first and most critical socializing agent. The young child learns that he or she is Catholic, Irish, Republican, or well-off, adopting the family's reference groups. Schools and churches also provide formative influences. Elementary school children are taught to salute the flag and to hold a mock election. They learn about the president from the first stories of George Washington, who could not tell a lie. They learn rules about equality and the value (within limits) of showing independence. They are, in short, learning political attitudes in an American social context, which would differ to greater or lesser degree in other national social contexts. Nevertheless, these same children undergo political learning from other social contexts: as part of a community and as a member of a family with a particular ethnic background, set of values, and occupational setting.

Adults also learn political attitudes in an American social context. They watch the same president and learn to recognize the same patriotic symbols. Many see the same top box-office movies and read the same best-selling books. At the same time, adults find themselves in diverse social settings. Some go to college, some move away from home, and some change their jobs. These experiences can bring new reference groups and new political opinions, reinforcing or challenging earlier learning. Socialization does not stop with maturity, although basic attitudes often resist change.

This process of socialization can help explain the consensus and diversity of opinion seen earlier in the chapter. No two people are influenced by the same socializing agents in the same way. Nevertheless, people with similar backgrounds will share learning experiences and develop similar attitudes. In addition, some of the socializing agents are more inclusive than others. Effects of elementary school teaching or mass culture reach most Americans whereas church, community, or peer influences differentiate one group of Americans from others. Hence we find differences in attitudes linked to differences in such characteristics as education, income, religion, and region of the country. As people vary in education, occupation, or other circumstances, they are subjected to different socializing agents.

One can see the effect of these agents of socialization by using the example of attitudes about war. These attitudes may have been shaped in the family by watching parents' responses to the experience of war. They may have been strengthened or challenged by church teachings, affected by war heroes one has seen, or by films about war. One's own peers may be in conflict with the larger community about joining or not joining in support for a war. Or one might support a president of one's own political party and so support the president's position on a war.

It should be enlightening to think back on how your own political opinions developed. What was the first major political event you experienced and what were others' responses to that event? When did you first think of yourself (or your parents) as associated with a political party, and what reference groups might have been important to that association? Have changes taken place in your attitudes and have they corresponded to changes in reference groups? Such informal political autobiographies can supply considerable insight into the socialization process.

Opinion Formation and Change

Many different theories are suggested as to how the complex process of opinion formation occurs. Most agree, however, that it involves three components: *exposure, comprehension,* and *acceptance.* Opinions include basic ideas about government as well as ideas on specific issues—how one feels, for example, about busing, defense spending, or nuclear plant safety.

Exposure varies with interest and information. The most interested people in the population are the most easily exposed (usually to communications from each other). Learning can be seen as a spiral process: information leads to interest, which in turn leads to further information. People interested enough to follow the news get more information and so on through the spiral. For the larger portion of the population, however, exposure is more difficult. Ideas move in a **two-step information flow,** from those most interested to the mass public. Some writers describe the process as a "trickle down" effect, while others speak of a "critical mass" of information necessary to cross the exposure threshold. For example, if the media concentrate on one subject long enough, a critical-mass effect can occur. This would not be a trickle but a flood.[24] Ideas move outward to the mass public from a small elite group, often called **opinion leaders**. Opinion leaders are those in a position to communicate with large portions of the population—government officials, journalists, leaders of various groups. Information moves from the opinion leaders to those most interested and, as the communication continues, outward to a larger audience. For the final portion of the population who are apolitical, exposure may not occur at all.

Suddenly people begin to discuss nuclear plant safety, the homeless, abandoned children, drug testing, or any of a number of issues. The problems are not new, but the exposure is new. The problem is written about, selected as the topic for a television interview show, or featured in a weekly news magazine. The idea has reached the mass public.

Exposure, however, is not sufficient for opinion formation or change. Comprehension varies with education, vocabulary, and language skills. Acceptance varies according to other political learning and the reference groups with which one identifies. In other words, people *choose* their sources of exposure as they choose what groups they want to identify with.[25] Psychologists speak of "reducing dissonance," or avoiding exposure to opposing points of view, in the face of potentially conflicting attitudes.

---

[24]For a good summary of these effects, see Neuman, p. 148. See also Thomas E. Patterson, *The Mass Media Election* (New York: Praeger, 1980).

[25]For some new evidence on the point, see Robert Huckfeldt and John Sprague, "Networks in Context: The Social Flow of Political Information," *American Political Science Review,* 81(1987), pp. 1197–1216.

Different pictures of war can influence public opinion and attitudes.
Platoon **(1986) was groundbreaking for its portrayal of the atrocities of**
the Vietnam War, while *Rambo, First Blood Part II* **(1985) reinforced the**
stereotype of the soldier as superhero.

One way to reduce dissonance is to select the source of information most in line with one's attitude. Another way is to listen or read selectively, "screening out" the potentially dissonant information. Still another way is to reinterpret or misinterpret whatever information is received. Surveys show, for example, that people who like particular candidates will see their views as close to their own, even when they are not close. These ways of dealing with information to fit one's own perceptions are called **selective perception.** People decide whether they will read a liberal or conservative newspaper or no paper at all. They are not merely the passive recipients of influence—they make choices as to what the influence will be.

So, controversies between the president and Congress occur frequently on defense spending. Many are decided before most people know they have occurred. Every now and then, however, a controversy gets exposure. People develop their own opinions from what they read and hear, as filtered by past attitudes toward defense or other opinions. These disputes may be decided differently because of the public opinion that has formed.

One consequence of these facts may surprise many readers. Does this mean that the most informed citizens are the most likely to have their attitudes changed? The answer appears to be yes; they have the exposure and comprehension necessary to receive information, and they may not want to risk seeming uninformed by screening out too many dissonant points of view. Studies find that the more exposure people have to the news media, the more likely they are to cite what the most important problems are and to suggest solutions.[26] When new issues arise in public debate, support for the issues is related to the political sophistication of the respondent.[27]

Support for democratic values is highest among the most informed voters and lowest among the apolitical. Whereas the population as a whole was fairly evenly divided among four basic ideologies as shown earlier, subgroups within the population vary greatly. Opinion leaders are concentrated in the upper two squares of Exhibit 3.6, while apoliticals are concentrated in the lower right square.[28] The opinion leaders are most likely to support democratic and capitalistic values. They will disagree, however, on which set of values is most important. The limits of influence and attitude change are apparent. Since the mass public is not concentrated in the top two squares, the "opinion leaders" are not influencing parts of the public into adopting their opinions.

Many writers say television has brought a "nationalization" of politics, with people attuned to the same issues and watching the same events. The facts about attitude formation and change, however, indicate nationalization is partial at most. Opinion leaders do read and watch the same information sources with some carry over to the less-interested mass public. But even the national media target specialized audiences in terms of age, education, and interests. (The term **narrowcasting** has been coined for this specialized kind of media targeting.)[29] Think of the television channels for music videos, sports, religious programming, health, and fitness. Beyond these influences, other agents of socialization—churches, communities, peer groups—keep opinion tied to localities and particular groups. These facts should be kept in mind when looking at the role and impact of the national news media.

PUBLIC OPINION AND THE MEDIA

Within the broad maps of one's political universe, more specific detailed information needs to be supplied. Most of this information is provided by the news media. Opinion leaders read the same newspapers and listen to the same interviews; journalists and editors read and watch each other. Most government officials read the *Washington Post* and *New York Times* each day and watch the same news programs. The officials, of course, can give interviews themselves or leak stories to reporters. Still, they do so at the media's invitation or acceptance. The media can start the flow of information out to the mass public, and they provide the exposure necessary for opinion formation and change.

[26]Alex S. Edelstein, *The Uses of Communication in Decision-Making* (New York: Praeger, 1974).
[27]See McClosky and Zaller, *op. cit.*, p. 241.
[28]*Ibid.*, pp. 249–52.
[29]The importance of this specialized targeting is the primary thesis of Nieburg's book, cited earlier.

Feeding frenzy: Reporters ask Republican vice-presidential nominee Senator Dan Quayle about his former military service in the Indiana National Guard.

Nevertheless, the role of the news media is complex and controversial. There is debate, often among journalists themselves, as to the importance of the news media and their influence and limitations.

The Media Elite

News media is a broad term that usually describes all national and local newspapers, television, radio, and weekly and monthly news magazines. It can also include film documentaries and reports to more specialized audiences. Seen this way, the media are multi-faceted, segmented, and diverse—there is no one "media" to talk about. It is true that local media are important to presidential primary candidates and to members of Congress who must keep in touch with their constituents. When we talk about media in national politics, however, we usually mean *a small elite portion of the national news media.* One study, for example, includes three newspapers (the *New York Times,* the *Washington Post,* and the *Wall Street Journal*), three news magazines (*Time, Newsweek,* and *U.S. News & World Report*), and the three national television networks plus the Public Broadcasting Service.[30] Any one source could be added or subtracted without changing the basic point. These media are read and watched because they are perceived to be

[30]S. Robert Lichter, Stanley Rothman, and Linda S. Lichter, *The Media Elite* (Bethesda, Md.: Adler and Adler, 1986), and esp. p. 11.

important, and they are important because they are read and watched by those who influence others' opinions as well as by the journalists themselves. It is this elite portion of the national news media that is referred to as "media" in the rest of the chapter.

Who are the people who make up this elite? What are they like and what kind of opinions do they hold? One study, published in 1986, conducted interviews with a sample of journalists from these same top enterprises, comparing them to other elite groups.[31] The print media sample included reporters, columnists, department heads, bureau chiefs, editors, and executives. The television sample included correspondents, anchors, producers, film editors, and news executives. The result is a group portrait that is homogeneous in several ways.

The journalists appeared similar in many ways to other elites found throughout American society and politics. The group was composed mainly of white males who were highly educated, well-paid professionals. Only one in twenty was nonwhite, and one in five was female. Almost all had college degrees and a majority had attended graduate school. There were few Horatio Alger figures found among the group. Most came from upper middle-class homes and described their family's income as above average when they were growing up. Forty percent were children of professionals—doctors, lawyers, teachers, or other journalists—and another forty percent described their fathers as businessmen. While the journalists were younger (primarily in their thirties and forties), more liberal, and more highly educated, they were not that different from the members of Congress, presidential candidates, and lobbyists they would be writing about.

The journalists were solidly within the American Ethos described in the preceding section. Most scored high on the Democratic Values and Capitalist Values scales. For example, about seventy percent agreed that "private enterprise is fair to workers" and three fourths agreed that American institutions did not need basic change. There were areas of disagreement, on subjects such as government regulation, foreign policy, and the role of the CIA, to mention a few. But the journalists were generally agreed in supporting the political and economic system that it would be their job as reporters to describe.

The point is often made that the media appeal to core American values already widespread and accepted: support for the institutions of government and private enterprise, for example. Evidently, many of these core values are their own.

Still, a story by Edward Epstein deserves retelling at this point. Epstein once asked eight NBC correspondents which black leader they admired most. Six of the eight mentioned Lou Smith, a Los Angeles black who had recently appeared on an NBC program. One month later, Epstein asked the same correspondents the same question, after Jesse Jackson had appeared

[31]*Ibid.,* see pp. 20–21.

on a program. No one mentioned Smith, and four mentioned Jackson.[32] Epstein was led to wonder how durable some of these opinions are. Perhaps journalists are caught in the magic of their own stories.

Studies of background and opinion presuppose a link between the media people and their handling of the news. But how much impact does this media elite have?

Media Influence

The case for media influence on the American public is very impressive. The news media *help to set the political agenda.* They focus attention on some issues rather than others and say what "problems" should be solved. Studies show a positive relationship between the amount of coverage devoted to issues and the degree to which the public regards those issues as important.[33] Unemployment reports or dramatic pictures of war casualties draw attention to these issues rather than others. It is generally held that the coverage of the Vietnam War by the end of the 1960s contributed to growing public opposition to the war. So, too, the continuing coverage of the Watergate scandal in the Nixon administration contributed to the loss of support for the administration and created a climate of opinion in which the congressional inquiry could go forward.[34] The "most important problems facing the nation today," as reported in the polls, are the continuing news stories of the day. People know these problems are important because they read and hear about them in the news.

The *negative side of this agenda setting* is equally important. If a protest demonstration occurs and is ignored by the media, its political impact has failed. In political terms it has not actually occurred. Issues that are not discussed do not become the "most important problems" cited in the surveys; hence members of Congress find little pressure to go about solving them.

Consider the media coverage of the AIDS epidemic, as documented by Randy Shilts in *And the Band Played On.* In 1981 evidence of an epidemic was first reported in an official medical publication. By the end of 1982, however, there had been only one network program and scant coverage in the nation's leading newspapers. By 1982, medical people knew that the virus could be transmitted through blood banks and from mother to child; most of the public did not know this. It was not until 1985, when film star

[32]Edward J. Epstein, *News From Nowhere* (New York: Random House, 1974), p. 203.

[33]W. Lance Bennett, *Public Opinion in American Politics* (New York: Harcourt, 1980), p. 305; Roy Behr and Shanto Iyengar, "Television News, Real World Cues, and Changes in the Public Agenda," *Public Opinion Quarterly,* 49(1985), pp. 38–57; and Donna Leff et al., "Crusading Journalism: Changing Public Attitudes and Policy-Making Agendas," *Public Opinion Quarterly,* 50(1986), pp. 300–15.

[34]See for example David Weaver et al., "Watergate and the Media: A Case Study of Agenda-setting," *American Politics Quarterly,* October, 1975, 458–72. And see Bennett, p. 306.

Rock Hudson died from AIDS, that it became a media story. According to Shilts, "Doctors involved in AIDS research called the Hudson announcement [that he was dying from the disease] the single most important event in the history of the epidemic."[35] The public began to be informed and Congress moved quickly to increase research funding.

The way a story is cast also affects the political agenda. Compare, for example, the treatment of the race riots in 1964 and 1968.[36] In 1964, the coverage was massive, emphasizing the need for urgent action and the potential for future violence. In 1968, by contrast, after the assassination of Martin Luther King, Jr., the riots were played down. Epstein cites the NBC evening news story:

> Los Angeles and New York City, scenes of the first big-city racial riots, were relatively quiet over the weekend. Though there were disturbances Thursday night in Harlem, Mayor John Lindsay stepped in quickly, and his intervention has been credited with helping prevent further trouble.

NBC did not include the fact that Lindsay's arrival on the scene brought more violence and he narrowly escaped by speeding away in his limousine. All of the networks had statistics available to show that the 1968 situation was at least as serious as the one four years before:

	1964	1968
Reported violent incidents	600	534
Arrests	465	491
Property damage (in millions)	5	15

The stories were not cast the same way, however. The 1968 message was clear: there was no need for further action and no cause for alarm.

The decision to report events on the front page, a back page, or not at all also affects opinion by changing the number of "don't know" responses. It also affects who has opinions and who does not, since interest and information vary with socioeconomic characteristics. Then, too, sustained reporting can override the public's selective perception and dissonance reduction. For example, one may have been socialized into believing that the president cannot tell a lie. Only sustained reporting that the president really was lying could challenge that deeply held belief.

The news media do more than shape the agenda. *They say who is winning and losing in the game of politics,* who is ahead in the polls, and who is leading and lagging. By interpreting the game to others, including the politicians, the media affect the outcome.[37] This effect is found in the early stages of the presidential nomination, as will be seen from the cases in Chapter

---

[35]Randy Shilts, *And the Band Played On* (New York: St. Martins, 1987). See esp. pp. 213, 579.
[36]Epstein, pp. 23–24.
[37]For example, see David L. Paletz and Robert M. Entman, *Media Power Politics* (New York: Free Press, 1981).

Five. One candidate is called the frontrunner, another is judged to be out of the race, another is barely mentioned. Since the chance of success shapes decisions about giving money, endorsements, and other support, the prophecy affects the outcome. This effect is seen also once candidates are in the White House. When the press focuses on presidential popularity polls, then presidents and members of Congress must do so too. A popular president, or one who is perceived to be, can propose more and win more in Congress. Therefore, media comment about a president's popularity can affect decisions throughout the government.

The media also *tell the public what the public thinks.* Networks and newspapers conduct polls of the public and then the poll results are reported as news. After televised debates and presidential press conferences, the announcers come on to say who won or lost, who was effective or weak. Two kinds of news are being reported in these cases: the initial event and the public's reaction (or expected reaction) to the event. After the 1988 presidential debates, most of the networks were careful to say that the viewers must judge for themselves. The *New York Times,* however, ran a front page story referring to Michael Dukakis's "loss" in the second debate. The reporting of the event becomes as important as the event itself to the presidential campaign.

A more extreme case occurred with the candidacy of Gary Hart for the 1988 Democratic nomination. Hart was caught carrying on an illicit affair by two *Miami Herald* reporters who staked out his home. When the news broke, the national media agreed that Hart was finished as a candidate, *even though the polls did not show that sharp a drop.* Many people evidently separated Hart's personal life from his qualifications for the White House. The story, however, continued to dominate the news, overriding a war in the Middle East. By the end of a week's coverage, Hart withdrew. When he decided to reenter, the same negative predictions continued. In a televised debate with the other Democratic candidates, Hart looked, according to one network commentator, "as if he really didn't belong there." *Time* did include some hard news: the public opinion polls showed Hart was still favored. However, the story ignored the polls for the most part, treating Hart's reentry as a joke.[38]

The media can have impact *in more direct ways* as well. As the Hart case illustrates, the medium can become the message, and stories can be editorials in disguise. Conservatives commonly see a liberal press bias, and the liberals see a conservative one, although no clear pattern of bias has been shown when the question is studied.[39] Recently, several writers have

---

[38]*Time,* December 28, 1987, pp. 14–20.

[39]C. Robert Hofsteter, *Bias in the News* (Columbus: Ohio State, 1976); Doris Graber, *Mass Media and American Politics* (Washington, D.C.: CQ Press, 1986), 2nd ed; Michael Robins, "Just How Liberal is the News?" *Public Opinion,* February/March, 1983, pp. 55–60.

also charged that the media's "consensus" values shape the content and tone of the news. One study summarizes:

> The media's routines, content, and impacts on the public are deeply imbued with consensus values and elite perceptions.... [Hence] stories omit, disparage, or dilute proposals and critiques that undermine the American ideology; they promote those moderate innovations most compatible with the system as it is.[40]

The media elite, themselves supporters of the American ethos, shape the stories in accord with their own values. Individuals can be criticized, but the institutions will be supported.

Limits on Media Influence

On the other hand, the news media are limited in at least two important ways. They are limited by people's use of *selective perception* in gaining information. People choose their media in accord with their own reference groups and pre-formed attitudes. For some people, then, it does not matter what the evening news says the most important problems are. They will not be watching. The media elite's own values are not those adhered to by the mass public: despite unanimous negative treatment of Hart, the public still favored him over other Democrats in the race.

The media are limited also by their own *job requirements*: to report the major events occurring and to sell their product, whether newspapers or air time. Some people and events "make news" of such impact that it must be transmitted—a press conference yields a dramatic revelation, government officials deliberately leak information, a foreign leader takes action affecting the United States. Even in the absence of major events, public relations firms stand ready to feed the ever-hungry news machine. Since reporters must rely on others for their regular flow of information, they can become dependent on them and their good will. The clearest example, although not the only one, is the White House influence on news content that will be examined in Chapter Seven. The White House Press Office has such control on content that Press Office staff in the Carter administration could predict with high accuracy what would be the leading news story of the following day—and Carter was not known as a great communicator. Two different perspectives on the job of covering the White House are shown in the box on pages 118–19.

Reporters must stay on good terms with their contacts and so refrain from transmitting critical information about them and honor requests about

[40]Paletz and Entman, pp. 251–52.

The Question of News Bias

Is the news biased in favor of any political views or candidates? At times in American politics, both liberals and conservatives have charged that a bias exists against their positions. Others suggest that whatever bias exists is a structural one, coming from the demands of the job. Thus reporters might emphasize conflict or scandal to produce more interesting news stories—the party or candidate associated with the scandal would not matter. Another structural bias is oversimplification and clichés: in the rush to produce a story and to make it intelligible to the audience, journalists might rely on stereotyping and oversimplified themes, thus distorting the facts.

Here to add to the debate are two accounts by journalists about the political reporting of the news. Jody Powell has seen the news from two points of view as journalist and press secretary in the Carter administration. He now writes a syndicated column and is a commentator for ABC News. Judy Woodruff covers the White House and the president for NBC's evening television news.

Powell talks directly about what he thinks is and is not biased. Woodruff's account is indirect. In showing how a television journalist puts together a story, her description raises other questions about structural bias in the news. In following Woodruff's day, ask yourself what kind of issues and story lines might be emphasized over others.

Jody Powell:

The principle problem with journalism is not political or ideological bias. It exists, but it just does not count for much. . . . In the first place, that is one disease that journalistic training seems to be successful in inoculating against. Reporters are taught to avoid partisanship and politics no matter what, that politics is a tacky business that decent folks don't bother with anyway; and if that's not enough, playing to a political preference is more likely to be spotted and punished than any other transgression.

Secondly, most journalists do not care that much about ideology. They are about as apolitical a group as you are likely to find anywhere. . . . They are interested in politics because the job requires it. But when it comes down to this or that political theory or party, they mostly just do not care.

The problem belongs in a more general category: the willingness to lie and deceive. It belongs there, because making things up and not telling the truth are means that journalists of various descriptions use to achieve a number of ends, the promotion of a political idea or party being one of the least common. The major bias in journalism, it seems to me, the one most likely to promote deception and dishonesty, has its roots in economics. The fact is that news has to sell, or those who report it and edit it will find themselves searching for a new job. And that creates a bias to make news interesting. There is nothing wrong with that on its face. The problems arise when the requirements of being interesting and being accurate part company. . . .

For journalists, the problem of identifying biases is complicated, or should be, by the fact that the sources of most stories are other subjective individuals. . . . If a reporter's source has a clear and identifiable stake in the outcome of the issue under discussion, the reader ought to be told, but usually is not. . . . To make matters worse, it is not unheard of for reporters to partially identify the source of a blind quote in a way that will give the quote a little extra zing and make the story more interesting and salable. [And one finds] the extension of the legitimate need to protect sources to include the questionable and all too common practice of promoting and rewarding them, for example. It is generally understood by Washington insiders that one of the best ways to keep your name out of the news in an unflattering context is to be a ready source of information, preferably unflattering, about others. Like other creatures, reporters tend not to bite the hand that is feeding them.

Judy Woodruff:

Rare is the day when the whole process doesn't come down to a race against the clock. Some days begin more slowly than others and lull you into thinking you have all the time you could possibly need. Then a story breaks late in the afternoon and suddenly you find yourself scrambling down to the wire to make your deadline. It's that kind of job.

Usually the first thing I do at the office is read or at least scan the *Washington Post,* the *New York Times,* and the *Wall Street Journal,* looking mainly for new leads worth pursuing that day on continuing White House stories. After the papers, I glance at the President's agenda for the day to see if any meetings have been added since the preceding late afternoon, when the White House press office distributes his schedule to the news media. Then I check in with NBC's Washington bureau. . . .

It's up to me to originate and select the stories I do, but it's the prerogative of the show's producers to decide whether to use them. Some days it's clear from the start that "Nightly" [NBC Nightly News] will want a piece from the White House, either because the President will be making news, or because an important announcement is expected from the Administration, or because of a development reported in the morning newspapers that demands a follow up. Other days, whether or not "Nightly" will want a White House piece depends on what news I am able to come up with by talking to sources. . . .

It's usually late morning, more than seven hours before the newscast, when the first videotape from the White House is delivered by courier to the Washington bureau. While I'm grabbing a sandwich at my desk, or working the telephones calling sources, or dashing from briefing to stakeout to photo opportunity, or pounding out the first draft of my script, the White House producer begins screening the first video cassettes. . . .

For me, the most challenging and frustrating aspect to making a story come alive on the screen is in the writing. To try to tell a complicated story in two hundred and fifty words or less—sometimes much less—requires a cool, decisive outlook. I'm not sure I'll ever grow entirely accustomed to leaving out information I think is important. But I have learned to grit my teeth when one of the show's producers tells me the script is too long and must be limited to ninety seconds or sometimes less.

Source: Jody Powell, *The Other Side of the Story* (William Morrow, 1984), 14–20.
Source: Judy Woodruff, *"This is Judy Woodruff at the White House,"* with Kathleen Maxa (Reading, Mass.: Addison-Wesley, 1982), 57–65.

how to treat a story. But this dependence can lead, in the words of Lance Bennett:

> ... To the emphasis of some issues over others, the direct transmission of politically 'loaded' information, and the subtle injection of political values into news reporting. In its more advanced forms [it] can result in the suppression of information, the concealment of political motives ... and the protection of sources who use the press to circulate strategic but unfounded political information.[41]

To do their job, reporters must often take the news pre-packaged from the newsmakers.

The job requirements also mean that the media must be attuned to public attitudes and tastes. They cannot afford to offend their audience or their sponsors. Sponsors with interests in Latin America, environmental issues, or covert CIA activities can influence the treatment or suppression of news on these subjects. Notions of public opinion itself shape what the public gets to hear, with stories geared so as not to offend major portions of the audience. Why, asks Randy Shilts, was information on AIDS, known since 1982, not reported as national news until 1985? If an epidemic was occurring on the lines of the projected estimates, it was the news story of the century. Shilts argues convincingly that homosexuality was not considered an acceptable subject for news. The "public" would be offended by the stories. It was not until the celebrity tie-in with Rock Hudson that the subject began to be publicized widely, usually in terms of the risks to heterosexuals.[42]

From this perspective, the flow of information appears complex and variable, taking at least four major forms, as shown in Exhibit 3.7. Each of these four major types can be traced using the example of the defense controversy previously mentioned.

In Type I, media decisions about coverage and treatment influence opinion leaders who in turn influence some segment of the mass public. The flow is *from the media* to the leaders to the mass. Reporters cover the defense controversy between the president and Congress because it makes a good news story. The coverage increases the flow of information which finally reaches the mass public.

The media also need the opinion leaders, however, and are dependent on them for information. Thus in Type II decisions made by opinion leaders (including government officials, industrial sponsors, and others) affect what the media report. The flow is *from the opinion leaders* to the media and on to other opinion leaders and mass public. Members of Congress and Pentagon officials talk about the defense controversy and feed this information to the media who then report it.

[41]Bennett, p. 323.
[42]Shilts, *op. cit.*

EXHIBIT 3.7	Four Types of Information Flow

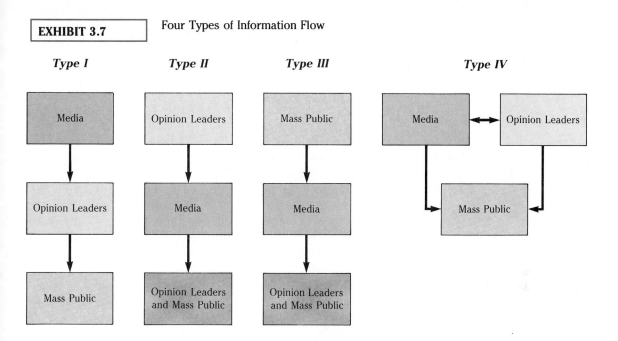

In Type III the mass public—or more accurately, perceptions about it—affect what the media report. Media, officials, and interest groups all gear their messages to the public tastes—for votes and support, audience, profit, and sales. The flow is *from the mass public* to the media and others. Public interest in a balanced budget or group protests about defense spending can give the story news appeal and increase the coverage. Public interest is affecting media coverage and therefore increasing the public interest.

In Type IV the flow is *from the media and opinion leaders in combination* to the mass public. Journalists and other opinion leaders share the same values and work closely in cooperation with each other. Everyone is reading and watching the same news. In this situation it may be impossible to separate the different influences.[43] The defense controversy is considered the leading issue of the day, because officials are talking about it and journalists are asking questions about it.

Even more subtle variations could be drawn for each of the four types. No one has tried to measure how frequently they occur, but cases can be found in support of each. When presidents and members of Congress manufacture news it is an illustration of Type II. The decision to treat Hart's affair as the top campaign story of the week is an example of Type I. The different

---

[43]See Benjamin I. Page, Robert Y. Shapiro, and Glenn R. Dempsey, "What Moves Public Opinion?" *American Political Science Review,* 81(1987), pp. 23–44. The authors suggest that the combined effect may not be able to be separated.

coverage given the president and Congress illustrates Type III—the media follows the public's interest in the president and lack of information about Congress. Many of the top stories of the week are probably cases of Type IV, where everyone begins to talk about the same subject.

On balance, how important is the news media in shaping public opinion? The media themselves gave increasing attention to this question in the months leading to the 1988 presidential nomination. It was debated in two MacNeil-Lehrer hours, ABC's *Nightline, Time, Newsweek,* and several *New York Times'* columns, among other occurrences (not to mention the success of the film *Broadcast News).* The news itself became a top news story. The question is not new, however. The press has long been called "The Fourth Branch of Government," and several nineteenth century politicians could claim that Gary Hart's treatment was not unique. The press grumbles about presidents censoring the news, and presidents grumble about the press. Perhaps the very durability of the debate is the best sign that the press has an impact.

People argue against the influence of the press by citing the limits on the news media. They show how news caters to mass values and is dependent on officials for handouts and leaks. Yet *all government decision-makers have limits.* Presidents need to cater to mass values, too, and are dependent on opinion leaders for much of their success. Showing the limits of media does not deny that a real influence exists. It is true that the public will not always follow the predictions made by the media. It is also true that competition and journalistic ethics can inhibit clear efforts to wield influence. Nevertheless, it is hard to deny the influence of this relatively small group of people, similar to each other in many ways, who can help set the agenda for national debate, say who is winning and losing in the game of politics, and tell the public what the public's opinion is.

"We the People," according to the Constitution, will establish a government to carry out a number of basic activities. The government will provide for the nation's defense, keep order at home, establish a system of law, courts, and justice, promote social and economic well-being, and protect the liberties of its citizens. Nevertheless, "the people" have varying interest in these activities and how they are carried out. Under some circumstances, interest is widespread and intense, but at other times the job of government is left to others—the people have their own jobs and interests to pursue. The people speak with many voices, reflecting areas of consensus and conflict within society; however, some voices are easier to raise and more likely to be heard than others. It is thus important to see how opinions are formed and who interprets what the people are saying. Two hundred years after the Constitution was written, the people remain the basis for what the government will be. They are thus watched by the journalists, pursued by the pollsters, and tirelessly sought by candidates and officials for their votes and support.

1. Public opinion is a collective term that refers to a wide variety of views held by many publics. It is often measured with great accuracy by polling carefully drawn random samples of the population.

2. Political interest and information is generally low, particularly for all areas beyond the presidential spotlight. Interest and information also varies with socioeconomic status. Thus people already disadvantaged in social and economic terms are the least likely to be attentive to politics. This leads to the vicious circle whereby those receiving less from society are less able to make their opinions heard.

3. There are at least three levels of public interest. The majority of the public, about 75 percent of the population, is only marginally interested in political issues. The apoliticals, approximating 20 percent, are not at all interested, while the remaining 5 percent, the activists, are very interested.

4. There is a consensus among most Americans on basic political and economic principles, such as support for democratic practices and the free enterprise system. However, there is disagreement about which principles are most important and how far they should be carried. Libertarians oppose government intervention in economic affairs and support expansion of personal freedoms, populists take the reverse positions, liberals support both, and conservatives oppose both. These internally consistent belief systems are called ideologies.

5. Socialization is the process of learning in a social context those rules and ways of thinking deemed most important for the success and survival of the individual and society. There are many socializing agents—families, schools, churches, work groups—but the family is probably most important.

6. Opinion formation and change requires exposure to information, comprehension of the information, and acceptance (or rejection) of the information. Exposure occurs as information moves from opinion leaders to the most interested citizens out to the mass public. Citizens are not passive recipients of information, however. By means of selective perception they can reject information offered or change it to accord with their own views. Thus, attitudes once formed can be difficult to change.

7. Much political information is provided by a small group of news media which includes key newspapers, television networks, and newsmagazines. By choosing to focus on some issues and not others, they help set the political agenda. They also declare winners and losers in the game of politics, and tell the public what it thinks. These media, however, are not the sole suppliers of information. Other opinion leaders as well as groups within the public can initiate the information flow.

KEY TERMS

public opinion

statistical theory of sampling

random sample

sample error

political efficacy

consensus

ideology

socialization

reference group

agents of socialization

primacy principle

structuring principle

two-step information flow

opinion leaders

selective perception

narrrowcasting

Interest Groups

S ome people are very interested in what the American government does. They not only have read or heard something about the candidates running for office, but they also know their records, watch what they are working on, and talk with them frequently. They have thought a lot about certain issues and have spent time, effort, and money trying to influence their outcome. They give as well as receive news releases. These people belong to interest groups. Interest groups can be large or small, regionally based or nationally organized, focused on a broad range of issues or on a single issue. Their one basic and distinguishing feature is political interest. In this, interest groups are similar to each other and unlike the broader American public.

Interest groups are collections of people with *shared attitudes* who are to some extent *conscious of their identity as a group* and the attitudes they hold in common. They *seek to influence government policy*, in a variety of ways, on the basis of these shared attitudes and so require a *concrete organization* to carry out their purpose. This definition can distinguish interest groups from those broad social categories that were called reference groups in the previous chapter. Reference groups need not have (1) conscious identity, (2) concrete organization, or (3) an engagement in any political activity. Many groups in society would not qualify as interest groups, even though their members might have a potential political interest in common. For one thing, they might not be aware of their identity. For another, they might not have the concrete organization or the opportunity to organize. And for another, even with consciousness and organization, they may not attempt any political activity.

Doctors, organized in the American Medical Association, constitute a political interest group that can influence government policy on Medicare or prescription drugs. Patients, although they have as much potential interest in the policy as the doctors, lack the organization and conscious identity for such a group. The category "women" supplies a reference group affecting the political attitudes and activity of some women. But other women may use other reference groups: race, age, occupation, or economic circumstances. They think of themselves as black, middle-aged, lawyers, or minimum-wage workers. A reference group is not necessarily an interest group. Only with the growing consciousness of a common interest did such women's interest groups as the National Organization of Women (NOW) and others become organized. The key words for identifying interest groups are *conscious identity*, *concrete organization*, and *actual political activity*.

Using these key words, it is possible to see why some interest groups would be more likely to form than others. People are socialized to think of themselves as belonging to various reference groups. If they are not taught to see themselves in certain ways—as women, for example, with common political interests—interest groups cannot form until "consciousness raising" has occurred. Some people are allied with organizations to start with, as in businesses or churches; others must try to form an organization before any interest group activity can begin. Doctors have an organization while patients would first have to form one. Political activity, too, will be easier for some kinds of people than others—those who can afford time from their work; those with education and training; and those who have been taught to feel they can make a difference to the world around them. Women who are single parents and minimum-wage workers have much to ask of the government. But if they are not aware of their common plight, are not part of an organization, and have no time for political activity, then they will not be forming the interest group that could help them.

THE VARIETY OF INTEREST GROUPS

Many people have an interest in oil, the environment, and Alaskan wildlife. (Top) A picture of the oilspill off the Exxon tanker *Valdez* in March 1989. (Bottom) A worker tries to save the life of an oil-soaked bird.

Even with the unequal advantages, an enormous range and diversity of groups are seen. They include labor unions, religious groups, trade associations, farm associations, business firms, ethnic and professional associations, cause and issue groups, foreign governments, and state and local governments. They range in size, budget, means of conducting political activity, and the amount of attention they devote to it. Political influence can be peripheral or central to the major goals of the group. A group like Common Cause organizes primarily for political activity, while a religious group turns to politics only as a side activity. Groups vary in size, cohesion, the status of their members, and the clarity of their goals. Each of these may be translated into political assets and combined in various ways. An association of shrimp fishers may have less social status and a smaller membership than an association of doctors, but it may have an advantage in the cohesion of its members and the clarity of its goals.[1]

It is important to keep this diversity in mind to help counteract the stereotype of the "big money" interest group, wining and dining all Washington and dangling members of Congress from its watch chain. Money, of course, can help, as can any kind of political resource. But there are many such resources: the number of people, the number of votes, threats of force and control over jobs, skills, and recognized social status. In many circumstances money will not be the most critical resource in deciding whether an interest group succeeds or fails in gaining the influence it seeks.[2] A later chapter will show, for instance, that congressional influence in any one policy area is concentrated in a small handful of members often representing similar regional and constituency interests. A regionally based interest group with a small budget does better in this setting than a nationally based, handsomely financed operation. So, the Biscuit and Cracker Manufacturers Association worked to end an American tariff on imported fig paste which was pushing up the price of fig bars and hurting sales. And the

[1]Mancur Olson Jr., *The Logic of Collective Action* (Cambridge: Harvard University Press, 1965), chapter 2.
[2]*Ibid.*

National Council for Monday Holidays (an alliance of travel agencies, unions, and travel-related companies) changed the way people celebrate their holidays. These are examples of interest groups—and very successful ones—but they are far from the stereotypes often depicted.

One staff person in a congressional office worked on legislation for the antibiotic uses of pigs. Never, he said, could he have imagined how many and varied were the pig lobbyists![3] So, it is not only the National Association of Manufacturers and the AFL-CIO one should have in mind when one thinks of interest groups. It is the pig lobbyists and the fig lobbyists too.

A look at the major interest groups on the American scene shows this diversity clearly. Groups can be divided according to their membership and the kind of benefits they seek.

Occupational Groups

Occupational groups are the oldest and most familiar kind of interest groups in America. Also called economic interest groups, these organizations work primarily to secure improved material benefits for their members. They include business groups, labor groups, and farm groups. They include unions with millions of dues-paying members and the U.S. Chamber of Commerce with more than seventy thousand membership firms and an annual budget of many millions. But they also include the Biscuit and Cracker people, the shrimp fishers, and other groups with a small budget and small membership base.

Farm.   Farm groups include such broadly based groups as the National Farm Bureau and the National Farmers' Union which typically take opposing positions to each other on many political issues. They also include the hundreds of special commodity organizations representing producers of a single product. The wheat growers and milk producers are two large and influential examples. These commodity organizations also find themselves lobbying against each other. Higher prices for feed grains mean lower profit margins for livestock; wheat subsidies hurt the market for feed grains. So, while there are many farm lobbies, and some very powerful ones, some of their efforts must be spent fighting each other.

Despite conflicts within and between groups, farmers have held their own in Washington for more than a century. In 1862 the Homestead Act promised free land for anyone who would settle for five years. Land grant colleges and farm extension programs were established to aid agriculture research. In 1916 credit programs were started, allowing farmers to receive loans at very low interest rates. Today, the federal government spends billions of dollars for farm programs including farm loans, export promotion,

[3]Larry Warren, "The Other Side of the Camera," *PS*, 19(1986), p. 86.

and price supports. (Price supports ensure farmers a congressionally mandated price for their products; if the market falls below the price, the government "buys" the product.) Other programs pay the farmer not to produce certain crops. By the late 1980s, support for the corn farmers alone averaged $12.3 billion a year.

There are about 250,000 beekeepers in the United States, many of them only hobbyists. Yet, by the end of the 1980s, the government was spending between $80 and $90 million a year on the beekeeping and honey producing industry. Two interest groups were hard at work for these programs: the American Honey Producers Association, representing primarily the large producers, and the American Beekeeping Federation.[4] Multiply honey by all the other commodities, no matter how small, and one has a sense of the size and activity of farm interest groups.

Labor.   Labor organizations are also important groups on the American political scene. The largest, the American Federation of Labor and Congress of Industrial Organizations (AFL-CIO), is a federation of some ninety independent national unions, each powerful in their own right and each with separate state and local chapters. Along with the United Automobile Workers, the Teamsters, and many other unions, the AFL-CIO has worked for the interests of labor in state and national government. COPE, the political arm of AFL-CIO, endorses candidates and contributes campaign money, organizes get-out-the-vote campaigns, spells out labor's position on issues, and lobbies government officials.

Labor's influence has diminished in recent years, with a decline in membership and increased opposition from business groups. While labor remains strong in many states of the Northeast and North Central regions, much of the work force in the South and Southwest is not unionized.[5] Internal rivalries and dissension have also hurt. Unions have held to their traditional ways, while much of the interest group world was changing around them.

Farm and labor groups remain a major force in American politics, but they have not kept pace in recent years with the rise of the business groups. In the view of many writers, part of the shift to the right in the politics of the 1980s can be explained by the changing trends in interest groups. The force and activity of the labor groups have waned. At the same time, new business groups have grown and old ones, such as the Chamber of Commerce, have been revitalized.[6]

---

[4]*Congressional Quarterly Weekly Report*, April 30, 1988, pp. 1149–52.

[5]Harry Holloway, "Interest Groups in the Postpartisan Era," *Political Science Quarterly* (Spring 1979), pp. 117–33.

[6]See Thomas Byrne Edsall, *The New Politics of Inequality* (New York: Norton, 1984). See also Kay Lehman Schlozman, "What Accent the Heavenly Chorus?" *Journal of Politics*, 46 (1984), pp. 1006–1032.

Business.   Many business groups, like the farm and labor groups, have been long-time participants in American politics. The Chamber of Commerce is an obvious example, as is the National Association of Manufacturers, which represents more than 10,000 corporations. Many trade and professional organizations have been active and influential since the nineteenth century. In recent years, however, a number of businesses have developed lobbying activity of their own, in part because of their dissatisfaction with the broader-based groups and in part because of competition from other interests. Thus, General Motors, which had no permanent lobbying organization in Washington in the 1960s, quickly developed one when challenged on the issue of car safety by consumer interest groups. The broader-based groups, too, began to improve and increase their lobbying activity.

A first step in the revitalization of business groups came in the early 1970s with the formation of the Business Roundtable. The Roundtable resulted from the merger of three groups: two had worked to restrict the bargaining power of unions (the Construction Users Anti-Inflation Roundtable and the Labor Law Study Committee), and an elite group (known as the March Group) was composed of the chief executive officers of major companies.[7] The groups kept their original purposes while broadening their goals to include regulatory, banking, and anti-trust issues. The Roundtable soon became known as the "political arm of big business."[8] It developed a lobbying strategy whereby the chief executive officers themselves would maintain close contact with the members of Congress whose states and districts contained the main facilities of the corporations. One corporate head could deal with the Texas Democrat while another talked to the New York Republican. The Roundtable also hired Washington law firms and public relations firms to supplement its own grass-roots lobbying efforts.

A second development came with the rejuvenation of the Chamber of Commerce. Described as a "sleeping giant" in the early 1970s, the Chamber woke up with a vengeance by the end of the decade, quadrupling its membership to 215,000 firms by 1983 and modernizing its lobbying organization.[9] The Chamber's computers can select from the 2800 state and local chapters and the 215,000 member firms which should be alerted—for major issues before the Congress which are perceived as a threat to the entire business community and for issues of concern to only some of its members. The Chamber also provides encouragement and a centralizing focus for the many ad hoc coalitions forming on specific issues.

The growth of these short-lived coalitions marks a third development in the revitalization of business interests. Hundreds of coalitions have formed,

---

[7]Graham K. Wilson, *Interest Groups in the United States* (New York: Oxford University Press, 1981), chapter 4.

[8]Edsall, p. 121.

[9]*Ibid.*, p. 123.

some lasting only long enough to lobby for or against a specific bill before the Congress, and some watching an issue year after year. For example, the Consumer Issues Working Group is an alliance of some 400 organizations that include corporate giants like Proctor and Gamble as well as small trade associations. Despite its name, the coalition has opposed consumer groups on a wide variety of issues and was chiefly responsible for the defeat of the Consumer Protection Agency.[10]

Business interests can be as internally divided as farm interests or labor groups. All have a potential for competition that can undermine their collective strength. The business groups formed in response to the threat posed by unions and other interest groups; these groups may now need to rally in response to them.

Nonoccupational Groups

The group universe includes many **nonoccupational groups** as well, groups that do not work primarily to secure material benefits for members. The number of these groups in existence has grown dramatically since the 1970s and the proportion with Washington offices has more than doubled. Nonoccupational groups may focus on single issues, work to help people (migrant workers, the homeless) who are not group members, or call themselves public interest groups. A **public interest group** has been defined as "one that seeks a collective good, the achievement of which will not selectively and materially benefit the membership or activists of the organization."[11] The benefits are not directed primarily to the members—there may not even be a membership in fact—and they are not primarily material. For example, a consumer group could claim to represent a public interest (all people, not only group members, are consumers) opposing the special interests of corporations, farm groups, or unions. Other public interest groups include the well-financed Common Cause, with a budget in the millions, which works for a variety of government reforms, and such environment groups as Friends of the Earth and the Sierra Club.

Other groups represent disadvantaged people in society, with social and legal improvements being the primary benefits sought. Examples include civil rights groups, women's groups, and senior citizen groups. These groups direct their efforts to helping people beyond any set of conscious, dues-paying members. Blacks or women can benefit from the efforts geared to their needs without seeing themselves as group members. Still other groups work for broad ideological positions that they see in the public interest (whether rival groups in that same public would agree or not). In the 1970s, a number of conservative groups joined together to use the direct-mail services of Richard Viguerie, forming the nucleus of what came to be

[10]*Ibid.*, p. 128.
[11]Jeffrey M. Berry, *Lobbying for the People* (Princeton: Princeton University Press, 1977), p. 7.

known as the New Right. Viguerie maintained computerized current addresses in his files of some two million people who contributed to right-wing groups or candidates. Other conservative groups, such as the Moral Majority, also came into being in reaction to what they saw as the overly liberal policies of the time.

At this point one can see that the term "public interest group" is something of a misnomer. Whose public interest and whose idea of public interest? Public interest groups are subject to as much rivalry and internal dissension as any of the farm groups or unions. Moreover, their positions are not necessarily more correct or less special than other opposing political positions. If some people in town want a new water resource project and others want to keep the trees, there is by definition no one public interest to be found. The public is divided as to what its interest is, and a *political* process which engages both sides will decide the outcome. The one real distinction between public interest groups and occupational groups is that the former are not concerned primarily with material benefits to members.

Among the many nonoccupational groups that have risen in recent years, single-interest groups have been prominent. As the name implies, these groups arise in response to one issue of the day; the lifetime of the group is usually only as long as the issue. There have been peace groups and stronger-defense groups, pro-choice and anti-abortion groups, groups for and against the Panama Canal Treaty and aid to the Nicaraguan Contras. These groups, too, would claim that they work for a public interest, even while they are opposed by other groups that claim the same. They are like the public interest groups in the kind of positions they take and the benefits they seek, but their efforts are directed at a narrower objective.

One can also find **issue networks**—fluid groupings of people who move in and out of policy areas, at times clustering toward one issue, at other times connecting several issues. These are not interest groups in the formal sense, but are rather groupings of individuals and groups who constantly move in and out of the network.[12] Since they link people in various groups and can contribute to any one group's goals, they form an important part of the activity that interest groups are involved in.

All this group activity is not a new phenomenon in American politics. In the nineteenth century, groups campaigned against slavery and for reforms in government. Tariff controversies as early as the 1830s mobilized local groups and a national interest organization. In this century, the Women's Christian Temperance Union (WCTU) and the Anti-Saloon League along with other groups mobilized so successfully that they actually won a constitutional amendment (the Eighteenth, prohibiting the sale of alcoholic liquor). This is more than any modern group can claim. Opposing groups then had to form to repeal the amendment. Among other examples, the Na-

---

[12]Hugh Heclo, "Issue Networks and the Executive Establishment," in *The New American Political System,* ed. Anthony S. King (Washington, D.C.: American Enterprise Institute, 1978), pp. 87–124.

tional Rifle Association (NRA) was founded in 1871 and an environment group, the Audubon Society, in 1905. The Audubon Society still exists and the NRA continues to be one of the most active and influential of the single interest groups. With modern communication technology, groups can form more easily now and reach their potential supporters, but they are the descendants of a very old political tradition.

Politics has been described as the process of "who gets what, when, and how." All of these groups are part of that process, whatever "what" they seek and "who" they seek it for. On occasion, public interest groups have taken on such giants as defense contractors and the American Medical Association, winning substantial victories.[13] The business groups have rallied in response, winning victories of their own.[14]

GROUP ACTIVITIES

Groups divide their efforts among many activities. Even while they seek to influence government, they must also spend the time and resources to maintain their own organization. Both kinds of activities can affect the success of the other.

Maintaining the Organization

A major task for an interest group is to maintain its own membership. It must rally the resources—in funds or numbers or enthusiastic workers—to do its job. Yet, for most people, politics is low on the list of priorities, and groups are joined only when there is a good reason for doing so. Why should people join an interest group? They may care about its policy, but they have many things to care about—and many worthy causes to contribute to. The problem is particularly severe for groups that seek benefits for people beyond their own membership. Why join the group if one can be a **free rider** and gain the benefits without the costs? A free rider is a person who benefits from the action of interest groups without expending effort or money for them.

Occupational groups, therefore, have an advantage since many can rely on a membership that goes with the job. Workers join the union; doctors join the American Medical Association. A few nonoccupational groups (such as church groups) can also count on a membership base. Even many of these groups, however, gain only partial support. One writer estimates that only 35 percent of the nation's farmers belong to any agricultural interest group, and 21 percent of the work force belong to unions.[15] A study of

---

[13]Michael Pertschuk, *Giant Killers* (New York: Norton, 1986).
[14]Wilson, *op. cit.,* esp. pp 80–82.
[15]*Ibid.*, pp. 33, 51.

public interest groups found that only 12 percent had a membership of over 100,000 and some 30 percent had no membership at all.[16]

Some groups solve their membership problem by offering **selective incentives.** These are rewards, independent of the policy goal being sought, that are given only to dues-paying members. The Farm Bureau offers low cost insurance rates as well as price breaks on seed, fertilizer, and cattle feed. Trade associations provide newsletters with valuable insider information. The National Wildlife Federation publishes several attractive magazines; thus the subscribers to the magazines become the interest group members. The closed-shop rule of many unions is a particularly strong incentive, since workers must pay dues and join the union in order to keep their jobs. In addition to providing incentives, groups must see that their strategies and goals work to attract members and do not drive them away. The policies they seek and the methods they use must be chosen with care. When the ACLU (American Civil Liberties Union) supported the right of a neo-nazi group to demonstrate in Skokie, Illinois, they lost members in droves. The ACLU had to choose between the issue of civil liberties and the overt anti-semitism of the nazi group. The choice kept faith with the ACLU's own policy goals, but it cost membership support.

How do groups sustain themselves without dues-paying members? Many of these groups, first established in the 1970s, were supported in large part by foundations. The Ford and Rockefeller foundations, among others, gave millions of dollars to consumer and environmental groups. One study indicates that about ninety percent of the nonoccupational groups received outside aid to begin.[17] Even the government has helped sponsor groups (that would in turn be lobbying the government). Senior citizen groups, for example, came into being *after* legislation was passed making money available to support their issues. The same process occurred in education and transportation policy. One scholar comments, "The formation of new groups was one of the *consequences* of major new legislation, not one of the *causes* of its passage."[18]

But foundations would not support the groups nor Congress pass laws to help them without some widespread public interest and support to start with. The groups' greatest triumph may have come before they were even established! Once again, the circle of interest and influence identified in Chapter Three is evident. Given public interest, groups could gain support from the foundations and government and be in a position to rally more interest and support. This circle helps explain why so many public interest groups came into being in the 1970s—the foundations and the government helped them. But it does not tell a group now how it can form in order to

---

[16]Berry, p. 28

[17]Jack L. Walker, "The Origins and Maintenance of Interest Groups in America," *American Political Science Review*, 77(1983), p. 398.

[18]*Ibid.*, p. 403.

mobilize public interest. And it raises the very interesting question of who is influencing whom. By giving or withholding money, the foundations and government are helping to say which groups can enter the political process and which cannot.

Maintaining an organization takes time and money. Selective incentives can be expensive, foundation grants must be applied for, and decisions will be taken with an eye to the membership rolls. While groups seek to influence the government, much of their time and resources must be spent simply to keep themselves going.

Influencing Government

Interest group activity ranges widely depending on the group's resources, goals, and the political context it must work within. Some activity is directed at influencing public opinion through publicity campaigns, demonstrations, special features offered to magazines and newspapers, advertisements, and computerized mailing lists. Other activity is focused directly on the government decision-makers. These two approaches have been called **outside** and **inside strategies**. The outside strategies seek to influence decision-makers indirectly through appeals to public opinion. The inside strategies target decision-makers directly—in Congress, the courts, or the executive branch.[19]

Inside Strategies.   Inside strategies in Congress can be general or specific. Groups spend time and money developing good will and favorable attitudes even when there is no issue of concern to them. As one farm lobbyist remarked,

> If I don't have an agriculture bill, you know, I won't see [two members of a House committee] for a while, except sometimes, I'll call them up and say, 'How are you doing,' or I will see them on the floor in the House and we'll have a cup of coffee downstairs. . . . You have to keep up your contacts.[20]

Good will is developed as lobbyists provide not only political and personal help, but specialized information needed by the official: position papers, facts and figures, and technical reports. They "create a dependency," in the words of one writer, when bureaucrats or members of Congress routinely look to them for something they cannot get elsewhere.[21] They also develop trust and credibility as the relationship is maintained over time. Groups attempt to influence specific decisions too. But at this point they can reap the benefits of all the general good will they developed before.

[19]Norman J. Ornstein and Shirley Elder, *Interest Groups, Lobbying, and Policymaking* (Washington, D.C.: CQ Press, 1978), pp. 82–83.
[20]*Ibid.*
[21]Jeffrey M. Berry, *The Interest Group Society* (Boston: Little, Brown 1984), pp. 122–123.

A good example of inside lobbying is the work done by Thomas Dine, head of the pro-Israel lobby known as AIPAC (the American Israel Public Affairs Committee). Dine's government experience included work for four Senate Democrats and for the Peace Corps, where he also lobbied in Congress. He is known for his technical knowledge of military questions—he once directed national security issues as part of his staff work for the Senate Budget Committee. Dine already has the good will, long-term relationship, and technical expertise to help his message get across to members of Congress.[22]

Inside strategies can be elaborately designed. Rockwell International, the company that produces B-1 bombers, devised an elaborate series of subcontracts to 5200 companies in 48 states. The fuselage was built in one congressional district and the electronic system somewhere else. When the controversial bomber runs into trouble in Congress, as it has periodically during the last thirty years, the members hear from the local industries that have the subcontracts.[23] Subcontracting, many critics say, reduces the efficiency and quality of production. It is, however, the strategy of choice for many interest groups because it ensures a broad base of support in Congress. The strategies are not limited to subcontracts. Any program or product that can be divided into 435 parts (the number of districts represented in the House of Representatives) has a good start in gathering congressional support.

Interest groups seek access and influence throughout the executive branch. Independent commissions, charged with regulating an industry in the private sector, are lobbied by the very interests they regulate. Bureaucrats in the departments and agencies of government are also lobbied. Later chapters will describe the operation of "subgovernments": the mutually supportive interaction between an interest group, a congressional committee, and an executive agency. In this tight interlocking system, the interest groups are working with the agency as well as with the committee members. Each part of the triangle supports the other. Thus as Rockwell International worked with Congress, it also sought support for its bomber among Pentagon officials in the Department of Defense. The Pentagon people helped Rockwell in persuading the Congress.

Groups seek access and influence in the White House as well. They vie to have their representatives selected for the special "Presidential Commissions" that are appointed from time to time. Presidential commissions, which study and make recommendations on a policy problem, are usually composed of people who already have an interest in the policy. The results of these commissions are rarely surprising—they can be predicted by seeing the members who are appointed. Groups also ask for meetings with the

---

[22]Congressional Quarterly, *The Washington Lobby*, 5th ed. (Washington, D.C.: Congressional Quarterly, 1988), pp. 81–82.

[23]*The Washington Monthly*, February, 1988, pp. 29–38.

president in the White House. While all presidents now maintain liaison staff with groups such as blacks, women, and the elderly, they vary in the attention they give the groups in personal encounters.[24] For example, blacks and women who were invited to the Carter White House complained of their lack of access during the Reagan years.

Interest groups engage in a different form of inside lobbying when they deal with courts. The judges on the lower courts and the justices on the Supreme Court are not personally approached by lobbyists. But interest groups promote their interests by sponsoring litigation, typically challenging governmental actions or trying to force government to take certain actions. Interest groups also participate in litigation by providing *amicus curiae* or friend of the court briefs. These are briefs filed by interested parties including interest groups who are not litigants in a suit but have a concern with the policy consequences of the outcome of the suit. These briefs offer the court factual information and legal arguments that in theory are supposed to help the judges but in reality attempt to persuade them to decide the suit in ways favorable to the groups that file the briefs. In the past, the ACLU and the NAACP have achieved many victories before the Supreme Court in cases they sponsored or in which they participated by filing *amicus curiae* briefs. In more recent years environmental groups, women's groups, and conservative groups have achieved some degree of success before the Supreme Court.

Outside Strategies.   Well-established groups, whatever their size or budget, may find inside strategies the most effective. They have been around as long as the bureaucrats, members of Congress, and Supreme Court justices and have developed credibility and good will. However, other groups, especially those newly formed or those representing people less well-known and trusted by the officials, need to turn to outside strategies. They take their case to the public or hire expensive public relations firms to make the case for them. The marches and demonstrations staged by black groups and women's groups were part of an outside strategy to change national policy. Neither group had enough access to decision-makers for an inside strategy. Indeed, the access was part of the reforms they were trying to get. The three-hour-long Gay Parade in New York City in 1988 was an outside strategy. It said to officials: "See how many people are willing to march in 90 degree heat in one city alone to show their support for gay issues." Other groups, even those not disadvantaged, can find outside strategies useful. In April 1989, the pro-choice march on Washington drew close to half a million people and was an outside strategy to persuade the Supreme Court, Congress, and state legislatures to retain a woman's right to choose abortion.

[24]John Orman, "The President and Interest Group Access," *Presidential Studies Quarterly*, 18 (1988), pp. 787–91.

One effective use of an outside strategy was carried out by nuclear protest groups in the 1980s. With good financial backing and some very prestigious scientists as spokespersons, the groups began to target middle-class, middle-aged America. They conducted polls on what people thought about the nuclear issue, held teach-ins at colleges and medical schools, sponsored books and articles, and encouraged other groups to do the same. One of its offspring, the Physicians for Social Responsibility, increased its membership from 3000 to 16,000 in one year and began to bring in four dollars for every one dollar spent on mailing.[25] This one group can be multiplied by the dozens of other sub-groups formed. So, while defense groups and military contractors have better access to Congress and the White House than the nuclear protest groups, the officials now know that the issue is controversial and a large segment of the public is concerned.

Some of the most advanced outside strategies have been developed by the religious fundamentalist groups.[26] The Moral Majority (now called the Liberty Foundation) maintains not only one of the largest direct-mailing operations, it also makes use of computerized phone banks that make up to 100,000 phone calls per week, with the message selected by issue, religious orientation, and even preacher loyalty. Supporters of the television ministries of Pat Robertson or Jerry Falwell would hear messages tied in to their own favorite religious leader. Christian Voice, a fundamentalist media group, which claims 350,000 members including 40,000 pastors, has direct access to the public through Christian television and radio stations. Christian Voice educates the television ministers, feeds them information, and warns them of upcoming legislation, and the ministers pass this on to the public. These groups claim that they can reach literally millions of constituents on issues opposing abortion and the Equal Rights Amendment and supporting school prayer.

Groups usually try to combine outside and inside strategies for maximum impact. They talk to the officials themselves and they tell their members to write to their representatives, saying how important the legislation is to them. The members of Congress will be hearing the case of the interest group while they are receiving mail from back home. On a recent controversy for a clean air bill, groups for and against the bill lobbied Congress and mounted major grass-roots campaigns to mobilize public opinion. The members of Congress were talking directly to the environmentalists and the unions and hearing from the public on both sides of the issue. The Concerned Women for America, a religious fundamentalist group, has evolved a two-track system in which a corps of women in Washington is linked to counterparts in the congressional districts. If a member of Congress cannot

[25]Fox Butterfield, "Anatomy of the Nuclear Protest," *The New York Times Magazine*, July 11, 1982.

[26]For the material in this paragraph, see Allen D. Hertzke, *Representing God in Washington* (Knoxville: University of Tennessee Press, 1988), pp. 50–51.

be persuaded directly, the counterpart in the home district goes to work to arouse public opinion.[27]

Groups are not only active participants in the political process, but vigilant watchers of it as well. Unlike the general public, interest groups monitor government activity. They keep informed about what is happening and what is likely to happen. They "rate" senators and representatives on the proportion of times they vote for or against the group's position on key votes in Congress. These ratings give group members a quick way of summarizing a legislator's general position and predicting how a decision in Congress is likely to go. An example of group ratings for one year for a selected list of U.S. Senators is provided in the box on page 140.

Finally, groups can affect the political process by election activity. If the decision-makers cannot be persuaded, and the ratings show the position is doomed to fail, then the logical recourse is to change the legislators, defeating the group's opponents and electing sympathetic members. One shuffles the pack and tries for a better deal.

POLITICAL ACTION COMMITTEES

Few recent trends in American politics have attracted more attention, or stirred more debate, than the rise of *political action committees* **(PACs)**. Political action committees are organizations set up by interest groups to raise and contribute money to campaigns in an attempt to elect or defeat candidates for office. Some PACs exist as special units within an interest group. While the group is concerned with all activities that affect national policy, the PAC concentrates on campaign contributions. These PACs are the electoral arm of the interest group. Other PACs have developed as independent entities. In effect, these independent PACs are new interest groups, concentrating on elections as their way of influencing policy.

Origins and Growth

PACs appeared and multiplied following the campaign finance reforms of the 1970s. According to law, unions and corporations could not use their own funds for campaign contributions, but they could administer a committee that would raise money from outside. In other words, the United Auto Workers could not contribute to campaigns, but they could form a PAC which would carry on the fund-raising and the contributions. Unions, corporations, trade associations, and other groups were quick to see how the law could be used to their own advantage, and PACs grew from 608 in 1974 to more than 4000 by 1984.[28]

---

[27]*Ibid.*, pp. 52–53.

[28]For background, see *Elections '86* (Washington D.C.: Congressional Quarterly, 1986), pp. 47–55. See also Michael J. Malbin, *Parties, Interest Groups and Campaign Finance Laws* (Washington, D.C.: American Enterprise Institute, 1980).

Senators' Policy Profiles

Groups keep track of how senators and representatives vote in Congress. The ratings show, roughly, the percentage of time the member of Congress votes "correctly" on key votes taken on group issues. In the following chart, for example, the conservative ACU rates Edward Kennedy as voting correctly ten percent of the time whereas Jesse Helms voted correctly all the time. Six groups are selected from the many that give ratings: their issues will be familiar to readers of Chapter Three. The liberal ADA and the conservative ACU are on opposite sides of many of the same issues. The ACLU opposes government infringement of personal freedoms and the CEI opposes government intervention in the economy. The LCV watches environmental issues while the NSI works for a stronger defense.

Ratings have been selected for a few of the most nationally visible senators. Many have been presidential and vice-presidential candidates. One, of course,

left the Senate to become vice-president. The ratings give a good capsule view of the senators' positions on a range of issues. Notice Lloyd Bentsen's position in relation to the other Democrats on the list and his very high defense score. William Cohen of Maine is also unusual in receiving high ratings for both environmental and defense issues. Since the ratings are available in many political science sources, all citizens, not only the group members, can make use of this information.

ADA   Americans for Democratic Action

ACU   American Conservative Union

ACLU American Civil Liberties Union

CEI   Competitive Enterprise Institute

LCV   League of Conservation Voters

NSI   National Security Index

	GROUPS RATE MEMBERS OF CONGRESS					
SENATORS, STATE, AND PARTY	ADA LIBERAL	ACU CONSERVATIVE	ACLU LIBERTIES	CEI ENTERPRISE	LCV ENVIRONMENT	NSI DEFENSE
Lloyd Bentsen, Tex. D	45	30	30	46	50	78
Bill Bradley, N.J. D	85	23	78	42	90	33
William Cohen, Maine R	50	52	64	56	83	88
Robert Dole, Kan. R	0	91	7	77	35	100
Albert Gore, Tenn. D	70	9	78	27	67	20
Jesse Helms, N.C. R	0	100	7	88	17	100
Edward Kennedy, Mass. D	80	10	100	31	78	0
J. Danforth Quayle, Ind. R	5	82	7	77	25	100

Ratings are based on the 1986 session; however, members' positions tend to remain stable over time.

Source: From *The Almanac of American Politics, 1988* by Michael Barone and Grant Ujifusa. Copyright © 1987 by National Journal Inc. All rights reserved. Reprinted by permission.

EXHIBIT 4.1

The Increase in
Political Action
Committees

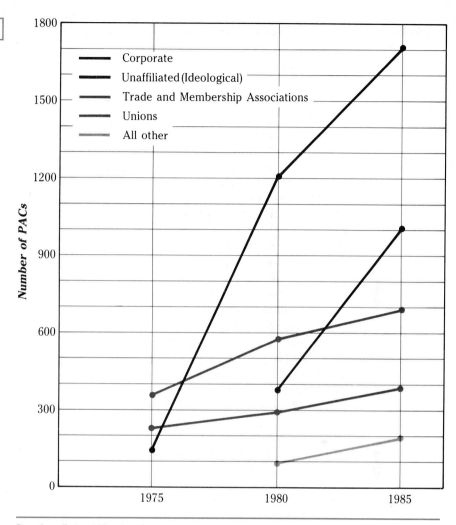

Based on Federal Election Commission Reports. The final "all other" category includes
government corporations that do not issue stock, and a small number of cooperative
groups.
Source: M. Margaret Conway, "PACs and Congressional Elections in the 1980s," in *Interest
Group Politics*, 2nd ed. (Washington, D.C.: CQ Press, 1986), p. 73.

Independent PACS soon joined the growing trend. They include the
now-famous National Conservative Political Action Committee (NCPAC),
the Fund for a Conservative Majority, and the National Committee for an
Effective Congress. While the unions were the first to develop political action committees, it soon became clear that corporate and ideological
groups might beat them at their own game. Through the 1970s and 1980s,
union PACs grew in number, but the others multiplied at a much higher
rate. By 1985 corporate PACs outnumbered union PACs by more than four
to one. (See Exhibit 4.1.)

EXHIBIT 4.2	POLITICAL ACTION COMMITTEE	AMOUNT CONTRIBUTED
Top-Spending PACs Among the Occupational Groups in Amount Contributed to Federal Elections	Realtors Political Action Committee	$2,782,338
	American Medical Association	2,107,492
	National Education Association	2,055,133
	United Auto Workers	1,621,055
	National Assoc. of Retired Federal Employees	1,491,895
	Letter Carriers Political Education	1,490,895
	D.R.I.V.E. (Teamsters)	1,457,196
	National Association of Home Builders	1,424,240
	Association of Trial Lawyers	1,404,000
	Machinists Non-Partisan Political League	1,364,550

Based on total spending in 1985–86.

Source: Federal Election Commission figures as reported in Harold W. Stanley and Richard G. Niemi, *Vital Statistics on American Politics* (Washington: CQ Press, 1988), p. 148.

PACs vary greatly in their size and budget, in the kinds of groups they affiliate with, and in the offices they maintain. While some PACS have large well-heeled Washington organizations, the majority do not. The Washington PAC is an exception to the rule. Millionaire PACs are also an exception. PACs contributing a total of $10,000 or less to campaigns make up about thirty-seven percent of the total, while those with budgets of more than $300,000 account for only two percent of all PACs.[29] Nevertheless, millionaire PACs do exist. The National Conservative Political Action Committee (NCPAC) spent over nine million dollars over a two-year period, while a real estate PAC spent six million and the American Medical Association's PAC spent five million. Many occupational groups, both unions and membership associations, spend more than one million for candidates in one election year alone. (See Exhibit 4.2.)

The Impact of Political Action Committees

Many people seeing the rise in number of PACs assume a corresponding importance. But how successful are these committees? Have they changed the way politics is conducted in this country and have they changed the results? The first studies of the subject suggest PACs have less impact than many people assume.

PACs work in a larger political environment where the candidates and parties continue to be active. Under the law, political action committees can give up to $5000 to any one candidate in a primary or general election

[29]See Theodore Eismeier and Philip Pollock III, "Political Action Committees: Varieties of Organization and Strategy," in *Money and Politics in the United States*, ed. Michael J. Malbin (Chatham, New Jersey: Chatham House, 1984), pp. 122–141; esp. p. 126.

race, although many contributions would be for less. Many PACs give little money at all, relying instead on **in-kind contributions**—that is, providing organizational or technical assistance to a campaign. While PACs can help a candidate, most of the money still must be raised at home in the states and districts. One political analyst estimates that no more than thirty percent of a campaign budget would come from the political action committee. The candidate would still need to find the other seventy percent.[30]

Moreover, candidates must be able to convince the PAC that they can run a viable race. They need to show the polls, local endorsements, and their own money-raising ability to justify the contribution. They have to raise money before they can go to a Washington PAC and raise money. "They have it backwards," one PAC director said, "if they think they can come to us first and then go back home and run the campaign. The real action is back home. . . . We're a lot more interested in how it plays in Peoria than how does it play in Washington."[31] The national parties, too, are playing an increasingly important role in PAC contributions. It is the parties that tell the PACs who is promising or vulnerable and the parties that help the PAC managers decide whether or not to give support. Parties provide money themselves to candidates and they also help the PACs decide where to give their money. Even with the PAC organization, the local connections are the most important. Officials in the Washington offices admit that the local recommendations of who is and who is not to be supported are approved between eighty and ninety percent of the time. As one national executive director put it, "If we have someone who raised 10,000 dollars at the local level, but wants to support someone who we don't think is especially deserving, we will usually go along with him. If we didn't, he might not raise that kind of money for us the next time around."[32] In short, political action committees work within the same political environment long considered important in winning elections. Local money raising, endorsements, an opponent's vulnerability, and party support are still basic to the candidate's success.

So, to what extent can PACs change the outcome of an election or the decisions taken by members of Congress? An important study by John Wright begins to provide some answers. Wright selects five PACs considered among the most influential: the American Medical Political Action Committee (AMPAC), affiliated with the American Medical Association; the Dealers Electoral Action Committee (DEAC), affiliated with the National Automobile Dealers Association; BANKPAC, associated with the American Bankers Association, the Realtors Political Action Committee (RPAC), and the Associated General Contractors Political Action Committee (AGCPAC).

[30]*Elections '86*, p. 55.
[31]*Ibid.*
[32]John R. Wright, "PACs, Contributions, and Roll Calls," *American Political Science Review*, 79 (1985), p. 405.

EXHIBIT 4.3			SENATE		HOUSE	
			WON	*LOST*	*WON*	*LOST*
Interest Groups and	ADA		44%	56%	59%	41%
Election Success,	Americans for Democratic Action (Liberal)					
1984 Races	COPE		54	46	64	36
	AFL-CIO, Committee on Political Education (Union)					
	NCEC		56	44	54	46
	National Committee for an Effective Congress (Liberal)					
	ACA		52	48	82	18
	Americans for Constitutional Action (Conservative)					
	BIPAC		50	50	64	36
	Business-Industry Political Action Committee (Business)					
	NCPAC		67	33	78	22
	National Conservative Political Action Committee (Conservative)					

Source: *Congressional Quarterly Weekly Report*, November 17, 1984, p. 2970.

He then looks at decisions taken in Congress that were seen by the PAC members themselves as most important to them. He finds no significant difference in support for the PAC position regardless of whether members of Congress received large contributions or received none at all.[33]

The same result is seen when looking for an impact on elections. Exhibit 4.3 shows the success rate for leading interest groups in the 1984 congressional elections. In Senate races, PACs do little better than 50–50 in helping their candidates get elected. In House races, the higher success rates reflect the fact that PACs give most of their money to incumbents. (Incumbents are those in office at the time of the election.) Since House incumbents are overwhelmingly likely to win their reelection bids, whether they receive the contributions or not, the PACs are not making a difference in these contests. NCPAC's high success rate in the table merely shows that it gave a lot of its money to these incumbents. The PAC contributions may be keeping the good will of the members of Congress, but they do not appear to be changing the outcome of the elections.

People continue to worry, however, about the growth of PACs and their influence in "buying" members of Congress. Certainly the candidates themselves think PACs are important and would like their help in campaign contributions. Presumably PACs have some impact about them; it is difficult to believe that so much money would be raised and spent without any positive return. Although, the claims made about them appear to be exaggerated.

[33]Wright, *op. cit.*, pp. 400–414.

A nineteenth-century protest by Thomas Nast against the power of big business groups: Liberty is captured by the trusts (monopolies) and the people's vessel sinks.

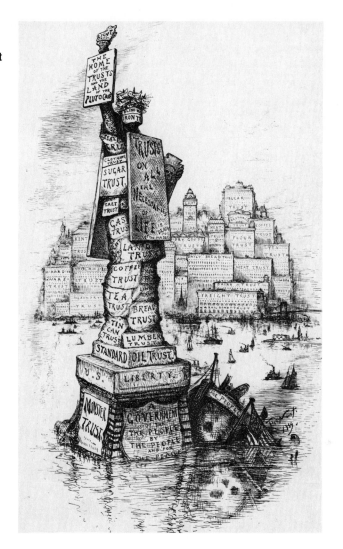

LOBBYING

One kind of interest group activity requires a closer look because of its importance, its place in political legend, and the number of misconceptions that have flourished around it. This activity is called lobbying. Since lobbies were the rooms of public buildings where citizens could talk with officials, lobbying came to mean working in these areas to influence policy. The word dates from the middle of the nineteenth century. (For an example of nineteenth-century lobbying, see the box on page 146.)

The Most Effective Lobbying, Nineteenth Century Style

Neither the practice of lobbying nor the attacks against it are new to the American political scene. Nineteenth century lobbyists, primarily representing business interests, grew so frequent that they were called the "Third House of Congress." The railroads lobbied, although in a somewhat disorganized fashion, and tariff and currency lobbyists set up permanent Washington offices. Historian David Rothman's description of the successful lobbyists of the 1890s, excerpted below, is strikingly similar to the picture of effective lobbying today. Notice how lobbyists establish a friendly relationship with sympathetic legislators and "create a dependency" by providing specialized information. Even the revolving door is very much in evidence. Defeated and retired senators were quickly hired by corporations to make use of their contacts and experience. In Rothman's account, "agents" are lobbyists and "rates" are taxes.

> [Lobbyists] devoted almost all their time and attention to public officials already sympathetic to their position, occasionally detouring to convince the doubtful but invariably ignoring known opponents. Agents typically answered the inquiries of interested senators, explaining the various proposals on the calendar and clarifying the pertinent but dull details of intricate bills. With regularity, they supplied information that only representatives of particular organizations could gather. Helping members of Congress to understand the increasingly technical legislation that came before the chamber, lobbyists became the experts in an era of specialization. . . .

Personal relationships with public officials were considered so vital that lobbyists would not bother to contact men they did not know. [An] agent for the sugar refiners explained that he discussed rates only with friends; with others "I presumed my views would not have had much weight." [A Texas senator] contended that corporations disliked great turnovers in office; their representatives could not form stable connections among constantly changing members.

The lobbying profession soon became an appropriate occupation for defeated or retired senators. Recognizing that ex-senators had access to friends who remained in office, corporations regularly hired them. The practice became so widespread that [one senator] proposed to alter the rules governing visitors' rights to the chamber floor. As a traditional courtesy, all former members were permitted to enter the Senate and mingle with their old associates. . . .

Nevertheless, . . . the chamber maintained its custom. Corporations naturally continued to hire former senators on the strength of their old connections.

Source: David J. Rothman, *Politics and Power: The United States Senate 1869–1901* (Cambridge: Harvard University Press, 1966), pp. 203–6.

Lobbying refers to communication aimed at a government decision-maker in the hope of influencing a decision.[34] Lobbying can be direct or indirect, pursued by anyone, and aimed at any official. Thus, presidents lobby Congress. This broad definition reflects the reality of politics where many people attempt to influence each other. Nevertheless, there is also a narrower definition that limits lobbying to communication by interest group

[34]See Carol S. Greenwald, *Group Power* (New York: Praeger, 1977), pp. 61–62.

representatives.[35] Group representatives who engage in such activity are called ***lobbyists.***

A law passed in 1946 (Title III of the Legislative Reorganization Act) requires lobbyists to register and report their expenses under the following conditions: if they seek direct communication with members of Congress on proposed legislation and if their money from fund-raising is used principally to influence the proposed legislation. It is easy to see the many loopholes in the law. Lobbyists seeking indirect influence through a representative's home district would not be included. Those working primarily on public opinion would not be included. Those whose expenses were only indirectly related to lobbying would also not be included. Congress has debated broadening the scope of the regulation, but has not yet succeeded in revising the 1946 law.

Lobbying is a major activity in the Washington scene. Individuals and organizations registering as lobbyists number in the thousands, and it has been called a "billion dollar industry" by a House committee.[36] Businesses, church groups, and large and small interest groups all lobby in Congress. The biscuit people and the travel agents lobby in Congress. Foreign governments with an obvious stake in American foreign policy—Israel, the Arab states, South Korea—also conduct lobbying, and so do major U.S. trading partners. Thus Swiss-Air, Singapore Airlines, the French Bankers' Association, and the Australian Meat Board are all registered as lobbyists. An illustration for one month of new lobbying registration is shown in Exhibit 4.4.

Lobbyists do more than try to influence proposed legislation. They often serve as initiators of the legislation and may even help to write it. Often they are the main source of information on the subject. They will also be experts in law, public relations, or the politics of Capitol Hill. The typical Washington lobbyist, for instance, is often a member of a large law firm or public relations firm or even a past member of the government. Ex-Senator James Abourezk (D-S.D.), after his retirement from Congress, became a lobbyist for Arab interests, and Ex-Representative Garry E. Brown (R-Mich.) practiced law and lobbied for the Michigan State Housing Authority. Ex-Cabinet members Dean Acheson (Truman administration), Clark Clifford (Johnson administration), Richard Kleindienst and William Rogers (Nixon administration), and Keith Clearwater (Ford administration) helped represent various foreign interests.

Notice that the lobbying for foreign governments is not carried out by mysterious foreign agents or people in colorful native dress. While foreign agents do register as lobbyists, foreign governments use many of the same people and firms as the domestic interests do. Arnold & Porter, one of

[35]A narrower definition is given by Lester W. Milbrath, *The Washington Lobbyists* (Chicago: Rand McNally, 1963).

[36]House Select Committee on Lobbying Activities, 81st Congress, Second Session, *General Interim Report*, p. 8.

EXHIBIT 4.4	GROUP	LEGISLATION
Lobbying in the 100th Congress—Selected Examples	BBC Inc.	Communication legislation
	Church of Scientology Int.	Religious Freedom Week
	Commodity Exchange Inc.	Tax code affecting futures trading
	Concerned Shrimpers of America	Endangered species
	Dow Chemical	Environmental issues
	Empire Resources Inc.	South Africa sanctions
	Greyhound Lines	U.S. Canadian Free Trade Agreement
	Hilton Hotels	Tax legislation
	International Association of Amusement Parks and Attractions	Assist Congress in developing legislation for the amusement park industry
	Mastercard International	Legislation affecting the credit card industry
	Midway Airlines	Airline Passenger Protection Act
	Morton Thiokol	NASA authorization and appropriation
	Shell Oil Co.	South Africa sanctions
	Time Inc.	Restrictions on Cable TV
	U.S. Gypsum Co.	Asbestos and Indoor Air Legislation
	Wilderness Society	National Forest issues; appropriations bills

New lobbyists must register with the government reporting the group they are working for and the subject of their legislative concern. Altogether, 145 lobbyists registered in the month of September, 1988, to join all the other lobbyists already at work. The table omits the names of the lobbyists giving only the group hiring them and the legislation they are concerned about.

Source: *Congressional Quarterly Weekly Report*, December 24, 1988, pp. 3586–90.

Washington's largest law firms, has worked for the London Commodity Exchange, the French Bankers, and the Swiss Government, as well as other foreign interests. Ruder & Finn, a New York public relations firm, went to work to change the image of the Spanish government in American public opinion. Greece and Chile, also unhappy with American images of their governments, have engaged American public relations firms.[37]

The Most Effective Lobbying

Studies of lobbying in Congress list three major requirements for success. First, the relationship would be indirect and socially based. The lobbyist and the government official would be friends or at least good acquaintances, entertained at home and welcomed in the office. Second, the communication would go in both directions—the lobbyist would do as much listening as talking. Third, the relationship would be with friendly officials, at

[37]See Congressional Quarterly, *The Washington Lobby*, 3rd ed. (Washington, D.C.: Congressional Quarterly, 1979), pp. 129–131.

least somewhat sympathetic to start with. The successful lobbyist would concentrate on the friendly legislators, be very careful with the neutrals, and avoid the opponents. In short, lobbying is most effective when it occurs as a *friendly, informal, long-term relationship* among people sympathetic to each other's concerns.

It follows that lobbyists are most successful with members of Congress when they represent concerns of the home district and are constituents themselves. The nationally based "Washington lobbyist" has much less impact. Why, asks one Washington reporter, could the soft-drink bottlers succeed in getting the House to exempt the industry from antitrust regulation? The exemption required a massive effort, supported by a large majority of members, to bypass the normal rules of the House. The bottlers were successful because "bottling is local," the reporter answers, "and in Congress these days so is lobbying." There were at least two bottling plants in every district, and it was a rare member of Congress who did not hear from a bottler.[38]

The same informal friendly activity recommended for Congress is seen in bureaucratic lobbying. The case, widely typical, is cited of the airline lobbyist who played golf frequently with the chairman of the Civil Aeronautics Board, joined him for part of his European vacation, lunched with all board members every two or three months and with staff members every two weeks.[39] Another agency head was known to be unapproachable through the usual lobbying techniques. One enterprising lobbyist, discovering that the man walked his dog at a particular time each day, got his own dog and proceeded to walk it in the same neighborhood. While far from the 1946 Lobbying Act, all this is a standard part of the lobbying business.

The importance of friendly informal lobbying can create a **revolving door** in government service whereby ex-government officials are hired at very high salaries to lobby their friends and former colleagues. From the standpoint of the interest group, these people offer invaluable contacts and experience. They know the inside story and continue to have lunch with the people they were having lunch with before. They are clearly earning their salaries. For the former official, the job offers high salary and status. After electoral defeat or a turnover at the White House, top level bureaucrats and members of Congress may find themselves out of a job. Former White House assistants have short tenure in office, often shorter even than the president's term. These are the people that keep the revolving door in motion. They leave government and turn around and lobby the government as part of their new job.

There is nothing necessarily illegal or unethical about these hiring practices as long as a few broad guidelines are observed. For example, officials cannot lobby on a particular matter if they participated "personally and substantially" in the issue while in office. They must wait two years

---

[38]*Congressional Quarterly Weekly Report*, May 30, 1981, p. 971. See also John W. Kingdon, *Congressmen's Voting Decisions*, 2nd ed. (New York: Harper and Row, 1981), p. 150.
[39]Greenwald, p. 230.

The revolving door: Former presidential aide Michael Deaver is called before a congressional committee for questions about improper lobbying after he left the White House.

before lobbying on any particular matter that they had general responsibility for. Senior government officials must also wait one year before lobbying at all in their former agency or department. Former White House assistant Michael Deaver violated these guidelines when he represented Canada on acid rain shortly after he helped make Reagan administration policy on the issue. He sat in on at least fifteen White House discussions of the issue, arguing for a special envoy to be appointed. Once out of government, he went back to meet the envoy he himself had nominated and to discuss the acid rain issue. Deaver was also representing South Korea, Mexico, Saudi Arabia, and Caribbean sugar producers in their lobbying with the Reagan administration. Since Deaver was a personal friend of the Reagans, he even kept his White House pass, had a copy of the president's personal schedule, and continued to play tennis on the White House courts.

Even when the guidelines are followed, however, there are other problems with the revolving door. One wonders whether the officials were thinking, *while in government*, of their possible future careers. Were they shown, indirectly but vividly, what a vice-presidency with Group X or a consultantship with Group Y would be like? At some point, the line of good ethics can be crossed, although it is difficult to say exactly when.

The Washington Lobbyists

While Washington lobbyists are not always the most effective ones, they are a major presence on the American political scene. Who are these people and where do they come from? What kind of social background and past experience do they bring to their jobs?

A profile of the Washington lobbyists is presented in Exhibit 4.5. The lobbyists are similar to the elected officials in representing a small social

EXHIBIT 4.5		**Percent**
	Sex	
A Profile of the Washington Lobbyist	Male	88
	Female	12
	Race	
	White	97
	Minority	3
	Education	
	College Graduate	91
	Prestige-college Graduate	28
	Father's Occupation	
	Professional/Managerial	53
	Blue Collar	29
	White Collar; other	18
	Previous Government Experience	
	National	45
	State or Local	9
	None	46
	Mean Age: 48.5	
	Mean Income (1982): $90,489	
	Mean Years with Current Organization: 12.0	

Source: Adapted from Robert Salisbury, "Washington Lobbyists: A Collective Portrait," in *Interest Group Politics,* 2nd ed., eds. Allan J. Cigler and Burdett A. Loomis (Washington, D.C.: CQ Press, 1986), pp. 151–55.

elite. They are white male college graduates for the most part, with women and minorities substantially underrepresented. More than half come from relatively advantaged family backgrounds, where the father's occupation was professional or managerial. More than a quarter graduated from elite colleges. They are middle-aged, earn very high salaries, and have spent a number of years with their current organization. *They are in fact very much like the members of Congress they are lobbying,* as Chapter Seven will show. Those members, too, comprise a white male social elite, predominantly college-educated and middle-aged. They, too, spend a number of years with their organization. So, if lobbying is most effective when it is informal and socially based, the shared background characteristics can make the job much easier. Earlier studies of lobbyists have reported the same kind of elite characteristics. The lobbying industry has grown and diversified in recent years, but the people doing the lobbying seem the same.[40]

The career patterns are also interesting. While more than half of the Washington lobbyists report some background in government, they have

[40]For the current portrait, see Robert Salisbury, "Washington Lobbyists: A Collective Portrait," in *Interest Group Politics,* 2nd ed. (Washington, D.C.: CQ Press, 1986), eds. Allan J. Cigler and Burdett A. Loomis, pp. 146–61; for the situation in earlier years, see Milbrath, *op. cit.* See also Schlozman, *op. cit.*, pp. 1006–32.

spent a good share of time in their current position. The "revolving door" is not constantly in motion. Even the outside consultants have spent more than ten years on the average in their current position. They are not jumping back and forth in and out of government. Still, almost forty percent of the lobbyists have worked at some time or other in Congress, the executive branch, or for a regulatory commission.

Other "Lobbyists"

Interest groups, however, are not the only lobbyists in Washington. If lobbying is defined broadly as any communication with a government official to attempt to influence policy, then group activity is only one part of a larger communication process. Executive branch bureaucrats and members of Congress seek assistance and influence from each other. Presidents seek support for their programs by lobbying individual members. Members of Congress, pursuing state and district interests, lobby the White House. Bureaucratic agencies, like interest groups, have public relations departments and public relations campaigns. The Air Force and Forest Service are not merely passive recipients of lobbying activity but active lobbyists themselves. Hence on any one issue, interest groups need not be the only voice or the loudest one to be raised.

Take the perennial issue of what should be done with the B-1 bomber or the MX missile. The White House is lobbied pro and con by agencies within the Defense Department and each of these is lobbied by interest groups. Members of Congress may be hearing from the groups and the agencies and receiving phone calls from the White House. They may even be lobbying each other. Interest groups are active lobbyists on defense issues, but many other people are lobbying too.

Even on the many less visible issues, interest groups are not the only ones trying to influence a decision. Members of Congress and government agencies, as shown in later chapters, face constraints from within their institutions. So, the House Ways and Means Committee, faced with interest group pressure for a particular tax break, will face other pressures from within the committee and from the House as a whole. The committee may be trying to make a particular kind of tax policy, or to maintain its influence in the House, or to support the House in its interaction with the Senate or the White House. These goals are independent of interest group activity and can override its effects.

One final point should be added. Members of Congress estimate that, of the decisions taken in one year, about thirty-five percent involve one active interest group, another thirty-five percent at least two active groups (not necessarily on opposing sides), and the remaining thirty percent involve no interest group activity at all.[41] If these estimates are even close (and mem-

---

[41]Kingdon, *op. cit.*, pp. 17–22, 139–167.

Lobbyists fill a row of telephone booths outside the House capitol and Senate capitol chambers to report the day's legislative activities.

bers may understate the amount of interest group activity), then *a majority of decisions could have been changed by more activity*. Decisions with only one active group might have become controversial with two. Decisions with no active group might have been redefined by the addition of one. So, for all the group activity and effort expended, there remains some fairly large slack in the process. Lobbying does not always produce a babel of voices— sometimes there is silence too. This means that if public opinion were mobilized on many issues, the policy outcome could be changed.

Lobbying as Communication

Notice the importance of *communication* in all of these descriptions of lobbying activity. As Carol Greenwald summarizes:

> Lobbying ... is a form of communication, on a par with input from media, research sources, political parties, colleagues' advice and opinion leaders in the community. Viewed in the context of a communication system, lobbying can be seen as a means to affect the behavior of individuals by supplying information.[42]

Viewing lobbying as communication makes a number of things clear. First, informal and indirect activity are important. Communication is not only the formal plea at a White House meeting or a call to a senator's office, but it is

[42]Greenwald, *op. cit.*, pp. 62–63.

also supplying technical background information, a magazine's special feature, and the small talk at a party or a golf game. Second, there are limits to interest group activity. Group representatives are not the only voices being heard. Presidents, bureaucrats, and members of Congress lobby each other. Finally, this activity will benefit some people and groups more than others. It helps to "speak the same language," move in the same circles, or be invited to the same clubs. It also benefits those groups that can persist in lobbying over a period of time—not only for one vote, one year, or one issue. A group organizing a massive lobbying campaign one year can find its gains erased the next year. A weapon system is cut from one budget and comes back in the next. "A good lobbyist," in the words of one group representative, "keeps in mind there'll be other issues, other battles, other times."[43] To be effective, the communication must continue.

INTEREST GROUPS AND PUBLIC INTEREST

Interest group activity takes place within the context of low public interest described in the previous chapter. How many people, when it comes right down to it, really care about fig tariffs? Or sugar, for that matter, or restrictions on sugar substitutes, or the Latin American foreign policy affected by sugar lobbies? Or if they do care, how many know when legislation is being considered in committee, how policy is made in the Food and Drug Administration, or when a controversial vote will be taken on the House floor? In one week in the House of Representatives, controversial votes occurred on potatoes, members' allowances, cherry marketing, the export-import bank, an arts foundation, hospital construction, urban housing, and fish protein. These were *controversial* votes. The representatives were divided and the vote could go either way. Evidently some people cared in order for these matters (as opposed to other matters) to be on the agenda for the week and to provoke controversy. Nevertheless, most people would not rank these high on their lists of the week's most serious problems.

The *Congressional Quarterly Weekly Report* tells people who can afford to subscribe to it (or read it in their college libraries) about what is going on in government. It reports the bills being considered in Senate and House committees, the kinds of difficulties they are expected to meet, and the different lines of controversy. It also reports the votes taken in Congress, the position of members, and the issues to be faced in the weeks ahead. In May, 1987, for example, an Agriculture subcommittee was debating a subsidy for the Farm Credit System, while another committee was debating how much compensation electric utilities would have to pay in the event of a nuclear accident. The Senate voted to repeal a law forcing industries to switch from oil and gas to coal—the repeal was seen as a way to help gas-producing

---

[43]Ornstein and Elder, *op. cit.*, p. 104.

states faced with an oversupply of natural gas. The House, meanwhile, was deciding whether to prohibit sightseeing flights that dip below the rim of the Grand Canyon and other national parks. The bill, supported by environmentalists, was expected to pass despite opposition from the Reagan administration and the tourist industry.

All of these issues involve interest groups; they are the "outcome" in a sense of what the groups are working for. Yet, very few of these issues are covered in the national news. So, even interested citizens, reading a national newspaper and watching the evening news, would not be aware of the upcoming decisions. Citizens are told to "write their representatives" on issues they care about. But if they care about nuclear accident compensation or Grand Canyon flights, they would not be aware of the need to write until the debate was over.

Groups are composed of people, too, of course—private citizens expressing opinions on government and working to bring policies in line with their opinions. In tracing the importance of public opinion on government, it is important to recognize that *interest groups are a part of this public opinion*—the most interested part. The term "special interest" misleads people into thinking groups are somehow separate from the rest of the public. But while groups are part of the public, they cannot be taken as synonymous with it. *Interest groups do not add together to equal the American people.* Allowing public opinion to be important—that is, building in a "democratic" influence—means that some people, depending on social, economic, and personal conditions, can more easily develop and express interest than others. Democracy and equality of influence, in short, do not necessarily go together.

There are two main responses to this problem in American political debate. One response, by people called **pluralists,** emphasizes the multiplicity of groups and group interest (plural meaning many, more than a few). Citizens have differences of opinion. They can organize in many different groups and compete for influence. If they do not do so, it can be assumed they do not have sufficient interest and have therefore yielded this democratic opportunity. Since the population is diverse and the opportunities for organization are good, so many groups will form and compete with each other that no one will have a dominant influence. Interest group representation, then, is central to the American political process: it shows democracy at work.[44]

A second response, from critics of pluralism, has been termed the **power elite** position. Associated with sociologist C. Wright Mills and followed by later writers, this argument emphasizes the lack of equality in the group representation process. These writers point out that everyone is not equally able to develop and express interest. There are socioeconomic biases in

---

[44]The classic description is provided by David B. Truman, *The Governmental Process,* 2nd ed. (New York: Knopf, 1971).

interest and information. Groups with the most resources (translated by power elitists as status and money) will be more successful than other groups. Surface competition masks a common interest, and interest group representation gives us government not by the many but the few.[45]

Both sides, it seems clear, emphasize important facts. Neither, however, is willing to confront the major points of the other. Pluralists do not confront the socioeconomic biases in interest and activity—the vicious circle whereby people already disadvantaged in a society are less able to make their interests known. Power elitists do not confront the variety of groups and the potential conflict between them. Many of the groups represent disadvantaged people, and many work in direct conflict with others. Group resources include but are not limited to social status and money. The power elitists ignore the importance of the other resources; the pluralists ignore the importance of power and money. Groups do not equal the American people, as the pluralists like to think, but neither are they somehow "special" and separate from the people. Pluralists stress the democratic nature of the process and power elitists stress the inequality. But democracy and equality need not go together. Both the importance of public opinion and the biases it can produce must be recognized.

This chapter has traced a system of interest group representation speaking for various kinds of people, following various strategies, and employing diverse resources. Some people are more advantaged by this system than others, as the power elitists point out. Nevertheless, as the pluralists maintain, the groups are both competitive and diverse. One cites the case of the WCTU and the Prohibition Amendment to argue for pluralism. One talks about the Business Roundtable and the overlapping of top corporate officials in government to show the power elite. Each side of the debate ignores important facts of the other side. How can groups show both democracy and inequality at work? Democracy and equality do not necessarily go together.

At the same time, interest group activity should not be exaggerated. When a House member said, "Most people back home don't realize it, but it's very easy to influence a congressman," he did not mean that bribes were passing back and forth and that hands were always out.[46] He meant that there was a large amount of slack in the system. There was room for more mail to come to the congressional offices, more groups to form, and more people to make their positions known.

CHECKLIST FOR REVIEW	1. Interest groups are collections of people with shared attitudes who are conscious of their identity as a group and who form a concrete organization to influence policy. They vary in size, cohesion, status, and clarity of goals. Occupational groups, also called economic interest groups, work

[45]C. Wright Mills, *The Power Elite* (New York: Oxford University Press, 1959). For a recent study, see Michael Useem, *The Inner Circle* (New York: Oxford University Press, 1984). See also Edsall, *op. cit.*

[46]Kingdon, *op. cit.*, p. 40.

to secure improved material benefits for their members. Nonoccupational groups—those that do not work primarily for members' material benefit—may focus on single issues, or work to help people who are not group members, or call themselves public interest groups.

2. Interest group activities are devoted to maintaining the group and influencing government. One way groups accomplish the former is through the use of selective incentives for members. They accomplish the latter by directly targeting key decision-makers or by appealing to public opinion (inside and outside strategies).

3. Political action committees are organizations set up by interest groups to raise and contribute money to campaigns in an attempt to elect or defeat certain candidates for office. They were formed in response to campaign finance reforms prohibiting the use of union and corporation funds as campaign contributions. Since candidates need to convince the PACs that they can run a good race, the candidates need to show their own money-raising, polls, and party support. It is the parties who tell the PACs who is promising or vulnerable.

4. Lobbying, narrowly defined, is communication by interest group representatives aimed at a government decision-maker in the hope of influencing a decision. The most effective lobbying involves a friendly, informal, long-term relationship: lobbyists work with their friends, not their opponents. Many lobbyists are former government officials, and most are similar in background to the officials they lobby. In the broader definition of the term, lobbying is done by anyone, even other officials, who communicate with decision-makers in the hope of influencing a decision.

5. The role of interest groups in democratic government can be interpreted in different ways. Pluralists point to the competition between a wide variety of groups and see this as democracy at work. Power elitists point to the importance of money and status and see a concentration of power where a few people have much more influence than others. Both interpretations avoid key facts of the other interpretation.

KEY TERMS

interest groups
occupational groups
nonoccupational groups
public interest groups
issue networks
free rider
selective incentives
outside and inside strategies

political action committees (PACs)
in-kind contributions
lobbying
lobbyist
revolving door
pluralists
power elite

Political Parties and Nominations

S tudents of American government cannot get far without finding a reference to *parties*. The word appears all over, used in many different ways. Parties describe groups of voters—people who call themselves Republicans or Democrats. But parties also describe organizations, such as the Republican or Democratic National Committee. Parties also describe people in government (a Democratic Congress, a Republican administration) and they are used to describe ideas as well. Students are confronted with a deluge of writing on the subject—on the importance of parties, their weaknesses, and predictions about their decline. So what are these parties that are pervading so much of the thinking and writing on American politics? What explains their central position in American political life?

PARTIES AND DEMOCRATIC GOVERNMENT

Parties, basically, are *organizing* devices, whether they organize people or ideas. Further, they are, at least in American politics, organizing devices concerned with the *electoral process*. They seek to influence government by nominating candidates for office and contesting their election. When parties name, or nominate, a candidate, they provide the party label for that candidate, a label that voters know and that many other candidates share. So, since organizations persist and names stick, parties become continuing, or *institutionalized*, forms of these organizing devices. They span voters, party workers, and candidates for office. They develop a life of their own and the means to continue their own existence.

Many political scientists do not define the word party, recognizing the great diversity of its forms. One scholar differentiates between the party in the electorate (that is, the party of the voters), the party in government, and the party as organization.[1] However, a working definition has the advantage of showing how these different varieties come together to work in American politics. It can also distinguish parties from other political groups.

Parties can be defined as organizations that seek to influence government by nominating candidates and contesting their elections. In so doing, they provide a label linking voters, workers, and candidates for office that can continue over time. (The word "can" in the definition simply recognizes that some parties may fail at continuing over time. They then cease to be parties.) Many groups, as shown in Chapter Four, seek to influence government and work to affect who is nominated and elected. The candidates have their own personal organizations to work for the nomination and election as well. None of these groups or individuals, however, provide a label that links voters, workers, and officials in the same way or to the same extent

---

[1]Frank J. Sorauf and Paul A. Beck, *Party Politics in America*, 6th ed. (Boston: Little, Brown, 1988).

Delegates gather in the 1868 Democratic Convention and the 1988 Republican Convention to select the party's nominee for president.

that parties do. Parties become continuing ways of organizing and describing the political world.

The Importance of Parties

This view of parties helps explain why they are seen as so important to democratic government.[2] First, parties organize and so simplify a complex political universe filled with many issues, many people, and many points of view. They organize public opinion about government and they provide an easy way to make one's vote count for people not as interested in politics as many other things. In short, parties help the voters.

Second, parties link the voters with the officials in government by supplying a label for both groups and by contesting for votes. In this way, parties organize support for the government in office and require it to be accountable to the citizens so it can win their votes again. The corruption of one Republican official can hurt the reputation of the party, not just the official. Hence the party will try to select candidates who will keep the party name in high regard. In other words, parties help the quality and the accountability of the government.

Third, parties offer a democratic and orderly way of criticizing the government in power and providing for government change. They offer a **legitimate opposition** to the current government.[3] It is an opposition because the party wants to win the election, toss the rascals out, and put its own people in. It is legitimate because it works through the process of demo-

---

[2]Two classic studies are E.E. Schattschneider, *Party Government* (New York: Farrar & Rinehart, 1942) and V.O. Key, Jr., *Politics, Parties, and Pressure Groups*, 5th ed. (New York: Crowell, 1964), chapters 1, 8.

[3]Richard Hofstadter, *The Idea of a Party System* (Berkeley: University of California Press, 1969).

cratic elections. Governments have the monopoly of force. They have the power to make laws and to jail or fine or bring to court those who disobey the laws. So who is going to criticize these people and cast them out of office? Who will be strong enough, and well enough known, to offer an alternative? Parties provide a way of changing the government without resorting to revolution. They thus support the continuity of democratic government.

It is not surprising, then, that parties have grown along with democratic governments. Imagine the following situation. A country has a revolution and creates a new democracy with regular elections. But how will the people know what the candidates stand for? Even if they like one candidate, how will they know which of the others, if elected, will help their person in government? Who will decide which candidates will run? If these questions are answered for one election year, they must still be answered again with each new election. Perhaps an Out party develops to contest against the Ins. Perhaps the Outs themselves split into two parties because of fundamental differences about government. Whatever the form and number of parties that develop, these organizations begin to provide the candidates and labels that guide the electoral process. Parties take their particular shape from the history and lines of conflict that develop in a country. Nevertheless, all democracies have parties of one kind or another.

American Attitudes Toward Parties

It is also not surprising that parties have a mixed reputation in the United States. As organizations engaged in contesting elections, parties are centrally involved in the business of politics. Indeed, the word *party* is commonly associated with *politics* and *politician*, all of which carry a negative connotation and hint of corruption. People speak negatively of a "party hack" or "party politician" and they say with pride that they "vote the man, not the party." The politicians themselves reassure the public that they are speaking not as Republicans or Democrats or from any low partisan motives. These attitudes can be found throughout American history. George Washington warned of the "evils" of party, and James Madison against the "mischiefs of faction." According to Austin Ranney, a leading twentieth century political scientist, a central theme in the history of American parties has been "the widespread belief that political parties are, at best, unavoidable evils."[4] They must be closely watched for hints of corruption and carefully controlled.

If parties are evils, they appear to be necessary evils. Madison, who warned against their mischief, was the co-founder with Thomas Jefferson of the first American political party. Modern-day Americans show the same ambivalence. They tend to identify with one party or the other and want

[4]Austin Ranney, *Curing the Mischiefs of Faction* (Berkeley: University of California Press, 1975), p. 22.

party labels kept on the ballot. On the other hand, they see parties as confusing issues, and they do not respect voters who vote in terms of parties or government officials who follow a party line. Such are the mixed attitudes about parties persisting from Madison's time to the present day.

Is the Party Over?

Many people say that parties are declining in importance in American politics. They point to the rise in **split ticket voting** (the tendency to vote for candidates of different parties), the importance of political action committees in funding candidates, and the increasing reliance of candidates on their own organizations and professional public relations firms. All these developments mean that parties no longer have a monopoly in the business of contesting elections—the candidates and interest groups are contesting too. They no longer have a monopoly over nominations either when states rely on primaries rather than state party conventions to nominate candidates. Primary elections mean that the voters, rather than the party officials, decide who will be the party's nominee.

Parties have lost the monopoly over nominating and electoral functions in the modern age of instant communication and mass mailing. But losing a monopoly is not the same as suffering a decline. Political action committees, as shown in Chapter Four, rely on the parties to tell them who is worth supporting. Some states, dissatisfied with the outcome of primary elections, have returned to the use of party conventions. And while voters often split their tickets for president or a well-liked congressional incumbent, more than two-thirds still identify themselves with one of the two major parties. They consider themselves Democrats or Republicans. Both parties have also begun to upgrade their organizations to keep step with the various kinds of competition.[5] So, as that great political philosopher Yogi Berra once said, "It ain't over til it's over."

■■■■ CHARACTERISTICS OF THE AMERICAN PARTY SYSTEM

Parties vary in their number and organization from one country to another. (The number and kind of parties in a country is described as a **party system**.) In fact, the American party system is unique among the major democracies of the world for the form it has taken. It can be characterized as dual, decentralized, and diverse. Each of these features, described in this section,

---

[5]See *Ibid.*, chapter 5; David Adamany, "Political Parties in the 1980s," in *Money and Politics in the United States*, ed. Michael J. Malbin (Washington, D.C., American Enterprise Institute, 1984), pp. 70–121; Leon D. Epstein, *Political Parties in the American Mold* (Madison, Wis.; University of Wisconsin Press, 1986), chapter 7; David E. Price, *Bringing Back the Parties*, (Washington, D.C.: CQ Press, 1984); Paul S. Herrnson, "Do Parties Make a Difference? The Role of Party Organizations in Congressional Elections," *Journal of Politics*, 48 (1986), pp. 589–615.

give American parties their own special character and help shape the kind of candidates elected to office.

Dualism: The Persistence of the Two-Party Form

One of the most striking things about the American party system is its dual form. Unlike most democracies, only two parties compete for office over time, persist as organizations, and fill the seats of government. Minor parties have existed throughout American history and have from time to time contested for national office. Nevertheless, the two major parties have been the only continuing serious contenders. **Minor parties** only rarely succeed in electing candidates to government. In contrast, the two major parties have continued across the years even through periods of losing elections.

Several reasons help explain the persistence of the two-party form. Third parties are discouraged by the electoral system, sometimes called the **single member-winner-take-all system** of allotting seats in the legislature. In a single-member system, the candidate winning the most votes in a state or district gets the seat; the losers, even if they win forty-nine percent of the vote, get nothing. This system works against minor parties since it rewards only the winners and encourages only those parties with a chance at winning. In contrast, a system of **proportional representation** is used in many democracies. Proportional representation allocates seats in the legislature according to the proportion of votes gained throughout the country. A party receiving forty-nine percent of the vote would get forty-nine percent of the seats. A new party might hope to win only ten percent of the vote, but it would come out of the election with ten percent of the seats. Such a system provides an incentive for minor party activity, whereas the single-member system does not.

Third parties are also hurt by the looseness and pragmatism of the two major parties, their capacity to be many things to many people.[6] The two major parties do not have clear and specific platforms. Hence they can absorb the most popular ideas of the minor parties whenever these show any great electoral appeal. The major parties go to where the voters are. If this means changing their position, then they are pragmatic enough to do it. The Democratic party absorbed many of the Progressive party's ideas, after the strong Progressive showing in the elections of 1912 and 1924. Republicans incorporated ideas from the States' Rights and American Independent parties of 1948 and 1968. Third parties, discouraged by the electoral system, are further discouraged if their best and most popular ideas are stolen away.

Institutions set up reinforcing factors of their own. Once the two parties come to government, they pass laws and adopt practices that help protect them from other challenges. The states' election laws, passed by legisla-

[6]Epstein, *op. cit.*, chapter 7.

tures composed of the two major parties' members, make it difficult for minor parties to get on the ballot and impede their activity in other ways. Rules in Congress, such as those governing committee assignments, penalize the rare independent member. Committee assignments for new members, as shown in a later chapter, are made by the two congressional parties. Who would take care of an Independent? The answer is no one— Independents would get their assignments after both parties have taken care of their own. Attitudes of the voters also reinforce the two-party system. People fear they will "waste a vote" by voting for a minor party candidate. Because minor parties have not won in the past, voters refuse to vote for them, which makes them not win in the present. If the voters think there are only two games in town, they will go to one or the other.

These reasons help explain why the two parties do not grow to three or four, but what keeps them from declining to one? What, after major electoral disasters and long years of defeat, keeps the second party going? The same kind of reinforcing factors contribute to a second party's support. If there are only two games in town and something happens to one (such as a major scandal or a depression), the second inherits the players. Voters toss the rascals out by turning to the other party. A second reason is also important. The number of separate power points in the American government helps the persistence of the two-party form. Winners take all, but there are many prizes for the winners to take—in Congress, in state governorships, and in state legislatures. Losing at one point (in one office or area of the country), the second party can win somewhere else. For years the Republican party dominated the presidency, before Franklin Roosevelt and the New Deal swept the nation in 1932. But the Democratic party kept running candidates and winning office in Congress and in many of the states. The Republicans did the same thing in the lean years after 1932. States and regions of the country vary widely in their degree of Republican or Democratic party strength. So even through long years of exile from the presidency, a party can carry on in Congress and govern in the states. In short, there are enough elections for both parties to win.

In years of active third-party races, the speculation arises about a permanent change in the two-party system. Maybe now, so goes the speculation, a major third or fourth party will develop. But four years later, that party has faded from national politics. In other years, there is the opposite kind of speculation: "Well, that's it now for the Republican (or the Democratic) Party. This is the end of the two-party system." People in 1948, in fact, were urged to vote Republican if only to support the continuation of the two-party system! And yet four years later, the party that was supposed to be in its dying gasps recaptured the White House. Those predicting change in the two-party form, and those who would like to achieve it, must recognize the reasons that have kept the two parties from multiplying or from dwindling away.

Two-Party Politics and the South.   The two parties, however, do not necessarily compete evenly across the nation: one party can dominate over the other in some regions and states. The clearest example is the Democratic dominance that held for years in the Southern states from the end of the Civil War to the years following World War II. The Republican Party was associated with Lincoln, the Northern cause in the Civil War, and the years of Reconstruction following the war. Hence Southern voters were overwhelmingly Democratic voters. Contests were waged over which Democratic candidate would be elected, since no Republicans could win. Southern politics, then, were virtually one-party politics—the South was solidly Democratic.

In the years following World War II, growing southern industrialization attracted northern residents. Republican presidential candidates wooed traditional southern voters. Southerners who had voted for Eisenhower or Nixon began to consider Republican voting more acceptable, and Republicans began to contest and win in state and local elections. The South is no longer the "Solid South" of one-party Democratic politics. In fact, at the presidential level it has become fairly solidly Republican. The example, however, has shown how the two major parties can vary in their strength from one region of the country to another.

Minor Parties in American Politics.   Although minor parties have not grown into major parties, they have existed throughout American history. Two broad categories of minor parties can be distinguished. One is the **doctrinaire party**. It is usually small in size, specific in program, and devoted in membership. Examples include the Socialist party, Vegetarian party, and Prohibition party. The Prohibition party won some 16,000 votes as recently as 1976 and a party called "Down with Lawyers" polled 1,718 votes in 1980. Altogether in 1984 more than ten minor parties ran candidates for president, totalling about 500,000 votes. Many of these parties show great durability across the years, despite the small number of votes polled. They do not expect to win elections; rather, they use the electoral process to publicize and dramatize their points of view.

A second kind of party is the **splinter party** or secessionist party, formed when a group within a major party splits off and forms a political party of its own. The Progressives split from the Republicans in 1912, the States' Rights (Dixiecrats) split from the Democrats in 1948, and the American Independent party split from the Democrats in 1968. The Dixiecrats made their break particularly dramatic by actually walking off the floor of the Democratic convention. These southern Democrats opposed the civil rights position that the party was attempting to adopt at the convention. When the Democrats succeeded in adopting the position as the official party policy, the Dixiecrats stood up and walked out. Like the doctrinaire parties, splinter parties want to publicize their point of view, but they also seek

EXHIBIT 5.1

The Leading Vote-
Getters Among the
Minor Parties

PARTY (CANDIDATE)	YEAR	POPULAR VOTE PERCENT	ELECTORAL VOTES
Anti-Masonic (William Wirt)	1832	8	7
Free Soil (Martin Van Buren)	1848	10	0
Whig (Millard Fillmore)	1856	22	8
Constitutional Union (John Bell)	1860	13	39
Southern Democrat (John Breckinridge)	1860	18	72
Populist (James Weaver)	1892	9	22
Progressive (Theodore Roosevelt)	1912	27	88
Socialist (Eugene Debs)	1912	6	0
Progressive (Robert La Follette)	1924	17	13
American Independent (George Wallace)	1968	14	46
Independent (John Anderson)	1980	7	0

The list includes only those parties receiving 5 percent or more of the popular vote.

electoral support. They want to show the popularity of their idea, bargain for it with the two major parties, and penalize the party that forced them away. Party unity is held to be important for winning elections. Hence dramatic breaks in unity hurt the party image and can do damage at the polls. Splinter parties also hope to gain enough electoral votes to force the election into the House of Representatives, where they could play a pivotal bargaining role. (See Chapter Six. A presidential candidate needs a majority of the states' electoral votes. If there is no majority, the election goes to the House.)

A listing of the biggest vote-getters among the minor parties is given in Exhibit 5.1. The Progressives in 1912 polled 27 percent of the presidential vote and 88 electoral votes, giving Woodrow Wilson and the Democrats the election. George Wallace's American Independent party in 1968 polled 14 percent of the vote, compiled 46 electoral votes, and only narrowly missed throwing the election to the House. Wallace's former party, the Democratic Party, did lose the election. While the Dixiecrats polled only 2 percent of the vote in 1948, they gained 39 southern electoral votes, with the Democrats only narrowly winning the election. From all these cases it is clear that the two major parties have to take third-party threats seriously.

Nevertheless, these splinter parties, for all their impressive strength in one election year, do not maintain that performance in a second election. They flare up, light the political sky, and quickly fade away. Their fortunes rise and fall with the fluctuations of public interest. When public opinion is mobilized around an issue, a third party gains support, momentum, and votes. But times change, public interest recedes, and the money and encouragement fade away. It is no coincidence that years of political unrest were also years of third-party strength. The year 1948 saw strikes and a painful post-war economic adjustment, while 1968 brought Vietnam demonstrations and racial unrest. By this view, third parties are an important but short-lived phenomenon in American politics. They are the exception to the two-party norm.

Decentralization and Diversity

Two other major characteristics of American parties need to be understood. One is decentralization. Party organization is primarily formed at the state and the sub-state level. Power is not concentrated at the national level but dispersed across—decentralized across—the states. A second characteristic follows from this decentralization and helps contribute to it: the parties' diversity. There is no one "Republican party" or "Democratic party," but fifty or more, each rooted in and responding to the politics of the states. This book is mainly concerned with national parties. To understand these, however, it is necessary to look first at how they work, and how they differ from one another, in the states.

Variation in Structure.
Parties are not mentioned in the Constitution since the framers considered them an evil to be avoided. Parties meant a partial interest—something less than the full public interest that elected leaders should pursue. So, when parties developed anyway (since people disagreed on what the public interest might be), it was left to the states to legislate for them. The great diversity of state and local party structures is the result. States vary from each other on two important dimensions. They vary on the method by which party officials are selected—by an election among the voters or by a meeting of designated party officials. States vary also by what organization unit gets to select the party committee at the state level, whether county committee members, town committee members, or individual voters in the primary.

There is a great diversity that results merely from these two differences in organization. In some states, power lies closer to the state committee, in others closer to the local committees, and in others it is dispersed even further to the level of the individual voters. All state parties are decentralized, but some are more decentralized than others.

Variation in Party Workers.
State parties vary also in the kinds of people they recruit. The people may be amateurs or professionals, the former attracted at a particular time for a cause or candidate, the latter working permanently for the party whatever the cause or candidate. They may be issue-oriented or job-oriented (that is, concerned with party patronage and other material benefits). They will be composed of various interest groups, depending on the social and economic makeup of the state. Parties in some states may be heavily supported by labor unions or a key industry, while parties in other states are tied up in ethnic politics and looking for the ideal nominee who is Irish Catholic with a Jewish wife, an Italian-speaking mother, and a Harvard law degree.

Amateurs are drawn to the party because of an issue or candidate, whereas the **professionals** work for the party regardless of the issues or candidates. As summarized by one political scientist:

> *Amateurs* ... [believe that] the party itself ... has no value and merits, no loyalty. Its only legitimate reason for being is to advance true ideals and good policies. The essence of politics is not the mere competition for office among parties and interest groups; it is standing up and being counted for what is right regardless of whether it is popular.
>
> *Professionals* ... have a substantial commitment to the party itself. They have served it before ... and expect to serve it after the election. Their morality requires the candidates and factions to compete in good faith and the losers to unite behind the winners. Winning the election is the party's prime goal, for it is indispensable for everything else it wants to do.[7]

Each party worker claims a value distinct from and higher than the other. To the amateurs, party regulars subordinate ideals to playing a game and winning an election. To the professionals, the amateurs undermine the rules of the game and do not see that negotiation and compromise help keep parties and governments in business.

Variation in Interparty Competition.   States vary also in the proportion of voters supporting the Republican and Democratic parties. Some states are fairly evenly divided in their number of partisans, producing very competitive elections. Others, less evenly divided, have a predominant majority party and a minority party, with one consistently winning more elections than the other. Exhibit 5.2 shows how the states varied in interparty competition in the 1980s, based on the number of victories won by the two parties in statewide elections. Parties in states with strong competition will face one kind of problem in nominating candidates and competing in elections, while parties in states with one dominant party will face another. Competitive parties must balance internal goals with the need to defeat the opposing party; thus an ideal candidate within the party may not be the most electorally competitive one. In states where one party dominates, the majority party will find its major conflicts occurring at the nomination stage, and the minority party will confront problems of keeping the organization together and recruiting candidates when no one is expected to win. To look at the national party organization, one needs to appreciate this very diverse and decentralized state and sub-state base.

National Party Structures.   Looking for national parties, one might say, "there aren't any." There are simply coalitions of state and local parties, and even some of these are coalitions of still smaller groups. Nevertheless, there are structures for party action at the national level that can be

---

[7]Ranney, *op. cit.*, pp. 138–41.

EXHIBIT 5.2

Party Competition in the American States

One Party Dominant

One Party Advantaged

Two-party

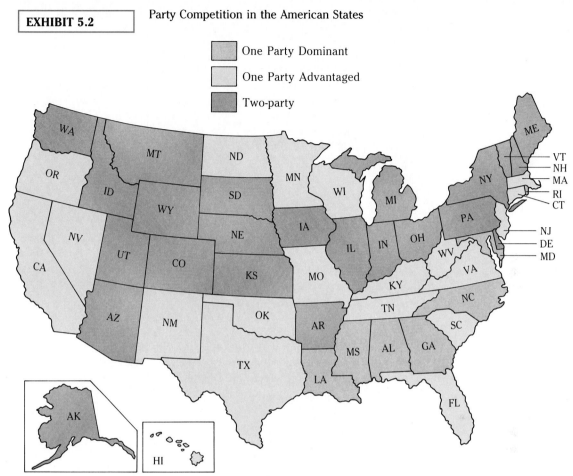

Source: Adapted from John Bibby, et al., "Parties in State Politics," in *Politics in the American States*, 4th ed., ed. Virginia Gray et al. (Boston: Little, Brown, 1983), p. 66.

studied in more detail. There is no single structure, but rather three distinct structures: the national committee, the elected national officeholders (the president and members of Congress), and the party delegates assembled in the national convention.

The national committee is formally the peak of the party organization pyramid, which begins in the precincts and rises through the county committees and state committees. But for much of the time of its history the national committee has been mainly a housekeeping organization: its major duties are fund-raising and arranging details for the national convention. The committee helps in the presidential election campaign, but the candidate's own organization typically runs the campaign. The national committee, then, does not play a very large part in the party's job of contesting elections. Nor is it at the center of the nominating activity, since the con-

Ronald H. Brown, Chairman of the Democratic National Committee.

vention is charged with that. It is true that the committee has an impact on the nomination, by making decisions on rules, delegate credentials, and other matters before the convention begins. Traditionally, its impact is great enough to make the selection of the national committee chairman an important event and at times a very controversial one. Nevertheless, this impact can be seen as subordinate to that of the convention. Serious disputes on the party's platform or convention rules will be fought at the convention itself. The committee is not particularly active in policy formulation either. Party policy, to the extent that it is worked out at all, is primarily the job of the elected officeholders.

Still, many writers see a growth in the committee's organizational strength and activity occurring through the past decade.[8] Both committees have become more active and aggressive in fund-raising, especially the Republican party. Both committees have attempted to hold the states to guidelines in delegate selection. Both have expanded their staff and budget and now even have grand new headquarters.

The national elected officeholders will be studied in later chapters. Here it is sufficient to see that this second national party structure is almost too diverse to be called a structure and too representative of the politics of the states to be called national. Congress comprises 435 representatives and 100 senators, each representing a district or state and each selected through the politics of that district or state. Although party organization

[8]Epstein, *op. cit.*, chapter 7; Adamany, *op. cit.*

exists in Congress and supplies its leadership, the congressional parties are very decentralized structures too. The president can be considered the head of one party, but who is head of the other? The party leaders in Congress do not really perform that role. They now give interviews regularly and make their own speeches after presidents address the nation. But even this activity is a relatively new development. No one would say, in 1989 for example, that Tom Foley was the leader of the Democratic Party. He was the leader in the House, while George Mitchell was the leader in the Senate, and while other Democrats tried to become leader by running for president in 1992.

The delegates assembled in the nominating convention make up the third and final national party structure. The number of delegates assigned to the states according to population, runs more than three thousand. Before 1972, the majority of delegates were selected in state party conventions, and the others were selected by state primaries. Since 1972 the majority have been selected by primaries, with slates of delegates pledged to vote for the candidates whose names appear on the primary ballot. The reforms of the 1970s tried to bring state delegate selection more into line with national party standards; hence some increased nationalization of the party convention has occurred. Most of the superdelegates of 1984 and 1988 were not only professionals, they were also nationally elected officials.[9]

These thousands of people convene once every four years for approximately one week. At this point they constitute the national party convention and within this structure, the party nominates the two candidates selected at the national level—the presidential and vice-presidential nominees.

There are, then, three different structures selected from the states, with no full coordination among them or overlap in membership. The one center and focal point is the president. However, for the party out of power (except for the brief time between nomination and election), no center exists.

The dualism, diversity, and decentralization have major consequences for the conduct of American politics. The dualism means that political conflict will be broadly and unclearly divided between the parties. Issues, electoral appeals, and talented candidates will gravitate toward—or be absorbed by—one of the two major parties. Their decentralization means that American national politics will be nourished by, and must return for success to, the politics of the states. The diversity means that within both of these broad and unclearly divided parties, there will be many different interests, channels of communication, and influential people. Can party pros, as in the cartoons, meet in smoke-filled rooms? Yes, but there have to be many rooms, and there would still be the problem of negotiating, communication, and combining the decisions made in each one. Parties are organiz-

[9]The changing profile of the delegates across the years is shown in William Crotty and John S. Jackson III, *Presidential Primaries and Nominations* (Washington, D.C.: CQ Press, 1985), chapter 5. See also Warren E. Miller and M. Kent Jennings, *Parties in Transition* (New York: Russell Sage, 1986).

ing devices, ways of organizing a complex political world. American national parties organize their universe loosely, and with visible state and sub-state markings.

A Comparison with Other Party Systems

American parties, therefore, are quite different from parties in many other democracies. Most countries have more than two parties; and even Britain, with two major parties and a third smaller one, is organized at the national level to define and enforce party positions. The national party selects the candidates for office who are in turn expected to support the party in the legislature. If the officials did not do so, at least on the most critical votes, they would no longer be party members—that is, they would no longer be able to stand for election with the party label. Contrast this situation with the diverse American parties where anyone can call themselves Democrats or Republicans, even if they vote consistently with the opposite party; they can win elections if they satisfy the voters in their own states and districts.

As parties attempt to win elections, they spell out positions to attract as many voters as possible. In a **multi-party system** (a country with more than two major parties), the parties carve out their own segment of the population, designing their appeal to this group. In a **two-party system**, in contrast, the two major parties competing for office must try to appeal to many groups who have diverse and conflicting opinions. They are said to **aggregate interests**, or combine them in a broad party appeal. Needless to say, the two-party systems cannot afford to be as clear and specific in their appeals as the multi-party systems are. If some of their targeted voters favor a policy and others oppose it, the parties could not take a position on that issue. The multi-party systems will have to compromise later when the various party members are elected to government; the two-party systems have worked out many of their compromises before in the process of aggregating interests and designing an appeal.

Nationally organized parties can be clearer in their appeals to the voters than the decentralized American parties are. In these more unified parties, candidates campaign on the positions that the parties are able to take and attempt to carry out the policies once they are in office. These have been called **responsible parties**, writers usually using the British parties as examples.[10] One would not find some Democrats campaigning on one position while others took the opposing position. American parties, therefore have been criticized by many writers—mainly Americans—for not being "responsible" enough. The British parties, however, are not necessarily as responsible as their American admirers might think. Members of Parliament can and do disagree with their party on many issues being decided in the chamber. In addition, the British legislators are part of a very different

[10]For a good review of the responsible parties thesis, see Epstein, *op. cit.*

| EXHIBIT 5.3 | Breadth of Appeals to Voters in Two-Party and Multi-Party Systems |

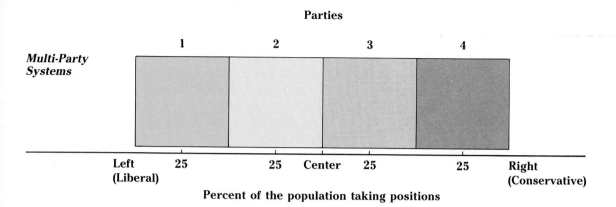

Multi-Party Systems

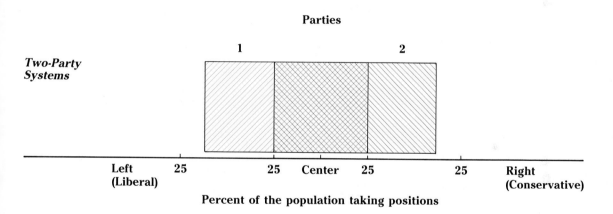

Two-Party Systems

kind of government. Party systems grow and adapt with the politics of a country—they cannot be changed by any formal decree.

Two-party systems are also criticized for showing "no real difference" between the parties. In their desire to win elections, both parties target the center of the political spectrum, that broad range of moderate opinions where most of the voters cluster.[11] (The contrast between two-party and multi-party systems in their appeal to the voters is shown in Exhibit 5.3.) This tendency can be seen at work in American parties by comparing the positions of party activists (those who hold office or serve as delegates to the national party convention) with the rank and file voters. Whereas about two-thirds of the Democratic activists call themselves liberal, only about

[11]The classic study is Anthony Downs, *An Economic Theory of Democracy* (Harper & Row: 1957).

one-third of the traditionally Democratic voters do. And while three-fourths of the Republican activists think of themselves as conservative, only about one-half of the traditionally Republican voters do.[12] Public opinion, as shown in Chapter Three, is concentrated in the middle of the liberal-to-conservative spectrum. Hence the activists in both parties modify their own positions to reach as broad a range of voters as possible. They sacrifice some ideological consistency to find broadly supported moderate positions.

Nevertheless, the two parties do differ in ideology, with Republicans identified with the conservative position and Democrats with the liberal position. These differences are seen among the party activists, the voters, and the elected office holders. Look back at the interest group ratings of senators as shown in the preceding chapter. The senators differ *by party* in their liberal and conservative group ratings, and also in their support for civil liberties, free enterprise, and a stronger defense. All Democrats will not support the same positions, given the diverse nature of the parties. But enough Democrats will support these positions—and oppose enough Republicans—that the policy consequences can be predicted merely by knowing the number of members of each party elected to Congress. Voters holding one ideology can vote for the party associated with the same ideology with the probability that their positions will be advanced in government. This, in its diluted American form, is the core of the "responsible parties" notion.

Beyond ideology, there are also differences in the groups the two parties appeal to. Traditionally, Republicans have been associated with upper-income earners, college graduates, and Protestants, while Democrats have appealed to union members, lower-income earners, blacks, Jews, newer ethnics, and those with grade school and postgraduate education. That these are not merely stereotypes of the parties is shown by the latest election results. The following groups showed higher-than-average support of Republicans and Democrats in both the 1984 and 1988 elections.[13] (Higher than average means support beyond that given by the voters nationwide.)

Republican Candidates *(Bush 1988, Reagan 1984)*	*Democratic Candidates* *(Dukakis 1988, Mondale 1984)*
White Protestants (traditional)	Blacks
White born-again Christians	Jews
White southerners	Union households
Income above $50,000	Income under $20,000
College graduates (men)	Grade school education
Nonunion households	Postgraduate education
Military veterans	Easterners

While both parties try to appeal to as broad a base as possible, they *can* be distinguished from each other.

---

[12]See Crotty and Jackson, *op. cit.*; see Miller and Jennings, *op. cit.*
[13]Based on exit polls by ABC News.

▬ PARTIES AND CONGRESSIONAL NOMINATIONS

How does the national party structure affect the kind of members elected to Congress? First of all, *the membership will be diverse.* The members have faced very different hurdles in gaining their initial nomination and winning their first election. Some have come from competitive two-party states and others from states where one party is dominant. They have gained different socialization and experience, succeeded at different things, and worked out different contacts by the time they begin to come together on Capitol Hill. Some have worked closely with professional politicians, while others have forged strong ties with interest groups. There is no one type of successful member selected. A large majority of the members of Congress have been born in the state they represent or were educated there, or served in a state elective office. (See Chapter Seven.) They need not have been elected in a state or local contest, but they will have shown in one way or another that they can deal with the politics of the states.

The decentralization of parties also affects Congress. Members are selected to a *national* legislature, but they have not been selected by a national party. They are charged with representing a state or district and are selected from that state or district. Once elected, however, they must act in and work for a national government. The leaders of Congress can try to persuade members to support a national party program, but it is understood that they may need to vote against their party on some issues, given their own state or local constraints.

Most states now nominate candidates for Congress through primaries rather than party conventions. This means that the state parties will have only limited influence on who gets the nomination: much will depend on the candidate's own resources and ability to raise money from various groups. The parties play even less of a role when a once-successful candidate seeks renomination. Incumbents (those in office at the time of the election) are overwhelmingly likely to be reelected, as will be seen in Chapter Six. Thus, since parties want to win elections, they will rarely interfere with a successful and popular incumbent. In fact, they frequently discourage potential candidates from running primary contests against them. Nevertheless, the state and local party officials will be consulted by interest groups and others as to who is vulnerable and who is strong.[14] So even the most successful incumbents, winners of several elections in a row, continue to make their trips home, do service for their constituents, listen to the state party people, and mend the occasional fence that might be broken along the way.

The initial nomination, like the initial election, is the one major hurdle; yet, it is difficult to generalize about it given the variety of state parties. In some states, where party influence is relatively concentrated, small numbers of party officials may have a decisive say on who gets the initial nomi-

[14]See Herrnson, *op. cit.* and Adamany, *op. cit.*

nation, who is being groomed for what office, and whose name is never to be mentioned, even in idle conversation. But in many states, no such clear point of decision exists; the money, endorsements, and other support must be welded together by the candidates themselves.[15] However the support is achieved, the winners of the initial nomination—and so the potential members of the national legislature—will be those who have succeeded best in the politics of the states.

PARTIES AND PRESIDENTIAL NOMINATIONS

In many elections, the choice of who will be president is made at the nomination stage. In all elections, the choice is narrowed by the nomination from a number of eligible candidates to each party's one nominee. How do these decentralized and diverse parties make such a choice? And to what extent are the parties themselves—as opposed to the candidates' organizations, the primary voters, and news media—critical to the choice that is made?

Although candidates begin work for the nomination two or more years in advance, the actual nominating process can be divided into three parts: (1) the first stage, which defines the "presidential possibilities" and "leading contenders"; (2) a second stage of primaries and state party conventions, where delegates who are pledged to, or who favor, various candidates are selected; and (3) the national party convention itself. Delegate selection (Stage Two) occurs from February through early summer of the presidential election year, leading to the convention (Stage Three) in July or August. Stage One, of course, begins as soon as the preceding nomination and election are over. Some of these stages involve more party activity than others. By the end of the process, a party's nominee will be designated—one bearing the party endorsement and inheriting the benefits of voters' party loyalty. For an illustration of these stages in the 1988 nominations, see the box on page 177.

Stage One: Presidential Possibilities and Leading Contenders

Well before the first primary in March of the election year, a critical narrowing down of potential nominees has occurred. Candidates test the waters to find what support and encouragement are available from party influentials, key money-raisers inside or outside the party, public opinion polls, and media commentary. All of these various factors, therefore, help decide who will be selected president by giving or withholding this essential early support. Candidates must find early financing for the enormously expensive

[15]See Marjorie Randon Hershey, *Running for Office* (Chatham, New Jersey: Chatham House, 1984), chapter 5; Louis Sandy Maisel, *From Obscurity to Oblivion*, rev. ed. (Knoxville, Tenn.: University of Tennessee Press, 1986), chapter 4.

The 1988 Nominations

We can trace the various presidential contenders in 1988 through Stages One, Two, and Three of the nominating process. Notice the kind of "results" that mark critical turns in the selection process and ask yourself who—the primary voters, the candidates, or the news media—causes these results to occur.

The Republicans: Seven Republicans were mentioned in the polls through much of 1987: George Bush, Bob Dole, Howard Baker, Jack Kemp, Pat Robertson, Paul Laxalt, and Pete du Pont. Baker withdrew and Laxalt and du Pont were not given much chance. Bush and Dole were favored, in the polls and media reports, at the end of Stage One.

After early wins in Iowa and South Dakota, Dole lost to Bush in the New Hampshire primary and never regained momentum. At the end of March, only seven weeks after the first Iowa caucus, Dole withdrew. While Robertson continued in the race, he ran poorly. In effect, by the end of March, Bush was the only survivor of Stage Two.

The one survivor of Stage Two was subsequently nominated at Stage Three—the convention.

The Democrats: Seven Democrats were mentioned frequently in the polls by the beginning of 1988: Gary Hart, Jesse Jackson, Michael Dukakis, Albert Gore, Richard Gephardt, Paul Simon, and Bruce Babbitt. Hart was the poll leader and early front-runner; Babbitt was not given much chance. After the scandal broke involving Hart, the news media predicted that he was finished as a candidate. While he would still enter primaries, Hart can be considered eliminated at Stage One. No clear front-runner emerged to take his place.

The Dukakis momentum began with his early wins in primaries. Gore did less well than expected in the southern primaries and Jackson did better. Gephardt also did well in several second and third place finishes. By the end of March, the race was considered a two-man race between Dukakis and Jackson. In early April, Dukakis won the Wisconsin primary, although Jackson showed impressive strength in a state with a relatively small black population.

Dukakis' victory in New York on April 19 effectively ended Stage Two although more than a month of primaries were still to be held. Dukakis had beaten Jackson at Stage Two.

The winner of Stage Two was subsequently nominated at Stage Three—the convention.

Two primaries figure prominently in this chronology: the Republican primary in New Hampshire on February 16 and the Democratic primary in Wisconsin April 6. Both primary results are given below, along with the relative standings of the Democratic candidates after Wisconsin.

New Hampshire Republican Primary

	Percentage of the Vote	Number of Delegates Won
George Bush	37.6	11
Robert Dole	28.4	7
Jack Kemp	12.8	3
Pierre du Pont IV	10.1	2
Others	11.1	0

Wisconsin Democratic Primary

	Percentage of the Vote	Number of Delegates Won
Michael Dukakis	47.5	44
Jesse Jackson	28.2	24
Albert Gore Jr.	17.4	13
Others	6.9	0

The Count After Wisconsin

	Percentage of the Total Primary Vote	Percentage of Total Delegates Won
Michael Dukakis	27.7	29.3
Jesse Jackson	27.1	27.9
Albert Gore Jr.	21.8	15.6
Richard Gephardt*	10.4	—
Paul Simon	7.5	6.8
Others; Uncommitted	5.5	20.4

*withdrew

nominating campaigns. Even more importantly, these early signs carry on the screening process. Some candidates gain momentum while others are eliminated. And since no one wants to back the wrong candidate at the beginning, all of the potential supporters are watching each other to see which candidates are gaining and losing support.

At the same time all this is occurring, there is continuous news media speculation and public opinion polling. The polls ask people their presidential preferences, typically supplying the respondents with a list of candidates to choose from. Speculation in news stories supplies names for the polls, and the poll results feed further speculation. In other words, the public and the media help to determine who receives support and when it is given. Indeed, a candidate with a clear lead in the polls can become the leading contender long before the primaries begin.

Where do the names come from and who gets on the list? New names can surface as potential candidates show early signs of money and support. A recent big election winner for senator or governor can be "mentioned" in the news media's speculation and will be added to the list. However, *most names on the list have been on the same list before*. Nixon's name appeared for twelve years (1960–1972) and Reagan's for sixteen (1968–1984). Among the Democrats, Hubert Humphrey's appeared for twelve years (1960–1972) and the various Kennedy's for at least twenty-four (1956–1980). People make the list by being major candidates for a past presidential or vice-presidential nomination or serious contenders. Thus a vice-presidential candidate, unknown four years previously, automatically becomes a part of the pool for the next presidential selection. By the time of the primaries, the list of serious presidential contenders is usually quite small.[16] A large part of the selection has already occurred.

What is expected of the candidates still in the running at the end of Stage One? First they need to generate some support within the party. Often they have been active in a nomination before, as a serious competitor or as a presidential or vice-presidential nominee. Second, they need to demonstrate public support, as shown in the polls, and preferably be the poll leader. Finally, they need to be taken seriously by the news media—the people who define who is a serious candidate and who is not. The major networks and national newspapers conduct their own polls (ABC-*Washington Post*, CBS-*New York Times*) and then proceed to interpret the results. Candidates gain or lose momentum as each of these influences affect the others. So, a good showing in the polls increases respect in the party and news media. Media speculation that support is falling can cause a further drop in support. Once in the White House, presidents will need support from the party and public as well as skill in dealing with the news media. Stage One allows the would-be candidates to test these skills and support.

[16]Donald Matthews, "Presidential Nominations: Process and Outcomes," in *Choosing the President*, ed. James David Barber (Englewood Cliffs, New Jersey: Prentice Hall, 1974), pp. 39–41; see also Stephen J. Wayne, *The Road to the White House*, 3rd ed. (New York: St. Martins, 1988).

Stage Two: Primaries, Caucuses, and the Selection of Delegates

The delegates who will vote in their party's national convention are selected in the states through primaries and caucuses. A **caucus**, or state party convention, is a meeting of party activists and officials from the state and a **primary** is an election by the voters of the state. Primaries can be **open** to all voters in the state or **closed**, that is, permitting only those voters who register as members of the party. Thus a closed Democratic primary is an election by registered Democratic voters. While people think of caucuses and primaries as selecting the candidates for president, they are actually selecting delegates who will vote for the candidates at the convention. Most of the caucuses and primaries are binding on the delegates through the first convention ballot. The delegates must vote for the candidate they have been selected to represent. The national party sets some of the guidelines for the selection of delegates, but the main choices are made in the states. The state parties decide whether they will hold primaries or caucuses and whether they will be open or closed. They set the date and compose the list of delegates, usually drawn from the leaders and active party workers in the state.

Changing the rules changes the game, people often say. Certainly, the choice of primaries or caucuses makes a critical difference to the presidential nomination. The primaries are now the major form of delegate selection. Before 1972, less than half of the delegates were selected by primaries; by 1980 about three-fourths were selected in this way. In the earlier years, a strong primary winner would not necessarily be a leader in delegate votes going into the convention. One could even sweep all the primaries and still have only a minority of delegates. In 1968, Eugene McCarthy, Vietnam war critic, ran against Hubert Humphrey, the vice-president and President Lyndon Johnson's acknowledged heir. McCarthy won primaries, while Humphrey won the delegates selected from the caucuses. Humphrey went to the convention as the clear front-runner in delegate votes and went on to win the nomination. In 1972, in contrast, the rules of the game had changed. Like McCarthy, George McGovern also ran on a platform against the war and also swept the primaries. But in so doing, McGovern went to the convention as the leader in delegate votes and won the nomination. Other newcomers to the national political scene—Jimmy Carter in 1976 and Michael Dukakis in 1988—also won heavily in primaries, led in delegates, and went on to win the nomination.

The change in delegate selection has changed the kind of characteristics important for successful candidates. Before 1972, support in the state parties was a necessary condition for surviving Stage Two. Candidates were required to show that they could win votes across the diverse party organizations of the fifty states. Winning primaries was nice and certainly might help, but failing to win them was not automatic cause for elimination. Since 1972, primary support among the voters has become the necessary condition. Presidents are required to show that they can appeal directly to the public and win votes. State party support is still important in order to generate momentum and money at Stage One, but a lack of support is not cause for elimination.

Other requirements follow from the emphasis on primary winning. The candidate's own organization and ability to raise money can make or break a primary campaign. Many of the leading candidates of 1988 had their own support groups outside the party: Pat Robertson drew support from religious fundamentalists; Jesse Jackson from the black community; Michael Dukakis from wealthy Greek-Americans. Media commentary is critical, as will be shown vividly later on. Gaining momentum is as important in Stage Two as it was earlier; hence the showing in early primaries is all-important. A poor showing or a dramatic victory for an opponent can spell an early end to the campaign. The best single predictor of primary success is the momentum gained from the previous primaries.[17] Iowa and New Hampshire, small in population but early in their primaries and caucuses, receive a disproportionate share of a candidate's attention. People have calculated the "cost per vote" in the states, based on the amount candidates spent in the contest and the number of people voting. (See Exhibit 5.4.) The cost per vote decreases steadily through the year. Candidates spend their money in the early primaries, knowing that if they do not succeed, there will be no need to spend money later on. They will have been eliminated at Stage Two.

So what has changed and what has not changed in this shift from caucuses to primaries? Primaries give the public a larger direct role, and party organizations a smaller role, in presidential selection; thus primaries appear the more democratic and popular method. A more attractive, popular outsider can now beat a less attractive insider, which was not the case before. The shift has also led to an increase in new names in nominating politics. The Dukakis and Carter phenomena—from nowhere to the presidential nomination—is more likely under a primary system. On the other hand, a candidate who is popular among partisan voters in the primary might not be popular among all voters in the November election. The parties thus have less control than before over selecting their strongest vote getter.[18] Still, both systems have produced some spectacular election losses. Barry Goldwater, nominated in 1964 through party conventions, received few votes outside Republican ranks. George McGovern, nominated in 1972 after winning primaries, was able to match Goldwater's dramatic election defeat.

For the immediate future, the primary route still seems likely to be the dominant one. While some states have returned to caucuses, a majority

---

[17]Larry M. Bartels, "Candidate Choice and the Dynamics of the Presidential Nominating Process," *American Journal of Political Science*, 31 (1987), pp. 1–30; Larry M. Bartels, *Presidential Primaries and the Dynamics of Public Choice* (Princeton: Princeton University Press, 1988).

[18]For an initial comparison of the two kinds of candidates, see T. Wayne Parent, Calvin C. Jillson, and Ronald E. Weber, "Voting Outcomes in the 1984 Democratic Party Primaries and Caucuses," *American Political Science Review*, 81 (1987), pp. 67–84.

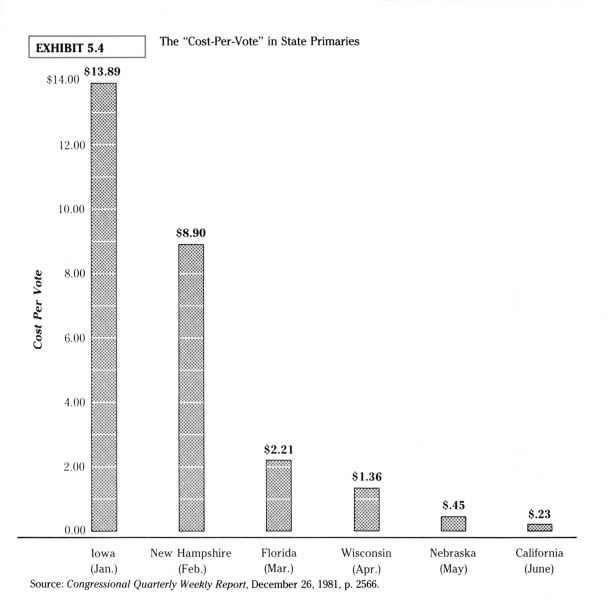

EXHIBIT 5.4   The "Cost-Per-Vote" in State Primaries

Source: *Congressional Quarterly Weekly Report*, December 26, 1981, p. 2566.

hold primaries. Nevertheless, the Democratic party has sought ways to allow the party to have more influence on the nomination. In 1984 and 1988
the Democrats reserved a number of slots for "superdelegates" at the nominating convention. These superdelegates, primarily members of Congress
and other party officials, are not bound to any particular candidate and are
free to negotiate as they see fit. Almost twenty percent of the convention
delegates were superdelegates: in 1988 they included all Democratic governors, about eighty percent of the Democratic members of Congress, and

such former office holders as Jimmy Carter, Walter Mondale, and former House Speaker Thomas (Tip) O'Neill. Superdelegates have been viewed as a way of keeping the primaries while returning to the parties an additional measure of control.

Despite the differences between caucuses and primaries, the two systems are similar in providing critical information. Both say, before the convention begins, who leads in delegate votes. They not only select the delegates, but they tell them who is most likely to win. Stage Three follows directly from this information.

Stage Three: The Convention

With bands, balloons, and gaudy demonstrations, national party conventions have long been a loud celebration of the American political process. The thousands of delegates gather as selected by the various states. They include governors, senators, mayors, and other political leaders. Most delegates, however, do not know each other. About half have never been to a national convention before. There is both superorganization and extensive confusion. This, oddly enough, is the national party meeting to nominate the president of the United States.

How do delegates in such a situation converge on one single candidate? Sense can be made out of much of the nominating process, past and present, by seeing the importance of any clear information around which the delegates can agree. In such a large and decentralized structure, any obvious cue becomes important. Thus *front-runners at the time of the convention have a decisive advantage.* This is not saying merely that candidates win who are expected to win, but that the perception itself leads to the victory. It becomes a self-fulfilling prophecy. Delegates rush to support the emerging nomination winner, producing the famous **bandwagon effect**.[19] Bandwagons occurred during the first ballot of many nominations through the middle years of the twentieth century. As a leading candidate emerged on the first ballot, the states rushed to support the likely winner and the nomination was over. In the most recent nominations, bandwagons are so swift that the balloting itself is merely a formality. The likely winner, on the eve of the convention, is automatically assumed to be the winner on the first ballot.

This means that campaigns at the convention to stop a front-runner are doomed to fail when they might succeed in other more centralized situations. **Dark horses** (little-known candidates who come from behind to win the nomination) are also highly unlikely. Perhaps the last dark horse to be nominated was Wendell Wilkie in 1940 and before that John W. Davis in 1924. (The 1924 Democratic convention, operating under different rules,

---

[19]A nice demonstration is provided in Donald S. Collat, Stanley Kelley, Jr., and Ronald Rogowski, "The End Game in Presidential Nominations," *American Political Science Review*, 75 (1981), pp. 426–35.

An actual campaign bandwagon is used for the Harrison-Van Buren contest in 1840.

went 103 ballots, with Davis's name first appearing on the ninety-fifth ballot.) These are part of the lore of American political conventions, but the facts of the convention structure argue against them. Given the difficulty of reaching any decision, only the most obvious and widely available information can be used.

The same argument helps explain other characteristics of the successful nominee, besides being a front-runner on the eve of the convention. First, nominees have frequently been selected from past convention nominees, even those who have been defeated in a previous election. They have demonstrated that they could win a nomination and that they could lose an election. For the delegates at the convention, the former fact appears to outweigh the latter in importance. Second, past vice-presidential candidates have recently emerged as leading contenders in presidential nominations. They are "the best known party leader short of the retiring president," in the words of one political scientist.[20] Also, they have demonstrated that they could get votes at a convention before. Third, the ideological position of the candidates can be shown to be important, with those seen as closer to the majority of delegates having an advantage over those to the right or left of the party majority. Those at the ideological center would be seen as the more acceptable candidates to the convention as a whole and therefore those most likely to win.

[20]Matthews, *op. cit.*, p. 45.

EXHIBIT 5.5	Presidential Nominees, 1948–1988

Democratic Nominees	Incumbent President	Front-Runner[a]	Past Nominee[b]	None of These
1948 Truman	■	■	■	
1952 Stevenson				■
1956 Stevenson		■	■	
1960 Kennedy		■		
1964 Johnson	■	■	■	
1968 Humphrey		■	■	
1972 McGovern		■		
1976 Carter		■		
1980 Carter	■	■	■	
1984 Mondale		■	■	
1988 Dukakis		■		
Republican Nominees				
1948 Dewey			■	
1952 Eisenhower				■
1956 Eisenhower	■	■	■	
1960 Nixon		■	■	
1964 Goldwater		■		
1968 Nixon		■	■	
1972 Nixon	■	■	■	
1976 Ford	■			
1980 Reagan		■		
1984 Reagan	■	■	■	
1988 Bush		■	■	

[a]Called the front-runner on a page-one story of the *New York Times* on the day before the convention
[b]Includes past presidential and vice-presidental nominees

In each of these cases, a candidate characteristic becomes information widely perceived by delegates (and perceived as being perceived), giving one candidate more advantage than others. The particular characteristic may be less important than the fact that it is clear and widely perceived as important. Conventions, then, are not merely occasions to ratify a choice made earlier, although they may seem to do this on the surface. They are critically important in their own right because they determine what kind of earlier information is important and how it is used. A different convention context, a different kind of national party convention, and other kinds of candidates could be selected. Changing the rules changes the game—and the winners and losers.

Exhibit 5.5 lists the recent nominees of the two major parties, with characteristics that would be known by all delegates. A front-runner is listed where one was named in front-page news reports on the day before the convention. Past nominees include presidential and vice-presidential nominees. Presidents are by definition either past presidential or vice-presidential candidates and are nearly always front-runners. In 1976, however, although Ford was considered a likely winner over Reagan, the race was too close to call before the convention. The final column of the table is the most interesting. With only two exceptions in forty years, all of the successful nominees have been either past nominees or named front-runners before the convention.

Conventions provide a structure that allows the nominees to be predicted in advance, thus eliminating the need to hold a convention! This poses a paradox and a question for the future. Bandwagons have become so swift that primary winners become the nominee. Even some of the vice-presidential candidates are known before the convention begins. In 1988, the Republicans postponed their vice-presidential announcement, it was said, to give some "suspense" to the convention. Indeed the controversial choice of Dan Quayle gave the convention its only dramatic moment. If both candidates are known before the party formally convenes, what is left for the convention to do?

Conventions now strike the opening note of the general election campaign with shows of unity and attacks on the opposing party. They build party morale for the days ahead by a week-long celebration that enlists film stars, past presidents, and other notables in their cause. On occasion, behind-the-scenes power struggles do occur. Fights on the convention rules can be staged by people still trying to stop the front-runner. In 1976 the Reagan forces came to the convention hoping to stop Ford, and in 1980 supporters of Ted Kennedy tried to stop Carter. (See the box on page 186.) Very little of this, however, has the makings of stirring political drama, and it is a far cry from the days when tension was built as the convention balloting began and the roll of the states was called. It is not surprising that the networks have cut the air time from gavel-to-gavel coverage to a few hours of highlights. Even so, much of the time in 1988 was spent rating the quality of the various speakers and talking about the city in which the convention was held. The change in media coverage has led one writer to speak of the "bifurcated convention," a convention split in two.[21] With the short selective media coverage, one convention exists for the delegates actually taking

[21]Byron E. Shafer, *Bifurcated Politics* (Cambridge: Harvard University Press, 1988).

At the Convention

Power struggles can occur even at modern conventions, when candidates try one last effort to stop the front-runner. Typically the struggle takes place over a vote on a rule in the first days of the convention. The rule itself is important mainly as a test of strength between the opposing sides. The accounts reprinted below tell of Senator Edward Kennedy's attempt to stop Carter in 1980 and Ronald Reagan's attempt to stop Ford in 1976.

The Kennedy forces wanted an "open convention," a phrase meaning that the primary delegates should be released from their pledged candidates to vote for anyone they wanted. They were pledged to Carter. The rule that bound them to their pledges was rule F3(c). Thus the Kennedy people tried to win on a vote overturning F3(c), hoping that the Kennedy magic would then stampede the convention.

The rule for the Reagan forces was 16-C, a rule defeated in the first meeting of the convention rules committee but due to be voted on again at the convention. The rule would require prospective candidates to name their vice-presidential running mates before the convention balloting. Reinstating the rule could be a sign of strength for the Reagan candidacy and further evidence that Ford's strength was not solid. Decisions in the Mississippi delegation were thought to be critical to the outcome of 16-C.

Neither attempt succeeded in stopping the front-runner. However, the accounts show that in the minds of many experienced politicians the convention outcome need not be a forgone conclusion. They also paint a vivid picture of the organization and confusion that exist, side by side, and show how the news media become part of the events that they are reporting.

Kennedy versus Carter

[T]he Carter command was prepared, with a mastery of convention technology that had developed over twenty years of politics and floor communication. Now, at this convention, the Carter off-floor headquarters was a circle of six trailers, about which buzzed the crowding press, while command by telephone and walkie-talkie went out to fourteen floor operatives, ten regional floor leaders, and some two hundred whips, all dressed in shimmering green vests.... [In] [t]he Kennedy command post ... one hundred twenty floor whips, recognizable by blue baseball caps, were assigned to shake loose the few uncommitted and a larger number of unhappy Carter delegates. One could follow the commotion on the floor as a clash of blue and green colors....

. . .

The Carter people, from the very beginning, had understood television better than Kennedy's team ... His staff had been studying the Republican convention and calculated that the cameras stayed on the podium for no more than eight minutes out of every hour, cutting away the rest of the time to famous personalities and floor reports. They had studied floor layouts, the movement of television's reporters down corridors and aisles, and now proceeded to strew dignitaries and cabinet members through the aisles on the floor. There, accidentally, the scurrying floor reporters would meet the people they had been seek-

part, while another exists for the voters and television viewers. Given the lack of newsworthy events, coverage may well be cut even further in the future.

Thousands of delegates, the most politically active people in the country, have a stake in the continued importance of these events. Nevertheless, these same people seek unity and an early resolution of their critical decision. It will be interesting to see what happens to the convention in the years ahead.

ing and could interview them forthwith, or send them off, if they were eminences, to be interviewed in the anchor booths. For the country press the Carter command had arranged specials. . . . What Carter could not control, however, was the live drama on the television time allotted to Kennedy. . . .

Source: Theodore H. White, *America in Search of Itself* (New York: Harper and Row, 1982), pp. 331, 336–337.

Reagan versus Ford

[T]he forces of Gerald Ford and Ronald Reagan had laid out costly and complex networks of phones, television monitors, walkie-talkies, beepers, and various other devices of the communications age to keep a firm grip on unfolding events. . . . Telephone lines went out from each trailer to the delegations and to floor leaders or whips in charge of dealing with problems as they arose in the various delegations. . . . The Ford trailer also had private lines into the anchor booths of NBC and ABC, high above the convention floor, in order to pass on information—and self-serving rumor, a service that CBS decided to do without.

. . .

All this electronic paraphernalia inevitably raised memories of Watergate, and so each campaign hired security men to guard the trailers and to sweep them daily for possible wiretaps or other bugs. Also, because the Ford trailer's telephone lines had to pass directly beneath Reagan's trailer, they were placed in a steel pipe to guard against sabotage or monitoring.

. . .

[Jim] Baker threw down a copy of the *Birmingham News* with a front-page headline that said: "Ford Would Write Off Cotton South?" The article . . . was an account of a breakfast that reporters had had with Rogers Morton [a Ford manager] where Morton had evidently said that Ford's campaign would concentrate on the big industrial states. . . . [T]he clear implication . . . was that the President intended to spend little time bucking Carter in Dixie.

Morton was on the floor at the time and Dan Rather of CBS collared him. He denied he had said Ford would write off the South. Whereupon Rather invited him to accompany him over to the Mississippi delegation to straighten the matter out—on live television. Someone in the Ford sky suite spotted Morton in Rather's grip and Morton was promptly ordered by walkie-talkie to get off the floor immediately. . . .

Copies of the newspaper, and word-of-mouth about the story, had already spread to the convention floor and especially within the Mississippi delegation. Talk of defections from Ford . . . floated up to the Ford sky suite. . . .

As the roll call on 16-C was proceeding, some of the Mississippians tried to commandeer a CBS trailer to caucus in, but then were thrown out by Mike Wallace when they refused to let their meeting be televised live.

Source: Jules Witcover, *Marathon* (New York: Viking, 1977), pp. 487–488, 497–499.

The News Media and the Nomination

The news media play a critical role in the selection process because they say what the "information" is that the delegates will be using. By announcing what is, they affect what will be: they set the self-fulfilling prophecies in motion. *New York Times* writer Russell Baker has given us the concept of the Great Mentioner, that mysterious Someone who announces in Stage One that so-and-so "is being mentioned" as a candidate. The Great Mentioner works in mysterious ways and has great power, sufficient to start or stop a campaign. Journalist David Broder agrees:

> At any given time in this country, there are several hundred persons who are potential candidates for nomination.... Who is it that winnows this field down to manageable size? The press—and particularly that small segment of the press called the national political reporters.[22]

The political reporters are not only mentioners, but they are handicappers too. They say who is leading, who is lagging, and who is likely to win. For Broder, this is the point where serious problems enter, since the reporters are clearly helping to make the news that they are supposed to be reporting. In 1968, front-runner George Romney told a television interviewer he thought he had been "brainwashed" by generals and diplomats about the war in Vietnam. The press pounced on the phrase, and Romney's "brainwashing" suddenly became the major news story. Would the phrase hurt Romney, the reporters speculated? When his support in the polls dropped following the speculation, this too was reported and speculated about. The spiral continued until by February 1968 Romney announced he was no longer a candidate for the nomination. An even clearer case occurred in 1988 when front-runner Gary Hart was reported to be "womanizing" while his wife was out of town. The report itself, by the *Miami Herald,* may have started events in motion, but the nationwide reporting of the story finished the job. "Was Hart through?" the press speculated, in every newspaper, magazine and television news show for a week. By the time the week was over, yes, indeed, he was.

But what was cause and what was effect? Did the events cause the polls to fall or did the press speculation that they would fall produce the very effect that was predicted? Broder, for one, sees the press responsible for such critical Stage One decisions.

In interpreting primary victories and delegate counts, the news media are also important in Stage Two. A major newspaper headline in 1976 proclaimed "Carter Wins" in large print after two primaries had been held on the same day, and Morris Udall came close to tying Carter in the one race both had entered. A different, though not less accurate, headline, "Carter Edges Udall," could have changed the course of the nomination. The actual news report effectively ended Udall's campaign, and the Carter bandwagon began to roll all the way to the convention. News reporting became even more pointed in 1988. The media announced that Gary Hart was through before the public had decided Hart's fate. Indeed, two-thirds of the American public who were polled thought the press had gone "too far" in its reporting of the Hart story.[23] The stories of Jesse Jackson's candidacy typically included the reporter's doubts that Jackson could win the nomination. CBS anchor Dan Rather got involved in such a heated exchange with George

[22]David Broder, "Political Reporters in Presidential Politics," in Charles Peters and Timothy J. Adams, eds. *Inside the System* (New York: Praeger, 1970), pp. 27–28.
[23]*Time,* November 30, 1987, p. 76.

Face to face: Candidate George Bush and television anchor Dan Rather engage in a heated exchange during the 1988 presidential campaign, as Rather asks Bush about his role in the Iran-Contra affair.

Bush that the public was subsequently polled to see which they supported—the candidate or the television personality!

Much of the reporting may lie well within the lines of responsible journalism. The reporters are following a story or building drama or making a prediction. And yet reporters read and watch each other, and the influential party people, contributors, and delegates read and watch them too. In any event, the problem remains of how much deciding is being done by those supposed to report the decision process of others.

Selecting the President

The nominating process selects the future president, narrowing the choice to two individuals. What kind of a selection process is it and what traits are the selections based on? Much of what happens before the convention, from the first polls through the last primary, can be seen as an information-accumulation process aimed at finding who is the most likely nominee. Since the most likely nominee may also be the most popular nominee (winning primaries and leading in public opinion polls), one can argue that the nominating process is democratic. The two parties' nominees are those who have won a number of popularity contests. Yet, given the importance of the self-fulfilling prophecy—the bandwagon momentum which accelerates so rapidly—any random occurrence can become decisive. If someone had gained one thousand more votes in an early primary. . . . If this news event was emphasized rather than another one. . . . The list could go on. In other kinds of decision-making structures, these random events could cancel each other. However, in this situation any stray fact or lucky push can start the bandwagon rolling. There may be, then, a fairly large chance factor (that we do not like to think about) in our selection of American presidents.

Moreover, this random momentum can produce a nominee that no one really likes. The selection is less a popularity contest than a process of elimination. Since the pool of potential candidates is small to start with at the beginning of Stage One, it does not take many eliminations to have only one candidate left standing. When early front-runner Hart was eliminated in 1988, the choice soon narrowed to Dukakis and Jackson, the two strongest candidates in the early primaries. Jackson, however, was perceived by many as unlikely to win the nomination because of his race. This is the negative side of the self-fulfilling prophecy. For the Democrats, then, early in Stage Two, there was really only one "likely" nominee. People did not know that much about him or whether he would be able to compete in an election campaign. Nevertheless, the choice had been made—the momentum could not be reversed.

The nominating process selects traits that appeal to a diverse and decentralized party. It favors moderators and compromisers or those who can appear to be so. And since 1972, it favors those who can demonstrate the broadest and clearest popular appeal in the polls and primaries—and so those who are skilled in using information and dealing with the news media. It also favors those who have been past candidates at a national party convention, whether as presidential or vice-presidential nominees. It screens out those who cannot rally or sustain financial and political support and those who do not have the organization or the good luck to avoid major public mistakes. Chapter Eight will show that this emerging profile of a democratically popular, information-using moderate who can be many things to many people is not a bad selection for what we in fact ask our presidents to be. But at the same time the process does not select for other traits that might be considered more important. Many people like to think of presidents as "honest" or "altruistic," concerned about others and willing to sacrifice themselves for the nation. Nothing in the selection, however, says that altruism is required, while honesty could easily cost a candidate the nomination.

▬ THE VICE-PRESIDENTIAL NOMINATION

On the last day of the convention, the delegates turn to the vice-presidential nomination. The same problem of finding one clear rallying point for the party exists, but it is complicated in several ways. First, the choice depends on the selection of the presidential nominee; hence it must wait until after that decision. Second, little information about vice-presidential candidates is available, since they are rarely major presidential contenders. Third, it is an anticlimax—the main event is over.

The choice, however, is more momentous than it might appear. Not only is a potential successor being named, in case of the death or disability of the president, but candidates are also being entered for a future presidential race. With only one exception, the recent vice-presidential candidates—Humphrey, Muskie, Mondale, Dole, Bush—have automatically been mentioned as leading contenders for president four or eight years after they were nominated as a vice-president. The only exception is Geraldine Ferraro. Studying vice-presidential nominations, therefore, tells us more about the influences on presidential selection.

It is commonly heard at convention time that "the presidential candidate selects the vice-presidential nominee." This, however, is a very recent precedent developing only since the 1960s. In earlier times, a presidential candidate would be able to veto a proposed running mate, as would (to a lesser extent) other individuals in the party. But the positive decision, within some pool of non-vetoed candidates, would be made by the convention delegates.[24] From 1960 on, the winning presidential nominee has "announced" the choice, and the convention has ratified the selection. So, in 1960, Nixon chose Henry Cabot Lodge and Kennedy chose Lyndon Johnson. The precedent continued: Carter chose Walter Mondale, Mondale chose Geraldine Ferraro, and Dukakis chose Lloyd Bentsen, to mention just a few.

Nevertheless, other people within the party can still veto an initial presidential choice. The new presidential nominee typically consults with various party leaders to see who is unacceptable. For example, a Democratic candidate unacceptable to labor groups, or a Republican who appeared too liberal for the majority of party members, could be eliminated at this stage. In 1968, the liberal and conservative wings of the GOP kept vetoing each other's candidates until the Nixon people looked for a "political eunuch" who had no ideological ties.[25] The choice of Spiro Agnew, therefore, was shaped by the presidential nominee plus the national Republican party.

The practice of consultation and veto affects the kind of candidate selected. It benefits those with no enemies among major segments of the party or those whose political profiles are less sharply drawn and less well-known than others. In 1944 it was common knowledge among party leaders that Franklin Roosevelt probably would not live out the term. Who, then, would be selected as vice-president? The choice of Harry Truman was described as follows: "The man with the fewest handicaps and with some tangible advantages was Harry Truman. He had a good record as a war investigator, he stood well with labor, he had voted with the New Deal, he came from a border state, and Roosevelt really had nothing very much against him."[26] These were the qualifications for the man who would probably become president.

[24]Michael Harwood, *In the Shadow of Presidents* (Philadelphia: Lippincott, 1966).

[25]Theodore White, *The Making of the President,* 1968 (New York: Atheneum, 1969), pp. 251–52.

[26]Cabell Phillips, *The Truman Presidency* (New York: Macmillan, 1966), p. 41.

The practice also puts a time constraint on the choice of the vice-presidential nominee. While presidential candidates consult in advance about likely running mates, the final choice has typically been made in late and highly pressured meetings at the national convention. Since the national party has a role to play in the selection, the final choice is delayed until the national party convenes. Even when presidential nominees were virtually assured of victory, they have waited until the convention to announce their running mates. The only two exceptions occurred in the Democratic party in the years 1984 and 1988, when Mondale chose Geraldine Ferraro and Dukakis chose Lloyd Bentsen before the convention. (It is interesting that Democratic superdelegates were appointed in these years, many of whom were members of Congress. Since the two vice-presidential nominees were themselves respected members of Congress, the process of consultation and veto could more easily occur before the convention.)

The vice-presidential candidate, then, is (1) screened as acceptable to the presidential nominee, not a personal or political rival, and one who is willing to work for the president in the campaign and for the next four years; (2) screened as having no powerful enemies in the party as far as this is known; and (3) often chosen from a list of finalists in a very short period of time. What else is known about these candidates? The answer is not much.

People often say that vice-presidents are selected as "ticket balancers." However, tickets can be balanced in any of a near-infinite number of ways. What, if anything, does this reveal about the kind of candidates selected?

Try this simple experiment. Take a roomful of people, such as a classroom, and draw names from a hat so that one person is designated president and a second person vice-president. If the group is diverse to start with, whatever two people are chosen by this lottery should have some characteristics that are different from each other. The two lottery winners might differ in sex, in race, in religion, or in family background. They might differ also in their friends and attitudes and future goals. We could say the ticket is "balanced," but we have achieved this result merely by drawing names from a hat. The observation that vice-presidents are selected as ticket balancers makes us think we know more about them than we actually do.

The one clear pattern that emerges is a balancing by region. With only occasional exceptions, the vice-presidential candidate will be from a region of the country different from that of the presidential candidate. (See Exhibit 5.6.) Thus the selection of a presidential candidate will tend to exclude from the second spot those candidates from the same region as the presidential nominee. There are, however, exceptions: for example, the Republican choice of the two midwesterners Gerald Ford and Robert Dole in 1976.

There is, however, little ticket balancing by ideology or political position. With one significant recent exception, vice-presidents are usually not selected from factions within the party representing clearly different political views from the presidential candidate. For some years liberal New Deal presidential candidates would be "balanced" by southern vice-presidential candidates, as in the Kennedy-Johnson ticket, but the southerners would be

---

EXHIBIT 5.6		Party Tickets—The Nominees

Year and Party		President and Vice-President	Region	Past Experience
1960	D	Kennedy-Johnson	East-South	Senator-Senator
	R	Nixon-Lodge	West-East	Senator-Senator
1964	D	Johnson-Humphrey	South-Midwest	Senator-Senator
	R	Goldwater-Miller	West-East	Senator-Representative
1968	D	Humphrey-Muskie	Midwest-East	Senator-Senator
	R	Nixon-Agnew	West-East	Senator-Governor
1972	D	McGovern-Shriver	Midwest-East	Senator-No elected office
	R	Nixon-Agnew	West-East	Senator-Governor
1976	D	Carter-Mondale	South-Midwest	Governor-Senator
	R	Ford-Dole	Midwest-Midwest	Representative-Senator
1980	D	Carter-Mondale	South-Midwest	Governor-Senator
	R	Reagan-Bush	West-South	Governor-Representative
1984	D	Mondale-Ferraro	Midwest-East	Senator-Representative
	R	Reagan-Bush	West-South	Governor-Representative
1988	D	Dukakis-Bentsen	East-South	Governor-Senator
	R	Bush-Quayle	South-Midwest	Representative-Senator

For region and past experience, the president is cited first and the vice-president second. Past experience refers to offices other than president and vice-president. Presidential candidates Nixon, Johnson, Humphrey, Ford, Mondale, and Bush had also served as vice-president.

known as New Deal supporters.[27] Conservative Barry Goldwater from Arizona was balanced by William Miller of New York State, but Miller was known to have strongly conservative views. While George Bush was not identified with the same conservative wing of the party as Ronald Reagan, his mix of moderate and conservative views could not accurately be seen as balancing. Perhaps the clearest exception to the rule in the twentieth century is a very recent one. Lloyd Bentsen, Michael Dukakis's running mate, was known as a very conservative Democrat. In fact, in his years in the Senate, he had voted with the Republicans as often as with the Democrats. He and Dukakis had different positions on several key foreign and domestic policy issues. Except for this one case, however, the running mate is usually not a rival in political views.[28]

[27]See Joel K. Goldstein, *The Modern American Vice Presidency* (Princeton: Princeton University Press, 1982). Goldstein agrees that there has been little ideological balancing, citing only three marginal exceptions in recent nominations: Johnson as less liberal than Kennedy, Mondale as more liberal than Carter, and Bush as less conservative than Reagan. These are matters of degree, however, and Bush's record in the House would place him closer to the conservative than the moderate wing of his party.

[28]The same point is made by Goldstein, pp. 74–75.

The rule against rivalry holds at the individual level as well. Many people believe that vice-presidential candidates are selected from major losing presidential candidates in order to unify the party after the nomination fight. This was one of the many arguments considered by the Kennedy people in offering the vice-presidency to Johnson in 1960.[29] Looking at major presidential candidates as those receiving more than their own state's votes at a convention, there are few vice-presidential nominees. No such candidates have been nominated for vice-president by the Republican party and only two have been nominated by the Democrats: Thomas Hendricks in 1876 and 1884 and Lyndon Johnson in 1960. (Reagan's selection of George Bush in 1980 could also be counted as an exception, although Bush, a serious candidate in the primaries, was not a candidate at the convention.) What the Kennedys seemed to think was the usual practice, and what they ought to do, was in fact a very rare exception. The major contenders against the presidential nominee are rarely selected as vice-president.

Few other patterns are apparent. There is some tendency to select vice-presidents from states largest in population, although there are many exceptions. There is also some tendency to select candidates from Congress, although governors have been chosen as well as candidates with neither congressional nor gubernatorial experience. Vice-presidents may be party leaders in Congress or people not known well at all. They may be old or young, or newcomers or oldtimers in national politics. Within a broad region of the country and a predominant ideology in the national party, many names are proposed—and many we have never heard of. Bentsen, Quayle, Ferraro, Mondale, Agnew—none were known to most American citizens before their selection was announced. It is impossible to predict who the nominees will be if we do not even know their names. And yet we vote for them when we vote for president. And the chances are good (about one in three, as will be shown in Chapter Eight) that they will become president themselves.

Parties no longer dominate the nominating processes of American politics. The candidates, the primary voters, and the news media also have a decisive influence. Yet, the labels still link the public and the elected officials and link one official with another across time. Parties, therefore, continue to be prominent features of American political life.

| CHECKLIST FOR REVIEW | 1. Parties are organizations that seek to influence government by nominating candidates and contesting their election. In so doing, they provide a label linking voters, workers, and candidates for office that can continue over time. Parties also offer a legitimate opposition, a democratic way to criticize the government and provide for change. |

---

[29]See, for example, Theodore Sorenson, *Kennedy* (New York: Harper and Row, 1965), p. 164.

O n the first Tuesday after the first Monday in November, in years divisible by four, the American people elect a president. At the same time, they elect the entire House of Representatives, one-third of the Senate, and many state and local offices. (The entire House along with another third of the Senate will face reelection two years later.) Elections are dramatic, decisive, and participatory; they show democracy at work. But how are the choices made and with what information? What do voters ask and what do they know about the individuals selected for office? How do their choices explain and predict who will be making the speeches of celebration and concession when election day is over?

A good place to begin is with the public, the actions they take, and the decisions they make about voting. One principle theme throughout this book is the impact of public opinion on government. Elections should constitute one major form of this impact. Voting occurs within the context of public opinion traced in Chapter Three and will set in motion forces of its own—in the kind of candidates selected and the conditions under which they hold office. As already shown, the general public's information about elections is low, that information varies with the socioeconomic status of the citizen, and it also varies between the presidential race and all other elections. This becomes the context for understanding why people vote the way they do.

THE AMERICAN VOTER

When choosing what to do during an election, people make two equally important decisions. Before they decide which candidates they will vote for, they must decide whether or not to vote. There are a variety of influences shaping each of these critical decisions.

Turnout

Many nations require citizens to vote: it is a legal obligation like paying taxes or registering for the draft. Other nations, many of which have strong religious traditions, stress the duty of voting; it is a moral obligation, something people should do, like going to church. Americans, however, are bound neither by law nor custom to vote. People are urged to do so by public-spirited messages. It is considered a good thing to do, but no penalties are attached to not doing it. Therefore, it is not surprising that Americans are among the lowest-ranked citizens of democracies in *turnout*—the percent of eligible voters who do vote. Americans prize the right to vote, but many do not avail themselves of the opportunity.

All American citizens of eighteen years or older are eligible to vote if they are not convicted felons, institutionalized for incompetence, or with-

out a residence. Only about half of the eligible voters, however, do in fact turn out to vote, and the proportion has been falling since the 1960s. The year 1988 brought a new record low for a presidential election when just 50 percent of the eligible voters turned out to vote. (See Exhibit 6.1.)

Turnout, the percent of eligible voters who actually vote, is affected by the excitement of the presidential race, as the graph in Exhibit 6.1 shows vividly. About fifty percent on the average vote in a presidential election year and about forty percent or lower vote in the off-year election held two years later. See the zigzag pattern in the congressional vote depending on whether or not the presidential candidates are running. Almost as many people vote for Congress in a presidential election year as they do for president; far fewer vote in the off-year election. Overall turnout is not affected by the competitiveness of the House race or by a Senate race being held simultaneously in the state. The effects of the rise and fall in turnout for congressional elections will be seen later in the chapter.

Turnout also changes with the age and education of the citizen, along with other socioeconomic characteristics: people in their 30s or older and those with more formal education show higher turnout rates than the

| EXHIBIT 6.1 | Turnout in Presidential and Congressional Elections |

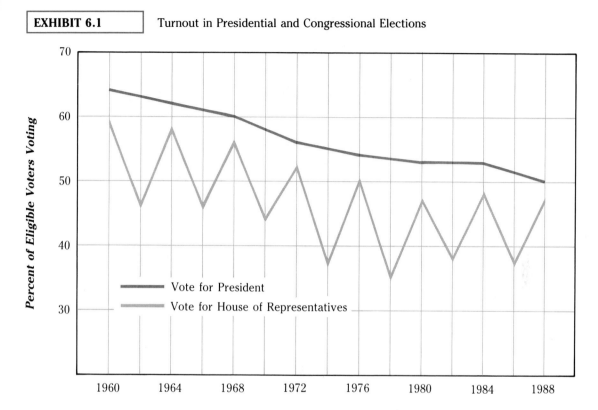

younger and less educated citizens. The citizen's race makes only a slight difference in turnout results and the citizen's sex makes no difference.[1]

Older and more educated people also have a stronger sense of efficacy, as was shown in Chapter Three, and a sense of one's duty as a citizen. Efficacy—the sense that one can have an impact on government—and civic duty both relate to the decision to vote. An interesting survey by ABC News shows these differences clearly. The survey compared those most likely and least likely to vote, each group making up about 10 percent at each end of the total sample. While the two groups differed in age and education, their answers showed as many similarities as differences. The least likely voters did not find the ballot "too complicated" any more than the most likely voters did. Nor did they complain much more that there was "no difference" between the candidates or that they did not like any of the candidates. About 40 percent of both groups said that the candidates did not take stands on issues important to them. The main difference between the groups was found in efficacy and civic duty. Those most likely to vote said

[1]Raymond E. Wolfinger and Steven J. Rosenstone, *Who Votes* (New Haven: Yale University Press, 1980), pp. 24–26.

they voted to "help a candidate win" and "to send a message to government." Almost three-fourths of the group admitted that they would feel guilty if they did not vote, and almost half said their friends or relatives would be disappointed in them. The comparable figures among the least likely voters were 31 and 29 percent. Only about one-third of the most likely voters agreed with the statement "Public officials don't care about people like me," whereas 60 percent of the least likely voters agreed with that statement.[2] Since officials facing reelection must think about who the voters are, the effect becomes circular: nonvoters would continue to feel that public officials do not care about them.

Institutional factors, too, affect the decision to vote—the difficulty of voter registration laws (which vary by state) and the scheduling of poll openings and closings. *Registered* voters are extremely likely to vote at rates above 80 percent.[3] States with easy registration laws, such as offering registration on the same day and the same place as the voting, show higher turnout rates. Clearly turnout could be improved by reforming registration and voting rules. This becomes a political problem, however, because the politicians who would reform the rules might not like the idea of waves of new voters entering the electorate. They are elected by the voters under the present rules. Reformed registration would bring new voters into the electorate, although people would still differ about their duty to vote and the difference that it makes.

Party Identification

Those who do vote face decisions for national, state, and local contests; many of the names are unfamiliar and the issues unknown. It is not surprising, then, that people seek ways of making good decisions with low information. The candidate's party, supplied on the ballot, becomes one obvious voting cue. The previous chapter showed that there are differences in ideology between the two parties and among the voters and the elected officials. Thus voters can argue that their own party's candidates will represent them better than the opposite party will. A party vote becomes one way of making a meaningful vote using very little information.

The voter's **party identification** is in fact an important influence on voting. Party identification refers to people's psychological attachment to a political party. When asked a question like "Generally speaking, do you consider yourself a Democrat, a Republican, an Independent, or what?" about 65 percent of American adults who are polled mention the Democratic or Republican party. This self-identification is what is meant by party identification.

Exhibit 6.2 shows the distribution of party identification over time. People who identified themselves as Democrats or Republicans are further dis-

[2]ABC News, *The 1984 Vote* (New York: ABC News, 1984), pp. 83–95.
[3]Frances Fox Piven and Richard A. Cloward, *Why Americans Don't Vote* (NY: Pantheon, 1988), see, for example, p. 262.

EXHIBIT 6.2	Distribution of Party Identification in the United States, 1966-1986

	NOV. 1966	NOV. 1968	NOV. 1970	NOV. 1972	NOV. 1974	NOV. 1976	NOV. 1978	NOV. 1980	NOV. 1982	NOV. 1984	NOV. 1986
Strong Democrat	18%	20%	20%	15%	18%	15%	15%	18%	20%	17%	18%
Democrat	27	25	23	25	21	25	24	23	24	20	22
Independent Democrat	9	10	10	11	13	12	14	11	11	11	10
Independent	12	11	13	13	15	14	14	13	11	11	12
Independent Republican	7	9	8	11	9	10	9	10	8	12	11
Republican	15	14	15	13	14	14	13	14	14	15	15
Strong Republican	10	10	10	10	8	9	8	9	10	12	10
Don't know; no answer	2	1	1	2	2	1	3	2	2	2	2
	100%	100%	100%	100%	100%	100%	100%	100%	100%	100%	100%

Source: Warren E. Miller and Teresa E. Levitin, *Leadership and Change* (Cambridge: Winthrop, 1976), p. 36, through 1972. 1974–1986 results were computed by the author from the biennial National Election Studies, Center for Political Studies, University of Michigan. The data utilized were made available by the Inter-University Consortium for Political and Social Research. Neither the original source or collectors of the data nor the Consortium bear any responsibility for the analyses or interpretations presented here.

tinguished as to whether they are strong or not so strong Democrats or Republicans; Independents are distinguished according to whether they say they lean toward either party. The table shows the stability of party identification across the years. Yet, within this stability, one can see the rise in the ranks of Independents (the three middle rows of the table) from approximately 25 percent to nearly 40 percent in the 1970s back down to about 33 percent by the end of the 1980s. The table also shows that the Democrats have the edge. More people are willing to call themselves Democrats than Republicans.

The table reveals both the importance and limits of party loyalty as an influence on voting. For over 60 percent of Americans (65 percent in 1986), an identification with one of the two parties can be used in voting across the years and for a number of different offices. On the other hand, for over 30 percent of the citizens, a party cue does not mean much at all. These voters would make their choice on other influences—and 30 percent is more than enough to swing an election.

Self-identification is important because it affects behavior. Party identification strongly influences one's vote in any one election, through time, and across a number of different offices. Thus one finds Democratic districts or Republican districts that tend to vote for their party's candidates or at least give them more votes than other states and districts. A Republican landslide election might give a Republican candidate a 65 percent margin in a Republican state or a 49 percent margin in a strongly Democratic state. Both have swung strongly for the Republican candidate, but they have done so from their own very different bases in party identification. Knowing

PERCENT GIVING A GOOD JOB RATING[a]

Party Identification	Democratic Representatives	Republican Representatives	Democratic President (Carter)
Strong Democrats	79%	58%	56%
Weak Democrats	66	54	40
Independents (D)	60	55	42
Independents	61	66	32
Independents (R)	62	78	21
Weak Republicans	54	70	17
Strong Republicans	54	84	16
Total	64	65	35

[a]The table can be read as follows: Of the strong Democrats in a district with a Democratic representative, 79 percent gave a good job rating. Of the strong Democrats in a district with a Republican representative, 58 percent gave a good job rating. Of all the strong Democrats, 56 percent gave President Carter a good job rating.

Source: Prepared from data from the 1978 American National Election Study, Center for Political Studies, University of Michigan. The data utilized were made available by the Inter-University Consortium for Political and Social Research. Neither the original source or collectors of the data nor the Consortium bear any responsibility for the analyses or interpretations presented here.

the partisan ratio of a state or district is a first step in predicting the election result.

Party identification can be a subtle, only partly conscious influence. Party loyalty acts as a perceptual screen, affecting the selection of information and perceptions of the candidates. People pick up favorable perceptions about the candidates of their own party and screen out unfavorable perceptions. They do the reverse for the opposing party's candidates, screening out the favorable and focusing on the unfavorable. So, someone can say, "I vote for the *candidates*, not the party—Nixon, Ford, Reagan, Bush." They like George Bush more than Michael Dukakis and remember hearing more favorable things about him. The same positive impression was gained about the other Republican candidates.

The power of this perceptual screen can be seen in Exhibit 6.3, showing the percentage of Americans polled who rated as "good" the job the president and their representatives were doing. The Democratic president was much less strongly supported than the representatives at the time. Nevertheless *the trend is the same* for all these officials. The evaluations rise and fall with the strength of party identification.

It is possible now to see more clearly why party identification influences the vote, as shown in Exhibit 6.4. Democratic identifiers are much more likely to vote for Democratic candidates, and Republican identifiers for the Republican candidates. The pattern is not perfect: see, for example, how the Independents who lean toward a party are often as likely to vote for the party as are the weak Democrats and Republicans. However, the

| EXHIBIT 6.4 | | Party Identification and the Presidential Vote |

Year/Candidate	Strong Demo-crat	Weak Demo-crat	Inde-pendent Demo-crat	Inde-pendent	Inde-pendent Republi-can	Weak Republi-can	Strong Republi-can	Total
1952								
Stevenson	84%	62%	61%	20%	7%	7%	2%	42%
Eisenhower	16	38	39	80	93	93	98	58
1956								
Stevenson	85	63	67	17	7	7	1	40
Eisenhower	15	37	33	83	93	93	99	60
1960								
Kennedy	91	72	90	46	12	13	2	49
Nixon	9	28	10	54	88	87	98	51
1964								
Johnson	95	82	90	77	25	43	10	68
Goldwater	5	18	10	23	75	57	90	32
1968								
Humphrey	92	68	64	30	5	11	3	46
Nixon	8	32	36	70	95	89	97	54
1972								
McGovern	73	49	61	30	13	9	3	36
Nixon	27	51	39	70	87	91	97	64
1976								
Carter	92	75	76	43	14	22	3	51
Ford	8	25	24	57	86	78	97	49
1980								
Carter	89	65	60	26	13	5	5	44
Reagan	11	35	40	74	87	95	95	56
1984								
Mondale	89	68	79	28	7	6	3	42
Reagan	11	32	21	72	93	94	97	58

Note: Results are from surveys in which voters are asked which party they identify with and who they voted for. The exact question is as follows: "Generally speaking, do you consider yourself a Republican, a Democrat, an Independent, or what?" If Republican or Democrat: "Would you consider yourself a strong (R/D) or a not very strong (R/D)?" If Independent or other: "Do you think of yourself as closer to the Republican or Democratic party?"

Source: Harold W. Stanley and Richard G. Niemi, *Vital Statistics on American Politics* (Washington, D.C.: CQ Press, 1988).

pattern is the same as the pattern for the job ratings in Exhibit 6.3, and it holds across all elections.

The table in Exhibit 6.4 also shows what is happening in such landslide elections as 1964 and 1972. While Independents are swinging strongly to the winning candidate—Johnson in 1964 and Nixon in 1972—a hard core of partisans is staying with their own party's candidate. In the landslide election of 1964, losing candidate Goldwater received 38 percent of the popular vote, while McGovern received 37 percent in 1972. These electoral minimums suggest that some voters in any election will vote for the candidate of their party regardless of who it is or what is happening at the time. Some Americans will make their decision with the party nomination: whoever is nominated, within some reasonable limits, will have their vote.

The limits of party identification must also be recognized. About one-third of the potential voters do not identify with a party and more than ten percent say they do not even lean toward a party. This is more than enough to swing the outcome of an election. Even more critically, people defect from their party to vote for the other party's candidate. These defections can be seen in Exhibit 6.4; one out of every four weak Democrats voted for Ford in 1976 and one out of every three voted for Reagan in 1984. People **split their ticket**, voting for a candidate of one party while at the same time voting for a candidate of the opposite party. The ticket is the ballot. People might vote for a Republican president and a Democratic representative, or split the ticket for the Senate and the House. The most recent studies show that about one-fourth of the voters split their tickets for national offices; even more do so when voting for national, state, and local offices.[4] Both sides of the picture need to be kept in mind. Party identification is an important influence on voting, but it is not the only one.

PRESIDENTIAL ELECTIONS

A presidential election is similar to that other fall classic, the World Series, in that it produces excitement and sustained attention, it captures the interest of those who do not follow the sport (politics, baseball) the rest of the year, and it is a major national event. At the height of a presidential campaign, anyone who leaves home, reads an occasional newspaper, or watches television would find it difficult not to know something about the contest. All this excitement, however, comes only at the last stage of a long selection process. Some hypothetical list of eligible candidates has been narrowed down to two—the nominees of the two parties. The election festivities take over at this point. They are important in their own right as long as we remember that much of the deciding has already been done.

In conducting a campaign, candidates must appeal to a national electorate. However, they must also appeal to state and regional populations, given the rules of the electoral college. Both of these requirements shape the final election result.

Voting for President

To understand presidential voting, it is important to distinguish between **long-term** and **short-term influences on the vote.** The long-term influence is the now-familiar party identification. It is independent of the candi-

[4]Harold W. Stanley and Richard G. Niemi, *Vital Statistics on American Politics* (Washington, D.C.: CQ Press, 1988), p. 112. The increase in split-ticket voting observable in the 1970s has stabilized and even fallen slightly in recent elections.

dates nominated, the campaign strategy, or the events in the world at the time of any one election. But clearly all these other things also influence voting. The short-term effects—people's perceptions of the candidates, the issues, and the parties at the time—also shape election results.

Thus, a simple model of four components makes it possible to analyze past elections and predict future ones:

Party Identification (Long-term)	+	Perception of the Candidates (Short-term)	+	Perception of the Issues (Short-term)	+	Perception of the Parties at the Time (Short-term)	=	**Vote**

In other words, the voters' choice will be affected by their basic predisposition toward one of the two parties, plus their specific perceptions of the candidates, issues, and parties at the time. They might find the Republican candidate more attractive, but find the major issues favoring the Democrats, in which case their choice might be decided by their basic inclination to vote with one or the other parties. Other voters, strongly Republican or Democratic, might make their decision on the long-term influence alone.

The Normal Vote. From this long-term force of party identification comes the idea of a **normal vote**. A normal vote is an abstraction—a hypothetical vote based on the percentage of people identifying with each of the two parties, plus an estimate of the likelihood that they will vote. It assumes that all who identify with a party will vote for their party's candidates and that Independents will split evenly, neither party having an advantage. In other words, the normal vote is the hypothetical vote that would occur if there were no short-term influences affecting the results. Studies have calculated the normal vote for recent years as 46 percent Republican and 54 percent Democratic.[5]

The normal vote thus provides a baseline of great value in analyzing elections. Comparing the difference between the normal vote and the actual election result, one can begin to measure the extent and direction of the various short-term influences operating in any one election. (See Exhibit 6.5 for an illustration.) For instance, taking the normal vote for the nation as 54 percent Democratic, a Republican victory of 54 percent, such as the victory won by George Bush in 1988, would show short-term effects at work. Some factor, *other than party*, would be helping the Republicans in that election. Similarly, if a Democrat won by 51 percent of the vote, as Carter did in 1976, one should not ask why that candidate won, but rather why the Republican opponent was actually advantaged. Ford gained more short-term effects than Carter, although he lost the election. A normal vote can be constructed for states or any population as long as the percentage of party identifiers is known.

---

[5]See Arthur Miller, "Normal Vote Analysis: Sensitivity to Change Over Time," *American Journal of Political Science,* 23 (1979), esp. p. 423.

| EXHIBIT 6.5 | Short-Term Effects and the "Normal Vote" in Presidential Elections |

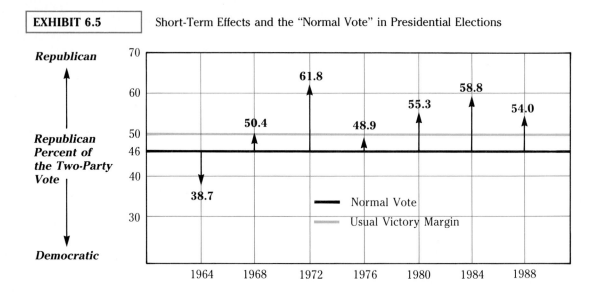

(Arrows show extent and direction of the short-term forces.)

The 1988 figure is based on unofficial returns.

Short-Term Effects.   With this understanding, we can look more close-ly at the short-term influences on presidential voting—the perception of the candidates, the issues, and the parties at a particular time. One candidate may be perceived as more attractive than the other, or the issues may favor one party more than the other, or a particular event (usually associated with the past administration—such as a scandal or major economic crisis) may hurt a party's image.

Candidate perceptions can be measured by what people in surveys say they "like" and "dislike" about the two candidates, calculating which one seemed to have the advantage. In some elections, the advantage is all on one side: Johnson over Goldwater in 1964, Nixon over McGovern in 1972, Eisenhower over Stevenson in 1956, Reagan over Mondale in 1984. In other elections, the perceptions are more evenly balanced: Nixon edged Kennedy in 1960 and won over Humphrey in 1968. Carter edged Ford in 1976, and Reagan won over Carter in 1980. In 1980, for the first time, *both* candidates were perceived negatively. Jimmy Carter was seen as doing a poor job as president, while Ronald Reagan made a number of people "uneasy," espe-cially about his ability to conduct foreign policy. As one writer described it, the electorate was being forced to choose "the lesser of the evils." Carter's rating overall was more negative than Reagan's; hence a small short-term effect favored the Republicans.[6] In 1984, Reagan led Mondale in all candi-

[6]Arthur Miller, "Policy and Performance Voting in the 1980 Election," paper delivered at the annual meeting of the American Political Science Association, September, 1981, esp. Figure 1.

date characteristics, except in intelligence, where the two were virtually tied.[7] The following list shows the candidate preferred by the voters for these candidate traits in both 1980 and 1984:

	1980	**1984**
Leadership	Reagan	Reagan
Imaginative Solutions to Problems	Reagan	Reagan
Puts Country Above Politics	Carter	Reagan
Likeable	Tie	Reagan
Sides with Average Citizen	Tie	Reagan
Intelligent	Reagan	Mondale
Moral	Carter	Reagan

Issue or party perceptions also create short-term influences. Law and order, the state of the economy, and the conduct of foreign policy have all been issues in recent elections. Economic issues often hurt the candidate associated with the past administration, causing people to decide, as they make their car payments or stand in the unemployment lines, that it is time for a change. Thus, when economic issues are seen as most important, the candidate associated with the party in the White House is often disadvantaged. A foreign policy crisis can help the party in the White House, with people rallying to the administration's support. In 1980, Carter was hurt by perceptions of his handling of the economy, although, as president at the time, he was favored over Reagan on foreign policy. By 1984, Reagan led Mondale in both foreign policy and economic issues.[8] In 1988, as the box on page 208 reveals, both economic and foreign policy issues favored the party in power, giving advantage to Bush and the Republicans.

Close and Landslide Elections.   In close elections, the short-term effects are contradictory or nonexistent. The elections of 1960 and 1976 are cases in point. In the 1960 Kennedy-Nixon race, the vote dropped close to the baseline: 49 percent Republican support compared to a normal vote of 46 percent. It is intriguing to see that surveys of the 1960 election showed no outstanding issues in the campaign and no net difference in party perceptions. Kennedy's Catholicism was mentioned in the candidate perceptions and worked both for and against him, though on balance appeared slightly on the negative side. Overall, Nixon only barely edged Kennedy in the candidate perceptions.[9] In short, almost no relevant short-term effects appeared to be operating in the campaign, and a normal vote or a vote only

---

[7]Gary King and Lyn Ragsdale, *The Elusive Executive* (Washington, D.C.: CQ Press, 1988), pp. 463–464. Cases where the candidates are within three percentage points of each other can be called a tie.

[8]See *ibid.* See also Paul R. Abramson, John H. Aldrich, and David W. Rohde, *Change and Continuity in the 1980 Elections* (Washington, D.C.: CQ Press, 1982), Chapter 7.

[9]This may surprise some people who think positively of the candidate killed in office and negatively of the one involved in a scandal. Nevertheless, the perceptions in 1960 were quite different.

Short-Term Effects in the 1988 Elections

Voter surveys can tap the short-term effects in an election by showing people's perceptions of the candidates and issues in a campaign. Especially valuable are the kind of open-ended questions that ask voters what they like or dislike about the candidates, thus showing the particular things that are on people's minds.

The following results are based on an ABC News exit poll. (An exit poll is a survey of voters taken at polling places across the nation, as they exit immediately after voting.) The poll asked people who they voted for and why they voted as they did, along with other questions. For example, people were asked if they thought they were better-off financially than they were in 1981, worse-off, or about the same. How people thought they fared under the Republican Reagan administration might affect their choice of party in 1988.

The results show the candidate and issue perceptions that the voters volunteered as their reasons for choosing a candidate. The figure that follows is the percent of people in the nationwide sample giving this particular answer. For example, 13 percent of the sample said they chose the candidate because of his leadership traits. Of these people, Bush was chosen by 54 percent and Dukakis by 46 percent. Only the most frequently cited reasons are listed at the end of the box.

Among other answers, foreign affairs was cited by 6 percent of the sample, with Bush heavily favored, while the budget deficit was cited by 8 percent, with Dukakis heavily favored. Bush's advantage on crime, cited by 4 percent, was balanced by Dukakis's advantage on jobs, cited by 5 percent. The combination of other answers did not advantage one candidate over the other.

Looking at the candidate perceptions, we see that no single impression dominates. The sample is divided into small proportions of people citing one trait or another. We see also that no one candidate is favored, as Reagan was favored in all traits in 1984. Bush is given experience and leadership, while Dukakis is given judgment and caring about people. The one net advantage concerns experience. More people cited this trait than any other and Bush was heavily favored.

Issue perceptions are even more closely divided. Bush's advantage on defense and taxes is balanced by Dukakis's on poverty and health. Notice, however, the close division on the national economy, splitting 53 to 46 percent for Bush. This is almost identical to the percentage division in the actual vote. Looking

slightly on the Republican side could be predicted. This is, in fact, what the results suggest occurred. The 1976 Ford-Carter race appears strikingly like the 1960 election. Few issues were perceived as favoring one candidate over the other, and both candidates were rated quite neutrally. Again, a result close to the normal vote could be predicted.

It is interesting that the first two televised debates between presidential candidates—with everyone scoring who "won" and who "lost" every round—occurred in 1960 and 1976, as if to provoke some difference between candidates or some debate on issues that otherwise seemed nonexistent or unclear. In 1976, people even scored the vice-presidential candidates in the debates, carrying the hunt for relevant short-term effects even further. Again, as in 1960, the Republican (Ford) edged the Democrat (Carter) in short-term effects, but not enough to overcome the normal vote disadvantage and win the election.

more closely at economic perceptions, 42 percent thought they were better-off than in 1981 and they went heavily for Bush; only 20 percent thought they were worse-off and they went heavily for Dukakis; 38 percent thought they were financially in the same position, and they split 57 to 42 percent in favor of Dukakis. On balance, it appears that economic perceptions were positive enough not to hurt the Republicans. Dukakis's potential advantage here, among those who were not better-off, did not become a major perception in the campaign.

A fuller analysis would need to separate these answers from party loyalties. Republicans might favor Bush because he was a Republican and simply find an answer—"experience"—to explain their vote. The importance of party identification can be a perceptual screen. Still, the results do offer some insights on the election. With many short-term effects fairly evenly balanced between the candidates, the Republicans gained from the sense of Bush's experience in the White House and a generally positive view of the national economy.

Candidate Percep- tions	Percent Deciding on this Trait	Candidate Favored (Percent)	
		Dukakis	Bush
Strong Leader	13	46	54
Good Judgment	12	55	44
Cares about People	16	87	12
Experienced	26	6	93

Issue Percep- tions	Percent Deciding on this Issue	Candidate Favored (Percent)	
		Dukakis	Bush
Best for National Economy	17	46	53
Best for Stronger Defense	16	13	87
Best for Poverty Problems	12	91	8
Lower Taxes	11	29	69
Health care	10	80	20

A **landslide** refers to an extremely large election victory in which the opponent is buried. In landslide elections, the short-term effects appear heavily on one side, pulling Independents and some partisans toward a particular candidate. This occurred most clearly in 1964 and 1972. In 1964 negative perceptions of Goldwater as too extreme and "unreliable" combined with the positive association of the Democratic party with the recently assassinated President Kennedy to swing the election to a Democratic landslide. In 1972 issues of law and order and perceptions of Democratic candidate McGovern as too extreme and subject to "weakness" and "bad judgment" swung the results to a landslide for the Republicans.

As the examples show, these short-term effects can be used to explain election results. But they can also be used to predict results before the election has occurred. In a year when people are worried about the economy or appear to like one candidate better than the other, the amount of these short-term effects can be estimated, adding them to or subtracting them from the normal vote, to arrive at a prediction.

The Electoral College

Constitutionally, the nation as a whole does not vote directly for president. The **electoral college**, composed of electors from each of the states, casts the official vote with each state allotted a number of electors according to its population. The candidate receiving the highest number of votes in each state (a plurality) is given all of the state's electoral votes. It is important to see that only a plurality, not a majority, of votes is needed, and to recognize the "winner-take-all" nature of the system. If one state splits 51 percent for the Republican candidate and 49 percent for the Democrat, all of its electoral votes are cast for the Republican. If another state splits 45 percent for the Democratic candidate, 44 percent for the Republican, and 11 percent for a third-party candidate, all of its electoral votes would go to the Democrat. Since states are allotted one electoral vote for each senator and each representative, even the states smallest in population will have three electoral votes. The District of Columbia also has three votes, granted it by the Twenty-third Amendment. Given the 538 votes in the electoral college today, a candidate must get 270 or more to win the election. The electoral college vote for president from 1960 to 1988 is shown in Exhibit 6.6.

Technically, a president is not elected on election day. The victorious slates of electors travel to their state capitals on the first Monday after the second Wednesday in December, where they cast ballots for their party's candidates and go home. The ballots are then sent from the state capitals to Congress, where early in January they are formally counted by the House and Senate leaders and the next president is announced. Since the vice-president, as president of the Senate, traditionally announces the result, Vice-President Richard Nixon declared his opponent—John Kennedy—to be president in 1961. In 1969, another vice-president, Hubert Humphrey, announced his opponent—Richard Nixon—the winner. But in 1989, Vice-President George Bush announced himself the winner.

If no candidate receives a majority of electoral votes, the election goes to the House of Representatives, where each state delegation casts one vote. (If a delegation is evenly divided, a state forfeits its votes.) Twice in American history the election has gone to the House, once in 1800 and subsequently in 1824, although people feared that it might happen again in 1968 if third-party candidate George Wallace received enough electoral votes to keep Nixon or Humphrey from a majority. The House will choose a president from among the top three candidates, taking consecutive ballots until one candidate wins a majority (26) of the state delegations.

The electoral college system was a compromise in the framing of the Constitution. It was felt that direct election would give an advantage to the most populous states, while a system without any reference to population would put them at a disadvantage. Therefore, in the electoral college sys-

EXHIBIT 6.6   The Electoral College Vote, 1960-1988

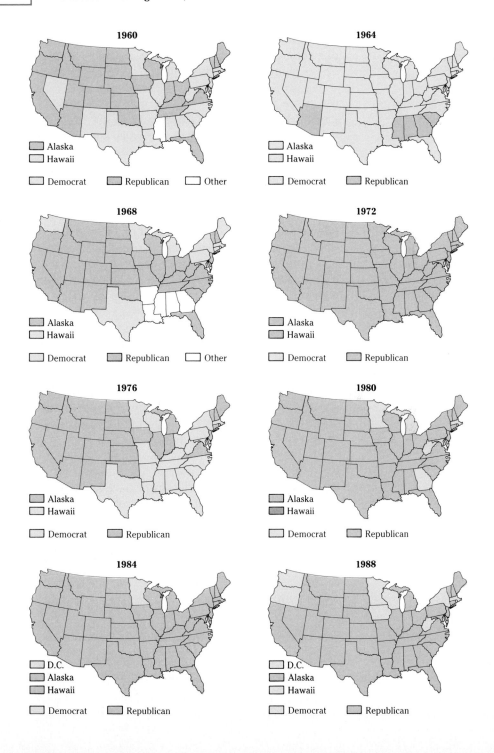

tem both state and population interests are preserved: the large states get electoral votes based on their population and the small states get the assurance of at least three electoral votes. In addition, the provision satisfied those who feared direct election of presidents and desired a more elitist set of electors than the public as a whole. (It was thought that the electors to be designated by the state legislatures would be distinguished citizens who would actually be electing the president and vice-president.) It also satisfied those who opposed the election of the president by the Congress, a method being considered seriously at the time. So, everyone got something—the large states, the small states, those who opposed direct election, and those who opposed election by Congress.

Like many compromises, however, the system may offer little in the way of logic or merit of its own. While eliminating one set of problems, it raises others. Critics point out that the "winner-take-all" rule allows a candidate who lost in the popular vote count to nevertheless win the election. This has occurred three times in American history, most recently in 1888. The same outcome might occur if the election went to the House: if the popular vote leader was Republican and the House was Democratic, then the Democratic candidate presumably would be elected. Some people claim that the system gives too much advantage to states with large populations; others claim that it overrepresents the smallest states; and others feel that it may hurt certain groups, such as blacks, who are concentrated unevenly across the states.[10] A direct election system would allow these groups to combine votes across the nation, thus posing a more formidable threat as a bloc of swing voters. One study indicates that the electoral college in fact overrepresents *both* large and small states, underrepresenting the middle states. It appears to overcount the vote of suburban residents and undercount rural residents. While it does not seriously underrepresent groups such as blacks, it can be argued that a direct election system would benefit them more.[11]

Debate on the question has waxed and waned in the twentieth century, typically becoming most intense after an electoral scare, such as in 1968, when the popular vote leader might have lost the election. It is likely, however, that no change will be made until people are clearer about who is actually hurt and who is helped by the system.

Whatever the consequences for representation, one impact of the electoral college is clear. It influences the campaign and the strategy of presidential candidates who must not only appeal to voters across the nation but must also put together a winning combination of states. This fact places a premium on those states with the largest number of electoral votes. In

[10]See Lawrence D. Longley and Alan G. Braun, *The Politics of Electoral College Reform*, 2nd ed. (New Haven: Yale University Press, 1975).

[11]Lawrence D. Longley, "The Electoral College and the Representation of Minorities," in *The President and the Public*, ed. Doris Graber (Philadelphia: Institute for the Study of Human Issues, 1982), pp. 172–204; and see George Rabinowitz and Stuart E. MacDonald, "The Power of the States in U.S. Presidential Elections," *American Political Science Review*, 80 (1986), pp. 65–87.

recent elections the eleven largest states—California, New York, Pennsylvania, Texas, Illinois, Ohio, Michigan, New Jersey, Florida, North Carolina and Indiana—together had a total of 271 electoral votes, enough to elect a candidate who lost all of the other thirty-nine states. It also gives priority to the highly competitive "swing" states that are capable of moving back and forth between the parties from one election to another. Thus states that are both large and competitive—such as New York, Pennsylvania, Michigan, Illinois, and Ohio—draw heavy attention from both candidates.

The two parties have developed areas where their presidential candidates are generally successful: the Republicans in the South and West and the Democrats in the Northeast. The once-solid Democratic South is Democratic no longer in presidential voting. The Republicans carried the South in 1972, 1980, 1984, and 1988. In 1980, in fact, Carter carried only his home state of Georgia. (See the box on page 214.) People point out the importance of a "southern strategy," observing that candidates who sweep the South need to pick up only a few large electoral-vote states in addition, whereas candidates who write off the South must carry almost all of the other large states. If the South stays Republican in the future, the loss of only a few large electoral-vote states spells defeat for the Democrats. Some writers go so far as to speak of an electoral college "lock" on the presidency for Republicans: claiming the South and West, along with such large states as Texas and California, the GOP would have half of the nation's electoral votes and almost enough for victory.[12]

Electoral college arithmetic dominates electoral strategy. Candidates must decide how much attention to give each region, adding up the states in various ways to reach more than one-half of the electoral college vote. The choice of a vice-presidential running mate can be crucial; candidates often choose a running mate from a state or region where they need additional strength. Thus, Michael Dukakis picked Lloyd Bentsen of Texas in 1988 in an attempt to break Republican dominance in the South and to capture the electoral votes of Texas, the adopted home state of Republican candidate George Bush. The Republicans turned to the Midwest, an area where Bush had run poorly in primaries, and selected the young Indiana senator Dan Quayle.

Decisions about where to campaign, based on electoral college arithmetic, are made at the highest levels of the campaign organization. To take one example, Carter's campaign manager during the 1976 successful election bid devoted no less than thirty-one pages of one memorandum to formulas to determine the relative effort to be spent in each state. States were assigned points under a "political-importance" formula using three criteria: the number of electoral votes, the state's potential for voting Democratic based on how many Democratic officeholders there were, and the amount of "campaign effort" needed, based on the time Carter had already spent in

[12]See for example William Schneider, "An Insider's View of the Election," *The Atlantic Monthly*, July, 1988, pp. 29–34.

The Unsolid South

The once-solid Democratic south is solid no longer. In fact, few generalizations hold across all of the states. When V.O. Key, Jr. wrote his classic work *Southern Politics* in the 1950s, he devoted a chapter to each of the states. In the 1990s the states still need their own individual treatment, as we can see by the following election results.

Election results are given for the 1960s and 1980s for the eleven states of the Confederacy. All of the states are now Republican in presidential voting, and yet each has come to this in its own way. Four states—Florida, Tennessee, Texas, and Virginia—went Republican as early as 1952, voting for Dwight Eisenhower. Arkansas waited until 1972. In the 1960 and 1968 elections, the states showed three different patterns: some states went Republican, some went Democratic, and some voted for third-party candidates.

The south, however, is clearly not solidly Republican either. Beyond the presidential election, most of the states continue to elect Democratic majorities to the House of Representatives. Virginia is the clearest exception. South Carolina and Arkansas, electing Republican majorities in the early 1980s, have since returned to the Democratic fold. As of 1988, six of the states have Democratic governors and all have Democratic majorities in both houses of the state legislature.

Thus southern voters go to the polls and split their tickets. They vote for Republican presidential candidates and for Democratic incumbents or new members who can build their own coalitions in the shifting politics of the state.

NUMBER OF TIMES STATES WENT DEMOCRATIC[a]

	Presidential Voting (3 Elections Each)		House Voting (5 Terms Each)		GOVERNORS, STATE LEGISLATURES, 1988
	1960s	1980s	1960s	1980s	
Alabama	1	0	4	5	Republican; Democratic
Arkansas	2	0	2	2	Democratic; Democratic
Florida	1	0	5	5	Republican; Democratic
Georgia	1	1	5	5	Democratic; Democratic
Louisiana	1	0	5	5	Democratic; Democratic
Mississippi	0	0	5	5	Democratic; Democratic
North Carolina	2	0	5	5	Republican; Democratic
South Carolina	1	0	5	2	Republican; Democratic
Tennessee	1	0	5	5	Democratic; Democratic
Texas	3	0	5	5	Republican; Democratic
Virginia	1	0	3	0	Democratic; Democratic

[a]A state that did not go Democratic could have voted Republican or for a third-party candidate. Going Democratic for the House means that a majority of the state delegation was Democratic.

the state and his popularity in the polls. The various campaigners were then allotted points—Carter's time was worth seven points, Mondale (his vice-presidential running mate) was assigned five points, and daughter Amy one point—so that the scheduled time would match the points developed under the political-importance formula.[13]

The Campaign

It is a maxim of campaign strategy that candidates should appeal to their traditional supporters and "get out the vote," attempt to attract uncommitted voters, and not try to convert traditional opponents. This strategy holds for presidential contests as well as other elections. In looking toward the popular vote and electoral college, candidates identify areas of traditional strength among party identifiers and specific groups, such as blacks, upper-income families, Catholics, or central city dwellers. The basic strategy is to appeal to these groups as a base and go on to target enough additional votes to win. As most students of American politics know, the Democrats have drawn largely from lower-income families, union members, blacks, Catholics, and urban dwellers, while the Republicans have worked from a base that is Protestant, white, non-poor, non-union, and non-urban.[14]

This strategy recognizes the importance of party loyalty among the voters. But candidates must do more than this, given the large bloc of Independents and the importance of short-term effects. To attract the necessary additional votes, they must devise ways of making their own image and definition of the issues as favorable to the voters as possible. The campaign, therefore, becomes a fight for the short-term component of the vote.

Issues are defined to win over uncommitted groups or to remind people of the opposing party's weakness. Enormous effort is spent on the candidate's own image, leading to the widely heard charge about "packaging the presidency." The past administration's record is debated by both parties. Incumbent presidents can take advantage of the awe surrounding the office and play the role of the statesman who is too busy with the cares of the nation to stoop to petty campaigning. Yet, incumbents can be hurt by the past record, too, by a poor economy or scandals in office. The studies cited earlier, for example, suggest Ford might have been helped by incumbency, and Carter hurt by it. Nevertheless, most presidents running for reelection have used their experience and the awe inspired by the office as an effective campaign technique. One of Carter's most effective commercials in 1980 showed him at work as night fell over the White House. A voice intoned: "The responsibility never ends. Even at the end of a long working day there

[13]John H. Kessel, *Presidential Campaign Politics*, 3rd ed. (Chicago, Ill.: Dorsey, 1988), p. 128.
[14]See for example Herbert B. Asher, *Presidential Elections and American Politics* (Homewood, Ill.: Dorsey, 1976), p. 294. See also the results of an ABC-*Washington Post* poll, *Washington Post*, November 8, 1984, p. A48.

is usually another cable addressed to the Chief of State from the other side of the world where the sun is shining and something is happening." As a light came on in the White House, the voice continued, "And he's not finished yet."[15]

Campaign studies find that Democratic candidates have tended to emphasize party appeals more than Republicans, given their advantage in party identification across the country. Republicans have been more likely to play down these appeals and even, as in the case of Reagan in 1980, to adopt some past Democratic history as their own. Reagan linked his campaign for changes in American society to the "New Deal" of Democratic president Franklin Roosevelt and the "New Frontier" of Democratic president John Kennedy. By 1988, however, George Bush could run on his Republican predecessor's popularity and the eight years of the Reagan record.

Television is the primary medium for presidential candidates to get their message across to the American public. The most popular and frequently used appeals are the short spots of thirty and sixty seconds which are interspersed with other commercials and the regular television programming. These short spots are cheaper to produce and air, compared with longer appeals, and tend to be viewed by a larger captive audience. Like any other commercial, they must be clear and memorable. They are designed by advertising professionals and tested on many target audiences. In 1984, the Reagan campaign effort hired forty top advertising executives to coordinate their media appeals. In all, the group produced forty-nine spots and one half-hour film that were aired, thirty commercials that were not shown, and about one hundred others that were written but not produced. The total cost was $27 million.[16]

The Debates.   Television debates have added a new dimension to evaluating the candidates. Encouraged by civic groups and the news media, the debates, begun in 1960 and continued in 1976, have now become a recognized part of the campaign. So in 1984, Ronald Reagan was virtually forced to debate Walter Mondale because of the pressure of public opinion, even though he stood little to gain and could have lost much by the event. George Bush, too, felt forced to debate in 1988, even though Michael Dukakis was felt to be the much better debater. The recent debates have drawn television audiences exceeding 100 million people. While these debates are free for the candidates, the networks donating their air time, they have inspired elaborate preparations on the part of the campaign staffs. There are briefings, strategy papers, media coaches, script coaches, and makeup coaches. Mock studios are built and full dress rehearsals are held, with someone on the candidate's staff playing the part of the opponent. (Reagan's budget adviser David Stockman played the part of Walter

---

[15]Stephen J. Wayne, *The Road to the White House*, 3rd ed. (New York: St. Martins, 1988), p. 215.
[16]*Ibid.*, p. 209.

Candidates George Bush and Michael Dukakis conduct the second of the 1988 presidential debates.

Mondale in one dress rehearsal.) Scripts are written and the candidates are coached in their responses to the opponent's hypothetical positions. In 1980, the Reagan staff even obtained (unethically) one of the Carter briefing books. They could thus rehearse their candidate on the response to the responses set forth in the Carter book.[17]

The debates, however, are not entirely within the candidates' own control. Network commentators have been willing to "score" the event, announcing who won and who lost and targeting particular areas of weakness and strength. Viewers of the Carter-Reagan debate might have thought Reagan did poorly, but at least one network announced that he had won. The debates are often followed immediately by viewer call-in programs in which some seven to ten people will say which candidate they thought did better and why. These announcements matter because studies show that public reaction moves through a two-step process to align itself with the announced interpretation. In step one, according to surveys taken immediately after the debate, opinion is influenced more by the audience's own perceptions and past dispositions. In the second stage, in surveys three or four days later, opinion has moved closer to the media consensus. For example, the percentage of people believing Reagan to be the victor over Carter almost doubled within four days of the debate.[18] In the Ford-Carter debates,

[17]*Ibid.*, p. 220.
[18]*Ibid.*, p. 223.

Ford made an error that was talked about afterwards as potentially damaging. (He implied that there was no Soviet domination of countries in Eastern Europe.) This error was emphasized so much in the post-debate commentary that opinion shifted from an 11 percent margin favoring Ford as the debate winner to more than thirty percent favoring Carter as the winner several days later.

This delayed reaction has been called the "spin" from the debates. Within minutes after the debates have ended, both campaigns deploy staff members to explain to television audiences and reporters why their candidate has won. These "spinners," which is how reporters refer to them, attempt to focus the public's attention on key errors in the opponent's debate and the strong points of their candidate's presentation. In 1988, the Bush staff measured the time it would take them to walk from the room in which they were watching the debate to the room where the reporters were gathered. The answer—three and one-half minutes—was deemed too long; so the spinners ran, with other campaign people stationed to clear onlookers from their path.

The year 1988 marked the fifth election year in which presidential debates were held (1960, 1976, 1980, 1984, and 1988). What could the debates claim and what were the problems remaining? In 1988, most observers agreed that the debates had been fair and had forced the candidates to discuss some substantive issues. A panel of reporters were selected to ask questions of the two candidates and a moderator imposed strict time limits on the answers; the candidates also had opportunities to respond to each other's remarks. Nevertheless, many people observed that the remarks often seem pre-packaged and over-rehearsed. The debates did not bring new material to the campaign, nor did they allow the candidates to react spontaneously. The voters heard what the briefing books and the dress rehearsals had prepared for. The problem of "spin" had also not been resolved. If debates are followed by viewer call-in shows or authorities scoring who won and who lost, a very few people can have a disproportionate impact in a closely contested race. Perhaps the rules of fairness followed during the debate could be practiced by the networks for the half-hour following it, allowing the 100 million viewers to make up their own minds before hearing other people's opinions. Since the debates appear to be a permanent feature for future presidential campaigns, these issues will probably be heard and discussed again.

The impact of the debates, like the campaign itself, must be seen in the larger context of how voters make decisions. Many people have made up their minds before the campaign actually begins:

- About 66 percent by the end of the two nominating conventions
- About 20 percent after the conventions but before the final weeks
- About 10 percent in the last two weeks
- About 4 percent on election day

"And as the campaign heats up, the latest poll shows the Dan Rather news team running slightly ahead of the Peter Jennings news team, with the Tom Brokaw team just two points back and gaining."

For perhaps two-thirds of the people, the campaign is not supplying information for a choice, although it may be encouraging or discouraging them to go to the polls and make their choice official. Still, elections can turn on that small percentage of people who decide their vote within the final weeks. Even if all the campaigning affected only that small percentage, the candidates would still think it worth the effort spent. The debates take their place as one kind of information, among many, supplied by the campaign.

Campaign Information.   In the quantity of information, presidential campaigns are impressive. But what is the quality of information given to the voters? What kind of decision is made on election day? If each party has equally competent campaign managers and public relations professionals, no blatant mistakes, and no major world disasters or economic crises occur, what decides the outcome? A normal vote could be predicted, with some voters quite reasonably using party labels as the only information available and the Independents splitting randomly. Assume that there is some major event—a scandal, a war, or a major economic crisis. In this case the short-term effects might well decide the outcome, but they would have little to do with the candidates themselves or the conduct of the campaign. Even with the best packaging possible, Alf Landon could have done little against Franklin Roosevelt in 1936. In some races, given events in the world, the candidate nominated by one party is virtually assured of the election.

What does all the campaign information produced tell us about likely presidential performance? Issues cannot be aired in thirty second television commercials or in scripted, rehearsed debates. A television ad for George Bush in 1988 showed him inspecting the pollution in Boston Harbor, right in Governor Dukakis's home state. But the ad did not tell voters about environmental issues, the Reagan-Bush record on the environment, or the likely positions of either candidate in the White House. It is an irony of recent American history that many Republicans defected from Goldwater to Johnson in 1964 on the perception that "extremist" Goldwater might involve us in another war. Johnson's escalation of the Vietnam War followed. Many Democrats defected from McGovern to Nixon in 1972—after the Watergate break-in and Nixon administration cover-up—because they feared that McGovern might show "bad judgment" in the White House. In both cases the voters could be said to be acting on the best information they had available.

CONGRESSIONAL ELECTIONS

We now turn away from the spotlight of the presidential race to voting for the United States Congress. People may pay little attention to the contest, care little about the outcome, and yet still manage to vote. How and on what information do they decide? Presidential elections can be analyzed as the result of long-term (party loyalty) and short-term forces involving perceptions of party, candidates, and issues at the time. Congressional elections can also be analyzed in terms of long- and short-term forces. But in this case, the short-term forces—and the vote fluctuations they produce—are less important, though they still exert a significant impact on the vote. Other influences include the importance of party loyalty (as in presidential voting) and the advantage of incumbency.

Party Loyalty

One major influence on congressional elections is party identification. As in presidential voting, people use party as a cue for voting choice, influencing their vote through time and across different offices. But unlike a presidential campaign, a congressional election offers few competing cues. The candidate's party is the one fact other than the candidate's name that ballots supply; thus a vote by party requires very little expenditure of interest and attention. Party affiliation thus becomes more influential in congressional than in presidential voting. Voting for both the Senate and the House is closer to a normal vote than presidential voting, since less information about short-term influences is available.[19] Thus with a nationwide normal vote slightly favoring the Democrats in recent American history, we

---

[19]In general, see John R. Petrocik, "An Expected Party Vote: New Data for an Old Concept," *American Journal of Political Science,* 33 (1989), pp. 44–66.

| EXHIBIT 6.7 | Party Control of the White House and Congress |

Republican Control   Democratic Control

find that Congress—both Senate and House—has been controlled by Democratic majorities almost exclusively since 1932. The exceptions are the years 1947–48 and 1953–54, when both houses were controlled by the Republicans, and 1981–1986 when the Senate, but not the House, was controlled by Republicans. (See Exhibit 6.7.)

Incumbency

A second major influence on congressional voting is the advantage of incumbency. An **incumbent** is a person holding an office; therefore, the **advantage of incumbency** means that the person holding the office is likely to be reelected over his or her opponent. House and Senate incumbents of each party have enjoyed success rates of 80 to 90 percent; that is, the incumbent who seeks reelection wins 80 to 90 times out of 100. In the House in particular the success rate has been spectacular, reaching as high as 99 percent in 1988. (See Exhibit 6.8.) Not only are House incumbents more likely to win, but their margin of victory is higher than that of successful nonincumbents. Incumbency alone, people have estimated, is worth about five percentage points of the vote.[20] That is the difference between someone winning 53 percent of the vote, for example, or losing by 48 percent.

[20]For a review of the many studies on incumbency, see Barbara Hinckley, *Congressional Elections* (Washington, D.C.: CQ Press, 1981), chapter 3; and Gary C. Jacobson, *The Politics of Congressional Elections*, 2nd ed. (Boston: Little, Brown, 1987), pp. 26–44.

| EXHIBIT 6.8 | | The Advantage of Incumbency in the House and Senate |

	HOUSE				SENATE			
YEAR	Seeking Reelec-tion	Defeated (Primary)	Defeated (Election)	Percent-age Re-elected[a]	Seeking Reelec-tion	Defeated (Primary)	Defeated (Election)	Percent-age Re-elected[a]
1946	398	18	52	82	30	6	7	57
1948	400	15	68	79	25	2	8	60
1950	400	6	32	91	32	5	5	69
1952	389	9	26	91	31	2	9	65
1954	407	6	22	93	32	2	6	75
1956	411	6	16	95	29	0	4	86
1958	396	3	37	90	28	0	10	64
1960	405	5	25	93	29	0	1	97
1962	402	12	22	92	35	1	5	83
1964	397	8	45	87	33	1	4	85
1966	411	8	41	88	32	3	1	88
1968	409	4	9	97	28	4	4	71
1970	401	10	12	95	31	1	6	77
1972	390	12	13	94	27	2	5	74
1974	391	8	40	88	27	2	2	85
1976	384	3	13	96	25	0	9	64
1978	382	5	19	94	25	3	7	60
1980	398	6	31	91	29	4	9	55
1982	393	10	29	90	30	0	2	93
1984	411	3	16	95	29	0	3	90
1986	393	2	6	98	28	0	7	75
1988	408	1	6	98	27	0	4	85

[a]Counting both primary and general election defeats.

Incumbents also tend to be even safer at the primary stage than they are in the general election. Few need to contest primaries and, of those who do, most win. Although the number of members seeking reelection has declined slightly in recent years, this decline does not change the overall success rates. So, in 1984, while people watched the presidential race and a few Senate contests, 392 of the 411 representatives running were returned to Congress. A new record was set in 1986, with 98 percent of the incumbents who sought reelection returned to office.

The advantage of House incumbents is not new. Since the late nineteenth century, the proportion of House first-term members has declined and the average number of terms served has increased. The House, originally designed to be the popular and responsive chamber, with elections every two years, has developed a stability to rival the Senate, where only one-third of the members stand for reelection at any one time.

Incumbents may have an advantage, but new members do get elected. Even if only fifteen percent of the House and Senate were new after each election, in six years almost half of the Congress would be changed. And in some recent Senate elections, barely half of the incumbents survived both primary and general election contests. Reasons for the incumbents' advantage must be able to explain the Senate as well as the House results.

The reasons cited for the advantage of incumbency deserve a closer look. For one, people cite the **perks** of the office—a slang term for perquisites, or the material support that comes with a job. These include the *franking privilege* which allows free mailing to constituents and local media, the paid staff for Washington and district offices, the distribution of government publications, and the use of the Congressional Research Service of the Library of Congress for issue research.

Second, incumbency provides its own rewards—the chance to build a record of service for constituents: for example, announcing a new construction project for the home district, maintaining an obsolete old one, plumbing the bureaucratic depths for someone's missing pension check, or arranging an emergency military leave. David Mayhew calls these "credit-claiming" activities. Mayhew points out how "advertising," "credit-claiming," and "position-taking" help the incumbent build a brand name. Incumbents can advertise and claim credit and they can select the issues to take positions on and avoid others.[21] The job becomes an extension of the congressional campaign. As one freshman member of Congress remarked:

> A lot of what you do as an office-holder is very similar to campaigning. I do town halls as a candidate and I do town halls as a congressman. I went to parades as a candidate, I go to parades as a congressman. I have meetings with interest groups as a candidate and I have meetings with interest groups as a congressman.[22]

A third reason is that success attracts money, and money helps success. Incumbents raise more money and spend more money on campaigns than nonincumbents, and PACs are much more likely to contribute to the incumbent's campaign than to the challenger's campaign. A **challenger** is a person running against an incumbent. Nevertheless, these nonincumbents include both strong and token challengers, the latter raising no expectations of making a serious bid for office. Serious challengers spend as much as or more than incumbents—often with notable success.

A fourth reason may be the most important. In the context of extremely low public interest in and information about Congress, the incumbent's

[21]David R. Mayhew, "Congressional Elections: The Case of the Vanishing Marginals," *Polity*, 6 (1974), pp. 295–317.

[22]*Congressional Quarterly Weekly Report*, November 2, 1985, p. 2229.

name is known. It may be all that is known, that and the party label on the ballot. This is not merely name recognition, but name recognition in a vacuum of other information. Most voters can recognize the names of incumbents in both the Senate and the House. While they can also recognize the Senate challengers, less than half of the voters recognize the House challengers. Since recognition usually carries a positive effect in these races, Senate incumbents who are known and liked by the voters are running against challengers who are also known and liked.[23] House incumbents do not face the same competition.

These explanations can be considered against the difference in Senate and House results. Senate incumbents, like House incumbents, possess advantages from being in office: material support and the chance to claim credit in the state. Senate incumbents, too, do their casework and constituency service and are generally liked by the voters. Senate incumbents, however, do not win elections the way that House incumbents do. And senators have one disadvantage not shared by their House colleagues—their opponents are recognized by the voters. Both money and name recognition are important, but it may be the *challenger's* money and visibility, rather than the incumbent's, that will be watched. A fifth reason, then, for the advantage of incumbency is the low visibility and activity of challengers.

All of these factors are reinforcing. If House incumbents are perceived to be safe, strong challengers do not enter the race or attract much money to contest it. Once a candidate is perceived to be vulnerable, strong competition follows. The effects are clear in the Senate: when both candidates are recognized by the voters, much of the advantage of incumbency disappears.

Why, then, do some incumbents attract strong challengers when others do not? The perception of vulnerability increases the likelihood of a strong challenge which in turn increases the likelihood of defeat. According to one study, the strongest challengers appeared in races where the incumbents could be predicted ahead of time to be vulnerable: either (1) their past electoral performance was weak, or (2) the national tide favored the party of the opponent, or (3) the incumbents were seen as too liberal or too conservative for their district.[24] Once the weakness appears in the incumbent's armor, strong challengers are attracted, money begins to come in, and money brings increased visibility. Three of the five factors used to explain the advantage of incumbents work together to show the limitations too.

On the other hand, the amount of casework and constituency service performed by incumbents did not appear to affect the strength of the challenge.[25] "Voters cannot be bought cheaply," one scholar concludes, referring to casework, mailings, and other service to the district.[26] The members

[23]Edie N. Goldenberg and Michael W. Traugott, *Campaigning for Congress* (Washington, D.C.: CQ Press, 1984), pp. 142–143.

[24]Jon R. Bond, Cary Covington, and Richard Fleisher, "Explaining Challenger Quality in Congressional Elections," *Journal of Politics*, 47 (1985), pp. 510–29.

[25]*Ibid.*

[26]John R. Johannes, *To Serve the People* (Lincoln: University of Nebraska Press, 1984), p. 211. See also Jacobson, *op. cit.,* p. 41.

of Congress and their staff people believe these things help, perhaps because all the time spent requires justification. However, service activities are best seen as minimum conditions expected of all incumbents. Weak casework does not necessarily bring a strong challenge nor does strong casework avoid one.

Both party and incumbency can be seen as low-information cues available to voters who have little other relevant information. The party label is supplied on the ballot and the incumbent's name is known. Either influence provides an easily justified cue for voting. Party identifiers can argue that the candidates of their own party will likely be better able than the candidate of the opposing party to represent them on issues in Congress. Other voters, whether party identifiers or independents, can argue that the incumbent they already "like" and know about is a better choice than the unknown challenger. It should not be surprising, then, that the two influences together can explain much of the congressional election results.

Party identifiers, as shown earlier, often defect and vote for the opposing party's candidate. About twenty percent do so in House races. Who are these party defectors? *They are partisans in districts where the incumbent is of the party opposite their own.*[27] Voters in districts with incumbents of their own party have not shown the same tendency. This fact, not well-recognized in the literature on voting, must be understood. The major limit on party voting in congressional elections is the influence of incumbency.

Of course, people may decide to vote for the incumbent or for their party's candidate after a careful study of qualifications and issues. These highly informed voters would appear to be following party and incumbency cues, while actually voting in terms of the candidates or issues. A liberal (who is also a Democrat) might vote for a candidate (who happens to be a Democrat) because the candidate stands for important liberal issues. Other voters might choose the candidate they like (who is also the incumbent) because they like his or her concern for the district. Some of what seems to be party and incumbency voting, therefore, can really be voting for candidates and issues.

Short-Term Effects

In a democracy, citizens ideally (1) will have information about both candidates contesting the election and (2) will choose between candidates on the issues or qualifications they consider most important. Campaign rhetoric takes this model seriously—candidates must discuss the issues and speak about their qualifications for office. Political commentators also follow this model; they speak of an issue or personal attribute as decisive to the election result. Many voters possess no information about one of the candidates in the race, however. Other voters do not have enough specific information about either candidate to make such an evaluation. Still, some voters ad-

---

[27]Albert D. Cover, "One Good Term Deserves Another," *American Journal of Political Science,* 21 (1977), pp. 523–42.

here to the model in all elections, monitoring an issue important to them, while other voters adhere to it when unusually clear information is presented. So, while issues and candidate qualifications are not the only or the most important influence on congressional voting, they do register a significant and independent impact.

Issues.   The extent and limits of issue voting in congressional elections can be summarized as follows. If one looks at the number of people informed about issues, one sees that the importance of issue voting is low. National surveys have asked people where they stood on major issues of the day and where the presidential candidates, the two major parties, and the congressional candidates stood. Most people can answer these questions until they come to the congressional candidates. Approximately 35 to 45 percent could not place the Senate candidates and about 50 to 65 percent could not place the House candidates, even when the position was available in the record.[28]

Nevertheless, issues can still be said to be important in congressional voting. Small numbers of people can make a difference in an election. Surveys show that about 15 percent of people cite issues as a reason for liking or disliking congressional candidates, and that these references are found to be significantly related to the vote, apart from party or incumbency effects.[29] Studies have also found that House members who take relatively extreme positions in Congress, compared to other party members, do less well at the polls than their more moderate colleagues.

In addition, the candidates' stands on issues may have effects that these measures cannot tap. In contrast to the general public, some groups of people are very aware of the candidates' stands on issues, and are willing to spend money to bring the winner's position more in line with their own. Some interest groups are concerned about single issues—gun control, abortion, labor legislation—that are high in controversy and prominent on the congressional agenda. Other groups are more broadly ideological, targeting conservative or liberal candidates expected to vote "right" or "wrong" on a wide range of legislation before Congress. Consequently, the specific positions and general ideology of candidates create indirect effects by provoking spending (for or against a candidate), which in turn affects visibility and the vote. Voters generally may be unaware of the liberalism and conservatism of two House candidates in a race, but the reason that there *is* a race—and a closely contested one—is that some groups are supporting the challenger or opposing the incumbent.

---

[28]Hinckley, pp. 101–4.

[29]Studies show issues affect the vote even after the effects of party and incumbency are taken into account. See Glenn R. Parker, "Incumbent Popularity and Electoral Success," *Sage Electoral Studies Yearbook*, vol. 6 (Beverly Hills: Sage, 1981); and Lyn Ragsdale, "The Fiction of Congressional Elections as Presidential Events," *American Politics Quarterly*, October 1980, pp. 375–98. See also Gerald C. Wright, Jr. and Michael B. Beckman, "Candidates and Policy in United States Senate Elections," *American Political Science Review*, 80 (1986), pp. 567–88.

Candidates.   Candidate qualifications, too, appear important in congressional voting, although the subject has received little study. What evidence there is can be summarized briefly.

Remarks about the candidates are cited more frequently than remarks about issues or parties when people explain why they vote as they do. This emphasis holds for incumbents, challengers, and candidates for open-seat contests. These perceptions, moreover, are significantly related to the vote, regardless of the voter's party identification and the presence or absence of an incumbent in the race.[30]

The impact of candidate qualifications is most clearly seen in cases of scandal. One study examined the voting impact of charges of corruption against House incumbents. Of a total of 80 representatives involved in scandals over a period of years, 65 ran for reelection and 49 won. The success rate for those running was 75 percent and the total return rate—that is, those returning to the House for the next term—was 61 percent.[31] In other words, incumbents facing scandals are less likely to win reelection than other House incumbents. Still, three-fourths do win reelection, and about 60 percent return.

The study also examined the effects of the scandal on the vote margin. On the average, incumbents charged with corruption lost from 6 to 11 percentage points of their expected vote margin. Morals charges brought the greatest vote losses, with bribery charges second. Conflict of interest charges did not bring a significant vote loss. Overall, the study shows that negative information about candidates can exert a significant impact on the vote.

Still, many of the claims about the importance of candidates' characteristics need to be treated with caution. For example, the age of candidates is often cited as important to the outcome of a contest. Commentators speak of a senator's advanced age as a major reason for defeat, ignoring all the equally elderly incumbents who are simultaneously winning reelection. Looking at Senate contests in recent years, it is possible to see if the age of the incumbent, the age of the challenger, or the relative effect of both ages made any difference to the results.

The answer appears to be no. Overall, the age of the incumbents, the challengers, and both in combination make no difference to the winning or losing of elections. The two populations, winners and losers, are virtually identical in age. Indeed, the very slight differences that exist are in the opposite direction: losing incumbents are on the average one year younger than winning incumbents, and winning challengers are slightly older than losing challengers. A majority of challengers are younger than the incumbents they oppose—on the average about ten years younger—whether they win or lose.[32]

---

[30]See studies by Parker, *op. cit.*, and Ragsdale, *op. cit.*

[31]John G. Peters and Susan Welch, "The Effects of Charges of Corruption on Voting Behavior in Congressional Elections," *American Political Science Review*, 74 (1980), pp. 697–708.

[32]Hinckley, pp. 87–88.

Sex, like age, is often thought to have political implications. Very few women candidates have been elected to Congress, and recent years show little improvement in the trend. But to what extent is this situation produced electorally rather than at other points in the selection process? Does the sex of the candidates affect the election results?

One study compared male and female House candidates for contested races. In the 1099 races, there were 91 women candidates. Overall, the results are striking in their similarities and not in their differences. Incumbents do well no matter what sex they are and no matter what the sex of their opponents; challengers do poorly; and open-seat candidates run in more closely contested races. Turnout also appeared unaffected by the candidacy of women, for both male and female voters. While some voters favored or opposed women candidates, both groups were overwhelmed by people with no opinions or recognition of the candidates. The women candidates shared obscurity with the men.[33]

Campaign contributions also show little difference for male and female candidates. Although women candidates raise slightly less money than men do—raising five dollars for every six raised by men—these differences can be traced to incumbency. Most incumbents are men. Controlling for incumbency, one finds that women challengers raise slightly more than men challengers do, and women incumbents raise slightly less. In effect, differences in candidates' money-raising ability are not related to sex.[34]

These examples point up the very large gap between popular commentary about elections and the actual election results. According to the popular accounts, age and sex (as well as other less easily measurable characteristics) are electorally relevant candidate traits, often cited as advantages or disadvantages in a campaign. Some people, for example, think voters are less likely to select women candidates or that women would have fewer contacts for money-raising than men. Others think women candidates are advantaged. There may seem to be more women candidates than there actually are since the media calls attention to the few that run. However, tested against the actual voting results, these characteristics appear to make no difference to the vote.

Presidential Voting.   One influence on congressional elections must still be examined—the impact of the presidential vote. Two separate observations are usually offered, each focusing on a different kind of election. Generations of political observers have noted the coattail effect, or "pulling power" of the presidential vote. As the vote for one party's presidential candidate increases state by state or district by district, the vote for that party's congressional candidates also increases. Or, expressed another way, the

[33]R. Darcy and Sarah Slavin Schramm, "When Women Run Against Men," *Public Opinion Quarterly*, 41 (1977), pp. 1–12.

[34]Carole Uhlaner and Kay Lehman Schlozman, "Candidate Gender and Congressional Campaign Receipts," *Journal of Politics,* February, 1988, pp. 30–50.

greater the vote for a party's presidential candidate, the less likely defeat is for its congressional candidates. They ride into office on the president's coattails. A **coattail**, then, can be defined as the extra votes the more popular candidate on a ballot is thought to give the other candidates, usually of the same party, who are running at the same time. This effect is distinct from partisanship.[35] Something beyond party identification apparently helps congressional candidates of the president's party win elections in presidential election years.

A second set of commentary focuses on the negative voting in the **midterm election**—the election two years after the presidential election when there is no presidential race. The midterm election is also called the *off-year election*. As a matter of historical fact, in this century in every midterm election but one, the president's party has lost seats in the House. (The exception is the election of 1934.) While the coattail argument explains the loss as a falling off of the coattails from the preceding presidential election year, the negative voting argument looks to the explanation within the midterm election itself. By this argument, the midterm election can be viewed as a mandate for the policies of the party in the White House. Some voters will always be dissatisfied with the president when the campaign hopes of the past are not fulfilled, hence the consistent loss of seats in the midterm election. Still, there will be more dissatisfaction in some years than others, and so the size of the loss varies greatly from one midterm election to another. Economic policies in particular, some writers contend, may provoke dissatisfaction with the party in the White House.[36] Therefore, according to the negative voting argument, the voters' reaction to the president's performance can help explain the congressional election results.

Both explanations emphasize presidential effects rather than the congressional races themselves. A third explanation is possible, which is called congressional autonomy. The results may say little about presidential impact; instead, they may record the influences in congressional races. The three explanations—presidential coattails, presidential negative voting, and congressional autonomy—can be looked at more closely.

First of all, it is important to consider both the presidential year and midterm elections and both votes and seats. While the president loses seats in the midterm election, it is also true that the president's party gains seats

---

[35]Coattails have been studied for more than twenty years. See, for example, Angus Campbell, "Voters and Elections: Past and Present," *Journal of Politics,* 26 (1964), pp. 745–57; Herbert M. Kritzer and Robert E. Eubank, "Presidential Coattails Revisited: Partisanship and Incumbency Effects," *American Journal of Political Science,* 23 (1979), pp. 615–26; George C. Edwards, III, "The Impact of Presidential Coattails on Outcomes of Congressional Elections," *American Politics Quarterly,* 7 (1979), pp. 94–108; Alan I. Abramowitz, Albert D. Cover, and Helmut Norpoth, "The President's Party in Midterm Elections," *American Journal of Political Science,* 30 (1986), pp. 562–76.

[36]See Edward R. Tufte, "Determinants of the Outcomes of Midterm Congressional Elections," *American Political Science Review,* 69 (1975), pp. 812–26. See also Samuel Kernell, "Presidential Popularity and Negative Voting: An Alternative Explanation of the Midterm Congressional Decline of the President's Party," *American Political Science Review,* 71 (1977), pp. 44–66.

EXHIBIT 6.9		Seats, Votes, and the President's Party in House Elections[a]

YEAR	PRESIDENT'S PARTY	HOUSE SEATS HELD (Democratic)	SEATS GAINED OR LOST (PRESIDENT'S PARTY) Pres. Year	Off-Year	HOUSE DEMOCRATIC VOTE % TWO-PARTY VOTE
1948	Democratic	263	+75		53.2
1950		234		−29	50.0
1952	Republican	211	+22		49.9
1954		232		−18	52.5
1956	Republican	233	−3		51.0
1958		284		−47	56.0
1960	Democratic	263	−21		54.8
1962		258		−5	52.5
1964	Democratic	295	+37		57.3
1966		247		−48	51.3
1968	Republican	243	+5		50.9
1970		254		−12	54.4
1972	Republican	239	+12		52.7
1974		291		−48	58.5
1976	Democratic	292	+1		56.9
1978		276		−16	54.4
1980	Republican	243	+33		51.4
1982		264		−26	56.2
1984	Republican	252	+17		52.9
1986		257		−5	54.5
1988	Republican	260	−3		
Total 1948-1988		Mean = 257 seats			Mean = 53.6%

[a]The president's party is the party of the winning presidential candidate. Since some congresses will have one or two independents, the number of seats gained or lost for one party will not always equal exactly the number of seats gained or lost for the other.

in almost every presidential election year. The midterm loss is only half of the curiosity that needs to be explained. The use of seats gained or lost is also a highly misleading measure, depending entirely on the number of seats held before the election. Seats are "gained" or "lost" only in relation to the seats held previously. It follows that the more seats held by one of the two major parties before the election, the larger the loss appears after the election, even if nothing else happens at all.

This is shown more clearly in Exhibit 6.9. The table lists the House seats held after each election, the seats gained or lost from the preceding election, and the nationwide percent of the Democratic vote cast for House candidates. Notice that behind the dramatic reversals in seats gained and lost, there is a very stable vote. Measured by seats, the voters were "saying" something quite different in 1948, 1966, and 1978 about the two parties. Measured by the actual *vote*, however, the results were almost the same. Nothing very different was being said at all.

Overall, the vote is extremely stable and close to the average vote in both the presidential year and off-year elections. These results accord with what is already known about congressional elections. Given the importance of party and incumbency, one would expect a stable vote for Congress despite a change in presidential voting. Congressional autonomy explains the congressional election results better than coattails or negative voting can, taken singly or together.

The table in Exhibit 6.9 can also be used to compare elections with each other and identify the unusual cases. The 1970 results, measured by seats lost, were interpreted by some people as "better than average" for a midterm election, while 1978 was called "about average." According to the actual vote, however, the two election results were identical. The post-Watergate election stands apart in its wide swing of votes against the president's party. Following the scandal in the Republican White House, Republican House candidates lost support at the polls.

Nevertheless, some small effects do remain—helping the president's party in the presidential election year and hurting it in the off-year. Both the coattail and negative voting arguments appear to have identified one-half of a pattern and missed the other half. The effects are small, averaging about two percentage points of the vote, but a two percentage point swing from one party to the other can make a difference in some races. This is the national trend people refer to, helping candidates of one party across the country because of the fortunes of the presidential race. The trend was Republican in 1972, Democratic in 1974, Republican in 1980 and 1984. The trend, however small, can defeat candidates in close races and contribute to that perception of vulnerability so important to the challenger's race.

The Campaign

From these major influences on elections comes a clearer perspective on the effects of the campaign. Most elections do not start with the first campaign activity. The two candidates do not line up and wait for the starting gun of the campaign, with the winner running the best race. Given the importance of incumbency, one candidate can have important advantages before the campaign begins. Choices can be made without campaign activity, due to party voting. People vote without having read or heard anything about the candidates in the race. Thus predominantly Republican states and districts tend to elect Republican candidates, and the same is true for the Democratic strongholds, regardless of the campaigns being waged. Still, candidates and issues can make a difference, beyond the effects of party and incumbency. Incumbents can be defeated. Scandals in office have an impact. In all of these situations, campaign activity can be important.

Homestyle: Congressman Romano Mazzoli keeps in touch with his constituents at an Italian-American function in Louisville, Kentucky.

Visibility may be the critical factor in all of these cases. Only a very visible communication cuts through the voters' low awareness of congressional affairs. An issue highly salient to the electorate has its own visibility. Scandals and other negative information get across to voters. Indeed, much of an incumbent's advantage may reduce to the fact that of the two candidates only one is visible to the voters. But visibility can be created through other means as well, through the effort and activity of the campaign.

Campaign Strategies.   The standard strategy of any campaign for political office is to strengthen existing support, activate potential support, and if possible convert some of the opponent's support. But as all realistic campaigners know, hoped-for conversion cannot be the mainstay of a campaign. Selective perception, as shown in Chapter Three, guards against opinion change. People tend not to expose themselves to sources that contradict their political predispositions. Democrats rarely read the editorials in a Republican newspaper. Also, even if exposed, selective perception screens out the contradictory impulses. Voters are more likely to see the good side of the candidate whom they already favor. Finally, even if some of the bad side is perceived, this information will be retained a shorter time than favorable items. The same tendencies work at the other extreme. Those most strongly in support of the candidate need little reinforcement.

By and large, the thrust of campaign energies is directed at activating and crystallizing latent support and at trying to reach those who are not easy to reach. Publicity is crucial. Face-to-face contacts, (such as coffees, speaking engagements, media advertising, general and special mailings, and house-to-house and telephone canvasses) are directed at least in part to this end. While a majority of senators and some representatives, especially those in competitive districts, hire professionals in public relations and advertising, they and their managers stress the importance of volunteer help and the candidate's personal organization.

Specific campaign strategies vary with the money available and the perceived chance of success. Consider the different kinds of congressional candidates that can be called Sure Winners (most incumbents), Vulnerables (vulnerable incumbents), Hopefuls (challengers running against vulnerable incumbents or candidates in open seat contests), and Sure Losers (other challengers).[37] Sure Winners tend to run limited campaigns focused on mobilizing loyal supporters to vote. They emphasize the candidate's personal characteristics, make appeals to party members in safe party districts, and deemphasize issues. Hopefuls and Vulnerables make broader appeals in the attempt to swing uncommitted voters. Issues become more important. Radio and television ads are used, where economically feasible, to reach as broad a public as possible. Vulnerable incumbents will often use a preemptive strategy, also called *inoculation*. They spend money early and attempt to set the terms of debate, in the hopes of discouraging strong challengers from entering the race. The Hopefuls can try preemptive strategies too, but their money tends to come later, and be spent later, than the incumbents' money. Sure Losers have little resources available to wage a strong campaign. They rely heavily on handouts and personal contacts with the voters, often running their own campaigns. Sure Losers may try to make broad appeals to the public and address a range of issues, but the appeals may not be taken seriously by the press or recognized by the voters. Whereas eighty-six percent of the incumbents, according to one study, had professional managers, only about half of the challengers did and half of the candidates in open seat contests. At the other extreme, very few incumbents or open seat candidates managed their own campaign, while thirty percent of the challengers did.[38]

Exhibit 6.10 shows the different information techniques used by the various kinds of candidates. Candidates are alike in their reliance on personal contact and campaign literature and different in their use of the more expensive direct mail and media advertising techniques. The vulnerable incumbents are more likely to use direct mail and radio and television ads than the Hopefuls they are running against. Not surprisingly, Sure Winners and Sure Losers are lowest in use of these expensive techniques.

Recent advances in campaign techniques can now be seen in perspective. Some campaigns do employ highly paid consultants and sophisticated media strategies. They use "tracking devices" whereby media ads can be instantaneously developed to respond to the opponent's ads and their own poll response. They spend money early and freely. While these sophisticat-

---

[37]The classification was developed by Goldenberg and Traugott, *op cit.,* pp. 183–184.
[38]Goldenberg and Traugott, *op cit.*.

EXHIBIT 6.10	Information Techniques Used by the Candidates[a]

| | PERCENT USING THE TECHNIQUE | | | | | | |
TYPE OF CANDIDATE	Personal Contact	Campaign Literature	Newspaper Ads	Direct Mail	Radio Ads	TV Ads	N
All Candidates	95	92	78	70	65	44	(149)
Incumbents							
Sure Winners	91	80	74	54	60	26	(46)
Vulnerables	100	100	88	100	81	75	(16)
Challengers							
Hopefuls	98	95	80	80	73	53	(40)
Sure Losers	88	92	65	46	42	27	(26)
Candidates in Open Seat Races	100	100	82	85	77	69	(21)

[a]As reported by campaign managers in the 1978 election. Cell entries are the percentages who mentioned using the technique in the campaign.

Sources: Goldenberg and Traugott, *op. cit.,* p. 116.

ed high-cost techniques are increasingly common in Senate races, they are less common in House contests. Some candidates may use tracking devices, but others are still out in the shopping centers hoping someone will recognize their name.

Campaign Spending. Support for all this campaign energy comes from three major sources, whose relative importance varies with the candidate's particular situation and the political environment. First, there is the party organization at the local, state, and national levels and the congressional campaign committees, which are affiliated with the national party committees. Congressional campaign committees are maintained by both parties in the Senate and the House.

Both parties, as shown earlier, can help candidates secure support from political action committees and provide a critical information link between the candidates and the various interest groups. Nevertheless, the amount of party support still varies considerably from candidate to candidate.

Second, there are the nonparty groups, some well-established and fairly permanent, others formed for one election or issue. Such groups may offer financial support directly to the candidate, general publicity, or assistance in mailings. The political action committees, or PACs, that proliferated in the 1970s sought to influence the election of candidates supporting the group's position. For example, BIPAC (Business-Industry Political Action Committee), one of the first political action committees formed, was organized to counter labor and liberal influence and to support conservative and business-oriented candidates. NCPAC (National Conservative Political Action Committee) claimed credit for the defeat of several liberal incumbents, particularly in the Senate through the late 1970s and early 1980s. (For the activities of political action committees, see Chapter Four).

Third, there is the candidates' personal organization and personal contacts. Because parties and nonparty groups must spread their support across a number of candidates, it is the personal organization—the candidate's own contacts for money, talent, and supporters—that bears the major burden of the campaign effort. In the years since 1974, when data on campaign funding and spending were first reliably collected, individual contributions comprise by far the largest source of campaign funding for both House and Senate races. Nonparty PACs are second, with the parties and the candidate's own financial resources making up the remainder.[39]

Who gets the campaign funding and what differences does it make? Money, it appears, helps some candidates more than others. Money is particularly important for nonincumbents and challengers especially. It significantly increases recognition and affects the vote. *Spending does not help incumbents.* Facing the same level of opposition from challengers, incumbents could spend a lot or a little money and find scant difference in the results. Challengers, in contrast, improve their recognition and their chance for electoral success with each increment of money spent. These findings hold for both the Senate and the House: *spending helps the challenger much more than the incumbent.*[40]

Money buys attention, not votes. Spending has its main impact on increasing the recognition of those candidates least visible to start with. Once the disadvantage is narrowed, candidates can campaign more equally with their more visible opponents, and provide a choice to the voters.

It follows that campaign contributors can have their greatest impact by giving to the challenger's campaign, and yet few contributors follow this strategy. Party committees support incumbents more than challengers, as do individual contributors and most of the political action committees. Money, of course, is typically spent only when there is some expectation of success. Senate challengers receive a larger proportion of funds than House challengers from all of these sources, but the Senate candidates were seen as more likely to win. Success draws money, and money helps success.

These facts about campaign spending have far-reaching implications. Given the many advantages of incumbents, campaign money may be the one chance challengers have—and they may need a lot of it—to bid for the election. Therefore, any reforms that limit spending, or otherwise curtail the congressional campaign, can have the effect of making incumbents even safer than they are. Reformers, then, may face a hard choice between increasing competition and limiting the role of money in congressional campaigns. Another point should also be considered: Senate challengers are nearly as well-known to the voters as the incumbents, whereas House challengers are not as well-known as the other House candidates. If campaign

---

[39]Michael J. Malbin, "Of Mountains and Molehills," in Michael J. Malbin, ed., *Parties, Interest Groups, and Campaign Finance Laws* (Washington, D.C.: American Enterprise Institute, 1980), pp. 154–155.

[40]Gary C. Jacobson, "The Effects of Campaign Spending in Congressional Elections," *American Political Science Review*, 72 (1978), pp. 469–91; Alan I. Abramowitz, "Explaining Senate Election Outcomes," *American Political Science Review*, 82 (1988), pp. 385–403.

spending helps recognition, then increased spending by House challengers may change that situation and bring House races more in line with the Senate results.

These facts are important, too, for groups in the population that would seek to improve their representation in Congress. Women and blacks, for example, are underrepresented in Congress compared to the population as a whole. While larger patterns of discrimination exist, the results suggest a shortcut through the broader discrimination. These groups, underrepresented in the past, need to defeat incumbents. Concentrated efforts at money-raising for the challengers is one way that works. Other groups may give money to the incumbent to resist the challenge, but money helps the challenger more than the incumbent.

████ DO ELECTIONS MAKE A DIFFERENCE?

What does it mean for the practice of American government whether Republicans or Democrats win the White House or Congress, that House incumbents are overwhelmingly reelected, or that particular candidates win rather than others? Some of the implications of these voting results can now be explored.

The importance of party voting has major consequences. Republicans and Democrats pursue different policies in office. Presidents find support in Congress primarily from members of their own party. The party that members of Congress belong to is a major influence on the positions they take on roll-call votes (see Chapter Seven). Thus the party voting we have identified helps shape cooperation and conflict between the president and Congress and influences the particular policies enacted.

This also means that presidents are limited—in what they may seek and in what they may get—by conditions beyond their control. Will Congress pass a president's budget request, or approve a Court nominee, or investigate high-ranking members of the executive branch? This depends in part on the party in control of Congress. Can presidents wait for major legislation until they gain experience on the job? No, because whatever strength they have at the beginning will be cut back by the midterm election halfway through their term. But can't presidents try to influence the congressional election results? They can *try*, but most of the influences on congressional elections are not presidentially inspired.

Party voting, however, is not the only influence on congressional elections. Senators and representatives are elected from states and districts whose interests may run counter to a particular party or presidential position. Incumbency and the short-term forces of candidates and issues in the campaign also affect election results. There are, then, many occasions when members of Congress do not follow party lines.

The incumbency advantage is also important. Incumbency affects Congress in two critically important ways. First, it ensures that the membership is stable, safe, and senior. A stable and senior membership, as will be shown in Chapter Seven, supports a "seniority norm"—a way of allotting influence in Congress in favor of those who have been there longest. A stable and senior membership, moreover, can develop long-term approaches to government policies, can oppose new presidential proposals, and can develop alliances with other people in government outlasting any one president's stay in office. Incumbency, then, strengthens Congress as a check on presidential power. Most members of Congress will still be on Capitol Hill when the president is gone.

These electoral patterns can also clarify the extent and limits of popular influence on government. Much of the influence on elections has little to do with the particular congressional members or their actions in Congress, and the members know this. Elections, then, allow a wide latitude for congressional behavior. Hence, it is to be expected that other influences, particularly from within the institution, will affect congressional behavior. And yet, because defeat is always possible and because voters do control the selection of members, there are boundaries to that latitude. Public opinion cannot be disregarded by incumbents who want to keep their jobs. Incumbents are not only recognized, they are liked and seen as doing a good job. Scandals lower the success rate. Given the electoral uncertainty, even the safest incumbents work hard, raise and spend money (even if it does not help), and worry about the next election. Politicians seldom take elections for granted. Then, too, perhaps the very safeness has been built from all that work and worry. A safe incumbent, running hard, discourages strong challengers from entering the race and limits the flow of money to the challenger's campaign.

Do presidential elections make a difference? The voters select which of two candidates will provide leadership for the nation and face the crises and decisions to come. So John Kennedy, not Richard Nixon, was in the White House when Russian-built missiles and launching facilities were discovered in Cuba. The event, known as the Cuban Missile Crisis, was acted on by one president rather than the other. Other evidence can be given for the difference elections make. Presidents try to fulfill their campaign promises: at least two thirds of their pledges tend to become White House proposals, although not all are enacted.[41] Republican and Democratic presidents develop different priorities and links to groups across the nation; hence some policies will change depending on whether Republicans or Democrats are elected. In addition, presidents will be appointing judges to the federal courts who will sit for life, thus influencing national policy long after the president's term is over. The appointments, as will be seen in Chapter Ten, tend to follow the party and political philosophy of the appointing president.

On the other hand, a large part of the selection is over before the election campaign officially begins. The voters choose between two candidates

---

[41]Jeff Fishel, *Presidents and Promises* (Washington, D.C.: CQ Press, 1985), p. 38.

only; much of the deciding has already been done. And even the decisions made must be based on poor information. Thirty-second commercials do not show the differences on issues, nor do the television debates with their elaborate rehearsals, briefing books, and press score cards show what the candidates are like.

It can be argued, however, that this information is useful—that winning elections requires the same skills that presidents will need in office. Once in the White House, presidents must also maintain an image that will elicit support from the American people and respect from world leaders. They will need to be briefed and rehearsed for their dealings with the press, who will continue to score their performance as they did in the television debates. Seen from this point of view, elections as well as the nominations described previously are rigorous training for the job that the candidates seek.

CHECKLIST FOR REVIEW	1. Turnout, the percentage of eligible voters who actually vote, averages about fifty percent for presidential elections and less than forty percent for off-year elections. Turnout generally increases with socioeconomic status, although there are many reasons that may influence the decision to vote.

2. Party identification, a voter's psychological attachment to a party, influences the perception of candidates and the actual voting choice. Party identification is a long-term influence on voting. This, along with short-term influences, can explain the election result. The short-term influences are the perception of candidates, issues, and parties at the time.

3. The normal vote is a hypothetical vote based on the percentage of people identifying with each of the two major parties, plus an estimate of the likelihood that they will vote. Deviations from the normal vote must be due to short-term influences. Thus the normal vote can be used to explain election results or, knowing the short-term influences, to predict them.

4. The presidential candidate who receives the most votes in a given state receives all of that state's electoral votes, and the candidate who wins a majority of the electoral votes is elected president. This system leads candidates to concentrate on states with many electoral votes or those with the potential to swing either way.

5. Campaign strategies are aimed at appealing to traditional supporters plus attempting to win over potential supporters. In presidential campaigns, television is a primary means by which candidates get their message across. In congressional campaigns, the specific strategies vary with the candidate's financial resources and likelihood of success. Campaign spending in congressional races helps visibility; thus spending helps the challenger much more than the incumbent.

6. Party voting, incumbency, and short-term effects are important influences on congressional elections. Incumbents who seek reelection are strongly advantaged, winning eighty to ninety percent or more of the time. The most important reason, among many, explaining the incumbents' advantage may be that they are much better known than their opponents. While short-term effects do have an influence, they are less important than in presidential elections, because of the low information available about the congressional contest.

KEY TERMS

turnout

party identification

ticket splitting

long-term influences on the vote

short-term influences on the vote

normal vote

landslide

electoral college

incumbent

advantage of incumbency

perks

challenger

coattails

midterm election

PART THREE

The Institutions of American Government

Congress

N ewspaper headlines tell us when a president sends a bill to Congress. We hear what its defenders and critics think about it and what it is intended to do. For many Americans, this means that something has happened, a policy decision has been made. For students of American government, however, nothing necessarily has happened at all. It is merely one opening step in a policy-making process of perhaps three to six years or more in duration, with the mysterious "Congress" of the headline to fire many rounds of its own. In the process, as the bill disappears behind all its committee and subcommittee doors (and disappears from the front page news), every part of the bill might be changed.

The *power* of Congress is the first fact to appreciate about this institution. In the original constitutional design, Congress was given some of the strongest independent checks on executive power ever assigned to a legislative body. It could tax, spend, and say when money should not be spent. It could have a say in making treaties and wars, in establishing executive agencies, and in agreeing to or turning down the president's appointments. The list of constitutional powers is shown in Exhibit 7.1. But Congress is also a *representative* assembly, charged with representing opinion in the states and districts of the nation. It must make national policy while it maintains its popular representational base. So, it is important to think not only of what Congress can do, but what it wants to do. And what Congress wants will be affected by what the people want in the 435 congressional districts and 50 states of the nation.

Congress can assert or ignore its war-making powers, obstruct or rubber stamp a president's proposal, and harass an agency to follow the congressional intent of a law or let the agency follow its own intent. But when will it decide to do one thing or the other and how will the decision be made? This chapter looks at how Congress combines power and representation, and at the members, the internal organization, and the kind of policy that is made.

MEMBERS AND THE JOB OF REPRESENTATION

Congress is not merely the name for a branch of government or a string of buildings on Capitol Hill. It is composed of people: 435 members of the House of Representatives and 100 members of the Senate. To understand Congress, it is necessary to understand what members of Congress are like and how they perceive the job of representation.

Characteristics of Members

One important characteristic of members of Congress is already known from the workings of elections described in Chapter Six: the membership is stable. Representatives are successfully reelected term after term. Since Senators serve for six years at a time, one successful reelection is all it

EXHIBIT 7.1

The Powers of
Congress

The powers of Congress are stated in Article I, section 8, of the Constitution and include the power to:

- Tax
- Borrow money
- Regulate commerce with foreign nations and among the states
- Establish uniform rules for naturalization and bankruptcy
- Coin money, set its value, and punish counterfeiting
- Fix the standard of weights and measures
- Establish a postal system and network of roads
- Issue patents and copyrights to inventors and authors
- Create courts inferior to (i.e., below) the Supreme Court
- Define and punish felonies on the high seas and crimes against the law of nations
- Declare war
- Raise and support an army and navy and make rules for their governance
- Provide for a militia
- Exercise power over the seat of government (Washington, D.C.) and all other federal facilities
- "Make all Laws which shall be necessary and proper for carrying into execution the foregoing Powers, and all other Powers vested by this Constitution in the Government of the United States or in any Department or Officer thereof."

takes to serve twelve years in office. In the House, the average representative has served for fourteen years; some, of course, have been there much longer. It is ironic that one of the original worries about the House, at the time of the framing of the Constitution (and one of the chief arguments for a Senate), was that its two-year term and popular election might make it too unstable. It might "yield to the impulse of sudden and violent passion" and pass laws too hastily and without due deliberation (see *Federalist* 62). In the twentieth century, however, the House has been criticized for being *too* stable and *too* unwilling to take any action. Rather than being swayed by the violent winds of passion, it has not seemed able to be swayed at all. What this stability means is that more than a decade of national policy will be made by the same congressional members. It also means that the average senator and representative have seen more than one president in and out of office. The members of Congress, along with the career bureaucrats, are the natives in town, who watch the presidential tourists come and go.

A second characteristic of the members is also important. Although they represent their constituencies, they do not reflect them in many social attributes held to have political significance. They are more highly educated and better-off financially than the population as a whole. According to a *Congressional Quarterly* report, most members of Congress could be financially secure without their government salaries. At the extreme, one-third of

the Senate could claim a net worth of $1 million or more each, although only about seven percent of the House members could.[1] Members are also considerably more likely to be lawyers, males, and Caucasians than the population as a whole. By the end of the 1980s, only 6 percent of the House were women and five percent were black. There were two women in the Senate and no blacks. More than two-thirds of the members of Congress were lawyers. At election time, a lot of attention is given to the few women candidates running, as if to say the times are changing. Nevertheless, in the early 1960s, before the Women's Movement, there were two women in the Senate. Twenty-five years later, the number was the same.

Congress is similar to other legislatures in overrepresenting an educational and social elite. In most Western democracies a highly educated national legislature is the norm. In wealth and social status, too, most other legislatures are unlike the population they represent. Men dominate the membership of foreign legislatures, although the United States has a poorer record than many in the number of seats held by women. In 1970, when women held four percent of the legislative seats in England, and fifteen percent in Finland and Sweden, they held two percent in the U.S. House of Representatives.[2] The United States Congress, then, is not unusual in the

[1]Congressional Quarterly, *Congressional Ethics,* 2nd ed. (Washington, D.C.: Congressional Quarterly, 1980), pp. 77–78.

[2]See Gerhard Loewenberg and Samuel C. Patterson, *Comparing Legislatures* (Boston: Little, Brown, 1979), p. 70; and J. Blondel, *Comparative Legislatures* (Englewood Cliffs, N.J.: Prentice-Hall, 1973), pp. 160–161.

problem of representation it poses—how an elite group of members can represent a much larger, less advantaged, and more diverse population.

A third characteristic, however, suggests how representation *can* work. Members of Congress are like their constituents in one very important regard. In their birth, education, and past occupation, they have grown up with them and share the same background socialization. This can be called the "hometown" orientation of the members, or what some people call congressional *localism* or *parochialism.* At the beginning of the 1980s, three-fourths of the senators had been born in the state that they represented, and two-thirds had received some higher education in the state or held a state elective office. Many senators had come from the House. Three-fourths of the House members were born in the state, three-fourths had some higher education in the state, and one-half had been elected to a state or local office. Those who had not held office had typically worked in the party, served in a state appointive position, or worked for a past congressional member. Only six percent in the Senate and seven percent in the House could be considered outsiders—that is, those who had neither been born, educated, or elected to office in the state.[3] Even the astronauts and ball players who have been elected to Congress did so by returning to their home-state base.

This local orientation is found throughout the members' congressional activity. It is reflected in the regional metaphors and local dialects sprinkled throughout debate and in the staff appointed. It leads to the much-criticized parochialism of Congress. How can a body make foreign policy, people ask, if a large portion of its members, excluding military service and their Washington stay, have never been out of the country and rarely out of the state? Yet it also helps to produce a membership that shares many of the beliefs and attitudes of the folks back home. Members of Congress repeatedly say that they "know their people," and they "know" the district because they have lived there. So, while there are few farmers in Congress, there are many people who claim to be able to represent a farm district because they grew up there. They know the people and what they need.

Groups in Congress

While individuals must represent their own states and districts, representation is carried on through group activity as well. Groups in Congress perform political as well as social functions, allowing like-minded members to work together to get results. Perhaps the largest and most important groups in Congress are the **congressional party caucuses.** There are four altogether, consisting of all Democrats and all Republicans in each chamber. Party caucuses have helped to make rule changes and to influence committee assignments. When the caucus becomes actively concerned about an issue,

---

[3]Barbara Hinckley, *Stability and Change in Congress,* 4th ed. (New York: Harper and Row, 1988), p. 86.

Materials of Political Science: CHARACTERISTICS OF PEOPLE IN GOVERNMENT

A Profile of the 101st Congress (1989–1990)

Congress, like most other national legislatures, is not descriptively representative: that is, it does not mirror the characteristics of the population as a whole. In the following profile, a picture emerges of an elite group quite similar to other elites in American society. They are like presidents and Supreme Court justices in many social characteristics and similar to the media elite discussed in Chapter Three.

Congress, however, must claim to represent people who are not middle-aged white lawyers and businessmen. Thus members develop a home style and show constituents that they keep in close touch with the folks back home.

		HOUSE	SENATE
Average age		52.1	55.6
Sex	Male	409	98
	Female	26*	2
Race	White	394	98
	Black	24	0
	Other[a]	17	2
Religion	Protestant (traditional)	248	66
	Catholic	120	19
	Jewish	31	8
	Other[b]	36	7
Leading Occupations[c]	Lawyers	184	63
	Business, Banking	138	28
	Education	42	11
	Agriculture	19	4
	Journalism	17	8

[a]Other includes Hispanics, Asians, and Pacific Islanders

[b]Other includes non-traditional Protestant, Greek Orthodox, Mormons, Seventh-day Adventists, and unspecified.

[c]Members can cite more than one occupation; hence the totals are higher than the total membership. The occupation of politics, which most members have served in, is excluded.

*Includes one woman elected in a special election in 1989.

Source: Based on data supplied by *Congressional Quarterly Weekly Report,* November 12, 1988, pp. 3243–45.

the leaders have to listen. Also important are the **state party delegations** in the House, particularly in states where the party holds a large number of seats. The delegations consist of all representatives from the party in the state. Some delegations meet frequently, discuss local and national issues, and seek to form a unified front in floor decisions. Most delegations supply information to members on upcoming votes in Congress and help new members to get committee assignments. Other groups consist of the various *classes* of newly elected members. A class refers to all members newly elected in the same year. Some classes meet regularly and have their own organization, while others are relatively inactive. One of the most famous classes, and one of the largest, was the freshman Democratic class of 1975, which played a major role in reforming House rules in the late 1970s.

Other groups have formed to advance particular policies or ideological positions. The Democratic Study Group (DSG), formed as an alliance of liberal Democrats in the 1950s, has an extensive organization, staff, and budget. The DSG produces study reports and policy papers, forms task forces to study issues, and raises money for congressional campaigns. Conservative southern Democrats have met regularly since the time of the New Deal to work out their own positions and to bargain with Republicans and northern Democrats. Termed "boll weevils" during the 1970s (after the insects that burrow into cotton plants), the group developed a more dignified title in 1981 and called itself the Conservative Democratic Forum. Moderate and liberal Republicans have also formed groups, although they have been smaller and less influential than the conservative Democrats. The Black Caucus, consisting of all black members of Congress, was first formed in 1969. The Caucus has a staff and budget, elects a chair, and develops an agenda on national issues as well as on specific legislation. The Caucus votes together, provides cues for other representatives on black issues, and has worked to build coalitions with other groups in Congress.

These are just some of the many groups that members can work with in Congress. The fact that such groups do form and join together for common purposes makes them a potential source of influence. There are currently about seventy of these groups working in Congress.

The Job of Representation

The concept of representation, like other political terms, is subject to many different and contradictory meanings. Hanna Pitkin distinguishes between two kinds of representation: *descriptive* and *substantive*. **Descriptive representation** involves the reflecting, or mirroring, of politically relevant characteristics of the citizens in the representative body. If questions of race, sex, or economic status have political implications, then a representative group of people would be those who showed the same proportion of these characteristics as the population at large. **Substantive representation** is defined by Pitkin as "acting in the interests of the represented, in a manner responsive to them." Representatives are not judged on who they are but on what they do.[4] Lawyers can represent farm districts and be substantively representative. They can act in the interests of the farmers even though they are not farmers themselves.

Still, there are many ways to act in someone's interests and different kinds of actions that can be performed. Are they all equally "representative" or are some more important for legislative bodies than others? Representatives can act in someone's interest by taking the role of a **delegate** or a **trustee.** Delegates try to follow the opinions of their constituents whether or not those opinions accord with their own. They try to do what the constituents want done. Delegates, for example, might oppose a tax bill after hearing complaints from local groups. Trustees, in contrast, try to do what they feel is in the best interest of the people, whether or not this accords with what the constituents want done. Unlike delegates, trustees do not look to the state or district for instructions—they act according to their own judgment. Trustees would be making up their own minds on the tax bill, not necessarily following the district. Some representatives, of course, vary these roles depending on the situation, acting at times as a delegate and at times as a trustee. One study of House members reported that about one-fourth thought of themselves as trustees, another one-fourth thought they were delegates, and one-half saw themselves as combining the two roles.[5]

Representatives can also act in people's interest by performing different kinds of activities. They can vote with a majority of their constituents on matters before the Congress. In other words, they represent their constituents on matters of *policy*, such as military aid to Central America or a tax increase. Representatives can perform *service* for constituents, answering their inquiries about government or assigning staff to help in the cutting of some bureaucratic red tape. They can help in the *allocation* of resources for their states or districts, saving an endangered local project or winning the contract for a new one. Or they can represent by *symbolism,* keeping in touch with their constituents by frequent newsletters and visits home. They are on hand for all the parades, ball games, and local festivals.[6] Members of Congress, in fact, do all of these things, although not necessarily with the same degree of effort or success.

Many people consider policy representation the most important job that their representatives should be doing in Washington. They believe that representatives should reflect their constituencies' opinion on policies facing the Congress. To what extent do the members of Congress perform this kind of representation? The answer, it seems clear, varies with the importance of the issue to the people back home. Studies of congressional deci-

---

[4]Hanna F. Pitkin, *The Concept of Representation* (Berkeley: University of California Press, 1967), esp. pp. 209ff.

[5]Roger H. Davidson, *The Role of the Congressman* (New York: Pegasus, 1969), p. 117.

[6]Heinz Eulau and Paul D. Karps, "The Puzzle of Representation," *Legislative Studies Quarterly, 2* (1977), pp. 233–54.

sions show that the correspondence between the decision and the opinion in the constituency varies greatly by issue area. On issues such as foreign policy, little constituency influence appears, but there may be little interest to represent. On other issues, such as agriculture or civil rights, constituency characteristics can explain a large part of the decisions taken.[7] So, if the Democrats put together a coalition of urban, farm, and labor interests, what do the Republicans do? The Republicans representing farm districts (or urban or labor districts) vote with the Democrats on these issues; the rest of the Republicans oppose the Democrats and vote on party lines. Hence a critic of the entire military budget makes an exception for an obsolete local naval base, or an opponent of price subsidies finds, after all, that the cranberry growers really do need help.

Does Congress succeed in its claim to be a representative institution? From all these terms and definitions, students of government must decide for themselves what the word "representation" should mean. Congress is clearly not descriptively representative. It does not reflect many attributes of the general population. Nevertheless, the very localism so criticized in members of Congress does give one kind of representational guarantee. They have been socialized in the attitudes of the states and districts that have elected them. They know the people and what they need. Moreover, the incumbents' very high reelection rates may be a sign of successful representation. Perhaps reelection means that members have done all that they were expected to do.

In short, perhaps the job of representing a particular state or district, as voters define it on election day, is not that difficult or demanding. Out of one hundred controversial decisions, there may be less than a half dozen where a substantial portion of the constituency cares about the outcome—or would care if they knew about it. There may be only a dozen or so more where interest groups of concern to the member would care about the outcome. Thus from the standpoint of representing a particular constituency, the representative or senator faces only a few issues with a "right" or "wrong" side. The others will be decided on other than constituency grounds—on one's own political judgment, a sense of national policy needs, a result of party influence, or other bargaining within the Congress itself.

In addition, representatives can work for a state or district in ways that have little to do with legislating. They can develop a **home style,** that shows they identify with their district, care about the people in it, and are good representatives.[8] This is the symbolic activity of representation. Representatives can claim credit for a federal construction project or perform other allocation. They can perform service for individual constituents when

[7]The initial and classic study is Warren E. Miller and Donald E. Stokes, "Constituency Influence in Congress," in *Elections and the Political Order,* eds. Angus Campbell et al. (New York: Wiley, 1966), pp. 351–72. See also Aage R. Clausen, *How Congressmen Decide* (New York: St. Martin's Press, 1973). The Clausen results hold through the congresses of the 1980s.
[8]Richard F. Fenno, *Home Style* (Boston: Little, Brown, 1978).

people seek advice, favors, information, or extrication from bureaucratic red tape. They can even initiate service from the legislative office itself, sending out newsletters, information brochures, and questionnaires. Representatives agree that service is the most time-consuming of their jobs and one of the most important. Needless to say, any one of these activities may be used to substitute for others.

All this suggests that members of Congress, given low public interest and information, work within a wide latitude of discretion. In the first place, the constituency may not ask that much by way of representation. Second, because of shared attitudes from the past, members may find little conflict between their own and their constituency's point of view. Third, even in cases of potential conflict, one big right vote, one local project, and heavy doses of service ensure that incumbents rarely disappoint their constituents.

THE ORGANIZATION OF CONGRESS

Because pressure from the constituency is not that firm, continuous, or demanding, other influences, especially from within Congress, can have a decisive impact on policy. These influences include the norms of Congress, its practices, and its forms of organization.

Congressional Norms

One important source of influence in Congress is provided by the norms of the institution itself. A **norm** is simply an unwritten rule of behavior in a social group. It expresses how things are done, and in so doing, it says how they ought to be done in the future. It is thus not only a description of behavior, but an influence on future behavior for people who want to stay in the group. Norms can be found in any number of groups and organizations. College students, for example, have norms of dress and behavior; one probably would not dress up to go to class, or talk too much about studying on Saturday nights. Congress is not unique in this nor are its norms particularly unusual. Congressional norms, however, have the power to affect behavior in the national legislature and so can affect the kind of policy that is made.

Four norms in Congress are particularly important. First is the norm of *seniority*. In its present form, the norm says that experience in Congress is valued, that the important lessons cannot be learned elsewhere, and that influence therefore should go to those who have been there longest. It is true that new members can now speak out more than before and even expect to have influence on subcommittees. Nevertheless, seniority is still upheld in selecting committee and subcommittee members and in distributing influence throughout Congress. New members do not have to be quiet, but they still have less influence than old members.

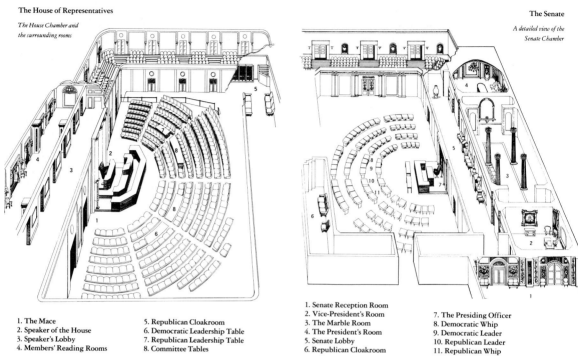

The House of Representatives

The House Chamber and the surrounding rooms

The Senate

A detailed view of the Senate Chamber

1. Senate Reception Room
2. Vice-President's Room
3. The Marble Room
4. The President's Room
5. Senate Lobby
6. Republican Cloakroom
7. The Presiding Officer
8. Democratic Whip
9. Democratic Leader
10. Republican Leader
11. Republican Whip

1. The Mace
2. Speaker of the House
3. Speaker's Lobby
4. Members' Reading Rooms
5. Republican Cloakroom
6. Democratic Leadership Table
7. Republican Leadership Table
8. Committee Tables

Courtesy The American University

A diagram of the House and Senate Chambers and their surrounding rooms.

If, for example, a new member comes to Congress with an economics degree and much experience in banking and monetary policy, he or she is no more likely to be appointed to the Banking Committee than any other new member. Since it is the experience *in Congress* that is valued, all new members are the same. When astronaut John Glenn was first elected to the Senate, there was a vacancy on the Aeronautics and Space Committee. Another freshman, Dale Bumpers of Arkansas, received the assignment; Glenn was assigned to Interior (its jurisdiction is public lands and Indian affairs). According to the norm, Glenn knew no more than Bumpers about space policy and much less than the senior committee members did. They were, after all, in Congress when Glenn was out orbiting the earth.

A second major norm is the norm of *specialization.* It says that members should not talk on all subjects; they should not even expect to have opinions on all subjects. They should specialize, presumably in some area of their committee work, and defer to other people's judgment on other committees. While the norm appears stronger in the House than in the Senate, it is important in both chambers in distributing influence widely across the membership. Everyone develops some area of expertise. The committee experts are deferred to, and committee recommendations are usually accepted on the floor. In some committees, the norm of specialization is carried down to the subcommittee level. So one can find an Appropriations subcommittee member who is czar of the School Lunch Program, or of the defense budget, or foreign aid. In these cases, following specialization, sub-committee recommendations will be accepted by the full committee and the full committee's recommendations accepted on the floor. (More on sub-committees appears later in the chapter.)

A third norm is *reciprocity*, or mutual accommodation. Often negatively referred to as "backscratching," the norm suggests that the accepted behavior is to help each other out in policy matters that mean much to one and not much to the other. In this way individual constituency claims can be put together into a majority vote. When the farm member supports the western water project and the western member comes out for corn subsidies, the two are following the norm of reciprocity. To say "I won't go along—I don't believe in this kind of backscratching," is breaking the norm.

A fourth norm is *institutional loyalty.* One should support the Congress, not allow it to be discredited, and join together against people, both within and outside Congress, who do not pay it the respect it deserves. What does this mean? It means that presidents or executive agencies that ignore a strong congressional sentiment may find themselves in trouble even with their usual supporters. Republicans, Democrats, liberals, and conservatives will all join together to support the norm. When then Vice-President George Bush once tried to lobby on the Senate floor for a Reagan administration program, the Senate Republicans met hastily to announce their unhappi-ness with the situation. They were so unhappy, in fact, that they hinted the president's program would be in trouble if such an action occurred again. An executive officer (even if he was also the President of the Senate) was claiming to tell U.S. Senators what to do. What else does the norm mean? It means that the congressional ethics committees will not be vigorous in in-vestigating the wrongdoings of members. According to the norm, issues for the committee to examine should not exist. On the other hand, a member already faced with public scandal or disgrace would have, by definition, broken the norm and would not be supported by the members.

The key word is *public.* Once a scandal becomes public, the norm has been broken, as the following examples show. Senator Joseph McCarthy was censured by his colleagues in 1954, not because he had destroyed indi-viduals' reputations by indiscriminately labelling them Communists or be-cause he had abused the congressional power of investigation. He was cen-sured, in effect, because he had attacked the integrity of the Senate. He insulted the Senate, calling a committee a "lynch bee" and a "handmaiden of Communist interests." After the Chappaquidick scandal (involving a car accident in which his female companion was killed), Senator Edward Ken-nedy was defeated for reelection to a top Senate leadership post. The pub-licity of the event—not the event itself—broke the norm. A late-night com-panion of prominent House member Wilbur Mills was photographed jumping into the Tidal Basin and was subsequently widely interviewed about her friendship with Mills. When the scandal intensified, Mills withdrew from his long-time chairmanship of the Ways and Means Committee, and said that he did not wish to be considered for reelection to the post. The very senior, highly specialized House member, a long-time supporter of the norms, knew when he had broken one.

Norms are not imposed on a group from outside or by some unrepresentative minority from within; by definition, they are supported by the majority of members. They are seen as good things, valuable to the group and to the individual members. Specialization gives everyone a say on some matter of national policy. Reciprocity makes things easier. And seniority means that people automatically gain influence if they only wait and keep getting reelected. Seen in this light, many of the reform proposals offered from outside Congress or from a minority of members are less than realistic. Abolish the seniority system? Not if it follows from the seniority norm, itself supported by a majority of members. Urge the party leaders to force a bill out of committee? Not without strong overriding cause, against the norm of specialization. Party leaders themselves are products of the norms and owe their leadership to them. Ask the ethics committees to be more active and powerful? Not when, according to the loyalty norm, there is not much for the ethics committees to do.

The Seniority System

The seniority system is a product of the broader seniority norm and, in turn, distributes influence of its own. It is a specific leadership selection device, a way of selecting who will chair the powerful standing committees of Congress. The **seniority system** refers to the practice of ranking committee members by party according to years of consecutive service on the committee (thus designating the chair of the committee). The member of the majority party having the longest consecutive service on the committee automatically becomes chair. If that person leaves the committee, the vacancy is filled by the majority party's next ranking member and so on down the line. New committee members are added only to the bottom of the party lists. If they choose to stay on the committee, they will automatically climb the seniority ladder.

Note that *consecutive* committee service is specified. If someone in line for a chair is defeated or retires (for example, to the vice-presidency) and returns later to Congress and to the same committee, the person is placed at the bottom of the list. The seniority system discourages members from making Congress anything less than a full career. Note also that the rule specifies consecutive *committee* service. Members who stay in Congress but who switch committees would also be placed at the bottom of the new committee ranking. They have gone against the norm of specialization, by changing from one area of expertise to another. Thus the simple provision simultaneously enforces three congressional norms: seniority, specialization, and institutional loyalty. The system, itself a product of the norms, becomes a means of reinforcing them.

EXHIBIT 7.2	DEMOCRATS	REPUBLICANS
Seniority on the Senate Armed Services Committee	Sam Nunn, Ga., Chair	John Warner, Va.
	J. James Exon, Neb.	Strom Thurmond, S.C.
	Carl Levin, Mich.	Gordon Humphrey, N.H.
	Edward Kennedy, Mass.	William Cohen, Maine
	Jeff Bingaman, N.M.	Pete Wilson, Calif.
	Alan Dixon, Ill.	Phil Gramm, Texas
	John Glenn, Ohio	Steve Symms, Idaho
	Albert Gore, Jr., Tenn.	John McCain, Ariz.
	Timothy Wirth, Colo.	
	Richard Shelby, Ala.	

Based on the membership in the 101st Congress (1989–90). Source: *Official Congressional Directory,* 1989 (Washington, D.C.: Government Printing Office, 1989).

An example of a committee list with its seniority rankings is shown in Exhibit 7.2 for the Senate Armed Services Committee. Note that Edward Kennedy has been in the Senate longer than James Exon or Carl Levin, but has been on the committee a shorter time. When Dan Quayle left the Senate for the vice-presidency, his place on the committee (under William Cohen) was taken by Pete Wilson. All the lower-ranked Republicans moved up one notch. With the Democrats, the majority party, Sam Nunn is the chairman. If the Republicans were to regain control, John Warner would become chairman.

The seniority system has long been one of the favorite targets of congressional reformers. Often called the senility rule, it has symbolized for many the lack of vigor and responsiveness of the Congress. It was also said to bias the leadership in favor of members from the safest seats. Liberals in particular thought that it favored southern conservatives from one-party districts. What the critics overlooked, however, was that most of the seats were safe in both the north and the south, and that a majority of the members kept supporting seniority. There have been only a handful of cases in the twentieth century when seniority was not followed in the committee rankings and fewer still when the violation affected the chair of the committee. Most of these involved members switching party or becoming Independents, thus losing their place in both parties' committee lists. In all other cases, for approximately forty committees in each congress, the seniority-ranked lists were ratified by the congressional party membership, voting together in caucus at the beginning of each new congress.

Even since the 1970s, when the Democrats began electing chairmen by secret ballots, the exceptions to the seniority rule have been few. In 1975, as part of the broader reform mood that swept the Congress, three committee chairmen were deposed; and in 1985 another, Melvin Price of Illinois, was defeated. All four were over 70 years of age. But through the same years the

Oliver North testifies in 1987 before a joint congressional committee investigating the Iran-Contra affair.

top-ranked members of all the other committees were being reelected. In short, since 1975, there have been 4 cases violating the seniority rule and about 270 cases when the rule has been followed.

The Committee System

Following the norm of specialization, legislation is distributed among some twenty-two House and seventeen Senate standing committees, each with jurisdiction in a given policy area. Policy formulation flows through the committees; hence, influence in a particular area will be found with the committee members, and especially the senior members and subcommittee chairs. Policy-making is therefore decentralized and broadly distributed among many House and Senate members. If one lives on a farm and one's representative is on the Judiciary Committee, he or she can help little on farm policy (except to vote the right way), but can help a great deal on gun control, abortion, or other issues within the Judiciary Committee's jurisdiction.

It is the **standing committees** that will be examined in this section. They are the power centers in Congress. They stay in existence from one congress to the next, and they alone have power to report legislation to the

EXHIBIT 7.3	HOUSE COMMITTEES	SENATE COMMITTEES
Standing Committees of the 100th Congress (1987–1988)	Agriculture	Aging
	Appropriations	Agriculture and Forestry
	Armed Services	Appropriations
	Banking, Finance, and Urban Affairs	Armed Services
	Budget	Banking, Housing, and Urban Affairs
	District of Columbia	Budget
	Education and Labor	Commerce, Science, and Transportation
	Energy and Commerce	Energy and Natural Resources
	Foreign Affairs	Environment and Public Works
	Government Operations	Finance
	House Administration	Foreign Relations
	Interior and Insular Affairs	Governmental Affairs
	Judiciary	Judiciary
	Merchant Marine and Fisheries	Labor and Human Resources
	Post Office and Civil Service	Rules and Administration
	Public Works and Transportation	Small Business
	Rules	Veterans Affairs
	Science, Space and Technology	
	Small Business	
	Standards of Official Conduct	
	Veterans Affairs	
	Ways and Means	

Source: *Official Congressional Directory,* 1987 (Washington, D.C.: Government Printing Office, 1987).

floor. Congress has other committees: **joint committees**, made up of both House and Senate members; **special committees**, formed to consider special problems or new legislation; and **conference committees**, appointed by the leadership to reconcile differences between House and Senate versions of a bill. One can have only one public law—not a Senate law and a House law—and so conference committees can be enormously influential. Nevertheless, when people say committees, they are usually referring to the standing committees, the "little legislatures" of the Congress. A list of the standing committees of the 100th Congress is seen in Exhibit 7.3.

Committee Power.   To understand committees in Congress, it is first necessary to appreciate their *power*. Committees are an initial and frequently decisive stage in the legislative process. (See Exhibit 7.4.) Upon submission in either house, bills are immediately referred to the relevant committee for study and recommendation. Committees rarely report bills negatively: they report them favorably, or in amended form, or they do not report them at all. Obviously, if bills are not reported from the committee,

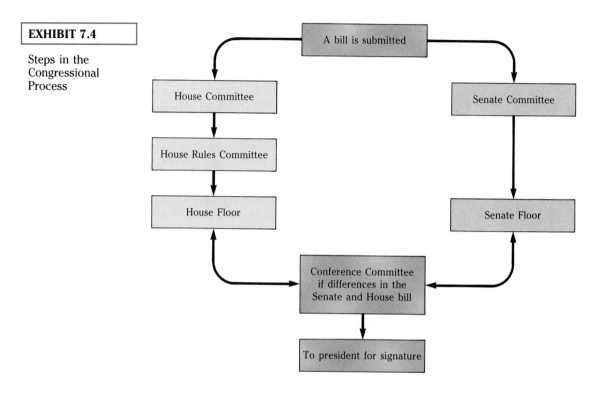

they cannot be voted on and become law. So, committee members do not need to criticize a bill they dislike or go on record as opposing it. Simply by ignoring it in favor of other business, they can bury the bill at the committee stage.

House bills face the additional obstacle of the Rules Committee. The crowded House, with its hundreds of members, unlike the much smaller Senate, requires a "rule" for bills specifying the time that will be allowed for debate and whether or not the bill may be amended. Hence the Rules Committee, which must supply that rule, can block a bill simply by keeping it in committee. The Rules Committee was famous, or infamous, during the 1950s and 1960s for blocking civil rights legislation. The chairman of the committee would be "away," meetings would not be called for weeks on end, and the civil rights bill would never go further. The Rules Committee no longer has the same independent power. It is now considered an arm of the party leadership to be described later in the chapter. So, the committee would no longer block a bill that the leadership wanted, but it still has the power to block other bills by keeping them in committee.

There are, then, three major committee stages at which a bill may be stopped: (1) the House committee, (2) the Senate committee, and (3) the House Rules Committee. Legislation can be killed merely by being stopped in any one of the three committees.

This negative power is well-known and supports the widespread notion of "obstructionist" committees somehow opposing the "will of Congress" as a whole. However, this power should be seen within the context of the norms already described. Members support the norm of specialization when they support a committee's decision, and expect to be supported themselves on their own committees. In other words, the will of Congress is usually the committee's will. Thus, while there are procedures for extricating a bill from committee, *if* a majority strongly oppose the committee's judgment, they are rarely invoked and even more rarely successful.[9] Bills that cannot pass the committee usually cannot pass on the floor.

Famous as committees are for their negative power, they have a positive power as well. A bill may have originated in planning sessions at the White House, but it is the *committee's* bill that is reported and the *committee's* judgment that weighs heavily with the other members of Congress. What this means is that committees can rewrite a bill; they can take out key provisions, create new exceptions, or rewrite the bill entirely. Carter sent an energy bill to Congress, but the gas provisions were rewritten in Ways and Means, the auto provisions in Commerce, and the House voted to pass the committee version, not the White House draft. Reagan wanted a tax reform bill, but the bill that came out of the committees bore little resemblance to the Reagan administration proposal. Members of both the House and Senate committees spent nearly two years on the bill. They consulted with other members of Congress and the leaders of both parties. They had interest group representatives lined up at their office doors. By the time the tax bill emerged from Congress, it had been almost entirely rewritten. Reagan signed the bill in 1986, but it was the Congress's bill he was signing.

The positive power extends further than gleefully gutting or amending an administration bill. Even the expectation of committee hostility can force presidents or others to negotiate with key senior committee members well in advance of the final committee drafting stage. The committee, then, or some influential and representative members, would be helping to formulate a bill that the committee would subsequently approve.

Committee Stability and the Assignment Process.   Committees are *stable.* Given the seniority system and the overall stability of members, there is very little turnover on most committees. Once appointed, a member who wishes to stay cannot be removed. Committee leadership, thanks again to the seniority system, is also stable. One can predict with good odds who will be the next committee chair and even who will be the chair after that. But what of the new members assigned to the bottom of the committee lists? Do they represent points of change, or do they duplicate the existing

---

[9]A detailed account of the various procedures is given in Lewis A. Froman, Jr., *The Congressional Process* (Boston: Little, Brown, 1967). See also Walter J. Oleszek, *Congressional Procedures and the Policy Process*, 3rd ed. (Washington, D.C.: CQ Press, 1988).

membership, holding the same points of view—and even the same constituencies—as the retiring members? To answer these questions, it is necessary to look at the influences on the committee assignment process.

The assignments are made by special committees for each congressional party (House Republicans, House Democrats, Senate Republicans, Senate Democrats) with the influence of the congressional party leadership. New members request assignments, and while they do not always receive what they ask for, the attempt is made to fulfill requests wherever possible.[10] Hence *self selection* is an important influence on the process. Given the norm of specialization, members seeking influence in a particular policy area will try to be assigned to the committee with jurisdiction in that area.

Members might seek Agriculture because of a local interest in peanuts or wheat or Armed Services because of a military base in the district or a belief in the need for a stronger defense. Such self selection means that like-minded members will tend to move toward the same committees, and these committees will tend to exhibit homogeneous points of view, consistent across the membership and across time. So, western members are predominantly on Interior committees, southern members are on the House Agriculture and the District of Columbia committees, and representatives from coastal states are on House Merchant Marine and Fisheries. Armed Services typically attracts conservative defense-oriented members, while the two foreign affairs committees attract liberals interested in international organizations and peaceful ways of conducting foreign policy. The result is a striking difference in the committees charged with military and foreign policy.

Constituency representation is a second influence on the assignment process. Where possible, new members are given assignments that correspond to a constituency interest to help the members win reelection.[11] Assignments often follow a same-state rule, giving a committee seat to a member from the same state as a retiring member. The same-state rule is followed in the Senate as well as in the House. When Armed Services member John Tower of Texas retired, new Texas senator Phil Gramm got the Armed Services assignment.

Assignments are also influenced by the *party leadership*. The House leadership has traditionally taken an interest in assignments to the most prestigious committees and may intervene in other assignments as well. Leaders may need to see that different interests are balanced on some committees and that particular points of view are represented. The committee assignment process need not produce a homogeneous membership, but it tends to produce a consistent one, reproducing over time a membership with the same constituency interests and policy concerns.

---

[10]Full studies of the assignment process are given in Kenneth A. Shepsle, *The Giant Jigsaw Puzzle* (Chicago: University of Chicago Press, 1978) and Steven S. Smith and Christopher J. Deering, *Committees in Congress* (Washington, D.C.: CQ Press, 1984). For a study of Senate assignments, see Charles S. Bullock, III, "U.S. Senate Committee Assignments," *American Journal of Political Science*, 29 (1985), pp. 789–808.

[11]*Ibid.*

Change, of course, occurs through the same assignment process. Members can seek assignments to challenge an existing policy. In the 1970s, "peace" Democrats (who wanted cuts in the defense budget and who had opposed the war in Vietnam) sought assignments to the Armed Services committees. Environmentalists tried to get assigned to the Interior and Public Works committees. The party leaders can facilitate change through their influence, allowing or denying requests or setting new criteria. Some years ago, so the story goes, the House Republican leadership grew concerned about the Foreign Affairs Committee. There were no real Republicans on the committee, it seemed, only atypical liberals who supported foreign aid bills just like Democrats. The subsequent shift to more conservative Republican appointees illustrates the possibilities for change through the assignment process. Nevertheless, any such new members would be outnumbered and outranked by old members. In Congress, change is slow.

One study focused on the ten committees most likely to have undergone change through the decade of the 1970s. Three committees showed some change: Ways and Means, which was brought more in line with the Democratic leadership, and Post Office and Government Operations, two very low-prestige housekeeping committees. Seven committees showed little change: Agriculture, Education and Labor, Commerce, Banking, Armed Services, Budget, and Rules. The results, the authors concluded, showed "the basic stability of congressional committee politics."[12]

The stability of committees—in membership, leadership, and the selection of new members—has profound effects on policy. First, committee power is power for the long haul—not for one but for many congresses. Second, policy-making becomes incremental: today's decision is based on what was done yesterday, and a problem is defined by how it was defined before. Third, policy-making becomes part of a continuing long-term interaction that limits the power of the president. Committee members, bureaucrats, and interest group representatives know that they will continue to make policy in a given subject area long after the president is gone.

The Variety of Committees.   A third fact to appreciate about committees is their *variety*. Committees vary in the subject matter they deal with—its degree of controversy or its relevance to a broad or restricted area of national policy. Committees vary by whether the membership is liberal or conservative, whether it represents like-minded or conflicting points of view, whether it is drawn primarily from one kind of constituency or it is a microcosm of the House or Senate as a whole. At one extreme, the House Agriculture Committee has been primarily composed of members representing farm districts in the South and Midwest, with a token New York City Democrat to represent the "consumer." At the other extreme, the House Education and Labor Committee exhibits diverse and sharply conflicting points of view. Pro-labor Democrats and pro-management Republicans fight

[12]Joseph K. Unekis and Leroy N. Rieselbach, *Congressional Committee Politics* (New York: Praeger, 1984), p. 115. See also Smith and Deering, *op.cit.,* p. 107.

out the labor bills; liberals and conservatives fight on the busing and federal-aid-to-education issues.

Committees also vary in prestige and in the stability and congressional seniority of their members. On the most prestigious committees (for example, Appropriations or Ways and Means), members once assigned tend to stay, while members on the least prestigious committees transfer as soon as possible. Few people see the Post Office or District of Columbia committees as at the heart of their congressional careers. The most prestigious committees, therefore, are the most stable and senior in membership; the least prestigious show the highest turnover rate and the highest proportion of junior members. Committees vary, too, in their importance as sites for resolving controversy. In some committees, conflict is resolved at the committee stage, in others it is channeled to the floor, and in others there is little conflict to be resolved.

Committees can also be classified by the primary goals of their members and their chief environments.[13] Members of Congress differ in their major goals. Some seek primarily to be reelected; others look beyond reelection to the making of good public policy, as they define it; and others seek congressional influence and prestige. This is not to say that all members do not seek reelection, but that some need to seek it more continually, more intensely, and with higher priority than others. The seven-term House incumbent, winning by margins close to seventy percent of the vote, probably does not lie awake nights worrying about term number eight. Committees attract members with these varying goals, depending on the committee's subject matter, its prestige in the institution, and the various clienteles it serves. Hence some committees (Interior, Post Office) attract reelection-oriented members; others (Foreign Affairs, Education) attract policy-oriented members; and still others (Ways and Means, Appropriations) attract those seeking institutional prestige. Students of Congress thus speak of *reelection, policy,* and *prestige* committees, distinct from each other in membership, strategy, and the kind of decisions made.

Committees also vary, independently of their members' goals, by the environment within which their business is conducted. These environments include: (1) the House or Senate; (2) the executive; (3) the parties; and (4) clientele groups (the interest groups directly affected by a committee's decisions). Some committees work closely with the White House, some look to the House or Senate leadership, and some work with interest groups or parties. For example, Foreign Affairs and Education would both be classified as policy committees, but Foreign Affairs works primarily in an executive envi-

---

[13]Richard F. Fenno, *Congressmen in Committees* (Boston: Little, Brown, 1973). Subsequent studies of member goals suggest the Fenno scheme can be used to classify committees. See Charles S. Bullock, III, "Motivations for U.S. Congressional Committee Preferences," *Legislative Studies Quarterly,* 1 (1976), 201–12, and Smith and Deering, *op.cit.,* p. 85.

ronment consulting with the president and members of the Department of State, while Education works largely in a party environment. The two committees will be similar to each other in some ways, but different in other respects because of the different political environments they work in.

This variety challenges many of the popular stereotypes about committees. Are committees little "baronies," as some writers have called them, closed-power centers against which neither presidents nor party leaders can prevail? They aren't if their major environments are the executive or the parties. Are committees enclaves of special interests, blinded to matters larger than their own district lines and following their own parochial points of view? This description fits some reelection committees that work with clientele groups, but it does not fit committees with other goals and other environments. If committees are at the heart of the congressional process, they are at the heart of the complexity and diversity of this process as well.

Subcommittees.   Specialization can be carried beyond the full committee to the subcommittee stage. Indeed, subcommittees have become a major fact of legislative life in the contemporary Congress. Some committees, such as House Agriculture and House Appropriations, have long relied on subcommittees for the bulk of their legislative work. Since the mid 1970s, however, subcommittees have sprouted in other committees, "like mushrooms," according to one observer, on Capitol Hill.

A subcommittee, as its name implies, is a division of the full committee. Its members are drawn from the committee and the ratio of Democratic and Republican members usually reflects that of the parent committee. The full committee determines who will serve on the various subcommittees. So, with the committee workload divided among its various subcommittees, influence over a particular subject matter will often reside with the subcommittee members.

House committees now routinely refer legislation to subcommittees where most of the work, of studying and rewriting the bill, is done. Whereas Armed Services referred approximately twelve percent of its legislation to subcommittee at the beginning of the 1970s, it now refers ninety-nine percent. Banking, Public Works, and Science show a similar increase. Three committees—Ways and Means, Foreign Affairs, and House Administration—depart somewhat from the typical House practice. While they refer the bulk of their legislation to the subcommittees, they reserve some of the most important for the full committee. Ways and Means, for example, has jurisdiction over tax, trade, health, and welfare policy. Ways and Means holds the tax bills for the full committee, and sends the other issues to the subcommittees.

In the Senate, by contrast, no consistent pattern is apparent. Some committees have increased the activity of their subcommittees, some have decreased it, and three committees—Budget, Rules, and Veterans Affairs—do not use subcommittees at all.[14] Senators have so many more committee and subcommittee assignments than representatives do that there may be less demand to create additional avenues of influence.

Specialization helps Congress represent its constituents. This effect seen for committees can be seen for subcommittees too. The same effect can be seen in subcommittees. The House Agriculture Committee, for example, divides its subcommittees by crop, with members who "represent" the various commodities assigned wherever possible to the relevant subcommittee. The following list shows the subcommittee jurisdiction along with the state of the subcommittee chair in a recent congress. You might cover the right-hand column and see if you can guess the state, or at least come close geographically. The more correct answers you get, the better you understand constituency representation in Congress.

Subcommittee Jurisdiction	State of Subcommittee Chair
Cotton, Rice, and Sugar	Mississippi
Tobacco and Peanuts	North Carolina
Forests and Energy	Oregon
Livestock, Dairy, and Poultry	Iowa
Rural Development	Tennessee
Foreign Agriculture and Research	California
Wheat, Soybeans, and Feed Grains	Washington
Consumer Relations	New York

This kind of representation does not occur on all subcommittees. Nevertheless, the fact that it does exist is worth attention.

The norm of seniority, too, can be seen at work at the subcommittee level, although less dramatically than in the selection of the full committee chairs. The members of the majority party in the House and Senate chair all the subcommittees; hence nearly half of the House Democrats and almost all of the majority party Senators are eligible for a subcommittee post. Given the number of prizes awarded, no selection system needs to be very visible or very exclusive. Before 1973, House subcommittee chairs were appointed by the full committee chair; since that time, they have been elected by the Democratic committee members. Nevertheless, both selection systems have produced the same result: the subcommittee chairs are given to the most senior members of the committee. In other words, if there are seven subcommittees, their chairs will tend to be the seven most senior members of the full committee. Few senior members are skipped over for more junior colleagues and left with no subcommittee chair. These skips can be called violations of the seniority norm. Under the old appointive system, such skips occurred only slightly more than ten percent of the time,

[14]Smith and Deering, *op. cit.,* pp. 134–135; see also pp. 149–152.

most of them occurring on the House Appropriations Committee. Under the new elective system, skips occur slightly less than ten percent of the time, with most of them still found in Appropriations.[15]

It is impossible to know, of course, if the members wanted the particular chair they received. They may have received it as a consolation prize after losing another chair to a less senior member. Members may not receive the chair that they want, but they will receive some chair, in both the old and the new selection systems.

Party Leadership

Thus far the focus has been on decentralization. The seniority and committee systems distribute influence widely across the Congress. All members hold some influence and can look forward to achieving more. Another structure, however, provides a degree of centralization, the *political party leadership*. In fact, parties supply the only real leadership that exists in Congress.

The House at the beginning of each new Congress elects a Speaker, with both parties nominating a candidate for that post. Since representatives almost always vote for their own party's nominee, the majority party's candidate wins the elections. Thus the **Speaker of the House** is actually the elected leader of the majority party in the House. The formal titles are deceptive in the Senate as well. Formally, the vice-president is the Senate's chief presiding officer, with a President Pro Tempore serving in the absence of the vice-president. Since early in the nineteenth century, however, the Senate made clear that vice-presidents need not inconvenience themselves by coming to Capitol Hill; the Senate could take care of its own presiding. The President Pro Tempore is simply an honorary position given to the most senior majority party member. The **majority** and **minority party leader,** in the Senate, elected by their own party members, become the actual leaders of the chamber.

There are, then, nine chief party leaders that see to the running of business in the Senate and House:

House Party Leaders	*Senate Party Leaders*
Speaker	Majority Leader
Majority Leader	Majority Whip
Chief Whip	Minority Leader
Minority Leader	Minority Whip
Chief Whip	

[15]The results for the congresses before 1973 are reported in Thomas Wolanin, "Committee Seniority and the Choice of House Subcommittee Chairmen," *Journal of Politics,* 36 (1974), pp. 687–702. For the results since 1973, see Hinckley, *Stability and Change in Congress*, 4th ed., pp. 167–169.

The **House Minority Leader** is the elected leader of the minority party and the losing candidate for Speaker. The **House Majority Leader** works with the Speaker, primarily in the role of chief lieutenant, as do the **whip organizations**. In both Senate and House, these organizations are charged with gathering information on members' positions on a vote of concern to the party and attempting to persuade them to the party's position. They must also see that the supporters of a bill are in the chamber for the vote. The title is derived from the British parliament, and was originally a fox-hunting term: the "whipper-in" was the person responsible for keeping the hounds from leaving the pack.

Leaders face a conflicting responsibility. On the one hand, they must see that the business of Congress runs smoothly, that legislation is scheduled, and that disruptive conflicts are avoided. On the other hand, they head one of the two opposing parties in Congress and need to fight for their own party's success. In addition, a leader of the president's party must balance working for White House programs while working for the interests and within the norms of Congress. Some party leaders have worked more closely with presidents than others, but all find their dual role a difficult one. Finally, the leaders must mediate between conflicting factions and points of view within their own party in Congress. Needless to say, in the face of all this balancing, leaders must be able to compromise and to call on considerable political skill.

The Powers and Limits of Leaders.

While the powers of leaders are by no means vast, they are sufficient to make them chiefs among equals in an otherwise decentralized assembly. Leaders control the scheduling of legislation and the course of debate. In cases of doubt, they can influence what committee might receive a bill and they rule on parliamentary procedure. They know what bill is coming when, who wants to speak on what, and what has to come after. Leaders can influence committee assignments and they can select the members of a conference committee. They can deploy and use the information of their extensive whip organizations. In all of these ways leaders find themselves at the center of the network of information in the House or Senate. This can become a substantial power in the hands of a skilled practitioner. The leaders are the generalists in an otherwise specialized political structure and the one point where 435 House members and 100 Senate members can be mobilized for a majority vote.

The leadership is limited, however, by the other structures of influence. Leaders are responsible for scheduling legislation, but any standing committee can change that schedule by keeping a bill from the floor. They can influence committee assignments only within the limits of the seniority system. They can bargain and persuade, but no one expects a member to vote against a clear constituency concern. They can formulate programs, but elections limit what programs will be proposed and what their success will be. Twenty more Democrats elected or defeated can make the difference in a welfare bill or a White House foreign aid request. A minority party proposes less, bargains differently, and wins less than a majority party. Leaders are

Majority Leader Lyndon Johnson uses his powers of persuasion on fellow Democratic Senator Theodore Francis Green.

limited by the election returns. They are also limited, finally, by the membership of the congressional party that elects them and that often disagrees about what being a Democrat or a Republican means. Leaders must reconcile serious splits within their party, keep in touch with various factions and with both senior and junior members, and support congressional norms. A good leader, in Congress and elsewhere, follows the norms of the group.

It is obvious why Republican leader Robert Dole called himself the "Majority Pleader." Congress is decentralized and will seek to remain so, because the members are ultimately responsible to the voters in 50 states and 435 congressional districts. Factions will differ within the parties, the two parties within each chamber, and the two chambers with each other and with the White House. Party leaders must work within these differences as best they can.

The Selection of Leaders.

Leaders are elected every two years, at the beginning of each new Congress. Yet while formally elective, the selection bears all the marks of a much more automatic procedure. Leaders stay in their posts for a number of congresses. New leaders are recruited from lesser leadership posts. Whip leads to majority leader and majority leader leads to Speaker. Exhibit 7.5 lists occupants of the top House and Senate leadership posts for three decades. Theoretically, each new Congress could bring an entirely new array of leaders. But instead, as the table shows, few changes take place for years at a time and a pattern of predictable advancement occurs as subordinate leaders move up to fill higher vacancies. It is, in fact, a kind of miniature seniority system in its stability and predictable route to power.

EXHIBIT 7.5	The Stability of Party Leaders, 1963–1989

Position in hierarchy	88th (1963–64)	89th (1965–66)	90th (1967–68)	91st (1969–70)	92nd (1971–72)	93rd (1973–74)	94th (1975–76)	95th (1977–78)	96th (1979–80)	97th (1981–82)	98th (1983–84)	99th (1985–86)	100th (1987–88)	101st (1989–90)
House Democratic Leaders														
1	McCormack	M	M	M	A	A	A	O	O	O	O	O	W	W; F*
2	Albert	A	A	A	B	O	O	Wright	W	W	W	W	F	F; Gephardt
3	Boggs	B	B	B	O'Neill	McFall	M	Brademus	B	Foley	F	F	Coelho	C; Gray
House Republican Leaders														
1	Halleck	Ford	F	F	F	F; Rhodes	R	R	R	M	M	M	M	M
2	Arends	A	A	A	A	A	Michel	M	M	Lott	L	L	L	Gingrich
Senate Democratic Leaders														
1	Mansfield	M	M	M	M	M	M	B	B	B	B	B	B	Mitchell
2	Humphrey	Long	L	Kennedy	Byrd	B	B	Cranston	C	C	C	C	C	C
Senate Republican Leaders														
1	Dirksen	D	D	Scott	S	S	S	Baker	B	B	B	Dole	D	D
2	Kuchel	K	K	Griffin	G	G	G	Stevens	S	S	S	Simpson	S	S

NOTE: An initial indicates the same person continues in a leadership post or is promoted to a higher post. With the exception of the first Congress listed, a last name indicates a new person elected to a leadership post. In the 101st Congress, Byrd resigned from the post and House Whip Lott was elected to the Senate.

*Wright resigned as Speaker in 1989 following an ethics investigation. Majority Leader Foley was elected as Speaker.

There are, of course, the exceptional cases when leaders are overturned. These usually involve a complex set of circumstances that have weakened their base in the congressional party. There may have been a severe defeat for the party in the previous election, creating a kind of psychological climate which can encourage revolt; or a loss of senior supporters through retirement or defeat or the addition of many junior members; or a growing sense that the leader has lost touch with an important segment of the party; or personal circumstances that weaken the incumbent leader in the eyes of the congressional party members.[16] Edward Kennedy's defeat as whip in 1971 followed the Chappaquidick scandal. House Democratic whip John McFall ran last in a field of four for majority leader in 1977 following his alleged involvement in a South Korean lobbying scandal. Both men broke the norm of institutional loyalty as described earlier. In addition, Speaker James Wright resigned his position in 1989 after an ethics committee investigation into his finances. While no other speakers have lost their leadership positions, some minority leaders have. Joe Martin was defeated by Charles Halleck in 1959, and Halleck in turn was defeated by Gerald Ford in 1965. Two Senate whips have been defeated in their bid to be the top GOP leader. Howard Baker defeated Robert Griffin in 1977, and Robert Dole defeated Ted Stevens in 1985.

These cases, however, remain very much the exception. There may be challenges and widely publicized threats of challenge, but in most cases when the dust clears and the votes are taken, the "insiders" are still in. The selection of leaders, then, is not a choice to be made with each new Congress. Party leaders, like the committee leaders and the members themselves, enjoy considerable job security.

Many people think of party leaders and committee leaders as natural enemies, fighting for influence in Congress from very different points of view. It has even been suggested that party leaders should appoint the committee leaders, thus eliminating the seniority rule. But a comparison of these two groups of leaders shows many characteristics in common. House party leaders from 1903 through 1974 had spent 20 years in Congress, on the average, before attaining their leadership post. They were as old as the committee leaders—almost 60 years of age—and had spent the same number of years in a leadership post.[17] So why would party leaders vote to keep the seniority system? Because *the same norm of seniority supports them*. The two groups of leaders may disagree about bills facing Congress, but there remains a strong basis for reciprocal support.

In 1985, Melvin Price was challenged and subsequently defeated for the chair of the House Armed Services Committee by fourth-ranked member Les Aspin. The issue was age and competence. The eighty-year old Price was no longer able to follow the business of the committee, much less lead it, and yet Speaker Tip O'Neill gave a passionate speech in defense of Price.

[16]See Robert L. Peabody, *Leadership in Congress* (Boston: Little, Brown, 1976). See also Garrison Nelson, "Partisan Patterns of House Leadership Change," *American Political Science Review,* 71 (1977), pp. 918–39.

[17]For these comparisons, see Peabody, *op.cit.,* pp. 32–37 and Hinckley, *op.cit.,* p. 195.

The same limits on conflict exist between leaders of the opposing parties. Major differences divide the parties, and much of the congressional agenda is devoted to them. A leader's reputation and support from the members depend in part on what is won and lost when the parties are opposed. And yet if half of a leader's business is partisan, the other half requires constant bipartisan consultation—the running, managing, and compromising of congressional business. The normal pattern is for majority party leaders to consult with the minority on scheduling, debate, committee ratios, and other procedures. Some opposing party leaders—Sam Rayburn and Joe Martin, Jerry Ford and Tip O'Neill—have been the closest of friends. "Conflict," observes Richard Fenno, "is the very life blood of a decision-making body in a free society. Yet it is amazing how much of the time and energy of . . . members is devoted to the business of avoiding conflict."[18]

Conflict does break out, of course. In 1985, Republicans angrily protested the lopsided party ratios on committees. They threatened to boycott the committee process if the ratios were not adjusted more in line with the newly elected membership in the House. Also in 1985, House Republicans staged a demonstration and marched out of the House chamber to protest the seating of a Democrat in a very closely contested election. The issue had already taken forty-five hours of floor debate—more than twice the amount of time being spent debating the MX missile. Republicans had kept the House in session all night on one occasion and had blocked legislative business for a full day. When the final vote was taken and the Democrats won as expected, the Republicans, led by Minority Leader Bob Michel, walked out the center aisle and down the east steps of the Capitol to the waiting television cameras.[19] Still, the party ratios were adjusted and Michel kept the respect of the Democratic leadership. The business of the Congress went on.

POLICY-MAKING IN CONGRESS

At this point, it is apparent how the membership and organization of Congress affect the kind of policy that is made. Action is taken in committee, on the floor, and at the oversight stage.

Committee Decisions

Much of the power of committees to affect policy has already been described. Committees can block legislation, with or without the support of party leaders, and keep it from debate and passage. Committees can change legislation, adding or subtracting key provisions, to the extent that it may be totally transformed. Committee members' opinions influence other

[18]Richard F. Fenno, "The Internal Distribution of Influence: The House," in *The Congress and America's Future*, 2nd ed., ed. David B. Truman (Englewood Cliffs, N.J.: Prentice-Hall, 1973), p. 89.
[19]*Congressional Quarterly Weekly Report,* May 4, 1985, p. 821.

members through the norm of specialization. Committee interest shapes the kind of oversight given to programs and so affects how they are implemented. Since other people in Congress and the executive branch know that committees have these powers, committees are consulted before policy is formulated. In short, committees affect policy both positively and negatively, and at points before, during, and after their own decision-making stage. The headlines tell us when a president proposes or signs new legislation. But before, during, and after the headline-making event, with little or no visibility, the congressional committees are at work.

Some committees do more than affect policy—they are the chief policy-makers. Think about those reelection committees working mainly with clientele groups (interest groups). Few people may know or care about the policies made in these committees: potato subsidies, a local contract, a flood control project for Elk Creek Lake. But the interest groups care, and the committee members care. They are allocating federal benefits to their constituents; they are "representing" them.

These are called **pork barrel policies,** a term and a practice that dates from the nineteenth century. The federal treasury is the barrel that members dip into for "pork"—the projects and spending for their own states and districts. So, the House Agriculture Committee, divided into crops, makes agriculture policy to a large extent, and the Congress supports the committee decisions. Jimmy Carter proposed eliminating thirty-two water projects from the federal budget. When the final budget reached his desk for signing, only nine had been eliminated. Ronald Reagan tried to eliminate Urban Development grants. The grants continued. He vetoed a mass transit bill including 120 special "demonstration" projects. The veto was overridden by Congress.

When people call the president the Chief Legislator, they do not cite these examples. In pork barrel politics, the committee is the chief legislator, supported by the other members of Congress. The members are following the norms of specialization and reciprocity. They are helping the committee members be reelected as they expect to be helped in turn. There is a conflict, of course, between a national interest and a multitude of local interests. The members of Congress are expected to make national policy *and* to be good representatives. With the calls for budget-cutting in recent years, more voices have been heard, even within Congress, for an end to pork barrel politics. But unless the voters say that good representatives should not allocate, the pork barrel is here to stay.

Floor Decisions

Committees report bills to the floor, that is, to the full body of the House or Senate assembled to consider legislation. Formally, the floor is used for debate and decision, the decision being made by a vote of the members. But informally, the floor also serves as a communication center for matters not necessarily related to the subject under debate. People "work the floor"—

that is, they rally support for positions through conversations with other members. There is much talking and moving around while a speech is being given, even in the fairly well-attended sessions. Attendance generally is very low, as it is in many other legislatures.[20] The chamber fills only when the roll call bells ring and members rush in to vote on the measures that have been debated.

What are the purposes of debate if no one is there to hear the arguments? Debate establishes a record for the legislation that is important in several ways. First, debate shows the congressional positions, pro or con, on an issue. Typical speakers are the sponsors and key committee members and the party leaders. People can then see in the record of debate what issues are being raised and who is aligned on each side. Second, debate provides a record of legislative intent that is important for later implementation or court decisions. The record will show what its supporters intended the bill to do. Finally, debate allows members to build a record with constituents or important interest groups. The speakers may be on the losing side of an issue, but they show they have fought the good fight for the people who are watching.

Bills do not flow automatically to the floor after a committee recommendation. For floor debate to occur, a bill must receive some positive action by either the leadership or a majority of members, or both. The House procedure is more structured and rule-bound than in the smaller and more informal Senate. For all major legislation, the House must first adopt the Rules Committee's recommendation of a rule for debate, including the time allotted and the number and scope of amendments. One of the longest times allotted for debate—ten hours—was given to the Civil Rights Act of 1964. The proposed Nixon impeachment debate was scheduled for twenty hours.[21] An *open rule* permits any number of amendments to any provision in the bill, a *closed rule* prohibits any amendments at all, and a *modified closed rule* specifies which particular provisions may be amended. Typically, a five-minute rule is in effect for debate; that is, each representative can speak no more than five minutes on an amendment. The Rules Committee recommendation is itself debatable for one hour, and the recommendation is then adopted or defeated by a majority vote. Although there are some exceptions that exist, the adoption of the rule is ordinarily a noncontroversial matter.

The Senate, in contrast, imposes no time limit for debate. Senators speak as long as they wish, yield the floor to other senators, and can resume speaking when the floor is given back to them. There is no five-minute rule in the Senate. Amendments can be considered and debated at any time and, unlike in the House, they need not be germane to the legislation in question. How then does the Senate ever get things done? In actual practice, the leaders of both parties consult with each other and agree on a tentative sched-

---

[20]David M. Olson, *The Legislative Process: A Comparative Approach* (New York: Harper and Row, 1980), pp. 392–393.

[21]*Ibid.*, p. 356.

ule which they announce to the chamber. What seems like a desultory debate is actually orchestrated and arranged by the floor leaders in each party. A widely used device to streamline the proceedings is the **unanimous-consent procedure**, a vote to bypass the rules if everyone in the chamber agrees. Under this procedure, debate can be limited or stopped by unanimous consent for the bill as a whole or for an amendment or group of amendments. As the term suggests, if one senator objects to a unanimous-consent agreement, the motion fails and debate continues. Nevertheless, most of the time debate proceeds under the guiding hand of the leadership and the senators' own sense of the importance of the accommodation. The Senate conducts much of its business by unanimous consent.

The Senate's rule of unlimited debate can result in a **filibuster**—the deliberate holding of the floor by a minority of senators to demonstrate opposition to a particular bill. Filibusters can be conducted by one senator or by many, all yielding the floor to one another and talking on any subject they wish. One senator included recipes for southern-style cooking and another talked about his fishing trips and his children. The record-holder for an individual filibuster is J. Strom Thurmond on a civil rights bill in 1957—24 hours and 18 minutes. Wayne Morse is the runner-up, speaking on an offshore oil bill in 1953 for 22 hours and 26 minutes. A filibuster can occur on the motion to consider a bill, as well as on the vote itself or on any amendment to it.

Filibusters became famous in the years following World War II when southern senators used them to block civil rights legislation. However, they had been used earlier in the century by outnumbered progressives and were rediscovered by liberals in the 1970s. Filibusters were waged against an antibusing bill, the supersonic transport (SST), the military draft, and a government loan to Lockheed Aircraft. In the 98th Congress (1983–84) filibusters were so common—used by liberals and conservatives, Republicans and Democrats, groups and individuals—that it seemed that the Senate would not complete its business for the term. The filibuster, in other words, is a weapon of any minority in the Senate to force the majority to consider its very strong feelings on an issue. Even the threat of a filibuster is often enough to gain concessions in the proposed legislation.

A filibuster can be stopped by the invocation of **cloture**, a resolution bringing an end to debate on a measure. Officially designated Senate Rule 22, the cloture rule has been modified several times since its adoption in 1917. Under the current rule passed in 1975, it takes *three-fifths of the full Senate membership*, or 60 Senators, to invoke cloture. This rule eases the cloture requirement from the previous rules, and makes filibusters easier to stop. Before 1975, a cloture attempt succeeded less than one time in four. Since 1975 it has succeeded about one time in two.[22] The rule change les-

---

[22]Before 1975, Rule 22 specified two-thirds present and voting to achieve cloture. Under this rule, 23 percent of the cloture attempts from 1960 to 1974 were successful. After the 1975 rule change, 47 percent of the cloture attempts from 1975 to 1980 were successful. See *Congressional Quarterly Almanac*, 1980 (Washington, D.C.: Congressional Quarterly, 1980), p. 14.

sens the potency of the filibuster threat, although members may be tempted to use the weapon more now that it is less devastating to Senate business.

Once debate is concluded, Congress is ready to vote. Most bills require a majority of members voting in favor of passage for the amendments and the bill as a whole. (Treaties, constitutional amendments, and votes to override a presidential veto, as described in Chapter Eight, require two-thirds majorities in both houses.) The important votes in Congress are taken by **roll call**; that is, when their name is called the members announce their position, either aye or nay. Electronic voting now allows the members to vote, if they wish, without leaving their offices. A defeat on the floor of either the Senate or the House kills the bill for the rest of the congress. The amendments decided here can change the bill entirely or weaken it beyond recognition. Individual members, too, are making a record for themselves by the positions they take. Thus the roll call stage is a critically important part of the congressional process.

Nevertheless, a roll call vote is only one stage in this process. Much has happened before it—in committee and in the meetings of party leaders—and much is still to come. If the Senate and House versions of the bill are different, a conference committee must be called. The conference committee, consisting of members from both Senate and House, is appointed by the party leaders. Members are drawn heavily from the two committees first reporting the bill. Conference committee members must compromise among themselves and find a version that the two chambers will be able to accept. Moreover, many of these decisions are being taken simultaneously. Committees look ahead to the roll call voting stage. The party leaders send their whips around to count the number of expected votes. Both the Senate and House are watching the progress of the bill in the other chamber. The decisions taken in committees and the cloakrooms can affect the roll call vote, and the expected vote tally can affect these decisions.

Influences on Roll Call Votes

Since most controversial and important votes are taken by roll call, students of Congress have long paid attention to roll call votes to determine the major influences on this part of the policy-making process.

Party.   One major influence on roll call votes is the influence of party. Since Republicans and Democrats vote differently on a wide range of legislation, simply knowing the party of the House or Senate member can, in most cases, supply a major predictor of the vote. For example, Democrats tend to vote on the liberal side of issues, and Republicans vote on the conservative side. This effect of party is shown in Exhibit 7.6 for the House and the 98th Congress. It also operates in the Senate and in other congresses. So, merely by electing Democrats rather than Republicans to Congress (or vice versa), people are affecting the number of votes that will be cast aye or nay when the roll is called.

EXHIBIT 7.6

Party Differences on
Roll Call Votes

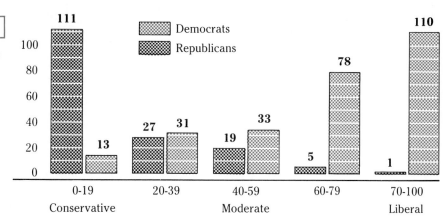

Ideological Voting Scores

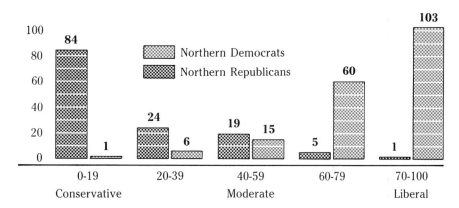

Ideological Voting Scores

Based on 1984 Americans for Democratic Action (ADA) scores for members of the House in the 98th Congress. ADA is a liberal group which rates members on the percentage of times they vote "correctly" on a wide range of liberal-conservative issues.

Party also influences particular issues. Congressional Republicans and Democrats have taken consistently opposing stands on a number of major issues in recent American history. Social welfare issues, such as education, housing, medical care, and poverty, found Democrats consistently favoring the program and Republicans opposing it. Fiscal policy, labor legislation, farm supports, and other issues involving the federal government's role also split the parties. Most of the controversial votes on war and defense in the late 1960s and early 1970s showed roughly two-thirds of the Republicans and two-thirds of the Democrats opposing each other, the Democrats voting against the war and for cuts in defense spending. The Panama Canal treaty, the extension of the ERA, aid to the anti-government forces in Nicaragua also were party votes. Do elections make a difference, then, in shaping the outcomes of congressional action? Merely by determining the number of Democrats or Republicans elected, they affect which programs can be considered and what the outcomes would be. Facing Democratic congresses, Democratic presidents can propose more and win more than Republican presidents can. Change the number of Democrats and there will be a different number of votes on one side rather than the other.

Both the importance and the limits of partisanship are apparent by looking at the members' voting on these party roll calls. Members vote with their own party between 70 and 80 percent of the time. These rates hold for both Republicans and Democrats in the Senate and House. In approximately three-fourths of the cases when the parties were opposed, individual members voted with their own party; in one-fourth of the cases, they voted against their party.

Party can be thought of as a kind of summary constituency measure—of the predominant "Republicanism" or "Democraticness" of the state or district. So it is not surprising that other influences on roll calls should also be the kind of constituency characteristics important to large numbers of House and Senate members.

Region.   One influence, nearly as important as party, is the region of the country that a member hails from. Region represents a constituency characteristic independent of party lines and is a second major predictor of the vote. Roll call studies show southern Democrats and eastern Republicans, who represent districts atypical of their national parties, often vote as frequently with the opposing party as with their own. These members are not saying, "Oh, I'm going to vote with my region on this." They are voting with their constituencies, which happen to be like other constituencies in the same region and unlike those in other regions.[23]

The famous **Conservative Coalition** in Congress is one such example of a regional influence. The Conservative Coalition is based on a regional bloc (the southern Democrats) crossing party lines and joining with Republicans to make congressional policy. The coalition originated in the 1930s in reaction to the New Deal. Traditionally, it has opposed increases in government spending and expansion of federal government activity. It opposed some social welfare legislation. In the 1960s and 1970s, the coalition expanded its area of activity, forming on defense votes, economic policy, farm policy, and even some public works bills—once the hard core of Democratic party legislation. In the 1980s, the Democratic leadership began to work out concessions that would bring the southerners back to the party fold.

---

[23]Most studies of roll call voting in Congress cite the importance of party and region. Standard studies include Clausen, *op.cit.,* and Barbara Sinclair, "Political Upheaval and Congressional Voting," *Journal of Politics,* 38 (1976), pp. 326–45. See also Aage R. Clausen and Carl Van Horn, "The Congressional Response to a Decade of Change," *Journal of Politics,* 39 (1977), pp. 624–66.

The southern Democrats are the pivotal member of the two potential coalitions. Depending on their negotiations with the leadership of both parties, conservative coalitions or party coalitions will form.

For all its importance, the Conservative Coalition is merely one example of a regional influence in Congress. What has occurred in the past in the South could occur elsewhere. Constituency influence, as reflected in a particular region, can produce voting across party lines.

Other Major Influences.   Other important constituency factors are also major influences on the vote. Urbanism, the influence of the state delegation, and the socioeconomic makeup of a district have been found to be important. It can be shown that taking merely five of these constituency measures—party, region, state, urbanism, and the percentage of blue collar workers in the district—can explain much of the variation in roll call voting on major issues.[24] In short, many decisions made at the roll call stage are responses to pervasive, long-standing constituency cues.

Cue Taking.   But what happens when there is little or no constituency interest, when the parties are not clearly opposed on the issue, and members have no positions of their own? Cue-taking studies, based on interviews with House members, report that representatives take voting cues from those whom they consider expert or knowledgeable in the area and especially from those they like, trust, and see as having views generally similar to their own. In one study, eighty-six percent of the respondents mentioned committee members as cue givers. Most frequent mention was made of chairmen and ranking minority members; the next most frequently mentioned were the other committee members. Other cue givers included the party leaders, members of the state delegation, and the president.[25] Notice how these responses correspond with the major influences already described. People who are "trusted" and seen as having generally "similar views" tend to be from the same party and the same kind of constituency. The cue-taking studies are merely another way of looking at these influences on congressional decisions. Notice also the importance of the committee members. Following specialization and seniority, those "expert" and "knowledgeable" in the area are the members of the committees dealing with the legislation, and particularly the senior members.

Predicting Roll Call Votes.   These influences together explain much of the variation in roll call voting. They hold over time and across a wide range of issues. In other words, the votes of individual members of Congress can be predicted merely by knowing their party and a few key charac-

[24]See Clausen, *op.cit.*

[25]John W. Kingdon, *Congressmen's Voting Decisions,* 2nd ed. (New York: Harper and Row, 1981) and Donald R. Matthews and James A. Stimson, *Yeas and Nays: Normal Decision-Making in the U.S. House of Representatives* (New York: Wiley, 1975), pp. 84–89.

teristics of their constituencies. To demonstrate, party and region can be used to "predict" two very visible votes of the recent past.

Take, for example, the voting on the Equal Rights Amendment in the fall of 1978. One key vote decided whether states that had already ratified the constitutional amendment would be allowed to rescind ratification (rescind, meaning take back, "deratify") during the remaining time that ERA had to be adopted. It was generally understood that allowing states to rescind would effectively kill any chance for final ratification of the amendment. Thus a yes vote would be a vote against the ERA; a no vote would be a vote for the ERA. The key Senate vote on the question was decided 44 (yes) to 54 (no) giving a temporary victory to the ERA supporters. A majority of all Democrats voted no (20–41), and a majority of Republicans voted yes (24–13). Southern Democrats, however, sided with the Republicans against ERA (15–4); and northeastern Republicans sided with the Democrats (2–8). If the vote had been predicted using only those two influences, and knowing nothing else about the issue, the predictions would have been right in 82 cases and wrong in 16.

For a second example, take the 1986 Reagan administration request for $100 million in military aid to the Nicaraguan contra rebels. The president pushed hard for the proposal; he even gave a major address to the nation on the eve of the House vote. The Democratic leadership in both the House and Senate opposed the request, and the Republican leadership supported it. The Democratic-controlled House defeated the president's proposal by a vote of 210 to 222. Of the 46 Democrats voting for the proposal, 39 were from the South. Only 16 Republicans voted with the Democrats and against the president; 11 were from the northeast. Using party and region, the predictions would have been right in 420 cases and wrong in 12.

The Republican Senate supported the proposal 53 to 47. Of the 11 Democrats voting with the Republicans, 9 were from the South. Of the 11 Republicans voting against the proposal, 6 were from the Northeast. Altogether, 7 of the 100 votes cast did not follow party and regional alignments. The predictions would have been wrong in these seven cases and right in the other 93.

There were exceptions, with some members voting against the predicted party and regional lines. Lobbying activity was intense on both issues, and only a few votes either way were needed to decide the outcome. Nevertheless, the importance of party and region can be seen. Whether Democrats or Republicans were elected to Congress and how voters in a particular region were seen to react helped decide the outcome.

Roll calls of the future can be given the same analysis. News reports will tell of the few undecided votes and the lobbying that is going on. But readers of this chapter should be able to predict the outcome with a good degree of accuracy, looking at the kind of constituencies the members represent.

Oversight Decisions

Once a law is passed, congressional policy-making does not cease. Besides legislating, Congress engages in **oversight**; that is, it supervises how executive agencies implement the laws it has passed and the programs it has funded. Constitutionally, the executive and legislature are independent branches that overlap in power. The president, as chief executive, is charged with seeing "that the laws are faithfully executed." But Congress, in passing legislation and supplying executive funding, shares this responsibility. And unlike the president, Congress is independent of the branch that it oversees. Its members are independently elected, independently assigned to committees, and protected by the seniority system from influences that might remove them from committees. Members of Congress, then, can investigate agencies, the White House, and the Army, protected as they are by this broader congressional support.

In the words of James Madison, writing in *The Federalist Papers, #51,*

> But the great security against a gradual concentration of the several powers in the same department consists in giving to those who administer each department the necessary constitutional means and personal motives to resist encroachment of the other.... You must first enable the government to control the governed; and in the next place oblige it to control itself.

Congressional oversight is one way to check executive encroachment, one way to make the government "control itself." If one feels that officials should be accountable to elected representatives, then the independence of Congress and its ability to conduct oversight should be of major concern.

Oversight may take many different forms, from a full-scale televised investigation to a routine committee hearing and report. It may be carried on merely by the threat of either of the above; agencies avoid the risk of harassment by staying close to the legislative intent. Oversight may also take the form of a kind of general watchfulness on the part of key members of a committee, or it may be carried on by the appropriations subcommittees as part of their annual review of budget requests. The major site of policy-making at this stage, then—after proposal, hearings, passage, and implementation—shifts back to the congressional committees.

There have been repeated urgings, from within Congress and without, for increased oversight activity. Long a major item on the congressional reform agenda, oversight was targeted by the reforms of the 1970s in both the Senate and House. Efforts were made to increase committee staff resources and information-gathering facilities. Committees were required to form an oversight subcommittee or designate an existing subcommittee for that purpose. A major Senate study of staffing and information was conducted. Nevertheless, reforms on paper need not make reforms in fact. Before the changes, oversight activity was characterized as generally low and infrequent. "The typical pattern of committee review," according to one scholar, was "one of no review at all for long periods of time . . . interrupted by a series of oversight bursts."[26] So, before speculating on the impact of the recent reforms, it should be asked why oversight was so infrequent and what seems to make those oversight bursts occur.

Perhaps the major condition is the *political and policy interests* of the relevant committee members. Oversight is frequently directed at changing the administration of a program or preparing for new legislation. Therefore, if members like the present policy and support the status quo, little oversight is likely to occur. For years, the House Banking Committee kept a critical eye on the Federal Reserve Board as part of the chairman's own personal crusade. At the same time the Senate committee, oddly enough, found no staff available to conduct oversight. What was going on? A majority of the Senate committee members supported the banking and monetary interests associated with the Federal Reserve. A study of the House Select Committee on Intelligence makes the same point. The study found that four of the thirteen committee members carried a disproportionately large share of the oversight activity; at the other extreme, three members showed very little involvement. The three inactive members all had strong records in support of defense issues, while three of the four most vigorous overseers were low in support.[27] A study of the House Foreign Affairs Committee shows the same pattern, with the most active overseers in the 1970s tending to be liberals and opponents of Republican administration policies.[28]

The interests of committee members can be affected by events. A public scandal, a breakthrough in Soviet technology, or a space shuttle disaster all focus public attention and bring corresponding congressional attention. Hence it is commonly joked that Congress in crisis is Congress at work. Following the 1986 explosion of the space shuttle *Challenger,* and the deaths of its entire crew, Congress was quick to initiate hearings on the National Aeronautics and Space Administration (NASA) and to criticize its own past laxness in overseeing the agency. One committee member admitted that Congress "may have been too trusting of NASA" and another member commented that "Congress must apply the same strong oversight to NASA that it does to any other government agency." Extensive hearings on the disaster were immediately begun.

But Congress had been following its *typical* pattern in not engaging in serious oversight of the space agency. The committees were composed of members with strong constituency interests in the program. For example,

[26]Seymour Sher, "Conditions for Legislative Control," *Journal of Politics,* 25 (1963), p. 540. See Morris S. Ogul, *Congress Oversees the Bureaucracy* (Pittsburgh: University of Pittsburgh Press, 1976), pp. 11–22. See also Lawrence C. Dodd and Richard L. Schott, *Congress and the Administrative State* (New York: Wiley, 1979), pp. 214–22.

[27]Loch Johnson, "The U.S. Congress and the CIA: Monitoring the Dark Side of Government," *Legislative Studies Quarterly,* 5 (1980), pp. 477–500.

[28]Fred Kaiser, "Oversight of Foreign Policy: The U.S. House Committee on International Relations," *Legislative Studies Quarterly,* 2 (1977), pp. 255–79.

Florida, home state of the Cape Canaveral shuttle launching base, had one representative who was chairman of the House Science and Technology Committee and another who was chairman of the space subcommittee. Other members also had constituency ties. NASA, for its part, had worked to build support in Congress. The two lawmakers who had previously been invited to fly on a shuttle were Jake Garn, chairman of the Senate Appropriations subcommittee in charge of NASA's budget, and Bill Nelson, who chaired the space subcommittee of the House Science Committee. Committee members, their spouses, and guests were flown to receptions and shuttle launches at Cape Canaveral. So while the event provoked a sudden oversight burst, the same argument suggests that when the space program fades from public view, the previous low levels of oversight will return.

A second major condition is the influence of *party*—specifically, whether Congress and the White House have same-party or divided-party control. **Same-party control** means that one party occupies the White House and has majorities in the Senate and House; **divided-party control** means that one party controls the White House and the other controls the Congress. Oversight, it is important to see, occurs more frequently when party control is divided. In the divided-party governments of the late 1940s and 1950s, the National Labor Relations Board was constantly being investigated: Republican congresses worried that the Truman-appointed board was overly friendly to labor, while Democratic congresses thought the Eisenhower-appointed board was too hostile to labor. In the 1950s, the famous Kefauver anti-crime investigations occurred under divided-party control, as did the investigations of Eisenhower aide Sherman Adams and of several regulatory agency officials. The Senate hearings on the Vietnam War, begun under the Johnson administration, took a leap forward in 1969 as the White House changed from Democratic to Republican and the Congress stayed Democratic. The Senate Watergate investigation in the Nixon years, the investigation of the CIA in 1974–75 and the inquiry into the Iranian arms deal in 1987 all occurred under divided party control. Even the less visible oversight activity is more frequent when the majority party, which chairs all the committees and subcommittees and hires the bulk of the committee staff, does not have ties of loyalty to the White House.

New legislation is helped by same-party control. The more members of the president's party there are in Congress, the more likely such policy innovation can occur. Oversight, in contrast, appears helped by the reverse condition. Thus people seeking *both* policy change *and* accountability through oversight will not find the two goals simultaneously attainable. Conditions that help one work against the other.

Another important condition is provided by *institutional loyalty:* specifically, the perception that presidents or bureaucrats are usurping congressional prerogatives or are too blatantly ignoring congressional intent. Such matters are most sensitive under conditions of divided-party control, although even under same-party control, agencies must take care to listen to what the committees are saying. Agencies that have built records of trust with Congress receive less oversight than other agencies.

A Critique of Congress, 1885

Congress is often criticized for being unresponsive to public opinion, so divided among itself and subject to corrupt lobbyists that it cannot govern. The criticism is exaggerated as many points in the chapter show. Nevertheless, it has been remarkably persistent. Everyone who wants to critique Congress says the same thing.

The quotation below shows just how long this kind of criticism has been occurring. Woodrow Wilson published *Congressional Government* when he was still a political scientist and long before he would have trouble from Congress himself, as president. The book as a whole is an argument against the powers of Congress and for a stronger presidential government.

Wilson's description has been used so often by later critics that they probably do not know how much they are quoting him rather than giving their own original account. Read the criticism without the date and one could think it was a contemporary account.

Congress has in our own day become divorced from the "general mass of national sentiment," simply because there is no means by which the movements of that national sentiment can readily be registered in legislation. Going about as it does to please all sorts of Committees composed of all sorts of men—the dull and the acute, the able and the cunning, the honest and the careless—Congress evades judgment by avoiding all coherency of plan in its action. The constituencies can hardly tell whether the works of any particular Congress have been good or bad; at the opening of its sessions there was no determinate policy to look forward to, and at the close no accomplished plans to look back upon. . . . A few stubborn committee-men may be at the bottom of the harm that has been wrought, but they do not represent their party, and it cannot be clear to the voter how his ballot is to change the habits of Congress for the better. He distrusts Congress because he feels that he cannot control it.

The voter, moreover, feels that his want of confidence in Congress is justified by what he hears of the power of corrupt lobbyists to turn legislation to their own uses. He hears of enormous subsidies begged and obtained; of pensions procured . . . of appropriations made in the interest of dishonest contractors. . . . There can be no doubt that the power of the lobbyist consists in great part, if not altogether, in the facility afforded him by the Committee system.

Source: Woodrow Wilson, *Congressional Government* (New York Meridian, 1956), p. 132. Originally published 1885.

In view of these conditions, efforts to improve staffing do not necessarily increase oversight activity. All the staff in the world will not produce oversight if the committees want the policy or the agency left alone. In fact, at times committee leaders have deliberately limited staff to discourage oversight; and committees have voted against giving themselves subpoena power for an investigation. At other times, committees that have long pleaded "not enough information" to conduct oversight suddenly and miraculously find it available when a policy goes against their interests. Note that decisions *not* to oversee are really decisions to continue existing policy. So, in deciding whether or not to conduct oversight, Congress also decides what the policy should be.

Congressional membership helps shape the organization of Congress and how policy is made. A safe senior membership supports a norm of seniority, a seniority system, and party leaders who are themselves safe and senior. And yet this membership may be safe in part because it keeps in touch with the people back home and distributes influence with an eye toward constituents' needs. Influence is distributed broadly across the membership; constituency interests are reflected in the committees, in the assignment process, and floor voting. Moreover, given low public interest and information in Congress, voters may not demand very much by way of representation. There may be considerable room—after the few "right" votes, one or two federal projects, and a lot of constituency service—for members to pursue their own goals, compromise and bargain across party lines, and make national policy.

Congress is not only a representative assembly, however, it is a powerful branch of government as well. The same practices that support constituency representation also support the independence of the congressional institution. Congress can bury a president's bill in committee, vote down another bill on the floor, and investigate executive branch personnel and activities. It can do so not only through constitutional provision but because its members are protected in their reelection, in their committees, and through the seniority system from influence concentrated at any external point (for example, at the White House). Congress can face expert executive witnesses or two-term presidents, claiming its own peculiar brand of expertise. It is the expertise from seniority and committee specialization. Members of Congress know the policy because they are the ones who have been making it for fifteen years or more.

If Congress is so powerful, why is it so often seen as sluggish, impotent, and unwilling to act even in view of the clearest national need? It waits for the executive branch to initiate legislation, it rubber stamps presidential requests, and its oversight is infrequent and half-hearted. Such responses can be seen within the context of representation. Congress often defers to presidents, but the public, whose opinion it represents, also defers to presidents. Oversight is not vigorous, but members often find that the constituency is best served by working with rather than against bureaucratic personnel. Congress has the power to do many things. It makes the laws and supplies government funding. It could vote itself all the staff, computer facilities, and much else necessary for any oversight it wished to do. It is not a matter of power, but a matter of will. And the "will" of Congress moves with the will of the people and the kind of government they are interested in.

CHECKLIST FOR REVIEW

1. While members of Congress are an elite group, in education and socio-economic status, they claim they can represent their constituents. Most come from the area that they represent and say they know the people and their problems. Members can represent constituents in many ways, by making policy, performing services, allocating resources, and engaging in symbolic representation, such as keeping in touch with the folks back home.

2. Four norms, or unwritten rules of behavior, in Congress are seniority (experience in Congress is valued), specialization (expertise in an area of committee work is deferred to), reciprocity (members help other members on matters important to them), and institutional loyalty (one supports Congress and protects its rights and reputation). While the seniority norm is weaker than in congresses before the 1970s, it still provides the basis for the seniority system.

3. The seniority system is a means of ranking members on a committee by years of consecutive committee service, with the top-ranked member of the majority party almost always selected as the chair of the committee.

4. Standing committees remain in existence from one Congress to the next and alone have the power to report legislation to the floor. When people speak of committees, they usually mean the standing committees. Committees have the negative power to block a bill from going any further, and they have the positive power to rewrite the bill, adding or deleting any provisions they choose. Committees are powerful, stable in membership, and varied in many ways.

5. The leaders of Congress are party leaders, elected by the full congressional party membership. While elected, they are like the committee

leaders in seniority and in holding their posts for many years. Leaders have some control over scheduling legislation and the course of debate, but they lead by persuasion and bargaining.

6. Most important and controversial floor decisions are taken by roll call vote. Party is a major predictor of how members will vote, with Democrats generally taking the liberal position and Republicans the conservative. Region of the country is also important as are other characteristics—such as urbanism—of the states and districts the members represent. The members themselves say they will take cues on voting from those they like and trust and see as having positions close to their own.

7. After a law has been passed, Congress can engage in oversight, or supervision of how executive agencies implement the bill. Oversight tends to be infrequent, but occurs most often in conditions of divided-party control, when institutional loyalty may be a factor, and when the committee members have particular interest in the policy.

KEY TERMS

congressional party caucuses
state party delegations
descriptive representation
substantive representation
delegate
trustee
homestyle
norm
seniority system
standing committees
joint committees
special committees
conference committees
Speaker of the House

majority and minority party leaders in the Senate
House Minority Leader
House Majority Leader
whip organizations
pork barrel policies
unanimous-consent procedure
filibuster
cloture
roll call vote
Conservative Coalition
oversight
same-party control
divided-party control

The Presidency

E veryone feels qualified to say something about the presidency. Indeed as citizens, people think they *should* be able to discuss this most important office of the government. They read about it every day in newspapers and discuss it informally in casual conversation. The president, the polls tell us, is "the best known American." It may be surprising, then, to find that the office is the least thoroughly studied by political scientists. There are more studies done about Congress and the courts and many more about the parties and the voters.

Why is this so? It is true that it is difficult to gain access to material— one cannot easily interview presidents and their advisers or sit in on decision-making in the White House. But the main reason may be that *people think they know more about the office than they do*. Journalistic information, so widely available, focuses on the immediate present and the current occupant of the White House. Hence, the problem of the moment becomes the problem of the presidency, and a knowledge of current events becomes a substitute for a knowledge of the office. This emphasis on the present makes us forget past administrations quickly and miss the patterns of the presidency that hold over time.

It is often said that Jimmy Carter was weak and ineffective, and yet his success in Congress was greater overall than Ronald Reagan's. It is also said that Reagan's style of decision-making allowed illegal actions to be taken by the National Security Adviser and the CIA (see Chapter Fourteen.) Reagan did not stay informed about what his subordinates were doing. But there is no reason to believe that other National Security officials and CIA agents under very different presidents were not carrying out the same kind of actions. People say that the office is too strong or too weak, looking at events at a particular time. There is, however, a more fundamental mixture of power that challenges all presidents and helps to explain what they do in office. It is these patterns of the presidency that are examined in this chapter: in the power and limits of the office; the work of presidents in dealing with the public, press, and Congress; and the kinds of decisions made in the White House.

THE PRESIDENTIAL OFFICE

The Constitution states that "the executive power shall be vested in a President of the United States of America" who shall hold office for the term of four years. Imagine someone reading this document who knows nothing about the actual American government. What *is* the office? What would it be like in practice? The answers are not provided in the Constitution. The office is left open and ambiguous.

To understand the office, it is necessary to look at its historical development: why "the executive power" was defined in this way; and how the definition led to the modern presidency.

The Problem of Power

Central to the problem of designing a government in 1787 was the issue of executive power. There would be no effective government without a strong executive, but there would be no ratification for the new government with one that was too strong or that hinted in any way of monarchy. The president had to be strong enough to govern, but not so strong as to threaten the liberties of the citizens the government was designed to protect.

The solution, built into the constitutional design, exists to the present day. First, *presidential power would be checked*, by a system of checks and balances and the authority of the other branches. In what was to be one of the strongest legislative bodies ever designed, Congress would share such traditional executive powers as war-making, taxing and spending, and the power to make appointments. To govern at all, presidential-congressional cooperation would be necessary. Each, like the holder of one-half of a hundred dollar bill, could do little without the other. There would be mutual cooperation or stalemate and tug-of-war. But second, *presidential power was left open*; it was left undefined. While the powers of Congress are enumerated in the Constitution, no such list and limits are given for the presidency. The president is to "see that the laws are faithfully executed," but how this is to be done is left for presidents and others to decide. In this sense, there are *no* limits on the office; the president would have adequate "vigor" and "energy," in the words of Alexander Hamilton, to do what needed to be done. The third part of the solution follows from the other two. *Presidential power was left ambiguous.* The first provision limits the power drastically, the second expands it to be whatever it needs to be, and the third provision says that both are correct. What are the president's war powers? It depends on what part of the Constitution and *The Federalist Papers* you read. What is the "intent of the framers" regarding presidential power? The intent appears to be to allow this ambiguity. The ambiguity is itself an answer, a way of saying: the president should be strong enough, but not too strong. The solution restates the problem by saying presidential power must be continually adjusted and attended to.

This question of power continued in American historical debate, often joined by the presidents themselves. Writing as a political scientist at the end of the nineteenth century, Woodrow Wilson severely criticized what he saw as the excessive power of Congress in tying the president's hands. He set forth a strong statement of the openness of presidential power: "The President is at liberty, both in law and conscience, to be as big a man as he can. His capacity will set the limit."[1] Theodore Roosevelt went further: "It was not only [the president's] right but his duty to do anything that the needs of the Nation demanded unless such action was forbidden by the Constitution or by the laws." The president should be "a steward of the people bound actively and affirmatively to do all he could."[2] William Howard Taft, president and later chief justice, directly contradicted Roosevelt's view. According to Taft,

> The president can exercise no power which cannot be fairly and reasonably traced to some specific grant of power or justly implied and included within such express grant as proper and necessary to its exercise . . . There is no undefined residuum of power which he can exercise because it seems to him to be in the public interest.[3]

Taft remarked on the "unsafe doctrine" that presidents should "play the part of a Universal Providence and set all things right." This notion of a Universal Providence will be mentioned again.

The same question of power has occupied modern writers on the presidency. People in the 1940s and 1960s were concerned that the president was not strong enough, especially in relation to the power of Congress. Presidents could come fresh from the people with a strong electoral mandate and find their programs blocked and their budgets slashed by aging members of congressional committees. Echoing Wilson, these writers saw Congress as too strong and the president as too weak, and the problem became how to strengthen presidential government. Richard Neustadt wrote a book on *Presidential Power* and how to get more of it in 1960, at the beginning of the Kennedy administration. But ten years later, writers were

[1]Woodrow Wilson, *Constitutional Government* (1908; reprint ed. New York: Columbia University Press, 1961), p. 70.
[2]*Theodore Roosevelt: An Autobiography* (New York: Scribner's, 1924), p. 357.
[3]William Howard Taft, *Our Chief Magistrate and His Powers* (New York: Columbia University Press, 1916), pp. 139–40.

concerned that the president was too strong. In *The Twilight of the Presidency*, George Reedy wrote of the dangers of unchecked presidential power, and Arthur Schlesinger, Jr. described *The Imperial Presidency*. Hence, students of American government in the 1960s would be very aware of the limits and highly skeptical of claims of excess power; students in the 1970s would be aware of the power and difficult to convince about the limits. For students of the 1980s the imperial presidency is merely a case of American history.

The *office*, however, has not changed over time, although events have highlighted one side of the tension as opposed to the other. It remains very limited and very much open to be anything it needs to be. To understand the office in the future, as the balance swings one way or the other, it is important to see the continuing potential for both.

Growth of the Office

The openness of presidential power has supported some of the strongest actions of the strongest occupants of the office. People have then expected presidents to act that way, and Congress has passed legislation to help them. Thus, there has been a growth in the presidential office resulting from this constitutional openness, from the precedents that have been established, and from the resulting expectations about the office held by the public and Congress. This growth can be seen in both domestic and foreign policy spheres.

No domestic policy powers are specifically assigned to presidents, other than reporting to Congress on the State of the Union, vetoing legislation (although the veto may be overridden), and seeing that the laws are faithfully executed. Nevertheless, presidents from the first have let Congress know about their policies and have attempted to mobilize support for them. The Great Depression of the 1930s brought Franklin Roosevelt's New Deal and an enormously expanded domestic policy role. Presidents were expected to be managers of the economy and solvers of a range of social problems. There followed the expectation that presidents would initiate such policy and also the legislation that gave them the office facilities and staff to do so. Congress might or might not accept the proposals, but presidents were expected to make them.

The same spiral of growth occurred in foreign policy and war-making. Constitutionally, the president is commander-in-chief, although Congress has the power to declare war and raise and support the military, whether eighteenth century militia or twentieth century missiles. Nevertheless, the president's war-making powers grew and were consolidated with each wartime administration, until the 1970s brought alarmed questions in Congress, the courts, and the press about what the limits of this power might be. When Wilson styled himself the "leader of the free world," many Americans questioned the idea, including the senators who defeated him on his League of Nations proposal. But once Wilson had taken that stand and Roosevelt had echoed it one world war later, people began to expect presidents to take that role. Today, any president who did not do so would probably be as suspect as Wilson was when he first claimed the role.

In each of these cases, legislation followed the rising expectations and further expectations followed the legislation. The Bureau of the Budget, established in 1921 (now called the **Office of Management and Budget**), gave the White House increased control in budget making vis-à-vis Congress and the executive agencies. The **Executive Office Act**, passed in 1939, empowered the president to form offices to implement all the new domestic and foreign policy responsibilities. **The Employment Act of 1946** created the Council of Economic Advisers to help the president formulate economic policy. **The National Security Act of 1947** created machinery at the White House level to coordinate the various military and national security agencies. So, the National Security Council and the Central Intelligence Agency were born. Each of these acts created new bureaucracies of its own. This machinery, in turn, whether or not it could be effectively utilized, created further expectations that the president would be in control, would be responsible for the budget and the economy, and would solve problems in foreign and domestic policy. After all, someone had to be in control, and if the president wasn't, who was?

Thus a spiralling of power occurs over time whereby *events and actions* of individual presidents lead to *expectations* by the public and others that presidents should act this way, which in turn leads to *legislation* by Congress empowering the president to do so. The legislation then leads to further expectations and further presidential action. Each component in the spiral leads to and reinforces the others.[4]

Powers and Limits

The result, in the second half of the twentieth century, is an impressively powerful office. Presidents can initiate legislation and are expected to do so. They can set budget priorities for the future and exercise discretion about how funds already budgeted will be spent. As commander-in-chief, they can call on the emergency war powers developed over a century and help to define when such an emergency exists. This means that they can claim national security for actions kept from the press and public. They can appoint, with senatorial approval, key executive officers, ambassadors, members of independent government commissions, and judges of the federal courts. They can solicit the entire range of executive branch resources from the Pentagon to the Internal Revenue Service, and they can recruit others outside the executive for any additional help. Few people refuse a request from the president or an invitation to the White House. Special presidential advisory commissions (on drugs, immigration, or any other issue) can thus

---

[4]A good description is found in Thomas E. Cronin, *The State of the Presidency*, 2nd ed. (Boston: Little, Brown, 1980), pp. 243–57.

attract public attention and stimulate new legislation. Presidents can gain immediate access to the American people through the news media—what they say, and when they choose to say it, automatically becomes news. No one can speak more immediately, more continuously, with more authority, or with more people simultaneously than American presidents. Perhaps most important, presidents are acknowledged as the leader of the nation by others—by the public, members of Congress, and representatives of foreign nations. They come to symbolize the nation and the American people, and are given the corresponding deference and support. Notice that only a few of the powers derive from a clear constitutional grant; the others have grown with the office over time. (See Exhibit 8.1.)

Besides the powers of the office, the limits also need to be understood. The president is a single individual with human limits on time and attention and so cannot use all resources or do all things at one time. Much is done "in the White House" or "at the presidential level" beyond any one individual's scope of attention. For every one or two things attempted by the president, others are done somewhere else or not at all. In contrast, executive bureaucracies and congressional committees are multiple structures ideally suited for attending to many things at once. Some kinds of policy are better suited to presidential influence than others; these include dealing with the crisis more than routine; front-page news as opposed to all other news or events not even reported as news; and symbolic policy (such as the president inviting a foreign political dissident to the White House) more than the practical and concrete. This further exaggerates presidential influence, since crises, front-page news, and symbolic policy are most likely to capture people's attention.

The limits of the office are most clearly seen in the strengths of the other branches. In Chapter Seven, for example, the importance of committees in blocking or completely overhauling presidential programs was shown. The president may be chief foreign policymaker, but a House appropriations committee can slash a foreign aid request in half or decide to add or drop a nation as an aid recipient. Presidents appoint department heads, but the heads need money to run their departments and so are as dependent on Congress as on the president. People look to the president for solutions to national problems, but each proposal faces a series of separate congressional obstacles, all of which must be successfully negotiated before the proposal becomes law. Finally, there are many ways in which Congress is independent of any presidential effects. Presidents can employ their prestige and their White House breakfasts, but the members of Congress are subject to other influences, many of them from within the Congress, and many are more important than the presidential influences.

The president as chief executive is by no means synonymous with the executive branch. In fact, the executive bureaucracy is a limit as much as a source of presidential power. The president, by all the manuals of executive organization, faces severe problems of administration and control. This chief executive cannot hire or fire subordinates, set their job assignments, pay their salaries, or protect their departments. Nor is the chief allowed to

	POWERS	LIMITS
EXHIBIT 8.1 The Powers and Limits of the President	*Constitutional Sources* The president is chief executive (head of the executive branch)	but Congress sets the mission and structure of the executive branch and funds all activity.
	The president is Commander-in-Chief..	but Congress has power to declare war and raise money for defense.
	The president appoints officials........	but the appointment is subject to Senate confirmation.
	The president selects ambassadors and negotiates treaties in foreign affairs....	but the selection and the treaties are subject to Senate approval.
	The president can veto legislation	but Congress can override the veto.
	The office vests power in one individual	but much of the power and supervision must be delegated to others.
	The president is the one official (along with the vice-president) elected by the nation as a whole.....................	but the President is elected for a limited term.
	Presidential power can be expanded by the Supreme Court's reading of the Constitution	but power can be limited by the Supreme Court's reading of the Constitution.
	Informal Sources The president is a symbol of the nation and the government	but presidents can be held responsible for events beyond their control.
	The president is the nation's top celebrity, with immediate access to the public.	but presidents are watched closely and criticized by the news media.
	Presidents are expected to propose legislation and conduct foreign policy	but Congress can block presidential policies and offer policies of its own.
	The president is the acknowledged head of the political party	but only until the time approaches for the next president to be elected.

stay long enough to learn the ropes and reshape things more to his or her own liking. The two-term constitutional limit keeps the top people in this "company" in transition and turnover. Presidents may attempt reorganization plans to control the resources for which they are supposedly responsible, but Congress determines the mission and structure of all executive departments and must pass on all presidential reorganization requests. Interest groups that are powerful enough to have gained access to the ex-

| EXHIBIT 8.2 | The President as Chief Executive |

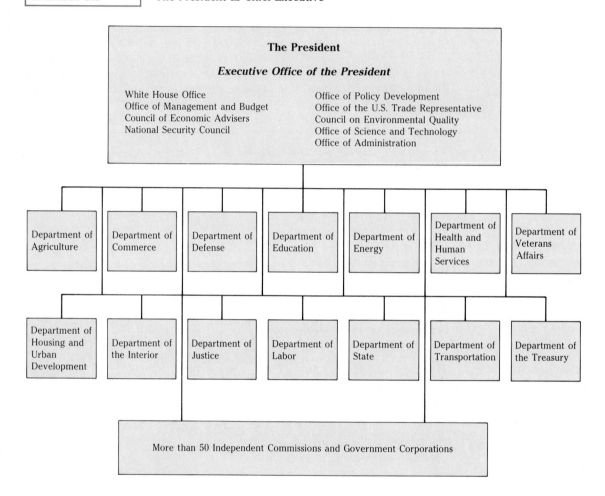

isting bureaucratic structures may also oppose these reorganization attempts.

Adding offices to the Executive Office of the President does not solve the bureaucratic problem. While they are staffed by people loyal to the president, they themselves become bureaucracies in need of supervision and control. What was going on in the National Security Council? people asked in the last years of the Reagan administration. The president did not know. Multiply the activity in one such office with all the offices shown in Exhibit 8.2 and one can begin to see the problem for all presidents, not merely Ronald Reagan. Many things can be done in the president's name without the president's knowledge. The Executive Office becomes a burden as much as a source of power.

Chapter Ten, on the judiciary, indicates additional limits. Presidents appoint Supreme Court justices only with the consent of the Senate, a consent that has not always been forthcoming. The justices, moveover, are appointed for life and have shown some marked differences from presidential expectations. They are subject to historical, professional, and collegial constraints and their own independent judgment. There are, in short, no presidential lieutenants on the Court. The Court, with good reason, is hesitant to oppose presidents. But it can do so—and has done so—with critical consequences for American government. "The President may be right in how he reads the Constitution, but he may also be wrong. And if he is wrong, who is there to tell him so?" This was the question in 1974 when Special Prosecutor Leon Jaworski argued the case before the Supreme Court for the subpoena of certain of President Nixon's taped conversations. Nixon felt he did not need to submit to the subpoena. Who can tell the president he is wrong? The answer that Jaworski had in mind, and the one to which the Court itself soon agreed, was the Supreme Court. The president is limited by the Constitution as interpreted by the Supreme Court. In *United States* v. *Nixon*, the Court unanimously ruled against Nixon and emphasized that the president is not above the law.

Presidents are limited beyond these constitutional checks by the very things said to be sources of power. They are the single leader, chief public celebrity, and symbol of government. But celebrities can be watched so closely and critically by the news media that they lose public support. And single leaders and symbols of government can be held responsible for events over which they have no control. The more power attributed to the office, the more chance of failure and public disillusionment when the expectations cannot be fulfilled.[5]

Seen one way, the office looks very powerful; seen another way, it is severely limited. Given the ambiguity designed into the office, both views are correct.

MANAGING THE WHITE HOUSE

Any chief executive—of a nation, firm, or other enterprise—must delegate power while maintaining control and organize information so that instructions can be carried out and so that feedback and new information can return. Presidents, therefore, face a problem common to other executives. Their problem is compounded, however, by the ambiguity of power surrounding the office and their sharing of authority with other political actors.

Two kinds of executive organizations can be characterized as the bureaucratic and palace politics modes. They are available to other execu-

---

[5]Cronin, *op. cit.,* p. 115. See also Hugh Heclo and Lester M. Salamon, eds., *The Illusion of Presidential Government* (Boulder, Colo.: Westview, 1981), p. 1.

tives as well as presidents and each has its own distinct problems and possibilities. A look at them in the presidential context suggests something of the difficulty of managing the White House.

The Bureaucratic Mode

Bureaucratic organization is hierarchical in structure, with a division of labor and specialization, and clear lines of communication and control. The president heads a vast federal bureaucracy, which in size and extent of specialization alone suggests great presidential power. However, the limits imposed by the bureaucracy, as shown earlier, are equally awesome. The president is notable for having less control over hiring, firing, promoting, or protecting than many chief executives. In addition, bureaucracies place high priority on routines and formal rules that can frustrate innovative chiefs. They develop internal practices of protection and support, which can restrict the flow of information and bias the kind of information transmitted. Instructions sent may not reach their destination. Information needed may not return. Chiefs may not count on subordinates having their interests at heart, their priorities in mind, or their undivided allegiance. As Richard Neustadt argues, bureaucrats may not "feel obliged on their responsibility to do what the President wants done." With all the resources available, the president may become not a leader, but a clerk.[6]

Presidents have help in their executive duties, of course, from people they have selected to work for them. They appoint, with the majority consent of the Senate, a cabinet consisting of heads of the various bureaucratic departments. They also appoint members of the Executive Office of the President. These appointees should feel obliged to do what the president wants done, but they pose other problems for a chief executive.

The President's Cabinet. Typically the first news to appear with a new administration is the news about cabinet appointments. Yet, these accounts, often heralded as signs of the incoming president's policies and style, can be extremely misleading. The names of the people announced daily in the news flashes are rarely heard again. Cabinet meetings will be brief, largely ceremonial, rarely called, and even more rarely used for advice on major policy directions. With some exceptions, most appointments will not be made from the president's circle of friends and advisers; they will instead provide a largely symbolic representation of various politically important groups in the country: labor, business, minorities, and others. Presidents, and recent presidents in particular, have not found the cabinet or its individual members an effective device for executive organization.

The cabinet, not provided for in the Constitution, consists of the heads of the major executive departments and any other officials that the president selects. The first cabinet was created when George Washington met

[6]Richard E. Neustadt, *Presidential Power: The Politics of Leadership*, rev. ed. (New York: Wiley, 1964), p. 8.

President Bush confers with aides in the Oval Office as his administration gets under way.

frequently with the attorney general and the secretaries of state, treasury, and war. The modern cabinet consists of the fourteen department heads, plus the ambassador to the United Nations, and a few other officials who are said to have "cabinet status." Reagan, for example, gave cabinet rank to the director of the Office of Management and Budget, since budget policy was to play such a large role in his administration. Bush gave cabinet rank to the coordinator of the war on drugs. Presidents often come to office saying that they will revitalize the cabinet. Carter held sixty cabinet meetings in his first two years in office, and then the regular meetings stopped. Reagan's cabinet meetings began to dwindle by the end of his first year. Cabinet members confessed that they would use the meetings to catch up on their weekly reading.

Formally, the cabinet is the link between the president and the federal bureaucracy; that is, the fourteen departments with all their divisions and subdivisions. The actual link, however, may be weak or nonexistent. Even with the best political skills, cabinet members face a conflict of loyalties that is often insurmountable. They owe their primary allegiance to the presidents appointing them, but they must deal effectively with the departments they head. Effectiveness with either can lead to loss of effectiveness with the other. The problems of department heads will be seen fully in the following chapter. Here, it is important to see primarily that the president's job as chief executive is not made easier by the cabinet connection.

The Executive Office of the President.   Presidents have their own bureaucracy which exists outside of the traditional departments and subdivisions of the federal executive branch. This is known as the **Executive Office of the President**, or the "institutionalized presidency." The Executive Office includes such famous agencies as the Office of Management and Budget, the National Security Council, the Council of Economic Advisers, along with other agencies and thousands of staff personnel. The office was designed to coordinate and bring closer to the White House activities also being pursued in the bureaucracy. So, the National Security Council deals with foreign affairs and matters of defense that are simultaneously being considered in the departments of State and Defense, in various corners of the Pentagon, and in other agencies. However, these offices have themselves become bureaucratic and specialized, posing additional problems of supervision. And since the traditional bureaucracy coexists with these new presidential agencies, supervision required may simply have doubled. Originally thought to be helping the president, the Executive Office may only have increased the burden of executive control.

In the Reagan administration, National Security Adviser Admiral John Poindexter and his assistant Colonel Oliver North were charged with diverting money from an Iranian arms sale to aid the anti-government forces in Nicaragua. The scandal became front-page news and prompted a full congressional investigation. The investigation concluded that the president did not know what his staff people were doing. One can ask, then, if this is a problem for one president, who chose to delegate a great deal of power, or a problem for all presidents?

The Palace Politics Mode

If the institutionalized presidency is not manageable, the bureaucracy is not loyal, or the cabinet is not effective, another mode of organization exists. This can be called the **palace politics mode**. Executives are linked to their subordinates in a fluid, personal, and nonhierarchical form. Assignment of functions, division of labor, and lines of authority are not formally drawn but exist at the chief's discretion. Bureaucracies are pyramids, but palace politics is more like a wheel with the executive's circle of helpers and advisers dependent on the hub. Or to change the metaphor, the executive is like a monarch with a court whose members are defined by and dependent on the royal pleasure. There are palace favorites, some fall from favor, and there is uncertainty as to who is closest to the King or who spoke with the president last. As the term suggests, palace politics is not new nor is it peculiar to presidents. Kings, corporate heads, and other executives have relied on a small set of personal advisers to maximize loyalty and organizational control.

Andrew Jackson had his famous Kitchen Cabinet, consisting of a small number of informal advisers whose loyalty was unquestioned. The Kitchen Cabinet existed simultaneously with the official cabinet; Jackson could use the services of either. John Kennedy used task forces, with varying members selected by him for specific jobs. A task force on health, for example, would work concurrently with the traditional health bureaucracies. One of the most famous task forces was the personally selected set of advisers who spent a week deciding the response to the Cuban Missile Crisis (see Chapter Fourteen). They included the president's brother, some personal aides, some selected members of the cabinet, and even private citizens. The group was picked by Kennedy for the problem at hand.

With some presidents, the court has narrowed in size to one or two favorites. Woodrow Wilson used Colonel House, a friend and adviser from the campaign days. Wilson consulted with House on domestic and foreign policy in the days before and during World War I. When one Secretary of State resigned, it was House who explained to the new Secretary what his duties would be, neglecting to mention his own European negotiations. Eisenhower used Sherman Adams—like House, a friend and adviser from the campaign. Adams's power and scope of authority were vast. No one, except Secretary of State Dulles, got through to see Eisenhower without the famous notation, "OK, SA." The joke circulated around Washington, "What if Adams should die and Eisenhower were to become president?" Nixon used aides John Ehrlichman and H.R. Haldeman, dubbed the "Palace Guard," and Reagan used Donald Regan. Each of these advisers suffered the fate of many palace favorites and fell from grace. House fell from favor. Adams was called before a congressional investigating committee on a conflict of interest charge and forced to resign. Ehrlichman, Haldeman, and Regan were also forced to resign during the scandals in their respective administrations.

The palace politics mode offers presidents loyalty, flexibility, and personal control, but it carries disadvantages too. The problem of bureaucratic control is not eliminated, it is merely displaced. Bureaucratic activity continues elsewhere, beyond the presidential circle. Such a circle, rather than increasing the chief executive's control, may narrow it severely, isolating the president from necessary information. It may build in a bias for certain kinds of information and against other kinds: since courtiers are dependent on presidential favor, those who agree with the president and report information in support of past decisions may fare better than others. At one point in the Vietnam debate, Lyndon Johnson reported that "all of his advisers" supported the present administration policy on the war. Left unsaid, however, was that those who did not support it were no longer his advisers. According to George Reedy's argument, the bias may go even further. Living in the palace surrounded by deferential courtiers, presidents may come to believe they are exempt from the laws governing ordinary human and political affairs.

Other questions need asking. Who are these aides who take action and make decisions in the president's name? What are they like and where have they come from? Some presidents delegate more responsibility to aides than others do, but all must to some extent rely on these people who are not elected, not known before the election, and not announced in the news of the president's cabinet. Given the importance of loyalty, the most trusted aides tend to be personal friends and associates from the campaign and the days before. "You don't get the best people," one presidential assistant commented. "You get the people you know."[7] Kennedy selected Harvard classmates and Johnson fellow Texans. Ehrlichman had been an advertising executive, and Carter's Hamilton Jordan was once a tour guide at Disneyland. All had worked in the presidential campaigns.

Managing the White House is a problem confronting each president, and the attempts at solutions and the success achieved will differ. Some presidents rely more on their bureaucracies and others on an informal circle of advisers.[8] Each form of organization, however, poses its own challenges and disadvantages. It is true that presidents have shown in their past careers that they can get others "to do what they want done." Still, the number and size of the organizations in need of managing make the president's problem especially difficult. The potential resources of the office are not necessarily on tap. It cannot be assumed that information will get to the president, that it will be sought, or that it will be acted on if received.

Who's in Charge Here?—The Problem of Information

Writers who urge for more power for the president have seldom asked about the quality of information that would be used in the exercise of power. Political scientists, however, have begun to look more closely at White House decision making in the wake of the Vietnam and Watergate experiences. Irving Janis cites numerous cases of presidential decisions to warn of the danger of **groupthink**—the kind of faulty thinking often found in groups where pressures for agreement override a look at the alternatives.[9] Alexander George uses recent cases to identify "malfunctions" of the decision-making process: for example, when advisers reach agreement too quickly; when the president is dependent on a single source of information; or when advisers see a problem but are unwilling to alert the president to it. Malfunctions can occur in bureaucratic or informal groups, although they are minimized by using more than one set of advisers. George argues for **multiple advocacy**—a system designed to encourage advice for alternative, and even opposing, positions.[10]

Things look different, however, from within the White House, according to what the *aides* say are the president's problems. (For the contrast, see Exhibit 8.3.) Multiple advocacy might be ideal, but the aides say "presidents don't have time for this." Premature agreement is a malfunction for George and Janis, but it is a rule of procedure among White House advisers. Debate stops at the first satisfactory alternative. In short, the kind of behavior en-

[7]Frederic Malik, *Washington's Hidden Tragedy* (New York: Free Press, 1978), p. 64.

[8]See Richard T. Johnson, *Managing the White House* (New York: Harper, 1974) for a description of five presidents and five different management styles.

[9]Irving L. Janis, *Groupthink*, 2nd ed. (New York: Houghton Mifflin, 1982).

[10]Alexander L. George, *Presidential Decisionmaking in Foreign Policy* (Boulder, Colo.: Westview, 1980), pp. 150–65.

EXHIBIT 8.3	FROM THEORIES OF DECISION MAKING	FROM PAST WHITE HOUSE AIDES
Advice to the President	• Avoid premature agreement.	• Take the first alternative. (The first alternative already has political support.)
	• Seek alternative and conflicting points of view (multiple advocacy).	• Move it or lose it. (Act early in the administration to take advantage of early suppport.)
	• Urge advisers to alert you to any problems.	• Avoid details.
	• Learn from experience.	• Learning must wait. (Presidents do not have time to further their education in office.)

couraged in the White House would be deemed most objectionable in an organization manual.[11] Presidents are running against the clock. They do not have time to seek multiple advocates or ask how a consensus was reached. They have enough disagreement; they do not need to look for more. At least, that is how the aides see it—and they are the ones in charge of the information.

Presidents need knowledge as well as power. They need to find the right information and identify alternatives. But the knowledge can be buried in the bureaucracy or caught within the rivalries of court advisers. Presidents cannot delegate too little information or too much. Somehow, they must learn to manage the White House and become chief executives in fact as well as name.

THE PUBLIC PRESIDENCY

From the first primary to the final proposal, presidents seek public support. Public opinion shapes what presidents are expected to do and their range of activities in office. This public opinion, however, is a mixed blessing. Like the Constitution itself, it can be a source of limits or strengths.

Public Support for Presidents

The public's view of presidents and support for them can be a reservoir of power which presidents are aware of and on which they can draw. This support is seen in children's learning about government, in adult perceptions, and in the historical continuity from the 1950s to the present day.

[11]Paul C. Light, *The President's Agenda* (Baltimore: Johns Hopkins University Press, 1982), pp. 218–23.

Studies of children's learning about government show how this support begins.[12] The child's initial point of contact with elected officials is with the president, more so than with mayors, governors, or anyone else. For the young child, the president *is* the government; other officials are learned about in terms of that basic orientation point. So, Congress becomes a group that "helps the president." The president, then, is the initial point of contact, the symbol of government, and the orientation point from which the rest of the government is perceived. Also, presidents are seen to be both powerful and benevolent—something like the child's parents or God. They are symbols of authority and power, and they are good. According to fourth-graders, the president "gives us things," "takes care of us," "does good things," and "tells the people what is good." In 1976, the Associated Press reported the responses of first-graders when asked by their teacher, "What should a president do for the people?" Among their replies were:

help ducks
sign papers
give poor people money
tell people where to go
keep people from stealing
feed birds
help a lost puppy
help us not die
work in the White House
help us build houses
save eagles
help boaters not crash

The president is seen as powerful and benevolent, acting like parents (supplying clothing, food, and shelter) and like God (watching over birds, boaters, and lost puppies). Two years after the Watergate crisis and Nixon's resignation, the next generation of Americans begins to form ideas about the president's job.

Adults, like children, see the president as the primary symbol of government, give support to the incumbent in office, and see the president as the predominant decision maker to which others—Congress and the public in particular—are subordinate. Presidents are far better known than other elected officials; their elections are followed with more interest and attention. On election day, Kennedy received barely fifty percent of the vote, but by his inauguration he had the "job approval" of sixty-nine percent of the people. When Ford assumed the presidency after Nixon was forced to re-

---

[12]The classic study is Fred I. Greenstein, *Children and Politics* (New Haven: Yale University Press, 1965). See also Cronin, *op. cit.,* chapter 3, and Fred I. Greenstein, "What the President Means to Americans," in *Choosing the President,* ed. James David Barber (Englewood Cliffs, N.J.: Prentice-Hall, 1974), pp. 121–48.

sign, seventy-one percent approved of the way Ford was doing his job. Most presidents have received strong support for how they were doing their job before they had any chance to do it. Studies show that people believe the president "stands for our country" and that they sleep better when a president they trust is watching over the country. Majorities believe that the public should support the president's actions, even if they personally believe the president is wrong. Majorities also agree that in times of crisis in domestic or foreign affairs, all citizens should support the president.[13]

Does an individual scandal in office hurt this general support? After the Watergate crisis, a majority of people polled agreed that the scandal had "reduced their confidence in the presidency as an institution." Elsewhere in the survey, however, no sign of the shaken confidence appeared. Two-thirds of the people still said that in times of domestic crisis, people should support the president's programs for dealing with the crisis; and one-half of the people polled agreed with the statement that "even though we may disagree with what the president asks us to do, it is our duty to obey him."[14] So, individual presidents can fail, but the support for the office continues. It is the office of Washington and Lincoln, not of Grant and Nixon, and individual failures can be kept separate in people's minds from the deeper symbolism.

One political scientist has summarized these findings in terms of the psychological needs that presidents fulfill for people. Presidents are used (1) as symbols of national unity and of the predictability of one's way of life; and (2) as outlets for affect—ways of feeling good about one's country and its government. They are used (3) as cognitive aids in that a single well-known individual can serve as an orientation point to simplify the confusion and complexity of government. These may be positive or negative orientation points. Presidents are also used (4) as a means of vicarious participation: through identification with presidents, people feel more effective and more a part of things occurring around them.[15] Families are spotlighted, presidential trivia is news, and a White House domestic event becomes an epic occurrence. The public learns things such as Ronald Reagan liked a special kind of jelly beans and they get to watch George Bush engage in all his athletic activities. Some nations separate these functions. In England, the Royal Family is the outlet for affect and symbol of the nation, while the Prime Minister is cognitive aid and lightning rod. In this country, however, the president carries the entire symbolic burden alone. An illustration of how this symbolism shapes the schedule of the president is shown in the box on page 304.

[13]Samuel Kernell et al., "Public Support for Presidents," in *Perspectives on the Presidency,* ed. Aaron Wildavsky (Boston: Little, Brown, 1975), pp. 148–81. For an early study, see Roberta S. Sigel, "Image of the American Presidency," *Midwest Journal of Political Science,* 10 (1966), pp. 123–37.

[14]Jack Dennis, "Dimensions of Public Support for the Presidency," Midwest Political Science Association Paper, Chicago, 1975, Table 2.

[15]Greenstein, *op. cit.,* "What the President Means to Americans."

The Burden of the Office

All official actions of the president are reported in *The Public Papers of the Presidents of the United States,* from George Washington to the present. If the president addresses a group in the Rose Garden, sends a message to Congress, gives an order, signs a paper, or engages in a question-and-answer session with reporters, these messages are included in *The Public Papers,* along with the time and place that they occurred. Informal actions, such as conversations with advisers or other activities behind the closed doors of the White House, are not included.

The following list details two weeks of Ronald Reagan's schedule, the weeks (in April, 1983) selected at random. Starred entries are oral remarks delivered in person by the president; all of the others are merely signed messages. Reagan and Carter include more proclamations and appointments in the official record than their predecessors do, but otherwise the schedule can be taken as an illustration for any of the contemporary presidents.

Notice how much of the activity is ceremonial: the greeting of foreign dignitaries, the giving of volunteer action awards, the messages to astronauts, and all the multitude of proclamations. There are weeks for crime victims and volunteers, days for mothers and American Indians, and months for cancer and arthritis control. Notice also how governmental activity, such as a nomination or a message to Congress, blends into other activity not associated with the government: the statements about Easter and Passover, for example, or the ceremonies in praise of volunteer work.

Many people feel that presidents should not try to be all things to all people or that they should not blend their political activity with religious statements. Yet, if presidents are expected to be the symbol of the nation, then they are increasingly drawn into all such affairs. Actions lead to expectations, and expectations lead to further action, in that spiral of growth described earlier in the chapter.

And if this is the official schedule, think of the Washington reporters covering the White House and trying to find some news in the day. (See Judy Woodruff's account in Chapter Three.) It is not surprising, then, that reporters must use the official White House handouts for news or try to capture a stray administration official who will say something interesting. The officials, of course, can allow themselves to be captured, and they can have their favorable stories already prepared.

April	1	Message to Congress on Heavyweight Motorcycle Imports
☆	2	Radio Address to the Nation on the Observance of Easter and Passover
	4	Statement Nominating an Ambassador
	4	Message to Space Shuttle Astronauts
	4	Proclamation Designating Swedish-American Friendship Day
	4	Proclamation Designating National Child Abuse Prevention Month
	4	Proclamation Designating Pan American Day and Pan American Week
	4	Proclamation Designating Prayer of Peace, Memorial Day
	4	Letter to Congress Concerning Proposed Export Act
	4	Executive Order Establishing an Emergency Board to Investigate a Railroad Labor Dispute
	5	Statement Nominating a Counsel for the Department of Transportation
	5	Statement Nominating Directors for the Communications Satellite Corporation
	5	Executive Order Extending the Presidential Commission on Drunk Driving
	5	Message to the Senate on the Indian Claims Settlement Bill
	6	Announcement of Members of the Emergency Board to Investigate a Railroad Labor Dispute
☆	6	Remarks and a Question-and-Answer Session with Students in Pittsburgh, Pennsylvania

The Cult of the Presidency

Public support for presidents is a major source of power, but it builds in weaknesses as well. The very idealized notion of the office creates disillusionment when the ideals cannot be fulfilled. The heavy symbolic burden adds to the difficulty. As symbols of the nation, presidents are loved; as symbols of the government, they are criticized; and as means of vicarious participation, they and their families are subjected to constant and relentless scrutiny. One kind of symbol works uneasily with the others. Yet, the public is not alone in this creation. Writers on the presidency, academics, and journalists have nourished it too. This has been called the **cult of the presidency,** one that readers of even an occasional news magazine will find familiar.

The cult of the presidency, as political scientist Thomas Cronin describes it, consists of three components: ascriptions of power, ascriptions of virtue, and personalization.[16] Presidents are assumed to be powerful, frequently (and incorrectly) "the most powerful individual in the world." They are assumed to be good—indeed, to be a kind of high priest and moral leader. The political leader becomes a moral leader after winning an election. It is not only the textbook writers or journalists who carry on the cult, however; the presidents themselves encourage it. A Kennedy aide commented that "our presidents today have to be a personal model, a cultural articulator, and a semi-priest or semi-tribal leader." And Carter remarked that the president must "set a standard of ethics and morality, excellence and greatness."[17] In speeches to the American people, presidents from Truman to Reagan cast political statements in religious or moral terms. Thus budget cuts call for a spirit of self-sacrifice, and God is cited more frequently than past presidents or current advisers.[18] Adults, like children, are being taught that the president is powerful and good.

At the same time that the power and virtue are emphasized, personal lives are kept under constant attention. We learn that one model and cultural articulator (Johnson) drove over the speed limit and picked up his dogs by the ears. The most powerful leader of the free world (Ford) stumbled on a ski slope and dropped a fork at dinner, and the wife of another of these most powerful beings (Reagan) consulted an astrologer. The first two components of the cult are in conflict with the third. The cult simultaneously creates a larger-than-life idol and then relentlessly spotlights the idol's feet of clay.

To see how this feels, imagine that one afternoon or evening you personally, as an individual, are burdened with a great exalted mission: who you are and what you do is of worldwide and historic consequence. But all

[16]Cronin, *op. cit.,* pp. 75–116.
[17]Cronin, *op. cit.,* p. 75.
[18]Barbara Hinckley, *The Symbolic Presidency* (Chatham, N.J.: Chatham House, 1989).

Ronald and Nancy Reagan pose for photographers in the White House.

the time you are pursuing this mission, you are subject to constant personal and trivial scrutiny. You frown, you have a drink, you wash your hair, drop a pencil, or yell at your dog. These events are recounted or photographed or speculated about. Does that mishap with the pencil mean you are fumbling in foreign policy? Have you lost your credibility with thousands of dog owners? Why, as a matter of fact, did you frown and yell at your dog, and what does that mean for the quality of leadership in the White House? A few hours into this exercise and you can see something of the psychic strain that the cult can produce.

George Reedy, past adviser to Lyndon Johnson and writer on the presidency, describes the effects of the cult on the White House. Reedy traces the idolatry and extreme deference of aides surrounding the president: "He is treated with all the reverence due a monarch.... No one speaks to him unless spoken to first. No one ever invites him to 'go soak your head' when his demands become petulant and unreasonable."[19] This artificial atmosphere, according to Reedy, isolates presidents from surrounding political reality, obscures their judgment, and harms their ability to make good decisions.

Since 1789, Americans have said we have "a government of laws and not of men," a statement against idolatry and cultism. No individual, including the president, is above the law, is privileged to break it, or should be exalted over it. So, when presidents and their advisers act beyond the law

---

[19]George E. Reedy, *The Twilight of the Presidency* (New York: World Publishing Company, 1970), p. 4.

and engage in cover-ups, lying, or diversion of funds, these events may not be isolated historical curiosities. The cult exalts a person and not a rule of law and creates a climate where such events can flourish.

The President and the Polls

While support for the office is high, the popularity polls for individual presidents show considerable variation. Hence public support can become a limit rather than a source of presidential power. Since presidents and their advisers watch the polls and consider them important and since other members of the Washington community also watch them as signs of presidential influence, an understanding of their fluctuation is important. The polls vary with events, but only some of these events are under a president's control.

Presidential popularity is a term used for a president's public support, often measured in the polls by a "job approval" question. Since the 1940s, the Gallup organization has asked on a monthly basis, "Do you approve of the way [president's name] is handling his job as president?" The percent approving becomes a measure of the fluctuations in popularity. It can be traced through any one president's term or compared across administrations. (See Exhibit 8.4.)

Three influences can be identified that are common to all administrations.[20] One is a *decline in popularity through the term.* The decline may not be steady or continuing, but the general direction is down. For most presidents, polls start at their high point and fall from there, with some increase at the beginning of a second term and again a decline. One Reagan aide was quoted as saying, "We're fighting the clock. We think about that all the time."[21] Presidents know they are running against time, and their time keeps getting shorter.

A second factor has been the *decline in popularity associated with economic hard times.* Most studies confirm that economic factors affect presidential popularity, although the measures used and the explanations offered for the effect differ. Bad economic news, about unemployment or inflation for example, is typically associated with a decline in presidential support. The clearest victim of this effect among recent presidents was Jimmy Carter. With the American economy suffering severely throughout his

[20]A very large body of writing addresses this subject. See, for example, John E. Mueller, "Presidential Popularity from Truman to Johnson," *American Political Science Review*, 64 (1970), pp. 18–34. Cliff Zukin and J. Robert Carter, Jr., "The Measurement of Presidential Popularity," in *The President and the Public,* ed. Doris A. Graber (Philadelphia: Institute for the Study of Human Issues, 1982); Samuel Kernell, *Going Public* (Washington, D.C.: Congressional Quarterly Press, 1986), pp. 173–210; George C. Edwards, III, *The Public Presidency* (New York: St. Martins, 1983); and Gary King and Lyn Ragsdale, *The Elusive Executive* (Washington, D.C.: C.Q. Press, 1988), pp. 277ff.

[21]Samuel Kernell, "The Presidency and the People," in *The Presidency and the Political System,* ed. Michael Nelson (Washington, D.C.: C.Q. Press, 1984), p. 256.

| **EXHIBIT 8.4** | Presidential Popularity from Truman to Reagan |

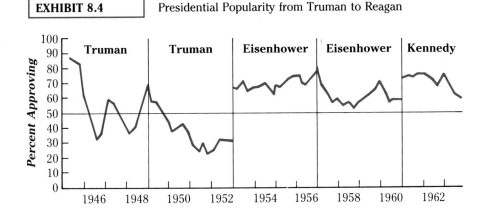

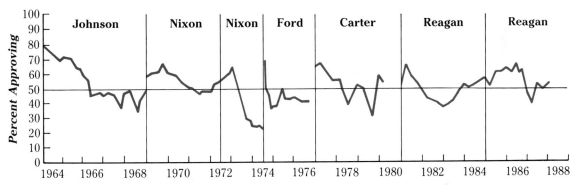

Note: The question asked was "Do you approve of the way _____ is handling his job as president?" The graph shows the percentage of people approving.

Source: George Gallup, *Gallup Poll Index, 1935–1971* (New York: Random House, 1972) and more recent Gallup poll results.

four years in office, his polls stayed low, no matter what else he did or did not do.

A third factor common to all administrations is the *increase in popularity in times of international crisis*—what has been called the **rally 'round the flag effect.** In an economic crisis, presidential support falls; in an international crisis, the support rises. Some of the clearest peaks in the polling results are associated with international events: the Russian attack on Afghanistan at the beginning of 1980, along with the first capture of American hostages in Iran, and the U.S. raid against Libya in 1986. This increase occurs even after the president's administration may have erred and helped produce the crisis in the first place. After the U-2 incident in 1960, involving the discovery of a secret American spying mission in Communist territory which caused the collapse of a summit meeting, Eisenhower's popularity rose six percentage points. After the Bay of Pigs disaster, a first major failure of the Kennedy administration, Kennedy's popularity rose ten percentage points. In Carter's case, the Russians and Iranians did the attacking—Carter did nothing—and yet his popularity jumped twenty points.

The rally effect is no minor matter, as the box on page 311 illustrates. When presidents appear before Congress and the American public to announce an international confrontation, they are given what they ask for—in support, troops, or a resolution of war. The rally effect has its limitations, however. If a crisis is prolonged—a war continues unsuccessfully, the hostages are not freed—then presidents lose the support they gained and risk even further losses. Look back to Exhibit 8.4 and see the wars in Korea and Vietnam reflected in Truman's and Johnson's public opinion polls.

These curiosities can be explained in terms of the earlier discussion of support. The president, as a symbol of the nation like the flag, is supported when the national interest is threatened by another nation. But as symbol of government and lightning rod, the president is held responsible even, as in the case of the economy, when the problem is beyond the action of any one head of state. If presidents are expected to "manage the economy" and "give us jobs," or as the fourth-graders said to "give us things" and "take care of us," then in economic recession and severe unemployment, they are clearly not doing their job. The same rationale helps explain the drop in support from the beginning of a term. Since the president is not a universal providence who can save the country from a host of assorted ills, the polls drop as the ills continue and the unrealistic expectations are not met.

Other influences on support can be traced to factors specific to a particular administration. Lyndon Johnson's polls fell below fifty percent and stayed there as the long and unsuccessful Vietnam conflict became increasingly unpopular. Richard Nixon's fell progressively with each revelation in the Watergate cover-up. Gerald Ford immediately lost his initial high support when he pardoned Richard Nixon. That action produced a massive drop of fourteen percentage points in the polls. Ronald Reagan's support fell with the uncovering of the Iranian arms scandal and the diversion of funds to Nicaragua.

One study of these major "presidential" events has been conducted by Michael MacKuen. MacKuen is concerned with separating these events from other trends, particularly economic trends, operating in an administration. Studying presidential popularity from Johnson through Carter, he identifies seventy-three "dramatic" events, including major speeches announcing policy changes, announcements about Vietnam and Watergate, Carter's Camp David summit meeting, and others. He finds that these events do have an impact as important as the economic trends. Their diminishment rate—that is, how long they continue to affect the polls—is about the same as the rate for inflation.[22]

---

[22]Michael B. MacKuen, "Political Drama, Economic Conditions, and the Dynamics of Presidential Popularity," *American Journal of Political Science*, 27 (1983), pp. 165–92. See also Samuel Kernell, "Explaining Presidential Popularity," *American Political Science Review*, 72 (1978), pp. 506–22.

The Power of the President

The president's power as symbol of the nation is especially important in international affairs when the national interest can appear to be threatened by another nation. In the following cases, presidents address Congress and the American people describing an international event that has occurred. Truman is asking for inflation controls to freeze prices and wages. Johnson asks for a resolution—it will be known as the Tonkin Gulf Resolution—permitting an escalation of the Vietnam War. Reagan explains why American troops invaded Grenada and are fighting in Lebanon. Reagan is merely asking for support. The Lebanon conflict has brought heavy American casualties, but the invasion of Grenada has suddenly intervened and is over.

None of these cases are clear cut. Truman is asking for emergency domestic powers so that the United States can help the United Nations fight a war in Korea. Johnson is pursuing a strategy on Vietnam that will become a classic case of poor decision making in the White House. In Grenada, Reagan imposed an unusual degree of press censorship, forbidding reporters into the invasion area. Thus the only evidence of why the invasion occurred is the evidence offered by the White House, widely disputed by observers on the scene.

Nevertheless, when the speech is over, each president gets what he is asking for. Truman and Johnson will have trouble later. The Tonkin Gulf Resolution will be repealed. But for the moment, the Resolution is passed almost unanimously, the controls go into effect, and the nation enters a new phase in the Korean and Vietnam wars. Congress grumbles a bit about Grenada, but goes little further in investigating what occurred. Reagan's popularity jumps, and American attention is diverted from the heavy casualties in Lebanon to the victory in Grenada.

As you read the speeches, watch for this symbolic presidential power, and ask yourself what you would do if you were a member of Congress listening to the president's words.

CASE 1   TRUMAN, KOREA, AND INFLATION CONTROLS (EXCERPTS FROM THE SPEECH OF DECEMBER 15, 1950)

I am talking to you tonight about what our country is up against, and what we are going to do about it. Our homes, our Nation, all the things we believe in, are in great danger. This danger has been created by the rulers of the Soviet Union.

. . .

In June the forces of Communist imperialism burst out into open warfare in Korea. The United Nations moved to put down this act of aggression, and by October had all but succeeded. Then, in November, the Communists threw their Chinese armies into the battle against the free nations. By this act they have shown that they are now willing to push the world to the brink of a general war to get what they want. This is the real meaning of the events that have been taking place in Korea.

That is why we are in such grave danger. The future of civilization depends on what we do—on what we do now, and in the months ahead. We have the strength and we have the courage to overcome the danger that threatens our country. We must act calmly and wisely and resolutely. Here are the things we must do:

. . .

[Truman outlines his policies to build up the armed forces, to impose price controls, and to stabilize wages. An office of Defense Mobilization will be established.]

All of us will have to pay more taxes and do without things we like. Think of this, not as a sacrifice, but as an opportunity, an opportunity to defend the best kind of life that men have ever devised on this earth. . . . Because of all these things I have been talking with you about, I will issue a proclamation tomorrow morning declaring that a national emergency exists. This will call upon every citizen to put aside his personal interests for the good of the country. All our energies must be devoted to the tasks ahead of us. No nation has ever had a greater responsibility than ours has at this moment. We must remember that we are the leaders of the free world. We must understand that we cannot achieve peace by ourselves, but only by cooperating with other free nations and with the men and women who love freedom everywhere.

. . .

The American people have always met danger with courage and determination. I am confident we will do that now, and with God's help we shall keep our freedom.

CASE 2   JOHNSON AND VIETNAM (SPEECH OF AUGUST 4, 1964)

As President and Commander in Chief, it is my duty to the American people to report that renewed hostile actions against United States ships on the high seas in the Gulf of Tonkin have today required me to order the military forces of the United States to take action in reply.

. . . The performance of commanders and crews in this engagement is in the highest tradition of the United States Navy. But repeated acts of violence against the Armed Forces of the United States must be met not only with alert defense, but with positive reply. That reply is being given as I speak to you tonight. Air action is now in execution against gunboats and certain supporting facilities in North Viet-Nam which have been used in these hostile operations.

In the larger sense this new act of aggression, aimed directly at our own forces, again brings home to all of us in the United States the importance of the struggle for peace and security in southeast Asia. Aggression by terror against the peaceful villagers of South Viet-Nam has now been joined by open aggression on the high seas against the United States of America.

The determination of all Americans to carry out our full commitment to the people and to the government of South Viet-Nam will be redoubled by this outrage. Yet our response, for the present, will be limited and fitting. We Americans know, although others appear to forget, the risks of spreading conflict. We still seek no wider war.

. . . I have today met with the leaders of both parties in the Congress of the United States and I have informed them that I shall immediately request the Congress to pass a resolution making it clear that our Government is united in its determination to take all necessary measures in support of freedom and in defense of peace in southeast Asia. . . .

It is a solemn responsibility to have to order even limited military action by forces whose overall

Smaller short-term gains and losses are seen in the polls as presidents make goodwill trips abroad or participate in international peace talks (the polls gain), a cabinet shake-up occurs or other conflict surfaces in the administration (the polls fall), or as unemployment rates rise or fall. Major addresses to the nation usually, although not always, cause a short-term gain. There are, however, only so many trips one can take or major speeches to make. While presidents can exert some control over the polls by these highly visible symbolic activities, they cannot alter the major trends in pop-

strength is as vast and as awesome as those of the United States of America, but it is my considered conviction, shared throughout your Government, that firmness in the right is indispensable today for peace; that firmness will always be measured. Its mission is peace.

CASE 3   REAGAN AND GRENADA (EXCERPTS FROM SPEECH OF OCTOBER 27, 1983)

. . .

These small, peaceful nations needed our help. Three of them don't have armies at all, and the others have very limited forces. The legitimacy of their request, plus my own concerns for our citizens, dictated my decision. I believe our government has a responsibility to go to the aid of its citizens if their right to life and liberty is threatened. The nightmare of our hostages in Iran must never be repeated.... We had to assume that several hundred Cubans working on the airport could be military reserves. Well, as it turned out, the number was much larger, and they were a military force. Six hundred of them have been taken prisoner, and we have discovered a complete base with weapons and communication equipment, which makes it clear a Cuban occupation of the island had been planned.... Grenada, we were told, was a friendly island paradise for tourism. Well, it wasn't. It was a Soviet-Cuban colony, being readied as a major military bastion to export terror and undermine democracy. We got there just in time.

I can't say enough in praise of our military—Army rangers and paratroopers, Navy, Marine, and Air Force personnel—those who planned a brilliant campaign and those who carried it out. Almost instantly, our military seized two airports, secured the campus where most of our students were, and are now in the mopping-up phase.

. . .

[Reagan tells the story of a dying Marine.] That marine and all those others like him, living and dead, have been faithful to their ideals. They've given willingly of themselves so that a nearly defenseless people in a region of great strategic importance to the free world will have a chance someday to live lives free of murder and mayhem and terrorism. I think that young marine and all of his comrades have given every one of us something to live up to.

They were not afraid to stand up for their country or, no matter how difficult and slow the journey might be, to give to others that last, best hope of a better future. We cannot and will not dishonor them now and the sacrifices they've made by failing to remain as faithful to the cause of freedom and the pursuit of peace as they have been.

. . .

God bless you, and God bless America.

ularity in their administrations. No trips or speeches halted the steady fall in Nixon's popularity, which continued until he resigned.

There are, then, two broad categories of influence on presidential public support. The first, common to all presidents, includes factors over which they have only limited control. They cannot control the growing disillusionment of hopes aroused by being elected. They cannot stop the clock. Only within limits can they influence the economy, shaped as it is by international processes and other American actors in the public and private sector.

They can emphasize or downplay international crises, but this effect is also limited by the international setting and has unpredictable long-term effects. Quick decisive action, as in the sending of troops to an international trouble spot, gains short-term support; but when the troops stay and are involved in a long, unsuccessful engagement, the drop in support far outweighs the previous short-term gain. The second category includes factors peculiar to a single administration, which presidents have more control over and which they are held responsible for. Some are major in impact and duration—the conduct of a war, a major scandal. Others, easily manipulated and largely symbolic, are short in duration and do not alter the other major trends.

The President and the Media

The public sees only what presidents appear to be doing, as reported through the news media. To understand the public presidency more fully, it is necessary to examine how presidents use the press and how the press treats presidents. ("Press" can be used here, as elsewhere, to include all news media—print, visual, and audio). Certainly, the relationship between presidents and the press has long been a stormy one. Journalists complain of news management and censorship, of press secretaries who are not credible, and of presidents who hide. Presidents for their part complain that the press is biased against them and that they are particularly badly treated in comparison with their predecessors. However, both presidents and the press need each other, and organizations have developed on both sides to accommodate and work daily with each other.

Reciprocal Needs.   To maintain their popularity and political reputation, presidents need the press. The media provide the link between the White House and the public, but journalists read and watch each other, too, and communicate with other political people. It follows that press reaction is a major preoccupation with White House officials and that a large part of the work of the White House Office is public relations.

The White House Office includes such separate units as the West Wing Press Office, which handles regular contact with reporters; the Office of Media Liaison, which deals with media based outside of Washington and with ethnic, regional, and other specialized publications; a News Summary Staff, which keeps presidents informed of the coverage they are receiving; and the White House Photo Office, which provides the White House's own pictures for distribution. It includes media advisers who assist on makeup and camera techniques. The First Lady's office has its own media consultants and public relations people; and the vice-president's office, with a total staff of about seventy, includes about thirty people handling press relations.

At the center of all this activity is the president's press secretary. The press secretary's office has its own staff and organization support. To be successful, press secretaries must be able to present the president effectively to the press, consult daily with top advisers, and be prepared for unexpected and undesired questions. They must also maintain credibility with reporters. Credibility involves both the appearance of honesty and frankness and the sense that they have access to and the respect of the senior White House officials. If they fail in either criterion, the press will give little credence to what they say. Finally, they must be able to communicate the media's needs to the White House, arrange interviews with senior staff members, hold background and informal briefings, and see to other accommodations. Johnson's press secretaries, for example, tried to convince him to issue advance information on his travel plans. When he refused, they provided it anyway and had it erased from the briefing record so that Johnson wouldn't see it.

This activity needs to be seen in the context of all the other public relations being carried on in Washington. Departments and agencies have their own press secretaries and their own large public relations staffs. Members of Congress devote extensive time and resources to maintaining communication with their constituents and key interest group representatives. They provide regular mailings to constituents, maintain home offices, make regular visits home, and provide news releases to local media. As Michael Grossman and Martha Kumar comment, the president must compete with the "advantages possessed by Congress, the bureaucracy, and interest groups, all of whom have better channels to communicate with their own group members or with particular segments of the public than does the president."[23] Presidents must try to hold their own in a town where public relations is serious political business.

On the other hand, the press needs the White House too. They need access to the president (the number one celebrity in the country) and daily briefings to report the national news. The national news typically is a White House story. In this sense, then, the press depends on the services of the White House to carry on their business. The White House is in a *monopolistic* position. Daily briefings provide the core of the day's news, information about appointments and resignations, decisions to sign or not to sign bills, future travel plans, and the White House reaction to events and issues. Background briefings and off-the-record interviews with "spokesmen" and "sources" are sought as the only way to get additional information. Background briefings help the White House, of course, by allowing information to be conveyed without the same responsibility as a quoted interview demands. Reporters need the White House to arrange schedules and transportation for presidential trips and to supply photographs and photo opportunities. Given the monopoly, presidents can set any rules they choose, as Ronald Reagan did when he prohibited questions from reporters during the photography sessions. In all of these cases, the White House can make sure that the information that is so highly valued shows the president in the most favorable way.

[23]Michael B. Grossman and Martha Kumar, *Portraying the President* (Baltimore: Johns Hopkins University Press, 1981).

James Fallows points out that the main news coverage of the day will tend to be that defined by the White House. He tells how during the Carter years the appointments staff would prepare weekly summaries of the president's schedule, listing for each day what the likely "news event" would be. Their predictions almost always came true.[24] The White House was not only predicting the news, it was shaping what the news would be.

The News Conference.   The news conference is often overrated as a meeting point between the presidency and the press. It is certainly good theatre—the president is on the spot and must field a range of questions from reporters on subjects of their choosing. Nevertheless, presidents do not like them and have developed other ways of reaching the public. And reporters agree that the conference is more stagecraft than substance, with control seldom out of the presidents' hands. One study summarizes: "The President decides when to hold a conference, how much notice reporters will be given, who will ask the questions, and what the answers will be."[25]

While most presidents since Theodore Roosevelt have met reporters for question-and-answer sessions, the modern press conference—with a formal meeting and all information on the record—can be traced to the Truman administration. Eisenhower added television filming, and Kennedy added live television coverage. The presidents after Kennedy, however, used the conference less than their predecessors and experimented with alternative techniques. Johnson, for example, would call meetings without notice, some on Saturday mornings, for informal walks around the White House grounds. Ford ruled against follow-up questions, a practice increasingly followed by his successors. It is difficult even to get a count of the number of press conferences held by the various presidents since they count them differently. Ford counted press conferences as including meetings at campaign stops and other conversations with reporters outside Washington. Omitting these informal meetings, Ford held fourteen conferences in his thirty months in office, rather than thirty-nine. Nixon, like Ford, held about one formal press conference every two months, although he steadily decreased their frequency through his first term. In fact, as Exhibit 8.5 shows, presidents from Nixon to Reagan have tended to use press conferences less than previous presidents.[26]

[24]James Fallows, "The President and the Press," in *The Presidency and the Political System, op. cit.,* p. 277.

[25]Grossman and Kumar, p. 244. See also Jarol B. Manheim, "The Honeymoon's Over: The News Conference and the Development of Presidential Style," *Journal of Politics,* 41 (1979), pp. 63–74.

[26]See Grossman and Kumar, *op. cit.,* pp. 245–46; and Jarol B. Manheim and William W. Lammers, "The News Conference and Presidential Leadership of Public Opinion," *Presidential Studies Quarterly,* 11 (1981), p. 61.

EXHIBIT 8.5	PRESIDENT	AVERAGE NUMBER OF CONFERENCES PER YEAR
The Decline of the News Conference	Truman	40
	Eisenhower I	25
	Eisenhower II	24
	Kennedy	22
	Johnson[a]	26
	Nixon I	8
	Nixon II	5
	Ford	19
	Carter	15
	Reagan I	6

[a]Johnson's conferences are counted from November 1963 through 1968.

Source: Gary King and Lyn Ragsdale, *The Elusive Executive* (Washington, D.C.: CQ Press, 1988), p. 268.

Although the number of press conferences has declined, other kinds of public activity have increased. Nixon held relatively few press conferences, but he appeared more often on prime-time television during his first eighteen months in office than did his three predecessors combined in a comparable period. Carter experimented with "town meetings" held in various locales around the country, and Reagan gave weekly radio talks to the American people. Presidents show an increase in recent years in the total number of speeches, the number of days spent on travel, and the number of public appearances. While the frequency of major addresses to the nation has remained stable, the number of minor addresses, given to specialized audiences and not nationally transmitted, has increased greatly. Minor addresses became more frequent in the Eisenhower years and continued to increase through the Reagan administration.[27] Presidents may try to adapt the news conference to their own purposes, but they can select other ways of reaching the public as well.

The Question of News Bias.   All the stagecraft in the White House cannot stop an independent press from criticizing the president or concentrating on embarrassing stories. What kind of stories are reported in the national news, and can a positive or negative bias be identified? A study by Grossman and Kumar gives some answers to these questions, based on a content analysis of three news sources: *The New York Times, Time* magazine, and the CBS evening news. The two print sources were analyzed for 1953–1978 and the three sources together for 1968–1978.

[27]Kernell, "The Presidency and the People," *op. cit.,* p. 242. See also Lammers, "Presidential Attention Focusing Activities," in *The President and the Public, op. cit.,* pp. 154–57; and Edwards, *The Public Presidency, op. cit.*

First, the treatment was consistent across the three news sources: it did not vary with the different editorial judgments. Second, the tone was predominantly positive, averaging about two positive stories to every one negative and one neutral story. The negative stories increased during the Johnson and Nixon years, reaching the point during Watergate where the negative stories outnumbered the positive in the three news sources. Positive coverage increased again in the Ford and Carter years, but did not return to the levels found in the Eisenhower and Kennedy administrations. The positive-to-negative ratio did not change with the party of the president in the White House.[28] The pictures accompanying the stories were even more positive. So, while all presidents complain of a press bias against them, the results suggest that their treatment is favorable overall.

Grossman and Kumar did find some differences in coverage and tone. For a third important finding, press treatment changed across the four-year electoral cycle. The greatest number of stories and the greatest number of favorable stories appeared during the first year, what is popularly called the "honeymoon" period. The lowest number of stories and the highest number of negative stories appeared in the final year.[29] Fourth, press treatment differed with the kind of story reported. News about the president's personal life tended to be positive, while stories about relations with Congress and the administration were more negative. The two print sources reported more personal news than coverage of Congress and the administration, while CBS News showed about even proportions.[30] Thus, to the extent that journalists carry on the cult of the presidency, emphasizing personality and downplaying the conflicts with Congress and within the administration, they contribute to a positive portrayal. It is therefore in the president's interest, too, to encourage the cult and play down interaction with other people in the government.

Other kinds of emphasis need to be considered, however. James Fallows argues that reporters shy away from the substance of government, looking to areas they feel more confident in writing about. He cites four:

- scandal or any hint of scandal
- dissension or rivalry in the administration
- the "gaffe," or blunder, made by presidents or high administration officials
- politics in its narrowest sense, as similar to sports handicapping

These can create negative impressions in ways not tapped by the content analysis. In another way, too, media coverage works to a president's disadvantage. Journalists focus on the new and the immediate, ignoring history and past administrations. This makes the current incumbent seem less

---

[28]Grossman and Kumar, *op. cit.,* esp. pp. 256–58.
[29]*Ibid.,* pp. 259–63.
[30]*Ibid.,* p. 269.

competent when he cannot solve long-standing, possibly unsolvable, problems.[31]

Still, through their nomination and election, presidents have already shown that they can deal with the media and communicate to the public. In fact, they may have been selected *because* they were better able to do these things than their competitors. The selection process ensures that the person in the White House will be a very skilled player in the continuing contest between the presidency and the press.

PRESIDENTS AND POLICY-MAKING

Just as *executive* does not mean *chief executive, policy* does not mean *presidential policy.* Presidents are very influential in some policies and totally uninvolved in others. Much of American government policy is made far from presidential attention—in the bureaucracy, courts, and committee rooms of Congress. Still, presidents can select the policies they are interested in and work for their success. They will achieve some of the things they set out to do. This in itself is a substantial power. This section looks at how presidents select issues and how successful they are in winning congressional support. It is then possible to see more clearly the range and limits of presidential policy-making.

Setting the Agenda

Presidents are known as the nation's priority setters. Some people, in fact, say that priority setting is what presidents do best. They focus the nation's attention on one or two issues, dramatize them in speeches to the American people, and require Congress to treat these issues seriously in making legislation. The Reagan administration focused on budget cutting, tax reform, policy toward Latin America, and an arms-limitation treaty with the Soviets. These issues became the featured news stories of the 1980s and came to dominate the congressional agenda too. Of course, presidents must react to external crises and the problems that continue from one administration to the next. Reagan and Carter had to give high priority to the nation's response to terrorism when American citizens were taken hostage by Iranian terrorists. Johnson's own priorities for domestic welfare programs were submerged by the ongoing crisis in Vietnam. While political realities limit what the agenda will be, presidents still can choose among many issues.

From all of the possible issues, how is the president's agenda determined? Interviews with the presidential aides themselves provide an insight into the agenda-setting process. Presidents and their staffs develop a consensus on the most important issues, *concentrating on one or two top issues*

---

[31]Fallows, *op. cit.,* pp. 272–76.

PRESIDENT	PROGRAM	PERCENT OF STAFF MENTIONING
Kennedy	Aid to Education	91
	Medicare	77
Johnson	Poverty	86
	Civil Rights	79
	Medicare	64
Nixon	Welfare Reform	75
	Revenue Sharing	65
Ford	Energy	79
	Inflation	50
Carter	Energy	84
	Inflation	63
	Welfare Reform	59

White House staff members were asked to name the most important domestic programs of their respective administrations. Respondents could give more than one reply. Programs mentioned by more than half of the staff are included in the table.

Source: Paul C. Light, *The President's Agenda* (Baltimore: Johns Hopkins University Press, 1982), p. 70.

during the term. "Everything else," said one adviser, "is icing on the cake."[32] Presidents have a wish list and a must list. The wish list is expressed in State of the Union messages and other speeches. But the must list, which is much shorter, consists of the one or two issues that will be given priority. The aides know what these issues are and so do the members of Congress. The top items on the domestic agenda in recent administrations, as identified by the advisers, are shown in Exhibit 8.6.

Where do the ideas come from? Presidents can bring their own ideas with them, as developed over the campaign and sponsored by the party and interest groups that have helped to elect them. They can draw advisers from outside the government—from business, universities, and other professions. Harvard's Henry Kissinger first came to the Nixon White House as National Security Adviser and stayed to be Nixon's (and Ford's) Secretary of State. Reagan hired Georgetown professor Jeane Kirkpatrick, a specialist in Latin American affairs. Contrary to the conventional wisdom, however, the aides suggest that *most issues enter the agenda from outside the White House.* Advisers cited Congress first as the source of ideas, then external events, and then bureaucratic proposals. Ideas coming from the staff, the campaign, the party, or the presidents themselves were cited less frequently.[33] In a turnabout of the usual notion—that the president proposes and Congress disposes—the advisers saw Congress as the primary hunting ground for ideas that could be remodeled as presidential programs. Why?

[32]Light, *op. cit.,* p. 71.
[33]*Ibid.,* p. 86.

Primarily, because support already existed for these programs, and some of the political wrinkles had been ironed out. The White House could adopt the programs as its own, revise them to its liking, and send them back to Congress with some assurance of success!

Some agenda items, of course, come from within the White House: Johnson's poverty program, Nixon's welfare reform, Reagan's tax and budget cuts in his first two years in office. Nevertheless, pressures of time require that alternatives be limited and that the sooner an item can be agreed on, the greater its chance for success. Presidents must spend their resources of power and popularity wisely; in facing Congress and the ever-watchful media, they need to maintain a reputation for winning. Hence, it is not surprising that old products will be put in new packages and issued from the White House, if these products have the greatest chance of success.

Presidents are limited in time, number of priorities, and the need to devise programs with a realistic chance of success in Congress. They have no blank slate to write America's future on. But they can make choices, and these choices can make a difference to the country and the world—this is the president's agenda-setting power.

Winning Support in Congress

With an agenda in hand, presidents must win support for their programs in Congress. That is not an easy task, as Chapter Seven makes clear. White House bills, like all other bills, must make their way through committees and subcommittees. They can be amended, defeated, or rewritten. Presidents, however, have powers of their own in this continuing battle. A large White House staff, the Office of Congressional Liaison, is devoted to following the bills through Congress and persuading members to adopt the president's position. Presidents can do their own persuading, inviting party members or key committee members to the White House. Most of all, presidents can address the American people directly, asking them to tell Congress what should be done.

Presidential success in Congress is typically calculated on the basis of the number of votes taken in Congress on which the president has announced a position. When Congress votes with the president's position, this is counted as a presidential success. Students should note that this is only one possible measure of support for presidential programs. It does not distinguish the must list from the wish list: presidents take positions on more than one hundred votes a year, but work hard for only one or two; nor does it distinguish bills close to the White House position from those that may have been drastically changed in the congressional process. Presidents might support a bill because it is the best they are going to get. Finally, this measure concentrates on the rate of success and ignores the ambitiousness of a program. Some presidents, Nixon and Ford for example, have taken positions on far fewer bills than other presidents do.

EXHIBIT 8.7   Presidential Success on Votes in Congress

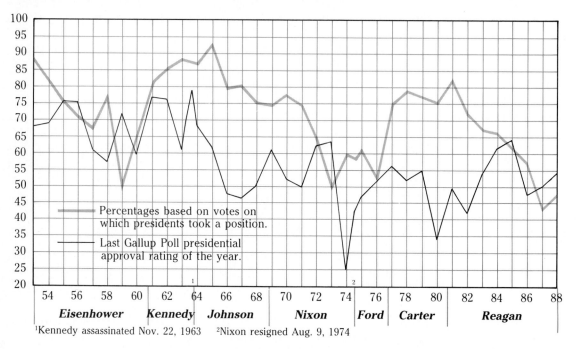

Source: *Congressional Quarterly Weekly Report,* January 7, 1989, p. 5.

Nevertheless, the measure does allow us to compare presidents and see the conditions most likely to ensure their success. Exhibit 8.7 shows the success rates of presidents from Eisenhower to Reagan. Immediately apparent is one political reality the White House must face: *success is highest for presidents facing congresses controlled by their own party.* Democratic presidents, all of whom faced Democratic congresses, enjoyed a higher success rate on the average than did Republican presidents Nixon and Ford, who also had to face Democratic congresses. Eisenhower and Reagan enjoyed more support in their first terms than they did later when the Democrats controlled both houses.

The importance of the parties for presidential programs can be seen in other ways as well. From the Eisenhower to the Reagan years, House and Senate Democrats supported Democratic presidents on the average about 65 percent of the time and Republican presidents about 45 percent. For Republicans, the situation was reversed. House and Senate Republicans supported Democratic presidents about 43 percent of the time and Republican presidents 65 percent.[34] Members of Congress vote with their party on

[34]George C. Edwards, III, *Presidential Influence in Congress* (San Francisco: Freeman, 1980). p. 162. The pattern holds for the Reagan years, although the Democrats gave Reagan only about 40 percent support.

EXHIBIT 8.8	PRESIDENT AND PARTY		PERCENT OF VICTORIES	SAME OR DIVIDED CONTROL
	Kennedy	D	84.6	Same
Presidential Victories on Votes in Congress	Johnson	D	82.6	Same
	Eisenhower I	R	79.0	Same (two years) Divided (two years)
	Carter	D	76.4	Same
	Reagan I	R	71.0	Divided[a]
	Nixon	R	67.2	Divided
	Eisenhower II	R	65.0	Divided
	Ford	R	57.6	Divided
	Reagan II	R	54.0	Divided[a]

[a]Reagan had a same-party Senate and a divided-party House through his first term and through the first two years of his second term.

Source: Based on the number of House and Senate roll calls on which the president took a position, as compiled from data in *Congressional Quarterly Almanac,* various years.

roll calls for many reasons, as Chapter Seven makes clear. They may be representing their states and districts, following congressional leaders, or reflecting their own belief in the party positions. They need not be thinking about the president. But whatever the motive, the effect is clear: presidents must look to their fellow partisans for the bulk of their legislative support.

The parties are not the only influence affecting the success of presidential programs, as Exhibit 8.7 shows. Look at the variation within each president's term and between presidents of the same party. Carter had more Democrats in the House than Kennedy did, but received less support. Success in Congress is affected by the president's popularity in the country. Members of Congress, listening to public opinion, appear less willing to oppose a very popular president and more willing to oppose an unpopular one. Since Congress has its own timetable for legislation (which does not follow the public opinion polls), no dramatic relationship should be expected. Nevertheless, some influence can be seen.[35] Overall, *presidents are helped when their party is in the majority in the House and Senate and when their popularity in the country is high.* (See Exhibit 8.8.)

Presidents cannot always control their popularity with the public and they cannot shape the membership of Congress either—most members win elections and reelections on their own. This means that presidents do not control the two influences most critical to the passage of their programs. Presidents are judged in part by their legislative success, but some presidents have a better chance at that success than others.

[35]*Ibid.* See also Jon R. Bond and Richard Fleisher, "The Limits of Presidential Popularity as a Source of Influence in the U.S. House," *Legislative Studies Quarterly,* 5 (1980), pp. 69–78; Charles W. Ostrom, Jr. and Dennis M. Simon, "Promise and Performance: A Dynamic Model of Presidential Popularity," *American Political Science Review,* 79 (1985), pp. 334–58.

The Two Presidencies. Is Congress more likely to support a president on foreign policy issues than on domestic policy issues? Are there "two presidencies," as many people believe, one for domestic policy and one for foreign policy? In a famous essay, Aaron Wildavsky argued **the two-presidencies thesis.** He pointed out the president's greater control of foreign policy information compared to Congress, and the public's relatively low interest in foreign affairs. He found, indeed, for one period of American history (1948–1964) that Congress was more likely to support presidents on foreign policy issues than on domestic policy issues.[36]

With the passage of time, however, the two-presidencies thesis was questioned. The Vietnam War made Americans and Congress more critical of foreign policy-making. The public no longer had a low interest in foreign affairs. A study comparing Wildavsky's results with a later time period (1965–1975) found little difference in the two policy areas. Presidents were only slightly more successful in foreign policy issues than those in domestic policy.[37] Another study cast even more doubt on the original argument. Looking only at key votes (the most important votes being taken in Congress), the study showed no difference in support for foreign and domestic policy in either time period.[38] If there is controversy on a bill, Congress will make its own decisions. On balance, the evidence suggests that congressional support does not vary with the policy area—there are not two presidencies, but only one.

Vetoes and Overrides. While Congress can vote down a president's bill, presidents can also stop a congressional proposal through the constitutional power of the veto. (See Exhibit 8.9.) Vetoes can be direct or indirect. A **direct veto** automatically nullifies the legislation unless it is overridden by a two-thirds vote in the House and the Senate. Presidents formally return the bill to Congress with a message stating their objections. An **indirect veto**, or pocket veto, has the same effect; presidents simply do not sign a bill received in the last ten days of a session, thereby killing the legislation. Even the threat of a veto is often sufficient to get Congress to change its mind, withdrawing the legislation or modifying it more to presidential liking. Historically, fewer than ten percent of the direct vetoes have been overridden by Congress, so Congress cannot take the threat of a veto lightly.

Presidents cannot treat vetoes lightly either. A veto indicates conflict with Congress and casts doubt on the president's power of persuasion. Popular presidents with strong party majorities in Congress rarely veto a bill,

---

[36]Aaron Wildavsky, "The Two Presidencies," *Trans-Action,* December, 1966, pp. 7–14.

[37]Lance T. LeLoup and Steven A. Shull, "Congress Versus the Executive: The Two Presidencies Reconsidered," *Social Science Quarterly,* 59 (1979), pp. 704–19.

[38]Lee Sigelman, "A Reassessment of the Two Presidencies Thesis," *Journal of Politics,* 41 (1979), pp. 1195–1205. Key votes have been defined by *Congressional Quarterly,* and can be found in yearly volumes of *Congressional Quarterly Almanac.*

	OPTION	PROCEDURE	RESULT
EXHIBIT 8.9	Sign bill	Affix signature within ten days of receipt	Bill is law
A President's Options When a Bill Is Passed	Do not sign	Let bill remain on desk for more than ten days	Bill is law
	Veto bill	Refuse to sign and return bill to Congress	If two-thirds vote to override in both House and Senate, bill is law If two-thirds do not vote to override, bill dies
	Use pocket veto	Hold a bill submitted with fewer than ten days left in the session	Bill dies

whereas those presidents facing hostile and active congresses might not veto for fear it would be overridden. (A **veto override** cancels the president's veto, thus making the bill become a law.) Vetoes and overrides are exceptions to the more normal, and less visible, conflict between the branches.

The number of vetoes and overrides has varied greatly across the years. George Washington vetoed two bills, but eight of the presidents from Adams through Taylor never used the veto. The veto leaders were Grover Cleveland and Franklin Roosevelt. Cleveland vetoed on the average one bill out of six, and Roosevelt vetoed one out of twelve. Among recent presidents, Truman, Eisenhower, and Ford used the veto most often; the other presidents, from Kennedy to Reagan, used it more sparingly. The overrides have varied too. Seven presidents had none of their vetoes overturned, whereas two—Pierce and Andrew Johnson—had a majority of vetoes overturned. Nixon, Ford, and Reagan had twenty percent or more of their vetoes overturned, while Eisenhower had very few. (See Exhibit 8.10.)

There are four types of veto patterns that can help to characterize the relations between the president and Congress.[39] Each type includes historical and recent examples:

Type 1 Cooperative and Successful (low in vetoes, low in overrides)
Examples: Lincoln, Kennedy, Lyndon Johnson

Type 2 Conflictual and Successful (high in vetoes, low in overrides)
Examples: Cleveland, Franklin Roosevelt, Truman

Type 3 Cooperative and Unsuccessful (low in vetoes, high in overrides)
Examples: Arthur, Nixon, Reagan

[39]Jong R. Lee, "Presidential Vetoes from Washington to Nixon," *Journal of Politics,* 37 (1975), pp. 522–46, develops the classification scheme. The authors have added the most recent examples.

EXHIBIT 8.10	**PRESIDENT**	**YEARS IN OFFICE***	**NUMBER OF VETOES**	**NUMBER PER YEAR**	**NUMBER OF OVERRIDES**	**PERCENT OF OVERRIDES**

PRESIDENT	**YEARS IN OFFICE***	**NUMBER OF VETOES**	**NUMBER PER YEAR**	**NUMBER OF OVERRIDES**	**PERCENT OF OVERRIDES**
Truman	7.5	180	24.0	12	7
Eisenhower	8.0	73	9.1	2	3
Kennedy	3.0	12	4.0	0	0
Johnson	5.0	16	3.2	0	0
Nixon	5.5	24	4.4	5	21
Ford	2.5	48	19.2	12	25
Carter	4.0	13	3.3	2	15
Reagan (first six years)	6.0	29	4.8	6	21

Direct Vetoes and Overrides, 1945–1986

*Half years are counted for Truman in 1945 and Nixon and Ford in 1974.

Source: Harold W. Stanley and Richard G. Niemi, *Vital Statistics on American Politics* (Washington, D.C.: CQ Press, 1988), p. 223.

Type 4   Conflictual and Unsuccessful (high in vetoes, high in overrides)
       Examples: Andrew Johnson, Ford

The pattern can change across a president's term. Wilson, for example, began with a Type 1 pattern, moved to a Type 3 after the midterm election of his first term, and ended the final years of his second term with a Type 4.[40]

For the historical and the modern cases, the party in control of Congress and the president's popularity help to explain the four types. The same factors already shown to affect congressional support also affect vetoes and overrides. Presidents are more likely to veto when they face congresses of the opposing party and when their electoral popularity is high (as seen from the results of their last election). Congress is more likely to override with presidents of the opposing party, in congresses after the midterm election, and in times of economic crisis or low military commitment. These are times when the president's popularity might well be low. Overrides are also affected by the size of the vote that was recorded in Congress when the bill was first passed. The larger the vote margin, the less likely the chance of a veto. Congressional leaders, then, who fear a veto to come are advised to build as strong a majority as possible on the first vote.[41]

Among the modern presidents, Lyndon Johnson had the greatest number of Democrats in Congress and the lowest number of vetoes. Ford

[40]*Ibid.*, p. 529.

[41]*Ibid.* and see David W. Rohde and Dennis M. Simon, "Presidential Vetoes and Congressional Response," *American Journal of Political Science,* 29 (1985), pp. 397–427.

had the smallest number of Republicans in Congress and very high vetoes and overrides. Republican presidents Nixon and Reagan were also high in overrides. With low levels of support in the public and in Congress, vetoes become more common, and so does the likelihood that the veto will fail.

The President as Policymaker

The American government has many policymakers. Presidents are actively involved in some foreign policy issues—those requiring military action and those affecting a few key areas of American interests around the globe. The remainder of policy will be carried on by Congress, the Departments of State and Defense, and other agencies. Latin American policy became a chief priority in the Kennedy and Reagan administrations, but was given lower priority by other presidents. In domestic policy, too, the role of the president varies greatly (as shall be explored in Chapter Eleven). Presidents set overall budget guidelines and make specific economic proposals. They let Congress know the must list for the domestic agenda. The rest of policy will be formulated by the other policymakers. Energy policy was raised to the White House in the Ford and Carter years; in other years it returned to the departments and the congressional committees. In addition, formulating a policy is not the same as enacting one. Presidential interest does not ensure presidential success.

So, should the president be given the names found so often in civics textbooks, such as Chief Legislator, Manager of the Economy, Guardian of the Nation's Welfare, Leader of the Free World, and Chief Foreign Policy Maker? These names were invented in the 1950s and have been carried on to the present day.[42] Many economists would say that the economy is not "manageable"—it can only be shifted and adjusted in limited ways. Congress, the real chief legislator, supports the president slightly more than fifty percent of the time. These labels are not *descriptions* of the office, but rather expectations, or wishes, about it. They are part of the cult of the presidency with its exaggerated views of the office.

To summarize, presidents can choose a few policies to work on with some likelihood of success. They are limited in the number of policies they can commit their resources to and by the steady ticking of the political clock. They are limited also by the party composition in Congress and the factors affecting their popularity over which they have only partial control. Nevertheless, they can choose and achieve some success. The flow of energy or welfare, relations with China or Latin America—all of these can be changed by the end of a president's term. Few other Americans could claim to do as much.

[42]They appear first in the work of Edward S. Corwin. See *The President: Office and Powers*, 4th ed. (New York: New York University Press, 1957). See also Clinton Rossiter, *The American Presidency*, 2nd ed. (New York: Harcourt, 1960).

J. Danforth Quayle is sworn in as vice-president as Justice Sandra Day O'Connor presides.

THE VICE-PRESIDENCY AND SUCCESSION

The vice-presidency is the second highest elective office in American government. It has supplied one-third of all presidents and more than one-third of the twentieth-century presidents. Vice-presidential candidates, as shown in Chapter Five, now become leading contenders for future presidential nominations: Humphrey, Mondale, Dole, and Bush are examples. Even Spiro Agnew, before the scandal that led to his resignation from office, was considered the front-runner for the presidential nomination of 1976. So if the office of president is considered important, it is necessary to look to the office from which so many presidents are drawn. The list of American vice-presidents is given in Exhibit 8.11.

Job Description: Nothing and Everything

John Adams, the first vice-president, gave a good description of the job. "I am nothing," he said, "but I may be everything." Vice-presidents are the presidents' understudies, the next in line in succession. Their job is to be ready, at presidential death or disability, to assume the duties of that higher office. As Article II of the Constitution states,

> In case of the Removal of the President from Office, or of his Death, Resignation, or Inability to discharge the Powers and Duties of the said Office, the Same shall devolve on the Vice-President.

The problem is that while they are waiting for the president to die, they have little of their own work to do. Benjamin Franklin opposed the idea of

EXHIBIT 8.11	The Vice-Presidents of the United States

VICE-PRESIDENT	STATE	PARTY	YEAR OF FIRST ELECTION	PRESIDENT	AGE	POLITICAL EXPERIENCE
Adams	Mass.	Fed.	1789	Washington, Va.	53	—
Jefferson	Va.	Dem.-Rep.	1796	Adams, Mass.	53	Cong.
Burr	N.Y.	Dem.-Rep.	1800	Jefferson, Va.	45	Gov.
Clinton	N.Y.	Dem.-Rep.	1804	Jefferson, Va.	66	Gov.
Gerry	Mass.	Dem.-Rep.	1812	Madison, Va.	68	Gov.
Tompkins	N.Y.	Dem.-Rep.	1816	Monroe, Va.	42	Gov.
Calhoun	S.C.	Dem.-Rep.	1824	J. Q. Adams, Mass.	42	Cong.
Van Buren	N.Y.	Dem.	1832	Jackson, Tenn.	50	Gov.
R. Johnson	Ken.	Dem.	1836	Van Buren, N.Y.	56	Cong.
Tyler	Va.	Whig	1840	W. Harrison, Ohio	50	Both
Dallas	Pa.	Dem.	1844	Polk, Tenn.	52	None
Fillmore	N.Y.	Whig	1848	Taylor, La.	49	None
King	Ala.	Dem.	1852	Pierce, N.H.	66	Cong.
Breckinridge	Ken.	Dem.	1856	Buchanan, Pa.	36	Cong.
Hamlin	Maine	Rep.	1860	Lincoln, Ill.	51	Both
A. Johnson	Tenn.	Rep.	1864	Lincoln, Ill.	56	Both
Colfax	Ind.	Rep.	1868	Grant, Ill.	46	Cong.
Wilson	Mass.	Rep.	1872	Grant, Ill.	61	Cong.
Wheeler	N.Y.	Rep.	1876	Hayes, Ohio	57	Cong.
Arthur	N.Y.	Rep.	1880	Garfield, Ohio	50	None
Hendricks	Ind.	Dem.	1884	Cleveland, N.Y.	65	Both
Morton	N.Y.	Rep.	1888	Harrison, Ind.	64	Cong.
Stevenson	Ill.	Dem.	1892	Cleveland, N.Y.	57	Cong.
Hobart	N.J.	Rep.	1896	McKinley, Ohio	52	None
T. Roosevelt	N.Y.	Rep.	1900	McKinley, Ohio	42	Gov.
Fairbanks	Ind.	Rep.	1904	Roosevelt, N.Y.	52	Cong.
Sherman	N.Y.	Rep.	1908	Taft, Ohio	53	Cong.
Marshall	Ind.	Dem.	1912	Wilson, N.J.	58	Gov.
Coolidge	Mass.	Rep.	1920	Harding, Ohio	48	Gov.
Dawes	Ill.	Rep.	1924	Coolidge, Mass.	59	None
Curtis	Kan.	Rep.	1928	Hoover, Calif.	69	Cong.
Garner	Tex.	Dem.	1932	F. Roosevelt, N.Y.	64	Cong.
Wallace	Iowa	Dem.	1940	F. Roosevelt, N.Y.	52	None
Truman	Mo.	Dem.	1944	F. Roosevelt, N.Y.	60	Cong.
Barkley	Ken.	Dem.	1948	Truman, Mo.	71	Cong.
Nixon	Calif.	Rep.	1952	Eisenhower, Kan.	40	Cong.
L. Johnson	Texas	Dem.	1960	Kennedy, Mass.	52	Cong.
Humphrey	Minn.	Dem.	1964	L. Johnson, Tex.	53	Cong.
Agnew	Md.	Rep.	1968	Nixon, Calif.	49	Gov.
Ford[a]	Mich.	Rep.	1973	Nixon, Calif.	61	Cong.
Rockefeller[a]	N.Y.	Rep.	1974	Ford, Mich.	66	Gov.
Mondale	Minn.	Dem.	1976	Carter, Ga.	48	Cong.
Bush	Tex.	Rep.	1980	Reagan, Calif.	55	Cong.
Quayle	Ind.	Rep.	1988	Bush, Tex.	41	Cong.

Note: Age is reported at the time of first election. "Political experience" is reported only for major elective office in Congress or a governorship or both.
[a]Appointed, not elected.

the vice-presidency and said that the holder of the office should be called "His Superfluous Majesty." Daniel Webster refused the vice-presidential nomination saying that he did not propose to be buried until he was already dead, and Theodore Roosevelt, who accepted it, said he was "taking the veil" and considered going back to finish law school to occupy his spare time. While the Constitution makes vice-presidents the president of the Senate, the Senate made clear early in the nineteenth century that it could take care of itself. The Senate elects its own leaders; the vice-president merely presides on formal occasions and casts tie-breaking votes.

Increasingly in the twentieth century, presidents have found uses for their vice-presidents as diplomats, heads of presidential panels, and general errand runners. Vice-presidents have made goodwill tours, attended functions, made speeches, and done things that presidents could not or did not wish to do.[43] Lyndon Johnson's vice-president, Hubert Humphrey, was assigned to speak around the country and explain the Vietnam War. Richard Nixon's vice-president, Spiro Agnew, was used as a critic of dissenters, intellectuals, and the news media. Nixon himself, when he was vice-president under Eisenhower, complained that he was the "Secretary for Catch-all Affairs."[44] George Bush and Walter Mondale were given a variety of jobs by their respective presidents. Mondale commented that he felt Carter had treated him better than any previous president had treated his vice-president, and Bush also was very visible in the Reagan administration.[45] And yet it is clear that the vice-presidential busy work could be easily given to other advisers, cabinet officials, or presidential aides. Further, the work is assigned at the pleasure of the president. "The president gives," said Humphrey, "and the president taketh away." Ultimately, it is the president's work—not the vice-president's—that is performed. Vice-presidents have none of their own work to do.

There have been famous accounts of presidents and vice-presidents, Woodrow Wilson and Thomas Marshall for example, who were not on speaking terms. Few vice-presidents are mentioned at any length in presidential biographies. Humphrey admitted that the only time he saw President Johnson was "when he ran out of people to chew on and raised hell with me."[46] Of all recent presidents, perhaps Kennedy needed the most from Congress in the form of an ambitious legislative program. His vice-president was a past leader of the Senate, widely recognized as a genius in the art of congressional persuasion. Yet, it was Kennedy's aide Larry O'Brien—not the former Senate leader Johnson—who devised the White House strategy that would be used on Capitol Hill. Johnson's name is rarely mentioned in the

[43]See Joel K. Goldstein, *The Modern American Vice Presidency* (Princeton: Princeton University Press, 1982), chaps. 7, 8. Goldstein lists six major vice-presidential roles: special commission chair, special envoy for foreign visits, presidential adviser, legislative liaison worker, party worker, and administration spokesman.

[44]Stephen Hess, *Organizing the Presidency* (Washington, D.C.: Brookings, 1976), p. 169.

[45]Letter, *New York Times,* March 13, 1981.

[46]Cronin, *op. cit.,* p. 225.

accounts of the great legislative battles of the time. The sharpest example of the vice-president's lack of preparation may have occurred with the transition to the Truman presidency. At the time of Franklin Roosevelt's death, Truman did not know of the existence of the atom bomb. Four months later he would need to make a decision about using it on a human population.

The contrast between the vice-president's actual and potential roles has supplied a rich source of American political humor. A Broadway musical of the 1930s, *Of Thee I Sing,* featured a fictitious vice-president by the name of Alexander Throttlebottom. Nobody in the play could remember his name. He spent his time feeding pigeons in the park and trying to find two people to supply references for a library card. Spiro Agnew jokes went the rounds when this unknown governor was first selected as Nixon's vice-president, just as Dan Quayle jokes were inspired by Bush's nominee. All comedy, however, has its very serious side. It must be asked whether people with the energy and talent for the presidency would agree to accept the vice-presidency, thus spending four to eight years of their lives doing nothing, and whether people who are willing to do so make good presidents. Moreover, the nation's comic office is also its symbol and reminder of presidential mortality. As an understudy in the wings, the vice-president is the foreshadow of the president's death. It may not be surprising, then, that presidents have not sought the presence and advice of their vice-presidents more frequently.

Still, the office may be becoming a more serious one. Both Mondale and Bush gained visibility from their years in the office. Bush was considered by the voters to have "experience," as shown in Chapter Six. The vice-presidential nominee is already considered a leading contender for a presidential nomination. So, if their years in the shadow of presidents begin to count as experience, vice-presidents may in fact become the second most important figure in American politics.

Succession

Despite the difficulties of the office, the vice-presidency has been successful in performing one basic function: it has provided an automatic and smooth transition in government at the time of a president's death. But even this feature came not from any constitutional clarity on the subject but from a working out of the tradition over time.

When William Henry Harrison died in 1841 after only one month in office, several questions arose. Would vice-president John Tyler become "acting president" only until a special election was called? If Tyler served the full remainder of the term, would he actually be president or be merely the vice-president serving as acting president? Did he need to take the presidential oath, since he had already taken the vice-presidential one?[47] The

---

[47]Ruth C. Silva, *Presidential Succession* (Ann Arbor: University of Michigan Press, 1951), shows the developing precedent on succession.

Constitution gave no clear answers, saying only that on the death of the president, the powers and duties "shall devolve on the Vice President."

Tyler made two decisions of the most fundamental importance for the office. First, he insisted on taking the presidential oath and asked for the cabinet's support in this decision. Second, he called himself the president of the United States. Fifty-three hours after the death of Harrison, Tyler took the presidential oath and delivered what he called his "inaugural address," saying, "I am called to the high office of president. . .to carry out the principles of the Constitution which I have sworn to protect, preserve and defend."

There was still some confusion. Some members of the press called Tyler "president," others called him "acting president," and others referred to him as "vice-president." The House passed a resolution calling Tyler president, and a Senate resolution followed, after some debate, by a vote of 38 to 8. The precedent gained strength in the next two successions, from Taylor to Fillmore and from Lincoln to Johnson, although Johnson was informed of the assassination in a note addressed to the "vice-president." By the fourth such transition, when Chester Arthur took office, it was considered automatic. Each succeeding vice-president has taken the presidential oath, and each with a steadily decreasing amount of time elapsing after the president's death. Tyler took the oath in fifty-three hours, Taylor on the following day, Coolidge in less than five hours, Truman in two and a half hours, and Lyndon Johnson within two hours. Each has been regarded by the public, by Congress, and by other governments as president of the United States. "Mr. President," Lyndon Johnson was informed, "the president is dead." Finally, in 1967, the Twenty-fifth Amendment spelled out that "the Vice President shall *become President*" (italics added), confirming the point that Tyler had made many years before.

When Garfield was shot, an old New York political crony of the vice-president was heard to gasp, "Good God. Chet Arthur—president of the United States!" The same reaction was heard when the Washington reporters first learned of the news of FDR's death: "Good God—Truman will be president!" The "Good God" in both cases was invoked against the double disaster of a president's death and the prospect of the vice-president becoming president. And yet as the next step in the ritual, the new president takes the oath of office and the Congress, press, and public give their support. The nation rallies around the person they could not imagine in the White House; they "approve of the way the president is doing his job." Throttlebottom is transformed into president of the United States.

The Disability Question

There are other problems of succession beside those of providing a swift and sure transition upon the president's death. The question of disability has emerged several times in American history: during Wilson's long illness, after Eisenhower's heart attack, in the days before Nixon's resignation; and

(Left) Harry S. Truman takes the oath as president in the White House after the death of Franklin D. Roosevelt. (Right) Lyndon B. Johnson is sworn in as president aboard Air Force One following the assassination of John F. Kennedy.

after the assassination attempt on Reagan. Exhibit 8.12 shows lengths of time the nation has been without a functioning president. The Twenty-fifth Amendment, ratified in 1967, attempts to provide a solution. The amendment states that either (1) the president, (2) the vice-president and a majority of the cabinet, or (3) others as Congress shall provide (for example, medical experts) could declare the president disabled. Upon receipt of this declaration in Congress, the vice-president becomes acting president. The president may challenge the claim or declare the disability corrected, but if those bringing the claim in the first place disagree, Congress must come into session within forty-eight hours and decide within the next twenty-one days whether or not the vice-president should continue to act as president. A two-thirds vote in both houses would be required to permit the vice-president to continue. Notice that all of the chief legislative and executive officers would be participating in these decisions.

The problem may not be solved, however, by the passage of an amendment. On the one hand, Americans do not want an incapacitated head of state; but on the other, they certainly do not want the threat of plots against a nonincapacitated president who might be charged with being incapacitated by political rivals in the vice-presidency, Congress, or White House staff. In an additional complication, the amendment assumes that the vice-president would be willing to act. Yet all of the vice-presidents involved in such a situation have shown a great unwillingness to do so. Arthur did not and Marshall did not through all the time that Garfield and Wilson lay uncon-

EXHIBIT 8.12	PRESIDENT	EXTENT OF DISABILITY
Presidents' Disabilities	William Henry Harrison	Bedridden for 7 days before his death
	Zachary Taylor	Bedridden for 5 days before his death
	Abraham Lincoln	Unconscious for 9.5 hours before his death
	James Garfield	Bedridden for 80 days before his death
	William McKinley	Bedridden for 8 days before his death
	Woodrow Wilson	Incapacitated for 280 days from a stroke before announced recovery
	Warren Harding	Incapacitated for 4 days before his death
	Dwight Eisenhower	Incapacitated for 143 days from a heart attack before announced recovery
	Ronald Reagan	Incapacitated for 20 hours after the attempt on his life
	Ronald Reagan	Incapacitated for 8 hours while under anesthesia for surgery

Source: Gary King and Lyn Ragsdale, *The Elusive Executive* (Washington, D.C.: CQ Press, 1988), p. 474.

scious. Nixon assumed only the more peripheral and ceremonial duties during Eisenhower's hospitalization. During the Nixon resignation crisis, Ford kept as much distance as possible from the White House. His loyalty and support of the president were evident throughout. To the extent that there is any precedent at all, vice-presidents do not seem to be encouraged by those around the president—and would be extremely reluctant themselves—to assume an active role in a disability decision. Finally, of course, the amendment assumes that the vice-president, members of Congress, and cabinet officials would *see* when the president was disabled. It does not consider the powerful protective abilities of the White House staff.

Overall, the role of vice-president follows from the characteristics of the presidency. There is no room in a system of checked and ambiguous power for any further sharing: there is no room for a number two. At the same time, there must be a number one, and so Throttlebottom inherits the cult of the presidency with all of its privileges and pressures.

It should now be clear that the power and limits designed for the presidency are very much a present reality. Presidents gain support merely by being in office. They become a symbol of the nation and are seen to be both powerful and good. Nevertheless, they cannot keep bees safe, give us jobs, or solve all the problems of the nation; they are not a universal providence. Thus unrealistic expectations lead to disillusionment—public support falls during the term and along with events over which presidents have only partial control.

The same mix of powers and limits is seen in managing the White House. Formally, the president is head of a vast expert bureaucracy and a large Executive Office. But the potential resources are not all actual resources; officials may not do what the president wants done. Even the loyal advisers offer a mixed blessing. In order to "protect the president," they can screen out vital information, leading to poor decision making in the White House that repeats itself over time. There is no reason to believe that a cover-up or a bungled decision is only the result of a particular circumstance or individual in office.

The same mixing of power is seen in legislation. Presidents are expected to propose legislation. They can work on their "must list" with some assurance of success. This in itself is a substantial power. But they may not be able to ask for much—or get all that they ask for. Presidential success in Congress follows party lines and the president's own popularity in the country. So, if presidents want to save eagles, help us not die, or build houses, they will need support in Congress, for Congress considers these policies part of its job too.

With power so mixed and ambiguous, there is only room for one president. Vice-presidents will do the presidential busy work, run unpopular errands, and wait their own turn at the presidential nomination. Hence they do not play an active role in any disability decision. Still, the vice-presidency has provided an automatic and swift transition of power in the event of the president's death. It does not matter who the vice-presidents are or what the public thinks about them; when they enter the office of Washington and Lincoln, the public approves of the way they are doing their job.

Finally, the office is open to develop with changing times and circumstances. Public expectations shape the office in very real ways, producing support in a crisis, a cult of the presidency, or anything else. This means that the public should think about the presidency they want, since they will probably get the one they ask for.

| CHECKLIST FOR REVIEW |

1. The power and limits of the presidency are built in by the Constitution. Power is checked by the other branches, left open to become what it needs to be, and left ambiguous. The openness has led to a spiral of growth in the twentieth century, in which events, expectations, and legislation follow each other in expanding the office.

2. Presidents can rely on formal (bureaucratic) or informal (palace politics) modes of organizing the White House. The bureaucratic mode is characterized by hierarchical structure, specialization and division of labor, and clear lines of communication and control. The palace politics mode is fluid, personal, nonhierarchical, and is typically used in the president's relations with aides and advisers. Each mode has its own advantages and limitations.

3. Public support gives presidents a reservoir of power on which they can draw, and yet it builds in unrealistic expectations and a cult of the presidency. The cult subjects presidents to intense scrutiny and yet simultaneously maintains that they are powerful and benevolent. While support for the office is high, the popularity of individual presidents shows great

fluctuation. Generally, popularity increases in time of international crisis, declines in economic hard times, and declines through the term.

4. Presidents need to use the press successfully to maintain their popularity, and the press needs the cooperation of the president to do its job. As a result, press coverage of the president tends to be favorable.

5. Presidents are expected to set an agenda, a list of priorities for Congress and the nation to focus on. Although most issues originate outside the White House, the president chooses which ones to emphasize. This in itself is a substantial power.

6. Presidential success in Congress is affected by the party in control of Congress and the president's popularity in the country. Presidents can veto legislation, but Congress can override the veto. Vetoes and overrides, too, are affected by popularity, the party in control of Congress, and the president's own style of pursuing conflict or compromise.

7. The vice-presidency is a strange contradiction of "nothing" and "everything." Vice-presidents are given work to do by the presidents, but they have no work of their own. The office has provided a swift and sure transition on the occurrence of a president's death, but it does not figure actively in disability decisions. Generally, vice-presidents would be extremely reluctant to question a president's right to hold office.

KEY TERMS

Office of Management and Budget	cult of the presidency
The Executive Office Act of 1939	presidential popularity
The Employment Act of 1946	rally 'round the flag effect
National Security Act of 1947	presidential success in Congress
The Executive Office of the Presidency	the two-presidencies thesis
palace politics mode	direct veto
groupthink	indirect veto
multiple advocacy	veto override

The Federal Bureaucracy

A new law is passed or a program is funded after its passage through Congress. But where did the details come from? And what happens now? Who decides how it will be interpreted and carried out, and whether it will be enforced or ignored? Much of the actual work of government is bureaucratic work; "governing" is in large part a bureaucratic activity.

The classic idea of a bureaucracy was explained by the German sociologist Max Weber. A bureaucracy has four key characteristics. It has specialization and division of labor—people work on specific tasks for which they are trained or selected. Bureaucracy also has a hierarchical structure and fixed lines of command and responsibility—power flows from the top down and responsibility from the bottom up. It has a set of rules and procedures, often very elaborate, to help carry out the communication among its various parts. And it is characterized by impersonality; all the rules are carried out and all the clients treated in the same way. The rules and procedures take precedence over any personal or special circumstances.[1] Hence, when the term **bureaucracy** is used, it usually means a form of organization characterized by specialization, hierarchy, detailed rules and procedures, and impersonality.

Weber stressed that bureaucracy was the "rational" way for modern society to conduct its business. Given the need for expertise, technical complexity, and the demands of dealing with large numbers of people, the bureaucratic organization would be the best for the job at hand. Bureaucracies are found in virtually all large organizations and many small ones: in school and church organizations, businesses, and national, state, and local government.

Yet, a government bureaucracy must work within a larger political environment where there are different rules and different lines of authority. Politicians are not experts except in the matter of politics, and impersonality is not as important as other values. Also, a bureaucracy in the American national government must work within an environment that emphasizes democratic and individual values and compromises between the chief governing institutions. Hierarchy and impersonality do not fit the usual idea of the American political process. So, how can bureaucracy be reconciled with principles of democratic government? How does it fit within the design of power balanced and blended between the president and Congress? The bureaucracy will be shaped by this larger political environment and will help shape it. National policy will be the result.

Therefore, it is necessary to see the importance of bureaucratic activity, its interdependence with the larger political environment, and the resulting diversity of this activity. There is no bureaucratic single-structure monolith, but a number of structures each capable of different relations with the many other parts of the government.

[1]See H.H. Gerth and C. Wright Mills, *From Max Weber: Essays in Sociology* (New York: Oxford University Press, 1958), Chapter 8.

**An Internal Revenue
Service worker
checks tax returns
against a computer.**

BUREAUCRATIC ORGANIZATION

The executive bureaucracy consists of three basic kinds of agencies: the cabinet departments with their many subdivisions, the independent agencies, and the independent regulatory commissions. Some of these agencies are more important than others, some overlap in their jurisdictions, and some are more closely connected than others to the chief executive. A good summary is provided by Richard Neustadt:

> Like our governmental structure as a whole, the executive establishment consists of separated institutions sharing powers. The president heads one of these; cabinet officers, agency administrators, and military commanders head others. Below the department level, virtually independent bureau chiefs head many more.[2]

According to Neustadt, the executive branch has many chiefs.

For a sense of the size and degree of specialization of these units, see Exhibit 9.1. The figure shows merely one of the fourteen cabinet departments, the Department of the Interior. Yet, there are twenty-nine separate offices within that department and many of these offices have their own sub-offices with their own bureaucracies. People who work for the National Park Service (in the lower-middle area of the figure) would know little about what is going on in the Bureau of Reclamation. An under secretary or an

[2]Richard E. Neustadt, *Presidential Power* (New York: Wiley, 1960), p. 39.

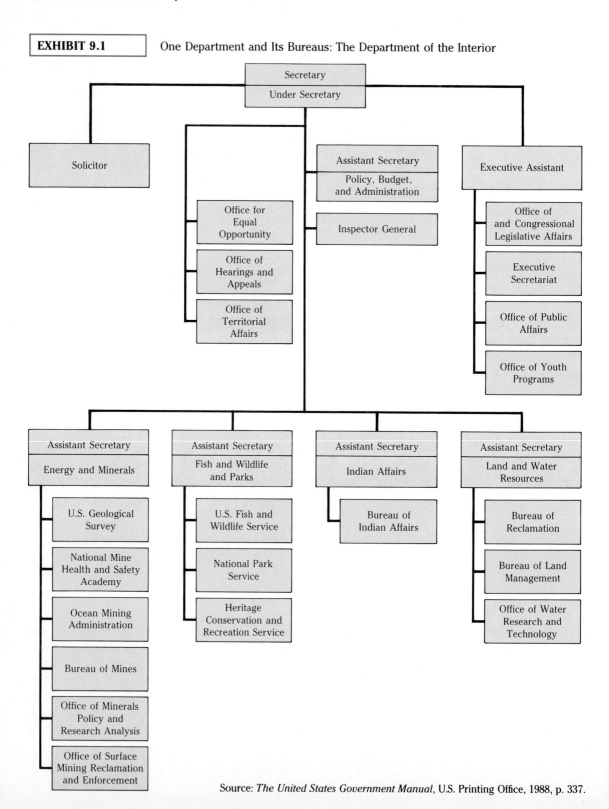

| EXHIBIT 9.1 | One Department and Its Bureaus: The Department of the Interior |

Source: *The United States Government Manual*, U.S. Printing Office, 1988, p. 337.

assistant secretary (the top middle area of the figure) also might not know what is going on in the Bureau of Reclamation, or in several of the other twenty-eight units. Multiply this diagram by all the other departments and agencies and one begins to see what a government bureaucracy is like.

Nearly three million civilian employees work for the federal government. They range from professional and technological experts to white-collar nonprofessionals and clerks. Counting the number of agencies within departments that have their own autonomy and chiefs as well as all the independent agencies outside the cabinet structure, there are probably upwards of 500 units carrying on the government's business, often on their own terms. The president cannot supervise all of this activity, and Congress finds it formidable too. Senator Dale Bumpers of Arkansas described the bureaucracy as "a 700 pound marshmallow. You can kick it, scream at it, and cuss it, but it is very reluctant to move."[3] Congressional oversight of the bureaucracy is typically slight. Thus the size and specialization make the bureaucracy an independent actor in the government. There is simply more going on than any of the other political actors can control.

The Cabinet Departments

The fourteen cabinet departments are the principal and oldest components of the executive bureaucracy. They carry out the bulk of the programs, spend most of the money, and employ most of the people. Each department is headed by a presidential appointee, appointed with the consent of the Senate, who is a member of the cabinet. Each is subdivided into a number of units (commonly called *bureaus* or *agencies*) and each has its own budget, staff, public relations departments, and liaison units to work with the other government participants.

The cabinet departments vary greatly in size, from Education, employing under five thousand, to Defense, employing over one million. They vary in budget from the relatively modest budgets of State and Justice to the gigantic budget of Health and Human Services. They vary in age. The departments of State, War (now called Defense), and Treasury were created in 1789 along with the new government, and other departments were added with the expansion of government activity, for example: in 1953, Health, Education and Welfare (HEW, now called Health and Human Services); in 1965, Housing and Urban Development, Transportation in 1966, Energy in 1978, Education in 1980, and Veterans Affairs in 1989. They vary in their relations with the president and Congress, in their orientation toward interest groups and public opinion, and in the importance of their department heads.

To highlight some of these differences, Thomas Cronin distinguishes between "inner" and "outer" cabinet departments. The inner cabinet includes State, Defense, Treasury, and Justice, and the outer cabinet includes all other departments. Heads of the inner cabinet, according to Cronin, tend

[3]Cited in George C. Edwards, III, and Ira Sharkansky *The Policy Predicament* (San Francisco: Freeman, 1978), p. 294.

to be distinctive in their role as counselors to presidents and in their interchangeability across several departments and several administrations. Douglas Dillon served Republican Eisenhower and Democratic Kennedy. Elliot Richardson moved from HEW secretary to Defense secretary to Attorney General. Cyrus Vance, Henry Kissinger, and Caspar Weinberger, among others, have served in more than one capacity and for more than one president. These quasi-permanent cabinet members are not strangers to government—in fact, they are valued precisely because they have shown they can find their way around town. Their influence, however, stems less from their cabinet position than from their own reputation and skill. Kissinger, for example, did not need to be a cabinet member to help Nixon conduct foreign policy.

Outer cabinet heads, in contrast, tend to take more of an advocacy than a counseling role. They tend to be less well-known by the president to start with, often selected to achieve better geographical, ethnic, or racial balance in the cabinet. They head departments, such as HUD or Labor, with strongly organized interest groups active in the policy-making process. Hence their interests may run counter to presidential interests and they may find themselves arguing *for* the interest group in the White House. They must take part in intense competition with one another for presidential access and budget support. According to Cronin and others, it is these departments that are most suspect to White House aides, most isolated from the president, and most likely to be caught in strong interest group or congressional pressures.[4]

Exhibit 9.2 gives a list of cabinet departments, ranking them from high to low in age, expenditures, and size of personnel. The inner and outer cabinet classification is also included.

The Independent Agencies

The independent agencies are also headed by presidential appointees and are formally under presidential control, although they are not part of any cabinet department. Despite their lack of cabinet status, many of these agencies possess great size and policy-making impact. The Veterans Administration, for example, with over two hundred thousand employees, was larger than many departments and finally in 1989 was raised to cabinet departmental status. The fifty or so independent agencies range from such famous establishments as the Civil Service Commission, the Board of Governors of the Federal Reserve System, and the National Aeronautics and Space Administration (NASA) to such little known ones as the American Battle Monuments Commission, the Delaware River Basin Commission, and the Soldiers' and Airmen's Home. Think of the range and extent of the policy

---

[4]Thomas E. Cronin, *The State of the Presidency*, 2nd ed. (Boston: Little, Brown, 1980), pp. 276–277. See also Richard P. Nathan, *The Administrative Presidency* (New York: Wiley, 1983).

EXHIBIT 9.2	AGE OF DEPARTMENT	SIZE OF BUDGET	NUMBER OF PERSONNEL	INNER OR OUTER RANKINGS
The Cabinet Departments Ranked on Four Dimensions[a]	1. State	1. HHS	1. Defense	*Inner:* State, Defense, Justice, Treasury
	2. Treasury	2. Defense	2. Veterans Affairs	
	3. Defense	3. Treasury	3. Treasury	*Outer:* HHS, HUD, Labor, Interior, Commerce, Agriculture, Transportation, Energy, Education, Veterans Affairs
	4. Interior	4. Agriculture	4. HHS	
	5. Justice	5. Labor	5. Agriculture	
	6. Agriculture	6. Veterans Affairs	6. Interior	
	7. Commerce	7. Transportation	7. Justice	
	8. Labor	8. Education	8. Transportation	
	9. HEW (HHS)	9. HUD	9. Commerce	
	10. HUD	10. Energy	10. State	
	11. Transportation	11. Justice	11. Labor	
	12. Energy	12. Interior	12. Energy	
	13. Education	13. State	13. HUD	
	14. Veterans Affairs	14. Commerce	14. Education	

[a]Departments are ranked from high (1) to low (14) on the first three dimensions.

Sources: Thomas E. Cronin, *The State of the Presidency*, 2nd ed. (Boston: Little, Brown, 1980), pp. 276–77; Fiscal 1990 Budget as cited in *Congressional Quarterly*, January 14, 1989, p. 77.

areas being governed: water resources, farm credits, Indian claims, space, commodity futures, and environmental protection, among many others. All of these are far from front-page news and from any one individual's knowledge or control.

Independent agencies are often formed to protect them from the red tape and biases of the traditional departments. So, Lyndon Johnson formed the Office of Economic Opportunity (OEO) to fight his War on Poverty rather than using such traditional departments as HEW and HUD. When the Nixon administration wanted to phase out the poverty programs, they were returned to the traditional departments. Some agencies, like OEO or the American Revolution Bicentennial Administration, come and go; others become permanent fixed objects in the political landscape. As such, like the traditional departments, they develop their own long-term relations with interest groups, members of congressional committees, and other bureaucrats. Just like the cabinet departments, they will vary in their importance and in their ties to the White House and Congress.

A special kind of independent agency is the **government corporation**. Examples include the Tennessee Valley Authority, the Federal Deposit Insurance Corporation, the Federal Home Loan Bank Board, and perhaps the most famous, the United States Postal Service, once a separate cabinet department. Government corporations are like private corporations in their structure and services, although, like the other independent agencies, they are subject to presidential and congressional control. By the Government Corporation Control Act of 1945, Congress authorized the corporate form of the organization and specified what it may and may not do. Congress can dissolve corporations, form new ones, or modify the authority and responsibility of existing corporations. The corporations are reviewed annually by the president, the Office of Management and Budget, and Congress. Corporations must submit budget programs annually, and Congress must supply working capital and authorize expenditures from corporate funds, although it need not appropriate funds. Corporate earnings may be retained and poured back directly into the operation. Government corporations, then, are considerably freer from budget controls than other government agencies, although they are still subject to Congress for their existence and annual budget review. Government corporations provide a service, typically at a lower cost than one would pay a private-sector corporation. Through COMSAT you can rent time on a space satellite for radio communications or with Amtrak you can ride on a government-subsidized passenger railroad.

The Independent Regulatory Commissions

The third component of the federal bureaucracy are the **independent regulatory commissions**. They conduct hearings, make rulings affecting individual firms and the industry at large, and operate under very broad congressional statutes that allow them to make supplemental laws of their own. They are, therefore, a kind of governmental hybrid—executive in organization, they perform law-making and judicial activities. They are hybrids also in their method of appointment. Like the cabinet secretaries, commission heads are appointed by the president with the consent of the Senate. But unlike the cabinet, these agencies are headed by several commissioners. By law these commissioners are from both political parties, serve for fixed terms, and are appointees of several presidents. Commissioners cannot be dismissed at a president's discretion. The major regulatory agencies include the following:

- *The Interstate Commerce Commission* (1887) eleven members; regulates and fixes rates for railroads, trucking companies, buslines, and other agencies of ground transport
- *The Federal Trade Commission* (1914) five members; regulates such practices as unfair competition, price fixing, deceptive advertising, and false packaging
- *The Federal Power Commission* (1930) five members; regulates electric utilities, natural gas companies, and hydroelectric projects

A nuclear power plant control room in Morris, Illinois.

- *The Federal Communications Commission* (1934) seven members; licenses and regulates television and radio stations; regulates frequencies used by police, aviation, taxicabs, and other operators; fixes rates for telephone and telegraph companies
- *The Securities and Exchange Commission* (1934) five members; regulates securities, investing, and information; regulates brokers and stock exchanges

Each of these agencies has its own extensive subbureaucracy, as shown in Exhibit 9.3. Within the cable television subdivision, for example, one finds four further subdivisions. Each has its own staff and special area of responsibility.

Other government agencies can do some regulating too. The National Labor Relations Board regulates unfair labor practices, and the Board of Governors of the Federal Reserve System regulates interest rates and banking practices. The Food and Drug Administration, located within Health and Human Services, has major regulatory functions. It inspects food processing plants, rules on the safety and effectiveness of all prescription drugs, and establishes quality and identity for food products. (When, for example, does orange juice become orangeade or even orange drink?) The independent regulatory commissions are not alone in this regulatory function, although they are unique in their structure and some of the political problems they raise.

EXHIBIT 9.3   The Federal Communications Commission

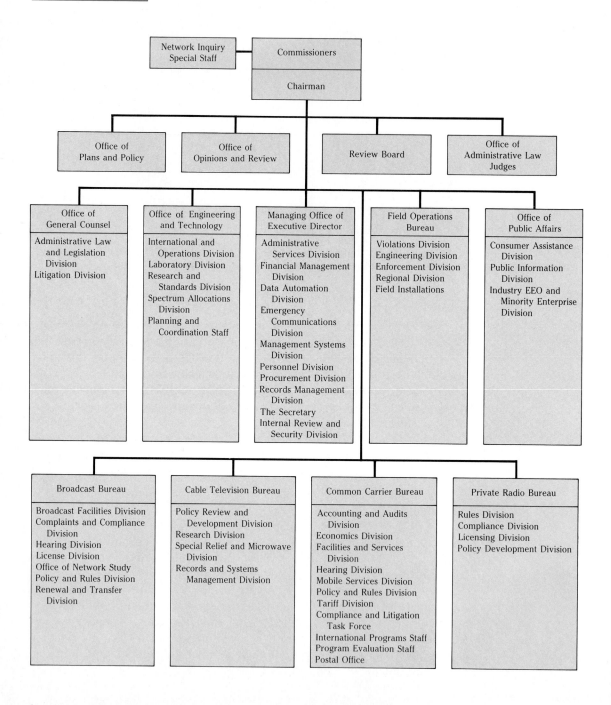

Source: *The United States Government Manual*, U.S. Printing Office, 1988, p. 539.

In establishing these very powerful regulatory agencies, Congress tried to protect them from political pressures: hence the fixed terms, bipartisan composition, and limits on any one president's appointments. These agencies were to oversee the "public interest" in matters involving private industry. Nevertheless, they must deal with such political questions as "who gets what"—who gets the $50 million license to operate a television station, and who wins and who loses in the regulation of gas rates or investment practices. Commissioners, just like other bureaucrats or members of Congress, are prime targets of interest group activity. The armies of lobbyists, lawyers, and public relations people descending on Washington include large numbers of regulated-industry representatives. All of the major radio and television networks have vice-presidents in Washington, and so do the railroads, truckers, and drug companies. The commissions, in short, are no more "independent" of the politics of national policy-making than are any other agencies.

In fact, their independence from the president and Congress can force a reliance on interest group support. The ironic result is that the protectors of the public interest in matters of private industry frequently become instead the protectors of the industry they are supposed to be regulating. Critics point to the "capture" of the regulators by those who are regulated—the agencies begin to take the clientele's point of view. Members of the commissions may be drawn from the industry or look forward to lucrative positions in the private sector later. All commissioners are not captured of course.[5] But isolated from Congress and the White House as they are, they may need to look to their own client group for political support.

If this is the executive structure that presidents inherit, what changes can they make? Most presidents have tried some reorganization plans—Nixon, Carter, and Reagan in particular—but few achieve very much success. *Congress* determines the mission and structure of the executive departments and must pass on all presidential reorganization requests. Since the congressional committees are organized to parallel the bureaucratic structure, members may not like to see their long-term relations disrupted. Given the importance of committee specialization, Congress looks skeptically at reorganization attempts. Interest groups, too, that have worked out their problems with the committees and the agencies often oppose reorganization. In the words of one former cabinet member, "It took [interest groups] years to dig their particular tunnel into the public vault, and they don't want the vault moved."[6]

[5]The standard argument for capture can be found in Marver H. Bernstein, *Regulating Business by Independent Commission* (Princeton: Princeton University Press, 1955), esp. p. 90. For a critique of the theory, see Paul J. Quirk, *Industry Influence in Federal Regulatory Agencies* (Princeton: Princeton University Press, 1981).

[6]Carol S. Greenwald, *Group Power: Lobbying and Public Policy* (New York: Praeger, 1977), p. 218. See also Richard L. Cole and David A. Caputo, "Presidential Control of the Senior Civil Service: Assessing the Strategies of the Nixon Years," *American Political Science Review*, 73 (1979), pp. 399–413.

■■■■ BUREAUCRATIC IMPACT ON POLICY

The president and Congress do not have the expertise or the numbers to gain the information, do the work, know the field, or carry out the job of policy-making in all its detail and complexity. They are the political experts. Policy expertise, in contrast, must be delegated to the bureaucratic agencies. What does this mean for the policy that results?

The bureaucracy (1) supplies information on which decisions are based. In making foreign policy decisions, for example, a president must rely on information supplied from military bureaucracies, Foreign Service officials, and others in national security agencies or at State Department desks. The bureaucracy (2) helps initiate new policy and defines its objectives and problems. A committee conducts hearings for new legislation or the White House formulates a new policy proposal. Each must turn sooner or later to bureaucratic expertise. The bureaucracy (3) supplies the specific interpretation for the general statutes that Congress passes and the president signs. It sets guidelines and uses discretion by taking action on some issues and not taking action on others. It decides what labor practices are "fair" and "unfair," how much of a contaminant is too much, and who gets the IRS audits and what the decisions will be. Finally, the bureaucracy (4) implements the policy—that is, it carries out the actions designed to achieve the general goals sought by the legislation. Implementation includes decisions on what agency resources to use, what actions should be taken and not taken, and how goals should be translated into operational rules of thumb.[7]

The importance of this power to interpret and implement can be seen in a few examples. A Civil Rights Act prohibits discrimination in employment by race or sex, but who will investigate when the employers break the law? What is an "adequate" attempt to follow the law by employers who say they cannot find qualified blacks or women? Product safety laws set general standards for handling and processing foods, but what does this actually mean for the meat packing plant or the potato chip factory? Who decides what meets minimum standards and when and where inspections shall be made? A welfare law requires able-bodied recipients to seek work or to take advantage of job-training programs, but who will decide who is able-bodied, and who will administer the training programs? Congress passes the general law and it is the members of the bureaucracy who will be interpreting and enforcing it.

Many times Congress leaves the language deliberately vague to avoid a controversy that would otherwise kill a bill. In one case, members of the House and Senate could not agree on whether to prohibit international

---

[7]For discussions of implementation, see Donald Van Meter and Carl Van Horn, "The Policy Implementation Process," *Administration and Society*, February, 1975, p. 447. See also Randall B. Ripley and Grace A. Franklin, *Policy Implementation and Bureaucracy*, 2nd ed. (Chicago: Dorsey, 1986).

loans to countries "violating human rights" (such as imprisoning people without a fair trial or torturing and killing them). The House wanted a strict prohibition and the Senate wanted more discretion as to which countries could receive loans. The final compromise language arrived at prohibited loans to countries violating human rights unless the programs were to be used to help the poor. Thus government officials would be deciding (a) whether a given country had violated human rights, and (b) even if it did, if the program would "help the poor."

The bureaucracy *implements, interprets, initiates,* and *informs*—not only in the few issues facing the president or the dozens under review in the committees, but for all the issues that make up ongoing governmental activity.

An illustration of this impact can be seen in foreign policy where presidents are traditionally considered dominant, with perhaps a John Foster Dulles or Colonel House or Henry Kissinger at their side. The foreign policy bureaucracy includes the Department of State with a billion dollar budget, over one hundred embassies abroad, and many thousands of employees, divided further into regional bureaus and still further into more than one hundred country desks with additional economic, congressional, public relations, and other bureaus. It includes the Defense Department with an even larger budget and a larger number of employees. Defense includes its own intelligence agency (the Defense Intelligence Agency, or DIA) and its own "little State Department," the Office of International Security Affairs. It includes the independent Central Intelligence Agency (CIA), with a budget that is conservatively estimated to equal the State department's, charged with coordinating the work of other government intelligence agencies. The foreign policy bureaucracy includes also the Agency for International Development (AID) and the U.S. Information Agency (USIA), as well as agencies within the Treasury Department, the U.S. International Trade Commission, the U.S. Arms Control and Disarmament Agency, the Overseas Private Investment Corporation, the Foreign Claims Settlement Commission, and the National Aeronautics and Space Administration. This is only a sample listing.

These foreign policy bureaucracies process and transmit information to other decision makers and, through media releases, to the American public. They provide the facts on military and economic trends, on what is going on in other countries, and on the strength of governments or rival factions. Information can be especially critical in the foreign policy field since few domestic sources of the same information are available. These bureaucracies also interpret and implement policy. As Richard Neustadt observes, there are few presidential "self-executing orders."[8] In other words, most policy decisions do not automatically translate themselves into the desired results. Bureaucratic characteristics can affect the translation process in

---

[8]See Neustadt, *op., cit.,* especially p. 25 and chapter 3.

several definite ways. The *routines* of bureaucracy make policy difficult to start and, once started, difficult to stop. The *size* multiplies the chance of leaks in secret negotiations, and the very fact that a piece of information is reported can change results. The *inertia* of bureaucracy means that in many cases nothing will be done. Inertia becomes a kind of bureaucratic veto. It is the ability to make things not happen. A famous example concerns Kennedy's problems with the United States missiles based in Turkey. Kennedy ordered the missiles removed, but nothing happened. He ordered the missiles removed a second time, and still nothing happened. He finally had to learn from the Russians, on the hot line during the Cuban missile crisis, that the missiles were still in Turkey.

There are, of course, limits on bureaucratic monopolies. Presidents can select advisers to support their own policy interpretations. Congress can hold hearings until it gets the information it desires. The bureaucratic agencies themselves may be at cross-purposes, supplying different and competing interpretations. Yet even in these cases, the information supplied—and the reality conveyed—originates with and is channeled through bureaucratic actors.

A different kind of illustration is shown by the work of the United States government during the week before President Nixon's resignation. It can be assumed that the president and his advisers were not giving certain issues the highest priority at the time. During that week, the Defense Department awarded sixty-one new contracts that would send three-quarters of a billion dollars to private industry. HUD officials lobbied in Congress on the issue of public housing subsidies. The Environmental Protection Agency carried out the first major effort to enforce compliance with air pollution regulations in metropolitan areas, while the Labor Department issued new regulations for the employment and training of migrant workers. Justice Department lawyers won indictments against government-licensed grain inspectors who had been charged with accepting bribes, while other Justice officials were lobbying in Congress against the forthcoming privacy act. Federal Energy Administration officials were studying ways to counteract efforts by oil companies to increase gas sales, and HEW officials were debating policy about where federally subsidized medical students might work.[9] These and other policies were going forward. Only the presidency was paralyzed; the rest of the work of government continued.

BUREAUCRATIC PERSONNEL

Given the importance of the job, how should members of the executive branch be selected? Do we want those most skilled or those most responsible to elected officials? What if the two criteria do not go together? The history of appointments in this country illustrates the problem.

[9]Hugh Heclo, *A Government of Strangers* (Washington, D.C.: Brookings, 1977), pp. 8–9.

The Civil Service System

George Washington claimed that his office holders should have "character and competence," as well as loyalty to the Constitution. But with the growth of popular democracy, many people pointed out that character and competence were a nice way of saying the privileged few. By 1828, Andrew Jackson argued that the administrative office had become "a species of property" for an elite group. Since democracy meant rule by the people, ordinary citizens could hold administration positions, appointed by elected officials. If the Democrats won the election, then the winning Democratic candidates would get to make the appointments. If the Whigs came to power (the name of the other major political party at the time), then the Whigs would toss all the Democratic rascals out. These appointments, available for distribution by public officials and political parties, are called **patronage**.

This system had its drawbacks, too, however, bringing incompetence and the buying and selling of offices. It became known as the **spoils system**. With offices awarded to the friends and supporters of the elected officials, the appointments were the spoils, or rewards, of victory. Pressure for reform grew following the Civil War and reached a critical point when President Garfield was shot by a disappointed office seeker in 1881. Congress passed the Pendleton Civil Service Act in 1883, modeled on the developing British civil service system. The Pendleton Act called for a **merit principle** in appointments: it provided for competitive examinations for prospective office holders and guaranteed job security with adequate performance. It serves as the basis for the **civil service system**, which exists to the present day.[10] Whereas the spoils system was based on patronage, the civil service system is based on the merit principle.

Under the Pendleton Act, perhaps ten percent of appointments were covered by civil service. Pressure to expand the system continued through the early twentieth century until by the 1930s some eighty percent of appointments were based on civil service. As more and more professionals and technical experts joined the government following the New Deal, these, too, became civil service appointees. Now, with the exception of the top political posts, virtually all bureaucratic personnel are appointed and promoted through the civil service or other special merit systems. (Military personnel, Foreign Service officers, and the FBI, for example, have their own merit systems.) The Civil Service Commission, called the Office of Personnel Management since 1978, establishes job eligibility and tests for application, job assignment, and salary. It sets broad guidelines for promotion, although the more specific decisions on promotion and duties will be set by the bureaucratic superior. Basing job qualifications on merit, the civil service removes personnel from political pressures, but in so doing it removes them from the direct control of elected officials.

---

[10]Paul P. Van Riper, *History of the United States Civil Service* (Evanston, Ill.: Row, Peterson, 1958).

"Let's switch. I'll make the policy, you implement it, and he'll explain it."
Drawing by Stevenson; © 1981 The New Yorker Magazine, Inc.

The Bureaucrats

"They have no brain," a character in a recent thriller says, "but a thousand arms to clutch at you and drag you down." This fictional bestseller is carrying on a stereotype of the modern bureaucracy—massive, faceless, and frightening. When bureaucrats are looked at more closely, however, they appear quite like elected officials. In general, members of the higher levels of the federal service are highly educated white males. As the level of the job rises, from GS 1 to GS 15, the proportion of blacks and women declines sharply, as shown in Exhibit 9.4. A majority of the top-level civil servants have entered government after completing their education and develop occupational specialties in the service. Those entering the higher ranks from outside also tend to have an occupational specialty tied to their job. Common professions are engineering, medicine, business, and law.[11]

Bureaucrats are like elected officials in many of their attitudes as well. They support democratic values and believe in open access to agency decisions for members of Congress and interest groups. They support the free enterprise system as opposed to a system of government control, and they hold abstract beliefs about government and policy similar to those of the public as a whole. They tend to be slightly more liberal in attitudes than the general public and more opposed to changes in the bureaucratic system. They also tend to develop the ideological tone of the agency employing

[11]See Joel D. Aberbach and Bert A. Rockman, "The Overlapping Worlds of American Federal Executives," *British Journal of Political Science*, January, 1977, pp. 23–47, and Joel D. Aberbach, Robert D. Putnam, and Bert A. Rockman, *Bureaucrats and Politicians in Western Democracies* (Cambridge: Harvard University Press, 1981). See also Ripley and Franklin, *Policy Implementation and Bureaucracy, op. cit.*, p. 51.

EXHIBIT 9.4			PERCENTAGE OF EMPLOYEES	
Blacks and Women in Civil Service Jobs[a]	LEVEL OF JOB	PAY (THOUSANDS)	BLACKS	WOMEN
	GS 1–4	8–15	24	74
	GS 5–8	13–23	20	61
	GS 9–12	19–37	9	34
	GS 13–15	34–61	5	9
	Executive	50 +	5	6

[a]To compare with these percentages, women comprise about 51 percent of the population and blacks approximately 12 percent.

Source: *Statistical Abstract of the United States*, pp. 335, 338. Government Printing Office, Washington, D.C., 1987.

them. In general, however, attitudes are similar to those found in Congress and the public.[12]

Bureaucrats have different motives and goals for their work in government service. They can be classified as *careerists, politicians, professionals,* and *missionaries.* Careerists identify their work and goals with the agency that employs them. They do not desire to move to other agencies or to leave government, and their most important concern is maintaining the agency's position and their own position within it. Politicians do expect to pursue a career beyond the agency, either in an elective or appointive office. In pursuing this goal, they seek to maintain good ties with a variety of sources external to the agency. Professionals look to others, both within and outside government, in the same profession or technical field as their own. Their most important concern is maintaining esteem with these other professionals and carrying on their own work interests. Missionaries are primarily concerned with specific policies or ideologies and work to see these policies carried out. They are less concerned with the agency itself, their personal future, or the approval of other professionals. Most agencies are dominated by careerists. The missionaries are the most rare.[13]

Agencies dominated by careerists will likely fight for their own programs and budgets and seek to maintain and increase their importance. Agencies dominated by politicians and professionals will be more concerned with the opinions of others and more susceptible to the influence of interest groups and members of Congress. The politicians and professionals may be seeking future careers among the very groups they are dealing with as government workers, but there is *no one agency dynamic or bureaucratic type.* The variety at work behind the single term "bureaucracy" will become even clearer in the following section.

---

[12]See Aberbach and Rockman, *op. cit.*; Ripley and Franklin, *op. cit.*, p. 52; Kenneth J. Meier and Lloyd G. Nigro, "Representative Bureaucracy and Policy Preferences: A Study in the Attitudes of Federal Executives," *Public Administration Review*, 36 (1976), pp. 458–69.

[13]Ripley and Franklin, *op. cit.*, pp. 52–53.

THE BUREAUCRACY AND ITS POLITICAL ENVIRONMENT

It has long been recognized that separating "administration" from "politics" can never be fully successful. Political currents blocked at one point will merely flow somewhere else. Bureaucrats, despite their nonpolitical appointment, work very much in a political environment. It consists of the president, Congress and its committees, court rulings, interest groups, parties, and the attitudes of the public at large. It consists also of the other bureaucratic agencies competing for such scarce resources as presidential attention or budget support. Agencies vary, however, in the particular environment that they find important.

Five Environments: Which Agency Where?

There are five major political environments. For some agencies, the *bureaucratic* environment is most critical, the key problem being one of maneuvering for position, program, or budget within the larger department. Rules and routines outweigh presidential innovation, and protecting a program means that information may not get to the White House or Congress. Presidents can say "do This, do That" and nothing will happen, for the major problems and incentives are closer at hand. Other agencies work primarily in a *presidential* or *congressional* environment: their programs depend on budget help, access, and reorganization. Poverty programs in the Johnson and Nixon years and energy programs during the Carter and Reagan years stood or fell with decisions in the White House. Bureaucrats in a relatively new agency or one without much public support need presidential allies against a skeptical Congress, while those in entrenched, long-favored programs need little in the way of presidential support. The FBI, the Forest Service, and the Soil Conservation Service, for example, have for years been congressionally favored. Officials in these agencies do not need to worry about who wins the next presidential election. Careerists may rely on their long-term relations with congressional and bureaucratic people, while the missionaries would be more likely to need sympathetic people in the White House.

Still other agencies find their major incentives and constraints in a broader work environment. In some cases a *professional* environment is most important, whether for meteorologists, space technicians, Latin American experts, or agricultural economists. The professionals are guided by their past training and experience, and the advice of their peers, in making policy decisions. In other cases, a *clientele* environment is critical. (A **clientele** refers to the client group or interest group in the private sector with which the agency must deal by providing services or regulations.) Agencies find help from their clienteles in their budget battles with Congress when they administer a popular program and one that is well-received by the groups concerned. Simply doing one's job requires good relations with the clientele that one must work with daily. At the extreme, one finds the prob-

The FBI building in Washington, D.C.

lem of **clientele capture**, in which bureaucrats begin to identify with the clientele that they are administering.

The dynamics of the clientele environment can be shown in more detail. Many officials look beyond their present job to high-paying and prestigious careers in their area of expertise. So, a Pentagon bureaucrat may want to become an industrial aircraft vice-president or a Securities and Exchange Commission official desires to join a Wall Street law firm. These people have highly valuable services to sell in the private sector—contacts, inside information, and experience in Washington. What is more, they know about this potential value for prospective employers even while working in the government. A Common Cause report showed that about half of those appointed to regulatory commissions came from regulated companies or the law firms that work for such companies. On leaving office, about half of the commissioners went to work for these companies or law firms. The same exchange of personnel was found for agencies dealing with federal energy, defense, food and drug regulation, and nuclear power. Subgovernments show examples of particularly strong clientele environments.

One study shows the problem of clientele capture in the Foreign Service. Reports to Washington describing the "enemy" were not referring to an enemy of the United States, but a country hostile to the country they were serving in. A Foreign Service officer assigned to an African nation watched one tribe commit genocide on another. Bodies, according to the account, were being carried past the embassy at the rate of a thousand per day, but the information was not sent to Washington. Why? It would hurt the country's relations with the United States and so undermine the work the official was doing.[14] The same problem is frequently cited in cases of regulatory policy. Thus bureaucrats in the Food and Drug Administration find that their key political environment consists of the major drug companies and the American Medical Association who stand to gain or lose financially by the policies set.

Besides these five environments—the bureaucratic, the professional, the clientele, the congressional, and the presidential—there are many combinations that also exist. Few bureaucrats single-mindedly pursue goals in only one environment, and few agencies include only like-minded bureaucrats. Goals keyed to one environment can be undercut by events (a mood for budget-cutting, a space shuttle disaster, an energy crisis), forcing agencies to look elsewhere for their source of support. The classification is not rigid, it merely shows the kind of variety that the bureaucracy is capable of. Agencies, like the committees of the preceding chapter, vary one from another depending on the goals of the members and the political environment in which they work.

[14]Roger Morris, "Rooting for the Other Team: Clientelism in the Foreign Service," in *Inside the System*, 3rd ed. eds. Charles Peter and James Fallon (New York: Holt, Rinehart and Winston, 1976), pp. 171–81.

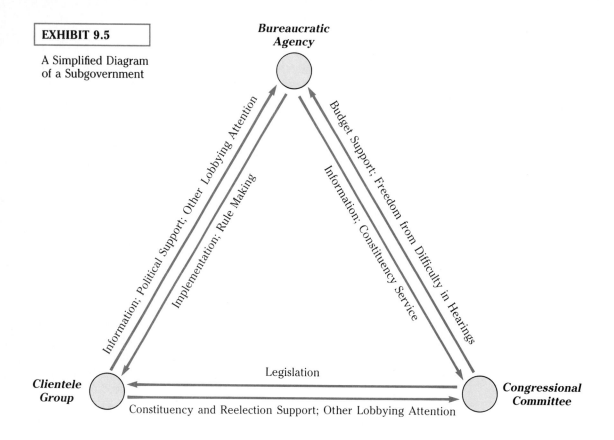

EXHIBIT 9.5

A Simplified Diagram
of a Subgovernment

The Case of Subgovernments

One way that agencies work with others in the political environment deserves more attention: that is, the mutual support between (1) an agency, (2) a congressional committee or subcommittee, and (3) a clientele group. This relationship is called a **subgovernment**.[15] All three units support each other and work for the same policy goals. Subgovernments have also been called "iron triangles," "cozy triangles," "triangular trading agreements," and "complexes" (as in the phrase the military-industrial complex). Each term, however, describes the same tripartite interlocking relationship, with the policy-making controlled by these particular political actors. It is a subgovernment, not a full government, since it excludes such key actors as the president, competing interest groups, and any broad public influence.

A simplified diagram of a subgovernment is shown in Exhibit 9.5, with the arrows indicating the nature and direction of this mutual support.

[15]For the term and examples, see Douglass Cater, *Power in Washington* (New York: Random House, 1964).

The agency gets congressional support for its program and budget as well as freedom from worrying about hearings or investigations. It gets predictable and friendly relations with the clientele group and the attentions of friendly lobbyists. It also gains technical information from the client—from laboratories, computer centers, or a highly paid staff—thus easing its own work load and improving performance. The committee members get information and help from the bureaucrats in performing their rounds of constituency service and they gain from the client group help in their reelection, support in their states and districts, and other lobbying attention. In exchange for all this money, attention, and political support, the clientele group gains the policy that it is seeking: the tax break, the preferred guideline, or the new legislation. All of the participants may believe in the policy they are making: one does not need to assume only narrow self-interest. Nevertheless, the policy-making is made easier—and pleasanter—by all this reciprocal support.

Examples of subgovernments have been documented from the 1950s to the present day.[16] Farm policy has been made by (1) the Extension Service (an agency in the Department of Agriculture), (2) both House and Senate Agriculture committees, and (3) the American Farm Bureau Federation. Soil conservation has been legislated by (1) the Soil Conservation Service, (2) the Agriculture subcommittee of the House Appropriations Committee, and (3) the National Association of Soil Conservation Districts. Water resource policy has been made by (1) the Corps of Engineers, (2) the Public Works committees, and (3) local groups interested in specific projects. Other subgovernments have been described for sugar policy, the military-industrial complex, and policy concerning native Americans.

Presidents can fight subgovernments at their own risk and at the cost of other interests. Some have done so, and with less than full success. Truman took on the sugar subgovernment, Kennedy fought some defense industries, and Carter battled the energy subgovernments. Carter tried to eliminate thirty-two water projects in the first year of his term and, after much effort, reached a compromise with Congress in dropping eighteen. The final bill that reached his desk restored all but nine of the projects. (Carter signed the bill.) But even if presidents achieve some limited success, where is the policy when their term is over? Who makes sugar policy in the Kennedy years or energy policy in the Reagan years? They are back in the subgovernments where they were before.

Subgovernments worry people who want a broad, popularly based policy-making process. If the farmers make farm policy, the defense contractors

[16]Cases of subgovernments have been documented from the 1950s through the 1980s. See, for example, Cater, *op. cit.*; Elizabeth Drew, "Dam Outrage," *The Atlantic*, April, 1970; Roger Davidson, "Breaking Up those 'Cozy Triangles': An Impossible Dream?" in Susan Welch and J.G. Peters, eds. *Legislative Reform and Public Policy* (New York: Praeger, 1977); "Pork Barrel Politics," *Congressional Quarterly Weekly Report*, October 24, 1987, pp. 2581–94.

make defense policy, and the doctors and drug companies make prescription medicine policy, clearly some broader kind of public interest is not being represented in the policy-making. The problem is compounded by bureaucratic size and the low visibility of many issues: while we know about the farm and the sugar and the water resource subgovernments, there are probably many more. The problem is further compounded by the lack of any broad public interest in politics. The orange juice producers are very interested in what percentage of water can be added to the orange juice before it must be called something else. The orange juice drinkers, on the other hand, do not worry about it very much, and the harassed FDA bureaucrat has many other things to do besides tasting orange-flavored liquids. Little wonder, then, that the few people who are interested are asked to get together and work it out.

Other Cases

Subgovernments, while common, are not the only kind of pattern that agencies must work within. They must often deal with diverse or conflicting client groups where no easy mutual accommodation is possible. In many policy areas, **issue networks** have grown up, consisting of very diverse groups that differ in their goals and their level of political activity. At any one point in time, several of these groups may be interested in a policy; at other times several other groups may be involved. In these cases, no clear arrangement can be worked out between the agency and the clientele groups, since the groups will be shifting and changing.[17]

Agencies must deal with very different kinds of committees, too, as Chapter Seven illustrated. Some committees—particularly reelection committees with very similar members—form subgovernments more easily than others. Some committees are deliberately shaped by the assignment process to build in opposing points of view. Even on potentially friendly or neutral committees, one or two senior members will often decide to conduct oversight as a kind of personal crusade. One critic of defense spending used to send a staff person to meet military aircraft and check the passenger lists to see who was riding at government expense. An illustration of two very different treatments of agencies by committees is shown in the box on page 359.

Cases of conflict between an agency and a committee occur with some frequency and are by no means a rare exception to the subgovernmental rule. At the end of the 1970s, the Federal Trade Commission began to make a series of decisions that were seen as pro-consumer and anti-business. Congress signalled the FTC to watch its policies more carefully. The Commerce committees began to hold back the agency's funding. Conflict increased. The committees pushed through a new law in 1980 increasing Con-

[17]Hugh Heclo, "Issue Networks and the Executive Establishment," in *The New American Political System*, ed. Anthony King (Washington, D.C.: American Enterprise Institute, 1978), pp. 87–124.

Agencies Face the Committees

Agencies must deal with the congressional committees who oversee their programs and make budget recommendations. Some agencies develop long-term relationships of trust and support, while others face committees who dislike their programs or who are skeptical of the way they are being carried out. In the following examples, taken from committee hearings, agency witnesses are testifying before the committee as part of the annual budget review. As the witnesses are questioned about their programs, it is very easy to see the variation in skepticism and support.

Example 1: Grilling the State Department

Committee Member: I find a gentleman here, an FSO-6. He got an A in Chinese and you assigned him to London.

Agency Official: Yes, sir. That Officer will have opportunities in London—not as many as he would have in Hong Kong, for example. . . .

Committee Member: What will he do? Spend his time in Chinatown?

Agency Official: No, sir. There will be opportunities in dealing with officers in the British Foreign Office who are concerned with Far Eastern affairs. . . .

Committee Member: So instead of speaking English to one another, they will sit in the London office and talk Chinese?

Agency Official: Yes, sir.

Committee Member: Is that not fantastic?

Agency Official: No, sir. They are anxious to keep up their practice. . . .

Committee Member: They go out to Chinese restaurants and have chop suey together?

Agency Official: Yes, sir.

Example 2: Supporting the FBI

Committee Member: How much did you ask the Budget for when you appeared before them?

Agency Official: They allowed $50,987,000, a reduction of $1,598,141 [from what the agency asked].

Committee Member: For what purpose were you going to use that extra money?

Agency Official: [We] were going to use that extra money . . . to try to cut down on the delinquency in our investigative work . . . Our backlog is increasing rather than decreasing.

Committee Member: So with that work in the security field, with the work in the atomic energy field, and with your tremendous backlog in fingerprint identification work, and with the increase in crime, is this cut . . . going to handicap you?

Agency Official: Most certainly it will.

Committee Member: I am very much disturbed about it.

Sources: House Committee on Appropriations Hearings as quoted in Aaron Wildavsky, *The New Politics of the Budget Process* (Scott, Foresman, 1988), pp. 110–111; and Richard F. Fenno, Jr. *The Power of the Purse* (Little, Brown, 1966), p. 375.

gress's role in overseeing the agency and permitting itself a veto of any FTC rules that did not need presidential agreement. At one point in the battle, the FTC actually had to close down for three days for lack of money. The conflict continued into the Reagan years. While both sides moderated their positions somewhat, Congress continued to watch FTC policy carefully.

One famous example of conflict between an agency and a committee occurred in atomic energy policy. The key committee in Congress (the Joint Committee on Atomic Energy) did not like the policy coming from the

Atomic Energy Commission. The Commission was working very much in a professional environment, stressing basic research and development, while the Joint Committee wanted to build as large a nuclear arsenal as possible in the shortest amount of time. For years, the Committee undertook vigorous oversight of the AEC and forced several commissioners to resign. It told the AEC it wanted to be fully informed of its projects and informed prior to the time they would be carried out. Hearings were constant, lengthy, and hostile, requiring hours of detailed preparation by AEC staff. The Committee saw itself as the "watchdog" of the AEC (Commission members called it the "hound dog"). The struggle continued for some fifteen years until presidents, giving up the battle, began to ask Congress who it would like to see as the commissioners.[18]

The example is particularly important because it occurred in an area of the highest secrecy and technical complexity. All of the information Congress was demanding had top national security classification. Such a policy is typically buried in bureaucratic secrecy on the grounds that oversight is neither feasible nor in the national interest. This is the argument made by the members of Congress themselves when they say they cannot oversee the Central Intelligence Agency or other defense agencies. And yet *when the congressional interest diverged from the bureaucratic interest*, even on an issue where secrecy had the highest priority, no such argument was heard. Congress demanded not only to be fully informed, but to be informed prior to the decisions being taken in this most technical and highly classified area.

The relationship between Congress and the Federal Reserve Board illustrates a different pattern. In theory, Congress can abolish the Federal Reserve Board or alter it in any way. In practice, however, Congress has limited its oversight to occasional skirmishes. The Fed has been particularly responsive to the banking community, especially the large banks and financial institutions. Many members of the Banking committees, too, are responsive to these interests, although some members are not. Consequently, there is a *mixed committee-agency relationship:* it is too conflictual for a subgovernment, but too supportive to allow any major oversight or policy change.

Less than happy with Federal Reserve policies, Congress has passed resolutions stipulating specific goals the agency must maintain. It has required the Fed to appear at semi-annual hearings and to report to the Joint Economic Committee twice a year with its predictions for the economy. With mounting interest rates in the early 1980s, criticism of the Federal Reserve Board increased. Bills were introduced to impeach the Chairman and the seven-member board of governors. Several bills were sponsored to restructure the entire Federal Reserve system, but they did not possess enough support to pass in Congress. A resolution was passed calling inter-

[18]See Harold P. Green and Alan Rosenthal, *Government of the Atom* (New York: Atherton, 1963). See also Richard Rhodes, *The Making of the Atomic Bomb* (New York: Simon and Schuster, 1986).

est rates "needlessly and destructively high." Meanwhile, the hearings and the semi-annual reports went on. Some said that the lowering of interest rates in 1982 was in part a response to these pressures. Overall, however, congressional control of the Federal Reserve Board remains weak.[19]

THE BUDGET PROCESS

The major contact point, or collision point, for these political and administrative worlds is the annual budget process. Departments, agencies, presidents, and congressional committees all take part.

The Participants

For presidents, the budget is a major tool for making policy and controlling the bureaucracy. In setting a target figure and priorities at the beginning of the budget process, presidents define broadly what the agencies can reasonably ask for. Assisting the president is the Office of Management and Budget (OMB) with its core of experts who review the requests from the various executive departments and agencies. After the gross budget figures are calculated by OMB, the president again reviews the estimates and adjusts them in line with the overall priorities. Some presidents have watched the budget for specific programs that they want increased or cut, while others, such as Reagan, have given the overall budget levels the highest priority. All presidents, however, can play a major role in the budget process, and are expected to do so by Congress. Whatever will happen later on, the presidents get to speak first.

While the Office of Management and Budget is a professional organization, it can be seen as an arm of the president in budget policy. First created as the Bureau of the Budget in 1921, it was transferred to the Executive Office of the President in 1939 and gained its present title in 1970. Since 1974, the director and deputy director of OMB are subject to Senate confirmation. OMB has become quite visible and controversial since the Nixon years, as presidents have used it for a variety of purposes in getting their programs through Congress. Carter's first appointee, Bert Lance, was investigated for his former banking practices and forced to resign, and Reagan's appointee David Stockman also attracted controversy and eventually resigned. Originally seen as a neutral group of experts who would help the president make budget policy, OMB has become very much a part of presidential politics.

Departments and agencies within departments also calculate their own budget requests, with an eye toward what is going on at the White House. Department heads submit a budget, deciding among the various agency pri-

---

[19]Lance LeLoup, "Congress and the Dilemma of Economic Policy," in *Making Economic Policy in Congress*, ed. Allen Schick (Washington, D.C.: American Enterprise Institute, 1983), p. 21ff.

orities, thus giving the cabinet secretaries a measure of control. But the agencies can look to their various environments for help in the budget battle. Thus agencies with popular programs and strong congressional support can ignore any department-level cuts. They know they can get the funds restored in Congress later on.

Congress independently reviews the executive budget requests through a series of separate decisions. The House and Senate Appropriations Committees and their subcommittees will conduct hearings on particular programs and agency requests. Given the norm of specialization, the subcommittees will be making the specific decisions, cutting one program or adding to another. Subcommittee recommendations will tend to be accepted by the full committee, and full committee recommendations will be accepted on the floor.

The Budget committees in the House and Senate set the overall target figures within which the Appropriations committees will work in the first budget resolution. The Budget committees were created by The Budget and Impoundment Control Act of 1974, which also established the highly expert Congressional Budget Office. The act marked an attempt by Congress to make broad budget decisions that could provide alternatives to the presidential budget. Congress would set its own targets, adjust priorities, and have its own professional staff. Thus the Budget committees, backed by the Congressional Budget Office, attempt to do for Congress what OMB is doing for the president; however, they set general figures only and do not evaluate specific requests. Specific decisions are left to the Appropriations committees. Under the new procedure, the budget committees receive reports from other committees and the CBO and then make their own recommendations which are introduced in a *concurrent budget resolution*. This resolution sets expenditure limits by overall categories, such as international affairs or agriculture, but not specific programs, although assumptions are made about their costs. A total appropriations target is specified, along with expected revenues and recommended new taxes. The resolution also spells out the gap between income and expenditures, which is the deficit. Key portions of the fiscal 1989 budget resolution enacted by the Senate are presented in Exhibit 9.6.

The evidence to date does not suggest any serious conflict between the Budget and Appropriations committees. One writer calls the Budget committees "adding machine committees."[20] They take the demands of the spending committees and impose as much restraint on them as the current congressional mood seems to call for. The Budget committees act as expected given the norms and distribution of influence in Congress. Both Budget and Appropriations will be consulting with each other and with the

---

[20]Dennis S. Ippolito, *Congressional Spending* (Ithaca: Cornell University Press, 1981), p. 104. See also Aaron Wildavsky, *The New Politics of the Budgetary Process* (Glenview, Ill: Scott, Foresman, 1988), p. 142. Wildavsky shows how Congress added new procedures while it kept the old ones intact.

EXHIBIT 9.6	BUDGET CATEGORY	SENATE BUDGET OUTLAYS
Budget Resolution Passed by the Senate in 1988 for Fiscal 1989 by Function (in billions of dollars)	Defense	$ 294.0
	Social Security	233.5
	Interest on the National Debt	151.9
	Income Security	138.3
	Medicare	86.9
	Health	48.9
	Education and Social Services	35.3
	Veterans' Benefits	28.4
	Transportation	27.9
	Agriculture	23.2
	International Affairs	16.2
	Natural Resources	14.9
	Science and Space	13.0
	General Government	9.4
	Commerce and Housing	9.1
	Justice	9.0
	Community Development	6.5
	Energy	4.2
	Offsetting Receipts	− 49.9
	TOTALS	$1,100.6
	Revenues	964.6
	Deficit	136.0

Source: Senate Budget Committee

leadership until the differences are worked out with a minimum of publicized conflict and a second resolution is passed.

The congressional leadership also has a role to play, together with the conference committees. Differences in House and Senate appropriations are expected, given the varying interests of the committee members. Hence the conference committees, appointed by the leadership to reconcile the differences, add their own input to the budget process. If an agency's budget is slashed in the House and reinstated by a friendly Senate, then the conference committee will be making the critical decision.

The Effects

Chronologically, budget formulation moves from the White House to agency and department requests, back to the White House and on to the multi-staged congressional process. (See Exhibit 9.7.) Nevertheless, in terms of actual formulation, each stage is recognized in advance by all the participants and simultaneously prepared for. An agency anticipating cuts at the

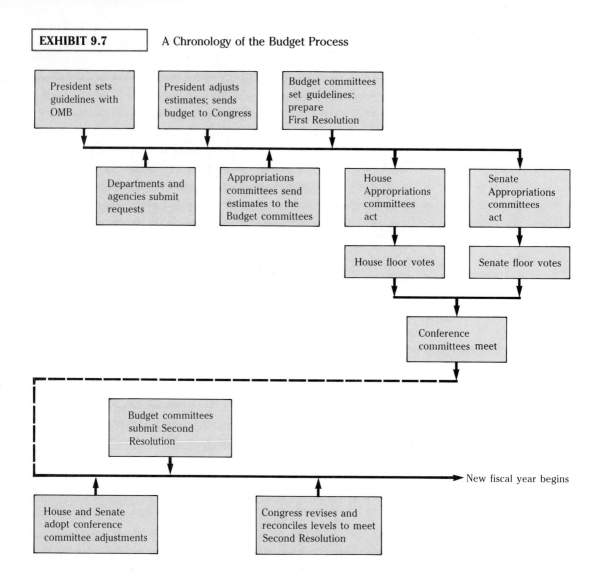

EXHIBIT 9.7   A Chronology of the Budget Process

White House will ask more than it expects to receive (although the White House will anticipate this anticipatory reaction). Presidents anticipate congressional reaction, and the House and Senate committees anticipate each other and the final conference committee stage. The House will agree to cuts knowing they will be restored in conference. This effect has been called **the law of anticipated reaction:** decisions are made with an eye toward what all the other participants will do.

In addition to the law of anticipated reaction, a process of **incrementalism** is also at work. Evaluating the programs and work of an agency is an enormously large and complex task. Therefore, agencies construct next year's budget request by adding an increment to the past and present base. The evaluators, in the White House and Congress, also focus on the increment. They judge its appropriateness rather than the program as a whole. It is the increment that is evaluated, cut, or preserved in negotiations.[21]

Incrementalism builds in an inertia and continuity to the policy-making process. Once accepted and funded, a program will tend to be continued, often outliving any original need. According to one study, more than eighty percent of the federal agencies existing in 1923 were still in existence fifty years later. Most of these had barely changed their status.[22] Other things being equal, old programs are more secure in budget negotiations than new programs. Incrementalism also limits any single president's control over the federal budget. Because federal money is limited, some new presidential programs will be sacrificed while others from the past are supported. The case was cited in Chapter Seven of the 120 urban highway programs that Reagan could not get out of the budget. Urban highway programs were already supported in Congress. Thus the president could try to cut the budget somewhere else.

The first years of the Reagan administration demonstrated that presidents can independently affect the budget. According to budget expert Allen Schick, Ronald Reagan succeeded by leaving alone the heavily supported programs and targeting cuts for those weakest in congressional support. Schick reports:

> [Reagan] deftly targeted his budget reductions against weak political interests, especially low-income groups. The White House strategy was to recapture control of the budget by defeating the weak interests.[23]

For example, welfare programs were cut while strongly supported public works programs were left alone. So, if presidents select programs in terms of their congressional support, Congress is helping to make policy even in the cases of presidential success. (See the discussion of the budget as domestic policy in Chapter Eleven.)

Finally, in addition to being incremental and interactive, the budget process is pluralistic: a number of different political actors make an independent effect. If committees split the difference between a high and a low estimate, the levels of the original estimates make a difference to the outcome. If presidents target programs weak in congressional support, both the president and Congress are shaping priorities. And if all the participants anticipate each other, all have an impact on the final result.

What counts most in helping an agency get the appropriation it wants? Most experts say that agencies should try to cultivate an active clientele and develop confidence among other government officials.[24] For some agen-

[21]Wildavsky, *The New Politics, op. cit.,* p. 78.

[22]Herbert Kaufman, *Are Government Organizations Immortal?* (Washington, Brookings Institute, 1976).

[23]Allen Schick, "The Problem of Presidential Budgeting," in *The Illusion of Presidential Government*, eds. Hugh Heclo and Lester M. Salamon (Boulder, Colo.: Westview Press, 1981), p. 109.

[24]Wildavsky, *The New Politics, op. cit.,* p. 101ff.

cies, finding an active clientele is no problem—the problem is how to avoid being captured by the clientele. Other agencies, however, serving groups without political influence (for example, prisoners, poor people, and most foreign nations) face more difficulty showing that their activities are needed and appreciated. Developing confidence is also easier for some agencies than others and easiest for those with long-standing reputations, administering programs that are already popular and known to produce results. New agencies as well as those administering controversial programs must hold on as well as they can.

The budget process, in short, is a microcosm of the larger political process. It is interactive, incremental, and pluralistic, and it is a process that the supposedly "apolitical" administrator must master in order to survive.

The Budget and Democratic Control

At this point, it is apparent how the budget process shapes much of the interaction between the bureaucracy and its various political environments. Whatever the individual bureaucrat's goals, the annual allocation of funds is a reality and a testing point that all must come to terms with—hence, the importance of good clientele relations, of access to the White House, and of good long-term relations with congressional committee members, as well as the importance of showing immediate concrete "results" and of defining public interest in terms of a broad distribution of clientele support. Many specific decisions and broader policy trends can be traced back to the need for budget support. The budget, therefore, becomes a major tool for bureaucratic control by elected officials—if they want to use it. But it is still necessary to ask whether the controls are sufficient and whether they produce policy that is in the public interest.

The question as to whether controls are sufficient must confront the problems of information seen in previous chapters, such as low public interest (Chapter Three), infrequent oversight (Chapter Seven), and difficulties in getting through to the president (Chapter Eight). The size of the bureaucracy and the need for success in the budget battle keep failures, illicit activities, and many other facts from being known. OMB budget examiners are not looking for substantive issues, and committee hearings, which could be used for this purpose, have been employed only sporadically and even then not for the most strongly supported agencies.

The second line of questioning asks whatever the controls, do they tend to produce policy in the public interest? If public interest is defined circularly as whatever the president and Congress (as elected by the public) will support, then the budget process is effective on that score. But other definitions suggest different answers. For example, subgovernments develop in part from the pressures of budget making, and subgovernments pursue special interests at the expense of a broader public interest. Or, for another example, the very devices necessary to protect the budget—such as secrecy and the continuation of old programs—go against the public interest by favoring certain kinds of policies over others.

All modern governments require bureaucratic specialization and expertise; but all democratic governments require controls by elected officials, themselves responsible to the people. The budget process gives one source of potential control. So it is necessary to think about how well the controls function and with what consequences for American government.

It is often too easy to caricature the bureaucracy with its inertia, impersonality, and glorification of routine. Adding in subgovernments and secret CIA adventures, one can visualize a kind of bureaucratic monster run amok, mindless but of superhuman power. Yet exaggerations provoke counterexaggerations and the too-easy justification that since the bureaucracy works in a political environment, and since budgets will be examined and reviewed, there are sufficient democratic controls. The critics of bureaucracy talk about clientele capture and subgovernment abuse; the defenders stress the pluralism and the budgetary controls. However, the chapter makes clear that neither exaggeration is adequate. Agencies vary in their political environments, their conflict with committees, and the rigor of their budget review. Some agencies fit the exaggerations, but many fall in the more complex and interesting range in between.

CHECKLIST FOR REVIEW

1. Bureaucracy refers to a form of organization, common throughout modern society, characterized by specialization, hierarchy, detailed rules and procedures, and impersonality. Since governments have bureaucracies, too, their role must be considered in the political process.

2. In American national government, the bureaucracy informs, initiates, interprets, and implements, thus shaping the policy made in the White House and Congress. However, the bureaucracy is not one powerful monolith. The various agencies differ in their impact depending on their relationships with the other government actors.

3. Five different political environments exist: bureaucratic, presidential, congressional, professional, and clientele. Some agencies look to the White House for support, some to the congressional committees, and others to fellow professionals or interest groups.

4. A subgovernment describes one particular relationship agencies can be involved in: that of mutual support between the agency, a congressional committee or subcommittee, and a clientele (or interest) group. Subgovernments are powerful, but they are not the only kind of pattern that agencies work within. Cases of conflict between an agency and a committee also occur with some frequency.

5. The budget process is a means by which elected officials can influence what the bureaucracy does. The budget process can be seen as incremental, pluralistic, and anticipatory, with each of the many participants calculating what the other participants will do. Nevertheless, as agencies differ in their political environments, they differ also in the rigor of their budget review.

KEY TERMS

bureaucracy

government corporation

independent regulatory
commissions

patronage

spoils system

merit principle

civil service system

clientele

clientele capture

subgovernment

issue networks

law of anticipated reaction

incrementalism

The Judiciary

T he judicial branch of government holds a special place in American government and politics. It is little known and widely misunderstood, a frequent scapegoat and source of political controversy as well as a potential savior for those who feel violated by government or wronged by private parties. It is a maker of public policy clothed in the largely inaccessible special language of law. At some lower levels in some localities it has been known to be corrupt, but elsewhere and especially at the highest levels it can soar above venality, pettiness, and partisanship and appeal to the enduring values and ideals of the American experience. This chapter examines the structure, processes, and politics of American courts with an emphasis on the federal courts and, in particular, the United States Supreme Court.

THE LITIGIOUS SOCIETY

Courts hear and decide disputes between two or more litigants, including government officials, who argue about their rights and responsibilities under law. Courts are established for the purpose of resolving conflicts that have been formed as legal questions. Did Jane Doe commit murder in the first degree? Did John Doe violate the terms of the contract he made with the finance company? Did the Worldwide Widget Company pollute the environment in violation of federal standards established under federal law? Does the state law imposing a processing tax only on widgets to be shipped out of state but not those for in-state use constitute a burden on interstate commerce and thereby violate the federal Constitution? Did the Worldwide Widget Company refuse to promote qualified women to middle-management positions on account of their gender and thereby violate federal civil rights law?

As these examples suggest, the American judiciary is heavily involved in processing disputes between particular parties, disputes that also have broader public-policy consequences. It is still as true today as it was over 150 years ago when Alexis de Tocqueville observed in *Democracy in America*, "Scarcely any political question arises in the United States that is not resolved, sooner or later, into a judicial question."[1] The judiciary is involved in disputes that are more or less "political" but that concern specific litigants with specific conflicts.

Today, millions of cases are filed each year in the state court systems alone. In 1987, for example, more than 25 million cases were filed (excluding juvenile and traffic matters). Most were **civil law cases** concerning economic relationships, personal status (such as divorce), personal injury, or

---

[1]*Democracy in America*, vol. 1, Phillips Bradley, ed., (New York: Vintage Books, 1954), p. 290.

property damage. Civil law does not involve the criminal law. In the federal trial courts that year, close to a quarter of a million civil cases and over 40,000 criminal cases began. The rate of litigation (cases per thousand in the population) has increased over time. In the federal courts, the litigation rate in 1902 was 20 cases filed per 100,000 persons. By 1972 it was 44 cases per 100,000 persons.[2] One commentator has even used the term "legal pollution" to describe this litigiousness.[3]

Yet this country may not be quite so litigious as we think it is. For one thing, other countries have higher litigation rates. For another, most disputes do not even go to court. A large chunk of court business consists of minor traffic offenses and routine bankruptcy actions. Our courts are busy, but the severity of litigiousness has been exaggerated.[4]

Kinds of Disputes and Dispute Processing

Courts decide three major kinds of disputes.[5] In *private disputes*, only private (non-governmental) parties are involved, such as individuals, businesses, and corporations. For example, a husband sues his wife for divorce, a contractor sues a subcontractor for breach of contract, an individual sues a corporation for damages as a result of injuries suffered because of faulty design of the corporation's product, a corporation sues another corporation for patent infringement, and so on.

In *public-initiated disputes*, federal, state, or local governments seek to enforce social norms through criminal and civil law and thereby regulate social behavior. Society, for example, has norms embedded in law against rape, murder, robbery, fraud, and exploitation of workers by employers. Criminal prosecutions constitute many of the public-initiated disputes.

In *public defendant disputes*, government is sued for allegedly violating certain individual rights, for violating the terms of a contract, or for seriously harming an individual or business. For example, a city may be sued if a municipal vehicle hits and injures a pedestrian and then careens out of control and crashes into the glass window of the corner convenience store. Or a poor person newly arrived in a state may find that the state has a nine-month residency requirement before being eligible for welfare benefits and may decide to challenge the law by suing the state. Disputes such as these

---

[2]Joel B. Grossman and Austin Sarat, "Litigation in the Federal Courts: A Comparative Perspective," *Law and Society Review*, 9 (1975), pp. 331–35.

[3]Thomas Ehrlich, "Legal Pollution," *New York Times Magazine*, February 8, 1976, pp. 17ff.

[4]Marc Galanter, "Reading the Landscape of Disputes: What We Know and Don't Know (and Think We Know) About Our Allegedly Contentious and Litigious Society," *UCLA Law Review*, 31 (1983), pp. 4–71.

[5]This section relies heavily on the analysis provided in Sheldon Goldman and Austin Sarat, eds., *American Court Systems*, Second Edition (New York: Longman, 1989), pp. 4–6.

are frequently conflicts over the exercise of government power and authority.

There are three major points to keep in mind about disputes and courts.

1. *Not all disputes are resolved in court.* Most disputes are resolved when one party decides to do nothing or informally works out the problem with the other party. For example, a student who feels that a mid-term examination was graded unfairly may simply accept the injustice or may ask the teacher to reconsider the grade. Some disputes are resolved privately and informally by a third party. The aggrieved student might go to the department chairperson, the Dean of Students, or a campus official whose job it is to resolve campus disputes. However, if the student were a woman and asserted that before the exam she turned down the professor's request for a date, a lawyer might advise that there is some basis for filing suit.

But even filing a suit does not mean that it will be heard and decided by a judge. The overwhelming majority of court cases are resolved without a trial. For example, if the student who complained that she was the victim of sexism filed a suit, the professor probably would agree to having the dispute decided out of court. The settlement might provide for another faculty member grading the exam and perhaps a cash payment to the student for emotional distress. The professor might be censured by campus administrators for sexual harassment.

2. *Courts do not resolve the underlying social issues contained in the disputes before them.* No court and no court decision can resolve the social problems in America, problems like racism, sexism, or poverty. Courts *can* deal with specific instances of racism, sexism, or unequal treatment of the poor. Within the context of cases brought before it, a court can order a school system to desegregate, order a business not to discriminate against women in hiring and promotion, or strike down a residency requirement for poor people to receive welfare benefits.

3. *Courts are distinctive institutions and process disputes in distinctive ways.* Unlike legislatures or administrative agencies, courts must wait for disputes to come to them. They cannot reach out and make decisions about issues that no one has brought before them.

Courts also require that a dispute take a particular form before it can be considered (these requirements are discussed in the section on organization of the judiciary). The rules of evidence, the form of argument, the citation of previous decisions, the mode of legal reasoning, and the use of legal words, phrases, and concepts (legal jargon to some) are all unique to the judicial branch. In making decisions, the judiciary is expected to observe distinctive standards. More than legislators, administrators, or presidents, judges are expected to be *neutral* towards the disputants, *unbiased* toward the issues, and *impartial* in fashioning a solution to the precise legal questions presented to the court.

The Growth of Litigation

Why has the business of the courts grown so much over the years? There is no shortage of possible explanations.[6]

First, it has been suggested that a changing, increasingly complex society is bound to generate disputes that can best be resolved by formal dispute-processing mechanisms. A complex economy, continuously developing high technology, the weakening of traditional industries, major population shifts, and other major social adjustments all may stimulate litigation to resolve the conflicts that inevitably arise.

Second, the family and church, institutions that once were the locus for much dispute resolution, have lost much of their clout. The family no longer exerts the authority over its members that it once did. The roles of family councils, family elders, and mothers and fathers have changed over the years. In our mobile society, children leave home for far-away colleges or jobs, grandparents resettle in warmer climates or distant retirement homes, and some parents divorce. Physical discipline of children today often is seen as child abuse. All of these changes have made the family less likely to resolve disputes. The church also has lost much of its force as a dispute-resolver, especially in domestic matters. Clergymen often met with estranged couples to help them resolve their problems. Religious leaders sometimes were called on to mediate business disputes among members of their congregations.

A third reason for increased litigation may be that Americans are more aware of their rights. The Supreme Court under Chief Justice Earl Warren (1953–1969) actively promoted and expanded civil rights and civil liberties and this in turn heightened people's expectations about their rights. For example, Clarence Earl Gideon, too poor to afford a lawyer when he was tried by the State of Florida for breaking and entering, was outraged when he was convicted. He believed that he had a *right* to a court-appointed lawyer to defend him. He petitioned the Supreme Court, which appointed a lawyer to argue on his behalf before it. In the landmark 1963 decision of *Gideon* v. *Wainwright*, the Court agreed with Gideon and held that poor people on trial for a felony are indeed entitled to a free lawyer provided by the state.[7] Increased rights consciousness also has led minorities and women to bring to the courts disputes over racial and sexual discrimination. Poor people can pursue their rights through the courts thanks to the federally funded Legal Services Corporation. Over one million disputes each year are handled by legal services lawyers.

---

[6]This section draws from Ralph Cavanagh and Austin Sarat, "Thinking About Courts," *Law and Society Review*, 14 (1980), pp. 371–420.

[7]The classic study of this case is Anthony Lewis, *Gideon's Trumpet* (New York: Random House, 1964).

" YOU GUYS ARE IN BIG TROUBLE. THIS IS MY LAWYER. I BURNED MY MOUTH ON YOUR PORRIDGE."

Fourth, the number of lawyers has increased. Today there are over 700,000 lawyers, and each year their ranks increase. The increase in lawyers probably is both a response to and a cause of the increase of litigiousness. As the numbers of lawyers increase, they compete for and stimulate business, and in so doing they contribute to the litigation rate.

Fifth, litigation may increase as government activity, including bureaucratic regulation, increases. New legislation creates new rights or obligations. The agencies of government inevitably must use the courts to enforce those rights. For example, various civil rights laws enacted in the 1960s established people's rights to be free from racial discrimination in employment, in their access to housing, in exercising their right to vote, and in their use of public accommodations such as means of transportation, hotels, motels, restaurants, and theaters. Civil rights laws also prohibited sexual discrimination. Various government agencies were created or empowered to enforce those rights and monitor their implementation. Likewise, government has increased its control over the economy, regulating not only working conditions but also business practices that have an impact on the environment. It also has assumed responsibility for a wide range of social problems including highway speed limits and a minimum nationwide drinking age. The result has been an increase in government regulation and an increase in the use of the courts by government. Between 1895 and 1910, for instance, only 20 percent of the cases in three of the largest federal appeals courts involved government. But between 1960 and 1975, over 60 percent of the cases involved government as a litigant.[8]

Sixth, increased use of the courts can likely be attributed in part to court decisions themselves. When courts are expansive in reading the Bill of Rights and generous in offering remedies to those whose rights have been violated, they stimulate litigation. For example, the Warren Court's decisions that gave new rights to the accused led to a dramatic increase in petitions from prisoners challenging the constitutionality of the procedures that had led to their conviction and imprisonment. Supreme Court decisions are considered by some experts as the primary cause of the expanding volume of disputes brought to the Court.[9]

ORGANIZATION OF THE JUDICIARY

As the structure of state courts was discussed in Chapter Two, discussion turns now to the structure, powers, and operation of the federal judiciary.

Federal Trial Courts

The structure of the federal court system is outlined in Exhibit 10.1. At the entry level lie the principal federal trial courts, the *United States District Courts*. Each state has at least one federal district court, and some have as many as four. Where states contain more than one district court, each district court is confined to specific geographic boundaries, as seen in Exhibit 10.2. For example, the state of Texas is divided into four geographic regions where the four district courts are located: Texas Eastern (the eastern part of the state); Texas Southern (the southern part of Texas); Texas Western; and Texas Northern.

There are 89 federal districts within the 50 states and one each in the District of Columbia and Puerto Rico. These 91 courts may hear only cases concerning federal law. In the states this means that violations of or matters concerning only state law that involve state residents exclusively may not be tried in federal court. For example, the burglar caught breaking and entering a Massachusetts convenience store is solely within the scope of Massachusetts state courts. In the District of Columbia and in Puerto Rico, purely local matters go only to the local courts and not to the federal courts.

The 89 federal district courts in the states are considered (and the federal district courts in the District of Columbia and Puerto Rico are treated as if they were) Article III **constitutional courts**, that is, established under

---

[8]Lawrence Baum, Sheldon Goldman, and Austin Sarat, "The Evolution of Litigation in the Federal Courts of Appeals, 1895–1975," *Law and Society Review*, 16 (1981–82), pp. 291–309.

[9]Gerhard Casper and Richard A. Posner, "A Study of the Supreme Court's Caseload," *Journal of Legal Studies*, 3 (1974), pp. 339–75.

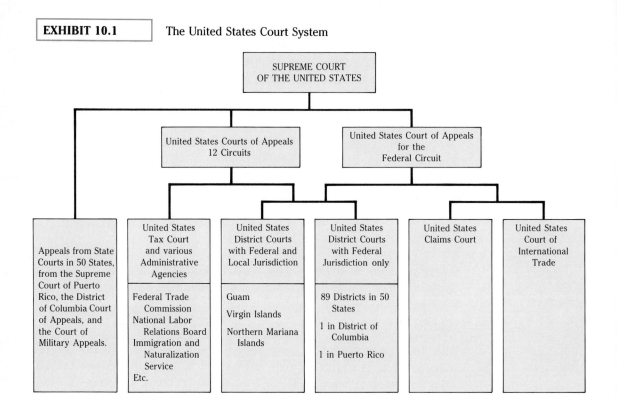

EXHIBIT 10.1   The United States Court System

SUPREME COURT
OF THE UNITED STATES

United States Courts of Appeals
12 Circuits

United States Court of Appeals
for the
Federal Circuit

Appeals from State
Courts in 50 States,
from the Supreme
Court of Puerto
Rico, the District
of Columbia Court
of Appeals, and
the Court of
Military Appeals.

United States
Tax Court
and various
Administrative
Agencies

Federal Trade
Commission
National Labor
Relations Board
Immigration and
Naturalization
Service
Etc.

United States
District Courts
with Federal and
Local Jurisdiction

Guam

Virgin Islands

Northern Mariana
Islands

United States
District Courts
with Federal
Jurisdiction only

89 Districts in 50
States

1 in District of
Columbia

1 in Puerto Rico

United States
Claims Court

United States
Court of
International
Trade

the Judicial Article of the Constitution. Article III specifies that judges are appointed for life ("good behavior" is the term used) and are guaranteed that their salaries will not be diminished while they hold office.

Three federal district courts deal with both federal and local concerns. These courts, in the federal territories of Guam, the Virgin Islands, and the Northern Mariana Islands, hear all cases arising within their borders whether they involve local law or federal law. They are considered **legislative courts** mandated by Article I of the Constitution, which empowers Congress to take responsibility for governing the territories. Judges in legislative courts are appointed for set terms of office (ten or fifteen years depending on the court) and are not afforded the protection given judges in constitutional courts under Article III.

Other courts of a specialized nature complete the trial court level of the federal system. The *United States Claims Court* hears only cases involving monetary claims made against the United States. The *United States Court of International Trade* hears only cases involving customs or tariffs concerned with foreign shipping. These courts have the status of constitutional (Article III) courts. The *United States Tax Court* has the status of a legislative court in that it was created to help carry out Congress's Article I enumerated power to collect taxes. Various federal administrative agencies, commis-

| EXHIBIT 10.2 | Geographical Boundaries of United States Courts of Appeals and United States District Courts |

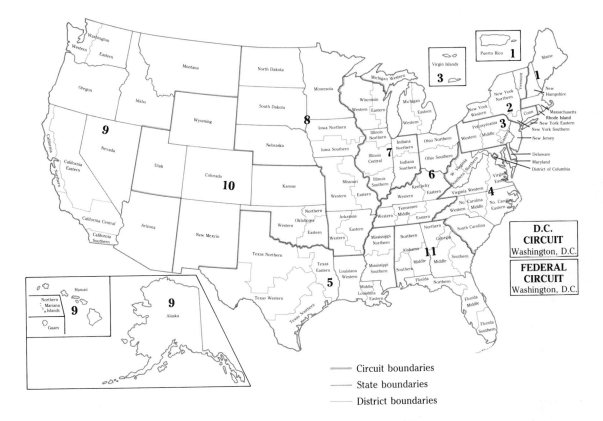

Circuit boundaries
State boundaries
District boundaries

sions, boards, and the like conduct their own in-house administrative hearings, which have a status analogous to that of district court proceedings.

Federal district courts hear and decide disputes brought before them. This process is sometimes referred to as the **adversary system**. Every case has at least two sides, adversaries at the bar, opposing each other. American trial judges are generally passive and leave it to the opposing lawyers to make their best arguments, question witnesses, present evidence, and establish facts. Only at the conclusion of proceedings does the judge take over and actively resolve the dispute through a ruling or, if appropriate, a sentence. Once the trial judge makes a ruling, the losing side ordinarily may make an appeal. The only exception to this is in criminal cases in which the defendant has been acquitted (found not guilty).

This is not to suggest that the trial judge is completely above the adversarial fray. In reality, the trial judge works behind the scenes with the opposing lawyers to resolve the dispute without going to trial. With criminal proceedings, the behind-the-scenes activity of the judge, prosecutor, and defense counsel may represent a collaborative effort to avoid a trial rather than embark on an adversarial process.[10] These work groups achieve some success and are responsible for much of the caseload that is resolved without trial. Overall, roughly eight out of ten criminal and nine out of ten civil cases filed in the district courts are settled without trial.

Why do the large majority of disputes fail to go to trial? In criminal cases either the prosecutor dismisses the charges or the defendant pleads guilty and gives up the right to a trial. Because it is unusual for a defendant to give up the right to a trial without something in return, a process known as **plea bargaining** frequently occurs. In plea bargaining, the defendant and the defendant's lawyer negotiate with the prosecution to reduce the charges and thus the maximum penalty to which the defendant may be subject. Part of the bargain may also involve a promise by the prosecutor to recommend that the judge impose a lenient sentence. Federal judges usually honor these agreements.

In civil cases, disputes sometimes are resolved without trial after negotiations in which the judge may be an active participant. This resolution is referred to as an out-of-court settlement. In a suit for damages, for example, the judge might tell the lawyers from both sides that in similar disputes the typical damage award has been $50,000 and they should try to convince their clients to accept that amount.

Federal Appeals Courts

When a case does go to trial and a federal district court renders a judgment, the defendant may take an appeal to one of the *United States Courts of Appeals*. There are eleven numbered regional circuits, each encompassing at least five district courts and at least three states (see Exhibit 10.2). The twelfth circuit is the District of Columbia Circuit, which hears not only appeals from federal district courts in the District of Columbia, but also appeals involving administrative agencies and other boards or commissions based in Washington, D.C. The *United States Court of Appeals for the Federal Circuit* is a specialized appeals court. It hears only claims and customs appeals from the United States Claims Court and United States Court of International Trade. It also hears patent, copyright, and trademark appeals from the district courts.

There are important differences between appeals courts and district courts. Almost all federal district trials are presided over by one judge. But appeals courts are **collegial courts**; most appeals are heard and decided by panels of three judges. Whereas the atmosphere of the trial court can be tense, crowded, and even noisy (as litigants, witnesses, friends, and curiosity seekers fill the courtroom), the atmosphere of the appeals court is far different. Voices are subdued, questions are polite and low-keyed, and tem-

[10]In general, see James Eisenstein, Roy B. Flemming, and Peter F. Nardulli, *The Contours of Justice* (Boston: Little, Brown 1988).

pers (ordinarily) remain calm. In appeals courts, there are no litigants or witnesses, and rarely are there onlookers. It is exclusively a professional's game; no amateurs are permitted to play.

The style of judicial decision making also differs in trial and appeals courts. Appeals court decision making tends to take a more scholarly approach. Trial court decision making is more spontaneous. Trial judges typically must decide on the spot to admit or exclude questions, testimony, and evidence. Written opinions by trial judges can be thoughtful and scholarly, but unless major statutory or constitutional claims are raised that cry out for judicial consideration, trial judges do not generally write opinions of any consequence.

The Supreme Court

The Supreme Court of the United States is at the very top of the federal judicial system. Although Americans like to think that every dispute is worthy of being heard by the Supreme Court (countless disputants have said "I'll take my case all the way to the Supreme Court"), the Supreme Court is under no obligation to hear most cases. This is one important way in which the Supreme Court differs from appeals courts.

Cases may come up to the Supreme Court from the twelve appeals courts and the specialized appeals court for the Federal Circuit. Although not pictured in Exhibit 10.1, there are an exceedingly narrow category of cases that may be decided by a three-judge district court and taken directly to the Supreme Court. The Supreme Court can also expedite hearing a case from a district court, thus bypassing the appeals court (but this is extremely rare). Cases from the highest state courts in the fifty states and from equivalent courts in Puerto Rico and the District of Columbia may also be taken to the Court. Since the Supreme Court is a unique institution, it will be examined in more detail later in this chapter.

Jurisdiction of the Federal Courts

John Troublemaker was nineteen years old and frequently lived up to his name. His last escapade, however, got him into deep trouble. He went to the local post office in Albany, New York, to buy some stamps. John found the lobby open but the postal windows closed; he had come some ten minutes after closing. In frustration, but also to obtain stamps, John kicked in a stamp machine, breaking the glass and grabbed all the stamps he could. A post office employee recognized the fleeing John. He was arrested by the local police, who turned him over to the federal authorities because he had violated federal law. John therefore came under the *jurisdiction* of the federal courts.

In order to understand how courts function, it is necessary to understand the concept of a court's jurisdiction. **Jurisdiction** means a court's authority to hear and decide the case. There are three criteria in deciding whether a court has jurisdiction—the subject matter of the case, the geographic origin of the case, and the legal origin of the case.

Subject Matter.   Of greatest importance is whether a court has subject matter jurisdiction, that is, the authority under law to hear the case. The federal courts have subject matter jurisdiction over all cases that raise questions of federal statutory law (acts of Congress), federal constitutional law (concerning a provision of the United States Constitution), a federal treaty, or disputes under **admiralty law** (concerning occurrences on the high seas) or **maritime law** (concerning shipping on rivers and waterways and occurrences involving ships to and from harbors). John violated federal statutory law and was thus subject to federal court jurisdiction.

Geographic Origin.   A court's jurisdiction encompasses those disputes that occur within the geographic boundaries serviced by the court. The prosecution of John Troublemaker occurred in Albany, New York, not in Boston, Santa Fe, or Los Angeles. However, under the federal courts' **diversity of citizenship jurisdiction**, a citizen of one state can sue a citizen of another state in the federal district court situated in either state (provided the amount at issue is at least $50,000). If John Troublemaker was a sleazy merchant based in Albany who sold over $50,000 worth of defective merchandise to a Boston firm and was then sued, the suit could be considered in federal court either in Albany or Boston.

Legal Origin.   In terms of legal origin, there are two types of jurisdiction: original and appellate. **Original jurisdiction** means that the court is the first court to hear the case. **Appellate jurisdiction** means that the court hears the case on appeal from a lower court. The federal district courts have original jurisdiction for most federal cases. They are the trial courts for the federal system, the courts of first instance. John Troublemaker would be prosecuted in a federal district court in New York under the court's original jurisdiction.

The appeals courts exercise mainly appellate jurisdiction; they hear cases on appeal from the district courts. If John Troublemaker were convicted, he could appeal to the circuit in which New York State is located, the Second Circuit. For certain administrative agency appeals, an appeals court is the first court to hear such cases.

The Supreme Court's jurisdiction is almost exclusively appellate. If John Troublemaker lost his appeal, he could petition the Supreme Court to hear his case under the Court's appellate jurisdiction. The Supreme Court also hears a handful of cases under its original jurisdiction, which is spelled out in Article III of the Constitution. For example, it has original jurisdiction in disputes between states.

Standing to Sue

To be heard by a court, not only must a case fall within the court's jurisdiction, but the litigants must have **standing to sue**, a legally recognizable basis for invoking the court's jurisdiction. Both Congress and the federal courts themselves have developed certain rules to determine whether a litigant has standing to sue.

First, there must be a genuine case or controversy. To have standing in federal court, there must be a genuine dispute subject to the court's federal jurisdiction. For example, if John Troublemaker contemplated kicking in the stamp machine in the post office but did not actually commit the deed, he would not be able to go before a federal judge and ask what his sentence would be were he to carry out his impulse. He would not have standing to sue.

Second, there must be some concrete relationship between the litigant and the dispute brought to the court. One cannot invoke the rights of others but not have a personal stake in the controversy. However, one *can* invoke one's rights *and* the rights of all others similarly situated (this is called a **class action**). For example, if John believed that Albany municipal officials discriminated against women in hiring and promotions in city government, he could not bring suit because he would not have a personal stake in the controversy. However, his sister Jane Troublemaker, an unsuccessful applicant for a municipal job, could sue the city either solely on her own behalf or as part of a class action suit.

Third, if governmental action is being challenged, that action must be sufficiently final to be what is known as *ripe for review*. For example, if Jane Troublemaker claimed that she was entitled to a benefit under social security but the local social security office denied her claim, she could not immediately file suit in federal court because the dispute would not yet be ripe for review. The Social Security Administration has its own internal procedures for hearing appeals from those like Jane Troublemaker who have been denied claims at the lower level of the agency. Only when those internal processes are exhausted can Jane and those like her go to federal court and argue that the agency has denied them their rights due under federal law.

Justiciable Disputes

For a dispute to be heard in a court, the dispute itself must be **justiciable**, that is, able to be resolved by the court. Certain types of disputes fall outside the realm of what courts believe to be legitimate judicial decision making, such as cases in which final authority lies with another branch of government. These cases raise what are called *political questions*. For example, questions of foreign policy have traditionally been considered political questions more appropriately resolved by the executive and legislative branches of government. The Supreme Court therefore avoided ruling on the constitutionality of the Vietnam War and has never considered stopping war-like activities in Nicaragua, the Middle East, the Persian Gulf, or elsewhere.

Beyond foreign policy, the question of what is and what is not a political question becomes cloudier. In practice, the federal courts have answered this on a case-by-case basis. For example, the issue of legislative malapportionment of state legislative and congressional election districts was once considered to be a political question. The Supreme Court took the position that an electoral scheme whereby some districts contain fewer voters than others yet elect the same number of representatives does not present a justiciable issue.[11] But in 1962, the Supreme Court reversed itself and ruled in the landmark case of *Baker* v. *Carr* that the issue of malapportioned election districts *is* justiciable because it raises a constitutional question that the courts *are* equipped to handle. More recently, in 1986, the Court ruled in *Davis* v. *Bandemer* that the issue of politically gerrymandered electoral districts is justiciable. This means that districts with equal population whose shapes were designed to give an advantage to the political party that constructed those districts is *not* considered to be a political question unsuitable for the courts to determine.

Other Supreme Court **precedents** (past judicial rulings that have the force of law until overruled) have considered as political questions such matters as whether a state has a republican form of government (as guaranteed by the Constitution) and the procedures by which constitutional amendments are to be ratified.[12]

A dispute is also not considered justiciable when a court judgment would have no effect on the original dispute because changes have occurred that make the case **moot** (hypothetical, no longer real). Perhaps a new law has been enacted that corrects the challenged situation, or the status of the litigants has changed, or the litigants themselves have already resolved the controversy. Finally, disputes in which a court can do nothing to remedy the alleged wrong are not considered justiciable.

Judicial Remedies

In what ways can courts right wrongs? In civil cases, people typically ask for money damages, that is, payments to recompense them for physical injury, financial loss, and possibly for psychological, reputational, or other damage done. Sometimes people also ask for punitive payments as a form of punish-

---

[11]The case was *Colegrove* v. *Green* (1946).

[12]The cases are *Luther* v. *Borden* (1849) concerning the republican form of government guaranty and *Coleman* v. *Miller* (1939) concerning procedures for the ratification of constitutional amendments.

ment for the person or entity responsible for the harm. Money historically is a **common law** (judge-made) remedy. Special remedies are available when money is not appropriate. These are remedies in **equity**. Historically, courts in equity were established to dispense justice and utilize remedies not available to the ordinary common law courts. Equitable remedies include the **injunction** (a court order instructing the party being sued not to do or to continue to do some action that causes harm to the complaining party) and the **writ of specific performance** (an order requiring the party being sued to do something that the party had agreed to do).

In recent years, the federal courts have used remedies that have been a source of controversy. For example, courts have ordered massive busing to desegregate school systems and have ordered the upgrading of prison and state mental hospital facilities. Courts have issued such orders after finding massive, long-standing, constitutional violations. The remedy is meant to right the constitutional wrong. However, critics argue that such remedies go beyond the wrong to be remedied and inevitably force the courts to make detailed rulings about matters beyond their competence—for example, concerning the day-to-day operations of complex institutions such as schools, prisons, hospitals, and fire and police departments.[13]

In criminal cases, if the defendant is found not guilty, the remedy is acquittal. If the defendant is convicted, the judge may order imprisonment, probation (regular contact with a probation officer), a fine, or a combination of these.

THE SELECTION OF FEDERAL JUDGES

How are federal judges chosen? What sorts of people become judges? On the surface, the process of selecting federal judges seems simple and uneventful. The attorney general recommends to the president an individual to fill a judicial position. The president submits the name of the nominee to the Senate where it is routinely sent to the Senate Judiciary Committee for its consideration. The Committee holds a hearing on the nomination and then typically votes to send the nomination to the floor of the Senate for a formal vote. If the person is approved (confirmed) by the Senate, the president signs the formal appointment papers and the individual is officially appointed a federal judge.

To understand why particular individuals receive or fail to receive judicial appointments, it is necessary to know a great deal about backstage maneuverings. At the heart of the politics of federal judicial selection is a

---

[13]See Phillip J. Cooper, *Hard Judicial Choices: Federal District Court Judges and State and Local Officials* (New York: Oxford University Press, 1988) and J. Anthony Lukas, *Common Ground: A Turbulent Decade in the Lives of Three American Families* (New York: Knopf, 1985).

negotiations process involving party organizations, key political officials who wish to exercise the power of patronage, interest groups who have policy concerns that may also be shared by public officials, and bar associations who may have their own professional agendas to promote.

The center of selection activity lies in the Justice Department, typically in the office of the deputy attorney general. The Reagan administration formalized the selection process even more than it had been by creating an Office of Legal Policy headed by an assistant attorney general whose major responsibility was the recruitment of judges. The Reagan administration created a special White House committee to make final decisions as to whom the president should nominate.

Participants in negotiations for district court judgeships include U.S. Senators and party leaders of the president's party from the state in which there is a district court vacancy. For courts of appeals judgeships, the senators of the president's party from the state from which the appointee will be chosen are consulted, but there is ordinarily more leeway on the part of Justice officials than there is with district court positions.

Since 1953, the American Bar Association's Standing Committee on Federal Judiciary has investigated and rated judicial nominees. The ratings go from "exceptionally well-qualified" (the summa cum laude of the legal profession) to "well-qualified," "qualified," and "not qualified." (Ratings for the appointees of Presidents Carter and Reagan are shown in Exhibit 10.3, which also presents information about the appointees' backgrounds.) There have been instances in which the A.B.A. has manipulated the ratings to influence the selection process. (See the box on page 386 for an example concerning Supreme Court Justice Harry Blackmun's first judicial appointment to the U.S. Court of Appeals for the Eighth Circuit.)

A senator of the president's party expects to be able to virtually pick the nominee for the federal district judgeship in his or her state. However, if the senator's choice is not acceptable to the Justice officials, if two senators of the president's party each favor a different person, or if there is disagreement among the senators and state party leaders, then the Justice officials must undertake extensive and sometimes delicate negotiations. This also results in delays in filling vacancies. The administration must not alienate senators of the president's party because a senator can seriously slow down senate consideration of a nominee or even kill the nomination.

Major Selection Variables

There are four major variables affecting the selection of federal judges. First are the *professional qualifications* of the candidates. Administrations usually are sensitive to the legal community's reception of their judicial nominees and do not want to antagonize the American Bar Association. Administrations also want to place qualified people on the bench because, as noted earlier, the government is the major litigant in federal court and unqualified judges can return to haunt the Justice Department when it tries cases before them.

BACKGROUND	DISTRICT COURT				COURTS OF APPEALS			
	REAGAN		*CARTER*		*REAGAN*		*CARTER*	
	%	*(N)*	%	*(N)*	%	*(N)*	%	*(N)*
Law School Education								
Public-supported	42	(123)	51	(102)	40	(31)	39	(22)
Private (not Ivy)	46	(132)	32	(65)	37	(29)	20	(11)
Ivy League	12	(35)	17	(35)	23	(18)	41	(23)
Experience								
Judicial	47	(135)	55	(110)	60	(47)	54	(30)
Prosecutorial	44	(128)	39	(78)	28	(22)	32	(18)
Neither one	28	(82)	28	(57)	35	(27)	38	(21)
Occupation								
Politics/government	13	(37)	4	(9)	6	(5)	5	(3)
Large law firm**	18	(51)	14	(28)	13	(10)	11	(6)
Moderate size firm	19	(56)	20	(40)	10	(8)	16	(9)
Small firm	10	(30)	14	(28)	1	(1)	5	(3)
Judiciary	37	(108)	45	(90)	55	(43)	46	(26)
Law professor	2	(6)	3	(6)	13	(10)	14	(8)
Other	1	(2)	1	(1)	1	(1)	2	(1)
Net Worth								
Millionaire	23	(67)	4	(6)*	18	(14)	10	(4)*
Party								
Democratic	5	(14)	93	(187)	—	—	82	(46)
Republican	93	(271)	4	(9)	97	(76)	7	(4)
Independent	2	(5)	3	(6)	1	(1)	11	(6)
Other	—	—	—	—	1	(1)	—	—
*Religion****								
Protestant	60	(174)	60	(122)	55	(43)	61	(34)
Catholic	30	(88)	28	(56)	31	(24)	23	(13)
Jewish	9	(27)	12	(24)	14	(11)	16	(9)
Ethnicity/race								
White	92	(268)	79	(159)	97	(76)	79	(44)
Black	2	(6)	14	(28)	1	(1)	16	(9)
Hispanic	5	(14)	7	(14)	1	(1)	4	(2)
Asian	1	(2)	1	(1)	—	—	2	(1)
Gender								
Male	92	(266)	86	(173)	95	(74)	80	(45)
Female	8	(24)	14	(29)	5	(4)	20	(11)
*ABA Ratings*****								
EWQ	4	(13)	4	(8)	17	(13)	16	(9)
WQ	50	(144)	47	(95)	42	(33)	59	(33)
Q	46	(133)	48	(96)	41	(32)	25	(14)
NQ	—	—	2	(3)	—	—	—	—
Average Age at Nomination	48.7		49.7		50.0		51.9	
Total number of Appointees	290		202		78		56	

EXHIBIT 10.3

Reagan and Carter Appointees to the Lower Federal Courts

*Figures available for 96th Congress only.

**A large law firm was defined as one consisting of 25 or more partners and associates; a moderate size firm was defined as one consisting of between 5 and 24 partners and associates; a small firm consisted of 4 or fewer members.

***There was also one Reagan District Court appointee classified as nondenominational.

****EWQ = Exceptionally Well Qualified; WQ = Well Qualified; Q = Qualified; NQ = Not Qualified.

The A.B.A. Helps Harry Blackmun Obtain a Judgeship

During the Republican Eisenhower administration, a vacancy occurred on the U.S. Court of Appeals for the Eighth Circuit and Justice officials determined that a Minnesota resident should fill it. A former Justice Department official who came from Minnesota and was then serving on the District of Columbia Circuit (future Chief Justice Warren Burger) recommended his old Minnesota friend Harry Blackmun, a distinguished lawyer who was serving as General Counsel for the Mayo Clinic. Blackmun, however, had not been politically active and did not have political backing from Minnesota Republican Party leaders (the Senators were both Democrats). The A.B.A. Committee forwarded to the Justice officials an informal report which was highly laudatory of Blackmun and contained a tentative rating of "well qualified." Justice officials came to the conclusion that Blackmun was superior to the candidates the Republican Party leaders were pushing and the Deputy Attorney General informed the Chairman of the A.B.A. Committee of the situation. The A.B.A. Chairman responded in a handwritten memo, "I am hopeful I can raise him [Blackmun] to an 'exceptionally well qualified' status." The A.B.A. Chairman subsequently sent a letter to a member of the Committee, a copy of which was sent to the Deputy Attorney General and placed in Blackmun's Justice Department (appointment) file. The letter said in part:

We should now encourage this type of nomination by giving him [Blackmun] our highest classification. I am impressed, too, by the fact that he is under serious consideration although he has never held political office or been active in the party. Since there is going to be such a scramble for this position, I have the feeling we ought to accord the top man our top classification if he deserves it.

The A.B.A. Chairman, after consulting with the Deputy, spoke with the editor of a leading Minnesota newspaper to persuade him that his newspaper should support Blackmun. According to the chairman, the editor was "most cooperative, showed a keen appreciation of the problem, demonstrated a willingness to be guided as to what should appear in the editorial." These efforts were successful and Harry Blackmun was nominated and confirmed. In 1970 Judge Blackmun was elevated to the United States Supreme Court.

Source: The documents and memos in the Justice Department Appointment File of Harry Blackmun, which were made available to Sheldon Goldman in the Spring of 1964.

Second are the *political party qualifications* of the contenders for judicial position. As Exhibit 10.3 shows, the large majority of appointments are made to members of the president's party. Historically, few administrations have named less than ninety percent of its nominees from the ranks of the president's party. Many of those selected have a background of party activity.

Third is the *approval of the senator or senators of the president's party from the state of the prospective nominee.* If these senators actively oppose a presidential nominee, they doom the nominations. In these cases the senators invoke what is called **senatorial courtesy**. They ask that their colleagues not confirm nominees whom they consider "personally obnoxious" (this is the term used). Another weapon in a senator's arsenal is the **blue slip procedure** of the Senate Judiciary Committee. Blue slips are forms that officially notify the senators from the nominee's home state that the nomination has been received by the Senate Judiciary Committee and invite the senators' written comments. Before 1979, any senator who opposed a nomination and withheld the blue slip could be assured that the chairman of the committee would bury the nomination by simply refusing to bring it before the committee. Since then, the committee has modified this practice and generally decides on its own whether to proceed with consideration of the nomination.

Fourth is the *policy and ideological outlook* of the candidate. Policy and ideological considerations have been less important during certain presidencies than others. In the last half century, Presidents Truman, Eisenhower, and Ford paid relatively little attention to this. In contrast, President Franklin D. Roosevelt's administration was concerned with placing economic liberals on the courts. President Richard M. Nixon was committed to naming law-and-order conservatives to the courts. President Ronald Reagan deliberately named conservatives not only to the Supreme Court but also to the appeals courts and federal district courts. In several publicized instances, the Reagan administration rejected potential nominees because they were not conservative enough. For example, one Republican woman lawyer, rated "well-qualified" by the A.B.A., was on the verge of being nominated for a position on the U.S. Court of Appeals for the Eighth Circuit but was abandoned by the Reagan administration after right-wing critics accused her of being "a strong feminist" and closet liberal.[14]

These four variables are not necessarily of the same importance for each administration. In general, party and senatorial considerations have been more important than the policy and ideological views of the candidates, which typically have been more important than professional qualifications. This was dramatically shown with the controversy over President Reagan's nomination in 1986 of Daniel Manion to the United States Court of Appeals for the Seventh Circuit. Manion had impeccable right-wing conservative credentials and strong party and senatorial backing but a weak professional record. Liberal groups opposed to Manion's extreme conservatism waged an all-out battle against Manion, who was nevertheless confirmed in a close senatorial vote. For the Reagan administration, policy and ideological considerations were given greater weight than perhaps any other presidency since that of Franklin D. Roosevelt.

One interesting wrinkle in the appointment process occurred during the administration of President Jimmy Carter. Carter sought to bring profes-

---

[14]Sheldon Goldman, "Reagan's Judicial Appointments at Mid-Term: Shaping the Bench in his Own Image," *Judicature*, 66 (1983), p. 343.

sional qualifications into greater prominence and also to open up the judiciary to women and racial minorities. He did this by establishing merit selection commissions to recommend the best available candidates for judgeships on the U.S. courts of appeals.[15] Senators established their own selection commissions for federal district judgeships in a majority of states.

Membership on the commission panels for the appeals courts was chosen by the White House and consisted largely of Democrats, many of whom were Carter loyalists. Studies found that a majority of the panelists were political liberals and that approximately forty percent were women and about thirty percent were black. Panels were concerned not only with professional qualifications, but also with the policy views of candidates.[16] For the first time in American history, however, the recruitment process was opened to women and racial minorities so that they not only had significant influence in selecting judges but they also were appointed to the courts in unprecedented numbers (see Exhibit 10.3). The appointees were also primarily Democrats, leading some observers to note that the selection commissions established merit selection of Democrats.

When Ronald Reagan became president in 1981, he disbanded the selection commissions. Republican senators were told that the White House had no objection if they wished to use or establish selection commissions for district court appointments. In practice, several Republican senators used selection commissions and to no one's surprise the end result was the merit selection of Republicans.[17]

Supreme Court Appointments

The death, retirement, or resignation of a justice of the Supreme Court is front page news, just as is the nomination of the successor. The Supreme Court makes news because editors and reporters as well as members of the public know that the Court is the nation's leading judicial policymaker. The kinds of people a president will appoint to the Supreme Court has in recent decades been a major presidential campaign issue.

Studies of Supreme Court appointments have found that while a different combination and weighting of circumstances and variables are needed to explain particular appointments, in general, presidents have considered such factors as personal friendship, party politics (for example, party affiliation, past service to the party, or the effect of the appointment on constitu-

[15]Executive Order No. 12,059 as cited by Elliot E. Slotnick, "Overview: Judicial Selection: Lowering the Bench or Raising it Higher," *Yale Law & Policy Review*, 1 (1983), p. 276.

[16]Larry C. Berkson and Susan B. Carlson, *The United States Circuit Judge Nomination Commission: Its Members, Procedures and Candidates* (Chicago: American Judicature Society, 1980) and Elliot E. Slotnick, "The U.S. Circuit Judge Nominating Commission," *Law & Policy Quarterly*, 1 (1979), pp. 465–96.

[17]See Gary W. Fowler, "A Comparison of Initial Recommendation Procedures: Judicial Selection Under Reagan and Carter," *Yale Law & Policy Review*, 1 (1983), pp. 299–356.

ent groups in the president's coalition), and ideological or policy orientation. Some or all of these considerations coalesce in certain candidacies. To give some examples, President John F. Kennedy appointed Byron White, a close associate who had helped direct Kennedy's presidential campaign in 1960 and was serving as Deputy Attorney General in the Kennedy administration when he was picked for the Court. President Lyndon B. Johnson named an old friend and adviser, Abe Fortas, a liberal Jewish Democrat to fill the vacancy created by another liberal Jewish Democrat, Arthur Goldberg.[18]

Ronald Reagan's selections for the Supreme Court also show these considerations at play. During the presidential campaign of 1980, Reagan pledged to appoint a woman to the Supreme Court. When Justice Potter Stewart retired from the Court in 1981, the president kept his pledge by naming a conservative Republican politician, Sandra Day O'Connor. O'Connor had been an Arizona state senator and had served as state senate Republican majority leader for two years. When Warren Burger retired from the chief justiceship in 1986, President Reagan elevated the most conservative associate justice on the Court, Republican William Rehnquist, to that position. To fill the associate justiceship vacancy created by Rehnquist's elevation, the president chose a conservative Republican intellectual, Antonin Scalia. Scalia is also the first Italian-American to serve on the Court and also a Roman Catholic, constituencies the Republican Party has cultivated.

When Lewis Powell retired in 1987, President Reagan nominated Robert Bork, who had previously served in the Nixon administration and who was a highly visible and combative conservative intellectual. A nationwide campaign led by civil liberties and civil rights groups led to Bork's defeat on the Senate floor. That the Senate in 1987 was for the first time during the Reagan presidency controlled by the Democrats was not insignificant. The vacancy was eventually filled by another conservative Republican, Anthony Kennedy, a Roman Catholic, who had a much lower profile than Bork and whose views were largely unknown but who was considered a likely member of the conservative wing of the Court.

Although senators tend to defer to presidential choices for the Supreme Court, they have not always done so. During the nineteenth century, close to one out of three nominations were not confirmed by the Senate. In the twentieth century, six nominations have failed to win confirmation by the Senate, with four of the six occurring during the 1968–1970 period and the latest being the defeat of Bork. When the Supreme Court is a center of controversy, the nominee is vulnerable on one or more grounds (professional, political, ideological), and the president is faced with formidable opposition in the Senate, the ingredients are present for a less than smooth confirmation process.

---

[18]See, Bruce A. Murphy, *Fortas* (New York: Morrow, 1988), pp. 160–85.

■■■ JUDICIAL BACKGROUNDS

What sorts of people become judges? There are a variety of background characteristics that have been examined by scholars including family background, professional experience and occupation at the time of appointment, partisanship, religion, race, and gender.

Family Background

Historically, federal judges have tended to come from the social and economic elite. A leading scholar calculated that close to ninety percent of Supreme Court justices came from economically comfortable families and the remainder from humble backgrounds.[19] Since the late 1960s, however, there has been a somewhat broader range of family backgrounds. The Court has contained the great-grandson of a slave and son of a country club steward (Thurgood Marshall), the son of poor Irish immigrants (William Brennan), and the son of a railroad worker (Warren Burger). Chief Justice Rehnquist's father was a salesman. However, aside from Rehnquist, President Reagan's other Supreme Court appointees came from more solidly middle class backgrounds. Sandra Day O'Connor's father was a rancher, Antonin Scalia's father was a college professor, and Anthony Kennedy's father was a lawyer. Historically, about two-thirds of all justices have come from politically active families. About one-third were even related to prominent judges. When judges from other courts are examined, the evidence suggests that most have come from the middle class or above.

Supreme Court justices and lower court judges tend to be extremely well-educated. A majority of those appointed to the Supreme Court have had the *best* legal education available. Studies of lower federal court judges suggest that their legal education also has tended to be distinguished.

Experience and Occupation at Time of Appointment

Many Supreme Court justices have held high political or judicial office or were prominent lawyers or law professors. For examples, see Exhibit 10.4 which offers key background information on the justices who served during part or all of the years between 1969 and 1989.

Only about one-third of lower federal court judges have no past experience as judges or prosecutors. The figures for the Carter and Reagan appointees in Exhibit 10.3 bear this out. Many federal judges served on the state bench. Many federal appeals judges served as federal district judges. Administrations often like to elevate a federal district judge to the appeals court because in that way they can make two appointments, one to the

[19]John R. Schmidhauser, *Judges and Justices: The Federal Appellate Judiciary* (Boston: Little, Brown, 1979), pp. 49–55.

| EXHIBIT 10.4 | Backgrounds of Supreme Court Justices Who Served During Part or All of 1969–1989 |

JUSTICE	PARTY	HOME STATE	YEARS ON COURT	FATHER'S OCCUPATION	OCCUPATION AT TIME OF NOMINATION	AGE AT NOMINATION
Hugo L. Black	Democrat	Alabama	1937–1971	farmer, storekeeper	U.S. Senator	51
William O. Douglas	Democrat	Connecticut	1939–1975	missionary, minister	Chairman, Securities & Exchange Commission	40
John M. Harlan	Republican	New York	1955–1971	lawyer; Mayor of Chicago	U.S. Circuit Court Judge	55
William J. Brennan	Democrat	New Jersey	1956–	labor leader	Associate Justice, New Jersey Sup. Ct.	50
Potter Stewart	Republican	Ohio	1958–1981	Associate Justice, Ohio Sup. Ct.	U.S. Circuit Court Judge	43
Byron White	Democrat	Colorado	1962–	branch manager, lumber supply	U.S. Deputy Attorney General	44
Thurgood Marshall	Democrat	New York	1967–	Chief Steward, country club	U.S. Solicitor General	59
Warren E. Burger (Chief Justice)	Republican	Minnesota	1969–1986	rail cargo inspector	U.S. Circuit Court Judge	61
Harry A. Blackmun	Republican	Minnesota	1970–	bank official	U.S. Circuit Court Judge	61
Lewis F. Powell, Jr.	Democrat	Virginia	1971–1987	businessman	Lawyer	64
William H. Rehnquist	Republican	Arizona	1971–1986	salesman	Asst. Att'y General	47
John Paul Stevens	Republican	Illinois	1976–	businessman	U.S. Circuit Court Judge	55
Sandra Day O'Connor	Republican	Arizona	1981–	rancher	State Court Judge	51
William H. Rehnquist (Chief Justice)	Republican	Arizona	1986–	salesman	Associate Justice	61
Antonin Scalia	Republican	New Jersey	1986–	college prof.	U.S. Circuit Court Judge	50
Anthony Kennedy	Republican	California	1988–	lawyer	U.S. Circuit Court Judge	51

appeals court and another to fill the vacancy created on the district bench. Elevation of district judges to the appeals courts also, in theory, rewards outstanding performance and reinforces the idea of a highly qualified, professional judiciary. In practice, elevations of district judges to the appeals bench are often governed by the same sorts of political and ideological considerations that were discussed earlier when examining judicial selection.

The judges' occupations at the time they were appointed is also shown in Exhibit 10.3. Many were in private practice. Since the Johnson administration, the trend has been to select fewer of those in a small law practice (that is, a practice with four or less lawyers).[20]

The judiciary itself is a fertile recruitment ground for the federal bench. At the appellate level, the majority of the Reagan appointees were already serving elsewhere as judges at the time of appointment. The Carter administration was unusual in that a majority of appeals court appointees were not sitting judges. Both the Reagan and the Carter administrations made several appointments to law school professors at a level unmatched since the administration of Franklin Roosevelt.

Knowing something about the economic backgrounds of the judiciary, what about their income levels when they were appointed? As Exhibit 10.3 suggests, close to one out of four Reagan appointees were millionaires compared to fewer than one in ten Carter appointees. These income differences suggest that there may have been a class distinction between the Republican and Democratic appointees, but the more significant fact is that the judges were drawn from a variety of middle-class backgrounds and not only from among the rich.

Partisanship

Judges are selected in a political process and it should come as no shock that many federal judges were politically active before their appointment to the bench. Anywhere from half to three quarters of the lower federal court judges appointed over the past thirty years were once active politically. As for political party affiliation, the typical pattern of nine out of ten appointments going to persons of the president's party held true for the Reagan and Carter appointments, as shown in Exhibit 10.3. The level of partisanship in the Reagan administration exceeded that of every president since Warren Harding for appeals court appointments.[21]

Religion, Race, and Gender

The religious origins or affiliation of judicial appointees has been of some interest because of what this tells about the similarities and differences between the pools of potential judges from which Democratic and Republican

---

[20]Sheldon Goldman, "Reagan's Judicial Legacy: Completing the Puzzle and Summing Up," *Judicature*, 72 (1989), pp. 321, 324.

[21]Goldman, "Reagan's Judicial Legacy," *op. cit.*, p. 325.

administrations draw. This also hints, to some extent, to what constituency groups an administration is appealing. The findings reveal that close to nine out of ten Supreme Court justices have been Protestants, and of these about eight out of ten have been from high-status denominations.[22] Low-status Protestants as well as Catholic and Jewish appointees have tended to be Democrats although the last two Reagan appointees were Catholic Republicans. Figures for the lower federal courts show that Republican Reagan appointed a larger proportion of Catholics than did Democrat Carter, a clear departure from the past. Democratic presidents once invariably appointed more Catholics than Republican presidents did, which reflected the religious composition of the parties themselves.[23]

In 1948, a student of American Government looking at a photograph of lifetime appointees on the federal judiciary would have found only one woman, no blacks, no one of Asian ancestry, and no one of Hispanic background in the composite. The judiciary then was a white male judiciary. Although there has been a significant change in the past decade, the large majority of the federal bench is still white and male.

The relatively few black Americans on the federal bench have been primarily appointed by Democratic presidents. President Truman named the first black American to an appeals court. President Kennedy named the first black to a federal district court plus three others and one (Thurgood Marshall) to an appeals court. President Johnson named Marshall to the Supreme Court, the first appointment of a black American, and Johnson placed five blacks on district courts and two on appeals courts. The Republican Nixon and Ford administrations combined appointed a total of nine blacks to the district courts and none to the higher federal courts. A major breakthrough came with the Democratic Carter administration. Carter, a southerner, appointed twenty-eight blacks to the district courts and nine to the appeals courts—an unprecedented number and proportion of appointees. President Reagan, however, returned to the Republican pattern of appointing few blacks.

Only in the past decade have women begun to be visible in the judiciary. The first woman appointed to a lifetime position on the federal district bench was appointed in 1949 by President Truman. The second was appointed by President Kennedy and President Johnson added two more. The Nixon and Ford administrations named a total of two women. The first woman appointed to a court of appeals was named by President Franklin Roosevelt.[24] Not until three decades later was another woman named to an appeals court (by President Johnson). President Carter broke with precedent and actively recruited well-qualified women for the federal bench. The

---

[22]Schmidhauser, *Judges and Justices, op. cit.*, pp. 62–68. The following are considered high-status Protestant denominations: Presbyterian, Episcopalian, Congregational, and Unitarian. Other Protestant denominations are considered low-status by sociologists of religion.

[23]Goldman, "Reagan's Judicial Legacy," *op. cit.*, pp. 322–23, 325–26.

[24]The judge was Florence E. Allen. See Beverly B. Cook, "The First Woman Candidate for the Supreme Court—Florence E. Allen," *Yearbook, Supreme Court Historical Society* (Washington, D.C.: Supreme Court Historical Society, 1981), pp. 19–35.

Carter administration named twenty-nine women to the federal district courts and eleven to the courts of appeals. President Reagan appointed the first woman in history to the Supreme Court, but he was less generous than Carter in placing women on the lower federal bench (see Exhibit 10.3). Overall, women account for about eight percent of the federal judiciary.

CONSEQUENCES OF THE RECRUITMENT PROCESS

Having seen the way federal judges are selected and read about their backgrounds, it is fair to ask what does a judge's background or the way the judge is chosen have to do with the decisions that individual makes? In answering this question it can be argued that the recruitment process has important consequences for the larger political system and for the administration of justice.[25]

Consequences for the Larger Political System

The background and recruitment of judges have several consequences for the larger political system. First, presidents can and do use their power of judicial appointment to further their policy agendas.[26] Most recently this was dramatically demonstrated with the presidency of Ronald Reagan. The Reagan administration had a social agenda that included opposition to abortion, support for prayer in the public schools, opposition to affirmative action programs that favor women and racial minorities, opposition to busing for the purpose of integrating public schools, opposition to many of the criminal procedural guarantees established by the Supreme Court particularly in the 1960s, and opposition to federal court policies and actions that in the view of the administration encroached upon states' rights and responsibilities. Needless to say, the social agenda was intimately tied to the actions of the federal courts and that meant that federal judicial appointments were of extreme importance to the administration.

The Reagan administration carefully picked judges, although it had to face the political realities of the role of senators of the president's party, particularly with selection of district court judges. The fight over the nomination of Robert Bork to the Supreme Court in the summer and fall of 1987 highlighted the use of the appointment power to shape the federal bench. The Senate Judiciary Committee and then the full Senate debated this concern at length and a majority of the Senate felt that Robert Bork's views were too extreme and that the administration went too far in its use of the

---

[25]The analysis in this section is drawn from Sheldon Goldman and Thomas P. Jahnige, *The Federal Courts as a Political System*, third edition (New York: Harper & Row, 1985), pp. 56–59.

[26]See Sheldon Goldman, "Judicial Appointments and the Presidential Agenda," in Paul R. Brace, Christine Harrington, and Gary King (eds.), *The Presidency in American Politics* (New York: New York University Press, 1989).

appointment power to shape the development of American law. Whether Robert Bork himself got a fair shake or not is another matter. The point is that the consequences of the appointment process for the larger political system were very much on the minds of senators and thrust onto the consciousness of the American public. Other presidents have also had a concern with the policy views of prospective appointees.

The political recruitment of judges, then, can be seen as furthering and promoting party responsibility. The judiciary, while not directly responsible to the electorate, can be kept in touch with popular sentiment through the process of political recruitment. Democratically elected administrations primarily choose judges who are members of their political party and who tend to be sympathetic to the administration's views and, indirectly, the views of the majority of the electorate. Thus political recruitment reaffirms party responsibility.

The political recruitment process has a second consequence for the larger political system. Because it is responsive to partisan considerations, over time the recruitment process has brought a diversity of social, economic, and political outlooks to the federal bench. It is questionable whether a less politically sensitive recruitment process would have or could have produced *when* it did the appointments of a black American and a woman to the Supreme Court or the current mix on the lower courts of labor lawyers, corporation lawyers, blacks, Hispanics, Asians, women, liberals, conservatives, and moderates. Political recruitment has tended to open up the judiciary for at least some members of all groups and classes in American society.

Sometimes political recruitment has unattractive consequences. Political pressures could mean that marginally qualified or even unqualified people are appointed. This is thought to be a problem that has been of concern to bar associations and other groups.[27]

Consequences for the Administration of Justice

Political recruitment also has consequences for the administration of justice. Whatever their party and whatever administration appoints them, federal judges have much in common. All have been socialized into the legal profession through their law school education and their practice of law. Most come to the federal bench with previous judicial experience or experience as a government lawyer. They are solidly middle or upper-middle class when they become federal judges. It is not unreasonable to believe that they share widely held American middle-class social, economic, and political values.

Yet, as shown earlier, there are some differences between the appointees of Democratic and Republican administrations. Do these differences

[27]See, for example, David M. O'Brien, *Judicial Roulette: Report of the Twentieth Century Fund Task Force on Judicial Selection* (New York: Priority Press, 1988).

affect how these judges decide cases? Are some backgrounds and attributes more important than others?

Central to answering these questions is the realization that judging is more of an art than a science. Judges must interpret sometimes vaguely worded statutory and constitutional provisions and make sense out of other written documents. They must apply certain generally phrased principles to specific instances. As a result, there is often room for honest disagreement on what the law is or how it should be applied in a specific dispute. In fact, if resolving legal disputes were clear-cut, people could just look up the solution in a reference manual and not bother with going to court unless there were other motives (such as harassing the opposing party, delaying carrying out an obligation, stubbornness, or the outside chance that a sympathetic judge would change the rules of the game). But the resolution of legal disputes is often not so clear-cut and judges frequently are in a position to decide in a variety of ways. Judges, in other words, exercise **judicial discretion**, and all judges do not use their discretion the same way.

Judges may differ on how a case should be decided largely because they have different hierarchies of political values and different ways (in part shaped by their differing personalities) of perceiving and evaluating reality.

Differences in their backgrounds and experiences are probably the key to understanding why judges exercise discretion differently. Some empirical evidence links judges' backgrounds to their decisions on the bench. Even stronger evidence links the appointing administration with differences in judicial behavior.[28] In sum, then, it is reasonable to conclude that the type of justice that judges dispense is intimately connected with the characteristics of the judges who do the dispensing.

OTHER JUDICIAL SYSTEM PERSONNEL

Judges are not the only people in the federal judicial system. The system is brimming with Justice Department lawyers, U.S. Attorneys, federal marshals, public defenders, magistrates, bankruptcy judges, law clerks, and juries. The Federal Bureau of Investigation (FBI) is formally located within the Justice Department and is concerned with investigating violations of federal law, gathering evidence, and apprehending the violators.

Over 22,000 lawyers work for the federal government. Many are involved in litigation. Some work for the regulatory agencies and others work in such government bureaucracies as the Social Security Administration. Most federal litigation is conducted by the Justice Department's six major legal divisions, by the Solicitor General's Office, and the offices of the United States Attorneys located in each of the ninety-four federal judicial districts.

[28]See, for example, Robert A. Carp and C.K. Rowland, *Policymaking and Politics in the Federal District Courts* (Knoxville, Tenn.: University of Tennessee Press, 1983) and C.K. Rowland, Donald R. Songer, and Robert A. Carp, "Presidential Effects on Criminal Justice Policy in the Lower Federal Courts: The Reagan Judges," *Law & Society Review*, 22 (1988), pp. 191–200.

Justice Department

The Justice Department headed by the Attorney General has six major legal divisions: Antitrust, Civil, Civil Rights, Criminal, Land and Natural Resources, and Tax. Each is headed by an Assistant Attorney General and staff lawyers who work closely with the U.S. Attorneys. Although the U.S. Attorneys' offices usually take responsibility for trying cases at the district court level, the Justice Department handles appeals to the courts of appeals and the appropriate division works with the Office of Solicitor General when cases are to be taken to the Supreme Court.

The *Solicitor General* has primary responsibility for briefing and arguing cases before the Supreme Court. When a case is of great importance for the federal government, the Solicitor General personally argues the government's position. Other cases are argued by staff attorneys serving under the Solicitor General. When a case before the Supreme Court is of major interest to, but does not directly involve, the government, the Solicitor General's office submits an **amicus curiae** (friend of the court) **brief**. The Solicitor General's office during the Reagan administration became a champion of the social agenda and demonstrated a degree of partisanship that critics considered unprecedented.[29]

U.S. Attorneys

The ninety-four *U.S. Attorneys* and their staffs are responsible for handling the bulk of the litigation involving the federal government before the district courts. Like key Justice Department officials (including the division heads and the Solicitor General), U.S. Attorneys are appointed by the president with the advice and consent of the Senate. Like federal district judges, U.S. Attorneys are typically appointed upon the recommendation or clearance of the senator(s) of the president's party from the state in which the district is located. They tend to have a record of party activism and to share the appointing administration's policy outlook.[30] Officially, the term of office of U.S. Attorneys is four years, but by custom they submit their resignations when a new president takes office.

Since the U.S. Attorney is a vital officer of the court, the Chief Judge of each federal district is authorized to fill a vacancy temporarily until the Senate confirms a new U.S. Attorney. The Attorney General formally supervises U.S. Attorneys and their assistants and can order them to try or not to try a case and discipline them even to the point of firing an assistant U.S. Attorney. Only the president can fire a U.S. Attorney.

U.S. Attorneys tend to have deep roots in their home states.[31] Being politically active, particularly in the winning campaign of a senator who

[29]See Lincoln Caplan, *The Tenth Justice: The Solicitor General and the Rule of Law* (New York: Knopf, 1987).

[30]See the discussion in James Eisenstein, *Counsel for the United States: U.S. Attorneys in the Political and Legal Systems* (Baltimore: Johns Hopkins University Press, 1978), pp. 35–48.

[31]*Ibid.*, p. 49.

belongs to the president's party, also helps. Most U.S. Attorneys have had previous government experience, usually as public prosecutors at the state or local level or as an assistant U.S. Attorney. The overwhelming majority of U.S. Attorneys are white and male, although the Carter administration named women and minorities in unprecedented numbers. The Reagan administration appointed fewer women and minorities.

Marshals, Defenders, Magistrates, and Bankruptcy Judges

There are other positions in the federal judicial system that deserve mention. The chief federal law enforcement agents for the federal districts are the United States Marshals. Like judges and U.S. Attorneys, they are appointed by the president with the advice and consent of the Senate. There are also federal public defenders in about one-third of the federal districts. They represent criminal defendants who cannot afford to hire a private lawyer. Federal magistrates are appointed by district judges and they perform the more routine pre-trial duties and are also authorized to preside over minor judicial proceedings. Bankruptcy judges appointed by the appeals courts for fourteen-year terms handle most routine bankruptcy actions and submit proposed findings of fact and conclusions of law in the more complex and controversial bankruptcy matters to the district judges themselves.

Law Clerks

Law clerks play a special part in the judicial system. They assist the judges for whom they work by doing legal research and even writing first drafts of opinions. Lower court judges typically have two to three law clerks who are recent top law school graduates frequently from major law schools. They generally serve for one year. Justices of the Supreme Court are authorized to hire up to four law clerks. The Chief Justice, in addition, has the help of the office of the Administrative Assistant to the Chief Justice that provides help in the special administrative duties the Chief Justice has in overseeing the entire federal court system. Almost all law clerks who serve Supreme Court justices now come to the Supreme Court after having served a lower court (federal or state) clerkship. Supreme Court law clerks can influence their justice's decisions about which cases the Court hears, a point that will be discussed at greater length.

A Note About Juries

There are two kinds of juries: the grand jury and the petit jury. The **grand jury** does not try cases. Rather it is an investigative body consisting of specially selected members of the local community who are presented testimony and other evidence by the prosecutor. The job of the grand jury is to determine whether a crime has been committed and whether there is a sufficient basis for bringing one or more individuals to trial for having committed that crime. If the grand jury agrees with the prosecutor, it hands down an **indictment** naming one or more individuals. Criminal prosecution then proceeds. The **petit jury** is the jury that actually tries cases and it is this kind of jury to which the following observations apply.

The jury has a role to play in the federal judicial system in the five to fifteen percent of all cases that have a trial by jury. The Sixth Amendment to the U.S. Constitution guarantees the right to a jury trial to all federal *criminal* defendants. Of course, defendants can waive their right to a jury trial by pleading guilty (as most do) or by having a **bench trial** heard and decided by the judge alone (less than half the defendants who go to trial choose this option).[32] For most federal *civil* cases, the Seventh Amendment guarantees the right to trial by jury. Only about two-fifths of the litigants whose civil cases come to trial (usually under seven percent of *all* cases) exercise their right to a jury trial, with the remainder tried by the judge alone.

Federal jurors are randomly selected from voter registration lists. This procedure builds in a bias against those at the lowest end of the socioeconomic scale because they tend not to register. But using voter registration lists is an improvement over what had been done until 1968, when prospective jurors' names were solicited from members of local business, social, and professional elites.

Researchers have been interested in how juries actually behave. Once the trial is over, the jury meets by itself and begins its deliberations. Jurors vote by secret ballot. Some findings suggest that juries are more willing than judges to bend the law in criminal cases so that "justice" is done.[33] Other findings have shown that when jurors' votes on the first ballot are evenly split, the final verdict is guilty as often as it is not guilty. In most instances where the jury is not unanimous on the first ballot, it eventually decides the way the majority voted on the first ballot. As the authors of a landmark study of jurors' behavior concluded, "with very few exceptions the first ballot decides the outcome of the verdict."[34] Another major study found that the practice in some states of allowing nonunanimous jury verdicts (as many as three out of twelve jurors can disagree) can make the jury's deliberations less thorough and even result in an incorrect verdict.[35]

Having examined the selection process by which federal judges are recruited for the federal bench and having looked at other personnel in the judicial system, it is now appropriate to focus full attention on the United States Supreme Court, how it functions, and the multifaceted nature of judicial decision making.

---

[32]*Annual Report, U.S. Courts, 1987*, Table C-7, p. 222.

[33]Harry S. Kalven and Hans Zeisel, *The American Jury* (Boston: Little, Brown, 1966), p. 495.

[34]*Ibid.*, p. 488.

[35]Reid Hastie, Steven D. Penrod, and Nancy Pennington, *Inside the Jury* (Cambridge, Mass.: Harvard University Press, 1983), pp. 227–33.

THE UNITED STATES SUPREME COURT

The Supreme Court of the United States lives up to its name. The Court's importance lies not in the actual number of cases decided, for it decides only about 250 to 350 cases each year out of the millions begun at the state level and the close to three hundred thousand started at the federal level. The Court's significance lies in the fact that it is the final arbiter of constitutional interpretation, the ultimate judicial policymaker for the nation. The Court is also important because it is so squarely in the public eye. Major shifts in judicial policy are headline news. Commentators are quick to react when the Court hands down its decisions. The Court is also important because it gives direction to the courts of the nation (although sometimes, for a variety of reasons ranging from ambiguity in the Court's decision to deliberate lower court evasion, it does not do this too successfully).

Yet the Court is still the least known of our major political institutions. In one survey twelve percent of the college-educated persons sampled thought the Supreme Court to be part of Congress.[36] Another survey found that over forty percent of those polled did not know anything the Court had decided in recent years.[37]

The Supreme Court is housed in what has been called a "marble palace," an imposing, ornate, marble structure completed in 1935. It stands across the street from the Capitol Building in Washington, D.C. Each of the eight associate justices and the Chief Justice has a suite of offices. The building also contains a law library, an inner courtyard (occasionally the site of coffee breaks), a public exhibition hall, a cafeteria, a private dining room for more formal occasions, and a gym.

The Supreme Court opens its term on the first Monday in October. In recent years, the Court has ended its term at the end of June or close to July 4. The term is designated by the year in which it begins. Thus the 1987 term began on October 5, 1987 and ended on June 29, 1988.

How Cases Come to the Supreme Court

As noted earlier, Article III of the Constitution provides for the establishment of the Supreme Court and specifies its jurisdiction. The structure of the federal judiciary including the Supreme Court along with the Court's powers and its appellate jurisdiction were provided for in the Judiciary Act of 1789. The appeals courts along the lines we know them today were estab-

---

[36]This was a Harris poll cited in *Confidence and Concern: Citizens View American Government* (Washington, D.C.: Government Printing Office, 1973), p. 250.

[37]Walter F. Murphy and Joseph Tanenhaus, "Public Opinion and the United States Supreme Court: A Preliminary Mapping of Some Prerequisites for Court Legitimation of Regime Changes," *Law and Society Review*, 2 (1968), pp. 360–61. Also see Gregory A. Caldeira, "Neither the Purse Nor the Sword: Dynamics of Public Confidence in the Supreme Court," *American Political Science Review*, 80 (1986), pp. 1209–26. In general, see Thomas R. Marshall, *Public Opinion and the Supreme Court* (Boston: Unwin Hyman, 1989).

The justices of the United States Supreme Court 1988–1989.

lished by the Circuit Court of Appeals Act of 1891 to ease the caseload pressures on the Court. However, caseload pressure persisted and eventually Congress enacted the Judiciary Act of 1925, which conferred on the Court control over a substantial portion of its docket. In 1988, the Supreme Court was given even greater control.

Today, almost all cases come to the Supreme Court by way of the **writ of certiorari** which is an order to the court whose decision is being challenged to send the records of the case to the Supreme Court so that the decision can be reviewed.[38] The losing party in the lower court asks the Supreme Court to issue the *writ of certiorari*. If the Court agrees, that means that the Court will hear the case. At least four justices must vote to grant the writ (this is known as the **rule of four**). Only a small portion of the petitions is granted, in recent years under ten percent. Petitions are placed on the **Appellate Docket**, which is reserved for lawyer-drafted petitions, generally about ten to thirty printed pages in length, or the **Miscellaneous Docket**, which is the repository for all other petitions including those filed by prisoners. At least three times as many more Appellate Docket petitions are granted than Miscellaneous Docket petitions and in some years the gap is even greater. In 1987–1988, about one percent of Miscellaneous Docket petitions and about eleven percent of Appellate Docket petitions were successful.[39]

---

[38]There are two other ways for cases to come to the Court. *Certification* of a case to the Court from a lower court occurs when certain questions of law that the lower court cannot answer are certified to the Court. *Extraordinary writ* cases are those whereby the Court intervenes directly into the activities of a trial judge by either ordering the judge to do something (known as a *writ of mandamus*) or not to do something (*writ of prohibition*) or by issuing a *writ of habeas corpus* which in practice means that the lower court must consider the argument of a prisoner that the imprisonment is in violation of law.

[39]*Harvard Law Review*, 102 (November, 1988), p. 354.

Before October 1988, some cases did not require a *writ of certiorari* to be heard by the Court. These were cases for which there was a legal right to appeal, such as when the highest state court upheld a state law in the face of a claim that it violated federal law. This meant that the Court was obliged to decide such cases, for they were considered to be within the Court's mandatory jurisdiction. However, 1988 legislation removed the Court's mandatory jurisdiction and these cases are now subject to the *writ of certiorari*. Thus the Supreme Court now has complete discretion to choose which cases to hear under its appellate jurisdiction.[40]

Why have the justices granted the *writ of certiorari* in some cases but not in others? Studies by political scientists have discovered that:

- The Court does not adequately explain why it grants or denies *certiorari*.[41]
- The Court is likely to take the case if the federal government is a party to the case and wants the Court to review the lower court decision, if there is actual conflict between two or more lower courts or with Supreme Court precedent, and an *amicus curiae* brief in support of *certiorari* is filed.[42]
- Between 1947 and 1957, organized labor in labor cases and civil rights and civil liberties petitioners were often granted *certiorari*. In the same period, issues of federalism concerning which level of government had authority over a particular dispute were often heard by the Court.[43]
- There were *no* instances during the Warren and Burger courts in the years examined in which *certiorari* was denied when all of the following were present: the federal government was involved and sought review, civil liberties or civil rights were at issue, and there was dissension either on the court below or between two or more courts.[44]

[40]The House of Representatives unanimously passed the measure, known as S. 952, on June 7, 1988. The Senate had passed it previously on March 18. President Reagan signed PL 100–352 into law on June 27, 1988.

[41]In general see Joseph Tanenhaus, Marvin Schick, Matthew Muraskin, and Daniel Rosen, "The Supreme Court's Certiorari Jurisdiction: Cue Theory," in Glendon Schubert (ed.), *Judicial Decision-Making* (New York: Free Press, 1963), pp. 111–32.

[42]S. Sidney Ulmer, "The Supreme Court's Certiorari Decisions: Conflict as a Predictive Variable," *American Political Science Review*, 78 (1984), pp. 901–11 and Gregory A. Caldeira and John R. Wright, "Organized Interests and Agenda Setting in the U.S. Supreme Court," *American Political Science Review*, 82 (1988), pp. 1109–27.

[43]These findings are from D. Marie Provine, *Case Selection in the United States Supreme Court* (Chicago: University of Chicago Press, 1980), pp. 85–100.

[44]This finding and the following three are from Virginia C. Armstrong and Charles A. Johnson, "Certiorari Decisions by the Warren & Burger Courts: Is Cue Theory Time Bound?" *Polity*, 15 (1982), pp. 141–50. Also see Donald R. Songer, "Concern for Policy Outputs as a Cue for Supreme Court Decisions on Certiorari," *Journal of Politics*, 41 (1979), pp. 1185–94; S. Sidney Ulmer, "Selecting Cases for Supreme Court Review: An Underdog Model," *American Political Science Review*, 72 (1978), pp. 902–10; and Saul Brenner, "The New Certiorari Game," *Journal of Politics*, 41 (1979), pp. 649–55.

- For the Burger Court, when the lower court decision favored the civil liberties decision, the Court was more likely to grant review than when the lower court decision had been opposed to the civil liberties claim.
- The Warren Court was more likely to accept for review conservative *economic* decisions particularly when the federal government petitioned for review, but the Burger Court displayed the opposite tendency giving a higher rate of review to liberal lower court economic decisions as opposed to conservative ones.
- Whether the lower court decision is liberal or conservative is a variable in determining whether review by the Court will occur.

Decisions about which cases to review are also influenced by the justices' law clerks. Because most justices do not have the time to read petitions for *certiorari* and all the accompanying documents, law clerks screen these materials. As Justice John Paul Stevens candidly revealed: "They [his law clerks] examine them [*certiorari* petitions] all and select a small minority that they believe I should read myself. As a result I do not even look at the papers in over 80 percent of the cases that are filed."[45] Other justices have their clerks prepare one-page memoranda summarizing the key issues in the petitions for review. The screening done by the law clerks undoubtedly accords with the overall interests and wishes of the justices for whom they clerk. But it is not unreasonable to expect that the clerks' own value systems subtly influence the screening that they do.

Mechanics of the Decision Process

The justices make their final decisions about which cases to accept or reject at their weekly conferences. When four of the nine justices vote to take the case, the next decision is whether the case should be argued by opposing lawyers before the justices (this is called *oral argument*) or decided on the basis of the materials already presented to the Court (this is called *summary judgment*).

Oral Argument.   If the case is to go to oral argument, each side of the case is given a half-hour in which to orally present its side and to answer any questions the justices may have. Lawyers for both sides (along with *amicus curiae*, if any) submit printed briefs before oral argument takes place. When oral argument begins, the courtroom is more like a graduate seminar than a trial in a court of law. The lawyer making the presentation before the justices is expected not to read a prepared statement but to summarize the gist of the argument found in the printed brief. The justices constantly interrupt the lawyer with questions. Sometimes they stimulate a dia

[45]"Some Thoughts on Judicial Restraint," *Judicature*, 66 (1982), p. 179.

A Court employee prepares the table for the Judicial Conference.

logue with the lawyer, sometimes among themselves. The give and take is informal. The justices frequently think out loud and explore various facets of the argument. After oral argument, the case is discussed by the justices at their Wednesday afternoon or all-day Friday conferences.

Judicial Conference. The judicial conference has both formal and informal aspects. There are traditions of long-standing. One in particular is that conference proceedings are confidential. Only the justices may be in the conference room during deliberations. No law clerk, confidential secretary, member of a justice's family, close judicial colleague from another court, or anyone else is permitted to observe. The most junior justice goes to the door of the conference room to receive messages. Another tradition is that when the justices enter the conference room they all shake hands to signify that they are members of the most elite judicial fraternity and are obliged not to take personally what might turn into heated debate.

When a case is discussed, the Chief Justice speaks first, followed by the others in order of seniority. Each justice states his or her views of the case and indicates how he or she will vote. In recent years it has been rare for a group discussion to follow the individual statements.[46]

[46]See the observations of Chief Justice Rehnquist and Justice Scalia as reported in the *New York Times*, February 22, 1988, p. A-16. Also see William H. Rehnquist, *The Supreme Court: How It Was, How It Is* (New York: Morrow, 1987), pp. 289–96.

When the Chief Justice votes with the majority, the Chief Justice is entitled to assign the writing of the Opinion of the Court, the Court's official decision, to any member of the majority, including himself. If the Chief Justice does not vote with the majority, the justice in the majority with the most seniority assigns the writing of the majority opinion. Studies of how Chief Justices have exercised their opinion assignment power have shown, for example, that Chief Justices tend to self-assign the major decisions and also strive to equalize the opinion-writing workload.[47] However, there is also an ideological pull at work so that, for example, Chief Justice Earl Warren tended to assign civil liberties opinions to those closest to his perspective but tended to use economic decisions to equalize the workload. In some delicate periods of judicial history, such as in the mid-1930s when the Court was at odds with the New Deal Roosevelt administration but also deeply divided itself, the evidence suggests that Chief Justice Charles Evans Hughes may have voted with the majority, in part, in order to control opinion assignment and that he assigned the Opinion of the Court in the most controversial cases to the most moderate of the justices in the majority or to himself.[48]

Majority, Concurring, and Dissenting Opinions. The majority that comes out of the conference, particularly if it is a majority of only five justices, is not necessarily a firm one. The justices exchange drafts of majority, concurring, and dissenting opinions. Sometimes a dissenting opinion is sufficiently persuasive to win over a majority justice, and a new majority forms.[49] But typically only about ten percent of the votes shift in the weeks or months between the first conference vote and the final vote in the case.[50]

Opinions of the Court tend to be group products. The majority justices work to produce an opinion that will be joined in by a majority. If a majority agrees on who should win the case but cannot agree on the reasons, there is only a judgment of the Court which states the bottom line disposition of the case. The Opinion of the Court is an attempt to demonstrate to the

[47]See David W. Rohde, "Policy Goals, Strategic Choices and Majority Opinion Assignments in the United States Supreme Court," *Midwest Journal of Political Science*, 16 (1972), pp. 652–82; Gregory James Rathjen, "Policy Goals, Strategic Choice, and Majority Opinion Assignment in the U.S. Supreme Court: A Replication," *American Journal of Political Science*, 18 (1974), pp. 713–24; Elliot E. Slotnick, "Who Speaks for the Court? Majority Opinion Assignment from Taft to Burger," *American Journal of Political Science*, 23 (1979), pp. 60–77; Elliot E. Slotnick, "The Chief Justices and Self Assignment of Majority Opinions: A Research Note," *Western Political Quarterly*, 31 (1978), pp. 219–25; and Harold J. Spaeth, "Distributive Justice: Majority Opinion Assignments in the Burger Court," *Judicature*, 67 (1984), pp. 299–304.

[48]David J. Danelski, "The Influence of the Chief Justice in the Decisional Process of the Supreme Court," in Goldman and Sarat (eds.), *American Court Systems*, second edition, *op cit.*, pp. 494–96.

[49]See J. Woodford Howard, Jr., "On the Fluidity of Judicial Choice," *American Political Science Review*, 62 (1968), pp. 43–57.

[50]See Saul Brenner, "Fluidity on the United States Supreme Court: A Reexamination," *American Journal of Political Science*, 24 (1980), pp. 526–35 and his follow-up study, "Fluidity on the Supreme Court: 1956-1967," *American Journal of Political Science*, 26 (1982), pp. 388–90.

judicial and legal profession, and sometimes to the public as well, that the Court's decision is the inevitable product of the correct application of previous precedents, sound legal principles, and recognized interpretations of statutes or the Constitution to the facts of the case. When the Court deliberately departs from precedent, as it did, for example, in the landmark case of *Brown* v. *Board of Education* (which overturned the separate-but-equal doctrine that had legalized segregation), it seeks to explain why it is necessary to do so and why departure reflects greater fidelity to the law than previous Court decisions. In *Brown*, the Court argued that separate can never be equal and therefore cannot be compatible with the guarantee in the Fourteenth Amendment of equal protection of the laws. Opinions of the Court contain many citations to previous Supreme Court and lower court decisions and sometimes incorporate quotations or references from law reviews and other scholarly (even social science) writings.

Dissenting opinions tend to be more personal and less inhibited. Unlike majority opinion writers, dissenters are under less pressure (subtle or otherwise) to be accommodating, particularly if their chances of winning over enough justices to form a new majority are slim. The dissent attempts to show how the Court has gone wrong, misinterpreted precedents, misconstrued the statute or the constitutional provision at issue, or missed the essential points of the controversy.

A concurring opinion is of a different order. Some concurrences essentially are postscripts to a majority opinion in which the concurring author joined. They are meant to highlight certain facets or point out the significance of what the majority has or has not done. Other concurrences argue that the majority may have arrived at the right place but got there by the wrong route. This kind of concurring opinion offers alternative legal reasoning, and the author may not join the majority opinion, but only agree with the result. Still another type of opinion is known as a concurrence in part and a dissent in part. Here the justice disagrees with part of the reasoning and/or part of the result.

When opinions are ready, they go to the Court's basement print shop for publication of what are known as slip opinions. The decisions and opinions are announced and occasionally even read in the courtroom.

Powers of the Supreme Court

As shown earlier, the Supreme Court wields power by deciding what *it* wants to decide. It can *never* be forced by any person, agency, or branch of government to decide an issue that it does not wish to decide. But when one considers the powers of the Supreme Court, it is the power of judicial review which first comes to mind.

Judicial Review. **Judicial review** is the power to review the legality of the actions of the other branches of government and to uphold or strike down those actions. When the interpretation of the Constitution is at issue, the Supreme Court has the final word. When the Court rules that an act of Congress, or a regulation of an administrative agency, or a state statute, or even a provision of a state constitution is in conflict with the federal Constitution, the Court's ruling can be reversed only by an amendment to the U.S. Constitution or by the Court at some later time changing its mind. Judicial review therefore means that the Court can legitimate or strike down the actions and laws of the states and the national government.

Curiously enough for a power so profound, judicial review is nowhere mentioned in the Constitution. What would the framers of the Constitution say about the Supreme Court striking down a Texas state law making it a crime to perform an abortion or a federal law conditioning spousal benefits for female members of the military upon proof of their spouse's dependency but requiring no such proof of dependency for spouses of male members of the military? It is hard to say what the framers would have said about judicial review much less these particular decisions because the framers did not debate the issue of judicial review. In fact, judicial review over the actions of the states came about by an act of Congress. Section 25 of the Judiciary Act of 1789 gave the Supreme Court jurisdiction to review state court decisions in which a federal claim is made.

By contrast, judicial review over congressional enactments was a power assumed by the Court in a cautious tentative way in the 1790s and boldly claimed by the Supreme Court in 1803 in *Marbury* v. *Madison.* But the Court thereafter, while exercising judicial review, did not strike down another act of Congress until 54 years later. It is in the twentieth century that there are the bulk of decisions striking down laws or parts of laws enacted by Congress. However, the Court has been cautious in the exercise of this power. In fact, the total number of decisions during the entire history of the Supreme Court in which acts of Congress have been struck down is less than 125. In contrast, the number of state or municipal laws invalidated by the Court is close to ten times that.

The Court does not interpret the Constitution like some delphic oracle without explanation or justification. It offers a variety of justifications for interpreting the Constitution. The first justification is the intent of the framers. The justices try to determine what the framers probably had in mind when they wrote a particular provision. They study the historical circumstance to which the framers were responding and examine congressional debates and debates over ratification to determine what the framers hoped to accomplish. They face the problem that different framers and different ratifiers had different intentions. Some constitutional phrases were worded vaguely to ensure wide support. The extraordinary difficulty of determining intent is a fundamental weakness of this approach to constitutional interpretation.

A second approach is to examine the meaning of the words in the Constitution. The justices must determine whether they are concerned with the plain meaning of the words—what they mean to reasonable people today or what they meant to the framers and ratifiers when the Constitution was written—or the implied meaning of the words. The latter requires the justices to examine the structure of the Constitution and where the constitutional provision is placed. Suppose the provision appears in the section on Congress's powers, as the Court found with "the necessary and proper" clause in *McCulloch* v. *Maryland* (decided in 1819). Then the provision would be considered a part of Congress's powers and would be broadly interpreted. If "the necessary and proper" clause had been placed in the section on the limits of Congress's powers, the implied meaning would have been to interpret the provision as a restriction on the powers of Congress.

A third approach is to use logical reasoning that applies widely accepted moral principles. Here things get even more subjective. Yet a justification for interpreting the Constitution in a certain manner can be made based on moral principles accepted as givens of our system of government. For example, in the early nineteenth century the Court interpreted the contract clause of the Constitution as applying to public contracts, grants, and corporate charters as well as to private contracts.[51] The Court reached this conclusion by the logical application of the principle that property rights are at the foundation of government and that when one party agrees to do something or grants something which is otherwise lawful, that party, whether a government or private individual or business, must keep its word *and* the government may not interfere or go back on *its* explicit word. It has only been since the 1930s that these principles and rulings have been substantially modified. A more recent twentieth-century example occurred when the Court established the right to privacy in a series of cases beginning in 1965 with *Griswold* v. *Connecticut*. The Court reached this conclusion by the logical application of the principle that individual privacy is a fundamental human right and that our system of government is based upon the government respecting the dignity of its people. The government has a heavy burden of justification for invasion of individual privacy. Only recently with the advent of a Court dominated by conservatives has the Court pulled back from this trend of decisions.

A fourth rationale that the justices apply in interpreting the Constitution is **stare decisis**, the rule of precedent. In practice, if the Court wishes to maintain an earlier interpretation of a provision of the Constitution, it merely recognizes the precedent and defers to it. When the majority wishes to evade a precedent, the Opinion of the Court can distinguish the present case from what otherwise would be the controlling precedent. Only rarely does the Court explicitly overturn precedent and establish a new policy.

Other Powers. The Supreme Court, like all other courts, has the traditional power of statutory interpretation. Long before judicial review was established, American courts exercised this power of applying relevant stat-

---

[51]Three leading early contract clause cases are: *Fletcher* v. *Peck* (1810); *Dartmouth College* v. *Woodward* (1819); and *Charles River Bridge* v. *Warren Bridge* (1837).

utes to the cases at hand. When the Supreme Court is called upon to interpret acts of Congress, it goes about this in ways similar to those used in interpreting the Constitution. The main difference is that a Court decision interpreting an act of Congress can be overturned by new legislation. For example, in 1988 Congress overturned a 1984 Supreme Court decision that interpreted Title IX of the 1972 Education Amendments as forbidding colleges and universities from practicing sexual discrimination *only* in programs or activities that actually receive federal aid.[52] Those programs or activities not receiving federal assistance were free to sexually discriminate if no other provision of federal law was violated. Before the Supreme Court's 1984 decision, if one program received aid, then the entire institution was forbidden to practice gender discrimination. Congress enacted legislation in 1988, over President Reagan's veto, overturning the Court's decision and explicitly returning the law to how it was understood and enforced before 1984.

The Supreme Court has other traditional powers. It can issue *injunctions* to prevent something from happening or continuing. It can issue *declaratory judgments* stating the rights and obligations of the parties involved in the case. It can issue a *writ of habeas corpus*, an order that those holding someone in custody bring the prisoner to the court so the legal basis for detention can be determined.

It can also be argued that the Court, by declaring some law or governmental action legal, performs a legitimizing function, which is a source of its institutional power. The other branches of government *need* the Court to say yes to their laws and actions. Whether the Court has a legitimizing function in the public mind, indeed, whether the public understands and follows what the Court does, is in doubt.[53] Nonetheless, by upholding a controversial action of government, the Court performs a positive function for at least some segments of the American polity, reassuring its citizens that they are a nation of law, committed to the enduring values and ideals embodied in the Constitution.

Limits on Judicial Power

While the Supreme Court has many powers, it is not all-powerful. There are formidable restraints on its exercise of judicial power.

Some of the restraints on the Supreme Court are institutional. The justices are limited to actual cases that fall under the Court's jurisdiction and for which the litigants have standing. The Court also is limited, by tradition, to ruling on issues that have been presented to it in briefs and oral argu-

---

[52]The decision was *Grove City College* v. *Bell* (1984).

[53]See the evidence and argument in David Adamany, "Legitimacy, Realigning Elections, and the Supreme Court," *Wisconsin Law Review*, (1973), pp. 790–846 and David Adamany and Joel B. Grossman, "Support for the Supreme Court as a National Policymaker," *Law & Policy Quarterly*, 4 (1983), pp. 405–37.

ment. Court rulings technically are legally binding only on the parties to the case (or when government officials are involved, their successors in office). For example, in 1954, in *Brown* v. *Board of Education*, the Court ruled that racially segregated school systems violated the equal protection of the laws guarantee of the Fourteenth Amendment. But that decision was legally binding on only the school boards involved in the case. Although other school boards in the South and border states were in violation of the new constitutional ruling, they were under no direct legal obligation to desegregate other than the obligation of all citizens to obey the Constitution. It took many years, many hundreds of law suits, and the threat of withholding federal aid, for *Brown* to be implemented in other school systems.

Other limits on the Court are inherent in the way the justices make decisions. Their decisions are group products, not the will of single individuals. The votes of a majority of the justices participating are needed for both a ruling and an Opinion of the Court. This means that when all nine justices are deciding a case, the votes of five are needed. Therefore, the justices must use sound legal arguments to persuade their colleagues.

This leads to another limitation that is of the utmost importance for understanding how courts work. The Court is a *judicial* institution, governed by the norms of behavior and decision making associated with legal institutions. It must justify its rulings by using accepted modes of legal reasoning. The Court cannot afford to convey the impression that it is legislating public policy. Rather, using the special language of law and forms of legal reasoning, the Court argues that a statute or constitutional provision is to be interpreted in a specified fashion because of a variety of reasons that the Court provides. The rule of precedent, *stare decisis*, usually limits the discretion of the justices, although precedent, too, can be played with. The judicial enterprise, then, that characterizes the Court as a court of *law* is a major institutional limit on the exercise of judicial power.

One final institutional limitation is a pragmatic one. The Court cannot physically enforce its decisions. It has no army of its own, no direct line to the F.B.I. or the military. It must depend upon the executive branch and the states for enforcement. Ultimately, it must depend upon the willingness of politicians, government officials, and the American public to obey the law.

The Court also operates under many political limits. Congress can use a number of powers against the Court. For example, Congress can impeach and remove a justice. (One Supreme Court Justice, Samuel Chase, was impeached by the House of Representatives in 1804 but was acquitted by the Senate the following year.) Congress can reduce the Court's appellate jurisdiction. (It did so in 1868 and has come close on a number of other occasions.) Congress sets the number of justices serving on the Supreme Court and can increase or decrease the Court's size. (Before 1869, Congress did so on several occasions. In 1937, President Franklin Roosevelt proposed an increase in the number of justices from 9 to a maximum of 15, but that plan died in the Senate.)

Congress controls the purse strings of the courts and has full financial control over the operations of the Court. The Constitution stipulates only that the salaries of the justices (and all other judgeships created under Article III) may not be lowered. But Congress is under no obligation to increase the pay of the justices. (Warren Court justices in the 1960s were denied salary increases for several years. Congress in 1989 denied a pay raise for the judiciary.)

Congress can regulate court procedure, as it did in the Judiciary Act of 1802. It manipulated the sessions of the Court to postpone consideration of *Marbury* v. *Madison*. With the Judiciary Act of 1925, Congress conferred upon the Court the discretion to grant or deny *certiorari*. In 1988, Congress extended this discretion by abolishing mandatory appeals.

The president has checks on the Supreme Court. He can refuse to order the enforcement of Supreme Court decisions. He can pardon people convicted of defying Court decisions. He can use the prestige of the presidency and the media attention it attracts to criticize publicly Court decisions. The president also can propose measures that use Congress's powers to check the Court.

These political checks are not often used. Historically, the Court, with few exceptions, has been sensitive to the limits to which it can go before these checks will be invoked.

Judicial Behavior and Decision Making

Despite the limits on the Supreme Court's powers, the justices have lots of room to maneuver in their decision making. The following are some of the most important influences on how justices make decisions.

Attitudes and Values. In theory, judges are not supposed to make decisions because of their ideology. They are supposed to be neutral arbiters of "the law," which they "find" in previous decisions and by proper reasoning. But research has persuasively demonstrated that Supreme Court justices vote *as if* their attitudes and values were largely responsible for their decisions. The patterns of votes can best be interpreted as corresponding to each justice's attitudes towards the issues of the cases and broader ideological concerns such as commitment to civil liberties versus the claims of government that freedom must be regulated in the public interest, commitment to equality for women and racial minorities versus claims that admirable ends should not be reached by questionable means, or commitment to the preservation of our economic system of regulated capitalism versus claims that regulation and free enterprise are incompatible.

Exhibit 10.5 presents the simple percentages of votes favoring civil liberties and civil rights claims of the justices during the 1981 through 1987 terms. The proportion of decisions favoring civil liberties and civil rights (with the exception of the 1987 term) is under 50 percent. In contrast, dur-

	TERM						
Justice	*1981*	*1982*	*1983*	*1984*	*1985*	*1986*	*1987*
Brennan	81%	76%	81%	84%	78%	95%	88%
Marshall	84	85	79	81	86	95	87
Stevens	53	68	58	63	62	72	70
Blackmun	56	58	40	49	66	70	69
White	37	33	29	34	32	25	43
Powell	28	28	28	40	33	36	—
O'Connor	29	25	24	34	30	28	37
Burger	15	26	22	29	21	—	—
Scalia	—	—	—	—	—	27	39
Rehnquist	16	15	19	22	14	14	30
Kennedy	—	—	—	—	—	—	47
COURT	40	36	30	45	37	43	52

ing the last two terms of Chief Justice Warren's tenure (1967-1969), over 75 percent of all civil liberties decisions decided with full opinion favored the civil liberties claim.[54] Note also the polarization on the Court with Justices Brennan and Marshall clearly the most liberal justices, followed by Stevens and Blackmun. In contrast, Justice Rehnquist was generally the most conservative justice both as Associate Justice and when he assumed the helm of the Court as Chief Justice in the 1986 term. Reagan appointees O'Connor and Scalia are also seen as clearly conservative. Justice Kennedy joined the Court in mid-term in February 1988, so any inferences about his voting behavior must be seen as tentative, although he appears to be following the conservative mold of his fellow Reagan appointees. Justice White, a Democrat and a Kennedy appointee, appears to be a solid member of the conservative bloc rarely supporting civil liberties more than one-third of the time.

Today it is publicly accepted that judicial decisions are associated in part with the attitudes and values of judges. Building on the pioneering studies of C. Herman Pritchett, several scholars have identified the major attitudes and values of twentieth-century justices.[55] One scholar, Harold Spaeth, at one time wrote a newspaper column in which he predicted Court decisions so accurately that he attracted media attention.[56] He identified three major values that influenced Supreme Court decisions during the Warren and Burger Courts: Freedom (including rights of criminal defendants and rights encompassed in the First Amendment), Equality (including rights to be free from political, economic, and racial discrimination), and New Dealism (including economic activity and government regulation).

Supreme Court justices' backgrounds, life experiences, and personal attributes help shape their attitudes and values. This has been statistically demonstrated by several researchers. For example, one analysis of the twenty-five justices who served on the Court between 1946 and 1978 showed that their decisions concerning issues of civil liberties and economic liberalism were strongly associated with their party affiliation, the party of the appointing president, and their prosecutorial and judicial experience.[57]

Facts and Decisions. Justices do not decide cases solely because of their attitudes and values. Their decisions also turn on the facts presented in the cases. However, there are more "facts" involved in litigation than commonly recognized. There are, of course, the facts of the dispute including what happened and which laws or constitutional provisions are invoked. These facts are almost entirely legally relevant; that is, they are acknowledged as bearing upon the determination of the law in the particular case. Next, there are the personal attributes of those who have brought the dispute, such as gender, race, age, social class, religion, and national origin. But most of these facts are *not* legally relevant. For example, the fact that an accused criminal is white or black is not officially recognized by the judicial system as legally relevant. Finally, there are the facts of how a case is processed, such as the type of lawyer handling the criminal defendant's case (hired by defendant, court-appointed, public defender) or whether a plea bargain was made. These facts also are ordinarily not legally relevant. But researchers have found that all three types of facts are linked to court decisions.[58] In other words, legally relevant facts *and* facts that are not legally relevant play a part in judicial decision making.

[54]Lawrence Baum, "Measuring Policy Change in the Supreme Court," *American Political Science Review*, 82 (1988), p. 910.

[55]C. Herman Pritchett, *The Roosevelt Court: A Study in Judicial Politics and Values 1937–1947* (New York: Macmillan, 1948) and *Civil Liberties and the Vinson Court* (Chicago: University of Chicago Press, 1954). See Glendon Schubert, *Quantitative Analysis of Judicial Behavior* (New York: Free Press, 1959), *The Judicial Mind* (Evanston, Ill.: Northwestern University Press, 1965), and *The Judicial Mind Revisited* (New York: Oxford University Press, 1974). Note the work of S. Sidney Ulmer, for example, his "Mathematical Models for Predicting Judicial Behavior" in Joseph Bernd (ed.), *Mathematical Applications in Political Science III* (Charlottesville: University of Virginia Press, 1967), pp. 67–95 and his "Selecting Cases for Supreme Court Review: An Underdog Model," *American Political Science Review*, 72 (1978), pp. 902–10. Also David J. Danelski, "Values as Variables in Judicial Decision-Making: Notes Toward a Theory," *Vanderbilt Law Review*, 19 (1966), pp. 721–40 and his "Causes and Consequences of Conflict and Its Resolution in the Supreme Court," in Sheldon Goldman and Charles M. Lamb (eds.), *Judicial Conflict and Consensus: Behavioral Studies of American Appellate Courts* (Lexington, Kentucky: University Press of Kentucky, 1986), pp. 21–49. Also see the work of Harold J. Spaeth, for example, Harold J. Spaeth and David J. Peterson, "The Analysis and Interpretation of Dimensionality: The Case of Civil Liberties Decision-Making," *Midwest Journal of Political Science*, 15 (1971), pp. 415–41 and Harold J. Spaeth and David W. Rhode, *Supreme Court Decision Making* (San Francisco: Freeman, 1976).

[56]See, for example, "Computer Helps Predict Court Rulings," *New York Times*, August 15, 1971, sec. 1, p. 75; "Court Handicappers: Computer Predictions of Supreme Court Decisions," *Newsweek*, 84 (August 12, 1974), p. 53.

[57]C. Neal Tate, "Personal Attribute Models of the Voting Behavior of U.S. Supreme Court Justices: Liberalism in Civil Liberties and Economic Decisions, 1946–1978," *American Political Science Review*, 75 (1981), pp. 355–67.

[58]See the discussion and citations in Sheldon Goldman and Thomas P. Jahnige, *The Federal Courts as a Political System*, third ed. (New York: Harper & Row, 1985), pp. 158–62.

The response of a justice to a particular combination of facts can be seen as representing the justice's attitudes toward those who bring disputes and attitudes toward the characteristics of cases. That judges decide on *all* the facts, not just those that are legally relevant, highlights the great discretion of the judiciary.

Judicial Role. Central to understanding judicial decision making by Supreme Court justices and lower court judges is the concept of judicial role. The concept of role is tied to the position the role player holds. The role of a judge may be defined as the "set of normative expectations concerning the official behavior" of the holder of a judicial position.[59] The judge's role behavior is that judge's acting out of his or her perceptions of what he or she *ought to* or *ought not to* do as well as *can* (in a pragmatic sense) and *cannot* do as a judge. The judge's attitudes and values can then be seen as filtered through a role screen.

What is expected from a Supreme Court justice? One does *not* expect to see the justices patronizing strip joints, being abusive, disorderly, and drunk in public, or smoking marijuana. One does *not* expect to see the justices campaign for presidential candidates (imagine the public reaction in 1988 if Chief Justice Rehnquist stumped for George Bush or Justice Brennan addressed rallies for Mike Dukakis). One does not expect the justices to be associated with political causes or engage in controversies that would call into question their impartiality. On the bench, the justices are expected to be dignified.

There are important aspects of the judicial role affecting decision making. The reasoning process and the Court's decisions are phrased in the special language of law. Thus, the language that is used and the concepts embodied in legal language may limit the range of discretion of justices.[60]

One role aspect that has attracted much public attention is that of judicial activism or its opposite, judicial restraint.[61] The judicial activist does not hesitate to use judicial discretion to promote policies the activist believes are beneficial to society—even if this means overturning actions, policies, or decisions of other branches of the federal government or of the states. Advocates of judicial restraint hold that courts ought to defer to the public-policy determinations of the popularly elected branches of government and not substitute judges' policy preferences for those of democratically elected public officials. But activism and restraint are sometimes difficult concepts to apply in particular cases when a justice may not view the matter as being activist or exercising restraint, but of doing his or her job to

[59]David J. Danelski, "Conflict and Its Resolution in the Supreme Court," *Journal of Conflict Resolution*, 11 (1967), p. 76.

[60]See John Brigham, *Constitutional Language* (Westport, Conn.: Greenwood Press, 1978). Also, in general, see John Brigham, *The Cult of the Court* (Philadelphia: Temple University Press, 1987).

[61]See the studies in Stephen C. Halpern and Charles M. Lamb (eds.), *Supreme Court Activism and Restraint* (Lexington, Mass.: Lexington Books, Heath, 1982).

interpret the Constitution. If a justice sees a constitutional violation, should that justice refuse to enforce his or her perception of the Constitution in order to win the praise of politicians advocating judicial restraint? Another point to keep in mind is that one can be "activist" on one issue and "restrained" on another.

Given all the factors that play a part in how judges make decisions, the words of political scientist James Gibson are illuminating: "Judges' decisions are a function of what they prefer to do, tempered by what they think they ought to do, but constrained by what they perceive is feasible to do."[62]

Small Group Dynamics.   What a justice thinks he or she ought to do, along with the justice's perception of constraints as to what is feasible and his or her own preferences, may be influenced by the small group setting in which Court decision making occurs. The justices interact not only during the formal judicial conferences but also in a variety of informal settings, such as at lunch, at occasional impromptu office visits, in exchanges of memos and drafts of opinions, and during phone conversations. During both formal and informal interactions, justices seek to persuade and negotiate over the wording of opinions. The Chief Justice particularly during the conferences may attempt to lead the group. The evidence suggests that the fact that the Supreme Court is a small group and that decisions are collective products may at times affect the kinds of decisions made.[63]

The personalities of the justices, the kinds of leadership offered by the Chief Justice, the perhaps differing role concepts among the justices, the clash of attitudes and values, and the kinds of issues before the Court all can be expected to affect the dynamics of the small group relationship on the Supreme Court.

CHECKLIST FOR REVIEW	1. American courts are actively engaged in resolving ever-increasing numbers and kinds of disputes. However we Americans are probably not as uniquely litigious as we think we are. Nevertheless, the fact does remain that many of our courts *are* overflowing with cases.

1. American courts are actively engaged in resolving ever-increasing numbers and kinds of disputes. However we Americans are probably not as uniquely litigious as we think we are. Nevertheless, the fact does remain that many of our courts *are* overflowing with cases.

2. The federal judicial system is comprised of federal district courts (the trial courts of the system), appeals courts (the intermediate level of the court system obliged to hear all appeals), and the Supreme Court (which can pick and choose which cases to decide). A court will not hear a case unless it has jurisdiction, the litigants have standing to sue, and the issue is justiciable. When a court decides a case, it has a variety of remedies available for resolving the dispute.

[62]James L. Gibson, "From Simplicity to Complexity: The Development of Theory in the Study of Judicial Behavior," *Political Behavior*, 5 (1983), p. 32.

[63]A landmark scholarly work and a major piece of journalism both attest to this. The works are Walter F. Murphy, *Elements of Judicial Strategy* (Chicago: University of Chicago Press, 1964) and Bob Woodward and Scott Armstrong, *The Brethren* (New York: Simon & Schuster, 1979). Also see the account by Chief Justice Rehnquist in *op cit.*, pp. 253–303.

3. The key personnel involved in the judicial selection process include the Justice Department, the White House itself, senators of the president's party, the Senate Judiciary Committee, and the American Bar Association's Standing Committee on Federal Judiciary. The four standards of judicial selection are the professional qualifications of the prospective nominees, their political party qualifications, their approval by senators from their home states, and their policy and ideological outlook.

4. When comparing Reagan appointees to the lower federal courts with Carter's appointees, about nine out of ten appointees belonged to the president's political party. While overall the appointees of both parties are typically from the middle class, have similar professional experience, and are white males, there are differences between the parties. More Democrats come from less well-off families than Republicans and Democrats have appointed more women, blacks, and Hispanics than Republicans.

5. Presidents can use their power of judicial appointment to promote their policies. Having a *political* recruitment process has, over the years, given us a diverse federal bench with judges who are politically liberal, moderate, and conservative and who have diverse professional and other backgrounds. There is evidence that links some backgrounds of judges to the way they exercise their discretion.

6. Judicial decisions are shaped by many complex forces. Justices of the Supreme Court behave within certain boundaries, boundaries shaped by the unique qualities of legal institutions as well as by the political and policy landscape of the country. Their attitudes, values, reactions to both legally relevant and legally irrelevant facts are filtered through the judicial role concept of individual justices, but are somewhat tempered by the dynamics of their small group setting. Justices may be political actors, but they are a special type of political decision maker operating within a unique context and occupying unique legal-political positions.

KEY TERMS

civil law case	diversity of citizenship jurisdiction
constitutional courts	original jurisdiction
legislative courts	appellate jurisdiction
adversary system	standing to sue
plea bargaining	class action
collegial courts	justiciable
jurisdiction	precedent
admiralty law	moot
maritime law	common law

equity

injunction

writ of specific performance

senatorial courtesy

blue slip procedure

judicial discretion

amicus curiae brief

grand jury

indictment

petit jury

bench trial

writ of certiorari

rule of four

Appellate Docket

Miscellaneous Docket

judicial review

stare decisis

PART FOUR

The Policies Produced by American Politics and Government

CHAPTER ELEVEN

Domestic Policy

$\mathbf{A}$ s has been shown in previous chapters, the story of American politics is largely about who gets what, when, and how.[1] **Public policy** is what emerges from this political process. Public policy is expressed in laws passed, executive orders issued by the president, regulations announced by government agencies, decisions handed down by courts, and actions taken by public officials. *Domestic policy* deals with the internal affairs of the United States. *Foreign policy* concerns the United States' relations with other nations (and is discussed in Chapter Fourteen).

Previous chapters have considered how the institutions of government—Congress, the presidency, the federal bureaucracy, and the judiciary—structure, generate, process, and implement public policy. The many participants make for a fragmented and difficult-to-coordinate policy process. This is the price paid for having a government with separation of powers and checks and balances functioning within a framework of federalism. This chapter focuses on domestic policy in all its variety and complexity. In so doing, the chapter will look at federal budget making as domestic policy and social welfare programs ranging from social security to aid to families with dependent children. It will be clear how our fragmented political system makes the policy process complex but not necessarily insurmountable.

■ VARIETIES OF DOMESTIC POLICY

Domestic policy is made and implemented every day, in matters ranging from the utmost importance to the seemingly trivial. It is made by governmental institutions at the national, state, and local levels. A state trooper who on his or her own initiative tickets only automobile drivers who exceed the posted speed limit by ten miles an hour is making policy. A local zoning board makes policy when it grants a variance to a local building contractor to build condominiums in a neighborhood zoned for single family dwellings. A state insurance commissioner makes policy when ruling that insurance companies may not require prospective policyholders to be tested for AIDS. Congress makes policy when it votes to continue to provide price supports for tobacco growers or when it votes to increase or decrease the funds available for student loan programs underwritten by the federal government. When the president presents Congress with a budget that provides for massive cuts in spending for some programs, increases in expenditures for others, and level spending for still others, this is policy-making on a grand scale.

In the national arena, policies are associated with every aspect of government and politics. Congress is the institution of national government whose formal task is to enact public policy. The judiciary, as previously

[1]Harold D. Lasswell, *Politics: Who Gets What, When, How* (Cleveland: Meridian Books, World, 1958).

shown and will be seen in greater detail in the following two chapters, plays a distinctive role in the making of public policy. In the executive branch, the president and his advisers develop an agenda of public policy concerns. The cabinet departments are also a center of domestic policy-making and policy-implementing activity. Each regulatory agency or commission makes and carries out policy. Although domestic policies show enormous variety, they can be categorized into four types: regulatory, distributive, redistributive, and symbolic policy.[2]

Regulatory Policy

Some domestic policy is regulatory. An example of such policy is the complex procedure used by the Food and Drug Administration before it permits a drug manufacturer to market a new drug. The extensive testing is designed to protect the public from medications that are harmful or that are not effective. Another example of regulatory policy is the procedure that corporations must follow before they are permitted to sell stocks and bonds to the general public. The Securities and Exchange Commission has this regulatory responsibility which is designed to protect the public from false claims. Occupational safety and health standards are yet another area of regulatory policy. They are determined by a federal agency created by Congress, the Occupational Safety and Health Administration (OSHA).

Some regulatory policy relates to the workings of the economy. For example, policy set by the Federal Reserve Board allows more or less money to circulate in the nation. Tightening the money supply cools down an overheated economy by making it more difficult (and costly) for businesses and individuals to borrow money. Inflation is curbed and unemployment may rise as businesses unable to afford loans cannot expand. The opposite policy may stimulate borrowing and help the economy expand.

The federal government, through its various departments, agencies, and commissions, regulates most aspects of our complex and interrelated economy and commercial life. For example, government determines minimum wages, maximum hours, and certain working conditions of American workers and oversees labor-management relations by protecting the right of workers to unionize and collectively bargain. It determines the various trade practices businesses may engage in as well as trade policy with other nations. Government contracts, grants, and other aid are used to regulate employment practices to prevent racial and sexual discrimination in hiring.

Distributive and Redistributive Policy

Domestic policy is distributive if it provides benefits to certain groups or classes of people. It is redistributive when it provides benefits for the less well-off at the expense of the better-off.

---

[2]The first three of these categories were suggested by Theodore J. Lowi, "American Business, Public Policy, Case-Studies, and Political Theory," *World Politics*, 16 (1964), pp. 689–715.

Examples of distributive policies include price supports for farmers and Social Security pensions for retired workers. Certain Defense Department policies such as the expansion of military bases and shipbuilding yards or multimillion dollar defense contracts distribute government funds. Public works contracts—a highway here, a bridge there, a dam elsewhere—all benefit the economy of the geographic area in which they are located and help the businesses and workers who will build them. Sponsors and supporters of distributive policies insist that the policies benefit the public as a whole and not "special interests."

Examples of redistributive policy include aid for dependent children of poor families, Medicaid (medical care) for the poor, and government grants to needy college students. Tax policy is often the means for funding distributive and redistributive policy.

Symbolic Policy

Some domestic policy offers no financial benefits. It offers symbolic value for one or more groups within the American polity. Symbolic policies may have positive value for some and negative consequences for others.

The Reagan administration's policies on several social issues were symbolic. As a candidate and as president, Ronald Reagan expressed his support for constitutional amendments that would overturn Supreme Court decisions that established a woman's right to abortion and prohibited prayer in the public schools. The Reagan administration also supported tough law enforcement policy and opposed long-standing Supreme Court decisions that excluded from a court of law evidence and confessions illegally obtained. Finally, the administration opposed affirmative action to correct the legacy of racism and sexism in the United States. George Bush also took similar stands when he successfully ran for the presidency in 1988. All of these symbolic policies were politically appealing to part of the electorate that the Republican Party cultivated. Such policies can hurt or benefit some groups or interests, but they do not, with the exception of affirmative action at the workplace, imply the distribution of material benefits.

THE MAKING OF POLICY

Abortion. Affirmative action. Environmental protection. Health insurance for workers. Catastrophic health care for the elderly. Issues like these become part of the national policy-making agenda through the interplay of private individuals, public officials, groups, the media, the shapers of public opinion, and political parties.[3] Some issues are part of the continuing business of the federal government, such as defense policy, trade policy, management of the money supply, supervision of public lands, and taxation policy.

[3]See George C. Edwards, III and Ira Sharkansky, *The Policy Predicament: Making and Implementing Public Policy* (San Francisco: W. H. Freeman and Co., 1978), pp. 87–117.

Medical care for the elderly is an issue whose time came in the 1960s and has remained on the policy stage into the 1990s.

Other issues may fester for so long that a gradual momentum builds, forcing them onto the national agenda. An example of this is catastrophic health care for the elderly. The problem faced by the acutely ill elderly facing massive hospital and doctors' costs not covered by Medicare was finally recognized by Congress and resulted in the enactment of the Medicare Catastrophic Health Care bill in 1988. But that took extensive lobbying by various groups and the strenuous efforts of several members of Congress, most notably Claude Pepper, who at eighty-seven was the oldest member of Congress at the time of the passage of the legislation. Even this extension of Medicare to cover catastrophic medical care does not provide for long-term nursing home care of the chronically ill. For example, a victim of Alzheimer's disease, a progressively incapacitating disease that destroys a person's mind and ability to function, is not entitled to nursing home care paid for by the government unless that person is destitute. That means that the victim and the victim's spouse must almost completely exhaust their assets before government will pay for nursing home care. The issue of home care and nursing home coverage is a continuing one, and, in fact, the catastrophic coverage act contained an amendment introduced by Representative Pepper that mandated a bipartisan study of how to finance nursing home care for the chronically ill.

Some issues are thrust onto the stage of public policy by people who write books that gain widespread attention. For example, the issue of the safety of automobiles was popularized by Ralph Nader in his book *Unsafe at Any Speed*, published in 1965, which eventually led to regulations requiring the installation of seat belts and shoulder harnesses, crash-resistant standards for bumpers, and various state laws requiring annual safety inspections of automobiles. Environmental pollution was dramatized as a national problem in Rachel Carson's book *Silent Spring*, published in 1962, which eventually led to environmental protection regulation including regulation of pesticides, toxic wastes, and industrial pollution. The extensiveness and misery of poverty in America was the subject of Michael Harrington's 1962 publication *The Other America*, which inspired the anti-poverty programs of the 1960s. To be sure, many of these problems remain with us in newly recognized forms (for example, the greenhouse effect caused by pollutants that deplete the earth's protective ozone layer or the issue of the poverty-stricken homeless). But such books give impetus for changes in public policy.

Issues are also brought to public attention by **public interest groups** organized to educate the public about certain issues such as environmental protection or consumer protection. These groups lobby for legislation, testify before legislative committees and regulatory commissions, and even bring law suits. Common Cause is one such national public interest group. Some groups that work to influence policy are linked with special interests—business, manufacturing, and trade associations, organized labor, education groups, farmers organizations, civil rights and civil liberties groups, and liberal and conservative research institutes (recall the discussion of interest groups in Chapter Four).

The platforms of the major parties are another way for issues to be placed on the national policy-making agenda. Every four years the Democratic and Republican parties hold their presidential nominating conventions. During the conventions, the parties adopt the platforms—statements of policies—on which their candidates will run. Sometimes these platforms are explicit. For example, the Republican platforms of 1980, 1984, and 1988 opposed abortion, while the Democratic platform of 1988 supported health insurance coverage for all people. Planks in the platform are designed to attract groups of voters. The Republican opposition to abortion was aimed not only at traditional Republicans, but also conservative working-class Democrats. Democratic support for health insurance coverage was aimed at winning back those working-class Democrats who had deserted the party in 1980 and 1984 by appealing to an important bread-and-butter interest.

The president is an important source of policy ideas and initiatives. He has power to set his own policy agenda and is in a unique position to place issues at the center stage of American politics. Other elected and appointed government officials also may have policy agendas of their own. Sometimes these officials simply react to the political pressures placed on them but do not initially assume a leadership role in the formation of policy. For example, in 1988 President Reagan signed the catastrophic health care bill, but neither he, his Secretary of Health and Human Services, or the Republican minority leadership in Congress initiated the legislation or assumed leadership roles in achieving its passage. At other times, government officials work with interested individuals and groups and provide political support and encouragement. On occasion a political figure may seize the initiative, develop policy, and see it through to its acceptance and implementation, as did Representative Pepper.[4]

In the tumult of American politics, hundreds, even thousands, of policies compete for governmental attention, for the attention of the media, and for the attention of other key players in the policy-making process. At any one time, some issues are just beginning to make their way onto the national stage. Others have moved into the spotlight. Still others have already exited from public view. And there are some issues whose time has yet to come.

The Contexts of Policy-making

Domestic policy is made within economic, cultural, political, and institutional contexts. The domestic policies emanating from a small coastal nation with an agrarian and shipping economy, as was the United States for the first several decades of its existence, are far different from those of a major industrial nation in an era of high technology, as the United States is today. The domestic policies that emerge from an economy based on private ownership and regulated capitalism (the United States) are far different from those that emerge from an economy based on state ownership, such as is found in socialist and communist countries. The economic context must therefore be recognized as shaping many of the kinds of public-policy issues that emerge within a political system.[5]

The political cultural context (the widely held attitudes and opinions about how politics should be conducted and what is expected from government) shapes the policy expectations of the American public.[6] Other aspects of popular culture also influence policy. For example, there is a long-running emphasis in American history on self-reliance and personal freedom associated with our agrarian heritage and even more so with the settlement of the West. In this century, these cultural factors have been reinforced and popularized by books, magazines, radio, motion pictures, and television. During the 1980s, the urban western (cops or private investigators versus criminals) replaced the cowboys versus Indians or outlaws, but in both kinds of drama, the same cultural values of self-reliance and personal freedom are disseminated. This may help explain why the National Rifle Association has successfully blocked strong gun control legislation, and why it took the United States longer than any other western democracy to enact social legislation such as Social Security, unemployment compensation, and minimum wage/maximum hour regulation. But of course the values of personal autonomy and responsibility clashed with the catastrophic

---

[4]In general, see Charles O. Jones, *An Introduction to the Study of Public Policy*, third edition (Monterey, Calif.: Brooks-Cole, 1984).

[5]See, Edwards and Sharkansky, *op. cit.*, pp. 213–32.

[6]*Ibid.*, pp. 234–36.

reality of the Great Depression which required the intervention and re-sources of the national community. Since the 1930s, the federal government's role and responsibilities have expanded.

The political context provides the partisan boundaries within which people generate, debate, and implement policy. In particular, elected officials have an eye on the next election, and the electoral process within the two-party system often encourages policy alternatives from challengers of incumbents.[7] At key points in American political history, the policy alternatives offered at national elections have significantly shaped the course of public policy.[8] For example, Ronald Reagan campaigned for the presidency in 1980 promising to scale back government and to cut taxes. His election began a massive shift in major areas of domestic policy. The activities of interest groups—lobbying, waging media campaigns, raising campaign funds for friendly candidates, campaigning to defeat their foes, and getting out the vote of their members and supporters—also shape the political context within which policy is made.

Finally, the institutional context affects public policy. That is, the institutions of government, their procedures, traditions, and histories must be understood. As previous chapters on Congress, the presidency, the federal bureaucracy, and the judiciary have suggested, public policy-making differs within these distinct institutions in part because of their individual institutional characteristics. Institutions of state government and their role within our system of federalism (recall Chapter Two) also affect how public policy is made and implemented.[9]

The President's Role

As shown in Chapter Eight, the president has an array of powers that he can use to promote his policies. The president can use his power of appointment, the preparation of the budget, his annual State of the Union address, executive orders, and proposed legislation to further the presidential agenda. He can also use presidential press conferences, speeches before special audiences and to the nation on radio and television, and exclusive interviews with reporters from the major newspapers and networks to push his agenda. His leadership role in his party also means that he has some political capital that can be used to further his policy goals.

The president may have a powerful arsenal when it comes to formulating domestic policy. But the president also has to face political reality. Newly elected presidents know that they have a limited amount of time and

[7]David R. Mayhew, *Congress: The Electoral Connection* (New Haven: Yale University Press, 1974).

[8]Benjamin Ginsberg, "Elections and Public Policy," *American Political Science Review*, 70 (1976), pp. 41–49.

[9]See, David C. Nice, *Federalism: The Politics of Intergovernmental Relations* (New York: St. Martin's Press, 1987).

must push quickly to turn policy into legislative results. Another political reality is that presidents have their own policy priorities and can only push so many issues at the same time. They need a good sense of what policy will win popular and political support and what faces rough going. President Lyndon Johnson's observations are particularly relevant:

> "A measure must be sent to the Hill at exactly the right moment and that moment depends on three things: first, on the momentum; second, on the availability of sponsors in the right place at the right time; and third, on the opportunities for neutralizing the opposition. Timing is essential. Momentum is *not* a mysterious mistress. It is a controllable fact of political life that depends on nothing more exotic than preparation."[10]

Another major political reality that all presidents must face in policy-making is the great weight of policies that they inherit from previous administrations and budgetary commitments that are fixed (for example, interest on the national debt and social security payments). Once in office, a president may find that there may be less room for policy innovation, particularly when it has a steep price tag, than he had thought on the campaign trail. President George Bush found this out in the first months of his presidency. A massive national debt and a near national consensus that the debt must be dealt with means that no matter what party occupies the White House, there are severe limitations on the introduction of costly new programs. New or increased spending in one policy area means decreased spending in another. For many presidents, the cost of much policy innovation is new taxes. George Bush promised in the presidential campaign of 1988 not to raise taxes, but he also promised to spend more money on education and child care. As president, George Bush found that something had to give.

Congress's Role

The policy-making role of members of the House and Senate is influenced by the needs of electoral politics and the desire to be good representatives. Even the most secure members of Congress will rarely affront their constituencies by sponsoring or supporting legislation that has wide opposition in the congressional district or state. Likewise the member who is concerned about political repercussions is unlikely to oppose legislation or programs for which there is overwhelming support among the constituents. A member of Congress representing a predominantly farm district or state will not oppose agricultural price supports. A member of Congress from a blue-collar, heavily unionized area will not push for anti-union or anti-labor legislation.

---

[10]As quoted in Doris Kearns, *Lyndon Johnson and the American Dream* (New York: Harper & Row, 1976), p. 226.

However, within the confines of constituency interests, members of Congress ordinarily have room to pursue other areas of domestic policy. Their influence in shaping policy may depend in part on their standing in Congress. Many factors affect a member's standing, including seniority, alliances forged in the past, and reputation for integrity, intelligence, and preparation. Additional factors include the policy-making role of the member's party, the member's interpersonal skills, the skills of the member's staff, whether the member belongs to the same party as the president, the level of interest group organization and activity within the member's district or state, and the member's own policy beliefs and preferences.

Committees in each house of Congress are organized by policy area, and domestic policy activity formally begins there. Within each committee are policy-specific subcommittees. These committees and subcommittees may hold hearings on certain domestic policy issues and issue committee reports. Recall the norms of specialization and seniority discussed in Chapter Seven. Members of Congress tend to specialize in certain policy areas, usually those that are important to their constituents. As the members gain seniority, they assume greater authority within their committees, for example, chairing an important subcommittee and perhaps eventually becoming chair of the committee. As policy experts within the committees and subcommittees, members of Congress may be able to exercise considerable influence in the drafting or shaping of domestic policy within their area of policy specialization.[11]

But members of Congress, like the president, also have political realities to face. Each house is organized by the majority political party and an individual member's policy agenda may be limited by that of the party.

The Bureaucracy's Role

The federal bureaucracy, as shown in Chapter Nine, is inextricably involved in the making and implementing of policy. The box on page 430 offers an example of environmental policy-making. Professional civil servants, aided by job security and anonymity (as far as the general public is concerned), are free to exercise some discretion in the policy arena. Political appointees, particularly heading departments, agencies, and commissions, play an even greater policy-making role. The government bureaucracy issues thousands of rules and regulations each year.

Bureaucrats may be powerful, but like the other actors on the stage, they are not free to make policy at will. The political appointees in the bureaucracy are expected to be responsive to the president's policy outlook and shape bureaucratic policy accordingly. These appointees may also be sensitive to pressures from the constituent groups supporting the presi-

---

[11]Barbara Hinckley, *Stability and Change in Congress*, 4th ed. (New York: Harper & Row, 1988), chap. 6.

The Environmental Protection Agency Moves on Water Pollution

On October 5, 1987, the Environmental Protection Agency (EPA) issued a press release announcing that it was establishing new rules to prevent toxic waste pollution of the nation's waters. The EPA's new policy was a direct result of a lawsuit brought by the Natural Resources Defense Council, an environmental public interest group. The EPA was under a court-ordered deadline to impose limitations on the discharge of toxic pollutants.

The sixty-six regulated pollutants include cancer-causing chemicals such as benzene and vinyl chloride and other organic chemicals and synthetic fibers. Polluters are obligated under the 1987 rules to use state of the art technology to eliminate the pollutants from discharged wastes. In 1987, EPA experts estimated that the cost to industry of controlling pollution might be as high as $500 million a year and might affect 1000 plants that manufacture more than 25,000 products. The greatest impact was expected to be felt by sixty-one chemical plants, employing 3300 workers, in Alabama, South Carolina, Virginia, and New Jersey. EPA officials acknowledged that these sixty-one plants might close if they could not absorb the costs.

If industry complied with the new regulations, the nation's waters would be spared some 23.6 million pounds of toxic pollutants and 108 million pounds of non-toxic pollutants. Water quality would improve, there would be clean water for irrigation, and other industries would benefit, including commercial fishing and the recreation industry. Although the regulatory policy would be costly to the chemical industry, the benefits, aside from health and aesthetic,might be as much as $330 million a year.

Source: Philip Shabecoff, "E.P.A. Adopts New Rules on Water Pollution," *New York Times*, October 6, 1987, p. A-20.

dent. Civil servants at all levels are aware that the president's budget requests for their agencies can mean expansion, contraction, or the status quo. The budget requests can contain funds, for example, for new equipment or larger quarters. Clearly it is not in the interest of government bureaucrats to act contrary to the president's policy or, if they are inclined to do so, to do it in a conspicuous fashion.

The government bureaucracy is also responsive to Congress, because Congress funds it, may investigate it, and may generally exercise oversight by way of a congressional subcommittee. Interest groups may influence the course of bureaucratic policy-making by bringing pressure on Congress, which in turn may use *its* leverage to shape the course of policy.

The judiciary may also affect bureaucratic policy-making by rulings in suits in which the agency is sued by an interest group that challenges its actions or inaction in light of its statutory responsibilities. The box on page 430 offers an example of this phenomenon.

As shown in Chapter Nine, government agencies seek political support by working with interested groups. It is sometimes unclear who has co-opted whom particularly when there is a convergence of goals and objectives. It has long been recognized that government agencies may become part of a policy network or subgovernment that includes interested members of Congress on key subcommittees and major interest groups.[12]

The Judiciary's Role

The federal judiciary plays an important role in national policy-making in several ways. It can, as the example in the box on page 430 suggests, through its power of statutory interpretation order government agencies to establish policy. The judiciary does this by interpreting acts of Congress and determining, for example, what these laws require federal agencies to do.

Sometimes federal courts use their power to interpret statutes to uphold an agency's policy determination, and here, too, the judiciary is often seen as a partner in policy. For example, in 1984, Judge Robert Bork authored an appeals court decision in *Oil, Chemical and Atomic Workers* v. *American Cyanamid Co.* In this case, the union was suing American Cyanamid, which had given its female employees of child-bearing age the choice of taking lower-paying jobs or being sterilized so that they could keep jobs that unavoidably exposed them to chemicals known to damage fetuses. In his opinion (joined by the other members of his panel), Bork ruled that the Occupational Safety and Health Review Commission had been correct in finding in favor of the American Cyanamid Corporation. Bork's critics later argued that he and his colleagues could have interpreted the law differently and prevented the women from facing the cruel choice of being sterilized or losing their jobs. However, if Congress feels a federal court has misinterpreted a federal statute or applied it incorrectly, Congress can enact a new statute clarifying its policy.

The judiciary also has the power to declare federal and state laws constitutional or unconstitutional. This power to legitimate a particular policy takes on special significance when a segment of the public or public officials have questioned a policy's legality. For example, in the 1964 case of *Heart of Atlanta Motel* v. *United States*, the Supreme Court affirmed a congressional policy when it ruled that Title 2 of the Civil Rights Act of 1964 was constitutional. Title 2 racially desegregated public accommodations such as hotels, restaurants, and theaters. Likewise, the Court in 1980 declared constitutional the minority business enterprise provision of the Public Works Employment Act of 1977 (*Fullilove* v. *Klutznick*). This provision required that at least ten percent of local public works projects financed by the act be used to buy services or supplies from businesses owned by minority group members. In 1987, the Court, for example, once again was a partner in policy-making when it upheld the constitutionality of a statute

---

[12]See, J. Leiper Freeman, *The Political Process: Executive Bureau-Legislative Committee Relations*, Revised Edition (New York: Random House, 1965).

Robert Bork was held accountable for his policy views before the Senate Judiciary Committee upon his nomination for elevation to the Supreme Court.

that gave federal judges the authority, under certain circumstances, to preventively detain those arrested by federal authorities. Preventive detention means that an arrested suspect is not offered the opportunity to be released on bail until the trial but instead remains in jail.

When the Court exercises its power to strike down federal and state laws as unconstitutional, its policy-making role becomes obvious. For example, in 1983, the Court struck down the **legislative veto** in *INS* v. *Chadha*. The legislative veto was a provision in nearly 200 federal laws and allowed either branch of Congress to invalidate a policy decision of the executive branch. In the 1986 decision in *Bowsher* v. *Synar*, the Court again made waves when it struck down a key provision in the Balanced Budget and Emergency Deficit Control Act of 1985 (better known as the Gramm-Rudman-Hollings Act). This law gave an official responsible to Congress the power, under certain circumstances, to automatically cut the federal budget and to have the cuts binding on the president. In recent years, there have been very few decisions striking down federal law.

Throughout its history, the Court has struck down at least ten times as many state statutes as federal statutes. When the Court strikes down state laws, it shapes policy in a negative sense. It tells the states what they may *not* do (and perhaps implies what they may do). Only rarely does the Court spell out a policy of what the states *may* do in the course of invalidating state law. This unusual kind of policy-making was evident in 1973 in *Roe* v. *Wade*, the landmark decision that recognized a woman's right, under certain circumstances, to have an abortion. It was also evident in the case of *Miranda* v. *Arizona*, the case that established the "Miranda" rights of those accused of a crime. (See the box on page 434 for excerpts from the Court opinions that spelled out these policies.)

Unlike Congress and the president, the federal courts are not free to take policy initiatives on their own. They must wait for issues to come before them. Of course, the Supreme Court has discretion in choosing cases to hear, but even so, it is limited to actual cases and how they frame legal issues. Sometimes issues are framed in ways that are not necessarily conducive to formulating a coherent policy.

The process of how issues are translated into policy and the various centers of policy-making in the federal government have been examined. There is fragmentation of power, many players, and built-in difficulties in establishing coherent public policy. This all comes to the fore in the most important domestic policy process the federal government engages in, enacting the federal budget.

THE FEDERAL BUDGET AS DOMESTIC POLICY

As the president, the bureaucracy, and Congress hammer together the federal budget every year, they in large part set domestic policy. Programs are added, eliminated, scaled down, scaled up, or modified in major ways. The federal budget determines who gets what, when, and how. It also contains policies that determine who pays for all that spending. The budgetary process is ongoing and complex and involves, as Chapter Nine showed, the president, the federal bureaucracy, and Congress. On occasion, the budget process has involved even the judiciary (as, for example, occurred when the Supreme Court invalidated a portion of the Gramm-Rudman-Hollings Deficit Reduction Act). Because American politics has become more polarized over the last two decades between the political left and right, the budget process has become increasingly controversial. As a consequence, in the words of Aaron Wildavsky, a leading scholar of the federal budget, "the new politics in a time of dissensus [disagreement] is about grand questions: How much, what for, who pays; in sum, what side are you on? . . . . The emergence of budgeting center stage signifies its increased dependence on shifting political alignments."[13] The complexity of the current process "unfortunately has become difficult to describe."[14] But difficult to describe or not, the budgetary process has important implications for domestic policy.

Rules of the Game

Every college student is familiar with living on a budget. There are certain **uncontrollable expenditures**, or fixed costs, of a college education—tuition, student activity fees, room and board, books and supplies, and health insurance, for example. Although the precise amounts for each of these expenses may vary from year to year (typically they increase), it is both possi-

[13]Aaron Wildavsky, *The New Politics of the Budgetary Process* (Glenview, Illinois: Scott, Foresman/Little, Brown, 1988), pp. xiv, xvi.

[14]*Ibid.*, p. xvi.

Supreme Court Policy-Making in Abortion and Criminal Procedures

In the famous 1973 decision of *Roe* v. *Wade*, the Supreme Court by a vote of seven to two announced its policy on abortion in an opinion written by Justice Harry Blackmun. The case concerned the constitutionality of a Texas criminal abortion law that made abortion a state crime if performed for reasons other than saving the life of the mother. This is the policy, as stated by Justice Blackmun in the opinion of the Court:

1. A state criminal abortion statute of the current Texas type, that excepts from criminality only a *life saving* procedure on behalf of the mother, without regard to pregnancy state and without recognition of the other interests involved, is violative of the Due Process Clause of the Fourteenth Amendment.

(a) For the stage prior to approximately the end of the first trimester, the abortion decision and its effectuation must be left to the medical judgment of the pregnant woman's attending physician.

(b) For the stage subsequent to approximately the end of the first trimester, the State, in promoting its interests in the health of the mother, may, if it chooses, regulate the abortion procedure in ways that are reasonably related to maternal health.

(c) For the stage subsequent to viability, the State in promoting its interest in the potentiality of human life may, if it chooses, regulate, and even proscribe, abortion except where it is necessary, in appropriate medical judgment, for the preservation of the life or health of the mother.

2. The State may define the term 'physician,' ... to mean only a physician currently licensed by the State, and may proscribe any abortion by a person who is not a physician as so defined. . . .

The Court also made policy in its famous *Miranda* v. *Arizona* decision of 1966. By a five to four vote, the Court announced in detail the procedures that law enforcement authorities must follow before they may interrogate a suspect in custody and have any statement or confession admissible in a court of law. These procedures were designed to give meaning to the constitutional guarantee against self-incrimination. Chief Justice Earl Warren delivered the opinion of the Court and said in part:

At the outset, if a person in custody is to be subjected to interrogation, he must first be informed in clear and unequivocal terms that he has the right to remain silent . . .

The warning of the right to remain silent must be accompanied by the explanation that any-

ble and necessary to plan ahead for them. The federal budget also has uncontrollable expenditures. They amount to at least seventy-five percent of the budget. For example, the federal budget must contain funds to pay the interest on the national debt. It must also pay the salaries of government employees, including the military. It must pay for **entitlement programs** (all those who qualify receive the benefit after properly applying for it) such as Social Security, medical care for the elderly (Medicare), medical care for the poor (Medicaid), other social welfare programs, veterans' compensation and pensions, and agricultural subsidies (or price supports). The budget must finance multiyear contractual obligations undertaken by the government to build or expand federal highways, erect federal office buildings, modernize harbors, construct dams, or create nuclear-powered submarines.

thing said can and will be used against the individual in court. . . .

The circumstances surrounding in-custody interrogation can operate very quickly to overbear the will of one merely made aware of his privilege by his interrogators. Therefore, the right to have counsel present at the interrogation is indispensable to the protection of the Fifth Amendment privilege under the system we delineate today. Our aim is to assure that the individual's right to choose between silence and speech remains unfettered throughout the interrogation process. . . .

Accordingly we hold that an individual held for interrogation must be clearly informed that he has the right to consult with a lawyer and to have the lawyer with him during interrogation under the system for protecting the privilege we delineate today. . . .

In order fully to apprise a person interrogated of the extent of his rights under this system . . . it is necessary to warn him not only that he has the right to consult with an attorney, but also that if he is indigent a lawyer will be appointed to represent him. . . .

Once warnings have been given, the subsequent procedure is clear. If the individual indicates in any manner, at any time prior to or during questioning, that he wishes to remain silent, the interrogation must cease. . . . If the individual states that he wants an attorney, the interrogation must cease until an attorney is present. . . .

If the interrogation continues without the presence of an attorney and a statement is taken, a heavy burden rests on the government to demonstrate that the defendant knowingly and intelligently waived his privilege against self-incrimination and his right to retained or appointed counsel. . . .

. . . . [S]tatements merely intended to be exculpatory by the defendant are often used to impeach his testimony at trial or to demonstrate untruths in the statement given under interrogation and thus to prove guilt by implication. These statements are incriminating in any meaningful sense of the word and may not be used without the full warnings and effective waiver required for any other statement. . . .

Some budget expenses are discretionary or **controllable expenditures**. For example, students can cut back or expand entertainment expenses. It is ordinarily not *essential* to order out for pizza when you have paid for the meal plan. Spending five dollars to see a movie at a local theater is not a *must* expense when cash is in short supply. The old car may not be worth the cost of upkeep and insurance no matter the convenience of having one on campus. Similarly, there are relatively controllable items in the federal budget. The president may want to further his policy agenda with new spending programs such as expanded child care for working mothers, public-service employment, or, the Strategic Defense Initiative (the "Star Wars" missile shield system).

Both the student budget and the federal budget require income or revenues. The student's revenues may come from summer and school-year jobs, savings, and parents. The federal government's revenues come from personal and corporate income taxes, excise taxes and duties, and other governmental fees. When expenses exceed income, student and government can either cut their expenses or increase their income.

Cutting expenses can be difficult. The student could change to a reduced meal plan, buy used textbooks instead of new ones, transfer to a less expensive school, or attend school part-time. These may not be pleasant choices to make. Analogously, the federal government can try to cut from uncontrollable expenditures by, for example, changing eligibility standards for certain social welfare programs, increasing deductibles for Medicare, tinkering with Social Security benefits, limiting the amount of subsidies paid to any one farm, or imposing a hiring freeze on government employment. The government could try to cut controllable expenditures, for example, by not going ahead with a new weapons system, scaling back or dropping a proposed new health, housing, or jobs program. Cutting expenses is never easy. At the federal level, it may be next to impossible politically, as the Reagan administration found in its first year when it tried and failed to make radical cuts across the board from ongoing domestic programs.[15] As Wildavsky has noted, "a good 90 to 95 percent of total spending is locked in as a consequence of past commitments and present promises."[16]

The other option to balancing a budget is to increase income. For the student, this might mean working more hours during the school year or taking a second job during the summer. For the government, it might mean raising taxes. (But politicians do not like to raise taxes. In fact, the centerpiece of President Reagan's economic program during his first year in office was to *cut* income taxes.) When income does not match expenses, the student or government must resort to borrowing. The government has borrowed very heavily in recent years. President Reagan cut personal and corporate income taxes which reduced revenues. Because it was politically impossible to drastically scale back entitlement and defense programs, the national debt during Reagan's presidency far exceeded the *total* amount of the national debt accumulated by *all* previous presidents.[17] (See Exhibit 11.1 tracing the deficits from 1945–1990).

The student is likely to plan his or her budget around the academic year. A family might plan a budget around the calendar year. The federal government operates on a **fiscal year**, which begins October 1 and extends through the following September 30. The fiscal year is known by the calendar year in which it *ends*. Thus, for example, fiscal year (or FY) 1989 began

[15]See, David A. Stockman, *The Triumph of Politics: How the Reagan Revolution Failed* (New York: Harper & Row, 1986).

[16]Wildavsky, *op cit.*, p. 29.

[17]See the discussion in Stockman, *op. cit.*, pp. 396–98. Also see, *Statistical Abstract of the United States 1988* (Washington, D.C.: U.S. Bureau of the Census, 1987), p. 355.

EXHIBIT 11.1   Federal Budget Deficit, 1945-1990 (in billions of dollars)

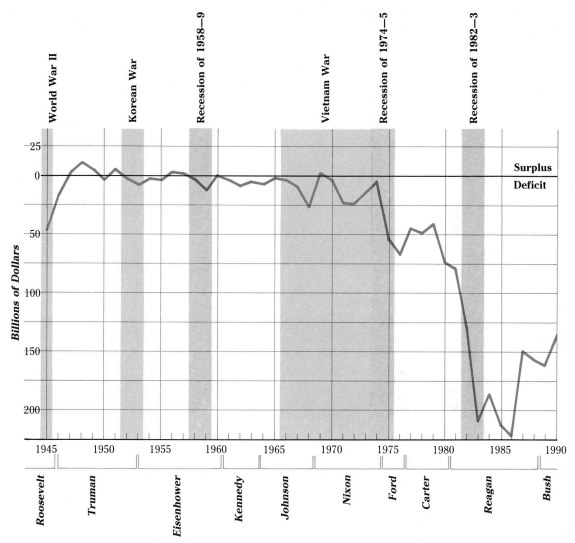

Sources: *Congressional Quarterly Weekly Report*, November 19, 1983, p. 2408; *Statistical Abstract of the United States 1988* (Washington, D.C.: U.S. Bureau of the Census, 1987), p. 291; *New York Times*, July 29 1988, p. A-9 and November 13, 1988, p. 31; *Congressional Quarterly Weekly Report*, January 14, 1989, p. 68.

The Federal
Government Dollar:
Income and
Expenditures
(estimates for fiscal
1989)

Borrowing **12**¢   Individual Income Taxes **38**¢   Social Insurance Receipts **32**¢   Corporation Income Taxes **11**¢   Other **4**¢   Excise Taxes **3**¢

Income: Where It Comes From

Direct Benefit Payments for Individuals **43**¢   National Defense **27**¢   National Debt Interest **14**¢   Other Federal Operations **5**¢   Grants to States & Localities **11**¢

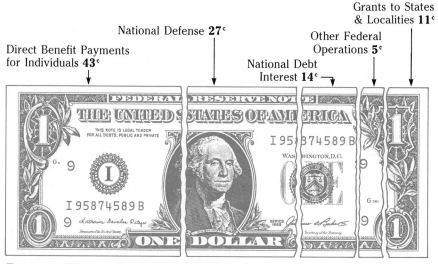

Expenses: Where It Goes

Source: Office of Management and Budget, February, 1988.

on October 1, 1988 and finished on September 30, 1989. The estimates for income and expenses for FY 1989 made by the Reagan administration are shown in Exhibit 11.2.

Budget Policy-making by the Executive Branch and Congress

President Reagan's first Director of the Office of Management and Budget (OMB), David Stockman, tried to establish firm White House control over the budget. Stockman clearly saw the link between the budget and policy. Programs disapproved of by the Reagan administration were cut back or even eliminated from the budget, as, for example, the Economic Development Administration and the Appalachian Development Program (Congress, however, later restored funds). The Reagan administration attempted to scale back entitlement programs by tightening eligibility standards and removing tens of thousands of people from benefit programs, and this, too, was built into the budget. Stockman, seemingly with Reagan's enthusiastic approval, had a grand plan to reduce the role of the federal government in substantial ways. These major reductions were designed to offset substantial tax cuts in personal and corporate taxes, which in turn would revitalize the economy.

In Congress, the budget resolution and reconciliation stages (recall the discussion in Chapter Nine) can become a major policy-making tool, as they did during the Reagan administration. When Ronald Reagan assumed office in 1981, he had pledged to cut personal and corporate income taxes, reduce domestic spending, increase defense spending, and to balance the budget. During the 1980 Republican primaries, George Bush, who was then challenging Reagan for the Republican nomination, called this "voodoo economics." Economic events later would prove Bush right—massive unprecedented deficits and stunning trade imbalances transforming the United States into a major debtor nation. But in order for this to come about, President Reagan had to first enact his economic policy and it was the budget resolution and reconciliation process that allowed him to do this quickly.

Riding on a strong victory in the presidential election, Ronald Reagan convinced Congress to enact the central elements of his program (tax cuts, increased defense spending, and reduced domestic spending) in a three year budget resolution. He also won a stunning victory with the enactment of the reconciliation bill for fiscal 1982. It cut domestic spending in hundreds of programs by about $35 billion.[18] By placing all the cuts in one legislative package, the Reagan administration avoided having to fight for each cut separately as the various authorization and appropriations bills moved through Congress, although there was a great deal of negotiating between the administration and key members of Congress.

Reagan's economic policy had serious consequences. The severe economic recession of 1982-1983 required additional social welfare expenditures that added further to the deficits. Of equal significance, in year after year Congress and the president had difficulty agreeing as to where budget cuts should be made. Members of Congress from both parties were protective of many domestic programs while the president was resistant to major defense spending cuts and tax increases. All this occurred while many were warning that massive budget deficits were a menace to the country's long-term economic health.

To try to cut the budget *and* minimize the political costs to members of Congress, Congress passed the Gramm-Rudman-Hollings Deficit Reduction

---

[18]Stockman, *op cit.*, pp. 193–94. For an examination of the impact of these cuts see Irene S. Rubin, *Shrinking the Federal Government: The Effect of Cutbacks on Five Federal Agencies* (New York: Longman, 1985).

President Reagan signs the Spending and Deficit Reduction package on December 22, 1987.

Act (officially entitled the Balanced Budget and Emergency Deficit Control Act of 1985). Under this legislation, there is a maximum deficit for federal spending for each fiscal year through 1991. If the deficit exceeds this maximum, across-the-board cuts in federal spending are required. Because Congress did not want to absorb the political costs of actually voting to cut funds from programs, the Act provided for automatic cuts administered by the Comptroller General, who heads the General Accounting Office (GAO). But this was ruled unconstitutional by the Supreme Court.

The Gramm-Rudman-Hollings Act contained a "fallback" deficit reduction process in the event that the automatic cutting provision was found unconstitutional. This process eliminated the Comptroller General's role and would have Congress vote on spending cuts. This, of course, was politically unsatisfactory to members of Congress. As a result, Congress revised the Act in 1987.

The revised Act still contains an automatic spending-cut process. But the Comptroller General is bypassed and the cuts that are mandated are ordered by OMB. This procedure was used in 1987. On October 20, 1987, automatic budget cuts of 8.5 percent in nonmilitary programs and 10.5 percent in defense spending went into effect to meet the $23 billion deficit reduction mandated by the law. Congress finally enacted a spending and deficit reduction package on December 22, which provided for $604 billion in spending for the remainder of fiscal 1988 and a $33.3 billion cut in the projected deficit for fiscal 1988 along with a cut of $45.9 billion for fiscal

1989. All sorts of policy decisions were contained in this legislation (see the box on page 442). But the federal deficit for fiscal 1988 was expected to remain close to the fiscal 1987 deficit of $148 billion (see Exhibit 11.1).

The required cuts under Gramm-Rudman-Hollings have a profound impact on public policy. They play havoc with domestic programs and make little sense. But it may be the only way to spur Congress and the president to cut the federal budget. The law says that by fiscal 1993 there must be a balanced budget. Given the political realities of the budgetary process, this is unlikely to happen.

IMPLEMENTING DOMESTIC POLICY

It would seem logical to assume that once a domestic policy program has emerged from the budget process with sufficient funds, the policy will be successfully implemented. That assumption may be logical, but it also can be wrong. At least six factors can make or break the implementation of a program: (1) the clarity of a program's goals; (2) administrative commitment; (3) administrative resources and authority; (4) cooperation among governmental units; (5) policy consensus with the target population; and (6) policy evaluation and program adjustment.

Clarity of Goals

The clarity of the goals of programs and policies is extremely important for their successful implementation. When policy goals are mixed or unclear, implementation can prove troublesome. The food stamp program, for example, began as a program with several goals. It was designed to aid farmers by expanding the market for agricultural goods, reducing government surpluses of food products costly to store, and helping to feed the poor. Thus the mixed goals of the food stamp program made it both an agricultural and social welfare program. Food stamps could only be used to purchase certain agricultural commodities that were in surplus. Not until the program was expanded in the 1960s and 1970s did it come to be considered primarily a social welfare program. Even so, it is still administered by the Department of Agriculture rather than the Department of Health and Human Services.

Medicare is another program with mixed goals. Medicare provides health insurance for those sixty-five and over. The federal government is the insurer and pays for most of the cost of hospital and physician care for those enrolled in the program. Medicaid is a related program that pays the medical care costs of all eligible poor people, including the elderly. The financial costs of Medicare and Medicaid combined have been enormous, with well over $100 billion spent in recent years. The government bureaucracy needed to administer both programs is immense.

Policies in the Budget Reconciliation and All Purpose Appropriations Legislation for Fiscal 1988

In the early morning hours of December 22, 1987, Congress enacted spending and deficit reduction legislation. This followed months of intense political activity, negotiations, and compromises both within the two houses of Congress and between Congress and the White House. Later that day, President Reagan signed the measures into law. The $604 billion spending bill ran to 1,085 pages; the bill on revenue-producing measures and ways to cut the deficit was 1,281 pages.[1] Within these statutes were scattered many domestic policies. Some had great significance, some minor. Some of these policies were controversial and caused debate in Congress. Others were slipped into the bills by influential members of Congress. Among the many policies contained within these measures were the following:[2]

- Smoking was prohibited on all domestic airline flights of two hours or less.

- Japanese companies were forbidden to receive contracts to participate in federally funded public works projects until Japan permitted American companies to receive contracts for Japanese public works projects.
- AIDS research, counseling, and testing was increased ninety percent over 1987 funding. The total amount appropriated for fiscal 1988 was $904.5 million.
- Reimbursements to physicians and hospitals under Medicare were tightened to save an estimated $2.1 billion in fiscal 1988 and $3.95 billion in fiscal 1989.
- Price supports to farmers for certain commodities were lowered and loan rates were changed, both of which were expected to save $1.5 billion.
- Taxes were increased for corporations and wealthy individuals that would raise $9.1 billion in fiscal 1988 and $14.1 billion in fiscal 1989 in additional revenues.
- Yucca Mountain in Nevada was named as the first permanent site for the deposit of high-level nuclear waste.

The federal government has tried to contain health care costs. But Medicare and Medicaid still are criticized as too costly, too bureaucratic, too subject to abuse by health care providers, too rigid in what is and what is not covered and in payment schedules (to hospitals and doctors). Medicare is criticized for not meeting the needs of the elderly who require long-term nursing home care. If the goal is to make medical care available to all, a national health service (socialized medicine where doctors are employed by the government and hospitals are owned and run by the government) probably would be less expensive than current programs. If the goal is to provide medical care for the poor, including the elderly poor, Medicaid should suffice. Under Medicare, however, *all* elderly, regardless of their means, are entitled *because of their age* (and because they pay premiums) to government medical benefits. The immense confusion in policy goals has thus led to a program that, while meeting real needs, does so at inordinate cost.

- The first twenty states to apply to the Federal Department of Transportation would be permitted to increase the speed limit to 65 miles per hour on rural state roads not within the federal interstate network but whose safety standards are the same. This was done despite the findings of a study conducted by the National Highway Traffic Safety Administration that deaths from accidents on interstate highways where the speed limit was raised to 65 increased by 52 percent.[3]
- Within the State Department's budget for refugees was an $8 million appropriation to build parochial schools in France. The State Department opposed this arguing that the North Africans in France for whom the schools were to be built were not refugees. But this budget item had been pressed by Senator Daniel K. Inouye and had been strongly recommended to him by one of his supporters.[4] (Six weeks later, Inouye reversed himself, apologized for his error in judgment, and the appropriation was rescinded.)
- Kellog, Idaho, got $6.4 million to construct a Bavarian-style ski resort to help the town re-

cover from the closing of the mine that had employed most of its population. This funding was placed in the bill by Idaho Republican Senator James A. McClure, a member of the Senate Appropriations Committee.[5]
- No appropriated funds could be used "to lobby for abortion."[6]
- Recognizing the financial difficulties of predominantly black colleges and universities, Congress increased aid by 50 percent over the previous year, for a total of $73.1 million.[7]

Clearly budget-making is the making of public policy.

[1]*New York Times*, December 24, 1987, p. A-12.
[2]Unless otherwise noted, these examples are drawn from the *New York Times*, December 23, 1987, p. B-8.
[3]*New York Times*, December 29, 1987, p. A-1.
[4]*New York Times*, December 31, 1987, p. A-26.
[5]*New York Times*, January 5, 1988, p. B-6.
[6]*Ibid.*
[7]*New York Times*, January 6, 1988, p. B-8.

Administrative Commitment

Successful implementation also depends on the commitment of the people charged with carrying out the policies.[19] Administrators who are unsympathetic to a program designed to carry out a policy may implement it halfheartedly. For example, President Reagan appointed several people to the Civil Rights Commission who opposed affirmative action programs designed to redress racism and sexism. These commission members eroded the policy of supporting affirmative action and supervising its use by public agencies and private organizations.[20] If the implementation of policy requires major change within the agency, implementation is less likely to be successful, particularly if there is a lack of enthusiasm for the policy.

[19]See George C. Edwards, III, *Implementing Public Policy* (Washington, D.C.: Congressional Quarterly Press, 1980), pp. 89–123.
[20]*Congressional Quarterly*, November 26, 1986, p. 2991.

Administrative Resources and Authority

The resources available to administrators and the authority given them are a third factor in the success or failure of policy implementation.[21] If agencies lack the personnel or money to carry out programs, the programs and the policies they embody will suffer. Regulatory agencies that are short on staff cannot be as effective as those with a full complement of employees. The continuing struggle over cutting the federal budget highlights this dilemma. Agencies prefer reductions in the dollar amount of benefits they expend to reductions in agency employees because with fewer people they are less effective at doing their job—that is, implementing policy.

A lack of authority also can prevent an agency's staff from implementing policy. An extreme example of this occurred with the professional staff of a small federal agency, the National Commission for Employment Policy, created by Congress to evaluate federal job-training programs.[22] In October 1987, the entire seven-person professional staff of the agency, all civil servants, were informed that their jobs would be abolished and the agency reorganized. The commissioners (who are political appointees) would select staff who would come to the agency from outside the federal civil service to serve for two-year fellowships. The agency would also contract with private policy evaluation firms. The commissioners asserted that the professional staff was not bringing a broad perspective to its task. The staff members countered that they were being fired for political reasons, that is, for not supporting the administration. The professional staff claimed that the commissioners wanted them to support administration employment policies instead of conducting non-partisan, objective analyses of the workings of federal job-training programs.

Cooperation Among Governmental Units

Successful implementation also depends on the extent to which it is necessary to secure the cooperation of other governmental units, and, if cooperation is needed, the extent to which the other units understand and share the goals of the policy. Cooperation may be difficult to achieve within the federal government. For example, welfare policy is contained in over one hundred federal programs spread over ten federal departments and agencies.[23] In 1978, President Jimmy Carter pointed out: "There are too many agencies, doing too many things, overlapping too often, coordinating too rarely, wasting too much money—and doing too little to solve real problems."[24]

Cooperation between different levels of government—federal, state, and local—may also be hard to accomplish. For example, an analysis of a feder-

---

[21]Edwards, *op. cit.*, pp. 53–87.
[22]*New York Times*, November 4, 1987, p. B-6.
[23]Edwards, *op cit.*, p. 134.
[24]As quoted in *Ibid*.

al program to create jobs for the unemployed in Oakland, California, showed that the coordination required among federal, state, and local officials and bureaucracies complicated implementation. Furthermore, whereas federal officials saw the program's goal as the creation of jobs for the unemployed, other governmental officials saw the program as a vehicle for the construction of public works.[25]

Policy Consensus with Target Population

Policies also succeed or fail depending on the extent to which the beneficiaries of the programs or their target populations understand and share the goals of the policies. For example, the Law Enforcement Assistance Administration (LEAA) was created with some fanfare in 1968. Its goal was to provide funds to state and local police forces to help them modernize, become more professional through the use of more effective training programs, and try innovative programs to improve the effectiveness of law enforcement. But the police forces, the target population, saw the program as a way to have the federal government pay for new police cars, police surveillance helicopters, and other hardware. The LEAA administrators bowed to the wishes of the target population, and the original policy goal was not implemented. Eventually, the LEAA was terminated. It is considered an example of failed policy implementation.[26]

Another example involved the federal government's Urban Development Action Grants (UDAG) and Community Development Block Grants. These were grants to states and localities intended to restore run-down inner cities, to provide funds for building housing for the poor or for renovating existing housing units, and to create jobs for the unemployed. In practice, some local governments spent their grants for parks, skating or other recreational facilities, or in other ways that did not materially improve the lives of the urban underclass. Instead the grant programs benefited the middle and business classes. In his scathing attack on the UDAG program and on the Reagan administration's unwillingness to end it in 1981, the Director of the OMB, David Stockman, sarcastically noted: "Four years later the Reagan Administration would be able to tell the American taxpayers with pride that their hard work had gone towards the construction of twelve new Hilton Hotels, six Hyatts, five Marriotts, four Sheratons, two Ramadas, one Albert Pick, and a Stouffers. . . ."[27]

---

[25]Jeffrey L. Pressman and Aaron Wildavsky, *Implementation* (Berkeley, Cal.: University of California Press, 1973).

[26]See Malcolm M. Feeley and Austin D. Sarat, *The Policy Dilemma: Federal Crime Policy and the Law Enforcement Assistance Administration 1968–78* (Minneapolis: University of Minnesota Press, 1980) and Thomas E. Cronin, Tania Z. Cronin, and Michael E. Milakovich, *U.S. v. Crime in the Streets* (Bloomington, Indiana: Indiana University Press, 1981).

[27]Stockman, *op. cit.*, p. 143. Also see, *New York Times*, December 1, 1987, p. A-27.

Policy Evaluation and Program Adjustment

Another factor that can determine the success or failure of policy implementation is whether implementation is evaluated and adjusted as necessary. Programs sometimes produce unintended consequences, such as with the LEAA and urban block grants. Because adjustments were not made so that implementation matched the original domestic policy objective, implementation was not successful.

Policy evaluation is not an easy task because it raises problems of both method and politics. Evaluating how a program is working and whether it is effectively implementing the underlying policy means that someone must accurately identify the policy objectives, measure policy performance, and interpret the findings skillfully and objectively. Another problem is that it is a challenge for government agencies to evaluate government programs in a non-partisan manner. Supporters and opponents of a policy try to influence policy evaluation. The National Commission for Employment Policy, described earlier, was supposed to evaluate federal job-training programs. The professional staff proposed evaluating policy by comparing the Reagan administration's Job Training Partnership Act of 1982 with the program it replaced, the Comprehensive Employment and Training Act (CETA). But the commissioners rejected this proposal, fearing unfavorable comparisons to the more ambitious and costly CETA program. The commissioners decided to evaluate the Reagan administration's program alone. To no one's surprise, the Commission's report praised it highly.

■ SOCIAL WELFARE POLICIES

As shown throughout this chapter, because there are many domestic policies and competing centers of policy-making, it is not easy to initiate policy, particularly policy that has a price tag. This chapter now examines some of the major social welfare policies that have been established by the federal government since the 1930s and that directly affect many millions of people. These policies provide the cornerstone for the modern welfare state, and the programs that implement them exceed the defense budget in annual expenditures. A long political struggle was required to enact them and they continue to encounter problems, but these policies are firmly woven into the social, economic, and political fabric of the nation.

Social Security

The Great Depression of the 1930s, with the collapse of the American economy and the widespread suffering of Americans, provided the impetus for a variety of policies that became known as the New Deal. One major piece of New Deal legislation was the Social Security Act of 1935, which created old-age and unemployment benefits programs. The old age benefits program is administered by the federal government, while the unemployment benefits program provides incentives to the states to create and administer their own programs that meet minimal federal standards.[28]

The idea of *social security* had been accepted and adopted decades earlier by the industrialized democracies of western Europe, but it took the national trauma of the Great Depression to produce the political support essential for the Act's passage. By providing workers aged sixty-five and older a guaranteed government income upon retirement, the old-age benefits program offered an incentive to older workers to retire from the work force and thus open up jobs for younger workers. In 1939, Congress extended Social Security benefits to dependents of retirees and surviving dependents of deceased workers. In 1956, Congress brought disabled workers and their dependents under Social Security and in 1965 enacted health insurance through Medicare as part of Social Security.

The old-age benefits program is an entitlement program. Every retired worker who has contributed to Social Security and has reached the statutorily defined retirement age is entitled to monthly benefits. Rich and poor alike receive benefits. The Social Security Administration administers the program, which is financed by a tax on employers and employees. This money goes into a separate trust fund that is used to pay the benefits. Workers of today, in effect, pay for the benefits of the retired and their spouses. The only workers who do not have to contribute to Social Security are state and local employees who belong to comparable state or local retirement systems.

Some observers have charged that Social Security is in precarious financial health. They point out that advances in medicine and healthier life styles have resulted in people living longer and collecting benefits for many years. They point to the automatic cost-of-living adjustments that also drain the Social Security trust fund. The unemployment rate, too, can strain the system. When unemployment is high, as it was in the 1970s and early 1980s, fewer workers contributed to Social Security. Likewise, the lower birth rates of the 1970s will produce a reduced work force in the 1990s. Will this reduced work force be able to sustain the Social Security system when the baby boom generation of the 1940s and 1950s retires?

In 1983, when the trust fund for old-age benefits was close to being depleted, Congress increased payroll taxes and reduced some benefits. But most observers expect that Social Security will face future crises. Some believe that in the future it may be necessary to institute a graduated benefits system so that those most in need will receive full benefits and those with less need will receive minimal payments. At some point, the Social Security trust fund also may have to receive infusions from the general treasury. Were that to happen, the pay-as-you-go principle on which Social Security

---

[28]Michael Morris and John B. Williamson, *Poverty and Public Policy: An Analysis of Federal Intervention Efforts* (Westport, Conn.: Greenwood Press, 1986), pp. 83–87.

is based will have been compromised, and the entire program would have to be redesigned. Politicians then would have to face the politically dangerous question of whether the old-age benefits program gives too much to those who don't need it and not enough to those who do. The fear of electoral retribution by middle-class elderly is likely to inhibit members of Congress and the president from boldly asking and answering this question.

Despite the continuing problems with Social Security, few would deny that the old-age benefits and related programs are a necessary component of a decent and just society. Social Security unquestionably keeps many millions (over 15 million in 1986) from lives of dire poverty and was found by a comprehensive study by the Census Bureau in 1988 to be the most effective of all anti-poverty programs.[29]

Medicare and Medicaid

Federally funded health insurance for the elderly, better known as **Medicare**, was the result of a long political struggle for national health insurance that began in the 1920s. This movement intensified in the 1930s, receded in the post Second World War and Cold War periods, when national health insurance was linked by its opponents to socialism and communism (although President Harry S. Truman supported it), and was revived in the 1960s by Presidents John F. Kennedy and Lyndon B. Johnson.

Social reformers had long pointed out that the United States lagged behind other countries. Germany adopted national health insurance in 1883, the United Kingdom in 1911, France in 1928, and by 1962, at least seventy-seven countries had some type of publicly funded health insurance.[30] The concept of national health insurance was vigorously fought by the American Medical Association (A.M.A.) beginning in 1920 when it was first seriously discussed by American social reformers.[31] In fact, until early 1935, the A.M.A. was completely opposed even to *private* health insurance.[32]

When it became clear by the late 1940s and early 1950s that it was politically impossible to enact national health insurance for the entire nation, supporters of health insurance began advocating national health insurance for the elderly as part of Social Security. Various bills were introduced in Congress including one in the Senate co-sponsored by then Senator John F. Kennedy from Massachusetts. The Eisenhower administration, conservative groups, and, in particular, the A.M.A. vigorously opposed this legislation as, in the words of President Eisenhower, "a very definite step in socialized

---

[29]*New York Times*, December 28, 1988, p. 1.

[30]Herman M. Somers and Anne R. Somers, *Doctors, Patients, and Health Insurance* (Washington, D.C.: The Brookings Institution, 1961), p. 224

[31]Odin W. Anderson, "Compulsory Medical Care Insurance, 1910-1950," *Annals of the American Academy of Political and Social Science* (January, 1951), p. 108.

[32]Edwin C. Witte, *The Development of the Social Security Act* (Madison, Wisconsin: University of Wisconsin Press, 1962), p. 183.

medicine."[33] With the election of John F. Kennedy in 1960, what came to be known as "Medicare" had a forceful advocate in the White House. The political battle intensified, but it was not until 1965, when Lyndon Johnson (another strong supporter of Medicare) occupied the White House, that Medicare was enacted and signed into law.

The Medicare program consists of two forms of insurance. The first is compulsory hospital insurance for those sixty-five years and older. Those who are retired pay premiums which are deducted from their Social Security benefits. Those who are still working have their premiums withheld by their employers and sent to the federal government. This is known as Part A of the Medicare program. Hospitals or comparable facilities are directly paid by the federal government for the services covered under the program. Close to 32 million people are currently enrolled in Medicare.

The second component of Medicare, Part B, is voluntary and provides insurance to cover the cost of physicians and other health care professionals. (Premiums are also paid for this coverage.) The government determines the reasonable fees for certain medical procedures and pays accordingly. Over 30 million people are enrolled in Part B.

In 1965, Congress also enacted **Medicaid** to provide medical care for poor people. Under Medicaid, the federal government finances health programs administered by the states. The elderly poor also benefit from Medicaid, which picks up the medical bills that Medicare does not cover. Over 20 million people receive Medicaid benefits.

It is only since the mid-1960s that the federal government has assumed so much responsibility for the health costs of Americans. Yet this is now a permanent feature of the welfare state and has achieved the same level of political importance in meeting pressing human needs as the original Social Security programs from the 1930s. In committing itself to financing medical care for so many Americans, the federal government does enormous social good. But these programs also create enormous problems with which policymakers and social reformers grapple.

The first problem is the enormous cost. The costs of medical care in the United States have steadily increased and in 1989 were expected to reach $590 billion. Between 1976 and 1989, the proportion of the gross national product spent by the nation on health care went from 8.5 percent to close to 12 percent. In 1987 alone, the federal government spent close to $80 billion in Medicare and over $25 billion in Medicaid. Exhibit 11.3 shows the rise of Medicare costs from 1970 to 1988. Some argue the costs may be too high in an era when most economists fear that massive federal budget deficits threaten the health of the American economy. In countries with nationalized health services for all citizens, hospitals are run by the government, and physicians and other health care workers are salaried government employees. These countries spend markedly less of their gross national prod-

---

[33]*Congressional Quarterly*, April 1, 1960, p. 588.

EXHIBIT 11.3	YEAR	NUMBER OF PARTICIPANTS	BENEFIT PAYMENTS
The Growth of Medicare, 1970–1988	1970	20,491,000	7 billion, 99 million $
	1975	24,959,000	15 billion, 588 million $
	1978	27,164,000	24 billion, 934 million $
	1979	27,859,000	29 billion, 331 million $
	1980	28,478,000	35 billion, 699 million $
	1981	29,010,000	43 billion, 455 million $
	1982	29,494,000	51 billion, 86 million $
	1983	30,026,000	57 billion, 443 million $
	1984	30,455,000	62 billion, 918 million $
	1985	31,083,000	70 billion, 527 million $
	1986	31,768,000	75 billion, 997 million $
	1987 over	32,000,000	close to 80 billion $
	1988 (est.)	33,000,000	86 billion, 900 million $

Source: *Statistical Abstract of the United States 1988*, p. 347. For 1987 estimates, *Congressional Quarterly*, November 28, 1987, p. 2934. For 1988 estimates, *Congressional Quarterly*, April 16, 1988, p. 1017.

uct on health care than the United States does. Great Britain, for example, spends some 6 percent of its gross national product on health care. (Western democracies that have national health services, including Britain, France, Sweden, Italy, Canada, and Australia, permit private hospitals and physicians in private practice for those who wish to purchase those services. But all citizens pay for the national health service through taxes.)

Second, because most health care facilities are not run by the federal government and most health care personnel remain in the private sector, the federal government has had to devise elaborate bureaucratic rules, regulations, and procedures to determine fair and reasonable costs for various medical services. The result has been a cumbersome, complex, and highly regulated system of medicine that must be administered by a large government bureaucracy.

Third, one result of a bureaucratized system in which billions of dollars changes hands is that unnecessary medical procedures are performed so that health providers can collect from the government. Some doctors have been known to adopt assembly-line tactics in treating Medicare patients to produce a high volume of financial reimbursements by the government. There have been instances of physicians and clinics billing the government for procedures or examinations never conducted. For example, in December 1987 it was revealed that a Miami-based medical center had defrauded the government of over $12 million. In February 1988, a study by the Department of Health and Human Services revealed that false Medicare claims submitted by hospitals cost the government more than $300 million each year.[34]

Fourth, there is the continuing problem of determining the quality of care provided to Medicare and Medicaid patients in the approximately 6,000 hospitals affiliated with Medicare and the close to 16,000 nursing homes in which Medicare and Medicaid patients are treated. The setting of standards and the policing of these facilities is a monumental task, particularly when private health-care facilities, including those run for profit, may have incentives to cut corners on medical care to the detriment of patients. Supervision of medical personnel presents even more difficult problems since the medical profession by tradition has insisted on policing itself.

Finally, there is the problem that despite the size and cost of Medicare and Medicaid, there are significant gaps in medical coverage. By 1987, some 17.5 percent of all Americans had *no* health insurance at all. Almost all of these people were the working poor whose employers did not provide health insurance and who could not afford it on their own. Within the Medicare system, costs for medical catastrophies were not covered until 1988 legislation. Catastrophic coverage provides for unlimited hospital stays and pays for certain out-of-pocket costs, including outpatient prescription drugs when those costs exceed a specified dollar amount in any given year. But there still remains a gap for Medicare patients who require long-term home care or custodial nursing home care, which is not covered by catastrophic insurance. These and other gaps in health coverage will continue to be issues as the battle for public policy continues in the White House, Congress, and by the activities of various interest groups.

Aid to the Needy

It is public policy in the United States that the poor shall receive help from government. There are two forms of public assistance to the poor. The first kind provides cash payments directly to those who fall below governmentally defined poverty levels. These are the programs that are popularly dubbed *welfare*. The second consists of non-cash assistance, called **in-kind benefits**, which consists of certain goods and services. Medicaid, or health care for the poor, is an example of an in-kind program of public assistance.

Money Payment Programs.   The major direct income programs for the needy are **Aid to Families with Dependent Children** (AFDC), **Supplemental Security Income** (SSI), Veterans' Pensions, and state and local government financed General Assistance. The underlying policy premise is

[34]See *New York Times*, December 16, 1987, p. A-21 about the Miami medical center and *New York Times*, February 11, 1988, p. 1, about the study that found false Medicare claims submitted by hospitals.

that the way to help people in need is to give them money so they can pay for the basic necessities of life. It should also be noted that four major social insurance programs that provide cash payments help prevent many people from becoming needy. These programs include Social Security, Unemployment Insurance, Workers' Compensation, and Veterans' Compensation.[35]

The most expensive, extensive, and controversial welfare program is *AFDC*. The program had its beginnings in various state programs established during the early twentieth century that provided some monetary assistance to widows and their children. The Social Security Act of 1935 contained a similar federal program. Over the years, the scope of the program expanded. By 1962, poor families with unemployed parents were covered. The federal government and the states together finance the program; it is administered at the state and local levels. The states have considerable discretion in determining who is eligible for AFDC and the amount of money a family is entitled to receive. As a consequence, there is wide variation from state to state. In 1985, the average monthly payment to a family ranged from $104 a month in Mississippi to $550 a month in Alaska. Within regions there also were variations; for example, in New England the average monthly payment ranged from $318 a month in New Hampshire to $450 a month in Connecticut.

AFDC has been charged with fostering a welfare dependency that extends from generation to generation. Critics argue that people become used to the idea that they do not have to work for a living and that children on welfare are raised with this belief. Opponents maintain that the programs have encouraged working fathers to desert their wives and children so that their families continue to receive welfare benefits. They also assert that because the more children a woman has the more welfare she receives, poor women are given an incentive to have large families.

The evidence reveals that these claims are either false or highly exaggerated. Half of all AFDC clients remain in the program for a relatively short time, under two years.[36] There *are* a substantial number of families whose average stay on welfare is over ten years. But there is no conclusive evidence that long-term AFDC clients would rather receive government handouts than be gainfully employed at a living wage. Similarly, the charge that the AFDC program encourages fathers whose jobs are low-paying to leave their families so that their wives and children can receive AFDC benefits is not much supported by the evidence.[37] Likewise, there is little evidence to support the charge that unmarried women have more children in order to increase their AFDC payments.[38]

---

[35]The discussion that follows draws heavily from Morris and Williamson, *op. cit.*, chap. 3. Also see Robert X. Browning, *Politics and Social Welfare Policy in the United States* (Knoxville: University of Tennessee Press, 1986).

[36]Morris and Williamson, *op cit.*, p. 56.

[37]*Ibid.*, pp. 58–60.

The AFDC program served 3.7 million families and a total of 11 million people in 1985 at a cost to the federal government of $7.9 billion (the cost to the states was also close to that amount). The Inspector General of the Department of Health and Human Services issued a report in December 1987 claiming that AFDC "fraud" cost the federal government as much as $1 billion in 1985. Eighty percent of the so-called fraud (the Inspector General included as fraud "unintentional misrepresentations of facts by clients" as well as deliberate misrepresentation) occurred with the initial applications for AFDC benefits, and the remainder occurred with the failure to remove from AFDC those whose circumstances changed, thus rendering them ineligible.[39] This report was issued less than two weeks before the House of Representatives narrowly approved a major welfare reform package designed to provide cash family support supplements and require state and local education, job training, and child care programs to enable welfare recipients to become permanently employed and eventually self-sufficient. Six months later the Senate enacted its own bill which was eventually reconciled with the House measure.[40] On October 13, 1988, President Reagan signed into law the new legislation known as the Family Support Act of 1988. The new welfare policy is that in exchange for cash assistance, ablebodied mothers and fathers must participate in job training programs. Child care and medical coverage are provided to enable the parents to train for jobs and to become fully employed.

The *SSI* program provides cash income to needy persons who are elderly but not otherwise covered by Social Security and to needy individuals who are permanently and totally disabled or blind. The federal government finances and administers SSI so that eligibility and cash benefits are standardized throughout the country. SSI provides a guaranteed annual income and SSI recipients, unlike AFDC clients, receive automatic cost-of-living increases. Over four million people receive SSI, and the majority are disabled.

The *Veterans' Pensions* program dates back to 1933 and covers needy wartime veterans who are at least sixty-five years of age or who are permanently and totally disabled, but not from injuries associated with their military service. Survivors of these disabled veterans also are eligible to receive benefits. These pensions are automatically adjusted to reflect cost-of-living increases and are paid for by the federal government and are now administered by the Department of Veterans Affairs.

State and local governments are responsible for *General Assistance* programs, which are supposed to fill in the gaps left by other programs. These programs differ from state to state, the number of people covered is relatively small (for example, 1.3 million in 1983), and the benefit levels tend to be low.[41]

---

[39]*New York Times*, December 7, 1987, p. A-25.

[40]For details of the House bill, see *Congressional Quarterly*, December 19, 1987, pp. 3160–65; for the Senate bill, see *Congressional Quarterly*, June 25, 1988, pp. 1764–69; for the bill that was finally enacted see *Congressional Quarterly*, October 8, 1988, pp. 2825–31.

[41]Morris and Williamson, *op. cit.*, pp. 74–75.

In-Kind Benefits.   Noncash benefits to the poor have increased markedly since 1965. By one accounting, the market value of goods and services
or in-kind benefits to the needy increased 800 percent from 1965 to 1984 as
compared to only a 56 percent increase in cash assistance programs during
that same time period.[42]

Cash benefits programs have as their basic policy assumption that what
poor people lack is money. Advocates of this policy approach argue that
government should give the poor enough money to meet their basic needs.
The in-kind benefits programs reflect a different policy view of how the
needy should be helped. This has caused some controversy.[43] Critics charge
that in-kind benefits deny the poor responsibility for managing their resources according to their own preferences. The Food Stamp Program, for
example, requires the poor to spend that benefit exclusively on the purchase of food rather than for clothing or household appliances. Critics also
argue that the in-kind benefits approach is paternalistic and assumes that
government knows best what the poor need. Critics further point out that it
is less economically efficient to provide in-kind benefits than direct cash
payments. In-kind programs require a complex bureaucratic structure that
is duplicated by different governmental agencies which administer the different in-kind programs. There is no coherent, unified policy. It is addition-
ally charged that there is a stigma attached to in-kind benefits. The individual who pays the supermarket bill with food stamps is immediately
identified as a welfare recipient. Cash customers are not.

Supporters of in-kind programs argue that it would be politically impossible to provide the poor with an equivalent dollar value of the in-kind benefits. Imagine the public outcry if a welfare family were to receive a monthly
check for $1500 even if that were the only governmental assistance provid-
ed. As a result, the poor would be worse off if in-kind benefit programs were
replaced by only cash assistance. Supporters point out that the public is not
enthusiastic about cash assistance welfare programs. This lack of enthusiasm is fueled by such reports as the one mentioned earlier of widespread
fraud adding up to billions of dollars over the years. By contrast, the in-kind
benefit programs have a more benign image (who can oppose giving food to
the hungry, shelter for the homeless, medical care for the sick?).

In-kind programs are supported politically by the suppliers of the goods
and services who are more effective lobbyists than are poor people. There
is also a bureaucratic vested interest at all levels of government in maintaining in-kind programs. The various government agencies that administer
in-kind programs would have to scale down their operations considerably
and employ far fewer workers if the in-kind programs stopped. Members of
Congress serving on the separate congressional committees and subcommittees that oversee and legislate these in-kind programs typically are sym-

[42]*Ibid.*, p. 91.
[43]The discussion in this and the next paragraphs draws heavily on *ibid.*, pp. 91–94.

**Food stamp client
using food stamps
on a shopping trip.**

pathetic to them. Supporters argue that in-kind food, housing, and medical benefits provide for a higher standard of living than would be obtained if cash payments were the only form of assistance. This is so because the poor may not be able to make the wisest purchasing choices in obtaining goods and services. Also the costs of these goods and services vary at different times and in different parts of the country. In-kind benefits hold out the promise that the poor will receive the essentials of life regardless of their cost.

The *Food Stamp Program*, as suggested earlier, is one of the major in-kind food programs for the needy. Although the program had its beginnings in 1939 during the Roosevelt administration, its modern form begins with the Kennedy and Johnson administrations of the 1960s. The Food Stamp Act became law in 1964 and the program was expanded in 1971 and 1974 during the Nixon administration. Food stamp allotments are determined in part by the amounts of cash payments under different state welfare programs. In states with less generous welfare benefits, the food stamp allotment is proportionately greater than in states with more generous welfare payments. In 1986, over nineteen million people received food stamps. The program spent over $10 billion.[44]

Another government food program is the *National School Lunch Program* which dates back to 1946. The federal government subsidizes this pro-

[44]*Statistical Abstract 1988, op. cit.*, p. 355.

gram in which private and public schools from nursery school through high school may participate. Needy children receive free lunches, the less needy pay reduced prices, and those not in need pay full price, although full price costs less than what can be bought in restaurants. Close to 24 million needy children were fed in 1986. This program reflects the policy that government ought to provide poor children with at least one nutritious meal a day. *Medicaid*, as discussed earlier, is the principal in-kind benefit program that pays for health care of the needy.

The oldest form of housing benefit (starting in 1937) is *federal public housing*.[45] The Housing Act of 1949 redirected this benefit to the neediest households. Under this program the federal government financed massive housing projects primarily located in urban areas. These projects eventually turned into slums and as a consequence little new public housing of this sort has been constructed over the past several decades.

Most in-kind housing benefits are directed through the Section 8 Existing Housing and Moderate Rehabilitation Program. Under this program, eligible participants receive a housing subsidy which makes up the difference between the rent paid (assuming that the rent meets the fair market value standard set by the Department of Housing and Urban Development for the locality) and thirty percent of the entire monthly income of the household. Housing shortages in many parts of the country and extremely high rents in some major urban areas have placed major strains on federal, state, and local agencies servicing the poor. In many places, poor people simply cannot find places to live on the rent subsidies they get. Poor families in cities like New York now often are housed in welfare hotels that are unsafe, crowded, festering with drugs, and dangerous for children. Rents, paid for by AFDC, may be $1500 a month or even more. The lack of coordination between the housing subsidy programs administered by the Department of Housing and Urban Development and the emergency housing assistance program of AFDC has been the subject of criticism.[46]

It should also be pointed out that there are numerous homeless individuals, some with severe emotional or psychiatric disorders, and some who are runaway or throwaway children, who do not come under the public assistance umbrella. They provide a continuing challenge for a society that aspires to be humane and progressive. Does a person have a civil right to sleep on park benches and live on the streets if that person so wishes? Should government forcibly remove these individuals from the streets and place them in shelters? Should government impose medical care on these people? These questions of public policy concerning the homeless have no simple answers.

---

[45]See the discussion in Morris and Williamson, *op. cit.,* pp. 112–21.
[46]See, for example, Sandra J. Newman and Ann B. Schnare, "Housing and Welfare: A Logical Link," *New York Times,* January 5, 1988, p. A-19.

There is also a public policy problem concerning the working poor who have been cut off from some programs in an effort to reduce the deficit.[47] There is considerable debate in the public arena over what standard of living should be guaranteed by the government.

The ongoing concern with deficits, repeated battles over the budgets, and conflicting priorities in the realm of public policy suggest that social welfare programs—their substance, their scope, and their costs—will continue to be a source of controversy.

Domestic policy encompasses a wide variety of policies and comes about through the workings of American politics. Policy is made directly when new programs or new rules and regulations are created. However, policy is also made within the context of budget decision making, and policy can be made or unmade at the implementation stage. Although the president and Congress often play the principal role in the realm of regulatory, economic, and social welfare policy, such domestic policy is made by all levels of government and by all branches.

CHECKLIST FOR REVIEW	content

CHECKLIST FOR REVIEW

1. Domestic policy emerges from the political process and can take several forms. It can be regulatory, distributive (benefits for certain groups of people), redistributive (taxing the well-off to pay for programs for the less well-off), or symbolic (when no material benefits are involved). All forms of policy have important political implications and consequences.

2. Public policy does not emerge spontaneously. First, there must be an issue. Then the transformation of issues to governmental policies involves a series of interactions between private individuals and groups and public officials at all levels and in all branches of government. It is also important to recognize that policy-making occurs within an economic, cultural, political, and institutional context.

3. The federal budget process is central in the making of domestic policy. There are inextricable links between budget decisions and domestic policy-making. The budget process in Congress, with its many committees and subcommittees, is in many respects cumbersome, inefficient, fragmented, and out of control. However, because budget-making *is* policy-making, it is no surprise to find that a party system that on many matters has been polarized produces a continuing series of prolonged battles over the budget.

4. Once domestic public policy is created, it does not necessarily follow that it will be successfully implemented. Six factors appear to be associ-

[47]According to 1986 Census Bureau statistics, two million full-time, year-round workers were poor. So were an additional 6.9 million individuals who worked less than full-time or who were employed full time for only part of the year. These figures and the trends concerning the working poor during the Reagan administration are reported in Robert Pear, "Increasingly, Those Who Have Jobs Are Poor, Too," *New York Times*, December 27, 1987, p. E-5.

ated with implementation. They include: (1) the clarity of the goals of the policy; (2) the extent to which the bureaucracy charged with carrying out the policy is committed to it; (3) the resources and authority available to the administrative units responsible for implementation; (4) the extent of cooperation among governmental units that is necessary to achieve implementation and the degree to which such cooperation is attained; (5) the extent to which the beneficiaries or the clients of the program understand and share the program's goals; and (6) the extent to which policy evaluation and subsequent program adjustment is made.

5. Social welfare policies demonstrate the complexity of policy-making and the problems of implementation. The major entitlement programs—Social Security, Medicare, and Medicaid—have had their problems as well as their successes. Aid to the needy is no different. The more prominent money payment programs include AFDC, SSI, and Veterans' Pensions. More popular, however, are in-kind benefits providing food (for example, the Food Stamp Program), medical care (such as Medicaid), and housing. There is some controversy over the plight of the working poor and the fact that some of their essential needs are unmet. A different policy problem surrounds the homeless, many of whom do not seek government help.

KEY TERMS

public policy
public interest groups
legislative veto
uncontrollable expenditures
entitlement programs
controllable expenditures
fiscal year

Medicare
Medicaid
in-kind benefits
Aid to Families with Dependant Children (AFDC)
Supplemental Security Income (SSI)

CHAPTER TWELVE

Civil Liberties

I magine what life would be like in the United States if it became a crime to oppose the policies of the president of the United States. How would you feel living in a country that told you that you must live and work where the government tells you? Would you be happy living in a country that forbade you to leave it? What would be your reaction if the government said that you could only worship the official state religion? Can you imagine what it would be like if the police could break into your home and search through your belongings at any time for any or no reason? Would it not be a nightmare if you were falsely accused of a crime, denied a lawyer, given no opportunity to confront the witnesses against you, given a poor excuse for a trial, and sentenced to twenty-five years of hard labor in the state penitentiary?

It *is* difficult for us to picture ourselves without civil liberties because our Constitution and our traditions tell us that we are indeed the land of the free. In 1991 we celebrate the bicentennial of the ratification of the Bill of Rights and congratulate ourselves that we are a free people. Yet the issues involved in civil liberties policy-making are complex and our institutions of government have not always been sensitive to the value of freedom when other values such as social order and national security have been involved. In particular, the decisions of the United States Supreme Court, the ultimate policymaker of just what constitutional rights Americans have, have not always been sensitive to claims of freedom.

The term *civil liberties* refers to two types of rights. First are the basic human freedoms that are associated with the condition of being free from governmental restraint. These include, as suggested earlier, the freedom to write, to talk, to criticize, to publish, to worship, to associate, to travel, to live and work where we want, to petition government, to try to persuade others, to organize, to run for public office, to have privacy in our home and in our person, and to make essential lifestyle decisions for ourselves. To enjoy such civil liberties means that we are free to engage in these activities without governmental restraints except those that are minimally necessary to prevent grave, immediate, widely recognized societal harm or those restraints minimally necessary to permit the orderly exercise of those freedoms by all members of society. These rights are **substantive rights.**

The second type of civil liberties are the **procedural rights** that we have when government seeks to deny us our liberty, property, or even our lives. These procedural guarantees are also known as *due process rights*. They include the rights to receive a fair and public hearing or trial, to be represented by a lawyer, to confront witnesses against us, not to be forced to incriminate ourselves, not to be subject to unreasonable searches and seizures, to have evidence obtained illegally excluded from trials, and to appeal unfavorable trial court rulings.

Both types of rights are guaranteed either explicitly or implicitly in state constitutions and in the federal Constitution, particularly the Bill of Rights and the Fourteenth Amendment. Within the Fifth and Fourteenth

Amendments is the guarantee that life, liberty, and property may not be denied without due process of law (this is the *due process clause*). This guarantee, found in both Amendments, protects *both* procedural and substantive rights.

Substantive rights are protected from state violation because the Supreme Court starting about a century ago chose to interpret the due process clause of the Fourteenth Amendment as incorporating certain specific rights as part of the liberty that cannot be denied without due process (such rights are known as **incorporated rights**). The Court began establishing the concept that statutes that infringed on such rights were inherently so unjust as to be a denial of liberty without due process of law no matter what procedures were specified in the law. This is the concept of **substantive due process** (that is, the due process clause is used to protect substantive rights). The Court first incorporated economic rights, but beginning in 1925 began to incorporate civil liberties.

This chapter first reviews the nature of Supreme Court policy-making and looks generally at the complexity of civil liberties issues. Attention then is given to civil liberties policy-making concerning freedoms of speech and press, the religion guarantees, various criminal procedural rights, and other civil liberties such as the right to privacy. The chapter concludes with an evaluation of the status and future of civil liberties.

THE COMPLEXITY OF CIVIL LIBERTIES

As noted in Chapter Ten, justices of the Supreme Court have a great deal of discretion. They must give meaning in specific cases to the Constitution's broadly phrased guarantees respecting due process of law, liberty, equal protection, freedom from an establishment of religion, freedom of speech and press, and so on. This means that the justices frequently must choose which precedent is applicable and how best to apply it, what interpretation of the constitutional provision at issue is valid, and how the statute or governmental action should be interpreted. The exercise of judicial discretion is the exercise of judicial power.

In exercising discretion, the justices inevitably promote certain values. These values may be associated with a judicial philosophy that, for example, views the judiciary as an active promoter of civil liberties or, conversely, a philosophy of judicial restraint and deference to the policies of democratic majorities. But whatever values individual justices may further through discretion, the decisions of the Court amount to policy-making. To be sure, criminal law and the workings of the justice system are traditional areas of court policy-making. But the Supreme Court has been active in policy-making in a wide variety of other civil liberties policy areas.

It seems so straightforward to say that Americans have the freedom to speak, publish, practice their religion, have a right to privacy, and a right to be protected against unreasonable searches and seizures. But issues of civil

"Oh, yeah? Well, I just happen to have a copy of the Bill of Rights with me." (Drawing by Charles Barsotti; ® 1981 The New Yorker Magazine)

liberties are usually complex. There are usually at least two sides to an issue. It is rare for there not to be competing values. For example, the argument that a woman has a right to determine whether or not to abort a fetus early in her pregnancy is countered by the argument that the fetus itself has a right to life. The publisher of a sex magazine who claims freedom of the press is challenged by the claim that sexual exploitation of women is a social evil that deserves no constitutional protection. The right of an accused to have evidence excluded from the trial if it was illegally obtained faces the competing right of society to punish those who are clearly guilty.

Not only are civil liberties issues complex, they are also among the most controversial issues in American politics. George Bush, running for president in 1988, favored the death penalty and specifically advocated its use for big-time drug dealers. His Democratic opponent, Michael Dukakis, opposed any use of the death penalty. Bush opposed liberal Supreme Court policies concerning criminal procedures such as the exclusionary rule; Dukakis disagreed. Bush opposed the Court's abortion policy and its policy forbidding prayer in the public schools; Dukakis did not.

The political attention that the Court's decisions generate is probably not lost on the justices. For example, in 1984, the Court allowed Pawtucket, Rhode Island, to sponsor a creche as part of the city's annual Christmas display. But that decision can also be viewed as an attempt to deflect criticism the Court continued to receive from its 1963 decision outlawing prayers in the public schools. It must be recognized that the Court always balances the competing interests and values inherent in the civil liberties disputes before it, but the Opinion of the Court may not necessarily reveal the strength of the losing claim. This does not mean, however, that such cases were easily decided. The nature of civil liberties issues is such that often their complexity and, at times, the politically charged controversy they generate ensure that most justices will not have an easy time finding constitutional solutions. This is amply demonstrated by the freedoms discussed in this chapter.

■ FREEDOMS OF SPEECH AND PRESS

The First Amendment to the Constitution guarantees freedom of speech and press against federal governmental restraints on the communication of spoken or written accounts, ideas, or views. In 1925, the Supreme Court agreed that these guarantees were part of the "liberty" that no state can deny without due process of law as specified in the Fourteenth Amendment. In other words, the Court incorporated freedom of speech and press as part of the substantive rights protected by due process. Thus, by the end of the third decade of the twentieth century, the states, too, were told they could not abridge fundamental First Amendment speech and press rights.

The justification for the guarantees of speech and press often rests on the marketplace analogy. A free society allows all ideas, like all businesses, to operate in the marketplace. In the competition of ideas, the good ideas will win favor and the bad ideas will be rejected. Truth will emerge from the competition, and society will be all the better for it. A free and open society will allow all members of that society to achieve their full potential and lead meaningful lives and this is surely the highest ethical good. An open society will ultimately reject the merchants of hate.

The marketplace concept is often associated with the concept of *pure tolerance*, whereby all ideas are entitled to be aired and their communication protected by government if need be. Those who argue for pure tolerance of freedom of speech and press recognize no difference in principle in protecting the right of the Democratic or Republican candidates for president to speak about the American Dream and the right of the Grand Dragon of the racist Ku Klux Klan to speak in favor of racial segregation. *All* speeches and speakers are equal under the law. The proponents of pure tolerance, such as the American Civil Liberties Union (A.C.L.U.), argue that it is better to protect *all* speech than to allow government censors to restrict *some* speech. In the words of Ira Glasser, the Executive Director of the A.C.L.U., "while today it might be the Nazis that are considered offensive, tomorrow it might be what I have to say, or what you have to say."[1]

Critics of the marketplace analogy point out that not all businesses are in fact permitted in the marketplace. For example, government does not allow into the marketplace businesses that sell marijuana, cocaine, or heroin and businesses that sell the services of children, women, and men for purposes of prostitution. Likewise, they argue, certain ideas should be con-

---

[1]As quoted in the *New York Times*, October 2, 1988, p. 26.

sidered so vile, contemptible, and socially harmful as to justify government's banning of them.

The reality of freedom of speech today and in the past is not pure tolerance. There never was and still is not an absolute, totally unregulated right of freedom of speech and press. There are many different types of speech and many issues surrounding them.

Political Speech

The First Amendment became part of the Constitution in 1791, but serious question as to its ability to protect political speech arose just seven years later when Congress enacted the **Alien and Sedition Acts**. This legislation was designed to curb the political opponents of President John Adams, whose party, the Federalists, controlled Congress. The law made it a federal crime to criticize the president or Congress with the intent of bringing either into "disrepute." Newspaper editors who supported the opposition, led by Thomas Jefferson, were prosecuted. But no one appealed to the Supreme Court because several Supreme Court justices in their capacity as trial judges had presided over Sedition Act convictions and had refused to entertain the argument that the Sedition Act violated the First Amendment guarantee of freedom of speech and press.

Not until the Civil War was the federal government again involved in limiting speech and press. But now the stakes were the highest, the survival of the nation, and the complexity of civil liberties was dramatically demonstrated. President Lincoln suspended the writ of habeas corpus and administration policy was to imprison those suspected of disloyal or treasonous acts and vocal opponents of the war. The government seemed to suggest that freedom of speech was a luxury the nation could not afford during wartime. In one instance when it could have ruled on the policy, the Supreme Court decided that it had no jurisdiction to hear the appeal because it came from a military court.[2] After the Civil War was over, however, the Court ruled that military courts could not try civilians as long as the civilian courts were open and functioning, but the Court did not take the opportunity to consider the freedom of speech implications of the government's actions during the war.[3]

It was another major war, World War I, that once again brought the actions of the federal government into conflict with the First Amendment. The *Espionage Act of 1917* made it a federal crime to interfere with military recruitment or the draft or to affect adversely military morale. Once again the value of freedom of speech collided with the value of national security. Under this law, the General Secretary of the Socialist party was convicted for publishing and distributing anti-war and anti-draft leaflets. The law and

[2]*Ex Parte Vallandigham* (1864).
[3]*Ex parte Milligan* (1866).

conviction were upheld by the Supreme Court in 1919 in *Schenck* v. *United States*. In this decision, Justice Oliver Wendell Holmes proposed a new policy, known as the **clear and present danger test**, to determine whether governmental restraint on speaking and writing is justified. The standard he proposed is that the government can invade our fundamental First Amendment rights only when speech and press pose an immediate danger of bringing about a substantive evil that government has an obligation to prevent. In this particular case, said Holmes, the nation was at war and the General Secretary's activities posed an immediate danger to the war effort. During peacetime, Holmes observed, such activities would not be dangerous.

The *Sedition Act of 1918* made it a federal crime to speak in "disloyal, profane, scurrilous or abusive language about the form of government, the Constitution, soldiers and sailors, flag or uniform of the armed forces." It was also a crime to speak favorably of the German Empire. The Justice Department vigorously enforced both the 1917 and 1918 laws and brought over 1500 prosecutions under them.[4] In 1919, the Supreme Court upheld the Sedition Act in *Abrams* v. *United States*.[5] Justice Holmes dissented and found no clear and present danger that justified such a violation of freedom of speech and press. Holmes' dissent is also a classic defense of freedom of speech and press using the marketplace analogy (see the box on page 466).

After the war was over, the Justice Department continued its campaign against radicals. The campaign reached its climax on New Year's Day of 1920 with mass arrests. President Wilson was seriously incapacitated and was unable to restrain these clear violations of constitutional rights. But the Attorney General thought that national security justified the abridgement of constitutional guarantees because these radicals wanted to overthrow the government and did not care about the Constitution. National security, protection against terrorists, prevention of espionage, and the war against drugs are some of the rationales used by those who support measures that conflict with constitutional guarantees. But the complexity of civil liberties issues is seen if violating our freedoms actually *would* make the nation more secure from those pushing for a different political and economic system as well as from terrorists, subversives, spies, drug dealers, and so on. Should we sacrifice our freedoms to be saved from these evils?

During the period between the world wars, the value of political speech gained momentum from Supreme Court decisions involving the states. At first the Court moved slowly, but it nonetheless incorporated freedoms of speech and press as part of the liberty the states must honor. The pace of protecting political speech quickened after 1937, when the Supreme Court elevated First Amendment freedoms to a position worthy of special protec-

[4]Richard Hofstadter, William Miller, and Daniel Aaron, *The United States: The History of a Republic* (Englewood Cliffs, N.J.: Prentice-Hall, 1957), p. 618.
[5]The story of the Abrams case is recounted in Richard Polenberg, *Fighting Faiths: The Abrams Case, the Supreme Court, and Free Speech* (New York: Viking, 1988).

Justice Holmes in Abrams v. United States (1919)

Mr. Justice Holmes dissenting: . . . .

I do not doubt for a moment that . . . the United States constitutionally may punish speech that produces or is intended to produce a clear and imminent danger that it will bring about forthwith certain substantive evils that the United States constitutionally may seek to prevent. The power undoubtedly is greater in time of war than in time of peace because war opens dangers that do not exist at other times.

But as against dangers peculiar to war, as against others, the principle of the right to free speech is always the same. It is only the present danger of immediate evil or an intent to bring it about that warrants Congress in setting a limit to the expression of opinion where private rights are not concerned. Congress certainly cannot forbid all effort to change the mind of the country. Now nobody can suppose that the surreptitious publishing of a silly leaflet by an unknown man, without more, would present any immediate danger that its opinions would hinder the success of the government arms or have any appreciable tendency to do so . . .

In this case sentences of twenty years imprisonment have been imposed for the publishing of two leaflets that I believe the defendants had as much right to publish as the Government has to publish the Constitution of the United States now vainly invoked by them. Even if I am technically wrong and enough can be squeezed from these poor and puny anonymities to turn the color of legal litmus paper; I will add, even if what I think the necessary intent were shown; the most nominal punishment seems to me all that possibly could be inflicted, unless the defendants are to be made to suffer not for what the indictment alleges but for the creed that they avow—a creed that I believe to be the creed of ignorance and immaturity when honestly held, as I see no reason to doubt that it was held here, but which, although made the subject of examination at the trial, no one has a right even to consider in dealing with the charges before the Court.

Persecution for the expression of opinions seems to me perfectly logical. If you have no doubt of your premises or your power and want a certain result with all your heart you naturally express your wishes in law and sweep away all opposition. To allow opposition by speech seems to indicate that you think the speech impotent, as when a man says that he has squared the circle, or that you do not care whole-heartedly for the result, or that you doubt either your power or your premises. But when men have realized that time has upset many fighting faiths, they may come to believe even more than they believe the very foundations of their own conduct that the ultimate good desired is better reached by free trade in ideas—that the best test of truth is the power of the thought to get itself accepted in the competition of the market, and that truth is the only ground upon which their wishes safely can be carried out. That at any rate is the theory of our Constitution. It is an experiment, as all life is an experiment. Every year if not every day we have to wager our salvation upon some prophecy based upon imperfect knowledge. While that experiment is part of our system I think that we should be eternally vigilant against attempts to check the expression of opinions that we loathe and believe to be fraught with death, unless they so imminently threaten immediate interference with the lawful and pressing purposes of the law that an immediate check is required to save the country. . . .

tion by the courts. This became known as the **preferred position doctrine**, the idea that First Amendment freedoms were placed by the framers at the head of the Bill of Rights to signify their crucial importance in a free society. Political free speech was upheld in one decision after another. The Court ruled that the right to peacefully picket was protected by the First Amendment. The clear and present danger test was used positively in 1937 to protect the political free speech rights of an African-American Commun-

Communist leader
Eugene Dennis
(second from right)
handcuffed with
fellow Communist
leader Benjamin
Davis, Jr., are led
away to begin their
sentences after the
Supreme Court
affirmed their
convictions in
Dennis v. *United
States*.

ist who believed that blacks should secede from the nation and form their own republic. In some cases, the Court did not accept free speech claims, but the tide of the Court's policy-making unmistakably had shifted.

Another war, however, was on the horizon, and Congress again made certain forms of political speech a crime. *The Alien Registration Act of 1940* or *the Smith Act* (named after its congressman sponsor) made it a federal crime knowingly to advocate, advise, teach, print, or distribute written material advocating, or knowingly to become a member of a group advocating, the overthrow or destruction by force and violence of any government in the United States. Conspiring to do any of these forbidden activities was also illegal. This legislation would not come before the Supreme Court until 1951 in the case of *Dennis* v. *United States*.

After World War II, the Soviet Union became the principal adversary of the West and through its vast espionage network stole secret information that enabled it to quickly develop nuclear weapons. Political free speech in the United States was seriously jeopardized by the onset of the Cold War and the growing anticommunist hysteria that reached fever pitch in the early 1950s. Within this context the Supreme Court had to decide the constitutionality of Smith Act convictions in the *Dennis* case. Eleven top Communist party leaders had been convicted of advocating and teaching (and conspiring to do so) the communist doctrine of the necessity of violent overthrow of the government in order to establish a communist dictatorship of the proletariat. They were not charged with having committed or even having conspired to commit any overt acts to bring about their communist utopia. They were theorists, not terrorists. But in 1951 the Supreme Court upheld their convictions. In so doing, for the first time in fourteen years, the Court used the clear and present danger standard to limit free speech. It did this by reinterpreting the test to discount the probable immediacy of the danger and to emphasize the seriousness of the evil. The majority seemed to suggest that these communist leaders could not be treated as harmless eccentrics when communism was a stark reality in the Soviet Union, Eastern Europe, and China, and nuclear secrets were stolen by communist spies in the United States.

In the early to mid-1950s, one of the main leaders of the anticommunist crusade in the United States was Senator Joseph McCarthy. He conducted investigations and his tactics included smearing the reputations of individuals by lies and innuendoes, bullying those called before his committee, and leaking false and damaging stories about individuals and government agencies including the State Department, which he portrayed as a hotbed of communist sympathizers. The Senator's tactics added a new word to the vocabulary of American politics—*McCarthyism*. But McCarthy overreached himself and falsely accused the United States Army of harboring communist sympathizers. Once McCarthy was discredited and gone from the scene, the Supreme Court, now under the chief justiceship of Earl Warren, became more sympathetic to political speech and the rights of dissenters. It even undermined, without reversing, the *Dennis* decision. Several federal and state statutes aimed at punishing Communists for their political beliefs were either struck down in whole or in part or moderated by Warren Court decisions. One of the last decisions of the Warren Court, *Brandenburg* v. *Ohio* (1969), resurrected the clear and present danger standard but with a new semantic cover. Political dissidents, under this precedent that is law today, cannot be punished for advocating illegal force and violence. They can only be punished for "incitement to imminent lawless action."

What is the status of political speech today? Courts are extremely liberal in allowing political speech as long as it is divorced from action. The pure toleration concept has been largely accepted in American constitutional law for such political speech. Political speech can only be regulated as to the time, place, and manner (such as the decibel level of loudspeakers), but not content. You have the right to hold a rally or a meeting on just about any political theme—abortion, apartheid, affirmative action, gay rights, and so forth. However, the Court in recent years has ruled conservatively on some peripheral issues of political speech. For example, the Court in 1972 and 1976 decided that the First Amendment does not operate in privately owned shopping malls. But in a later case it ruled that *states* are free to protect such speech under their own constitutions.[6]

Symbolic political speech has raised some provocative issues and has met with mixed reactions from the Court. The Warren Court defended the right of school children to wear black armbands in school to protest the Vietnam War. But that same Court upheld an act of Congress that made it a

[6]*PruneYard Shopping Center* v. *Robins* (1980).

crime for men of draft age to burn or otherwise mutilate or destroy their draft cards. The destruction of draft cards had been a popular way of symbolically protesting the war. The Rehnquist Court in 1989, however, ruled that the First Amendment protects the burning of the American flag in a peaceful political protest, thus invalidating the federal flag desecration law and similar state laws. But this decision provoked a move to overturn it with a constitutional amendment.

Artistic Free Expression

Political free expression is the basis of a democratic political order. That right is pushed to the limit by those who would deny political free expression to others or who promote bigotry and violence. Artistic free expression, on the other hand, touches other raw nerves of a culture, particularly in its representation of sexual behavior. At stake is not the debasing of the political system but the debasing of the society's ethics, morals, and culture.

Most large cities in the United States today have movie theaters that show hard-core pornography and video stores that rent hard-core videotapes. These films are generally characterized as sexual exploitation films and typically women are exploited as sex objects. The message of these films is that women are to be used for the pleasure of men. Women say "no" when they mean "yes." Women like to be treated rough. The natural order of life is for the male to dominate. While there is no clear-cut evidence that men who watch these movies or read magazines with similar content rush out and commit rape, such films and magazines clearly promote sexism and encourage promiscuity, and thus may indirectly share some responsibility for the spread of sexually transmitted diseases including AIDS. Do such films and magazines deserve to be protected by the First Amendment? Does society have a right to protect itself from the social harm these ideas cause?

As is typical with issues of civil liberties, the issues are complex. Some defenders of pornography argue that it depicts a vital part of human existence about which most people have an intense curiosity. Defenders argue that there is nothing wrong with having erotic fantasies and willingly exposing oneself to material that is a sexual turn-on. Sex therapists even see therapeutic value in some uses of pornography. Even if one believes that hard-core pornography serves no social purpose and may cause harm, civil libertarians argue that freedom of speech and press is meant to protect *all* ideas, no matter how repugnant they are. Defenders of the First Amendment argue that censorship raises many questions: What is the definition of obscenity? What representations of sex deserve to be suppressed? Who makes the decisions? Why should adult Americans be told what they can and cannot read, hear, and see? What makes films of explicit sex acts more reprehensible than films that glamorize violence, glorify war, and encourage racial hatred? If First Amendment freedoms are grounded on the concept of the marketplace of ideas, how can censorship of sexually oriented material be justified? The marketplace concept is based on faith in the ultimate good sense and intelligence of Americans to reject bad ideas, and the First Amendment is based on the premise that government has no business telling Americans what they may and may not think and believe.

Traditionally, however, obscenity was a crime and not considered an exercise of freedom of expression. The Supreme Court in 1957 explicitly ruled that obscenity is *not* protected by the First Amendment.[7] But the Court sought to define obscenity and in so doing gave some protection to sexually oriented material. Nevertheless, the Court found it difficult to be precise (try yourself to define obscenity in a way that distinguishes between legitimate artistic expression with a sexual content and hard-core pornography). By the mid-1960s, for a work of art, a book, a magazine, or motion picture to be adjudged "obscene," it had to be "utterly without redeeming social value," something quite difficult to show. The 1960s was a decade of massive social change and part of that change included a liberalization of artistic standards in the representation of sexual behavior and language. The strict privately enforced codes that once governed motion pictures were replaced by a rating system in which "R" rated films could have uncensored language, nudity, and simulated sex acts. Books no longer were self-censored or subject to prosecution, as written descriptions of sexual behavior met with what appeared to be absolute constitutional protection. Photographic representation of sex, although somewhat more troublesome, passed the muster of the Warren Court's looser standards.

To some people, artistic free expression had become altogether too free. In 1973, the Burger Court undertook to reverse the liberal policies on artistic free expression. It offered a new definition of obscenity in two key cases—*Miller* v. *California* and *Paris Adult Theatre* v. *Slaton*. Under the Court's new obscenity policy, local communities could impose their own standards of what representations of sex were patently offensive and appealed to a prurient interest in sex. State statutes were to be explicit and precise about the representations of sex to be considered "obscene." And the Court directed that no longer must the challenged work be *utterly* without redeeming social value. Instead, a work can be considered legally obscene if the work *as a whole* lacks artistic, literary, scientific, or political value. The Court's more permissive attitude toward the suppression of sexually oriented material has not resulted in a nationwide crackdown on the billion dollar pornography industry, but the legal tools are there if and when public opinion and government officials decide something should be done.

With the rise of the women's movement in the 1970s, the issue of artistic free expression assumed a new perspective. As suggested earlier, the hard-core sex industry has consistently degraded women's bodies, often equating sex and violence. Some civil libertarians have rethought their positions on censorship. They have sought to distinguish erotic, nonsexist ma-

[7]*Roth* v. *United States* (1957).

terial from exploitative, sexist, violent pornography. But defenders of the pure tolerance view of the First Amendment respond that censors cannot make such distinctions (one person's erotica is another's pornography). Furthermore, they emphasize that adults should be free to decide what they wish to read, see, or hear as long as they are not imposing their choices on others or otherwise impinging on others' rights.[8]

An additional complexity concerning artistic free expression is the issue of children's access to sexually oriented material and the protection of the rights of adults who do not want to be confronted with such material. This is relevant for the broadcast media (radio and television) as distinct from the print media, live theater, and motion pictures that are theatrically exhibited. Because children and adults can tune in and out of radio and television broadcasts, the airwaves are subject to certain content control in the realm of sex and language by the Federal Communications Commission. The Supreme Court has upheld this.

Another issue surrounding artistic free expression is the use of children as participants in sexually oriented materials. This is considered child abuse and several states have attempted to strike at what has been called the kiddie-porn industry. In 1982, the Court unanimously upheld a New York law which punished the distributors of sexually oriented materials that used children under the age of sixteen. Liberals and conservatives alike recognized that the curbing of sexual abuse of children overrides any incidental effect on First Amendment freedoms.[9]

Freedom of the Press

The right of the news media to publish or broadcast goes to the heart of an open, democratic society. Without a free and independent press, democracy cannot flourish. Total control of information and state control of the media are hallmarks of a totalitarian political system. Americans traditionally pride themselves on the freedoms they enjoy, particularly a free press. But the press in the United States has grown so powerful and influential, with control of the media in relatively few hands, that the press itself has become an issue in recent years. The power of the press is such that it is sometimes referred to as "the fourth branch" of government. What is the constitutional nature of the press' freedom, and how free is the press?

The First Amendment states unequivocally that Congress may not abridge freedom of the press. This guarantee has been interpreted by the Court to mean that only in extraordinary circumstances (such as in wartime, when a newspaper is about to publish top secret troop movements) may government literally stop the presses. The freedom to publish free

---

[8]For a full discussion of the women's movement and this issue see Donald A. Downs, *The New Politics of Pornography: The First Amendment's Encounter with a Dilemma* (Chicago: University of Chicago Press, 1989).

[9]*New York* v. *Ferber* (1982).

The first day of the publication of the Pentagon Papers.

ew York Times

NEW YORK, SUNDAY, JUNE 13, 1971

75¢ beyond 50-mile zone from New York City, except Long Island. Higher in air delivery cities.

Vietnam Archive: Pentagon Study Traces 3 Decades of Growing U. S. Involvement

By NEIL SHEEHAN

A massive study of how the United States went to war in Indochina, conducted by the Pentagon three years ago, demonstrates that four administrations progressively developed a sense of commitment to a non-Communist Vietnam, a readiness to fight the North to protect the South, and an ultimate frustration with this effort—to a much greater extent than their public statements acknowledged at the time.

The 3,000-page analysis, to which 4,000 pages of official documents are appended, was commissioned by Secretary of Defense Robert S. McNamara and covers the American involvement in Southeast Asia from World War II to mid-1968—the start of the peace talks in Paris after President Lyndon B. Johnson had set a limit on further military commitments and revealed his intention to retire. Most of the study and many of the appended documents have been obtained by The New York Times and will be described and presented in a series of articles beginning today.

> Three pages of documentary material from the Pentagon study begin on Page 35.

Though far from a complete history, even at 2.5 million words, the study forms a great archive of government decision-making on Indochina over three decades. The study led its 30 to 40 authors and researchers to many broad conclusions and specific findings, including the following:

¶That the Truman Administration's decision to give military aid to France in her colonial war against the Communist-led Vietminh "directly involved" the United States in Vietnam and "set" the course of American policy.

¶That the Eisenhower Administration's decision to rescue a fledgling South Vietnam from a Communist takeover and attempt to undermine the new Communist regime of North Vietnam gave the Administration a "direct role in the ultimate breakdown of the Geneva settlement" for Indochina in 1954.

¶That the Kennedy Administration, though ultimately spared from major escalation decisions by the death of its leader, transformed a policy of "limited-risk gamble," which it inherited, into a "broad commitment" that left President Johnson with a choice between more war and withdrawal.

¶That the Johnson Administration, though the President was reluctant and hesitant to take the final decisions, intensified the covert warfare against North Vietnam and began planning in the spring of 1964 to wage overt war, a full year before it publicly revealed the depth of its involvement and its fear of defeat.

¶That this campaign of growing clandestine military pressure through 1964 and the expanding program of bombing North Vietnam in 1965 were begun despite the judgment of the Government's intelligence community that the measures would not cause Hanoi to cease its support of the Vietcong insurgency in the South, and that the bombing was

Continued on Page 38, Col. 1

from censorship is almost, but not quite, absolute. There is a heavy burden on government to demonstrate that a story should not be published or a news program broadcast. The guarantee of freedom of the press is what the courts call the guarantee against **prior restraint** or stopping the press from publishing (censorship). But if the press publishes something and in so doing violates a law against, say, obscenity or libel, it is subject to what is known as **subsequent punishment**, that is, being brought before a court and tried for violating the law. The editor or publisher may, if found guilty, be heavily fined and/or sent to prison. But the presses may not be stopped.

This view of freedom of the press was articulated by Chief Justice Charles Evans Hughes in the landmark 1931 decision in *Near* v. *Minnesota*.[10] Forty years later, a series of events led to the Court's reaffirming *Near* v. *Minnesota*'s presumption against prior restraint in the Pentagon Papers case, known more formally as *New York Times Co.* v. *United States*. What happened was that a former Pentagon official gave the *New York Times* and

---

[10]For a full account of the events behind the *Near* case, see Fred W. Friendly, *Minnesota Rag* (New York: Random House, 1981).

the *Washington Post* copies of a classified forty-seven-volume study conducted by the Pentagon on how the United States became involved in the Vietnam War and what went wrong. The newspapers' top reporters read, digested, and prepared selections and summaries from what became known as the Pentagon Papers. The *Times* and *Post* began publishing their series in June of 1971 and the federal government quickly sought to stop publication, arguing that national security was jeopardized. The federal government's efforts, however, proved unsuccessful as the Court found that the government had not met the heavy burden of showing justification for the imposition of prior restraint.

Because the press is so important to an open society, shouldn't the press have special access to the institutions of government so it can report to the American people how their institutions are working and what policies and practices are being implemented in their name? Wouldn't this special access strengthen public debate over policy, alert government policymakers to problems, stimulate better alternatives, and strengthen the democratic process? These questions have come before the Supreme Court. But the Court has decided that the press has no *special* right of access to such governmental institutions as prisons and courts.[11] The Court has also decided that the First Amendment free press guarantee contains no presumption that the identities of news sources should remain confidential, even though without such confidentiality the ability of journalists to investigate and report the workings of American institutions may be seriously impaired. The Court has refused to recognize the right of a reporter to protect sources by withholding information from a grand jury. In one case involving a college newspaper, the Court held that if there is probable cause to believe the newspaper office contains evidence concerning the commission of a crime by third parties, law enforcement officials do not need subpoenas to get that evidence. They need only get a search warrant and search the newspaper office.[12] This decision outraged the nation's press and led to legislation prohibiting this practice.[13]

As difficult as it is to face complex issues concerning freedom of the press, it can be even more difficult to know what is right when freedom of the press is in direct conflict with another civil liberty, such as the right of an accused to a fair trial. For example, in 1966 the Supreme Court overturned a murder conviction on the ground that sensationalistic newspaper reporting made a fair trial impossible.[14] But the Court has not been sympathetic to lower court orders forbidding the press from publishing details of criminal cases. The Court eventually recognized that the public and the press have a First Amendment right to attend trials and pretrial criminal

[11]See *Houchins* v. *KQED* (1978) (prisons) and *Gannett Co., Inc.* v. *DePasquale* (1979) (courts).

[12]*Zurcher* v. *Stanford Daily* (1978).

[13]The statute, PL 96–440, passed Congress October 1, 1980. See *Congressional Quarterly Weekly Report*, October 4, 1980, p. 2897.

[14]*Sheppard* v. *Maxwell* (1966).

hearings. States may even permit broadcast coverage of criminal trials. The Court has emphasized that the burden of providing a fair trial falls on the judge, and can be accomplished without banning the press from the courtroom or censoring its reporting.

The First Amendment guarantees freedom of the press, but this freedom at the same time confers an obligation not to print or broadcast falsehoods that can damage the reputations of individuals or businesses. In other words, freedom of the press does not mean the right to **libel**. A publisher who is convicted of libel may have to pay money damages to the victim of libel both for the harm done and as a punishment. In 1964, however, the Warren Court in *New York Times Co.* v. *Sullivan* changed the law of libel concerning public figures. In order for a public figure to win a libel suit, that individual must prove that not only was a falsehood published or broadcast, but that the newspaper or broadcast station *knew* it to be false when it published or broadcast the falsehood or showed reckless disregard for whether it was true or false.[15] This is known as **actual malice**. The Burger Court in several rulings emphasized that private individuals, including convicted criminals, are not public figures and therefore *can* sue for libel without having to prove actual malice. Private individuals need only prove that the press was negligent in publishing a defamatory story (for example, the reporter did not check all the relevant facts or follow through on all the relevant leads). The Court also ruled that in libel suits involving a public figure, it was legitimate in order to determine "actual malice" to question reporters and editors as to their state of mind, including their conversations and beliefs, at the time they made the editorial decisions that resulted in the alleged libel. However, in 1988 the Rehnquist Court reaffirmed *New York Times Co.* v. *Sullivan* and ruled in *Hustler Magazine* v. *Falwell* that a public figure cannot collect damages for the press' intentionally inflicting emotional distress. The Reverend Jerry Falwell was mercilessly lampooned in a *Hustler Magazine* parody that was vulgar and cruel. But the First Amendment protects even *Hustler Magazine.*

The First Amendment may appear to offer absolute blanket protection of speech and press, but in practice it does not. The First Amendment says *Congress* shall make *no* law abridging these freedoms. But in fact, on a few occasions, Congress *has* made laws abridging freedom of expression and the Court, in the past, generally approved. Furthermore, obscenity and libel traditionally have not been considered protected by freedom of speech and press. Yet America's political ideology makes much of the First Amendment freedoms that do exist and that distinguish the United States as an open society. If we are to be a free society, we must continue to protect the freedoms of those with whom we disagree. If this overview of freedom of speech and press tells us anything, it is that these freedoms must be vigorously defended and infringements must be challenged. Complacency may be the true enemy of these rights.

[15]For interesting case studies, see Renata Adler, *Reckless Disregard* (New York: Knopf, 1986).

■ THE FIRST AMENDMENT'S RELIGION GUARANTEES

An early tenet of the Mormon religion was polygamy, which meant that Mormon men were encouraged to have multiple wives. But this violated laws in every state and made Mormons with multiple wives subject to prosecution. Did such laws deny Mormons their religious freedom? Are believers in a religion that requires the smoking of marijuana denied their religious freedom by being prosecuted for violating federal drug laws? Is it a denial of religious freedom to prohibit animal sacrifices as part of religious rituals? Is religious freedom denied when children are forbidden to participate in organized religious prayer in the public schools, even a moment of *silent* prayer? Does government really *establish* religion when it subsidizes the salaries of teachers of geometry and physics in parochial high schools of all denominations?

As the above examples suggest, complex issues of civil liberties are raised when the religion guarantees of the Constitution are examined. These guarantees—that Americans may freely exercise their religion and that there shall be no governmental establishment of religion—were placed by the framers of the First Amendment at the head of the Amendment. Indeed, religious freedom played a crucial role in the founding of the colonies. Many of the colonists had fled religious persecution when they came to America and religious freedom was considered by the framers to be a fundamental right. The two religion guarantees were linked in that the framers believed that an established church, that is, a state-sponsored religion, would inevitably jeopardize the free exercise of religion and shackle religious freedom. But the First Amendment does not tell us what happens when the exercise of one's religion clashes with other societal values, and it does not tell us precisely what constitutes the establishment of religion.

The Supreme Court's policy decisions in the religion sphere first dealt with the free exercise guarantee, but over the last three decades the establishment guarantee has occupied much of the Court's attention. Keep in mind that these two rights are sometimes merged in the Court's decisions. Occasionally, a free exercise claim has been decided as a more generalized First Amendment claim.

Free Exercise of Religion

The Jehovah's Witnesses were involved in several cases that came to the Supreme Court in the early 1940s. These cases established certain principles of free exercise and religious freedom that hold true today. The Court incorporated the free exercise guarantee as part of the liberty that states may not deny in the 1940 decision of *Cantwell* v. *Connecticut*. In this case, the Court struck down a state statute that required a state certificate of approval before people could solicit funds for religious or charitable causes, holding that this interfered with the free exercise of religion. In a similar vein, the Court protected the Jehovah's Witnesses' free exercise

---

Materials of Political Science: SUPREME COURT DECISION

The Court Affirms First Amendment Freedom in West Virginia State Board Of Education v. Barnette (1943)

Mr. Justice Jackson delivered the opinion of the Court: . . . .

This case calls upon us to reconsider a precedent decision, as the Court throughout its history often has been required to do. . . .

The freedom asserted by these [Jehovah's Witnesses] appellees does not bring them into collision with rights asserted by any other individual. It is such conflicts which most frequently require intervention of the State to determine where the rights of one end and those of another begin. But the refusal of these persons to participate in the [flag salute] ceremony does not interfere with or deny rights of others to do so. Nor is there any question in this case that their behavior is peaceable and orderly. The sole conflict is between authority and rights of the individual. The State asserts power to condition access to public education on making a prescribed sign and profession and at the same time to coerce attendance by punishing both parent and child. . . .

There is no doubt that, in connection with the pledges, the flag salute is a form of utterance. Symbolism is a primitive but effective way of communicating ideas. The use of an emblem or flag to symbolize some system, idea, institution, or personality, is a short cut from mind to mind. Causes and nations, political parties, lodges and ecclesiastical groups seek to knit the loyalty of their followings to a flag or banner, a color or design. . . .

It is also to be noted that the compulsory flag salute and pledge requires affirmation of a belief and an attitude of mind. . . . To sustain the compulsory flag salute we are required to say that a Bill of Rights which guards the individual's right to speak his own mind, left it open to public authorities to compel him to utter what is not in his mind. . . .

Struggles to coerce uniformity of sentiment in support of some end thought essential to their time and country have been waged by many good as well as evil men. Nationalism is a relatively recent phenomenon but at other times and places the ends have been racial or territorial security, support of a dynasty or regime, and particular plans for saving souls. As first and moderate methods to attain unity have

rights to distribute and sell religious tracts without having to pay for a municipal license. The Court also invalidated a broadly written statute that was used to punish a Jehovah's Witness from ringing doorbells or otherwise summoning the occupants to their doors so that they could receive an announcement of a prayer meeting.

Perhaps the most famous of the Jehovah's Witnesses cases from this period concerned the compulsory flag salute in public schools. Saluting the flag violates the religious beliefs of Jehovah's Witnesses who hold that the Bible's command against worshipping a graven image must be taken literally and that saluting the flag is worship of a graven image. In the 1940 decision of *Minersville* v. *Gobitis*, the Court upheld the compulsory flag salute as a valid measure to promote national unity which is necessary for national security. In the clash of values, said the Court, national security must be considered superior to the free exercise claims of the Jehovah's Witnesses. But several of the more liberal justices had second thoughts on the matter

failed, those bent on its accomplishment must resort to an ever-increasing severity. . . . Those who begin coercive elimination of dissent soon find themselves exterminating dissenters. Compulsory unification of opinion achieves only the unanimity of the graveyard.

It seems trite but necessary to say that the First Amendment to our Constitution was designed to avoid these ends by avoiding these beginnings. There is no mysticism in the American concept of the State or of the nature or origin of its authority. We set up government by consent of the governed, and the Bill of Rights denies those in power any legal opportunity to coerce that consent. Authority here is to be controlled by public opinion, not public opinion by authority.

The case is made difficult not because the principles of its decision are obscure but because the flag involved is our own. Nevertheless, we apply the limitations of the Constitution with no fear that freedom to be intellectually and spiritually diverse or even contrary will disintegrate the social organization. To believe that patriotism will not flourish if patriotic ceremonies are voluntary and spontaneous instead of a compulsory routine is to make an unflattering esti-

mate of the appeal of our institutions to free minds. We can have intellectual individualism and the rich cultural diversities that we owe to exceptional minds only at the price of occasional eccentricity and abnormal attitudes. When they are so harmless to others or to the State as those we deal with here, the price is not too great. But freedom to differ is not limited to things that do not matter much. That would be a mere shadow of freedom. The test of its substance is the right to differ as to things that touch the heart of the existing order.

If there is any fixed star in our constitutional constellation, it is that no official, high or petty, can prescribe what shall be orthodox in politics, nationalism, religion, or other matters of opinion or force citizens to confess by word or act their faith therein. If there are any circumstances which permit an exception, they do not now occur to us.

We think the action of the local authorities in compelling the flag salute and pledge transcends constitutional limitations on their power and invades the sphere of intellect and spirit which it is the purpose of the First Amendment to our Constitution to reserve from all official control. . . .

and two new justices came to the Court over the next several years. In 1943, a new majority reversed itself in *West Virginia State Board of Education* v. *Barnette* in an opinion that is a ringing affirmation of the virtues of First Amendment freedoms (see the box on pages 476 and 477). The free exercise of religion was placed in a broader First Amendment context by Justice Robert Jackson, author of the Court's opinion. In 1977, the Burger Court reaffirmed this precedent in a case involving New Hampshire Jehovah's Witnesses who had been convicted of obscuring the state motto "Live Free or Die" on their license plates in violation of New Hampshire state law.[16] The Witnesses argued that the state motto conflicted with their political and religious beliefs and the Court struck down the convictions, relying heavily on *West Virginia* v. *Barnette*.

[16]*Wooley* v. *Maynard* (1977).

When free exercise claims compete with other claims, the Court has at times ruled against them. For example, the Warren Court found that Sunday closing laws, which made no exception for proprietors who celebrated a different sabbath day, did not violate the guarantee of the free exercise of religion. The Court found a valid secular purpose in government's establishing Sunday as a day of peace and tranquility. The majority could not see any inhibition on the free exercise of religion of those whose sabbath fell on a different day of the week. Similarly, in the 1986 decision of *Goldman* v. *Weinberger*, the Burger Court rejected the free exercise claim of Air Force Captain Goldman, an orthodox Jew, that an order forbidding him to wear a yarmulke (a religious cap) infringed upon the exercise of his religion. The Court found that the Air Force dress code was reasonably and evenhandedly administered and served the interest of military uniformity and discipline. Goldman was not prevented from praying or celebrating his holy days. Here, again, it is seen that civil liberties claims raise complex issues and competing interests that must be judicially decided.

Establishment of Religion

As already shown, at times the guarantee of free exercise of religion conflicts with the guarantee against the establishment of religion. The question arises, what may government do to enable persons to freely exercise their religion? There is little doubt that government's payment of chaplains for the armed forces is permissible. The Court has also said that students can be released from school to go to religious instruction off school premises because this arrangement does not establish religion and, by implication, promotes the free exercise of religion. But does a moment of silent meditation in public schools help children freely exercise their religion or does it represent state establishment of religion in violation of the First Amendment? Clearly there are tensions between the religion guarantees of the First Amendment, and underlying them are the uncertainties surrounding the establishment clause.

The Supreme Court, in the 1947 decision of *Everson* v. *Board of Education*, ruled for the first time that the establishment guarantee of the First Amendment was an obligation on the states through the Fourteenth Amendment due process clause. The Court said that there must be a wall separating church and state. But at the same time it said that New Jersey parents of parochial school students could be reimbursed by the state for the costs of transporting their children to school. This did not violate the establishment guarantee and did not breach the wall of separation. With this ruling, the Court became involved in practices and programs of the states that concern religion.

It is not an easy matter to determine what constitutes establishment of religion. The historical evidence suggests that the framers of the First Amendment were primarily concerned that no official state church be established, but they were also wary of state support of religion.[17] The language of the establishment guarantee is general and is not limited to the formal establishment of a state religion. It has been a challenge for the Supreme Court to develop standards for determining when an action of the state *establishes* religion. Some of the Court's decisions have been inconsistent, a result of shifting majorities, and the Court has had some difficulty determining what type of aid may be given to school children attending parochial schools.

When the promotion of religion was clearly the motivating factor behind government legislation, the Court has generally taken an unfavorable view. For example, in 1968 the Court invalidated as constituting establishment of religion an Arkansas statute that forbade the teaching of evolution in the public schools.[18] In 1987, the Court similarly struck down a state law, this one from Louisiana, that required that whenever evolution was taught in the public schools, "creation-science" (the Bible's account of creation) also be taught.[19]

The most controversial line of establishment decisions has concerned prayer in the public schools. The Warren Court first announced its school prayer policy in 1962 when it invalidated a bland, nondenominational prayer approved by the New York State Board of Regents for use in public schools. The next year the Court made a broader ruling in the **Abington School District v. Schempp** decision when it struck down as a violation of the establishment clause the reading of the Lord's Prayer and passages from the Bible as part of religious ceremonies in the public schools. Even if students are not forced to take part, the Court found prayer in the schools amounts to state-sponsored religion. This school prayer policy remains the law of the land. In 1985 the Court struck down an Alabama statute whose clear and unambiguous purpose was to bring prayer to the public schools through a moment of silent meditation. However, the Court hinted that state moment-of-silence laws enacted to advance a secular purpose (such as to promote a moment of quiet and relaxation) might be given Court approval.

In the 1971 decision of *Lemon* v. *Kurtzman*, the Burger Court set down a policy to determine under what circumstances an action of government violates the establishment clause. The Court offered what is called *the Lemon three-pronged test*. For a law not to violate the establishment clause, (1) it must not have a religious purpose; (2) its effect on religion must be neutral, that is, it must neither promote nor inhibit religion; and (3) it must not be seen as fostering excessive government entanglement with religion. If a law or other governmental action does not meet all three standards, it is invalid. By using this test, the Court said that states cannot subsidize the salaries

---

[17]Leonard W. Levy, *The Establishment Clause* (New York: Macmillan, 1985).
[18]*Epperson* v. *Arkansas* (1968).
[19]*Edwards* v. *Aguillard* (1987).

"BOY, DID I GET INTO TROUBLE. I FELL ASLEEP AND HE THOUGHT I WAS PRAYING!"

of teachers in parochial schools even if they teach only nonreligious subjects. The state would have to monitor the schools and teachers to make sure state money was not used to teach religion, and parochial schools would be encouraged to continually lobby the state legislatures for subsidies. Thus, such a program would foster excessive government entanglement with religion. Applying this same test, however, the Court upheld federal aid to church-related colleges and universities by way of construction grants to build secular academic facilities. This, reasoned the Court, would not foster excessive entanglement since these are one-time building grants.[20]

In one of the most controversial and widely publicized establishment decisions, the Court in 1984 in the case of *Lynch* v. *Donnelly* ruled that the city of Pawtucket, Rhode Island, did not establish religion by sponsoring a creche in the context of a Christmas display in a city park. In the Opinion of the Court, written by Chief Justice Burger, there was the clear suggestion that the three-pronged test was useful as a guide but need not necessarily be mechanically or rigidly applied in every case. The majority rejected the view of the four dissenters that there was a religious purpose behind Pawtucket's sponsorship, that the city-sponsored creche advanced the Christian religion, and that it raised the specter of excessive entanglement with

[20]*Tilton* v. *Richardson* (1971).

non-Christian religions asking for city-sponsored religious displays. The majority reasoned that Christmas is a national holiday and has, in large measure, assumed a secular status. The creche, as part of a Christmas display, portrays the historical basis for the holiday and is not strictly a religious symbol, particularly within a holiday panorama featuring reindeer, carolers, a Santa Claus figure, animals, and so forth.

The First Amendment guarantees both the free exercise of religion and freedom from state-established religion. But these rights do not prevent government from playing any role in the religious life of Americans. The wall of separation, in fact, often *is* breached. The application of the three-pronged policy is open to differing interpretations, and there are different views of the justices as to the meaning of the religion guarantees themselves. The Supreme Court of the future could follow the suggestion of former Chief Justice Burger in *Lynch* v. *Donnelly* that the establishment guarantee should be taken as preventing the imposition of *one* official religion, not the fostering of all religion. Were it to do so, then the law of church and state would change in some fundamental ways.

Religion has long been a powerful, worldwide force in politics. In United States history, the influence of religion on politics has ebbed and flowed. Is the United States in or about to enter a new cycle? Will the Supreme Court adopt a more permissive policy as to what constitutes the establishment of religion? Will religion soon be blessed by Court rulings?

▬▬ CRIMINAL PROCEDURAL GUARANTEES

The framers of the Bill of Rights knew that sometimes government actions can deprive people of their liberty, property, or even their lives. How were citizens to be protected from unreasonable intrusions? How were those accused of crimes to be guaranteed fair and just treatment? To answer these questions, the Bill of Rights includes *procedural guarantees*—guarantees of fairness on the part of government when government seeks to deprive us of our lives, liberty, or property. Procedural guarantees are applicable to both criminal and noncriminal processes, but it is in the criminal sphere that the Constitution provides the most detailed and explicit inventory of rights to ensure fairness. In interpreting these guarantees, the Supreme Court, just as with other areas of civil liberties, has made policy that is sometimes highly controversial. The constitutional guarantees, the policies based upon them, and their applications in specific cases have raised troubling questions. One question that deeply disturbs most Americans is whether the guilty should go free on "technicalities." This is particularly an issue with the Fourth Amendment search and seizure guarantee and the Fifth Amendment guarantee against self-incrimination, but it also is applicable to other guarantees. Can a mass society in an age of violent crime and terrorism afford procedural rights? Can a free society continue to be free without them?

The Guarantee Against Unreasonable Searches and Seizures

The Fourth Amendment guarantees "The right of the people to be secure in their persons, houses, papers, and effects, against unreasonable searches and seizures." It specifies that no warrants shall be issued by magistrates to law enforcement officials "but upon probable cause, supported by Oath or affirmation, and particularly describing the place to be searched, and the persons or things to be seized." Clearly the Fourth Amendment contains both a substantive right of privacy and a procedural guarantee concerned with the circumstances under which searches can be conducted, evidence seized, or persons arrested.

In 1914 in the case of *Weeks* v. *United States*, the Supreme Court adopted an important policy designed to implement the search and seizure guarantee. The Court ruled that evidence seized in violation of the Fourth Amendment cannot be introduced as evidence in a federal trial court. This is the **exclusionary rule**. The Court strongly suggested that the exclusionary rule must be considered part of the Fourth Amendment because without it, the Amendment would be worthless. In 1961, the Court in *Mapp* v. *Ohio* ruled that the exclusionary rule was applicable to the states through the Fourteenth Amendment due process clause. The states and the federal government must respect the requirements of the Fourth Amendment. If either does not, any evidence so obtained must be thrown out of court—even if that means that a guilty person will go free.

The theory of the exclusionary rule is that government must not profit from violating the Constitution. There must be no incentive for law enforcement officers to violate rights. The privacy and security of the innocent can only be protected by throwing out of court illegally obtained evidence implicating the not-so-innocent and thus discouraging illegal actions by public officials. Of course, when a law enforcement officer is in hot pursuit of a criminal or sees an offense being committed, no warrant is needed. No warrant is needed if someone would destroy evidence in the time it would take to secure a warrant. But otherwise, law enforcement officers must obtain a warrant from a neutral magistrate or judge. Without that requirement and the exclusionary rule, police abuses would be inevitable and innocent people would be subject to arbitrary and lawless behavior by those charged with enforcing the law.

Some critics argue that the exclusionary rule lets criminals get off on a "technicality." The Court has been asked to make a good faith exception to the exclusionary rule and allow evidence illegally seized to be used as evidence in court as long as the police acted in good faith, that is, believed that they were obeying the law. In 1984 in the case of *United States* v. *Leon*, the Court established a good faith warrant exception to the exclusionary rule. This means that evidence taken by use of a defective warrant that the police in good faith thought was valid is admissible in a court of law. Civil libertarians saw the decision as a major first step towards a general good faith exception rule and the eventual end of the exclusionary rule. Significantly, the majority in the 1984 decision refused to see the exclusionary rule as an integral part of the Fourth Amendment guarantee.

When the Fourth Amendment was ratified as part of the Bill of Rights in 1791, transportation was by horse and ship and communication was by written word or face-to-face conversation. Two hundred years later, people are transported by plane and automobile, communicate by telephone and by computer, and live in a world of technology that the Framers could not have imagined. It has been up to the Supreme Court to adapt the Fourth Amendment to the age of technology. At first, however, the Court was reluctant. In 1928, the Court had to decide whether tapping telephones to gather evidence came under the Fourth Amendment's requirements for search and seizure. The Court said it did not, giving as its reason that wiretapping did not involve a *physical* search and seizure.[21] The evidence was gathered strictly by the use of hearing. The Fourth Amendment applies only to that which can be physically searched and seized. This was Court policy for almost forty years. Finally, in 1967, the Court reversed itself and ruled all eavesdropping devices were subject to Fourth Amendment criteria.[22] The Fourth Amendment protects people wherever they have a reasonable expectation of privacy.

The automobile has posed problems when it comes to search and seizure. Is a person's automobile a private place like a home? Under what circumstances can an automobile or its occupants be searched and evidence seized without a search warrant? These questions have been difficult for the Court to answer. After some confusing and contradictory decisions, the Court came up with a policy for stopping, searching, and seizing. In a 1982 decision, the Court ruled that where there is probable cause to believe that an automobile is carrying something illegal, it may be stopped without a search warrant and places or containers in the automobile may be searched that might contain the contraband. If the police are looking for illegal aliens, they cannot search the glove compartment or open suitcases or containers. But if they are looking for drugs, then they may do so.[23]

What about searching the occupants of an automobile without a search warrant? If an automobile is stopped for even a minor traffic offense and the driver arrested, a full field search of the driver may be conducted. This means that even the contents of a package of cigarettes can be examined. Of course, the situation is different when the police have no authority to search. Whenever a person consents to be searched or consents to a search of his or her home, automobile, or possessions, that individual, by consenting, has waived his or her Fourth Amendment rights.

The Court has emphasized that the Fourth Amendment applies where an individual has a reasonable expectation of privacy. This means that a

---

[21]*Olmstead* v. *United States* (1928).
[22]*Katz* v. *United States* (1967).
[23]*United States* v. *Ross* (1982).

warrant must be obtained based on probable cause to search a home (but not a mobile home), or to make a routine arrest in a person's home, or to bug a person's telephone or a phone booth from which a person is making a call. But the Court has ruled that an open field, even when fenced in and marked by no trespassing signs, does not qualify its marijuana-growing owner for Fourth Amendment protection, because in an open field there is no reasonable expectation of privacy. The same is true for a barn or a fenced-in backyard on a person's property. A person who grew marijuana in his backyard which was protected by a high fence could not claim a Fourth Amendment violation when his backyard was viewed and photographed by police officers from an airplane. The photographs provided the justification for obtaining a search warrant and the seizure of the marijuana. In 1988, the Court ruled that there is no reasonable expectation of privacy in garbage bags left outside the home for trash pickup. Law enforcement officers can search the trash for evidence without first obtaining a search warrant. Prisoners also do not have a reasonable expectation of privacy in their cells and consequently are not protected by the Fourth Amendment from surprise searches.

The Warren Court extended the guarantees of the Fourth Amendment while the Burger and Rehnquist Courts have pulled back. Nevertheless, the Burger Court justices unanimously rejected the Nixon administration's argument that the Fourth Amendment did not apply to domestic security matters.[24] Although the post-Warren Court has given the benefit of the doubt to law enforcement authorities, it still has protected a bottom-line Fourth Amendment guarantee.

The Guarantee Against Self-Incrimination

The Fifth Amendment contains several criminal procedural guarantees, but none has been more controversial than the guarantee against self-incrimination, and, in particular, the Warren Court's policy for enforcing that guarantee. At first glance, the guarantee against self-incrimination seems quite straightforward. The Fifth Amendment states unequivocally that no one shall "be compelled in any criminal case to be a witness against himself." But what about a person who confesses during an interrogation but later claims that the interrogation was psychologically coercive? Isn't the use of the statement or confession at the trial turning the person into "a witness against himself?" On the other hand, how can *any* interrogation of a suspect *not* be psychologically coercive? Interrogation is a necessary investigative technique and as long as there is no physical coercion why shouldn't law enforcement officials be allowed to do their job? The historical evidence suggests that the principal concern of the Framers was to prevent physical torture and that the rationale for the guarantee is that a confession pro-

---

[24]*United States* v. *United States District Court* (1972).

duced by torture is unreliable.[25] Why should criminals be given protection not explicitly required by the Constitution?

The Warren Court took the reasonable position that the Fifth Amendment guarantee does not spell out a right restricted to instances of physical torture. The Court looked at a confession or a statement used as evidence at the trial of the person who made it as "a witness against himself" which the Fifth Amendment forbids unless it was not "compelled," that is, unless it was voluntary. In the landmark case of *Miranda* v. *Arizona*, decided in 1966, the Warren Court spelled out the conditions under which a confession or statement can be considered voluntary. These **Miranda rules** were designed to ensure that any statement or confession made by a suspect is truly voluntary (and by definition not compelled) and made with full knowledge of his or her constitutional rights.[26] When taken into custody, before questioning can begin, the suspect must be told

(1) of the right to remain silent;
(2) of the fact that anything said can be used against the suspect in a court of law;
(3) of the right to the assistance of a lawyer;
(4) of the right to have a lawyer provided and paid for by the state if the suspect cannot afford a lawyer;
(5) of the right to have one's lawyer present during interrogation;
(6) of the right to stop the questioning at any time.

The Court also made clear that if questioning occurs without an attorney being present and a statement is taken or confession made, "a heavy burden rests on the government to demonstrate that the defendant knowingly and intelligently waived his privilege against self-incrimination and his right to retained or appointed counsel." Statements or confessions made in violation of the *Miranda* policy are considered to be "compelled" and may not be used in *any* manner at the trial. Chief Justice Warren in his opinion for the Court pointed out, "In fact, statements merely intended to be exculpatory by the defendant [intended by the suspect to demonstrate innocence] are often used to impeach his testimony at trial or to demonstrate untruths in the statement given under interrogation and thus to prove guilt by implication. These statements are incriminating in any meaningful sense of the word and may not be used without the full warnings and effective waiver required for any other statement."

The Burger and Rehnquist Courts, which followed the Warren Court, were not sympathetic to the *Miranda* policy and in some instances undermined it. Early in the Burger Court era, the Court ruled that statements made without the *Miranda* warnings could nevertheless be introduced at a

---

[25]See Leonard W. Levy, *Origins of the Fifth Amendment* (New York: Oxford, 1968).
[26]For an account of the Miranda decision and the controversy surrounding it, see Liva Baker, *Miranda: Crime, Law and Politics* (New York: Atheneum, 1983).

Ernesto Miranda (on the right) with his attorney during his retrial on kidnapping and rape charges following *Miranda* v. *Arizona*, which overturned his first conviction. Miranda was subsequently convicted again.

trial to impeach the credibility of the defendant's testimony.[27] The *Miranda* v. *Arizona* statement to the contrary, quoted in the previous paragraph, was considered a mere judicial aside and not a controlling precedent. Thus, *Miranda* v. *Arizona* was not overruled, but rather distinguished—and undermined. The Court subsequently handed down rulings that with only few exceptions took a narrow view of the *Miranda* policy.

In 1984, the Court made a major departure from the *Miranda* policy when it ruled in *New York* v. *Quarles* that when the public safety is immediately and directly threatened, the *Miranda* warnings need not be given before questioning a suspect. This public safety exception to *Miranda*, like the good faith warrant exception to the exclusionary rule, is a milestone down the road whose end is the overturning of Court precedent. This does not necessarily mean that *Miranda* will be overturned in the near future. But the logic of a public safety exception could be stretched to other situations, for example, the questioning of suspected terrorists, suspected murderers, suspected violent rapists, all of whom, it could be argued, represent a grave threat to the public safety. Imagine a captured terrorist or a deranged person who has planted a time bomb in a crowded public place set to explode in a matter of hours. Why should the police have to read that person his "rights" if that would deter the individual from revealing where the bomb is planted? Why should a suspected mass murderer be read the Miranda warnings when it is in the interest of public safety to have that individual talk and help convict himself? But what about the innocent peo-

---

[27]*Harris* v. *New York* (1971).

ple who were coerced into falsely confessing before the *Miranda* policy? The *Miranda* policy raises complex issues of public policy and can be expected to remain controversial.

The Right to Counsel

The Sixth Amendment offers Americans many specific guarantees to ensure a fair trial. Among them is the right "to have the Assistance of Counsel." This guarantee was the first of the criminal procedural guarantees to be incorporated and made applicable to the states through the Fourteenth Amendment. When it was incorporated in the 1932 decision of *Powell* v. *Alabama*, the Court agreed that if the accused is denied the assistance of a lawyer at a criminal trial, fundamental unfairness can result. Our system of justice is an adversarial one—prosecution and defense are locked in combat. For one side not to have a lawyer is a major handicap. In the *Powell* case, African-American defendants in Scottsboro, Alabama, were charged with raping two white women, a *capital crime* (punishable by death). The accused were illiterate teenagers too poor to afford a lawyer. The Court ruled not only that the Constitution guarantees the accused the right to hire a lawyer to defend them in court, but that defendants such as these, on trial with their lives at stake, are entitled to a lawyer provided free of charge by the state. This was, indeed, a major new policy.

It is hard to believe that a policy of providing poor defendants free lawyers would be controversial, but for a long period of time it was. The *Powell* policy only applied to defendants who potentially faced the death penalty. The Court in 1942 refused to extend the policy to poor criminal defendants accused of non-capital offenses, reasoning that as long as the trial is a fair one, the state need not be financially burdened with providing free lawyers.[28] But this decision was inconsistent with the rationale behind the *Powell* policy. The Warren Court explicitly recognized this inconsistency and in 1963 overturned the 1942 decision in the landmark case of *Gideon* v. *Wainwright*.[29]

Gideon v. Wainwright established the right under the Sixth and Fourteenth Amendments of any indigent state criminal defendant accused of a felony to a free court-appointed lawyer. In a companion case, the Court also ruled that poor people are entitled to a free lawyer, paid for by the state, when they first appeal a criminal conviction. The Burger Court extended the right to counsel when it ruled that a poor person is entitled to a free lawyer when accused of a misdemeanor punishable by a jail sentence (*Gideon* applied only to felonies).[30] But the Court later made clear that the state need not appoint a free lawyer if the defendant would not be sentenced to jail.

[28]*Betts* v. *Brady* (1942).

[29]The classic study of the Gideon case is Anthony Lewis, *Gideon's Trumpet* (New York: Random House, 1964).

[30]*Argersinger* v. *Hamlin* (1972).

Thus, any judge refusing to appoint counsel for a poor defendant in a misdemeanor trial cannot then impose a jail sentence as punishment. By so ruling, the Court ignored the potential negative consequences of a misdemeanor conviction other than imprisonment, such as a damaged reputation or future employment prospects.

The right-to-counsel cases in recent years have raised several troubling questions. Should the state be constitutionally required to give poor people the same advantages the better-off can afford? The Court has generally said no, for example, ruling that the state has no obligation to provide a free lawyer so that the poor convicted defendant can appeal to the United States Supreme Court. Are poor people entitled to a competent lawyer? The Court has said yes to this question. Are poor people entitled to a free court-appointed lawyer when they are in jeopardy of losing custody of their children or losing their homes? The Court has answered no, arguing that the states are *required* by the Constitution to provide a poor person with the assistance of counsel *only* when the indigent faces loss of physical liberty.

Guarantees Against Excessive Bail and Cruel and Unusual Punishment

The Eighth Amendment guarantees that "Excessive bail shall not be required, nor excessive fines imposed, nor cruel and unusual punishment inflicted." But what is "excessive?" What is "cruel and unusual?"

The Eighth Amendment guarantee against excessive bail is applicable to the federal government but not to the states. It is one of the few guarantees in the Bill of Rights that has not been incorporated through the Fourteenth Amendment due process clause. This means that state judges are free to impose excessive bail as a form of preventive detention. That is, if they want to keep an accused person locked up until tried because they believe the accused to be dangerous, they can set bail so high that it cannot be posted.

But even low bail may be "excessive" for poor people. If the poor person cannot afford bail, that individual must remain in jail until trial. While a prisoner, he or she is subject to such prison practices and rules as strip searches, including inspection of body cavities, after contact with outside visitors, prohibition of packages or books from private parties, sharing a cell originally meant for one, and surprise searches of cells. If the accused is later found innocent or the prosecutor drops the charge, the accused will have suffered the months in jail for no other reason than poverty. His or her only "offense" was being too poor.

Another issue is that of **preventive detention** itself. In 1984, Congress enacted a Bail Reform Act which permits federal judges to refuse to set bail and to hold suspects for whom certain objective criteria would suggest that they pose a potential menace to the community.[31] While this is more

---

[31]For a discussion of the law's provisions, see *Congressional Quarterly Weekly Report*, October 20, 1984, pp. 2752–58.

straightforward than using high bail to preventively detain, it raises serious constitutional issues. Civil libertarians argue that preventive detention imposes a punishment on someone who is legally innocent until proven guilty. If the preventively detained individual is subsequently acquitted or the charges dropped, then a grave injustice will have been committed. But these arguments were rejected in 1987 by the Rehnquist Court, which held that pretrial (or preventive) detention does not violate the Constitution.[32]

The cruel and unusual punishment guarantee was incorporated in a 1962 case involving the conviction of a drug addict for violating a California law that made it a crime to *be* an addict.[33] The Court ruled not only that this guarantee was part of due process of law required of the states by the Fourteenth Amendment, but that the California law violated that guarantee by punishing a person merely for being ill.

Most of the controversy over the guarantee against cruel and unusual punishment concerns the death penalty. Have we reached that point in the development of American civilization that the death penalty itself should be considered cruel and unusual punishment? Is it cruel for government to execute mass murderers, big-time drug dealers, or ordinary killers? Is it cruel to execute those whose crimes were committed when they were young teenagers or who have the mental age of young children? When the Supreme Court began tackling the issue of the death penalty in 1972, the justices ruled that the capricious and arbitrary manner in which the death sentence was imposed and the lack of uniform nationwide standards for its imposition *did* make it cruel and unusual punishment.[34] But in 1976, the Court ruled that the death penalty in and of itself did *not* constitute cruel and unusual punishment.[35] The Court suggested, however, that laws that required the death penalty but did not consider mitigating circumstances indeed violated the guarantee against cruel and unusual punishment, while laws that *did* consider mitigating circumstances *were* constitutional.

In subsequent death penalty decisions, the Court clarified its policy. It ruled that the death penalty may not be imposed for the crime of rape and that only a person who kills, intends to kill, or tries to kill can be punished by the death penalty. Death penalty statutes must take into account a wide variety of mitigating circumstances (for example, the defendant was coerced into participating in the crime) and must be precise and not vaguely written or interpreted by state courts. But state courts are under *no* obligation to review the cases of others convicted of the same crimes to determine if consistency and fairness in the imposition of the death penalty is taking place. The Court also rejected as irrelevant statistics that show that

---

[32]*United States* v. *Salerno* (1987).

[33]*Robinson* v. *California* (1962).

[34]*Furman* v. *Georgia* (1972).

[35]*Gregg* v. *Georgia* (1976); *Jurek* v. *Texas* (1976); *Proffitt* v. *Florida,* (1976); *Woodson* v. *North Carolina* (1976); *Roberts* v. *Louisiana* (1976). For a strong argument against the death penalty, see Franklin E. Zimring and Gordon Hawkins, *Capital Punishment and the American Agenda* (New York: Cambridge University Press, 1987). For a defense of the death penalty see Walter Berns, *For Capital Punishment* (New York: Basic Books, 1979).

**The electric chair
used by Florida.**

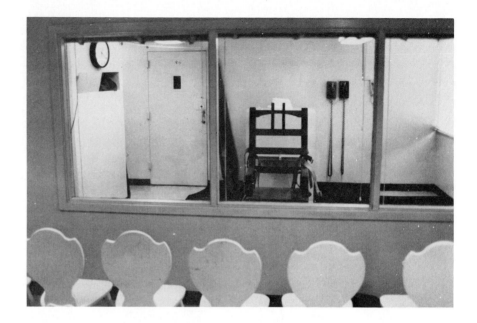

blacks convicted of killing whites have a much greater chance of receiving the death penalty than whites convicted of killing blacks.[36] In this case, the Court found that the defendant had received a fair trial and was convicted under a valid death penalty statute.

Eighth Amendment guarantees in practice appear to be tied to class and race. The middle and upper classes do not waste away in jail because they cannot afford the money to post bail. The middle and upper classes ordinarily do not receive the death penalty. Blacks are more likely than whites to be sentenced to death. The Eighth Amendment guarantees as presently implemented by the policies of the Supreme Court permit discrepancies in the treatment of the accused based on class and race. These issues are part of the unfinished business of a society that aspires to liberty and justice for all. The death penalty itself, because of its dreadful finality, does not recognize that mistakes can be made and that the person executed might be innocent after all. Opponents argue that the death penalty is murder by the state. What this means is that the complex issues surrounding the Eighth Amendment promise to continue to be controversial.

OTHER CIVIL LIBERTIES

American citizens have a variety of other civil liberties, including the right to procedural due process in civil law, the right to travel, and the right to privacy.

---

[36]*McCleskey* v. *Kemp* (1987).

The Right to Procedural Due Process in Civil Law

The right to procedural due process in civil law means the right to be noti-fied when government plans to affect one adversely, the right to a fair hear-ing, and other procedural safeguards. In an important decision with major implications for the rights of those who receive benefits from government, the Court ruled that welfare payments may not be discontinued unless re-cipients first are offered a hearing.[37] At the hearing, welfare recipients should be able to appear personally, with or without a lawyer, before the official who determines whether they are eligible for welfare, and should be able to present written or oral evidence and to confront or cross-examine adverse witnesses. People also have the right to a hearing and a judicial determination before their property can be repossessed by creditors. Public school students have the right not to be suspended from school without first being afforded notice and a hearing. However, the Court in one decision in 1977 ruled that public school students were not entitled to notice and a hearing prior to the imposition of corporal punishment (in this case, pad-dling on the buttocks).[38]

People who are mentally ill are also entitled to due process. The Court in 1975 adopted a policy that the mentally ill cannot be confined against their will if they are not violent and if they can live safely in freedom.[39] Before people can be committed indefinitely to a mental institution, the due process clause requires that the state provide proof that the mental illness necessitates institutional confinement so that the patient is no danger to him or herself or to others. The standard of proof to be used must be more strict than the "preponderance of the evidence" measure ordinarily used in civil law but less strict than the "beyond a reasonable doubt" required in criminal law.[40]

The Right to Travel

Totalitarian states do not permit their citizens to leave the country or to freely travel or resettle within the country without special governmental permission. Restrictions on the right of Americans to travel—abroad or within the country—would be bitterly opposed. Yet there have been times when state laws have discouraged travel or resettlement, and the Supreme Court has had to confront this issue. For example, in 1941 it struck down a California law aimed at keeping out-of-state poor people from entering Cali-fornia.[41] In the 1969 decision in *Shapiro* v. *Thompson*, the Court struck

---

[37]*Goldberg* v. *Kelley* (1970). Civil servants are also entitled to a pretermination hearing to re-spond to charges that threaten their employment. See *Cleveland Bd. of Education* v. *Loudermill* (1985).

[38]*Ingraham* v. *Wright* (1977).

[39]*O'Connor* v. *Donaldson* (1975).

[40]*Addington* v. *Texas* (1979).

[41]*Edwards* v. *California* (1941).

down a one-year residency requirement for welfare assistance eligibility as interfering with the right to travel. The Court has also ruled that a durational residency requirement for voting, that is, a set time a person must live within the jurisdiction in which he or she wishes to vote, must be only for the minimum time necessary to establish accurate voting lists. The Court found not only a burden on the right to vote but a fundamental infringement on the right to travel. So, too, was the right to travel invoked by the Court when it struck down a one-year residency requirement as a condition for receiving nonemergency hospitalization or medical care at county expense. The right to travel abroad, subject only to minimal reasonable restrictions on travel, has been recognized by the Court, but the Court upheld President Reagan's restrictions on tourist travel to Cuba as a reasonable exercise of presidential power under statutory law.[42]

The Right to Privacy

The right to privacy includes those rights that inhere in our being persons worthy of being treated with dignity by our government.[43] The right to be secure in the privacy of our own homes, as integral to our personhood, is explicitly recognized in the Constitution in both the Third and Fourth Amendments. The Third Amendment says that the government cannot invade people's homes against their will for the purpose of sheltering soldiers (an issue of immediate concern to the Framers, who had experienced the time when the British forcefully quartered soldiers in colonists' homes). The Fourth Amendment, as shown earlier, guarantees our right to be secure against unreasonable searches and seizures. The Thirteenth Amendment goes to the heart of personhood and privacy by abolishing slavery. Involuntary servitude is also prohibited except as a legally imposed punishment for someone convicted of a crime.

In recent years, the right to privacy has been expanded to encompass some of the most personal decisions anyone can make, decisions concerning sexual reproduction and activity. The leading Supreme Court decision is **Griswold v. Connecticut**, decided in 1965. In that case the Court struck down a Connecticut law that made it a crime for any person, married or unmarried, to use "any drug, medicinal article or instrument" for the purpose of birth control. It was also a crime to provide any person with birth control information. The Court found that various guarantees in the Bill of Rights "have penumbras formed by emanations from those guarantees that help give them life and substance." The specific guarantees of the First, Third, Fourth, Fifth (self-incrimination clause), and Ninth Amendments cre-

---

[42]See *Aptheker* v. *Secretary of State* (1964); *Zemel* v. *Rusk* (1965); *Regan* v. *Wald* (1984).

[43]For a formulation of rights of personhood that define a fundamental privacy right, see Laurence H. Tribe, *American Constitutional Law* (Mineola, New York: The Foundation Press, 1978), chapter 15. For a consideration of the broad issues concerning privacy, see Richard F. Hixson, *Privacy in a Public Society: Human Rights in Conflict* (New York: Oxford, 1987).

ate zones of privacy. The right to use contraceptives goes to the heart of the intimate decisions made within a marriage relationship, suggested the Court, and is a constitutionally protected manifestation of privacy. The Burger Court went even further and in a subsequent decision ruled: "If the right of privacy means anything, it is the right of the *individual*, married or single, to be free from unwarranted governmental intrusion into matters so fundamentally affecting a person as the decision whether to bear or beget a child."[44] Even the state regulation of the sale of contraceptives to keep them from persons under sixteen and that permits them to be sold to those above that age only by licensed pharmacists was invalidated.

The most controversial reproductive autonomy decision based on the right of personal privacy was the **Roe v. Wade** abortion decision of 1973.[45] The key point of that decision is that it is the woman's *right*, as long as the fetus cannot live outside the mother, to determine for herself whether or not to bear a child. A more private right involving the essentials of personhood is hard to imagine. Yet the fact that a decision to abort means the taking of an innocent potential life makes this decision poignant and troublesome. The Court decided that such a personal decision must remain with the woman and not legislative majorities. But starting in 1989, with a new Court majority, the Court began to approve legislative restrictions on abortion, signaling an end to the *Roe* v. *Wade* policy.

The right of sexual privacy has been limited to heterosexual relationships. In 1986, in the decision of *Bowers* v. *Hardwick* (see the box on page 494), the Court ruled that consenting adult homosexual activity is not protected by a constitutional right to privacy. There is no constitutional right to adult sexual preference that has been recognized by the Court.[46]

Critics of the Court's privacy decisions assert that nowhere in the Constitution is the term "privacy" to be found. They argue that the *Griswold* decision and the decisions that built on it have no constitutional foundation. Sexual privacy and a generalized privacy right are creations of judges, not the Framers of the Constitution or of the legislative branches of government. This argument was made by Robert Bork before the Senate Judiciary Committee during the hearing on his ill-fated nomination to the Supreme Court in 1987. The Senate rejected Bork's narrow reading of privacy and apparently much of public opinion is sympathetic to some constitutional protection of privacy. This is an area of policy that promises continued controversy. Clearly the privacy concept is a crucial civil libertarian concern and can be expected to be deeply involved in the evolving jurisprudence of rights.

[44]*Eisenstadt* v. *Baird* (1972).

[45]See Marian Faux, *Roe v. Wade: The Untold Story of the Landmark Supreme Court Decision that Made Abortion Legal* (New York: Macmillan, 1988).

[46]See Tribe, *op. cit.*, pp. 941–48. Also see John Brigham, *Civil Liberties and American Democracy* (Washington D.C.: C.Q. Press, 1984), pp. 144–46.

The Court on Homosexual Rights in Bowers v. Hardwick (1986)

Michael Hardwick, a 29-year old homosexual living in Atlanta, brought a civil suit in federal district court. The suit grew out of the following facts. On August 3, 1982, a police officer went to Hardwick's home to serve a warrant for failure to pay a fine for public drunkenness. The man answering the door was not sure if Hardwick was at home but allowed the officer to enter and pointed the way to Hardwick's bedroom. The officer walked down the hall to the bedroom where he found the door partly open and he observed Hardwick and another man engaged in oral sex. The officer then arrested both men and charged them with sodomy, an offense under Georgia criminal law punishable by a prison sentence as long as twenty years. Hardwick challenged his arrest as a violation of his rights and the District Attorney decided not to submit the charge to the grand jury unless there was additional evidence. This was unsatisfactory to Hardwick who believed that the District Attorney could, at his discretion, reinstitute the charges. Hardwick then decided to challenge the Georgia sodomy law under which he was originally arrested. The federal district judge dismissed the suit. The Court of Appeals reversed and remanded, holding that the Georgia statute violated Hardwick's fundamental rights. The Attorney General of Georgia, Michael J. Bowers, took the case to the Supreme Court, which rendered its anti-civil liberties decision by a vote of five-to-four.

Justice White delivered the opinion of the Court: . . . .

[R]espondent [Hardwick] would have us announce, as the Court of Appeals did, a fundamental right to engage in homosexual sodomy. This we are quite unwilling to do. It is true that despite the language of the Due Process Clauses of the Fifth and Fourteenth Amendments, which appears to focus only on the processes by which life, liberty, or property is taken, the cases are legion in which those Clauses have been interpreted to have substantive content, subsuming rights that to a great extent are immune from federal or state regulation or proscription. Among such cases are those recognizing rights that have little or no textual support in the constitutional language . . . [such] as . . . the privacy cases. . . .

Striving to assure itself and the public that announcing rights not readily identifiable in the Constitution's text involves much more than the imposition of the Justice's own choice of values . . . , the Court has sought to identify the nature of the rights qualifying for heightened judicial protection. . . . [I]t was said that this category includes those fundamental liberties that are "implicit in the concept of ordered liberty," such that "neither liberty nor justice would exist if [they] were sacrificed." A different description . . . categorized . . . those liberties that are "deeply rooted in this Nation's history and tradition." . . .

It is obvious to us that neither of these formulations would extend a fundamental right to homosexuals to engage in acts of consensual sodomy. Proscriptions against that conduct have ancient roots. . . . In fact, until 1961, all 50 States outlawed sodomy, and, today, 24 States and the District of Columbia continue to provide criminal penalties for sodomy performed in private and between consenting adults. Against this background, to claim that a right to engage in such conduct is "deeply rooted in this Nation's history and tradition" or "implicit in the concept of ordered liberty" is, at best, facetious. . . .

Even if the conduct at issue here is not a fundamental right, respondent [Hardwick] asserts that there must be a rational basis for the law and that there is none in this case other than the presumed belief of a majority of the electorate in Georgia that homosexual sodomy is immoral and unacceptable. This is said to be an inadequate rationale to support the law. The law, however, is constantly based on notions of morality, and if all laws representing essentially moral choices are to be invalidated under the Due Process Clause, the courts will be very busy indeed. Even respondent makes no such claim, but insists that majority sentiments about the morality of homosexuality should be declared inadequate. We do not agree, and are unpersuaded that the sodomy laws should be invalidated on this basis. . . .

THE STATUS AND FUTURE OF CIVIL LIBERTIES

Although the Supreme Court has the last word on matters of constitutionality, the status of our civil liberties *in practice* cannot necessarily be determined from Court decisions. It is one thing for the Court to speak, but quite another for the Court's policies to be implemented. At the lower federal court and state court levels, Court policies may or may not be faithfully followed. Compliance with Court policies depends on individuals being willing to go to court to assert their rights. State and local officials have opportunities to ignore Court policy. Indeed, officials at every level of government can be sensitive or insensitive to civil liberties. Ultimately, the reality of our day-to-day exercise of civil liberties depends more on the actions of thousands of governmental officials, particularly in the law enforcement and intelligence communities, than on the pronouncements of the Supreme Court.

The last point deserves special emphasis. Congressional investigations in the mid-1970s implicated several government agencies in illegal surveillance of citizens thought to constitute security risks. For three decades the FBI had conducted clearly illegal activities in its zeal to protect the country from elements that its director, J. Edgar Hoover, considered "subversive" or potentially harmful to the country. An extensive Senate committee investigation revealed that the FBI had spied on, harassed, and even manipulated the lives of a wide variety of Americans. Some victims of this zeal were members of the Communist party, some were members of potentially violent groups, but vast numbers were merely exercising their First Amendment rights, particularly in opposition to the Vietnam War or in favor of civil rights for black Americans. The FBI started files on over half a million Americans whose only offense was the exercise of freedom of speech. The Senate committee found that, between 1956 and 1971, the FBI counterintelligence program violated "federal and state statutes prohibiting mail fraud, wire fraud, incitement to violence, sending obscene materials through the mail and extortion."[47]

In 1969, journalist Joseph Kraft reported that the United States had expanded the Vietnam War by bombing Cambodia. The government denied this because the bombing was a classified secret for Americans. However, it was no secret to the Cambodians. As a result of Kraft's reporting, the Nixon White House ordered Kraft's home phone to be wiretapped. Kraft was not alone in receiving this treatment. In its zeal to find who leaked the information on the Cambodian bombing, the White House ordered some seventeen wiretaps.[48]

---

[47]Senate Select Committee to Study Governmental Operations with Respect to Intelligence Activities, *Final Report*, Book II (Washington, D.C.: Government Printing Office, 1976), p. 216, as quoted in Robert Justin Goldstein, "The FBI and American Politics Textbooks," *PS*, vol. 18, no. 2 (1985), p. 239. Also see William W. Keller, *The Liberals and J. Edgar Hoover: Rise and Fall of a Domestic Intelligence State* (Princeton: Princeton University Press, 1989).

[48]David Wise, *The American Police State* (New York: Random House, 1976), pp. 3–10, 19–21.

Wiretapping, opening mail, and other information collection about private citizens not accused of crimes have been documented since the early 1960s. The White House, FBI, CIA and IRS have all been implicated in these activities.[49] During the Vietnam War, college students also were spied on by the federal government. At the request of President Nixon, the CIA conducted surveillance on college campuses. When then CIA Director Richard Helms had agreed to this undertaking, he wrote in his memo to the White House: "This is an area not within the charter of this Agency, so I need not emphasize how extremely sensitive this makes this paper. Should anyone learn of its existence it would prove most embarrassing for all concerned."[50] The rationale for undertaking these illegal activities was the belief that these actions were necessary to protect national security.

Perhaps the most famous victim of such activities was Nobel Peace Prize winner Reverend Martin Luther King, Jr., who was subject to bugging of his phones, offices, and places of residence.[51] He was a victim of FBI harassment that included mailing him a tape recording of phone conversations that allegedly would have embarrassed him and damaged his public image if they had been released to the press. According to the Senate committee report, the note that came in the package with the tape suggested that suicide would be a way of avoiding public disclosure. This kind of behavior goes to the heart of civil liberties. Federal law enforcement officials who break the law and make life difficult for those exercising their First Amendment rights subvert the very Constitution they are sworn to uphold.

Despite the FBI's activities, both the civil rights and antiwar movements flourished in the 1960s. Hundreds of thousands of Americans exercised their rights. How many more would have done so had it not been for the FBI is impossible to know. After the revelations from the Senate Committee, the FBI underwent extensive reform of its intelligence operations. Today it is supposed to focus only on those who break federal law, including terrorist groups that actually engage in violent, illegal activities.[52] But the line between legitimate activities of the FBI (such as tracking down suspected spies for the Soviet Union) and trampling on the rights of law-abiding Americans may be difficult to draw. For example, in 1988 it was revealed that the FBI had a Library Awareness Program under which it tried to recruit librarians to help identify Soviet spies. Librarians in many engineering and science libraries on university campuses were asked by FBI agents to report the names of "suspicious-looking persons"

---

[49]Wise, *op. cit.*; U.S. Senate, 94th Congress, *Final Report of the Select Committee to Study Government Operations with Respect to Intelligence Activities* (Washington, D.C.: U.S. Government Printing Office, 1976); Athan Theoharis, *Spying on Americans* (Philadelphia: Temple University Press, 1978).

[50]Theoharis, *op. cit.,* pp. 15–16.

[51]Keller, *op. cit.*, chap. 3.

[52]See John T. Elliff, *The Reform of FBI Intelligence Operations* (Princeton, New Jersey: Princeton University Press, 1979). Also see, in general, Gary T. Marx, *Undercover: Police Surveillance in America* (Berkeley: University of California Press, 1988).

American citizens of Japanese descent and lawfully residing Japanese resident aliens waiting to be processed for evacuation to detention camps in April 1942.

and those with "East European or Russian-sounding names" who had an interest in certain scientific subjects. The agents were also interested in what books and journals were checked out by such persons. Civil liberties groups attacked the program as harassment and an invasion of privacy of library users. A spokesman for the FBI defended the program as an effort "to make library employees aware of this threat from a hostile intelligence operation" and to seek their cooperation in helping to protect national security.[53]

The activities of the FBI also point up the fragility of our civil liberties in practice. They are subject not only to the misguided actions of law enforcement officials or agencies at every level of government, but to political pressures and national crises. For example, shortly after the Second World War began, all those of Japanese ancestry living on the West Coast (over 120,000 American citizens and lawfully residing aliens) were imprisoned in internment camps. College students were forced to leave school, businessmen their businesses, farmers their farms, and families their homes and possessions. Their only "crime" was belonging to the same ethnic group as a country with which the United States was at war. This massive violation of civil liberties was justified at the time as necessary because some persons of Japanese ancestry might be saboteurs (none were ever so proven). The

[53]*Los Angeles Times*, June 3, 1988.

Supreme Court upheld the constitutionality of these actions.[54] Finally, in 1988, the nation officially apologized in a law that also gave those who were interned $20,000 in tax-free lump sum payments.

Civil liberties are also fragile because it is the configuration of justices on the Court that determines which civil liberties shall be protected as a matter of constitutional law and which shall not. And even here, unless people are willing to exercise their rights and even become involved in litigation, we run the risk of losing our liberties from disuse.

Civil liberties may be fragile but they also evolve and change. For example, the constitutional concept of the right to privacy today is very different from the concept of privacy of a half century ago. The right of women to make personal decisions concerning birth control or abortion was not seriously discussed as a constitutional right as recently as thirty years ago. The rights of racial minorities to equality and women to be free from discrimination based on gender (both discussed in the next chapter) have evolved over the past half century.

New concepts of rights are beginning to emerge as society becomes sensitized to issues long hidden from view. There is growing recognition that spouses and children have the right to be free from violence and sexual abuse. Another emerging concept is that of a right to adult sexual preference. Still another is the right to die, that is, the right of an individual to end life or have help ending his or her life, when, for example, the person is terminally ill and suffering. It is not inconceivable that at some point in the future the right to breathe clean air, drink pure water, and enjoy the unspoiled wilderness will assume constitutionally protected status. The courts of tomorrow will be grappling with new views of civil liberties and government officials will be acting or refraining from acting in ways that will determine how Americans enjoy old and new-found rights.

Civil liberties claims are constantly before the courts, and our freedoms are in their hands, the hands of the government, and ultimately our own hands.

CHECKLIST FOR REVIEW

1. The term civil liberties encompasses substantive and procedural rights. These rights are spelled out in the Bill of Rights as guarantees against the actions of the federal government. The United States Supreme Court made most of them applicable to the states. These rights were incorporated individually over many decades in separate decisions.

2. Civil liberties issues are both complex and controversial. This is demonstrated by examining First Amendment freedoms of speech and press. During wartime, political free speech has been most controversial and the Supreme Court has had a mixed record on defending political speech. However, the trend since 1937 has been to expand protection.

[54]See Peter Irons, *Justice at War* (New York: Oxford, 1983).

Artistic freedom also raises complex and controversial First Amendment issues, particularly that of censorship of works with a sexual content. The Supreme Court under Chief Justice Warren adopted a permissive artistic expression policy, however, the Burger and Rehnquist Courts have been more conservative.

3. Freedom of the press has generally been protected by the Supreme Court over the past six decades. The Court has drawn the distinction between prior restraint and subsequent punishment. Prior restraint violates the guarantee of freedom of the press under virtually all circumstances. Subsequent punishment holds the press accountable in a court of law for violating the law, for example, the law of libel. But freedom of the press raises complex issues when, for example, it conflicts with the right of a criminal defendant to a fair trial.

4. The First Amendment's religion guarantees have raised numerous questions which have led to a number of Supreme Court policies. The policies concerning the free exercise guarantee have generated less controversy than those concerned with establishment of religion.

5. Criminal procedural guarantees cover a number of rights and have been the focus of clashes between the forces of law-and-order and the advocates of fair procedures. The Warren Court liberalized the procedural guarantees in the Bill of Rights and incorporated almost all of them through the due process clause of the Fourteenth Amendment. These liberal criminal justice policies were for the most part narrowed and to some extent eroded by decisions of the Burger and Rehnquist Courts.

6. There are other areas of civil liberties policy-making including procedural due process rights in civil law, the right to travel, and the right to privacy. The right to privacy has generated considerable controversy, particularly as the Court applied it to protect a woman's right to choose to have an abortion. The Court, however, has not extended the right of sexual privacy to homosexuals. Furthermore, the Rehnquist Court has begun to withdraw protection of a woman's right to reproductive choice in favor of the protection of potential life.

7. The civil liberties we enjoy define the extent to which we are free in a free society. But every civil liberties claim can be countered by a claim from government—that national security requires curtailment of a civil liberty, or that prevention of a great moral or ethical harm requires restraint on civil liberties. When civil liberties claims conflict, the situation becomes even more difficult. Civil liberties can be seen as fragile but they also can be seen as continually evolving and developing.

KEY TERMS	

substantive rights

procedural rights

incorporated rights

preferred position doctrine

prior restraint

subsequent punishment

libel

actual malice

Abington School District v. *Schempp*

substantive due process

Alien and Sedition Acts of 1798

clear and present danger test

exclusionary rule

Miranda rules

Gideon v. *Wainwright*

preventive detention

Griswold v. *Connecticut*

Roe v. *Wade*

Minorities, Women, and Equality

H ow would you feel to be told that you could not stay in a hotel or eat in a restaurant because of your race or religion? Would it be fair for an employer to refuse to hire you because of your gender? Wouldn't you be outraged if a law were passed that you could not drink from public water fountains, use public bathrooms, patronize public libraries, stay in bus station waiting rooms, or attend public schools unless those facilities were specially designated for persons of your race?

If you were the victim in situations such as these, you would claim that your rights were violated. But the rights you would be claiming are different from the civil liberties examined in Chapter Twelve. Civil liberties concern the "freedoms from" or "freedoms to" that are considered essential to a free society. They include freedoms of speech, press, and worship as well as the right to procedural fairness or due process whenever government wishes to take from us life, liberty, or property. But the rights you as victim in the above examples would claim are rights to equal treatment often called *civil rights*. The civil right of equality includes the right of all persons to equal treatment by government. This means that if government must distinguish among its people, it may not do so in irrational ways. The civil right of equality also suggests that government is obliged to enforce equality in the institutions of society.

In this chapter, types of equality and equality as a legal concept are considered. The focus then is on the evolution of civil rights policy, particularly as it concerns the struggle of black people throughout American history to achieve racial equality. Sexual equality policy and policy concerning political and economic equality are also looked at.

CONSIDERATIONS OF EQUALITY

Many groups have claimed the right to equal treatment by society and have pushed for government to adopt policies to guarantee that right. Dominating American history and politics has been the struggle for *racial equality*, in particular, for black Americans. Other racial or ethnic groups including Hispanic-Americans and Asian-Americans have also battled for equal treatment. Women, too, have faced many barriers to achieve *sexual equality*. A contemporary permutation is the claim of the right not to be discriminated against because of sexual preference.

Another form of equality claim, in some respects the oldest historically, is that of *political equality*, that is, the right to have one's vote count the same as all other votes and the right to have an equal chance to exercise political power. The lack of political equality of adult American males as compared to Englishmen was one factor that led to the American Revolution. Still another claim of equality is that of *economic equality*, that is, the claim that government should treat poor people the same as those who are not poor in terms of government services such as police protection, road repairs in their neighborhoods, and public schools for their children. These types of equality do not exhaust the claims of equal treatment that various segments of society have made or will make, only those that have received the most consideration from government. Ultimately, political and judicial processes determine civil rights policy, that is, which claims of equality are taken seriously and how rights are enforced.

Equality claims often are those in which government is asked to take action to ensure equal treatment. Liberty claims generally ask government to stop interfering with the exercise of a freedom. Thus, equality claims ask the government to *do* something while civil liberties claims ask it *not* to do something or simply to keep order so that all people can enjoy their freedoms.

Equality and liberty contain other fundamental contradictions. For example, a racial or sexual equality claim can conflict with the exercise of a liberty, such as freedom of association or the right to advocate racial or sexual discrimination. Or an economic equality claim can conflict with the economic freedoms of a capitalist economic system. There is a tension between liberty and equality, and issues of equality in the context of this tension have been a part of American politics. Since most demands for equality are legal claims, it has been the courts (and since the Civil War the United States Supreme Court) that have sorted out these claims. Therefore, discussion of policies concerning minorities, women, and equality must include consideration of leading Supreme Court decisions. But other branches of government have also dealt with equality issues and their policies are also considered in this chapter.

The federal Constitution of 1787 does not contain a guarantee of equal treatment. To the contrary, the Constitution recognizes, although in disguised language, the existence of slavery. The Constitution also accepts political inequality with its formula for representation in the United States Senate whereby each state is entitled to two senators regardless of the state's population. You will not find in the Constitution that ringing phrase from the Declaration of Independence that "all men are created equal," which taken literally is itself a sexist assertion. Not until the adoption of the Fourteenth Amendment in 1868 did the term "equal protection of the laws" appear in the Constitution.

Until 1868 the individual states had, with few exceptions, exclusive authority to treat their citizens unequally, discriminating, for example, on the basis of race, gender, and wealth. The framers of the Fourteenth Amendment, however, intended to change this by preventing states from discriminating against black Americans. The Fourteenth Amendment prohibits states from impairing the privileges or immunities of United States citizenship, from denying life, liberty, or property without due process of law, *and* from denying any person *equal protection of the laws*. For the first time, protection of concrete individual rights and the guarantee of equal treatment became a federal government responsibility. Although the equal protection clause was intended to protect the newly freed slaves from racially discriminatory state laws and practices, the guarantee is broadly phrased and not limited to one race. Congress has full power under the Fourteenth Amendment to enforce the guarantees with appropriate legislation. In fact, both before and after the ratification of the Fourteenth Amendment, civil rights statutes *were* enacted by Congress. The policy of military reconstruction (occupation of the South by the army) was justified, in part, as necessary to ensure that the substantive, procedural, and equality rights of black people were honored by the southern states.

With the end of Reconstruction, the restoration to power of the white elites of the old South, and a series of Supreme Court decisions, the promise of equality to blacks became an empty one. Equal protection of the laws for black Americans became, for several generations thereafter, an almost meaningless platitude. Not until the 1950s was the equal protection clause to become a meaningful guarantee against racial discrimination. Since 1954, the states and the federal government have been obliged to provide equal protection of the laws. As will be shown later in this chapter, during the 1960s and 1970s Congress enacted various statutes to promote not only racial equality, but sexual equality and equality for others.

■ RACIAL EQUALITY: THE HISTORICAL RECORD

The story of America's treatment of black people is not a pleasant one.[1] By the time of the writing of the federal Constitution, slavery was an established institution. Some framers thought that slaves were property and one purpose of a new constitution was to protect property rights. Others viewed slavery as morally wrong. This disagreement among the framers was pragmatically resolved by having the Constitution neither approve nor disapprove of slavery. Slavery was referred to in the Constitution (although not the terms "slavery" and "slaves") in the provisions for counting of the population for the census, for determining the number of representatives in the House of Representatives, and for imposing direct taxes. The Constitution specifies that enumeration for these purposes shall be "determined by adding to the whole number of free persons ... three fifths of all other persons."[2] Other provisions related to slavery established an end to the foreign slave trade by 1808 and a policy for the return of runaway slaves (referring to them as persons "held to service or labour").

Black people who were not slaves were racially discriminated against by the states and by the federal government. They were treated as second-class citizens in the states and subjected to political, economic, and social discrimination. At the national level, for example, Congress enacted a Natu-

---

[1]Neither is America's treatment of native American Indians. But their struggle, unlike that of black Americans, was one for sovereign autonomy and not, for the most part, waged within the context of America's political and legal system.

[2]Article I, Section 2, paragraph 3.

ralization Law in 1790 and limited the right of becoming citizens "to aliens being free *white* persons" (emphasis added). Congress enacted a Militia Law in 1792, which specified that each "free able-bodied *white* male citizen" be enrolled in the militia (emphasis added). Blacks were excluded by an 1810 federal law from being mailmen. Free blacks, with few exceptions, were unable to receive passports until after the Civil War.[3]

During the first six decades of the nineteenth century, state courts and occasionally the federal courts grappled with cases involving slavery. But despite the occasional actions of a few abolitionist judges who resolved benefits of the doubt in favor of freedom, the institution of slavery was never struck down because it *was* legal under the federal Constitution as well as under many state constitutions.[4] The United States Supreme Court infrequently heard cases involving slavery, and when it did, it typically was more sympathetic to property rights than to human rights.[5]

By the time the Supreme Court decided **Dred Scott v. Sandford** in 1857, slavery was a major issue in American politics. The controversy over slavery had become a north-south issue and the various compromises that Congress had enacted, particularly concerning slavery in the federal territories, were unacceptable to both supporters and opponents of slavery.

In the *Dred Scott* decision, the Court majority in an elaborate opinion by Chief Justice Taney, sought to spell out the legal status of slaves and free blacks. Taney's opinion is correctly seen as racist, but it was also in fact a detailed account of institutionalized racism in the United States. Taney ruled that the framers of the Constitution considered all black people, not just slaves, inferior and therefore not eligible for United States citizenship. Congress had never provided for the naturalization of black people, who were treated as property. Slaves, being property, argued Taney, could not be taken from their owners by an act of Congress. This meant that the Missouri Compromise of 1820 prohibiting slave owners from bringing their slaves into certain of the federal territories was unconstitutional. Slave owners, said Taney, had an absolute property right in their slaves.

While Taney's account of the status of black people at the time of the framing of the Constitution and during the early years of the Republic had the ring of truth, he failed to recognize the evolution of civilized opinion regarding slavery in the United States, as well as the clear-cut constitutional power of Congress to regulate the federal territories. That free black persons who were citizens of the free states were not also citizens of the

---

[3]See Leon F. Litwack, *North of Slavery* (Chicago: University of Chicago Press, 1961), pp. 31 ff. and in general. Also see, Leonard P. Curry, *The Free Black in Urban America 1800–1850: The Shadow of the Dream* (Chicago: University of Chicago Press, 1981).

[4]In general, see Robert M. Cover, *Justice Accused: Antislavery and the Judicial Process* (New Haven: Yale University Press, 1975) and A.E.K. Nash, "Reason of Slavery: Understanding the Judicial Role in the Peculiar Institution," *Vanderbilt Law Review*, 32 (1979), pp. 7–223.

[5]See, for example, *Scott* v. *Negro Ben* (1810); *Mima Queen and Child, Petitioners for Freedom* v. *Hepburn* (1812); *The Antelope* (1825); *Groves* v. *Slaughter* (1841). But compare *LeGrand* v. *Darnall* (1829) and *United States* v. *Schooner Amistad* (1841).

Dred Scott and his family pictured in a newspaper account of the Supreme Court decision concerning him.

United States was untrue despite the fact that they endured, for the most part, second-class national citizenship. The Civil War and the constitutional amendments it spawned overturned the *Dred Scott* decision and changed the constitutional status of black Americans.

From 1864 until 1876 Congress was controlled by a faction of the Republican party known as the Radical Republicans. They were committed to changing the South's social and political structure through a policy of military occupation and "reconstruction" and protecting the newly freed slaves. The Joint Committee (of both houses of Congress) on Reconstruction was established to frame legislation and to propose constitutional amendments to secure the rights of blacks. This was all the more urgent because once the Civil War ended, the southern states enacted laws that became known as *black codes*, which severely limited the rights of blacks and treated them as noncitizens or even semi-slaves. Congress responded by enacting the Civil Rights Act of 1866 and the military Reconstruction Acts of 1867, and proposing the Thirteenth, Fourteenth and Fifteenth Amendments, which within a five-year period became part of the Constitution.

The Thirteenth Amendment was ratified in 1865 and outlawed slavery and nonpunitive involuntary servitude. Congress was explicitly given the power to enforce this by enacting appropriate legislation.

The Fourteenth Amendment became part of the Constitution in 1868 and is the most complex, longest, and in some ways the most ambiguous of the Civil War amendments. The first section of the amendment requires the states to set their own standards of rights and apply them equally (the equal protection clause), and provide minimal procedural standards (the due process clause) and minimal substantive rights (the privileges or immunities clause). Citizenship is defined in the first sentence of section one and specifically overturned the *Dred Scott* ruling that had claimed that black people were not citizens of the United States. The opening words of section one are "All persons born or naturalized in the United States, and subject to the jurisdiction thereof, are citizens of the United States and of the State wherein they reside." Black people were incontrovertibly black *Americans* with full rights of citizenship, the Fourteenth Amendment promised.

The framers and ratifiers had no consensus as to *what* "privileges or immunities" were protected by section one, although some framers thought it included basic rights contained in the Bill of Rights. Also, the due process and equal protection rights were guarantees to "persons" and not just citizens. This meant that aliens and blacks who had not been born in the United States (typically those brought over during the slave trade before 1808) were also to be given procedural and equality rights. Section five of the Amendment gave Congress enforcement powers, which meant that if a state did not voluntarily comply, Congress could assume authority over the internal affairs of the state to enforce the guarantees of the first section.

The Fifteenth Amendment, ratified in 1870, explicitly guaranteed, "The right of citizens of the United States to vote shall not be denied or abridged by the United States or by any State on account of race, color, or previous condition of servitude." Significantly, the Amendment said nothing about gender or age; thus states were free to restrict the vote to males (which they continued to do) who attained a certain age (typically twenty-one years of age).

The Radical Republicans lost control of Congress in the 1874 congressional elections. Before the new Congress took control, one last piece of civil rights legislation was enacted. The Civil Rights Act of 1875 outlawed racial discrimination in public accommodations. This was to be the last federal civil rights law for over eighty years. A series of Supreme Court decisions as well as actions of various state legislatures effectively robbed that act, other civil rights acts, and the Civil War amendments of their ability to protect the rights of blacks. There was fundamental indifference, if not hostility, to black rights on the part of presidents, much of Congress, and the majority of white America.

Whether the Supreme Court could have politically resisted the weakening of the statutory and constitutional guarantees made to black people between 1865 and 1875 could be the subject of endless speculation. That the Supreme Court *should have* is a moral certainty from our vantage point today. But what in fact happened was that, in a series of decisions, the Supreme Court interpreted the key provisions of the Fourteenth Amendment so that it lost its effectiveness as a protector of the rights of blacks. In the *Slaughterhouse Cases of 1873*, the Court narrowly interpreted the privileges or immunities guarantee of the Fourteenth Amendment as not adding new substantive freedoms. In the *Hurtado* v. *California* decision of 1884, the Court interpreted the Fourteenth Amendment's due process clause as not incorporating any of the criminal procedural rights explicitly granted in the Fifth Amendment and, by implication, the other procedural guarantees of the Bill of Rights. These decisions, while having serious negative implications for the rights of blacks, also applied to whites. But in a series of other cases dealing directly with legislation affecting the rights of blacks, the Court in most instances came down firmly on the anti-black side, striking down antiracist federal legislation and upholding racist state statutes. Some of the highlights of this series of decisions are presented in Exhibit 13.1. The climax of this trend was the **Plessy v. Ferguson** decision, in which the Court gave its constitutional blessing to what were known as **Jim Crow laws**, laws requiring racial segregation (apartheid) and treating violations of those laws as *criminal* offenses. Separate but equal facilities, said the Court, satisfy the equal protection guarantee.

By the turn of the century, the South and border states had successfully and legally placed black Americans in semi-slave status. With the complicity of the state and federal courts, the "equality" portion of the separate-but-equal formula was ignored. Black Americans were economically exploited and often subjected to harsh violence when they sought to exercise such elementary rights as the right to vote. Blacks who failed to be servile towards whites were punished. The law, rather than protecting black Americans, was the instrument of their oppression. To be an "uppity" black, not knowing one's place at the low rung of the status ladder, was a cardinal sin that sometimes attracted the vicious retribution of the Ku Klux Klan or other lawless vigilante groups. The promise of federal law and the Civil War amendments was quickly broken and constituted a series of empty rights and toothless guarantees.

Blacks outside the South and border states were not subject to such virulent racism, although the Klan operated in southern portions of several Midwestern states. While the North generally did not have state laws requiring racial separation, racism nevertheless flourished. Blacks and whites lived in separate neighborhoods, were typically educated apart, and led, for the most part, segregated lives. But as the twentieth century progressed, particularly after the Second World War, more and more northern states enacted state legislation prohibiting various forms of racial discrimination. The economic status of blacks was generally low but tended to be superior to that of their southern brothers and sisters. The North offered a greater range of economic opportunities than the South although the growing craft union movement sought to keep blacks from the trades. Organized labor

	Case	Ruling
EXHIBIT 13.1 Key Supreme Court Decisions That Denied Black Americans Their Rights	*U.S.* v. *Cruikshank* (1876)	Enforcement Act of 1870 cannot be used to prosecute racist white hoodlums who used violence to break up a political meeting of Louisiana blacks. Scope of act is limited.
	U.S. v. *Reese* (1876)	Enforcement Act of 1870 provision for federal supervision of the electoral process in the states to ensure that black Americans could vote and providing federal penalties for those impairing the right to vote is unconstitutional. Regulation of suffrage is a state concern. Fifteenth Amendment means only that states may not enact laws that prohibit black Americans from voting. If private persons interfere with blacks attempting to vote, that is solely concern of the state, not Congress.
	Hall v. *Decuir* (1878)	State law forbidding public carriers from racially discriminatory practices is an unconstitutional burden on interstate commerce.
	U.S. v. *Harris* (1883)	Major provisions of the federal Third Enforcement Act (also known as the Ku Klux Klan Act) are unconstitutional.
	Civil Rights Cases (1883)	The public accommodations provisions of Civil Rights Act of 1875 are unconstitutional. The equal protection clause of the Fourteenth Amendment applies only to the explicit actions of state authorities, not private persons.
	Pace v. *Alabama* (1883)	Alabama's antimiscegenation law prohibiting blacks and whites to marry did *not* violate equal protection since it applied equally to *both* blacks and whites.
	Plessy v. *Ferguson* (1896)	State law requiring separation of the races in separate but equal public facilities and services meets constitutional requirement of equal protection.

was primarily concerned with bettering the lot of white workers, and cheap black labor was seen as an economic threat.

Blacks in the North could vote and usually received a piece of the political pie in the form of patronage to local black politicians and their party organizations. The vision and dreams of these black politicians were as narrowly materialistic as those of their white counterparts. *Defacto segregation*

(segregation as a matter of practice, *not* state law), particularly residential housing segregation, was a way of life in the North.

The Struggle for Racial Equality

By the turn of the century, progressive whites and their black colleagues saw an urgent need for national collective action to improve conditions for black people. In 1910, the National Association for the Advancement of Colored People (the **NAACP**) was founded by a joint effort of blacks and whites. It became the principal vehicle for bringing the plight of black Americans to the attention of white Americans and their elected representatives.

The NAACP operated on many fronts. The organization was committed to attracting both blacks and whites to its ranks, and to educating blacks to work within the American political system. After all, the system had once worked during Reconstruction, when Congress enacted statutes and constitutional amendments to protect the rights of blacks. During that period, and in some parts of the South until the start of the twentieth century, blacks could and did vote. In fact, not only had blacks been elected to state legislatures, but between 1870 and 1902 twenty blacks were elected to the U.S. House of Representatives. In 1870 and 1874 two black Mississippians were elected to the U.S. Senate. The NAACP's message to blacks was that there *was* the potential for regaining rights but that also a long hard struggle *within the system* would be necessary. Organization was a prerequisite for that struggle.

The NAACP was at the same time committed to educating the public about the evils of racism and changing white America's perception of black America. It publicized the achievements of blacks in the arts, sciences, and playing fields of the nation. A new positive image of patriotic, hardworking, high-achieving black America was promoted. The NAACP also acted as the racial conscience of the nation, publicly protesting racial injustices.

Efforts on the part of the NAACP and other civil rights oriented groups to enact new statutory protection for blacks fell on more responsive ears at the northern state level, but Congress was dominated by segregationists who stifled federal civil rights legislation. The NAACP and black leadership in the country sought access to the White House, but not until the presidency of Franklin Roosevelt did black America have a loyal, dedicated friend in the White House—and that was the First Lady, Eleanor Roosevelt.

President Roosevelt was faced with a vexing dilemma at the start of the Second World War. He believed that racial segregation was wrong but also that the armed forces of the nation needed to be an effective fighting machine. The highest priority was to win the war. Thus the United States fought a war against the monstrously racist Nazi regime with a racially segregated army that included separate black combat units. On the home front, as noted in Chapter Twelve, those of Japanese ethnicity including thousands of American citizens living in certain areas of the West Coast and

**Segregated water
fountains.**

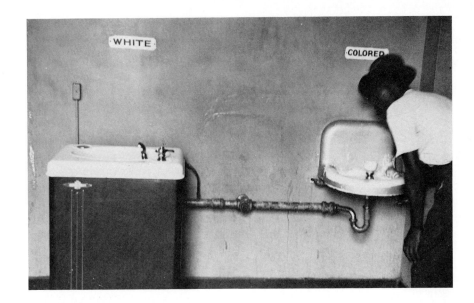

Arizona, were forcibly evacuated from their homes and herded into internment camps because their loyalty could not be immediately established.
These racist policies were also at odds with the concept of equal protection. However, President Roosevelt forbade racial discrimination in the defense industry, while the Supreme Court, although declaring the internment
policy constitutional, ordered the unconditional and immediate release of
Japanese-Americans and others of Japanese descent whose loyalty was established. After the war, President Truman desegregated the armed forces.

The New Deal coalition that Franklin Roosevelt put together included
the strange bedfellows of northern blacks and white Southerners. Ultimately
black Democrats insisted that the Democratic party make good on its implicit promises to black America. On February 2, 1948, President Truman
presented to Congress a comprehensive civil rights program which was
promptly suffocated by the segregationists in control of Congress. Five
months later, the 1948 Democratic party convention adopted the strongest
civil rights plank in the party's history, calling for new and effective civil
rights laws. That, in turn, precipitated the walkout from the convention of
numerous southern white Democrats, who then formed the States' Rights
party. President Truman won the 1948 election. Although Congress would
not enact the civil rights legislation he again introduced after the election,
Truman made some highly visible gestures towards black America, including appointing William Henry Hastie the first black American named to a
United States Court of Appeals judgeship.

Civil rights organizations were to a great extent concerned with pressing the rights of blacks in American courts. They never gave up on the
United States Supreme Court and in fact saw occasional modest successes,

which became more frequent in the late 1930s and 1940s and culminated in the landmark 1954 school desegregation decisions.

Although the Supreme Court during the first three and a half decades of the twentieth century did nothing to disturb the racist doctrine of *Plessy* v. *Ferguson*, it gave some evidence of moving away from its previous hostility to black rights. For example, in 1914 the Court struck down a state law that authorized intrastate railroads to provide white passengers but not black passengers with sleeping and dining cars. This law, said the Court, violated the equal protection guarantee of the Fourteenth Amendment.[6] Also in the 1920s and 1930s the Court expanded criminal procedural rights in cases which involved shockingly racist injustices against southern blacks.[7] However, the Supreme Court did not upset the legal basis for America's racial apartheid. For example, the Court as late as 1935 ruled that black Americans could be excluded from voting in Democratic party primaries because the party primary was an activity of a private organization and did not involve the action of the state. Because there was no *state* discriminatory action, the Court ruled that the equal protection guarantee of the Fourteenth Amendment was not violated.[8] Of course, at that time the Democratic party primary in the South was the functional equivalent of the general election and this ruling legitimized the "white primary" whereby white Southerners maintained their political monopoly.

The Supreme Court, during 1937 and after, began paying more attention to civil rights and civil liberties. In 1938 the Court, in a major decision involving law school education in the state of Missouri, ruled that the "equal" of the "separate-but-equal" formula must be honored within the boundaries of Missouri. This meant creating a law school for qualified blacks of equal quality to the white University of Missouri law school.[9] Another key decision was made in 1944, during the Second World War, when the Court overturned its previous white primary decision from 1935 and ruled that the party primary is an integral part of the electoral process. The Fifteenth Amendment thus prohibits excluding blacks from voting in primaries.[10] Blacks, at least as a matter of constitutional law, could no longer be legally disfranchised (what happened in practice was something else).

In still other decisions concerning racial equality, the Court in 1946 struck down a Virginia law that required the racial segregation of interstate passengers. The state law was considered to be an unconstitutional burden on interstate commerce.[11] Ironically, the rights of blacks in this case were equated with the free flow of commerce, an uncomfortable reminder of the

---

[6]*McCabe* v. *Atchison, Topeka & Santa Fe Railroad* (1914).

[7]See, for example, *Moore* v. *Dempsey* (1923); *Powell* v. *Alabama* (1932); *Norris* v. *Alabama* (1935); and *Brown* v. *Mississippi* (1936).

[8]*Grovey* v. *Townsend* (1935).

[9]*Missouri ex rel Gaines* v. *Canada* (1938).

[10]*Smith* v. *Allwright* (1944).

[11]*Morgan* v. *Virginia* (1946).

time when blacks were treated as articles of commerce in the domestic and foreign slave trade. But the decision itself furthered racial equality. In the late 1940s, the Court ruled that state courts cannot enforce restrictive covenants entered into by homeowners not to sell property to blacks. For the state courts to enforce such covenants (agreements) would amount to state action in violation of the Fourteenth Amendment.[12]

Separate-but-equal graduate and law school education was at issue in decisions in 1948 and 1950 and the Court strongly suggested that separate professional schools for blacks and segregated treatment of blacks in "white" schools were inherently unequal.[13] Armed with these precedents, the NAACP decided to wage an all-out legal assault on separate-but-equal in public elementary and high school education, hoping that the end of separate-but-equal education would upset the legal underpinnings of racial apartheid. The NAACP's gamble and strategy was ultimately successful in the landmark **Brown v. Board of Education** decision of 1954. If *Brown* did not launch the civil rights movement, it gave it a legitimacy and a momentum that eventually resulted in a new era in race relations, changing the social and political landscape of the nation.

Brown v. *Board of Education* **and the Civil Rights Revolution**

Brown v. *Board of Education* (see the box on pages 514 and 515 for excerpts from the decision), announced on May 17, 1954, consisted of school segregation cases from four states. The accompanying decision in *Bolling* v. *Sharpe* concerned school segregation in the District of Columbia (a federal territory). These decisions were not reached swiftly or lightly. The justices were sensitive to the impact and massive problems of implementing the decision to end separate-but-equal in public education. Fortunately, the Supreme Court was led by a great Chief Justice, Earl Warren, who patiently persuaded his colleagues to join his opinion of the Court explicitly reversing *Plessy* v. *Ferguson* in public education.[14] The *Brown* decision fatally undermined the legal basis for racism in all areas of social life, even though only public school education was at issue.

The lead case was a suit by Oliver Brown to require the Topeka, Kansas, Board of Education to admit his eight-year-old daughter Linda to a white school only five blocks from their home. Linda had been traveling twenty-one blocks to an all-black school. Under the permissive Kansas state law, Topeka had imposed the dual school system on its schools whereby there were separate but presumably equal school systems for each race. In the *Brown* case and the three others from the states (South Carolina, Virginia, and Delaware), the Court found that separate was inherently *unequal*. State-

[12]*Shelley* v. *Kraemer* (1948).

[13]*Sipuel* v. *Board of Regents of the University of Oklahoma* (1948); *McLaurin* v. *Oklahoma State Regents* (1950); *Sweatt* v. *Painter* (1950).

[14]The leading study of the *Brown* decision and its political, historical, and legal context is Richard Kluger, *Simple Justice* (New York: Knopf, 1975).

Chief Justice Warren's Opinion in *Brown* v. *Board of Education*

Chief Justice Warren delivered the opinion of the Court:

These cases come to us from the States of Kansas, South Carolina, Virginia, and Delaware....

In each of the cases, minors of the Negro race, through their legal representatives, seek the aid of the courts in obtaining admission to the public schools of their community on a nonsegregated basis. In each instance, they had been denied admission to schools attended by white children under laws requiring or permitting segregation according to race. This segregation was alleged to deprive the plaintiffs of the equal protection of the laws under the Fourteenth Amendment. In each of the cases other than the Delaware case, a three-judge federal district court denied relief to the plaintiffs on the so-called "separate but equal" doctrine announced by this Court in *Plessy* v. *Ferguson*. Under that doctrine, equality of treatment is accorded when the races are provided substantially equal facilities, even though these facilities be separate. In the Delaware case, the Supreme Court of Delaware adhered to that doctrine, but ordered that the plaintiffs be admitted to the white schools because of their superiority to the Negro schools.

The plaintiffs contend that segregated public schools are not "equal" and cannot be made "equal," and that hence they are deprived of the equal protection of the laws....

In approaching this problem, we cannot turn the clock back to 1868 when the Amendment was adopted, or even to 1896 when *Plessy* v. *Ferguson* was written. We must consider public education in the light of its full development and its present place in American life throughout the Nation. Only in this way can it be determined if segregation in public schools deprives these plaintiffs of the equal protection of the laws.

Today, education is perhaps the most important function of state and local governments. Compulsory school attendance laws and the great expenditures for education both demonstrate our recognition of the importance of education to our democratic society. It is required in the performance of our most basic public responsibilities, even service in the armed forces. It is the very foundation of good citizenship.

required racial separation in the public schools in and of itself violated the equal protection guarantee of the Fourteenth Amendment. In the case involving public school segregation in the federal territory of the District of Columbia, the constitutional basis for the Court's decision was the Fifth Amendment due process clause (the Court could not use the equal protection clause of the Fourteenth Amendment because it applies only to the states).

The Court ruled that equal protection is an explicit responsibility of the states and a responsibility on the federal government implicit in the Fifth Amendment's due process clause. These decisions established the proposition that racial equality is *both* a state and federal obligation and that, at least in public education, separate can *never* be equal and must be struck down as violating the equality guarantees of the Constitution. However, in its 1954 opinions the Court did not explain how school desegregation was to occur.

Today it is a principal instrument in awakening the child to cultural values, in preparing him for later professional training, and in helping him to adjust normally to his environment. In these days, it is doubtful that any child may reasonably be expected to succeed in life if he is denied the opportunity of an education. Such an opportunity, where the state has undertaken to provide it, is a right which must be made available to all on equal terms.

We come then to the question presented: Does segregation of children in public schools solely on the basis of race, even though the physical facilities and other "tangible" factors may be equal, deprive the children of the minority group of equal education opportunities? We believe that it does.

. . . .To separate them from others of similar age and qualifications solely because of their race generates a feeling of inferiority as to their status in the community that may affect their hearts and minds in a way unlikely ever to be undone. The effect of this separation on their educational opportunities was well stated by a finding in the Kansas case by a court which nevertheless felt compelled to rule against the Negro plaintiffs:

"Segregation of white and colored children in public schools has a detrimental effect upon the colored children. The impact is greater when it has the sanction of the law; for the policy of separating the races is usually interpreted as denoting the inferiority of the Negro group. A sense of inferiority affects the motivation of a child to learn. Segregation with the sanction of law, therefore, has a tendency to retard the educational and mental development of Negro children and to deprive them of some of the benefits they would receive in a racially integrated school system."

Whatever may have been the extent of psychological knowledge at the time of *Plessy* v. *Ferguson*, this finding is amply supported by modern authority. Any language in *Plessy* v. *Ferguson* contrary to this finding is rejected.

We conclude that in the field of public education the doctrine of "separate but equal" has no place. Separate educational facilities are inherently unequal. Therefore, we hold that the plaintiffs and others similarly situated for whom the actions have been brought are, by reason of the segregation complained of, deprived of the equal protection of the laws guaranteed by the Fourteenth Amendment. . . .

The following year, the Court announced its enforcement policy, which was to turn implementation over to local school authorities and local federal courts with the clear understanding that flexibility and sensitivity to local needs and conditions would be taken into account by the courts. But, said the Supreme Court, there must be "a prompt and reasonable start toward full compliance." The federal district courts were authorized to retain jurisdiction of the cases during the period of transition from a discriminatory dual school system to a racially nondiscriminatory unitary school system. They were empowered to "enter such orders and decrees . . . as are necessary and proper to admit to public schools on a racially non-discriminatory basis *with all deliberate speed* the parties to these cases" (emphasis added). By its enforcement opinion and its use of the "all deliberate speed" terminology, the Court recognized that desegregation would not occur at once, but would be gradual.

Paratroopers from the 101st Airborne Division protecting nine black students at Central High School in Little Rock, Arkansas.

With *Brown* v. *Board of Education*, America's unjust treatment of black America was thrust before white America. The eloquently written opinion by Chief Justice Earl Warren was headline news. It was as if white America were a sleeping giant just awakening from the nightmare of racial injustice. However, the awakening process was unsettling. The white South was at once outraged, fearful, and defiant. The desegregation of over 2,200 public school systems in the South and border states clearly would not come about by voluntary compliance. This meant that civil rights forces, principally the NAACP and the NAACP Legal Defense Fund, had to finance numerous suits to force local authorities to end racial segregation in the public schools.

While black America had the moral force of its position and a favorable Supreme Court ruling to give it comfort, it had little else. President Eisenhower neither praised nor openly supported the *Brown* decision (privately he thought it a mistake), and he was unwilling to take the initiative to use the full force of the federal government's power to secure region-wide compliance.[15] However, events in Little Rock, Arkansas, several years later placed President Eisenhower in the position of having to choose whether to permit open defiance of a specific federal court order desegregating Little Rock's Central High School. The president ordered federal troops to protect black high school students at the desegregated high school, thus enforcing

[15]Piers Brendon, *Ike: The Life and Times of Dwight D. Eisenhower* (London: Secker & Warburg, 1987), pp. 279–81.

the court decision. The Supreme Court, a year later, affirmed the desegregation decision of the appeals court that the president had in fact enforced.[16]

During the late 1950s and early 1960s, school desegregation lawsuits occupied much of the time of southern federal courts. Eventually, the Warren Court lost patience with evasion, delay, and subterfuge. In 1964 the Court pointed out, "There has been entirely too much deliberation and not enough speed."[17] By 1968, it exhorted "delays are no longer tolerable."[18] The next year the Burger Court firmly and vigorously ruled that "all deliberate speed" as a standard for desegregation "is no longer constitutionally permissible." The Court insisted that "every school district is to terminate dual school systems at once...."[19]

Of all the institutions of government, the Supreme Court led the way in efforts to achieve racial equality. At the other extreme, most southern politicians opposed desegregation. In 1956, some 101 southern congressmen signed what became known as the *Southern Manifesto* (significantly, in light of the major civil rights role he would one day play as president, then Senator Lyndon B. Johnson was one of the few Southerners who did not). The Manifesto attacked the *Brown* decision as "a clear abuse of judicial power" and pledged "to use all lawful means to bring about a reversal of this decision which is contrary to the Constitution." While the signers of the Manifesto may have been alluding to a possible effort to pass an amendment to the Constitution overturning *Brown* or the appointment of anti-*Brown* justices, the Manifesto was a signal that massive resistance and defiance were justified because the Court's decision was lawless.

The Southern Manifesto was all the more significant because southern congressmen held key legislative positions and were able to use their power to stifle attempts at enacting civil rights laws. Nevertheless, the new urgency given racial equality and the recognition of racial injustice in the United States led to a congressional breakthrough in 1957 when Congress enacted the first civil rights law in eighty-two years. The legislation was more important for its symbolism—that Congress was able to act in the civil rights sphere—than for its modest accomplishments. The new law established the Civil Rights Commission and vested it only with investigatory powers. It created the Civil Rights Division within the Justice Department and empowered it to seek injunctions when citizens were denied the right to vote. After the congressional elections of 1958, when Democrats gained forty-nine House seats and seventeen Senate seats (most of whose occupants were sympathetic to civil rights), Congress enacted the Civil Rights Act of 1960, which strengthened the powers of the Civil Rights Commission and enhanced the role of the Justice Department in instances where there was denial of the right to vote.

[16]*Cooper* v. *Aaron* (1958).
[17]*Griffin* v. *Prince Edward County School Board* (1964).
[18]*Green* v. *School Board of New Kent County* (1968).
[19]*Alexander* v. *Holmes County Board of Education* (1969).

Rosa Parks riding in the front of a Montgomery, Alabama bus following the Supreme Court decision striking down segregation on municipal buses.

The Court's decision in *Brown* had an electrifying effect on the nation's African-Americans. The NAACP had shown that, with patience and persistence, black Americans could accomplish something by working within the system. But the message of *Brown* also held out hope that the moral and legal wrong of racism was doomed in *all* its vestiges.

Black America began losing patience in the months that followed *Brown* when nothing much actually changed. This was dramatically illustrated by events in Montgomery, Alabama, in 1955, when a middle-aged black seamstress, Rosa Parks, tired after a day's work, defied the city's Jim Crow law that required blacks to sit at the back of municipal buses. She sat down on the first available seat and refused to surrender her seat to a white person. Her arrest sparked a boycott of the buses by Montgomery's blacks that was led by Martin Luther King, Jr., the minister at Mrs. Parks's church. The boycott was effective and lasted over a year, until the buses were desegregated following a Supreme Court ruling striking down as a violation of equal protection the municipal regulation requiring segregated seating on municipal buses. The boycott also thrust the Reverend King into national prominence.

The late 1950s saw the increased use of boycotts to attack racial discrimination. The civil rights movement used other forms of protest, including the sit-in (which originated in 1960 at a lunch counter in North Carolina), picketing, freedom marches, mass demonstrations, freedom rides (to desegregate interstate buses, trains, and airplanes and their waiting rooms), and sometimes outright civil disobedience.[20] Black leaders formed or rein-vigorated civil rights groups and pressed on a variety of fronts—the state and local levels, Congress, the presidency, and particularly the federal courts. Success was greatest at the Supreme Court level until Congress passed the Civil Rights Act of 1964. The Warren Court used *Brown* as prece-dent and equated separate with unequal in violation of equal protection. This was the constitutional basis for striking down segregation in all public facilities, not only municipal buses, but municipal golf courses, public swimming pools and beaches, libraries, publicly owned athletic facilities and stadiums, private restaurants in municipally owned buildings, and state and local courthouses and courtrooms.

With the election of John F. Kennedy in 1960, black America had a friend in the White House who was prepared to actively support racial equality. The Kennedy administration protected the freedom riders, en-forced desegregation of facilities at bus and railroad terminals, began aiding black petitioners in school desegregation suits, and instituted numerous suits to protect the voting rights of blacks. President Kennedy, towards the end of 1962, signed an executive order prohibiting racial discrimination in federally subsidized housing, including housing guaranteed by federal mort-gages. However, the administration bowed to political pressures from southern Democratic senators and appointed some racists to the southern federal courts.[21]

During the early 1960s, the civil rights movement accelerated, with cri-sis after crisis vividly reported by television, radio, and the print media, dramatically demonstrating the viciousness of racism. President Kennedy, after one such crisis involving Alabama Governor George Wallace, gave a television address to the nation in which he eloquently described the plight of black America in words aimed to affect the hearts and minds of white America. Kennedy said, in part:

> "If an American, because his skin is dark, cannot eat lunch in a restaurant open to the public; if he cannot send his children to the best public school available; if he cannot vote for the public officials who represent him; if, in short, he can-not enjoy the full and free life which all of us want, then who among us would be content to have the color of his skin changed and stand in his place? . . . .
> [T]his nation, for all its hopes and all its boasts, will not be fully free until all its citizens are free.
>
> We preach freedom around the world, and we mean it. And we cherish our freedom at home. But are we to say to the world—and much more importantly to each other—that this is the land of the free, except for the Negroes; that we have no second-class citizens, except Negroes; that we have no class or caste system, no ghetto, no master race, except with respect to Negroes?"

[20]See Aldon D. Morris, *The Origins of the Civil Rights Movement: Black Communities Organizing for Change* (New York: Free Press, 1984).
[21]Victor S. Navasky, *Kennedy Justice* (New York: Atheneum, 1971), chap. 5.

| EXHIBIT 13.2 | Highlights of the Civil Rights Bill Introduced on June 19, 1963 |

The civil rights bill drafted by the Kennedy administration and introduced in Congress on June 19, 1963, included the following provisions:

- enforcement of the constitutional right to vote;
- desegregation of public accommodations (in hotels, motels, restaurants, theaters, and local transportation systems);
- extended authority of the Commission on Civil Rights to investigate denial of equal protection on account of race, color, religion, or national origin;
- created Commission on Equal Employment Opportunity with powers to enforce the ban on discrimination by employers and labor unions;
- prohibited discrimination in federally assisted programs;
- strengthened the authority of the Justice Department to sue state and local governments whose laws and practices perpetuated racism in the public schools and other public facilities.

On June 19, 1963, President Kennedy introduced the most comprehensive civil rights legislation ever presented to Congress (see Exhibit 13.2 for highlights of the bill). But simply offering such legislation, although a milestone, was hardly enough as opponents had the power to stall legislation in committee or filibuster it to death—unless a large majority of members of Congress were committed to the bill's passage. Kennedy campaigned for national support for the bill to bring pressure on Congress. The civil rights movement, led by Dr. Martin Luther King, Jr., also began a series of nationwide activities to maintain the pressure. The climax of this campaign was a massive *March on Washington* to show support for federal action to end racism. On August 28, 1963, an estimated 200,000 people, black and white, from all parts of the country, walks of life, and age groups, gathered on the Mall in a peaceful rally, in which the high point was Dr. King's now famous "I have a dream" speech. Dr. King, evoking the idealism of the nation and the deepest hopes and dreams of black Americans, said in part:

> "I have a dream that one day this nation will rise up and live out the true meaning of its creed. . . .
>
> I have a dream that one day . . . the sons of former slaves and the sons of former slaveowners will be able to sit down together at the table of brotherhood. . . .
>
> I have a dream that my four little children will one day live in a nation where they will not be judged by the color of their skin but by the content of their character. . . ."

Despite the strenuous efforts of the Kennedy administration and the Civil Rights movement, Congress did not budge. Only after the assassination of President Kennedy on November 22, 1963, was President Lyndon B. Johnson, by combining political pressure and moral fervor, able to successfully push for enactment of the Civil Rights bill as a memorial to Kennedy.

Johnson, himself a Southerner, prodded his former southern congressional colleagues and others, pulling out the stops until victory came. The **Civil Rights Act of 1964**, signed into law on July 2, was not only a major breakthrough in the struggle for racial equality. During the congressional consideration of the measure, sexual discrimination was added making the Act of even additional historic importance. Also in 1964, the Twenty-Fourth Amendment was ratified outlawing the poll tax.

Title 2 of the Civil Rights Act of 1964 contained the public accommodations provisions forbidding racial discrimination in hotels, restaurants, theaters, and any public accommodation if "its operations affect commerce." A constitutional challenge to Title 2 was rejected by the Supreme Court in 1964 and the Court in another case dismissed the numerous state criminal trespass prosecutions of sit-in demonstrators who tried to desegregate public accommodations.[22] By enacting Title 2, said the Court, Congress abated all sit-in prosecutions.

The Civil Rights Commission's reports vividly reminded the nation that black Americans, particularly in certain parts of the South, were still being denied the right to vote. Civil rights leaders urged federal supervision of the state electoral process to protect the voting rights of black Americans. The Reverend Martin Luther King, Jr., led a series of marches in 1965 to dramatize the urgent necessity of federal action. During one march, on Selma, Alabama, civil rights demonstrators were attacked and beaten. The violence directed at the black and white marchers captured the media's attention and forced white America to confront the issue of brutal racism. President Johnson kept up the momentum and successfully pressed for enactment of the **Voting Rights Act of 1965**. That Act provided for federal supervision of elections in states violating the Fifteenth Amendment. It also eliminated literacy or other educational tests used to discriminate racially. The Supreme Court upheld the law's constitutionality.[23] It also invalidated the poll tax for elections to state and local office.[24]

The Johnson administration also tackled the problem of racial discrimination in the sale or rental of housing. The Civil Rights Act of 1968 was enacted and included Title 8, containing the fair housing provisions. Tragically, it was the assassination of Dr. King in 1968 that provided the momentum needed to push the bill through Congress. The Supreme Court revived an older fair housing policy in a 1968 case in which it ruled that a section of the Civil Rights Act of 1866 prohibiting all public and private racial discrimination in the sale or rental of property was constitutional and still in effect.[25]

---

[22]*Heart of Atlanta Motel* v. *United States* (1964) (upheld Title 2); *Hamm* v. *City of Rock Hill* (1964) (dismissed trespass convictions of sit-in demonstrators).

[23]*South Carolina* v. *Katzenbach* (1966) and *Katzenbach* v. *Morgan* (1966).

[24]*Harper* v. *Virginia State Board of Elections* (1966).

[25]*Jones* v. *Mayer Co.* (1968).

■ RACIAL EQUALITY TODAY

Many black Americans today, on the whole, have much better lives—in terms of economic opportunities, material well-being, protection of their legal rights, and integration in white America—than thirty years ago and earlier. But this does not mean that they no longer face racial prejudice in their everyday lives. Even more to the point, the issue of racial equality is not how far black Americans have come in their treatment by white America, but how black Americans compare with white Americans in such matters as being able to exercise their voting rights as citizens, to enjoy employment opportunities, to live where they like, and to have opportunities for a quality desegregated education. These issues raise a number of questions:

- What should be the role of government in securing racial equality for black Americans? Should it be one of aggressive enforcement of antidiscrimination laws? Should it include withholding government funds from those who practice racial discrimination?
- What are the appropriate remedies for correcting the effects of past racial discrimination? In education, is massive busing of school children the appropriate remedy? In employment, should racial quotas be used to increase the proportion of black employees? Should **affirmative action**, that is, an aggressive search for qualified blacks and other groups that have been victims of discrimination, and set goals be required? Should colleges and universities be allowed to set aside a certain number of places in entering classes for qualified minorities who, although qualified, may not be *as* qualified as some white applicants who are denied admission?
- What are the ultimate goals of racial equality—equality of opportunity, which may mean shutting one's eyes to the disabling effects of past racial discrimination on many of those in the group discriminated against, or equality of result, which may mean giving preference to minority individuals who themselves may not have been victims of discrimination over whites who themselves may be innocent of any discriminatory wrongdoing? Is it enough to say "no more discrimination," or is more needed to raise the discriminated-against group to a level where its members can equally and fairly compete?
- Is the equality of results argument racially patronizing and does it trivialize the historic and current accomplishments of African-Americans in every field of endeavor? Is equality of results a reasonable criterion by which to determine that racial discrimination is no longer practiced?

These issues cannot be resolved here, but some of them can be examined when considering the status of racial equality today. Primary attention is paid to African-Americans, but some of the discussion is relevant for Hispanic-Americans and others who face discrimination.

Voting Rights

Who would deny that the right to vote is basic to a democratic society and that the federal government should protect its citizens when they seek to exercise that right? The Voting Rights Act of 1965 and its extensions in 1970, 1975, and 1982 were designed to protect the voting rights of black Americans in those southern states in which they had been, for the most part, denied the vote. For example, in 1940 only 5 percent of eligible black Americans were registered to vote in the eleven states of the old Confederacy.[26] Although the Civil Rights Acts of 1957, 1960, and 1964 brought federal government involvement in securing the vote for blacks, the burden was on the federal government to prove in individual law suits that racially motivated practices resulted in denial of the vote. Even with this time-consuming legal process, by 1964 some 38 percent of voting-age blacks in the South were registered; however, registration rates varied by state.[27] For example, by early 1965, only 7 percent of Mississippi voting age blacks were registered, compared to 70 percent of whites.[28] Alabama, Georgia, Louisiana, South Carolina, and Virginia also had major discrepancies by race. In Virginia 38 percent of the blacks were registered, compared to 61 percent of the whites. All these states came under the Voting Rights Act of 1965 (see Exhibit 13.3 for the key provisions of the Act).

The 1970 extension of the Voting Rights Act continued the original provisions of the Act with some modification for another five years. The 1975 renewal was for an additional seven years and Spanish speaking and other language minority groups were brought under the Act's coverage. The 1982 Voting Rights Act continued the "preclearance" (approval by government of any changes in the voting laws) provisions for another twenty-five years but stipulated that a state or county could be released from federal supervision if it could satisfy a three judge district court that it had not impeded the right of voting age blacks or other minorities to register and to vote during the previous ten years.

One important aspect of the 1982 Voting Rights Act was that it liberalized a 1980 Supreme Court decision that an electoral scheme must offer black voters equal access to the ballot but need not provide for equality of results. Only if it could be proven that the *intent* of the electoral scheme was to make it difficult for blacks to win electoral office would that electoral scheme be struck down.[29] The 1982 Voting Rights Act extension provided that private individuals *can* challenge an electoral scheme by showing that

---

[26]Richard Scher and James Button, "Voting Rights Act: Implementation and Impact," in Charles S. Bullock III and Charles M. Lamb, eds., *Implementation of Civil Rights Policy* (Monterey, California: Brooks/Cole, 1984), pp. 39, 41.

[27]*Ibid.*, p. 41.

[28]These figures and those that follow are from *ibid.*, p. 42.

[29]*City of Mobile, Alabama* v. *Bolden* (1980).

| EXHIBIT 13.3 | Key Provisions of the Voting Rights Act of 1965 |

The Voting Rights Act of 1965 provided that:

- entire states or counties within states would automatically come under the provisions of the Act if, as of November 1, 1964, they employed literacy tests for voting *and* less than 50 percent of the voting age population had either registered or voted in the 1964 election;
- most qualifications for voting were suspended for five years with the exception of proof of citizenship, age, residency, and achievement of a sixth grade education as proof of literacy;
- federal voting examiners could be sent to suspect counties to determine the eligibility for voting of unregistered voting-age residents and to list those eligible who previously had been illegally refused registration by local officials. Federal observers could be assigned to the polling places to assure that those registered to vote would be able to exercise their right;
- any changes in the voting laws of the states and counties subject to the Act had to be approved by the Attorney General or by the United States District Court for the District of Columbia (known as *preclearance*).

it consistently results in racially biased or skewed outcomes. Courts were directed to examine the totality of circumstances when considering whether the Voting Rights Act was violated.

What have been the results of the voting rights legislation and its implementation? The evidence suggests that while there have been some inconsistencies in Justice Department enforcement policies which varied in part by which political party was in power (Democratic Presidents Johnson and Carter's administrations were somewhat more vigorous enforcers than Republican administrations), there has been overall success.[30] Of course, the massive and strenuous efforts of civil rights groups to register black voters and to protect the exercise of their franchise has been instrumental in the increase of black electoral participation.[31] For the South as a whole, by 1980 some 59 percent of eligible blacks were registered to vote, compared to 66 percent of whites.[32]

In some southern states the gains in black registration were dramatic. By 1972, the gap between black and white registration had been lowered considerably. For example, in Mississippi from a 1965 gap of 63 percent there was a drop by 1972 to a gap of 10 percent. Georgia went from a 1965 gap of 35 percent to a 1972 gap of 3 percent. Alabama went from a 50 percent to a 24 percent gap. In Arkansas and Texas black registration was even proportionately greater than white registration in 1972.[33] Other figures show

[30]Scher and Button, *op. cit.*, pp. 31–37.

[31]In general see Hanes Walton, Jr., *Invisible Politics: Black Political Behavior* (Ithaca, N.Y.: State University of New York Press, 1985).

[32]Scher and Button, *op. cit.*, p. 40.

[33]The statistics on registration gaps between blacks and whites in 1965 and 1972 are from Scher and Button, *op. cit.*, p. 42.

Black voter registration in Memphis, Tennessee in 1968.

that in eleven southern states the numbers of blacks registered to vote increased from 2.1 million in 1964 to 5.6 million in 1984.[34]

The evidence suggests that today whatever differences exist in registration rates between blacks and whites is not as much due to racially discriminatory electoral practices as socioeconomic factors.[35] There are still millions of poor blacks and whites who do not participate in the electoral process. There are also millions of non-poor who choose not to participate, but they are proportionately fewer than the poor. When voting participation in presidential elections nationally is close to 50 percent of those of voting age, there are obviously problems in addition to poverty and ignorance. However, it appears that today, with possibly isolated exceptions, African-Americans are not denied the right to vote on account of their race.

The true test of black electoral participation is the ability of black voters to elect blacks to public office and to influence white officials who need their votes. Here there also appears to be progress over the past two decades. In 1968 there were a total of 248 black elected officials in the South. By 1981 there were 2535 and by 1987 the figure stood at 4287. Most black elect-

[34]As cited in the *New York Times*, March 4, 1985, p. A14.
[35]Raymond E. Wolfinger and Steven J. Rosenstone, *Who Votes?* (New Haven: Yale University Press, 1980), pp. 90–92 as cited by Scher and Button, *op. cit.*, p. 44. But see the argument in Frances Fox Piven and Richard A. Cloward, *Why Americans Don't Vote* (New York: Pantheon, 1988).

EXHIBIT 13.4	YEAR		
Position	*1970*	*1978*	*1987*
Mayor	48	170	303
State Legislatures:			
State Senator	31	56	89
State Representative	137	238	311
U.S. Congress:			
Senator	0	1	0
Representative	10	16	23
All elective offices	1479	4544	6646

Black Elected
Officials: 1970, 1978,
and 1987

Source: Joint Center for Political Studies as reported in *New York Times*, February 29, 1988, p. B-8 and U.S. Bureau of the Census, *Statistical Abstract of the United States: 1988* (108th edition) (Washington, D.C.: 1987), p. 247.

ed officials were at the local level and included black mayors of Atlanta and New Orleans. At the state legislative level there were a total of 200 southern black legislators serving in 1987, up from 23 serving in 1968.[36] Nationally, by 1987, there were 23 black members of Congress, 400 members of state legislatures, 303 mayors, and, in total, 6646 black elected officials (see Exhibit 13.4).

The evidence suggests that blacks are underrepresented least at the local level and most at the state and national levels. Whether blacks have their fair share of elected public officials or not, it *is* clear that the black vote has had a profound impact on politics. Southern Democratic senators owed their elections in 1986 to the black vote. When civil rights organizations opposed Robert Bork's nomination to the Supreme Court and mobilized the black electorate, these senators were attentive. When most southern Democratic senators came out against Bork, the nomination was doomed. In 1987 and 1988, Jesse Jackson was a serious candidate for the presidency, winning millions of votes in primaries and caucuses. He became the runner-up to Michael Dukakis, the eventual nominee of the Democratic party. After the election, African-American Ronald H. Brown was elected the Chairman of the Democratic National Committee thus becoming head of the national party organization.

No longer do white candidates in the South vie with each other as to who can be more racist. Black votes are now courted by white politicians and black citizens are treated far differently than in the era of segregation. Symbolic of this change were the events that occurred in Selma, Alabama, on March 3, 1985. Just two decades earlier, Selma had been the site of a bloody attack by state law enforcement officials on peaceful civil rights

[36]Scher and Button, *op. cit.*, p. 45; U.S. Bureau of the Census, *Statistical Abstract of the United States: 1988* (108th edition) (Washington, D.C.: 1987), p. 247.

protesters marching to call attention to the lack of voting rights for blacks. The nationwide media coverage of the brutality provoked widespread revulsion and led to the passage of the Voting Rights Act of 1965. Twenty years later a civil rights march commemorating the events of 1965 was conducted through the streets of Selma, but this time the mayor, who had been mayor twenty years earlier, presented the keys to the city to the leaders of the 1985 march, Jesse Jackson and Joseph E. Lowery.[37] It is true that white residents of Selma did not line the streets cheering and throwing flowers. Most stayed home, but the racial climate clearly had changed. The ability of blacks to exercise freely their right to vote was largely responsible for the change.

Equal Rights in Employment

While the right to vote free from racial discrimination required enforcement policies that were relatively noncontroversial as far as most of the nation was concerned (but not, of course, in the affected localities), the right to employment free from racial bias has caused more dispute. The dispute has not been over whether racial discrimination in employment practices is wrong (most people today think it is). Rather, the dispute has been over the remedies used or proposed to correct abuses of the past.

The legacy of racism is apparent in the figures for median family income for 1987. Nationwide for white families it was $32,274, but for black families it was $18,098. Hispanic families fared only slightly better than black families ($20,306 median family income).[38] In the South, close to two-thirds of black workers have employment as unskilled, semi-skilled, or lowest-status service workers such as maids and waiters, as compared to about one third of white workers. Outside the South, about half of black workers are employed in such jobs.[39]

The challenge has been and continues to be what can government do to prevent racial discrimination at the workplace. Presidents Kennedy and Johnson issued executive orders prohibiting racial discrimination by federal contractors. Johnson extended the ban to subcontractors and unions doing work on any federal project. His executive order created the Office of Federal Contract Compliance Programs to enforce and monitor compliance. In 1968, that office required affirmative action programs with specific timetables and goals. Congress, too, acted with the Civil Rights Act of 1964, which created the *Equal Employment Opportunity Commission* (**EEOC**) to enforce Title 7 which prohibits private employers or unions with a mini-

---

[37]This account is drawn from *New York Times*, March 4, 1985, pp. A-1, A-14.

[38]These figures are from the Census Bureau and were reprinted in *USA Today*, September 1, 1988, p. 3A. Also see Harrell R. Rodgers, Jr., "Fair Employment Laws for Minorities: An Evaluation of Federal Implementation," in Charles S. Bullock III and Charles M. Lamb, eds., *Implementation of Civil Rights Policy* (Monterey, California: Brooks/Cole, 1984), pp. 93-117.

[39]*New York Times*, April 6, 1985, p. 7 and February 29, 1988, p. B-8. Also see Rodgers, *op. cit.*, p. 103.

mum of twenty-five workers from engaging in racial discrimination in hiring and employment. The Civil Rights Act of 1972 expanded the authority of the EEOC, allowing the agency to sue in federal district court. The Act also gave the EEOC wider jurisdiction to cover all businesses or unions containing a minimum of fifteen workers *and* state and local government employees (in 1978, federal employees were added).

The EEOC used affirmative action as the cornerstone of its nondiscrimination plans. This usually meant setting aside a given proportion of *new* jobs for minorities or ensuring that black employees would have access to a given proportion of job training opportunities. Opponents of this form of affirmative action argued that by reserving a set number of jobs or training opportunities for blacks, or other minorities, or women (all of whom were protected by the civil rights acts), employers would be practicing unlawful discrimination against white males.

The legality of affirmative action programs, whether imposed by the EEOC or voluntarily adopted by labor and management on their own without government instigation, was decided by the Supreme Court in the 1979 decision of *United Steelworkers* v. *Weber*. In that case, the national steelworkers union and Kaiser Aluminum and Chemical Corporation negotiated a collective bargaining agreement that included an affirmative action job training program for black employees so that they would be eligible for the higher paying craft jobs. Because of past racial discrimination, almost all craft workers were white. Under the plan, 50 percent of openings in craft-training programs were to be reserved for black employees until the percentage of black craft workers in a plant would approximate the proportion of blacks in the local labor force. Brian Weber, a white production worker, was refused admission to the craft-training program and instituted a suit on behalf of himself and all others in his situation. Weber worked at the Kaiser plant in Gramercy, Louisiana, where less than 2 percent of the skilled craft workers were black, although 39 percent of the workforce in the area was black. Black workers with less seniority than Brian Weber were selected for the program and Weber argued that this was discrimination in violation of Title 7 of the Civil Rights Act of 1964. But the Supreme Court disagreed. Title 7, said the Court, does not prohibit private, voluntary race-conscious affirmative action plans meant "to break down old patterns of racial segregation and hierarchy." Title 7 was meant to open employment opportunities for blacks in occupations which have traditionally been closed to them. The Court suggested that to meet the requirement of the law, affirmative action plans such as this one should be temporary measures to correct a racial imbalance due to past racism and not be used to perpetuate a racial balance or to require the firing of white workers so that blacks can be hired.

The Reagan administration actively opposed affirmative action programs that used numerical goals and quotas to remedy past racism and sexism and to ensure equal employment opportunities. The administration asked federal courts to modify affirmative action plans imposed by the courts on state and local governmental units by removing goals and quotas.

These same plans had been devised or accepted by the Justice Department of previous administrations.[40] The Reagan administration made it clear that its goal was the end of all affirmative action programs, whether voluntary or court-ordered.

In 1984 the Supreme Court handed down a decision in *Firefighters Local Union No. 1784* v. *Stotts* in which it ruled that courts could not interfere with seniority systems in order to protect blacks from job layoffs. This case involved the Memphis Fire Department, which had hired blacks under a court-ordered affirmative action program. But the black employees, being the most recently hired, were subject to being laid off first. Civil rights groups believe that affirmative action programs would be severely undermined and gains for black workers eroded if they did not receive some protection from job layoffs. But the Court ruled that seniority rights have the higher priority. The Reagan administration then took the position that the Court's decision meant that *all* preferential treatment of blacks, other minorities, and women must end and that no longer could group-based remedies be used to correct past discrimination. The Reagan administration insisted that only when individuals can prove that they personally were victims of discrimination would they be entitled to relief. This extreme position, however, was rejected by the Court in 1986.

In a series of decisions, including *Local 28 of Sheet Metal Workers* v. *EEOC*, the Supreme Court drew a distinction between *hiring* and *layoffs*. At the hiring stage, employers *can* use (or be ordered by a court to use) the group-based remedy of affirmative action to correct past discriminatory abuses. This is also true for promotions. The impact on white males is much less than using preferential treatment rather than seniority for determining who is to lose jobs. To lay off white workers because of their race violates their guarantee of equal protection of the laws. In subsequent cases the Court emphasized that even subjective or discretionary employment practices may be analyzed in terms of their discriminatory impact on black workers.[41] However, in several decisions in 1989, the Court made it more difficult to prove discrimination and invited white males to file reverse discrimination suits challenging Court-approved affirmative action plans.[42]

What are the results of government's effort to end racial discrimination in employment and to provide for fair employment opportunities? The figures contrasting the proportions of blacks in different occupations in the year 1958 compared to 1977 are striking. The proportion of blacks employed in professional and technical occupations tripled over this time period.[43] The proportion of black women working as domestics fell from 37 percent in 1958 to 9 percent in 1977, but, in contrast, the proportion work-

---

[40]*New York Times*, April 3, 1985, p. A-16.

[41]*Watson* v. *Fort Worth Bank and Trust* (1988).

[42]*Wards Cove Packing Co.* v. *Antonio* (1989); *Martin* v. *Wilks* (1989); *Patterson* v. *McLean Credit Union* (1989).

[43]These and the figures which follow are from Rodgers, *op. cit.*, pp. 102–3.

EXHIBIT 13.5		MALE		FEMALE	
	Occupation	*Black*	*White*	*Black*	*White*
Employed Persons in 1986 by Occupation, Race, and Gender (in percentages)	Executive-Managerial	6.2%	13.9%	6.0%	10.0%
	Professional	6.6	11.9	10.7	14.6
	Technician	2.0	3.0	3.1	3.2
	Sales	5.2	11.9	8.7	13.7
	Clerks	8.6	5.4	26.5	29.8
	Domestic (private household)	0.1	0.1	4.3	1.6
	Firefighter/Police/Security Guard	4.2	2.4	0.8	0.4
	All other service workers (food/ health/janitorial/personal services)	13.4	6.0	23.2	14.9
	Mechanics/Construction/Repair/ Precision	16.0	20.7	2.6	2.3
	Machine operators/assemblers/ inspectors	11.0	7.4	10.6	5.9
	Transportation and material moving occupations	10.8	6.5	0.1	0.8
	Freight, stock, material handlers and laborers	12.2	5.9	2.1	1.5
	Farming, forestry, fishing	3.7	4.9	0.4	1.2

Source: U.S. Bureau of Labor and Statistics findings as reported in *New York Times*, February 29, 1988, p. B-8 and U.S. Bureau of the Census, *Statistical Abstract of the United States: 1988* (108th edition) (Washington, D.C.: 1987), pp. 376-77.

ing as clerical workers increased from 7 percent to 26 percent. In general, by 1977 there were higher proportions of black males in white-collar and skilled blue-collar jobs than in 1958. Despite these gains, blacks still are not at the same occupational and income levels as whites. The figures for 1979 nationally showed that while 52.5 percent of whites were white-collar workers, only 35.2 percent of blacks worked in such jobs. This improved somewhat by 1986, but there are still disparities in the jobs of blacks and whites and also men and women, as shown in Exhibit 13.5. The unemployment rate for black adults is typically at least twice that for white adults.

The income gains of blacks have been greatest for black husband-wife families and least for older blacks and black teenagers. Among two-spouse families where only the husband was employed, the median income for black families was 58 percent of that of white families in 1959 but 74 percent in 1980. For two-spouse families where both the husband and wife were employed, the median income for black families was 64 percent of that of white families in 1959 but 88 percent in 1980.[44] Clouding the income gains for blacks has been the increase in black female headed families (between 1970 and 1980 an increase of more than 80 percent). In 1986, over two out of five black families were headed by women as opposed to only one out of

[44]Rodgers, *op. cit.*, p. 106.

eight white families. In 1970, the median income for blacks was about 61 percent for that of whites. In 1986, the median income for blacks was about 58 percent of the median income for whites.

Job discrimination does not account for all the income disparity between blacks and whites. The culture of poverty which makes it difficult to acquire the values and skills necessary for advancement and the accompanying lack of education place heavy burdens on poor blacks who are unemployed or want to do better than work at low-paying jobs. Sexism also continues to affect adversely black as well as white women. It is a continuing challenge for government to devise policies that will narrow the differences based on race, ethnicity, and gender in employment and family income.

Equal Access to Housing

The right not to be racially discriminated against in the sale or rental of housing has been very difficult to enforce, although the law is quite clear. Title 6 of the Civil Rights Act of 1964 forbade discrimination on grounds of race, color, or national origin in any federally financed program, including housing. The Civil Rights Act of 1968 contained Title 8, with its fair housing provisions prohibiting racial discrimination in the sale or rental of housing. Yet residential segregation continued. In 1988, Congress enacted a new fair housing law with severe penalties for violators. Penalties include fines from $10,000 to $50,000 for those who discriminate in the sale or rental of housing because of race, color, gender, religion, or national origin. If alleged violators are found guilty in suits brought by the federal government, they can be ordered to pay damages to the victims in amounts ranging from $50,000 to $100,000. It is too early to assess the effectiveness of this law.

Racial ghettos have remained in America's cities in part because of persistent poverty and the social ills that are associated with poverty, including high crime rates that discourage whites from living there. Many of those who would like to leave the ghetto cannot afford better housing. The black and Hispanic middle class who can afford better housing escape as soon as they are able.

The sad fact is that most of America lives in racially segregated neighborhoods. This is apparently so because many whites and some minorities prefer this. But even more importantly this is because most banks, real estate agents, and governmental agencies at the national, state, and local levels have helped to maintain patterns of residential segregation. The techniques used to accomplish this have been used nationwide and include:[45]

- *Exclusionary zoning* laws, while not overtly racial, keep most blacks, Hispanics, and lower-class whites out of white middle-class and upper-class neighborhoods by requiring that lots be a certain minimum

---

[45]This discussion draws heavily on the data and analysis offered by Charles M. Lamb in "Equal Housing Opportunity," in Charles S. Bullock III and Charles M. Lamb, eds., *Implementation of Civil Rights Policy* (Monterey, California: Brooks/Cole, 1984), pp. 150–51.

size and that houses be a minimum square footage. Such laws also effectively exclude federally subsidized housing or other low-income housing.

- *Racial steering* by real estate agents, although illegal, is widely practiced. This means that real estate agents show blacks, Hispanics, and other racial minorities rental and sales properties only in black or Hispanic neighborhoods, in those whose racial composition is changing, or in run-down or otherwise undesirable areas.

- *Blockbusting* is another illegal technique that promotes residential segregation. It typically involves a real estate agent selling a home in a white lower-middle-class area to a minority family, usually at a greatly inflated price. Then the real estate agent visits the white families in the neighborhood and uses scare tactics to pressure them to sell their homes. The agent warns that the neighborhood is "turning" and that property values will decline. The white homeowners are urged to sell while they can still make a profit or at least break even. Like a set of dominoes, the whites sell, the neighborhood turns from white to minority, and the real estate agents and banks make a great deal of money.

- *Redlining* also involves the actions of banks and mortgage companies. A redlined neighborhood is one in which banks refuse to give mortgages for either all housing or houses over a certain age or they charge higher interest rates on mortgages and require a large down payment. Some neighborhoods are redlined only for blacks and Hispanics, that is, the banks refuse to give mortgages to prospective minority homeowners for fear that property values will be adversely affected.

- *Nonenforcement by government of fair housing laws*, including the actions of government itself, helps perpetuate residential segregation. The U.S. Commission on Civil Rights noted in 1975 that the federal government itself has been "most influential in creating and maintaining urban residential segregation." The Federal Housing Authority (FHA) issues mortgage loans. From the 1940s to 1960 only about 2 percent of FHA-insured loans went to black homeowners. The Veterans Administration (VA) offers low-interest home mortgage loans to veterans. In 1976 over 96 percent of loans went to white applicants, whose loan acceptance rate was higher than for blacks.[46] Whites received, on the average, larger loans than blacks, even though the average income of blacks and their average assets were higher than for whites. Whites also had, on the average, ten more months to repay their loans than did blacks.

A 1985 study of federally subsidized housing projects found that most of these projects are segregated by race, with whites living in better maintained and serviced facilities than blacks and Hispanics. None were found to

[46]Lamb, *op. cit.,* p. 168.

be completely integrated. The Department of Housing and Urban Development (HUD) is responsible for this housing and apparently has chosen to ignore the racial segregation practiced by local housing authorities and federally financed private developers.[47] The study concluded that there is a distinct and widespread pattern of government sponsored racial segregation in housing. At the same time, the enforcement budget of HUD to ensure compliance with Title 8 of the Civil Rights Act of 1968 has never been large and under the Reagan administration the enforcement staff was cut. The Reagan administration cut back on federal prosecutions of housing discrimination; indeed, the Justice Department failed to file a single suit during 1981.[48]

Another facet of housing policy and racial discrimination can be seen in the plight of the homeless. Although statistics are hard to come by, one study of homeless people in Chicago found that 63 percent were black and 12 percent Hispanic. Half of those surveyed claimed they had been evicted by landlords from their places of previous residence and the rest said they were homeless because they had argued with the persons with whom they had lived, the building in which they lived was destroyed, or they had received a court order for eviction. It is difficult to pinpoint the underlying causes of homelessness, but racism is probably a contributing factor, along with substance abuse, mental illness, criminal behavior, sexism, and, of course, poverty.[49]

There are, however, a few bright spots in the housing picture. High income blacks, Hispanics, and other minorities, particularly professionals, generally do have access to high quality housing in upper-income neighborhoods. There have been modest reductions in residential segregation in several cities. However, the widespread residential segregation that exists and the continuation of racially discriminatory practices by individuals, businesses, and governmental agencies suggest that this is one area in which racial equality is most lacking. If there is ever to be full racial equality in access to housing, there must be a national commitment for this goal accompanied by vigorous enforcement. The 1988 Fair Housing Act provides the tools for enforcement. Whether they will be vigorously used remains an open question.

Equality in Education

The current extent of racial equality in education has come about as a result of many factors. Supreme Court decisions and follow-up decisions at the lower court levels have been important. So have federal laws and actions of federal authorities to enforce them and state and local governments to comply with them. At the level of Supreme Court policy, one of the most

[47]*New York Times*, February 11, 1985, p. A-15.
[48]Lamb, *op. cit.*, p. 172.
[49]"Homeless in Chicago," study conducted by the School of Social Service Administration of the University of Chicago, 1988, as cited in *Christian Science Monitor*, September 2, 1988, p. 4.

significant decisions after *Brown* v. *Board of Education* was the decision in *Swann* v. *Charlotte-Mecklenburg Board of Education* (1971). In *Swann*, the Court gave its approval to court-ordered busing of school children as one of several appropriate remedies for the constitutional violations that had been brought about by racial segregation. Another major decision was *Keyes* v. *School District No. 1, Denver* (1973), in which the Supreme Court for the first time held the North accountable for racial discrimination in public education. The *Keyes* decision made it clear that racial discrimination on the part of school authorities or other public officials that resulted in the separation of the races in public schools would be treated in the same way that state-required segregation in the South was treated by the Court. Neither is constitutional and the busing of school children is a valid remedy in both situations.

But the Court made clear in yet another busing decision, *Milliken* v. *Bradley* (1974), that *only* school systems in which it has been proven that the authorities took official actions to keep the races apart can be subject to desegregation plans. The remedy, typically a busing plan, may *not* be imposed on innocent school systems as part of a metropolitan area-wide busing program. In this case an area-wide busing program to desegregate the Detroit public schools was struck down and Detroit was told that the busing remedy must be limited to the city of Detroit. Nevertheless, in subsequent cases the Court has emphasized that where past discrimination has been proven, busing is a reasonable remedy.

The most significant decision involving higher education concerned the legality of affirmative action admissions programs. In the 1978 decision of *Regents of the University of California* v. *Bakke*, a badly divided Supreme Court confronted this issue. Justice Powell was the swing vote and the ruling that emerged from this case was his compromise position that race can be considered in admissions decisions along with other attributes and qualities of applicants, but that racial *quotas* violate the Fourteenth Amendment.

Of course, after the Supreme Court makes its constitutional rulings there must be implementation by the other branches. Congress and the Executive Branch acted decisively in the mid-1960s to desegregate the nation's school systems. The Civil Rights Act of 1964 specified in Title 6 that federal funds shall not go to institutions that racially segregate. The Act also authorized the Justice Department to take segregating school systems to court on behalf of black students and to join private plaintiffs who initiate school desegregation suits. The Department of Health, Education, and Welfare (HEW) was armed with a strong weapon, the threat of a cutoff of federal aid, when it negotiated with local school systems over their plans for desegregation. The threat of a lawsuit was another weapon. Although the pace of negotiations was not swift, much was accomplished until the Nixon administration stopped HEW from cutting off federal aid to noncomplying school districts. Later, Congress itself stopped HEW from ordering school systems to bus. Only the courts could order busing to remedy a constitutional violation. But this, too, became a source of intense controversy. The Reagan administration opposed all court-ordered busing.

The greatest amount of school desegregation occurred in the late 1960s and early 1970s. In the southern states there was practically no desegregation for a full decade after *Brown*. In 1964, only 2.25 percent of black students attended school with whites.[50] This began to dramatically change in the mid to late 1960s, so that by the 1972–3 school year 86 percent of southern black students attended schools with whites. In the border states, the proportions of black students attending school with whites ranged from over 69 percent in Missouri to 100 percent in Oklahoma. During this same period the proportion of black students attending virtually all-black schools was only 8.7 percent in the South and 11.2 percent nationwide. However, particularly in the North, the majority of black students attended schools in which blacks constituted a majority of the student body. Furthermore, some resegregation has occurred *within* officially desegregated schools with black students disproportionately placed in separate remedial classes.

The struggle for racial equality has been a long and complex one filled with victories and defeats, sometimes with intense commitment on the part of courts, presidents, and congresses and other times with indifference, if not thinly veiled hostility. Despite the tortuous path, the overall trend has been positive, with greater protection of civil rights and movement toward full racial equality. That lower-class blacks, Hispanics, and other minorities face the problems of poverty and sexism along with the historic legacy of racism and its residual effects today cannot be denied. For them, full equality of opportunity remains to be attained.

SEXUAL EQUALITY

Although white women were not subject to slavery (black women were because of their race), the legal status of all women until well into the twentieth century was that of second-class citizenship.[51] Not until the Nineteenth Amendment became part of the Constitution in 1920 were the states prohibited from preventing adult women the right to vote on account of their gender. Women were restricted in their property and other legal rights. In marriage they were legally subservient to their husbands, as symbolized by the woman's legally adopting the husband's surname and dropping her own, a practice that has outlived the legal inferiority it once represented. Indeed,

[50]Charles S. Bullock III, "Equal Education Opportunity," in Charles S. Bullock III and Charles M. Lamb, eds., *Implementation of Civil Rights Policy* (Monterey, California: Brooks/Cole, 1984), p. 65. The other figures cited in this paragraph are from this source, pp. 68–73.

[51]See Albie Sachs and Joan Hoff Wilson, *Sexism and the Law* (New York: The Free Press, 1978), pp. 67–132.

during much of the nineteenth century, as noted by Justice Brennan in the leading women's rights decision of *Frontiero* v. *Richardson* (1973):

> "[T]he position of women in our society was, in many respects, comparable to that of blacks under the pre-Civil War slave codes. Neither slaves nor women could hold office, serve on juries, or bring suits in their own names, and married women traditionally were denied the legal capacity to hold or convey property or to serve as legal guardians of their own children."

Even when women began making progress in fashioning careers for themselves, sexist practices and traditions discriminated against them in the professions and workplaces. Under the guise of paternalistic laws designed to "protect" women, women were treated unequal to men.

All branches of government reflected deep-seated, long prevailing institutional sexism until what is sometimes referred to as the second women's rights movement emerged in the 1960s to mobilize the attack on sexism. (The first women's rights movement began in the middle of the nineteenth century and had as its focus winning for women the right to vote.) The first victories for the women's movement were the enactment of two pieces of legislation that had great import for women's rights: the 1963 Equal Pay Act and **Title 7 of the Civil Rights Act of 1964** (see Exhibit 13.6).

The addition of "sex" to Title 7 was apparently a ploy by a conservative southern congressman who opposed the Civil Rights Act and hoped that the addition would kill the bill.[52] It didn't, and it provided the legal basis for a major attack on sexism. In 1967, President Johnson issued an executive order prohibiting gender discrimination by companies or institutions receiving federal government contracts over $10,000. Also in that year Congress enacted the Age Discrimination Act, which is of immense importance to older women entering the labor force for the first time.

Congress has enacted several other pieces of legislation designed to end discriminatory treatment of women (see Exhibit 13.6). In 1972, Congress passed by more than a two-thirds vote the **Equal Rights Amendment (ERA)**, which stated simply: "Equality of rights under the law shall not be denied or abridged by the United States or by any State on account of sex." This proposed constitutional amendment was then sent to the states for ratification. Thanks to the vigorous efforts of women's groups, including the National Organization of Women (NOW), ratification of the ERA occurred in thirty-five states by the fall of 1977. But that fell short of the necessary thirty-eight states needed for ratification, and in the face of vigorous opposition by the Reagan administration, the ERA died on June 30, 1982.[53] However, sixteen states have equal rights amendments in their state constitutions and numerous state laws forbid sex discrimination.

---

[52]Sachs and Wilson, *op. cit.*, p. 210.

[53]See Mary Frances Berry, *Why ERA Failed: Politics, Women's Rights, and the Amending Process of the Constitution* (Bloomington: Indiana University Press, 1986).

EXHIBIT 13.6	LEGISLATION	WHAT IT PROVIDES
Key Legislation Protecting Women's Rights	*The Equal Pay Act of 1963*	Requires that those who do the same work be paid the same. Prohibits wage discrimination on the basis of race, color, religion, national origin, *or* sex.
	Title 7, Civil Rights Act of 1964	Prohibits discrimination at the workplace on the basis of race, color, religion, national origin *or* sex.
	Age Discrimination Act (1967)	Protects workers of both sexes aged 40 to 70 from being discriminated against by employers because of age.
	Title 9, Education Amendments of 1972 Act	Forbids discrimination on the basis of sex by colleges and universities receiving federal aid.
	The Equal Credit Opportunity Act of 1974 (amended 1976)	Prohibits creditors from discriminating in giving credit on the basis of such attributes as gender, marital status, race, age, or that one receives public assistance.
	The Housing and Community Development Act of 1974	Makes illegal sex discrimination in the sale, rental, and financing of housing.
	The Pregnancy Discrimination Act of 1978	Outlaws employment discrimination on the basis of pregnancy, childbirth, or pregnancy-related conditions (a woman unable to work because of a pregnancy-related medical condition must be treated like any other disabled worker; if able to work, she must be allowed to continue).

The Supreme Court actively entered the sexual discrimination arena in the 1971 decision of *Reed* v. *Reed*, which questioned the rationality of state statutes that discriminate on the basis of sex. In that decision, the Court struck down as unconstitutional an Idaho law that required that preference be given to men when persons of both sexes are equally qualified to administer estates. The Court found this to be an arbitrary legislative choice that did not bear a rational relationship to a legitimate state objective, thereby violating the equal protection guarantee of the Fourteenth Amendment.

One of the landmark sexual equality decisions of the Supreme Court was, as suggested earlier, *Frontiero* v. *Richardson* (1973). The Court by a vote of eight to one ruled that the military's different treatment of women members of the military as to dependent's benefits was unconstitutional. What makes this case of special interest is Justice Brennan's sweeping plurality opinion that sought to make a dramatic advance in the constitutional adjudication of sexual discrimination claims. Because a majority did not join the opinion, it did not become Court policy. Brennan argued that classifications based on sex should be considered "inherently suspect," analogous to classifications based on race. This would then justify a standard of "strict judicial scrutiny" of the compelling interest asserted by the government that supposedly justifies the classification. Had a majority accepted the use of "strict scrutiny" as the standard for examining sexual classifications, a difficult burden would have been placed on government to provide convincing evidence that there is a compelling governmental need for such classification. However, in a subsequent sex discrimination case, *Craig* v. *Boren* (1976), a majority accepted an intermediate level scrutiny somewhere between *no* scrutiny and strict scrutiny.

The Court has rejected numerous statutes that called for placing one sex or the other at an advantage. The United States Jaycees, the Rotary Clubs, and many other private clubs were told that government can require that they admit women. But not all sexual classifications have been struck down by the Court. Indeed, numerous state and federal laws that provide sexual classifications have met with the Court's approval, including draft registration for males only.

In a significant decision in 1984, *Grove City College* v. *Bell*, the Court interpreted Title 9 of the 1972 Education Amendments to forbid sexual discrimination *only* in the program or activity actually receiving federal aid. Programs or activities of the college or university *not* receiving federal assistance were free to sexually discriminate insofar as no other provision of federal law was violated. Before this decision, if one program received aid, the entire institution was forbidden to practice sex discrimination. As a result of this decision, it became difficult to eliminate all forms of sexual discrimination.[54] Congress in 1988 enacted, over President Reagan's veto, civil rights legislation that overturned the Grove City decision.[55]

A constitutional issue concerning women that is highly emotionally charged is the issue of women's reproductive rights, that is, the right to have an abortion. The Supreme Court in **Roe v. Wade** (1973) ruled that women have a constitutional right to privacy that protects their choice whether to abort a nonviable fetus. The intense political controversy following the abortion decision led the Court to back off somewhat on the periphery of that issue by ruling that neither the federal government nor the states were compelled by the Constitution to pay for abortions of poor women under medical assistance programs.

The abortion issue became more intensely political with the Reagan administration's commitment to overturning *Roe* v. *Wade* and its efforts to appoint judges opposed to abortion. The party platforms in 1988 reflected the sharp partisan battle with the Democrats favoring pro-choice (allowing women to choose abortion) and the Republicans opposing abortion. From the standpoint of the women's movement, the right of a woman to choose how her body is to be used is a fundamental right. Opponents see abortion

[54]See *Congressional Quarterly Weekly Report*, Vol. 43, No. 15, April 13, 1985, pp. 682–83.
[55]See *Congressional Quarterly Weekly Report*, Vol. 46, No. 13, March 26, 1988, pp. 774–76.

*"No, I'm not a secretary, I'm a lawyer.
Are you a secretary?"*

as the taking of human life. In 1989, a new Court majority began to seriously undermine the *Roe* v. *Wade* policy thus ensuring that this controversy will be in the political and legal arenas for some time to come.

Women have made progress towards the goal of sexual equality, but much remains to be done. In employment, there has been a history of sexual stereotyping. As late as 1978, women were channeled into such jobs as secretarial positions (99 percent of these jobs were held by women), nursery and kindergarten teaching (99 percent women), housekeepers (97 percent women), telephone operators (95 percent women), keypunch operators (93 percent women), and bookkeepers (90 percent women).[56]

Because of federal laws and affirmative action programs either voluntarily adopted to avoid a suit, negotiated with the government, or ordered

[56]These statistics are cited in Susan Deller Ross and Ann Barcher, *The Rights of Women*, Revised Edition, (New York: Bantam Books, 1983) p. 18, which is taken from U.S. Department of Labor, Bureau of Labor Statistics, *Employment and Earnings*, 153–54 (January 1978).

By 1987, women accounted for 7.6 percent of local law enforcement officers nationwide.

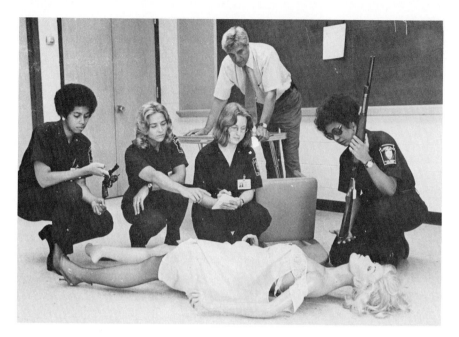

by a court, professions that once were closed to women have been opened to them. For example, in New York a court decree specified as a reasonable goal that 10 percent of entrants to the state police academy should be women.[57] As a result of an affirmative action program, the Philadelphia police department went from no women police officers to 450. Other court decrees involved police and fire departments as well as other governmental agencies, and the private sector as well.

From 1970 to 1980 the proportion of women in managerial positions increased from 10 to 19 percent and in professional positions from 25 to 38 percent.[58] From 1975 to 1985 the proportion of women in the legal profession jumped from 7.1 percent to 18.2 percent.[59] The number of women holding public office in 1987 was over 17,000 (including 15.5 percent of state legislators).

Despite these gains, women still do not earn as much as men. In 1987, the median income of women was $16,909 but that of men was $26,008. Women's median income was only 65 percent that of men. This was as true for women college graduates as compared to male college graduates as it was true for female and male high-school dropouts. Clearly, the struggle for gender equality is a continuing one.

[57]*New York Times*, April 3, 1985, p. A-16.
[58]As cited in the *New York Times*, April 20, 1985, p. 22.
[59]As cited in the *New York Times*, July 26, 1987, sec. 4, p. 6.

OTHER EQUALITY CLAIMS

Among the many other claims of equality, political equality, or the right to have one's vote count the same as another's, has had special appeal. The concept of one person, one vote, has a pleasing egalitarian ring to it, although at the federal level the Constitution explicitly rejects that principle for voting for the U.S. Senate (each state, no matter its population, elects two senators) and in the provisions of the electoral college. The Constitution leaves the drawing of congressional as well as state legislative district boundaries to the state legislatures. As a result, particularly in the first half of the twentieth century in which major population shifts from rural to urban areas occurred, malapportionment of state legislative and congressional districts increased.

In the landmark case of **Baker v. Carr**, decided in 1962, the Supreme Court ruled that malapportionment raised a Fourteenth Amendment equal protection issue that can be adjudicated by the courts. *Baker* concerned the state of Tennessee, in which 37 percent of the voters elected over 60 percent of the state Senate and 40 percent of the voters elected 64 percent of the members of the state House of Representatives. In subsequent cases the Court announced the standard of one-person-one-vote for elections to the U.S. House of Representatives and both houses of state legislatures.[60] The Court rejected the federal analogy for the state Senate, pointing out that the creation of the United States Senate was a unique political compromise necessary for the founding fathers to form the new United States government. The Court also extended the one-person-one-vote principle to elections for local government office.[61]

While the Warren Court insisted that districts be as mathematically equal as possible, the Burger Court permitted state legislative districts (but not congressional districts) to depart from mathematical equality if the legislature advanced a rational state policy. One of the last decisions of the Burger Court was *Davis* v. *Bandemer* (1986), in which the Court took the position that it could consider equal protection challenges to purely partisan gerrymandering of equally apportioned election districts. The Court suggested that such electoral schemes are constitutional as long as they do not "consistently degrade a voter's or a group of voters' influence on the political process as a whole." But the Court was unclear as to what would constitute the "consistently degrade" standard that would move the Court to strike down partisan gerrymandering.

The evidence suggests that nationwide reapportionment of legislative and congressional districts has resulted in more equitable representation

---

[60]*Wesberry* v. *Sanders* (1964) (U.S. House of Representatives) and *Reynolds* v. *Sims* (1964) (both houses of state legislature).
[61]*Avery* v. *Midland County* (1968).

and has had profound political consequences.[62] In the state legislatures and in the House of Representatives, political power has shifted from rural America to urban-suburban America.

Equality claims of poor people have met with a more mixed reception from the Supreme Court. The Warren Court ruled that state residency requirements for welfare benefits violated equal protection.[63] But the Burger Court took a different view of equal protection for the poor. The Court ruled that financing public schools through local property taxes, even though poorer school districts had less money to spend on education, did not violate the Fourteenth Amendment.[64] The majority was concerned that, were it to find a constitutional violation, "then it [local taxation] might be an equally impermissible means of providing other necessary services . . . including local police and fire protection, public health and hospitals, and public utility facilities of various kinds." By implication, the state would then have to assume responsibility not simply for a minimum standard of living for the poor, but a standard *equal* to the nonpoor. Other more narrowly drawn decisions have concerned the rights of the poor, and some of these decisions, such as a free lawyer for a poor person accused of a serious crime, are based on other parts of the Constitution (recall Chapter Twelve). The fundamental economic disparities that exist within American society have remained virtually untouched by constitutional law.

It is possible to cite a variety of other claims for equal treatment, some of which have been the subject of federal or state legislation or court rulings. These include the claim not to be discriminated against on the basis of age, the status of being an alien, illegitimacy, being handicapped, or sexual preference. Current views of the equal protection clause have raised the consciousness of various groupings in society as to their rights. For the courts, unequal treatment must, at the very least, serve some rational purpose to accomplish a legitimate governmental objective. The decisions of the courts over the years expanding the concept and scope of equal protection no doubt gave hope to those who felt that they were singled out for unequal treatment. But the Rehnquist Court and a lower federal judiciary dominated by conservatives offers little hope for expansion of equal protection and the constant threat of serious contraction.

---

[62]See, for example, Roger A. Hanson and Robert E. Crew, Jr., "The Policy Impact of Reapportionment," *Law and Society Review*, 8 (1973), pp. 69–94; Matthew D. McCubbins and Thomas Schwartz, "Congress, the Courts, and Public Policy: Consequences of the One Man, One Vote Rule," *American Journal of Political Science*, 32 (1988), pp. 388–415.

[63]*Shapiro* v. *Thompson* (1969).

[64]*San Antonio Independent School District* v. *Rodriguez* (1973).

	NAME AND DATE OF APPOINTMENT		PRESIDENT	PREVIOUS GOVERNMENT POSITION
	John Foster Dulles	1953	Eisenhower	Truman Administration
	Christian Herter	1959	Eisenhower	Hoover, Eisenhower Administrations; House; Governor
	Dean Rusk	1961	Kennedy	Truman Administration
	Dean Rusk	1965	Johnson	Truman Administration; Kennedy Secretary of State
	William Rogers	1969	Nixon	Eisenhower Attorney General
	Henry Kissinger	1973	Nixon	Nixon Administration
	Henry Kissinger	1974	Ford	Nixon Administration; Nixon Secretary of State
	Cyrus Vance	1977	Carter	Kennedy Administration; Johnson Administration
	Edward Muskie	1980	Carter	Senate
	Alexander Haig	1981	Reagan	Nixon Administration
	George Shultz	1982	Reagan	Nixon Secretary of the Treasury
	James Baker III	1989	Bush	Reagan Secretary of the Treasury; Ford Administration

EXHIBIT 14.1

The Secretaries of State, 1953–1989

The Secretary of State

As head of the Department of State and a member of the cabinet, the secretary of state has traditionally been the president's chief foreign policy adviser since the post was created in 1789. The secretary's actual role, however, fluctuates greatly with the presidents and the secretaries' own skills in the palace politics of the White House (see Chapter Eight). Some presidents like to conduct their own foreign policy, at least for one area of the globe that they may be interested in. And some secretaries are more adept than others at White House infighting. Secretary of State John Foster Dulles was the one person who could get to see Eisenhower when presidential aide Sherman Adams kept everyone else at bay. Secretaries of state for some other presidents have found themselves advisers in name only since they never saw the person who would be asking their advice.

The full listing of secretaries of state since the Eisenhower years is shown in Exhibit 14.1, along with their previous experience in government. These are the inner cabinet members as described in Chapter Eight: they are a senior group of men (the average age is about sixty) with years of Washington experience. All but one of the secretaries had worked in the executive branch for a previous president before becoming secretary of state. Five of these men had previous cabinet posts.

Still, the secretaries must compete with others who also have Washington experience for the prize of the president's attention. The problems of the secretary of state are nicely illustrated by Alexander Haig in his book

Caveat. Haig was secretary during the first term of the Reagan administration. Time and again, Haig would be left thinking that *he* was pursuing a policy for the president while the White House aides were pursuing another policy. Haig would finally get to see Reagan, always described as "amiable" and "relaxed," and would be assured of his support, only to find things continuing just as before. He was shocked to see that aides sat in on National Security Council meetings at the table along with the actual members of the council and often led the discussion and framed the options. According to Haig, he was not considered the chief spokesman for the president's foreign policy; he did not even have easy access to the president; and there was no agreed upon structure for the role of the secretary. Every president since Eisenhower had signed a document outlining such a structure, but Reagan did not, although he always "amiably" promised to do so.[8]

Haig's successor, George Schultz, complained of the same lack of structure in the Reagan administration, admitting he did not know of the policy to arm the Nicaraguan guerrillas. The secretary was not informed of what the National Security Council was doing. The problem is not limited to the Reagan White House, although Reagan may have delegated more responsibility to aides than some other chiefs have done. Woodrow Wilson's aide Colonel House conducted the European negotiations on the brink of World War I, while the secretary of state was left in the dark. When Carter's secretary of state and National Security adviser disagreed over the attempt to rescue the hostages in Iran, Carter sided with his adviser. In the aftermath of the failed rescue attempt, the secretary of state resigned. Henry Kissinger directed foreign policy during the Nixon years both when he was secretary and when he was National Security adviser. Few people remember that William Rogers was Nixon's first secretary of state.[9]

The Secretary of Defense and the Joint Chiefs of Staff

The secretary of defense advises the president on defense and national security matters and must coordinate the policy of the various service branches (army, navy, air force, marines). The head of Defense is in effect the deputy commander-in-chief. But defense secretaries, like their counterparts at State, have varied greatly in their influence within an administration, depending on the personalities and politics of the White House. Robert McNamara, for example, played a much larger role in the Kennedy administration than Caspar Weinberger did during the Reagan years.

The link between the highest civilian authorities and military is provided by the Joint Chiefs of Staff. The five Joint Chiefs (one heading each of the major service units and a chairman) are technically under the secretary of defense, although a 1958 statute gives them the right to report directly to

[8]Alexander Haig, *Caveat* (New York: Macmillan, 1984), esp. pp. 344–345.
[9]Joseph G. Bock, *The White House Staff and the National Security Assistant* (Westport, Conn.: Greenwood, 1987).

the president. The Joint Chiefs need to be good politicians as well as good military men. They must not only represent their own services and reach compromises with each other, but they must also advise the president and Congress on some of the most controversial matters of defense. Carter, like other presidents, sought the Joint Chiefs' support on a controversial issue when he was lobbying for his Panama Canal Treaty in Congress. At other times the Joint Chiefs themselves need to lobby for increased congressional support.[10]

In the American tradition, the military is subordinate to the civilian authorities (the politicians and policymakers). But military judgments have policy implications and need to be made with an eye toward national and international politics. Just how the Joint Chiefs should balance policy and military expertise has been the subject of much debate. *Purists* argue that military advisers should confine themselves to the purely military aspects regardless of administration policy at any time. *Fusionists* argue that the two must be combined, that the military advisers must possess knowledge in nonmilitary fields and see issues in their broader perspective.[11] Most would agree that military experts need to be good soldiers first and policy analysts second. But the debate continues on where the line should be drawn in adding broader policy judgments.

The National Security Council

Neither cabinet post—Defense or State—gave presidents the flexibility they sought in foreign policy making or a structure to coordinate at the White House level the various strands of policy. Thus the National Security Council was created by the National Security Act of 1947. The *National Security Council* (NSC), located within the Executive Office of the President, is the arm of the president for foreign policy making. The NSC formally consists of the president, vice-president, secretary of defense, and secretary of state, with the director of the CIA and the Joint Chiefs of Staff serving as statutory advisers. The main work of the NSC, however, is carried out by a special assistant for national security affairs, called the National Security Advisor, and as many NSC committees and staff units as the president decides to employ.

The president determines the mission of the National Security Council staff and the relationship with the National Security Advisor. Recent presidents have granted this assistant a large degree of independence. Hence the National Security Advisor can carry on a policy unknown to the secretary of state and even unknown to the president. It is important to see that presidents have encouraged this independence. So, Rear Admiral John

---

[10]Amos A. Jordan and William J. Taylor, *American National Security*, rev. ed. (Baltimore: Johns Hopkins University Press, 1984), pp. 165–67. See also Lawrence Karb, *The Joint Chiefs of Staff: The First Twenty Five Years* (Bloomington: Indiana University Press, 1976).

[11]A good discussion of the issue is found in Jordon and Taylor, pp. 169–73.

Poindexter, Reagan's national security advisor, could claim the president did not know of the illegal aid being supplied to the Nicaraguan guerrillas. Money from a secret arms sale to Iran was diverted to support the antigovernment forces in Nicaragua. The president had repeatedly asked Congress for Nicaraguan aid and his requests had been refused or severely limited. When the affair came to light, prompting a full congressional investigation, Poindexter took responsibility for what his staff did. The scandal hurt the Reagan presidency, causing a drop in his pubic opinion polls and further difficulties with Congress. Either the president did know, people said, and he was using the NSC to evade the law, or he did not know and so was not in control of his own appointees. However, Reagan was not the first president who allowed the staff to pursue activities he would rather not be aware of. Like so many of the "powers" of the president, an independent National Security Council can be a burden or a blessing in disguise.

This mixed blessing can be seen more clearly by looking at the concept of **plausible denial**. Plausible denial is a strategy that allows someone, such as the president, to deny knowledge of covert action being carried out by the government. The president should not know the details of the covert action; thus the United States could (plausibly) deny responsibility for the action. Indeed, when people talk of giving presidents "flexibility" in foreign policy, they often mean plausible deniability. The term, and the practice, is a standard part of the conduct of foreign policy, not limited to the United States government. Achieving plausible deniability is a challenge for presidents quite different from the usual challenge of managing the White House. They cannot oversee too closely the agencies pursuing foreign policy or they would lose their deniability, but they have to be able to use the agencies to secure major objectives. One scholar cites Eisenhower, with his military background skills, as the best at achieving this difficult balance.[12]

The Reagan-Poindexter affair, therefore, was an example of plausible denial at work. Reagan could claim he did not know of the illegal actions being taken at the same time his National Security Adviser was pursuing the policies the president wanted carried out. Covert actions, of course, are not supposed to come to light; therefore most of the time presidents will not suffer the embarrassment of having to deny them.

The Central Intelligence Agency

The National Security Council is not the only arm of the president for foreign policy making. *The Central Intelligence Agency* (CIA), created along with the NSC as part of the National Security Act of 1947, is a presidential agency designed to coordinate and bring to the White House level matters of intelligence and national security affairs. The CIA is responsible to the president and the National Security Council. Congress legislates and oversees its activities from the Armed Services Committees, traditionally

---

[12]John Prados, *Presidents' Secret Wars* (New York: Morrow, 1988), pp. 108, 410.

EXHIBIT 14.2

From the CIA
Charter

The CIA shall have no police, subpoena, law-enforcement powers, or internal security functions.

The CIA shall perform such functions and duties related to intelligence affecting the national security as the National Security Council may from time to time direct.

The CIA shall perform, for the benefit of the existing [other] intelligence agencies, such additional services of common concern as the National Security Council determines can be more efficiently accomplished centrally.

The Director of the CIA shall be responsible for protecting intelligence sources and methods from unauthorized disclosure.

Source: The National Security Act of 1947.

---

staunch supporters of the defense establishment. The basic charter of the CIA, outlining its mission and activities, is shown in Exhibit 14.2.

The CIA was a postwar baby, and yet it owed much to its predecessor, the Office of Strategic Services (OSS) which achieved glory in World War II. Many of the methods and procedures of OSS, as well as some of the personnel, would become part of the new peacetime unit.[13] There was opposition to the forming of the unit at first. Many in Congress opposed it, as did J. Edgar Hoover, the powerful director of the FBI, who did not fancy the idea of a rival intelligence unit. President Truman at first opposed the idea of the agency, saying he did not want a "Gestapo" in the United States.[14] Soon, however, the developments of the Cold War made Truman change his mind. Congress supported the president and the CIA was formed.

As founded, the agency would have three different kinds of functions: first, to coordinate other intelligence activity; a second, its analytical function, to gather and analyze intelligence on its own; and a third, to carry on other covert activities. Its coordinating function never developed strongly, because intelligence agencies are not especially willing to share information with each other. Both analytical and covert activities proceeded, although experts suggest that the covert activity came to dominate early in terms of personnel and budget.[15]

Thus the CIA not only gathers intelligence to influence policy decisions, it also engages in covert actions around the globe, in effect "making" foreign policy as it does this. At least 81 covert actions were initiated in the Truman administration by the director of Central Intelligence on his own authority; 104 were approved in the Eisenhower years and 163 were approved in the three years of the Kennedy administration.[16] Covert activities include supporting a government against rebel factions and supporting the

---

[13]William M. Leary, ed. *The Central Intelligence Agency: History & Documents* (University of Alabama Press, 1984), p. 4.

[14]*Ibid.*

[15]*Ibid*, p. 5.

[16]See Prados, pp. 35, 80, 230.

factions against the government, as well as creating circumstances favorable to one government or the other. Iran, Guatemala, Cuba, Iraq, Vietnam, Laos, Cambodia, Chile, Angola, Italy, Portugal, Madagascar, the Congo, Nicaragua, Chad, and Libya are countries where CIA activity has been documented.[17] It has occurred in all presidential administrations from Truman to Reagan.

Covert activities *outside* the U.S. are considered within the CIA's mission as broadly defined. (See Exhibit 14.2.) Nevertheless, the agency has also engaged in activities beyond its charter. It was active in bringing former Nazis to work for the CIA, often forging papers to allow them to become U.S. citizens. (The immigration laws forbade citizenship to Nazis.) These included war criminals, and one who was held personally responsible for the murders of 128,500 people. The intelligence agency said merely that it did not "know" of the war crimes record, although at least two of the war criminals recruited had already been tried in abstentia by tribunals and sentenced to death.[18] Among other illegal activities, the CIA burglarized a psychiatrist's office for damaging material on an American journalist leaking Nixon administration secrets to the press. From the 1950s to at least the mid-1960s, the agency conducted experiments using psychoactive drugs such as LSD and other substances. The experiments were performed on Americans in college campuses, prisons, and hospitals. The subjects, needless to say, were not informed of their role in these experiments. The agency was looking for drugs to serve two purposes: one to "discredit" people who would unknowingly have taken the drug; and two, to provide subconscious programming that could later be triggered to action.[19]

One theme pervades all these activities: a commitment to fighting the Cold War and stopping the spread of communism. Thus dictatorships were supported, as long as they were anticommunist; new democracies were undermined if vulnerable to takeover. The Nazis were valuable because they were strong anticommunists who already had good "cover" and who could work knowledgeably in the European arena.[20] The drug program was perceived as part of a war for the mind that the U.S. was fighting with Russia. Many of the agency's directors were strong anticommunists: Allen Dulles (Eisenhower), Richard Helms (Johnson), William Casey (Reagan). However, the concept of plausible deniability does not allow for the separation of the actions or motives of the directors from those of the president and his advisers. Allen Dulles was the brother of John Foster Dulles, Eisenhower's secretary of state. President Truman approved the illegal immigration program

[17]See Prados. See also John Ranelagh, *The Agency: The Rise and Decline of the CIA* (New York: Simon and Schuster, 1986).

[18]Christopher Simpson, *Blowback* (New York: Weidenfeld and Nicholson, 1988), esp. pp. 168, 257, 258.

[19]John Marks, *The Search for the Manchurian Candidate* (New York: New York Times Books, 1979) and Morton H. Halperin et al., *The Lawless State* (New York: Penguin, 1976).

[20]Simpson, p. 35.

as long as only "nominal" Nazis would enter. In other words, the anticommunism of the agency was found in the State Department, the White House, and the National Security Council too. Clearly the CIA is a major foreign policy actor, although all of its independent actions cannot be separated from those directed, at least generally, from the White House.

Congress, like the president, does not want to know all that the CIA is doing. Congress wants plausible denial too. For much of its lifetime, the agency has been free of congressional oversight. Its budget is buried in the Defense Department's budget so that it cannot be reviewed. Questions about its activities are rare. Even the one major investigation occurring in 1975 and 1976 was deliberately limited in scope. CIA activities had already come to light during the Watergate scandal. The congressional investigation followed, limiting questions to activities occurring before the 1970s. The Senate report was published, but the more detailed House report was kept secret by a vote of the House members themselves. (It was subsequently leaked to *The Village Voice* for publication.) As a result of the investigation, Congress established special oversight committees to watch the CIA and added legislation to restrict the charter. It said, for example, that the agency should not attempt to overthrow foreign governments or conduct experiments on unwitting subjects.

In the 1980s, the oversight committees continue, although the restrictive legislation was repealed at the request of President Carter. Covert operations, cut back after the investigation, were reemphasized. Reagan Director William Casey hired back most of the 800 agents let go during the housecleaning of the 1970s. Congress investigated the agency again for its covert activity in Nicaragua, at a time when Congress opposed the Reagan administration policy in that country. Most of the time, however, little oversight occurred. The budget remained buried and the oversight committees found little to do.

The CIA, of course, is not the only member of the intelligence establishment. The military branches conduct their own intelligence; the Department of Defense has its own agency as do the departments of Treasury and State. Someone once counted more than forty government agencies doing intelligence work. They regulate the conduct of immigration and drug enforcement, deal with trade, currency, terrorists, and revolutions. All help to carry out the foreign policy of the United States, although, by definition, their work is hidden from public view.

The agency heads are subject to presidential appointment and Senate confirmation, thus theoretically responsible to the elected office holders. All but the CIA are subject to the annual accounting in the congressional appropriations process. Yet, the size of their operations and the number of subordinates give great autonomy and independent influence. So, the NSC officials supplied aid to the Nicaraguan rebels even though Congress had forbidden government agencies from doing this. Their justification was that they were part of the White House and *not a government agency*. They claimed presidential protection even while they argued that the president was not informed. Even these events came to light only because Congress felt so strongly about the particular policy. Most of the time Congress leaves these foreign policy makers alone. The president, too, may not know, or want to know, or may be protected from knowing, what they are doing.

In a recent cartoon, a little boy, holding an axe, was shown saying to his father, "I cannot tell a lie. The CIA made me do it." The very independence of the intelligence agencies allows foreign policy to be carried on outside constitutional and legal boundaries. Presidents can find this a benefit when they are restricted from pursuing the policy in other ways. So, the CIA budget, unexamined by Congress, is treated gingerly in the White House as well. In the Carter years, for example, a majority of the OMB examiners assigned to oversee the budgets of the CIA and other intelligence agencies had previously worked in the very agencies they were to oversee.

To these chief bureaucratic actors, add all of the subordinates—in the NSC committees or at State Department desks—who carry out foreign policy every day. They make decisions about what actions shall be taken, what news shall be leaked to the press, and what information shall be passed upward or withheld. Like Allen Dulles or William Casey, these are people with their own incentives and objectives. They may work for what the president wants or they may work for themselves: most of the time no one knows. Seen from this perspective, statements that "the president makes foreign policy" seem naive and misleading at best.

Congress

Another major participant in foreign policy making remains to be accounted for. Congress clearly has the power to engage in foreign policy making if it chooses to use that power. The Constitution makes Congress a partner to the president in foreign policy. It states that the Senate can accept or reject a treaty or attach reservations and amendments as the price of its support. The Senate can also confirm or reject all presidential appointments of ambassadors, ministers, and other high-level officials. It gets to rule on foreign service appointments and promotions. While the president is commander-in-chief, the Constitution gives Congress the power to declare war and to raise and support armies. Its legislative power means that presidents' bills can be stopped or rewritten in committee, voted down or amended on the floor. Most important, however, is the power of the purse. Congress, through its powerful appropriations committees, decides how the taxpayers' money will be spent. This means that even those agreements that are not treaties and those military actions that are not wars require congressional support. The White House can try to find the money elsewhere—thus the illegal diversion of funds to Nicaragua—but it risks trouble in Congress when it does so.

Supplementing its formal powers, Congress has found ways to ensure its independence from executive pressure and expertise, as shown in Chapter Seven. Committee members become "specialists" in foreign policy. Safe in their reelection and protected by the seniority system, the congressional foreign policy makers outlast any one president's term. One prospective secretary of state, facing the Senate Foreign Relations Committee for a confirmation hearing, heard the chairman tell of the six secretaries of state he had worked with thus far. (He had such good relations with these six that he was looking forward to working with the new nominee.) The point of the story was clear.

However, Congress is also a representative assembly, watchful of its own constituents' points of view. If members hear about the economy and local issues as they keep touch with the folks back home, they will tend to these issues in Congress, allowing foreign policy to be made somewhere else. When foreign policy issues become salient to the public, they become more salient to Congress too.

So what is the "role" of Congress in foreign policy making? The role will vary depending on the circumstances and the issues of the time. But issues can be created or ignored by press coverage. Circumstances are changed by what the public hears and what interest groups are mobilized for action. Hence it follows that the media, interest groups, and the broader public are also participants in foreign policy-making.

THE MANY KINDS OF FOREIGN POLICY

Foreign policy is not a category consistent in itself and distinct from domestic policy. There are many different kinds of foreign policy engaging many different people with different results. This can be shown by contrasting four kinds of foreign policy: military action, diplomacy, foreign aid, and defense. The particular focus will be on the role of the president and Congress in this policy-making.

Military Action

Decisions on the use and threat of force have followed a consistent pattern in American foreign policy, spanning a number of years and diverse circumstances. A list of major U.S. military actions since World War II is provided in the box on pages 562 and 563.

The Predominant Pattern. Most of the time when presidents have gone to Congress to ask for declarations of war or mobilization of troops and arms, *they have received what they asked for—with speed, little debate, and virtual unanimity*. This holds for undeclared wars and other more limited military action. White House declarations of a military emergency have produced immediate congressional support, even when details could not be provided and the scope of subsequent necessary action remained undefined. This was the case with the 1964 Tonkin Gulf Resolution, which initiated the wider American involvement in Vietnam. And it has remained the case, even since the 1973 passage of the War Powers Act.

Major U.S. Military Interventions, 1946–1986

Much of the time since World War II, American troops have been engaged in hostile, or potentially hostile, situations somewhere in the world. The following list does not include U.S. participation in multinational peacekeeping forces. So, the fighting in Lebanon in 1983, which brought heavy U.S. casualties, is not included (although the Korean War, fought under the auspices of the United Nations, is included). Covert actions are also not on the list nor are military engagements designed by the United States but using foreign nationals. For example, the Bay of Pigs attack on Cuba, sponsored by the Kennedy administration and using Cubans as the attack force, is not included. In other words, the list greatly understates the actual military involvement occurring. The use and threat of force is one major part of American foreign policy.

Each of these actions ultimately is the decision and responsibility of the president as Commander-in-Chief. Nevertheless, the decisions are shaped in the military and intelligence bureaucracies and filtered through White House advisers. (See Chapters Eight and Nine.) Information is collected and choices are made about the particular troops and their strength and their numbers. Some of these military actions are more successful than others. Yet, with only a few exceptions—Korea, Vietnam, and the aborted helicopter rescue of the hostages in April 1980—these events have brought support from Congress and the public. The president's popularity rises in times of international crisis. Very few of these actions have been subjected after the fact to any widespread or visible review.

This list, therefore, can provoke questions about the role of military policy making in democracies. On the one hand, there are strong arguments for military secrecy and expertise. On the other, there are strong arguments for the responsibility of elected officials. How can the claims be balanced and what kind of line can be drawn between the two? This is not an occasional problem, as the list makes clear, but a continuing one to be faced in the years ahead.

JULY - AUGUST 1946. President Truman sends U.S. naval units to Trieste, anticipating attack from Yugoslav-Soviet forces. After U.S. Army transport planes are shot down, reinforcements arrive in Italy.

AUGUST 1946. To counter Soviet threat to Turkish control of Bosporus Straits, Truman dispatches a powerful carrier force.

SEPTEMBER 1946. One U.S. carrier is stationed off Greece during attempted Communist takeover.

JANUARY 1948. Marine reinforcements are sent to the Mediterranean as a warning to Yugoslavia.

APRIL 1948 - NOVEMBER 1949. U.S. Marines are sent to Nanking and Shanghai to protect the U.S. Embassy and to aid evacuation of American nationals in wake of Communist takeover of China.

JUNE 1950 - JULY 1953. Korean War.

JULY 1954 - FEBRUARY 1955. Five U.S. carriers arrive at Taiwan to evacuate Americans and others threatened by Communist Chinese bombing.

FEBRUARY 1957. Marines are poised to protect Americans during revolt in Indonesia.

JULY 1957. Four U.S. carriers are sent to defend Taiwan during Chinese Communist attack.

JANUARY 1958. When mob violence breaks out in Venezuela, the *U.S.S. Des Moines*, with one company of U.S. Marines on board, is stationed nearby.

MARCH 1958. A Marine company, attack squadron and helicopter squadron are deployed with the Seventh Fleet off Indonesia to protect U.S. citizens.

JULY - OCTOBER 1958. Following civil unrest in Beirut, President Eisenhower sends 5,000 Marines to Lebanon to "protect American lives" and to "assist Lebanon in preserving its political independence." Eventually 14,000 U.S. soldiers and Marines occupy areas in Lebanon.

JULY 1959 - MARCH 1973. Vietnam era. Sent as troop trainers, the first U.S. military are killed in South Vietnam in July 1959. In October 1961, President Kennedy decides to send Green Beret "military advisers." In August 1964, Congress passes Gulf of Tonkin Resolution. In March 1973, the last U.S. troops withdraw.

NOVEMBER 1961. U.S. Navy planes and ships arrive off the Dominican Republic as show of force.

MAY - JULY 1962. A Marine expeditionary unit of 5,000 lands in Thailand to support the government against threat of outside Communist pressure.

OCTOBER - DECEMBER 1962. Challenging a Soviet introduction of missiles into Cuba, President Kennedy orders 180 Navy ships and a B-52 bomber force carrying A-bombs into the Caribbean to effect a quarantine.

MAY 1963. A U.S. Marine battalion is positioned off the coast of Haiti.

NOVEMBER 1964. U.S. transport aircraft in the Congo carry Belgian paratroopers in an operation to rescue civilians, among them 60 Americans, held hostage by antigovernment rebels.

MAY 1964 - JANUARY 1973. Beginning as retaliation for the downing of American reconnaissance planes flying over Laos, U.S. Navy jets attack Pathet Lao Communist strongholds. Air attacks on Laos continue into the 1970s.

APRIL 1965. Following Communist-leaning revolt in the Dominican Republic, President Johnson dispatches 21,500 U.S. troops to protect Americans and offer supplies and military assistance to locals.

JUNE 1967. During the Arab-Israeli War, President Johnson sends the U.S. Sixth Fleet within 50 miles of Syrian coast as a warning to the Soviet Union against entering the conflict.

JULY - DECEMBER 1967. Responding to an appeal from Congolese President Mobotu, President Johnson sends three C-130 transport planes to aid government forces.

APRIL - JUNE 1970. U.S. ground troops attack Communist sanctuaries in Cambodia.

MAY 1975. President Ford sends combined force of Navy, Marine, and Air Force to rescue crew of 39 from U.S. merchant ship *Mayaguez*, which had been captured by Cambodian Communists.

APRIL 1980. Ninety-man U.S. commando team in Iran aborts effort to rescue American hostages held in U.S. Embassy in Tehran. Eight die in collision between transport plane and helicopter.

OCTOBER 1983. U.S. Marines and troops from neighboring eastern Caribbean nations invade island of Grenada.

MARCH 24, 1986. The U.S. Sixth Fleet ventures across the "line of death" over the Gulf of Sidra. Libyans fire SA-5 missiles at U.S. planes. The *U.S.S. America* fires A-6 harpoon missiles and sinks Libyan patrol boat. U.S. military operations lead to a temporary shutdown of the Sirte radar station, the sinking of two Libyan patrol boats and the disabling of a third.

MARCH 26, 1986. Fourteen U.S. military helicopters ferry Honduran soldiers to near the Nicaraguan border to repel an incursion by Nicaraguan government forces. Approximately 50 U.S. pilots and crew members take part in the mission.

Source: *Congressional Quarterly Weekly Report*, April 1986, p. 700.

Further, when recent presidents have reported on *prior* actions taken or decided to take action without congressional authorization, *they have received support for what was already done.* The Korean decision of 1950 is a case in point. After President Truman had reached his decision to commit United States troops to South Korea, he discussed the decision with some congressional leaders. These included Senate and House party leaders and some senior members of the Foreign Relations, Foreign Affairs, and Armed Services committees—fourteen members of Congress in all. But Congress was not formally asked its advice or consent. Even the congressional leaders were given only a superficial briefing, and they were told the decision at the same time as the press. The other members of Congress read about it in the newspapers. Another case occurred with President Kennedy's decision to sponsor the attack by anti-Castro Cubans on Cuba's Bay of Pigs at the beginning of his administration. The only member of Congress consulted before the event was William Fulbright, chair of the Senate Foreign Relations Committee. Fulbright, incidentally, was reported to be the only one who objected to the plan.

An extreme case, showing even less consultation, occurred during the 1962 Cuban missile crisis. After Russian-built missiles were discovered in Cuba, Kennedy decided to blockade ships entering Cuban ports in lieu of more drastic military action, and to send an ultimatum to Russia to remove the missiles. Kennedy reached his decision after a week of deliberation and consultation with a number of advisers, about twenty in all. (See the box on pages 566 and 567.) However, no congressional members were included. Although conditions of crisis prevailed, making speed and secrecy of the gravest importance, there was still time and opportunity for such consultation. The decision was arrived at and a speech drafted. On Sunday, the British ambassador and the president's press secretary were informed. Congressional liaison head Larry O'Brien was told to round up a number of congressional leaders for their first briefing on the subject. On Monday, Kennedy held more conferences, briefed the congressional leaders at 5 P.M., and at 7 P.M. addressed the nation.[21]

In each of these cases of military action, there is presidential involvement in selecting advisers, executive branch participation, and little congressional role. The pattern has been one of presidential decision and congressional support, with or without consultation.

One caution is in order. When speaking of "presidential decisions," presidents are limited by the information, the interpretations, and the advisers that they choose. A large bureaucratic apparatus in affairs of state and defense provides information and so defines options and interprets events, in Cuba, Korea, the Kremlin, or anywhere else. Bureaucratic incentives frequently differ from presidential incentives. Some kinds of informa-

[21]Theodore Sorensen, *Kennedy* (New York: Harper & Row, 1965), pp. 672–703; Elie Abel, *The Missile Crisis* (Philadelphia: Lippincott, 1966); and Robert Kennedy, *Thirteen Days* (New York: W.W. Norton, 1969).

tion may be deliberately withheld from the White House and other kinds of information cast so as to make bureaucratic objectives seem inevitable. Although it was "Truman's decision" to drop the atom bomb a few months after he became president, the decision was heavily shaped by information from the War Department, where the Manhattan Project was being administered, and from the Air Force. Similarly, it was "Kennedy's decision" to attempt the Bay of Pigs landing in the early days of his administration, although the plan and the argument supporting it had evolved within the bureaucracy. Recall the difficulties of presidential advice and information as seen in Chapter Eight. Even when world events allow time and experience in office before making major decisions of war, the problem remains of how much presidential decisions are—or ought to be—constrained by bureaucratic objectives or by other advisers in the White House.

The Exception—Controversy. Exceptional cases occur when Congress disputes the course of administration policy. In fact, the birth of the Republic was immediately followed by a clash between the first president and the first Congress over who was to conduct foreign affairs and also whether the newborn nation would immediately go to war. In 1793, as President Washington issued a proclamation of neutrality in the war between Britain and France, Jefferson and others in Congress (who sided with France and the French Revolution) protested that Congress, not presidents, was given the power to declare war. The newly evolving political parties widened the debate: the Federalists in the White House favored Britain and neutrality; the Jeffersonian Republicans in Congress supported the French Revolution and American aid to France.

Washington and the neutralists won on the issue, establishing the first precedent for the president's dominance in war making. Nevertheless, the fact of the controversy is itself worth notice because it introduced a debate that would occur many times again. Congress and presidents have since disagreed at several points in American history over whether wars should be waged and who had the constitutional right to decide on the waging of them. Among other examples, they disagreed on the Spanish-American War and on U.S. involvement in World War II. In the case of the Spanish-American War, President McKinley lagged behind a more belligerent Congress; in World War II, President F. Roosevelt led a more reluctant Congress until the Japanese attack on Pearl Harbor. In each case Congress clearly helped "make" foreign policy, accompanied by considerable public opinion and interest.

The same conflict occurred in the late 1960s over disengagement in the Vietnam War. As the war dragged on without success and American casualties mounted, Congress became increasingly critical of the "president's war." Hearings in the Senate Foreign Relations Committee were held in a Democratic Congress against a Democratic president (Johnson) and grew even more vocal and critical when the Republican president (Nixon) took office. From 1969 to 1971 opposition in Congress widened until both houses

The Cuban Missile Crisis—The President's Advisers

Presidential biographies provide the inside accounts of what went on in a particular administration. They offer keys to the president's personality, priorities, and ways of making decisions. They tell also about the people around the president, their access to him and their various roles in the palace politics of the White House. These materials have to be used carefully, however. The accounts can be self-serving, biased for or against the president, concerned less with presenting facts than offering up praise or blame. It can be especially helpful when there are two or more accounts of the same events—each provides some check on the other.

The following list of President Kennedy's advisers in the Cuban Missile Crisis is supported by the many books and articles that have been written on the event. Particularly helpful are two biographies that list the president's advisers. The author of one, Theodore Sorensen, was himself one of the advisers; Arthur Schlesinger, the author of the other, was in the Kennedy White House and close to many of the participants. They agree in their accounts in almost all particulars, although Lyndon Johnson, mentioned as a participant by Sorensen, is not mentioned in the Schlesinger account.

The critical week in October began very early one Tuesday morning when aide McGeorge Bundy brought Kennedy confirmation of the photographs of Russian missile silos being built in Cuba. Kennedy knew a decision had to be made and immediately asked Bundy to round up a group of people. They would become known as the "Executive Committee" of the National Security Council, although they were not formally or comprehensively selected from that council. They were instead the people Kennedy wanted to help make the decision.

It is interesting to see whom Kennedy chose. Some of the advisers were in formal positions—in State, Defense, and the CIA—and others were not. Overall, one-third of the group had no direct formal connection with the issue. Aides Sorensen and O'Donnell were simply old friends who had been brought to the White House from the touch-football days and had worked on the 1960 Kennedy campaign. The President's brother was included in the list. There were even three private citizens, from that group of six "wise men" who were so influential in American foreign policy in the years following World War II. (See footnote 3 on page 550.)

It is equally interesting to see who was not chosen: most particularly, any members of Congress. Frequently, presidents would consult with a few senior members of the foreign relations committees. William Fulbright, chair of the Senate committee, had been consulted by Kennedy in the earlier Cuban Bay of Pigs invasion, and in fact warned against going through with what turned out to be a disaster. Nor could it be said that the few committee members would violate the necessary secrecy of the plans. There were, after all, some twenty members already

had debated resolutions and restrictions against the war. The Tonkin Gulf Resolution was repealed: twice, in fact. The controversy formed along party lines with two-thirds of the Democrats opposing two-thirds of the Republicans on votes in Congress on Vietnam. In 1970, as in 1790, both president and Congress could debate, on constitutional grounds, their relative responsibilities in war.

Both Congress and the public support presidents in times of immediate crisis. But if the war continues without success, the support can be withdrawn, as the public opinion polls in Chapter Eight show dramatically.

included. Their staff people—legal, diplomatic, military—knew enough of the event to work out the details. One gathers, from other accounts, that Kennedy did not particularly like most members of Congress, and he evidently decided that he did not want them in on the decision-making.

The group met for a week, often forming subgroups. The recommendation that Kennedy finally accepted was to blockade Cuban ports from any incoming Russian ships. The blockade included 180 ships and a bomber force carrying atomic bombs. The blockade was chosen over other stronger options, such as bombing the bases, and over weaker options, such as merely warning the Russians to disband their equipment and leave. The blockade worked, the Russian ships turned back with the silos uncompleted, and the Cuban Missile Crisis was over. Many people felt, at the time and since, that the U.S. and Soviet Union could have been close to nuclear war.

With the success of the decision, there is a tendency to praise the decision makers. And yet there are remaining questions. What if the silos were built three or six years later? Would Johnson's advisers, or Nixon's, make the same decision? Would other relatives or private citizens be included? The president was the only elected official, along with the vice-president, in the group. Should a few members of Congress be consulted? Or would Johnson or Nixon or any other president have the decision to make alone?
Representatives from the Department of State
Secretary Dean Rusk
Under Secretary George Ball

Latin American Assistant Secretary Edwin Martin
Deputy Under Secretary Alexis Johnson
Soviet expert Llewellyn Thompson
Representatives from the Department of Defense
Secretary Robert McNamara
Deputy Secretary Roswell Gilpatric
Assistant Secretary Paul Nitze
General Maxwell Taylor, Chairman of the Joint Chiefs of Staff
Representatives from other government posts with direct relevance to the issue
CIA Deputy Director Marshall Carter
CIA Director John McCone (on his return to Washington)
U.N. Representative Adlai Stevenson
USIA Deputy Director Donald Wilson
Vice-President Lyndon Johnson
Representatives from other government posts with less direct relevance to the issue
Attorney General Robert Kennedy
Treasury Secretary Douglas Dillon

Other participants
Presidential aides McGeorge Bundy, Theodore Sorensen, and Kenneth O'Donnell
Former state officials and then private citizens Dean Acheson, Robert Lovett, and Charles Bohlen

Source: Theodore Sorensen, *Kennedy* (New York: Harper and Row, 1965), pp. 674–75. See also Arthur M. Schlesinger, Jr., *A Thousand Days*, (New York: Houghton Mifflin, 1965), pp. 802–8.

Truman's popularity fell steadily during the Korean War and Johnson's fell during the war in Vietnam. The change in the domestic environment is shown in Exhibit 14.3. As more and more people decided the Vietnam War was "a mistake," Congress became increasingly active in policy-making.

The War Powers Act.   The Vietnam experience and increasing congressional dissatisfaction with presidential war-making policy brought **the War Powers Act of 1973.** The act restricts presidential authority to employ forces on a sustained basis to a sixty-day period (with a short exten-

| **EXHIBIT 14.3** | Public Opinion and Congressional Action on the Vietnam War |

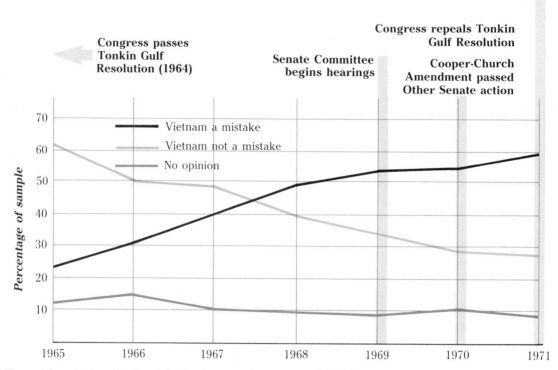

The question asked was "In view of the developments since we entered the fighting in Vietnam, do you think the United States made a mistake in sending troops to fight in Vietnam?"

Source: Public opinion data provided by the American Institute of Public Opinion (AIPO) poll, compiled by John E. Mueller, *War, Presidents and Public Opinion* (New York: John Wiley, 1973), pp. 54–55.

sion possible) within which the Congress must act either to validate or invalidate the presidential action. Congress has forced itself to take *some action* either to stop or continue the hostilities. The act also requires presidents to report to Congress within forty-eight hours of any such initial commitment and urges them to undertake prior consultation whenever possible.

Passed by bipartisan and extraordinary majorities in the two houses over a Nixon veto, the act on paper suggests a strong assertion of congressional war-making powers. Nevertheless, the context of the legislation must be kept in mind. It was passed in a Democratic Congress with a Republican president; with a president (Nixon) whose credibility and public support had been severely damaged by the ongoing reports of the Watergate cover-up; and at a time when the public was still mindful of Vietnam. So the War Powers Act, seen as a striking exception to the past pattern of support, was passed under highly exceptional circumstances of its own. Whether the act will be enforced at some future time with the same-party control, with the public supporting the president, and with Vietnam a matter of history remains an open question. Under the War Powers Act, it should be noted, Congress can still follow its typical pattern and give the president its unquestioned support.

The War Powers Act had its first test under the Ford administration in 1975. On May 12, Cambodian Communist troops captured the American merchant ship *Mayaguez* and its crew of thirty-nine. President Ford responded with combined forces of Marine, Navy, and Air Force units who on May 14 succeeded in retaking the ship and rescuing the crew. The Defense Department estimated the cost of the rescue at $9.5 million; in the engagement thirty-eight American soldiers were killed, with three others missing and presumed dead. The White House liaison staff had telephoned congressional leaders before the Marines landed on May 14, to notify them of the action but not to consult them. Ford reported to Congress on May 15 the nature of the incident, the action taken, and the outcome.

Reaction in Congress to Ford's decision was generally favorable. Members agreed that the show of American strength was important; few questioned that the rescue was hardly an unqualified military success. The Senate Foreign Relations Committee followed with a resolution of support. House and Senate members who had been instrumental in drafting the War Powers Act said that they felt the law had worked satisfactorily. Notice, however, the similarity between the *Mayaguez* incident and the cases occurring before the act was passed. Ford's actions differed little from Kennedy's or Truman's as commander-in-chief.

The cases since that time show a mixed record in presidents' willingness to follow the formal provisions of the act. Ford did report to Congress on *Mayaguez*, although he was slightly over the forty-eight hour limit in doing so. Months would pass before Congress had an accurate picture of the events and decisions that had taken place. He did not report on forces used to assist the 1975 evacuation from Vietnam, arguing that the congressional recess made consultation impossible. When Carter ordered U.S. transport aircraft to support French and Belgian troops with the airlift in Zaire in 1978, he did not follow the act. When he conducted the unsuccessful helicopter rescue attempt of the Iranian-held hostages in 1980, he did report to Congress two days after the attempt, but made no mention of the War Powers Act. The mission, he said, "was ordered and conducted pursuant to the president's powers under the Constitution." Congress had not been consulted before the rescue attempt. Reagan followed the War Powers Act in military action in Grenada and in the raid on Libya, but did not follow it in actions in El Salvador or Lebanon. Presidents, it appears, are deciding when they will do so and when they will not.

U.S. soldiers and tanks proceed down the streets of Grenada in November 1983.

The raid on Libya, like *Mayaguez*, was not a military success. Of the bombers on the mission, one was lost and its crew presumed dead, several returned without completing their mission, and at least one bombed a civilian target by mistake. Nevertheless, no voices were raised in Congress criticizing the Reagan administration's decision. Congress and the public supported the president.

Does the War Powers Act make a difference to the conduct of military policy? Some people believe that the act is important in alerting presidents to Congress's view that it should have an active role in military decisions. Further, the reporting requirements may influence the kind of decisions presidents will make. Yet, it is also true that nothing looks very different from the past. Presidents appear to be doing what they have done since the late 1940s in going to Congress after the fact and asking for support. Congress, too, appears to be doing what it has done before in supplying the support that is asked for. The predominant pattern in military action remains one of presidential decision and congressional support even after the War Powers Act.

Diplomacy

There is a second kind of foreign policy: namely, the conduct of diplomacy, as seen in the making of treaties and other international agreements.

Treaties. Making peace seems the logical reverse of making war, and yet there are differences between these two kinds of foreign policy. In peace as in war, the president is the one looked to for leadership by Congress and the American people. In peace as in war, the bureaucracy provides information, defines the options, and interprets events. The Constitution gives Congress peace-making as well as war-making powers: treaties require a vote of two-thirds or more of the Senate. (A **treaty** is an agreement, legally binding in international law, that is formalized by two or more nations after negotiation.) However, Congress has been much more willing to assert itself in matters of peace than in war. A number of cases illustrate the point.

The most famous case is peace making after World War I. President Woodrow Wilson exerted world leadership in designing the Treaty of Versailles (the peace treaty) and the new League of Nations. But Congress refused to sign the treaty, since it opposed the League. This would be the American "foreign policy" on the question. It is an extreme case, but a difficult one for presidents to forget.

In preparing for the Japanese Peace Treaty of 1952, President Truman was determined not to make Wilson's mistakes. Ambassador Dulles met frequently with the Subcommittee on Far Eastern Affairs of the Senate Foreign Relations Committee, the committee that would be reporting the treaty for a vote on the Senate floor. The subcommittee participated in the treaty-making to the extent of discussing and selecting from alternative proposals that Dulles presented. Truman, however, could still not take the Senate support for granted. When the treaty was due to come to a vote, concern developed that Japan might negotiate a separate treaty with the communist government of China, which the Senate did not want the United States to recognize as a legitimate government. Fifty-six senators advised the president that unless Japan gave assurances that it would not sign such a treaty with the Chinese, they would oppose the peace treaty in the Senate. Truman had to go back to the Japanese negotiators and get their assurance, bring in the subcommittee members and the fifty-six senators again, and read them the result. Truman got his treaty, but at some cost of White House time and attention.

Kennedy's nuclear test ban treaty provides another example. Kennedy aide Theodore Sorensen comments that from Kennedy's perspective the United States Senate posed as large a problem as the Russians in negotiations. Both required continued and simultaneous discussions.[22] Kennedy consulted with the favorable Senate Foreign Relations committee, but faced the threat of losing the required two-thirds vote on the Senate floor. A "Citizens Committee for a Nuclear Test Ban" was organized from the White House to mobilize public support, conduct nationwide newspaper and television advertising, and to lobby specific undecided senators. In the resulting roll call, a total of eighty senators finally voted yes, and nineteen voted no. Kennedy won his treaty, but at a high cost of time, lobbying effort, and legislative attention.

The case is similar to the Panama Canal Treaty negotiated in the Carter administration. Carter, too, faced serious Senate questioning in committee

[22]Sorensen, pp. 736–737.

and on the floor; Carter, too, mounted a major lobbying effort, contacting individual senators and engaging in extensive negotiations with those undecided. He even had Vice-President Mondale and former president Ford working the phones. When undecided Senator Edward Zorinsky of Nebraska told Carter it wasn't he but his constituents the president had to convince, Carter asked for a list of names. A whole delegation of Nebraskans got invited to the White House and Carter shook hands with every one. (Zorinsky ultimately voted against Carter and the treaty.) Carter, like Kennedy, won his treaty, although more narrowly and at the cost of two conservative compromise amendments. In contrast, Reagan faced less Senate opposition over his arms-limitation treaty with the Russians; nevertheless, he, too, had to work at gaining support.

In these cases, presidents have defined the issues, set constraints for debate, and won all or some of what they wanted. Their control is clearer and their success rate better than in many domestic policy cases. However, compared to the military action, the difference is clear. Presidents have had to fight for what they wanted, count the votes on the floor, and work with the committees and party organizations in Congress. Presidents have to ask Congress for its advice and consent. Support cannot be taken for granted.

Executive Agreements.   Just as wars are not always declared, international agreements are not always made by treaty. **Executive agreements** with other nations negotiated by the president and State Department officials require no Senate consent. Although not provided for in the Constitution, the use of executive agreements has multiplied in the years since World War II, while the number of treaties has remained fairly stable. Criticism, in Congress and elsewhere, has grown accordingly. Critics argue that the changing form of international commitments erodes the powers of Congress in foreign policy. Moreover, even when Congress is involved in the foreign policy process, the issues it considers are relatively less important than those handled unilaterally by the executive. One senator complained that "the Senate is asked to convene solemnly to approve by a two-thirds vote a treaty to preserve cultural artifacts in a friendly neighboring country. At the same time, the Chief Executive is moving American military men and material around the globe like so many pawns in a chess game."[23] Executive agreements were reduced in number in the Carter and Reagan years, as the graph in Exhibit 14.4 reveals. Nevertheless, any full study of congressional foreign policy making must look beyond the power to reject or amend treaties.

One such study suggests that Congress retains an important role, at least quantitatively, in the making of international agreements. The authors

[23]Loch K. Johnson and James McCormick, "The Making of International Agreements," *Journal of Politics*, May, 1978, p. 470. And see Loch K. Johnson, *The Making of International Agreements* (New York: New York University Press, 1984). For other commentary, see Arthur M. Schlesinger, Jr., *The Imperial Presidency* (New York: Houghton Mifflin, 1973), pp. 310–19, and J. William Fulbright, *The Crippled Giant* (New York: Random House, Vintage Books, 1972), pp. 216–27.

| EXHIBIT 14.4 | Treaties and Executive Agreements from Truman to Reagan |

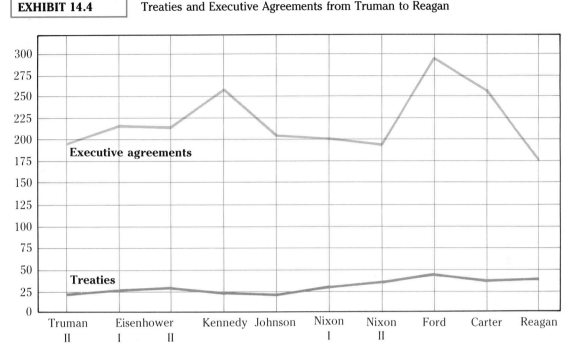

Source: Gary King and Lyn Ragsdale, *The Elusive Executive* (Washington, D.C.: Congressional Quarterly Press, 1988), p. 143, for years 1949–1983.

separated all agreements into three categories: treaties, executive agreements requiring the president's signature only, and executive agreements requiring some kind of statutory provision—that is, legislation passed through both houses of Congress. The authors found that the overwhelming majority—from 80 to 93 percent—of executive agreements are made by statutory provision. The results hold across five presidential administrations. It is the *statutory agreements* that have been increasing in the years since World War II. In other words, much of recent American diplomacy has involved government spending, in the form of economic or military aid, and government spending requires Congress.[24] The use of executive agreements are not presidential devices to evade Congress as much as choices of a different kind of diplomacy.[25] If the agreement requires government spending, Congress must be faced in its committees, appropriation process, and votes on the House and Senate floor.

Presidents retain some discretionary authority to allocate funds on their own. Some agreements, then, can be signed without facing the con-

[24]Johnson and McCormick, pp. 468–78.

[25]The same point is made by Gary King and Lyn Ragsdale, *The Elusive Executive* (Washington, D.C.: CQ Press, 1988), p. 114, in their comprehensive analysis of treaties and agreements.

gressional process. As part of the same mood that prompted the War Powers Act, Congress passed legislation in 1972 requiring the executive branch to submit to Congress the texts of all international agreements. Congress may thus see the agreements but has no power to veto them. Legislation giving Congress a veto power has several times been initiated in the Senate but has not passed the House. *It is Congress that is deciding the congressional role in foreign policy making.*

Foreign Aid

Beyond war and peace, a major part of contemporary American foreign policy has been maintained through the politics of foreign aid. Questions of who will receive what aid with what restrictions and under what conditions profoundly affect the American role in international relations, upholding governments against revolutions, cementing some alliances and discouraging others. Each year as part of the federal budgetary process, Congress will authorize an amount of money for foreign and military aid, after considering the president's budget request. As distinct from an isolated executive agreement, this is a continuing process of foreign policy making and one that the Congress is very interested in.

The use of foreign aid as a major tool of American foreign policy can be traced to the aftermath of World War II and the beginning of the Cold War. Faced with the problem of European economic recovery, President Truman, Secretary of State Dean Acheson, and other advisers saw American economic aid as a major defense of a "free Europe" against communism. The American decision makers, ironically, accepted the logic of Karl Marx that economic conditions produce political effects. Thus a poor Europe was ripe for Communist coups and American economic aid became a major weapon in the containment policy of the Cold War. The Truman Doctrine and the Marshall Plan followed, executive in design and implementation, through which aid was given to Greece, Turkey, and Western European nations. In the years that followed, American strategy would widen beyond Europe and attempt to distinguish between various Communist regimes. Nevertheless, the basic defensive rationale for the aid program remained. A major part of the new cold-war diplomacy rested on the politics of foreign aid.

Aid, however, requires money, and money requires Congress. Foreign aid had the drawback from the congressional point of view of representing taxpayers' money spent for no clear constituency benefit received. Presidents, therefore, have been dependent on Congress for one major tool of contemporary foreign policy making. The foreign aid programs have been executive in inspiration and direction, but Congress has shown no reluctance to add or subtract—dollar amounts, countries, restrictions—from the executive requests. The president as "Leader of the Free World" has a bankbook only in a joint account and a credit limit, through the annual appropriation process, of only one year.

**American corn and
grain is unloaded
from a freighter as
aid to Somalia.**

So, throughout the years from the late 1940s to the present, foreign aid has been controversial. Vote counting, White House breakfasts for key committee members, and other efforts of presidential persuasion became routine. These efforts, occasional in matters of peace making and exceptional in matters of war, became the regular and expected events in foreign aid policy. And so also foreign governments would not only pursue negotiations through State Department channels, they would lobby in Congress as well. They would hire American public relations firms to improve their image and bring their case to the American public. In other words, foreign aid is closer to some domestic policy controversies than to some other foreign policy making.

From the late 1940s the controversies in Congress followed party and regional lines. A majority of Democrats supported and a majority of Republicans opposed presidential aid requests, no matter which party the president belonged to. Southern Democrats and Northeastern Republicans tended to vote with the opposing party. Hence presidents would win or lose key requests depending on the number of defections that occurred and how many of their own partisans they had to start with.

Presidents since Nixon have increasingly worked military aid components into the foreign aid package in the attempt to bolster congressional support. Nevertheless, controversy has remained and has primarily followed party lines. Indeed, looking at all foreign aid roll calls from 1974 through 1987, there is a striking pattern of continuity with the earlier period. Of ninety-one roll call votes taken in the Senate and House, (1) most of the votes (90 percent) are controversial, showing less than three-fourths of the members voting on one side. (2) Most of the votes follow the party lines evident in the earlier period. Eighty-eight percent of the controversial votes are also party votes: that is, votes in which a majority of one party opposes a majority of the other party. (3) While presidents win much more than they lose, their success is by no means assured. On slightly more than three-fourths of the controversial votes, Congress voted with the president's position, and on about one-fourth of the votes Congress opposed the president. It is not known, of course, how much the legislation was already compromised from the original administration position.[26]

Congress has set qualitative as well as quantitative limits to the aid programs. *Since presidents have had to bargain for aid programs*, Congress has been able to set specific restrictions and even specific recipients. By denying presidential requests for long-term borrowing and insisting on annual appropriations, it has forced the White House into a year-by-year process of bargaining and review and forced foreign economies into short-term planning. Congress has at times required one-half of aid shipments to be transported by American-flag vessels. It has dictated the currency for repayment of loans, set Export-Import Bank lending policy, and frequently suggested to foreign nations the kinds of uses to which aid funds should be directed and the conditions under which they might be expected to be continued. Originally casting the program to Congress as a defense against communism, presidents subsequently found it difficult to propose aid policies that did not follow the same bipolar world view. Over strong White House opposition, Congress authorized aid to anticommunist Spain under the dictatorial Franco regime and denied aid to Communist Poland. Aid went to Spain and did not go to Poland. That was American "foreign policy" on the question. Congress has selected other aid recipients, prohibiting aid to nations (such as the United Arab Republic) preparing for military action against other nations (Israel) and cutting off assistance to Indonesia and Turkey. It has required the State Department to evaluate and report on the treatment of human rights in nations proposed as aid recipients.

The practice of **earmarking** portions of the aid budget also shows the importance of executive-congressional negotiations. The committees traditionally have earmarked—that is, have written into law—portions of the aid budget, leaving the remainder open to the president's discretion. The president can then change the aid allocations within that remaining portion, switching them from one country or program to another. In return, the committees expect to be consulted when the changes are made. Congress has earmarked substantial amounts of aid for some countries, Israel and Egypt in particular, often at levels higher than the administration proposed.

[26]See Barbara Hinckley, *Stability and Change in Congress*, 4th ed. (New York: Harper and Row, 1988), pp. 303–7.

At the same time, it has typically cut the overall aid budget, thereby putting an especially tight squeeze on the programs and countries not singled out for congressional attention. President Reagan relied on his ability to reprogram funds in providing military aid to El Salvador, against expressed congressional disapproval. The action became an issue in the following year's debate on foreign aid, when Congress cut the overall budget further and added to the earmarking.

In all of these cases, American foreign policy is made. Relations with other nations are guided or constrained or redefined. The result is not merely a matter of White House decision or State Department action but a combined product of many people's decisions. The problem of aid to the Nicaraguan contras, so important to the Reagan administration, can be seen from this perspective. (The contras were the name of the Nicaraguan guerrillas fighting against the Sandinista government.) The president gave the issue high priority, lobbying in Congress and speaking around the country in its support. Since the administration itself was split on the issue, one group of advisers had convinced the president against the opinion of other advisers. Congress was skeptical about the value of the aid, and public opinion, even after Reagan's speeches, was not supportive. Thus Reagan's requests for aid from Congress met with very little success. Some proposals passed in the Senate were voted down by the Democratic House. Other proposals were amended to restrict the aid to humanitarian (nonmilitary) aid, or to limited amounts for limited times. The result was that Reagan was not getting the Nicaraguan policy he wanted from Congress.

It is in this context that the actions of the National Security Council referred to earlier in the chapter can be seen. The NSC advisor Admiral Poindexter and subordinate Lt. Colonel Oliver North arranged for a diversion of funds from a secret arms sale to Iran, the money to be spent on the Nicaraguan contras. The CIA Director William Casey was also aware of the diversion of funds and was helping to implement the Nicaraguan rebellion. A policy blocked by some of the foreign policy makers was being carried on by others. Things might have stopped there, but the news media also became participants, publicizing the disclosures of the illegal actions and giving the story continuing high priority. An investigation followed in the Democratic-controlled Congress, with members sharply critical of the actions of Poindexter and North. The scandal hurt the president's popularity and his bargaining power with Congress.

The case illustrates several points about American foreign policy making. It shows the power of the president, who can tap resources in a vast bureaucracy and cloak the actions with the secrecy required by "national security." But it also shows the power of Congress and the limits of the president as foreign policy maker. In addition, it shows the power of, and the problems with, the bureaucracy that can work in secrecy and take actions in the president's name. These particular illegal actions happened to be disclosed. There is no reason to believe that other actions in other administrations did not also occur.

Should the president have flexibility in pursuing policy even against the will of Congress? Or should there be more responsibility in government and more accountability to Congress and the public? What line should be drawn and balance made between the two? The questions have surfaced before, during the Watergate investigations in the Nixon White House and they certainly will again.

Defense Policy

Both defense and foreign aid are major kinds of American foreign policy. Both are complex, heavily dependent on bureaucratic expertise, and subject to annual congressional legislation. Both help to shape the American role in the world and image abroad. Despite these similarities, the contrasts in policy-making are striking. Like the cases of military action, widespread debate and controversy are the exceptions. But like many kinds of domestic policy, much of the policy is made far from the White House; it is made in the Pentagon bureaucracy, in subgovernments, or in secret intelligence agencies.

The development of nuclear weapons, the choice of preferred weapon systems, and negotiations for limiting weapons have been issues of the highest visibility since the dawn of the atomic age in 1945. Presidents have taken positions on these issues and have received mixed support in Congress. For example, both Kennedy and Carter tried to get a test ban treaty ratified in Congress: Kennedy succeeded and Carter did not. Reagan did not succeed in gaining the support he asked for his Star Wars defense system. The overall level of defense spending has also been visible and controversial. The defense budget was cut in the 1970s in comparison with past levels and increased in the 1980s. (See Exhibit 14.5.)

Beyond these issues, however, are many other areas of defense policy: conventional weapons systems, manpower standards, priorities for research and development, and tactics for guerrilla wars. The budget makers in the White House and Congress set the general guidelines for these policies, but the specific policy choices are made by the military experts, subject to their own negotiations and lobbying. The presidents themselves are lobbied about what kind and level of weapon system is to be preferred. The military branches, private sector lobbyists, and defense contractors lobby Congress too. A typical defense budget (see Exhibit 14.6) can give a sense of the kind of decisions that must be made. How much will be spent for research versus military construction, the army versus the navy, or strategic forces versus general purpose forces? Presidents will not usually be making these decisions.

It is in the low-visibility issues where the *subgovernments* are found, as described in Chapter Nine. Committees, defense agencies in the Pentagon, and interest groups all support the same policy and help each other. Jokes were made about key committee members from Georgia and South Carolina, saying that if the states received one more military installation added to all the ones they had already, they would sink. More typically, however,

EXHIBIT 14.5

The Defense Budget

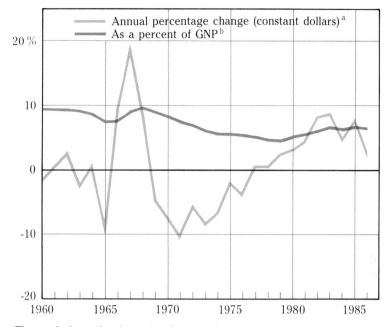

[a]The graph shows the change in relation to the previous year's spending. Thus a minus figure means the budget was cut that much of a percent from the previous year's level. Using constant dollars corrects for inflation and makes the years comparable.

[b]The graph shows the percentage of the gross national product (a measure of the nation's income) spent on defense.

Source: Harold W. Stanley and Richard G. Niemi, *Vital Statistics on American Politics* (Washington, D.C.: CQ Press, 1988), p. 302.

defense spending is spread across the states and districts of the nation. All members of Congress can support a policy that benefits their own constituents.

"Who are we to say no to the military?" a House Appropriations Committee member asks rhetorically. (It is a question not asked for other complicated and technical subjects: Congress does not say "Who are we to say no to the economists, or the space agency, or the State Department?") Congress's deference to the military agencies is actually a way of saying that *they support the policy of the agencies.* Hence, Congress helps make low-visibility defense policy by supporting decisions made elsewhere.[27] In the exceptional cases when Congress objects to a policy, it says "no" very readily.

[27]The congressional committees' support of defense agencies shows considerable stability over time. See Lewis Dexter, "Congressmen and the Making of Military Policy" in Robert L. Peabody and Nelson W. Polsby, eds. *New Perspectives on the House of Representatives*, 2nd ed. (Skokie, Ill: Rand McNally, 1969); and Bruce Ray, "The Responsiveness of the U.S. Armed Services Committees to Their Parent Bodies," *Legislative Studies Quarterly*, November, 1980, pp. 501–15. See also *Congressional Quarterly Weekly Report*, March 31, 1984, pp. 729–36.

EXHIBIT 14.6

Three Ways of
Looking at a Defense
Budget

ITEM	AUTHORIZATION (BILLIONS OF DOLLARS)
By Title:	
Military Personnel	68.9
Operation and Maintenance	78.2
Procurement	96.8
Research and Development; Evaluation	31.5
Military Construction	5.5
Military Family Housing	2.9
Revolving and Management Funds	1.7
Receipts and Deductions	−0.6
Total	284.7
By Component:	
Department of the Army	74.4
Department of the Navy	96.5
Department of the Air Force	99.9
Other Defense Agencies	13.0
Other (Defense-wide)	1.0
Total	284.7
By Program:	
Strategic Forces	27.8
General Purpose Forces	120.6
Intelligence and Communications	25.1
Airlift and Sealift	7.0
National Guard and Reserve	15.7
Research and Development	24.6
Central Supply and Maintenance	24.4
Training, Medical, and Other Personnel	33.1
Administration	5.9
Support of Other Nations	0.5
Total	284.7

Source: Aaron Wildavsky, *The New Politics of the Budgetary Process*, p. 351. The budget is for Fiscal Year 1985.

So, a congressional committee (the Joint Committee on Atomic Energy) conducted vigorous oversight of the Atomic Energy Commission when it felt the latter was not sufficiently zealous in building a nuclear arsenal. It demanded to be kept informed of everything the commission was doing, including matters with top secret classifications. It did not say it did not have the expertise, or it could not keep the secrets, or it could not say no to the executive. And so Congress battled President Kennedy, who wanted cuts in the defense budget, and fought President Reagan, who wanted increases at the expense of some domestic programs. President Nixon battled the Congress for more than two years for an ABM system (antiballistic missile system), winning only after some of the most extensive lobbying of his administration and by the narrowest of votes. Presidents Carter and Reagan also fought Congress for an MX missile system: Carter cut the program and Reagan put it back again.

Each event became an issue, made the news, and could be followed and debated. But by the same token, when the concerns of the various participants shift elsewhere and the momentary conflict recedes, no such events occur. In the absence of those exceptional conditions producing conflict among defense decision makers, the subgovernments return.

If we ask, then, who makes defense policy, we must answer that many people do, with the particular cast of characters dependent on the circumstances of the time. Presidential interest can raise a routine policy question to White House level. A committee can hound an agency until it gets a policy to its liking. Issues can gain public attention and new interest groups can form, transforming a cozy subgovernment into an arena for debate.

Draft legislation, like other issues of defense, illustrates the role of many different policymakers. The draft is an issue of immediate concern for citizens between the ages of eighteen and twenty-six. It is thus more comparable to issues of unemployment, Social Security, or civil rights in confronting the citizen directly with the national government than to some other defense issues: for example, the location of a distant missile base or the abstract issue of the total defense budget. The draft is sensitive to public opinion also in tapping public attitudes toward war. Compulsory enlistment in military service is supported to the extent the nation's security is seen to be threatened. If the credibility of the threat or the rationale for a war is questioned, the draft also loses support.

Nevertheless, the issue shares one important characteristic with the other defense issues: the advantage of military bureaucracies in using often-classified sources of information.[28] Presidents, members of Congress, and other participants in the defense debate are in large part forced to rely on specific bureaucratic information for defense capabilities, military threats, or fighting capacity of the United States or other nations. Thus, if a draft decision depends on the perception of a national security threat or "preparedness" issue as weighed against the capability of U.S. forces to meet the threat or achieve the preparedness, the military bureaucracies are often the main and uncheckable source of this kind of information.

---

[28]For cases of bureaucratic policy-making, see Morton H. Halperin and Arnold Kanter, eds., *Readings in American Foreign Policy: A Bureaucratic Perspective* (Boston: Little, Brown, 1973). See also Irving L. Janis, *Groupthink*, 2nd ed. (New York: Houghton Mifflin, 1982); and Charles M. Hardin, *Presidential Power and Accountability* (Chicago: University of Chicago Press, 1974).

The nation's first peacetime draft was enacted into law on the eve of World War II by the Selective Training and Service Act of 1940. New legislation was passed in 1948 and again in 1951, on the eve of the Korean War. The 1951 act (the Universal Military Training and Services Act) was subsequently extended by Congress five more times until July 1973. From 1973 until 1980, there was no draft and no registration for the draft.

The 1973 date of the end of the draft is clearly important. It followed public and congressional opposition to the Vietnam War and the broader antiwar movement of the period. But the cries of "never again" of the Vietnam period had faded seven or eight years later. Potential antiwar groups had moved on to other, more publicly visible issues.

Increasing pressure, however, came from senior Pentagon officials who believed the all-volunteer system would not be adequate to the nation's security needs, even during a limited war. Larger numbers would be needed. President Carter was persuaded to support registration for the draft. Carter then used a time of heightened military activity, with Americans held hostage in Iran and a Russian move into Afghanistan, to ask for draft registration. He also asked Congress to relax restrictions on the CIA. By the summer of 1980, peacetime registration for the draft had returned.

Public opinion, aroused to end the draft, was then appealed to by a president to reinstate it, at least insofar as concerned registration. The president and Congress followed the advice of the military bureaucracies. The "normal" policy returned.

Domestic Policy Parallels

Not only are these four kinds of foreign policy—war, diplomacy, foreign aid, defense—different from one another, they also resemble cases of domestic policy. Foreign aid, for example, is like social welfare policy, with its debates over welfare levels, housing, and poverty programs. Both policies are controversial in Congress and both find the parties on opposing sides. There have been annually recurring budget battles in both policies and restrictions added in Congress. Congress has added provisions to welfare programs as it added restrictions to the foreign aid programs. Agencies administering both policies need the president's support in facing a skeptical Congress. Thus the policy outcome will change depending on the interest of the president and the number of members of the president's party in Congress.

Defense, in contrast, suggests other domestic policy parallels, especially those where subgovernments are active. Federal spending is distributed broadly across the nation, as in many agriculture and public works programs, so that all member of Congress have a share of the federal pie. Members of the Armed Services committees support the defense agencies just as the members of the Agriculture or Public Works committees support their respective agencies: they make public policy while they allocate goods and services to their constituents at home. (See Chapter Seven.) Conflict can occur and subgovernments can be disrupted, but only with exceptional effort. Kennedy fought the defense subgovernments as Carter fought the energy policy subgovernments, each to little effect. The FBI in a Republican administration (Reagan's) investigated charges of corruption and payoffs made in awarding defense contracts in a Democratic-controlled Congress. But what happens to all these policies when a new president is inaugurated? They are back in the subgovernments where they were before. One might expect, therefore, in defense issues, as in agriculture and energy policy, considerable stability across several presidential terms.

Although cases of military action and diplomacy are more distinctive, there are domestic policy parallels, too. Information will be gathered by bureaucratic officials; it can be selected, transformed, or withheld from presidents entirely. The news media can focus on issues of foreign or domestic policy, ignoring an event or giving it continued attention. The most visible issues are more likely than others to reach the president. Thus the site of decision and the kind of decision made will vary in domestic and foreign policy cases with visibility, bureaucratic politics, and White House interests. Presidents can be very influential in some military and diplomatic decisions. But how have they chosen which policies to focus their attention on? Who have they selected as advisers? Who supplies them with the information? As shown in Chapter Eight, presidents will concentrate on one or two issues in the domestic agenda. They can concentrate on only one or two military or diplomatic issues as well. The other matters of war and peace will be decided by other foreign policy makers.

When treaties are visible and controversial, other domestic parallels appear. Presidents attempt to mobilize broad public and congressional support, as they might do for a Supreme Court nomination or a tax reform plan. Congress becomes involved and the committees are active. Debate widens out from a narrow executive decision-making site to engage the public and interest groups. Some treaties, like some domestic policies, require extensive compromises; they are not forged by the White House alone. Other treaties are like the unanimous resolutions waved through Congress periodically in favor of cancer research, Mother's Day, or a war against drugs.

Four different kinds of foreign policy have been discussed, each with domestic parallels and each showing a different role for the president. No, it cannot be said that the president "makes foreign policy." The president is more involved in some foreign policy areas than others, and more successful in some areas than in others. At the same time, many other people are making foreign policy too.

Seeing the parallels between foreign and domestic policy can help to better understand both policy areas. As the site changes—from the White House to the committees to a secret agency—the decisions also change. But what explains why one site becomes critical rather than another? Three influences appear important from the foreign policy cases looked at in this chapter: the perceived *importance* of the issue to the nation's security; the *visibility* of the issue; and the *time frame* posed by the situation.[29] Visibility allows the influence of public opinion and increases the chance of controversy and debate. The time frame also affects the chance of controversy. When a military action has time to become political, Congress deals with the politics of war as with the politics of peace. When a conflict drags on without success, presidents lose support from the public and Congress. This occurred not only in the wars of Korea and Vietnam but also in the Lebanese conflict in Reagan's first term in office. Members of Congress said they were hearing their constituents say to bring the Marines home. In contrast, the Reagan administration policy in Grenada quickly closed off the criticism that was beginning. While the White House explanations of the event were found not to be factually accurate, the mission was swiftly over and successful. The raid on Libya and the *Mayaguez* affair, as noted before, showed military and strategic flaws. Both, however, were over so quickly that criticism was closed off. Visibility and importance can also affect the time frame. News reports can stay with a story, thus extending the chance for controversy, or turn to other stories. If issues are perceived to be important, they are presumably brought to the White House; but the same issues, six months or a year before they become important, are decided somewhere else.

---

[29]For a typology of foreign policy situations, see Barry B. Hughes, *The Domestic Context of American Foreign Policy* (San Francisco: W.H. Freeman, 1978).

The president is expected to be involved in the most important issues; the president, Congress, and the public in the most visible ones; and Congress and the agencies in issues with the longest time frame. Thus advisers who make decisions on what is "important" and the news media that decide on visibility are influencing policy decisions. In both domestic and foreign policy, changing the name changes the game and the number of players.

These cases of foreign policy should be sufficient to raise a number of observations. First, American foreign policy is not a category consistent in itself and distinct from domestic policy. There is not one but many kinds of foreign policy, raising different issues and engaging different sets of participants. Second, even within any one foreign policy category, there are variations and exceptions. And so, third, it is important to push beyond the usual statements on the subject to find the reasons for these variations.

Doing so leads back to influences discussed in earlier chapters: the importance of public opinion and the role of the news media; the importance of party voting in Congress and the activity of subgovernments; the problem of presidential information and the role of advisers. The same influences affecting domestic policy are found in this chapter as well. Both foreign *and* domestic policy vary in their visibility, time frame, and perceived importance, and so will be decided by different policymakers. There is one president, not two, who enjoys variable influence in policy-making, whether foreign or domestic. And there is one Congress, not two, which decides its own involvement. As part of its "constitutional role," it can rubber-stamp a presidential request or be a hard-line bargainer; it can hound an agency or let it alone.

"We must not bother the president," Eisenhower aide Sherman Adams used to say. "He is trying to keep the World from war."[30] Questioning the mystique of the foreign policy category leads to some bigger questions. Claims of national security have been used to justify many things—from illegal activities in the White House to press censorship and harassment to suppression of public dissent in the Vietnam War. The illegal acts are not restricted to one president's administration or to the activities of one CIA Director. Nevertheless, it is clear that speed, secrecy, and decisiveness in foreign policy cannot be sacrificed. What should the role of the president and Congress be in balancing the need for secrecy and the need for responsibility? How can the line be drawn between illegal and justifiable acts of government power? If the contemporary international condition is, as Richard Neustadt asserts, one of "continuing crisis,"[31] American institutions must accommodate but not bend with such crises. Seeing foreign policy not as a distinct category of problems and powers but part of a larger set of political influences can lead to clearer thinking on this issue of continuing concern.

---

[30]See Robert Donovan, *The Inside Story* (New York: Harper and Row, 1956), p. 71.

[31]Richard E. Neustadt, *Presidential Power*, rev. ed. (New York: Wiley, 1964), chapter 3.

1. Foreign policy, a country's relations with other nations, is shaped by events in several contexts: by events at home and abroad, by historical memories and continuities, and by individual's choices. There are many kinds of American foreign policy and many foreign policy makers.

2. The National Security Council and the Central Intelligence Agency are designed to bring White House control and flexibility to foreign policy. They also allow plausible deniability, the strategy that allows someone, such as the president, to deny knowledge of covert action being carried out by the government. This means that neither the president nor Congress may want to oversee too carefully what the NSC and CIA are doing.

3. One kind of foreign policy involves military action and the use or threat of force. In military actions, presidents generally receive support from the public and Congress. This predominant pattern holds for undeclared wars and other more limited action and it is seen before and after the passage of the War Powers Act. The exceptional cases of controversy have occurred largely when military action is protracted and unsuccessful.

4. Congress has been more willing to assert itself in matters of diplomacy. Presidents can still get what they ask for, but they pay a price in time spent persuading Congress and bargaining for its support. Contrary to popular wisdom, most executive agreements do not allow presidents to avoid dealing with Congress, since the majority of agreements require money to be legislated and spent. Congress treats money decisions very seriously.

5. Foreign aid is a third kind of foreign policy, one quite similar in many ways to domestic policy conflicts. Decisions often involve conflict between the White House and Congress and conflict across party lines. In contrast, defense policy is usually not controversial, but like other domestic policy cases, it is often made far from the White House—in the subgovernments and military departments. Congress sets general spending levels, but the military usually makes specific policy choices and is adept at lobbying Congress for its cooperation.

6. The variety in these foreign policy cases suggests that decisions will be made in different ways and by different people depending on the importance, the visibility, and the time frame of the issue.

foreign policy

bipolar

interdependent

isolationist

plausible denial

the War Powers Act of 1973

treaty

executive agreements

earmarking

The Declaration of Independence
In Congress, July 4, 1776

The unanimous Declaration of the thirteen united States of America,

When in the Course of human events, it becomes necessary for one people to dissolve the political bands which have connected them with another, and to assume among the Powers of the earth, the separate and equal station to which the Laws of Nature and of Nature's God entitle them, a decent respect to the opinions of mankind requires that they should declare the causes which impel them to the separation.

We hold these truths to be self-evident, that all men are created equal, that they are endowed by their Creator with certain unalienable Rights, that among these are Life, Liberty and the pursuit of Happiness. That to secure these rights, Governments are instituted among Men, deriving their just powers from the consent of the governed. That whenever any Form of Government become destructive of these ends, it is the Right of the People to alter or to abolish it, and to institute new Government, laying its foundation on such principles and organizing its powers in such form, as to them shall seem most likely to effect their Safety and Happiness. Prudence, indeed, will dictate that Governments long established should not be changed for light and transient causes; and accordingly all experience hath shown, that mankind are more disposed to suffer, while evils are sufferable, than to right themselves by abolishing the forms to which they are accustomed. But when a long train of abuses and usurpations, pursuing invariably the same Object evinces a design to reduce them under absolute Despotism it is their right, it is their duty, to throw off such Government, and to provide new Guards for their future security.—Such has been the patient sufferance of these Colonies; and such is now the necessity which constrains them to alter their former Systems of Government. The history of the present King of Great Britain is a history of repeated injuries and usurpations, all having in direct object the establishment of an absolute Tyranny over these States. To prove this, let Facts be submitted to a candid world.

He has refused his Assent to Laws, the most wholesome and necessary for the public good.

He has forbidden his Governors to pass Laws of immediate and pressing importance, unless suspended in their operation till his Assent should be obtained; and when so suspended, he has utterly neglected to attend to them.

He has refused to pass other Laws for the accommodation of large districts of people, unless those people would relinquish the right of Representation in the Legislature, a right inestimable to them and formidable to tyrants only.

He has called together legislative bodies at places unusual, uncomfortable, and distant from the depository of their Public Records, for the sole purpose of fatiguing them into compliance with his measures.

He has dissolved Representative Houses repeatedly, for opposing with manly firmness his invasions on the rights of the people.

He has refused for a long time, after such dissolutions, to cause others to be elected; whereby the Legislative Powers, incapable of Annihilation, have returned to the People at large for their exercise; the State remaining in the mean time exposed to all the dangers of invasion from without, and convulsions within.

He has endeavoured to prevent the population of these States; for that purpose obstructing the Laws for Naturalization of Foreigners; refusing to pass others to encourage their migrations hither, and raising the conditions of new Appropriations of Lands.

He has obstructed the Administration of Justice, by refusing his Assent to Laws for establishing Judiciary Powers.

He has made Judges dependent on his Will alone, for the tenure of their offices, and the amount and payment of their salaries.

He has erected a multitude of New Offices, and sent hither swarms of Officers to harass our people, and eat out their substance.

He has kept among us, in times of peace, Standing Armies without the Consent of our legislatures.

He has affected to render the Military independent of and superior to the Civil Power.

He was combined with others to subject us to a jurisdiction foreign to our constitution, and unacknowledged by our laws; giving his Assent to their acts of pretended Legislation:

For quartering large bodies of armed troops among us:

For protecting them, by a mock Trial, from Punishment for any Murders which they should commit on the inhabitants of these States:

For cutting off our Trade with all parts of the world:

For imposing taxes on us without our Consent:

For depriving us in many cases, of the benefits of Trial by Jury:

For transporting us beyond Seas to be tried for pretended offences:

For abolishing the free System of English Laws in a neighbouring Province, establishing therein an Arbitrary government, and enlarging its Boundaries so as to render it at once an example and fit instrument for introducing the same absolute rule into these Colonies:

For taking away our Charters, abolishing our most valuable Laws, and altering fundamentally the Forms of our Governments:

For suspending our own Legislatures, and declaring themselves invested with Power to legislate for us in all cases whatsoever.

He has abdicated Government here, by declaring us out of his Protection and waging War against us.

He has plundered our seas, ravaged our Coasts, burnt our towns, and destroyed the lives of our people.

He is at this time transporting large armies of foreign mercenaries to compleat the works of death, desolation and tyranny, already begun with circumstances of Cruelty & perfidy scarcely paralleled in the most barbarous ages, and totally unworthy the Head of a civilized nation.

He has constrained our fellow Citizens taken Captive on the high Seas to bear Arms against their Country, to become executioners of their friends and Brethens, or to fall themselves by their Hands.

He has excited domestic insurrections amongst us, and has endeavoured to bring on the inhabitants of our frontiers, the merciless Indian Savages, whose known rule of warfare, is an undistinguished destruction of all ages, sexes and conditions.

In every stage of these Oppressions We have Petitioned for Redress in the most humble terms: Our repeated Petitions have been answered only by repeated injury. A Prince, whose character is thus marked by every act which may define a Tyrant, is unfit to be the rulers of a free people.

Nor have We been wanting in attentions to our British brethren. We have warned them from time to time of attempts by their legislature to extend an unwarrantable jurisdiction over us. We have reminded them of the circumstances of our emigration and settlement here. We have appealed to their native justice and magnanimity, and we have conjured them by the ties of our common kindred to disavow these usurpations which, would inevitably interrupt our connections and correspondence. They too have been deaf to the voice of justice and of consanguinity. We must, therefore, acquiesce in the necessity, which denounces our Separation, and hold them, as we hold the rest of mankind, Enemies in War, in Peace Friends.

We, therefore, the Representatives of the united States of America, in General Congress, Assembled, appealing to the Supreme Judge of the world for the rectitude of our intentions, do, in the Name, and by authority of the good People of these Colonies, solemnly publish and declare, That these United colonies are, and of Right ought to be Free and Independent States; that they are Absolved from all Allegiance to the British Crown, and that all political connection between them and the State of Great Britian, is and ought to be totally dissolved; and that as Free and Independent States, they have full power to levy War, conclude Peace, contract Alliances, establish Commerce, and to do all other Acts and Things which Independent States may of right do. And for the support of this Declaration, with a firm reliance on the Protection of Divine Providence, we mutually pledge to each other our Lives, our Fortunes and our sacred Honor.

The Constitution of the United States of America

We the People of the United States, in Order to form a more perfect Union, establish justice, insure domestic Tranquility, provide for the common defence, promote the general Welfare, and secure the Blessings of Liberty to ourselves and our Posterity, do ordain and establish this Constitution for the United States of America.

ARTICLE 1

Section 1.

All legislative Powers herein granted shall be vested in a Congress of the United States, which shall consist of a Senate and House of Representatives.

Section 2.

The House of Representatives shall be composed of Members chosen every second Year by the People of the several States, and the Electors in each State shall have the Qualifications requisite for Electors of the most numerous Branch of the State Legislature.

No Person shall be a Representative who shall not have attained to the Age of twenty five Years, and been seven Years a Citizen of the United States, and who shall not, when elected, be an Inhabitant of that State in which he shall be chosen.

Representatives and direct Taxes shall be apportioned among the several States which may be included within this Union, according to their respective Numbers, which shall be determined by adding to the whole Number of free Persons, including those bound to Service for a Term of Years, and excluding Indians not taxed, three fifths of all other Persons.[1] The actual Enumeration shall be made within three years after the first Meeting of the Congress of the United States, and within every subsequent Term of ten Years, in such Manner as they shall by Law direct. The Number of Representatives shall not exceed one for every thirty Thousand, but each State shall have at Least one Representative; and until such enumeration shall be made, the State of New Hampshire shall be entitled to chuse three, Massachusetts eight, Rhode-Island and Providence Plantations one, Connecticut

---

[1]"Other Persons" being black slaves. Modified by Amendment XIV, Section 2.

five, New-York six, New Jersey four, Pennsylvania eight, Delaware one, Maryland six, Virginia ten, North Carolina five, South Carolina five, and Georgia three.

When vacancies happen in the Representation from any State, the Executive Authority thereof shall issue Writs of Election to fill such Vacancies.

The House of Representatives shall chuse their Speaker and other Officers; and shall have the sole Power of Impeachment.

Section 3.

The Senate of the United States shall be composed of two Senators from each State, chosen by the Legislature thereof, for six Years; and each Senator shall have one Vote.

Immediately after they shall be assembled in Consequence of the first Election, they shall be divided as equally as may be into three Classes. The Seats of the Senators of the first Class shall be vacated at the Expiration of the second Year, of the second Class at the Expiration of the fourth Year, and of the third Class at the Expiration of the Sixth Year, so that one third may be chosen every second Year; and if Vacancies happen by Resignation, or otherwise, during the Recess of the Legislature of any State, the Executive thereof may make temporary Appointments until the next Meeting of the Legislature, which shall then fill such Vacancies.[2]

No Person shall be a Senator who shall not have attained to the Age of thirty Years, and been nine Years a Citizen of the United States, and who shall not, when elected, be an Inhabitant of that State for which he shall be chosen.

The Vice President of the United State shall be President of the Senate, but shall have no Vote, unless they be equally divided.

The Senate shall chuse their other Officers, and also a President pro tempore, in the Absence of the Vice President, or when he shall exercise the Office of President of the United States.

The Senate shall have the sole Power to try all impeachments. When sitting for that Purpose, they shall be on Oath or Affirmation. When the President of the United States is tried the Chief Justice shall preside: And no Person shall be convicted without the Concurrence of two thirds of the Members present.

Judgment in Cases of Impeachment shall not extend further than to removal from Office, and disqualification to hold and enjoy any Office of honor, Trust or Profit under the United States: but the Party convicted shall nevertheless be liable and subject to Indictment, Trial, Judgment and Punishment, according to Law.

Section 4.

The Times, Places and Manner of holding Elections for Senators and Representatives, shall be prescribed in each State by the Legislature thereof; but the Congress may at any time by Law make or alter such Regulations, except as to the Places of chusing Senators.

[2]Provisions changed by Amendment XVII.

The Congress shall assemble at least once in every Year, and such Meeting shall be on the first Monday in December, unless they shall by Law appoint a different Day.[3]

Section 5.

Each House shall be the Judge of the Elections, Returns and Qualifications of its own Members, and a Majority of each shall constitute a Quorum to do Business; but a smaller Number may adjourn from day to day, and may be authorized to compel the Attendance of absent Members, in such Manner, and under such Penalties as each House may provide.

Each House may determine the Rules of its Proceedings, punish its Members for disorderly Behaviour, and, with the Concurrence of two thirds, expel a Member.

Each House shall keep a Journal of its Proceedings, and from time to time punish the same, excepting such Parts as may in their Judgment require Secrecy; and the Yeas and Nays of the Members of either House on any question shall, at the Desire of one fifth of those Present, be entered on the Journal.

Neither House, during the Session of Congress, shall, without the Consent of the other, adjourn for more than three days, nor to any other Place than that in which the two Houses shall be sitting.

Section 6.

The Senators and Representatives shall receive a Compensation for their Services, to be ascertained by Law, and paid out of the Treasury of the United States. They shall in all Cases, except Treason, Felony and Breach of the Peace, be privileged from arrest during their Attendance at the Session of their respective Houses, and in going to and returning from the same; and for any Speech or Debate in either House, they shall not be questioned in any other Place.

No Senator or Representative shall, during the Time for which he was elected, be appointed to any civil Office under the Authority of the United States, which shall have been created, or the Emoluments whereof shall have been encreased during such time; and no Person holding any Office under the United States, shall be a Member of either House during his Continuance in Office.

Section 7.

All Bills for raising Revenue shall originate in the House of Representatives; but the Senate may propose or concur with Amendments as on other Bills.

Every Bill which shall have passed the House of Representatives and the Senate, shall, before it become a Law, be presented to the President of the United States; If he approve he shall sign it, but if not he shall return it, with his Objections to that House in which it shall have originated, who shall enter the Objections at large on their Journal, and proceed to recon-

[3]Provision changed by Amendment XX, Section 2.

sider it. If after such Reconsideration two thirds of that House shall agree to pass the Bill, it shall be sent, together with the Objections, to the other House, by which it shall likewise to be reconsidered, and if approved by two thirds of that House, it shall become a Law. But in all such Cases the Votes of both Houses shall be determined by yeas and Nays, and the Names of the Persons voting for and against the Bill shall be entered on the Journal of each House respectively. If any Bill shall not be returned by the President within ten Days (Sundays excepted) after it shall have been presented to him, the Same shall be a Law, in like Manner as if he had signed it, unless the Congress by their Adjournment prevent its Return, in which Case it shall not be a Law.

Every Order, Resolution, or Vote to which the Concurrence of the Senate and House of Representatives may be necessary (except on a question of Adjournment) shall be presented to the President of the United States; and before the Same shall take Effect, shall be approved by him, or being disapproved by him, shall be repassed by two thirds of the Senate and House of Representatives, according to the Rules and Limitations prescribed in the Case of a Bill.

Section 8.

The Congress shall have Power To lay and collect Taxes, Duties, Imposts and Excises, to pay the Debts and provide for the common Defence and general Welfare of the United States; but all Duties, Imposts and Excises shall be uniform throughout the United States;

To borrow Money on the credit of the United States;

To regulate Commerce with foreign Nations, and among the several States, and with the Indian Tribes;

To establish an uniform Rule of Naturalization, and uniform Laws on the subject of Bankruptcies throughout the United States;

To coin Money, regulate the Value thereof, and of foreign Coin, and fix the Standard of Weights and Measures;

To provide for the Punishment of counterfeiting the Securities and current Coin of the United States;

To establish Post Offices and post Roads;

To promote the Progress of Science and useful Arts, by securing for limited Times to Authors and Inventors the exclusive Right to their respective Writings and Discoveries;

To constitute Tribunals inferior to the supreme Court;

To define and punish Piracies and Felonies committed on the high Seas, and Offences against the Law of Nations;

To declare War, grant Letters of Marque and Reprisal, and make Rules concerning Captures on Land and Water;

To raise and support Armies, but no Appropriation of Money to that Use shall be for a longer Term than two Years;

To provide and maintain a Navy;

To make Rules for the Government and Regulation of the land and naval Forces;

To provide for calling forth the Militia to execute the Laws of the Union, suppress Insurrections and repel Invasions;

To provide for organizing, arming, and disciplining, the Militia, and for governing such Part of them as may be employed in the Service of the United States, reserving to the States respectively, the Appointment of the Officers, and the Authority of training the Militia according to the discipline prescribed by Congress;

To exercise exclusive Legislation in all Cases whatsoever, over such District (not exceeding ten Miles square) as may, by Cession of particular States, and the Acceptance of Congress, become the Seat of the Government of the United States, and to exercise like Authority over all Places purchased by the Consent of the Legislature of the State in which the Same shall be, for the Erection of Forts, Magazines, Arsenals, dock-Yards, and other needful Buildings;—And

To make all Laws which shall be necessary and proper for carrying into Execution the foregoing Powers, and all other Powers vested by this Constitution in the Government of the United States, or in any Department or Officer thereof.

Section 9.

The Migration or Importation of such Persons as any of the States now existing shall think proper to admit, shall not be prohibited by the Congress prior to the Year one thousand eight hundred and eight, but a Tax, or duty may be imposed on such Importation, not exceeding ten dollars for each Person.

The Privilege of the Writ of Habeas Corpus shall not be suspended, unless when in Cases of Rebellion or Invasion of the public Safety may require it.

No Bill of Attainder or ex post facto Law shall be passed.

No Capitation, or other direct, Tax shall be laid, unless in Proportion to the Census of Enumeration herein before directed to be taken.

No Tax or Duty shall be laid on Articles exported from any State.

No Preference shall be given by any Regulation of Commerce or Revenue to the Ports of one State over those of another; nor shall Vessels bound to, or from, one State, be obliged to enter, clear, or pay Duties in another.

No Money shall be drawn from the Treasury, but in Consequence of appropriations made by Law; and a regular Statement and Account of the Receipts and Expenditures of all public Money shall be published from time to time.

No Title of Nobility shall be granted by the United States; And no Person holding any Office of Profit or Trust under them, shall, without the Consent of the Congress, accept of any present, Emolument, Office, or Title, of any kind whatever, from any King, Prince, or foreign State.

Section 10.

No State shall enter into any Treaty, Alliance, or Confederation; grant Letters of Marque and Reprisal; coin Money; emit Bills of Credit; make any

Thing but gold and silver Coin a Tender in Payment of Debts; pass any Bill of Attainder, ex post facto Law, or Law impairing the Obligation of Contracts, or grant any Title of Nobility.

No State shall, without the Consent of the Congress, lay any Imposts or Duties on Imports or Exports, except what may be absolutely necessary for executing its inspection Laws: and the net Produce of all Duties and Imposts, laid by any State on Imports or Exports, shall be for the Use of Treasury of the United States; and all such Laws shall be subject to the Revision and Controul of the Controul of the Congress.

No State shall, without the Consent of Congress, lay any Duty of Tonnage, keep Troops, or Ships of War in time of Peace, enter into any Agreement or Compact with another State, or with a foreign Power, or engage in War, unless actually invaded, or in such imminent Danger as will not admit of delay.

ARTICLE II

Section 1.

The executive Power shall be vested in a President of the United States of America. He shall hold his Office during the Term of four Years, and, together with the Vice President, chosen for the same Term, be elected, as follows:

Each State shall appoint, in such Manner as the Legislature thereof may direct, a Number of Electors, equal to the whole Number of Senators and Representatives to which the State may be entitled in Congress: but no Senator or Representative, or Person holding an Office of Trust or Profit under the United States, shall be appointed an Elector.

The Electors shall meet in their respective States, and vote by Ballot for two Persons, of whom one at least shall not be an Inhabitant of the same State with themselves. And they shall make a List of all the Persons voted for, and the Number of Votes for each; which List they shall sign and certify, and transmit sealed to the Seat of the Government of the United States, directed to the President of the Senate. The President of the Senate shall, in the Presence of the Senate and House of Representatives, open all the Certificates, and the Votes shall then be counted. The Person having the greatest Number of Votes shall be the President, if such Number be a Majority of the whole Number of Electors appointed; and if there be more than one who have such Majority, and have an equal Number of Votes, then the House of Representatives shall immediately chuse by Ballot one of them for President; and if no Person have a Majority, then from the five highest on the List the said House shall in like Manner chuse the President. But in chusing the President, the Votes shall be taken by States, the Representation for each State having one Vote; A quorum for this Purpose shall consist of a Member or Members from two thirds of the States, and a Majority of all the States shall be necessary to a Choice. In every Case, after the Choice of the President, the Person having the greatest Number of Votes of the Electors shall be the Vice President. But if there should remain two or more who have equal Votes, the Senate shall chuse from them by Ballot the Vice President.[4]

The Congress may determine the Time of chusing the Electors, and the Day on which they shall give their Votes; which Day on which they shall give their Votes; which Day shall be the same throughout the United States.

No Person except a natural born Citizen, or a Citizen of the United States, at the time of the Adoption of this Constitution, shall be eligible to the Office of President; neither shall any Person be eligible to that Office who shall not have attained to the Age of thirty five Years, and been fourteen Years a Resident within the United States.

In Case of Removal of the President from Office, or of his Death, Resignation, or Inability to discharge the Powers and Duties of the said Office, the Same shall devolve on the Vice President, and the Congress may by Law provide for the Case of Removal, Death, Resignation or Inability, both of the President and Vice President, declaring what Officer shall then act as President, and such Officer shall act accordingly, until the Disability be removed, or a President shall be elected.

The President shall, at stated Times, receive for his Services, a Compensation, which shall neither be encreased nor diminshed during the Period for which he shall have been elected, and he shall not receive within that Period any other Emolument for the United States, or any of them.

Before he enter on the Execution of his Office, he shall take the following Oath or Affirmation:—"I do solemnly swear (or affirm) that I will faithfully execute the Office of President of the United States, and will to the best of my Ability, preserve, protect and defend the Constitution of the United States."
Section 2.

The President shall be Commander in Chief of the Army and Navy of the United States, and of the Militia of the several States, when called into the actual Service of the United States; he may require the Opinion, in writing, of the principal Officer in each of the executive Departments, upon any Subject relating to the Duties of their respective Offices, and he shall have Power to grant Reprieves and Pardons for Offences against the United States, except in Cases of Impeachment.

He shall have Power, by and with the Advice and Consent of the Senate, to make Treaties, provided two thirds of the Senators present concur; and he shall nominate, and by and with the Advice and Consent of the Senate, shall appoint Ambassadors, other public Ministers and Consuls, Judges of the supreme Court, and all other Officers of the United States, whose Appointments are not herein otherwise provided for, and which shall be established by Law: but the Congress may by Law vest the Appointment of such inferior Officers, as they think proper in the President alone, in the Courts of Law, or in the Heads of Departments.

[4]Provisions superseded by Amendment XII.

The President shall have Power to fill up all Vacancies that may happen during the Recess of the Senate, by granting Commissions which shall expire at the end of their next Session.
Section 3.

He shall from time to time give to the Congress Information of the State of the Union, and recommend to their Consideration such Measures as he shall judge necessary and expedient; he may, on extraordinary Occasions, convene both Houses, or either of them, and in Case of Disagreement between them, with Respect to the Time of Adjournment, he may adjourn them to such Time as he shall think proper; he shall receive Ambassadors and other public Ministers; he shall take Care that Laws be faithfully executed, and shall Commission all the Officers of the United States.
Section 4.

The President, Vice President and all civil Officers of the United States, shall be removed from Office on Impeachment for, and Conviction of, Treason, Bribery, or other high Crimes and Misdemeanors.

ARTICLE III

Section 1.

The judicial Power of the United States, shall be vested in one supreme Court, and in such inferior Courts as the Congress may from time to time ordain and establish. The Judges, both of the supreme and inferior Courts, shall hold their Offices during good Behavior, and shall, at stated Times, receive for their Services, a Compensation, which shall not be diminished during their Continuance in Office.
Section 2.

The judicial Power shall extend to all Cases in Law and Equity, arising under this Constitution, the Laws of the United States, and Treaties made, or which shall be made, under their Authority;—to all Cases affecting Ambassadors, other public Ministers and Consuls;—to all Cases of admiralty and maritime Jurisdiction;—to Controversies to which the United States shall be a Party;—to Controversies between two or more states;—between a State and Citizens of another State;—between Citizens of different States;—between Citizens of the same State claiming Lands under Grants of different States, and between a State, or the Citizens thereof, and foreign States, Citizens or Subjects.

In all Cases affecting Ambassadors, other public Ministers and Consuls, and those in which a State shall be Party, the supreme Court shall have original Jurisdiction. In all the other Cases before mentioned, the supreme Court shall have appellate Jurisdiction, both as to Law and Fact, with such Exceptions, and under such Regulations as the Congress shall make.

The Trial of all Crimes, except in Cases of Impeachment, shall be by Jury; and such Trial shall be held in the State where the said Crimes shall have been committed, but when not committed within any State, the Trial shall be at such Place or Places as the Congress may by Law have directed.

Section 3.

Treason against the United States, shall consists only in levying War against them, or in adhering to their Enemies, giving them Aid and Comfort. No person shall be convicted of Treason unless on the Testimony of two Witnesses to the same overt Act, or on Confession in open Court.

The Congress shall have Power to declare the Punishment of Treason, but no Attainder of Treason shall work Corruption of Blood, or Forfeiture except during the Life of the Person attainted.

ARTICLE IV

Section 1.

Full Faith and Credit shall be given in each State to the public Acts, Records, and judicial Proceedings of every other State. And the Congress may by general Laws prescribe the Manner in which such Acts, Records and Proceedings shall be proved, and the Effect thereof.
Section 2.

The Citizens of each Sate shall be entitled to all Privileges and Immunities of Citizens in the several States.

A Person charged in any State with Treason, Felony, or other Crime, who shall flee from Justice, and be found in another State, shall on Demand of the executive Authority of the State from which he fled, be delivered up, to be removed to the State having Jurisdiction of the Crime.

No Person held to Service or Labour in one State, under the Laws thereof, escaping into another, shall, in Consequence of any Law or Regulation therein, be discharged from such Service or Labour, but shall be delivered up on Claim of the Party to whom such Service or Labour may be due.
Section 3.

New States may be admitted by the Congress into this Union; but no new State shall be formed or erected within the jurisdiction of any other State; nor any State be formed by the Junction of two or more States, or Parts of States, without the Consent of the Legislatures of the States concerned as well as of the Congress.

The Congress shall have Power to dispose of and make all needful Rules and Regulations repecting the Territory or other Property belonging to the United States; and nothing in this Constitution shall be so construed as to Prejudice any Claims of the United States, or of any particular State.
Section 4.

The United States shall guarantee to every State in this Union a Republican Form of Government, and shall protect each of them against Invasion; and on Application of the Legislature, or of the Executive (when the Legislature cannot be convened) against domestic Violence.

ARTICLE V

The Congress, whenever two thirds of both Houses shall deem it neccessary, shall propose Amendments to this Constitution, or, on the Application of the Legislatures of two thirds of the several States, shall call a Convention for proposing Amendments, which, in either Case, shall be valid to all Intents and Purposes, as Part of this Constitution, when ratified by the Legislatures of three fourths of the several States, or by Convention in three fourths thereof, as the one or the other Mode of Ratification may be proposed by the Congress; Provided that no Amendment which may be made prior to the Year One thousand eight hundred and eight shall in any Manner affect the first and fourth Clauses in the Ninth Section of the first Article; and that no State, without its Consent, shall be deprived of its equal Suffrage in the Senate.

ARTICLE VI

All Debts contracted and Engagements entered into, before the Adoption of this Constitution, shall be as valid against the United States under this Constitution, as under the Confederation.

This Constitution, and the Laws of the United States which shall be made in Pursuance thereof; and all Treaties made, or which shall be made, under the Authority of the United States, shall be the supreme Law of the Land; and the Judges in every State shall be bound thereby, any Thing in the Constitution or Laws of any State to the Contrary notwithstanding.

The Senators and Representatives before mentioned, and the Members of the several State Legislatures, and all executive and judicial Officers, both of the United States and of the several States, shall be bound by Oath or Affirmation, to support this Constitution; but no religious Test shall ever be required as a Qualification to any Office or public Trust under the United States.

ARTICLE VII

The Ratification of the Conventions of nine States shall be sufficient for the Establishment of this Constitution between the States so ratifying the Same.

AMENDMENT 1 [1791]

Congress shall make no law respecting an establishment of religion, or prohibiting the free exercise thereof; or abridging the freedom of the press, or the right of the people peaceably to assemble, and to petition the Government for a redress of grievances.

AMENDMENT II [1791]

A well regulated Militia being necessary to the security of a free State, the right of the people to keep and bear Arms, shall not be infringed.

AMENDMENT III [1791]

No Soilder shall, in time of peace be quartered in any house, without the consent of the Owner, nor in time of war, but in a manner to be prescribed by law.

AMENDMENT IV [1791]

The right of the people to be secure in their persons, houses, papers, and effects, against unreasonable searches and seizures, shall not be violated, and no Warants shall issue, but upon probable cause, supported by Oath or affirmation, and particularly describing the place to be searched, and the persons or things to be seized.

AMENDMENT V [1791]

No person shall be held to answer for a capital, or otherwise infamous crime, unless on a presentment or indictment of a Grand Jury, except in cases arising in the land or naval forces, or in the Militia, when in actual service in time of War or public danger; nor shall any person be subject for the same offense to be twice put in jeopardy of life or limb; nor shall be compelled in any criminal case to be a witness against himself, nor be deprived of life, liberty, or property, without due process of law; nor shall private property be taken for public use, without just compensation.

AMENDMENT VI [1791]

In all criminal prosecutions, the accused shall enjoy the right to a speedy and public trial, by an impartial jury of the State and district wherein the crime shall have been committed, which district shall have been previously ascertained by law, and to informed of the nature and cause of the accusation; to be confronted with the witnesses against him; to have compulsory process for obtaining witnesses in his favor, and to have the Assistance of Counsel for his defence.

AMENDMENT VII [1791]

In Suits at common law, where the value in controversy shall exceed twenty dollars, the right of trial by jury shall be preserved, and no fact tried by a jury, shall be otherwise re-examined in any court of the United States, than according to the rules of the common law.

AMENDMENT VIII [1791]

Excessive bail shall not be required, nor excessive fines imposed, nor cruel and unusual punishments inflicted.

AMENDMENT IX [1791]

The enumeration in the Constitution, of certain rights, shall not be construed to deny or disparage others retained by the people.

AMENDMENT X [1791]

The powers not delegated to the United States by the Constitution, nor prohibited by it to the States, are reserved to the States respectively, or to the people.

AMENDMENT XI [1798]

The Judicial power of the United States shall not be construed to extend to any suit in law or equity, commenced or prosecuted against one of the United States by Citizens of another State, or by Citizens or Subjects of any Foreign State.

AMENDMENT XII [1804]

The Electors shall meet in their respective states, and vote by ballot for President and Vice-President, one of whom, at least, shall not be an inhabitant of the same state with themselves; they shall name in their ballots the person voted for as President, and in distinct ballots the person voted for as Vice-President, and they shall make distinct lists of all persons voted for as President, and of all persons voted for as Vice-President, and of the number of votes for each, which lists they shall sign and certify, and transmit sealed to the seat of the government of the United States, directed to the President of the Senate;—The President of the Senate shall, in the presence of the Senate and House of Representatives, open all the certificates and the votes shall then be counted;—The person having the greatest number of votes for President, shall be the President, if such number be a majority of the whole number of Electors appointed; and if no person have such majority, then from the persons having the highest numbers not exceeding three on the list of those voted for as President, the House of Representatives shall choose immediately, by ballot, the President. But in choosing the President, the votes shall be taken by states, the representation from each state having one vote; a quorum for this purpose shall consist of a member or members from two-thirds of the states, and a majority of all the states shall be necessary to a choice. And if the House of Representatives shall not choose a President whenever the right of choice shall devolve upon them, before the fourth day of March next following, then the Vice-President shall act as President, as in the case of the death or other constitutional disability of the President.—The person having the greatest number of votes as Vice-President, shall be the Vice-President, if such number be a majority of the whole number of Electors appointed, and if no person have a majority, then from the two highest numbers on the list, the Senate shall choose the Vice-President; a quorum for the purpose shall consist of two-thirds of the whole number of Senators, and a majority of the whole number shall be necessary to a choice. But no person constitutionally ineligible to the office of President shall be eligible to that of Vice-President of the United States.

AMENDMENT XIII [1865]

Section 1.

Neither slavery nor involuntary servitude, except as a punishment for crime whereof the party shall have been duly convicted, shall exist within the United States, or any place subject to their jurisdiction.
Section 2.

Congress shall have power to enforce this article by appropriate legislation.

AMENDMENT XIV [1868]

Section 1.

All persons born or naturalized in the United States and subject to the jurisdiction thereof, are citizens of the United States and the State wherein they reside. No State shall make or enforce any law which shall abridge the priviliges or immunities of citizens of the United States; nor shall any State deprive any person of life, liberty, property, without due process of law; nor deny to any person within its jurisdiction the equal protection of the laws.
Section 2.

Representatives shall be apportioned among the several States according to their respective numbers counting the whole number of persons in each State, excluding Indians not taxed. But when the right to vote at any election for the choice of electors for President and Vice-President of the United States, Representatives in Congress, the Executive and Judicial offices of a State, or the members of the Legislature thereof, is denied to any of the male inhabitants of such State being twenty-one years of age and citizens of the United States, or in any way abridged, except for participation in rebellion or other crime, the basis of representation therein shall be reduced in the proportion which the number of such male citizens shall bear to the whole number of male citizens twenty-one years of age in such State.
Section 3.

No person shall be a Senator or Representative in Congress, or elector of President and Vice President or hold any office, civil or military, under the United States or under any State, who, having previously taken an oath, as a member of Congress, or as an officer of the United States, or as a member of any State legislature or as an executive or judicial officer of any State to support the Constitution of the United States, shall have engaged in insurrection or rebellion against the same, or given aid or comfort to the enemies thereof. But Congress may by a vote of two-thirds of each House, remove such disability.

Section 4.

The validity of the public debt of the United States authorized by law, including debts incurred for payment of pensions and bounties for services in suppressing insurrection or rebellion, shall not be questioned. But neither the United States nor any State shall assume or pay any debt of obligation incurred in aid of insurrection or rebellion against the United States, or any claim for the loss or emancipation of any slave; but all such debts, obligations and claims shall be held illegal and void.

Section 5.

The Congress shall have power to enforce, by appropriate legislation, the provisions of this article.

AMENDMENT XV [1870]

Section 1.

The right of citizens of the United States to vote shall not be denied or abridged by the United States or by any State on account of race, color, or previous condition of servitude.

Section 2.

The Congress shall have power to enforce this article by appropriate legislation.

AMENDMENT XVI [1913]

The Congress shall have power to lay and collect taxes on incomes, from whatever source derived, without apportionment among the several States, and without regard to any census or enumeration.

AMENDMENT XVII [1913]

The Senate of the United States shall be composed of two Senators from each State, elected by the people thereof, for six years; and each Senator shall have one vote. The electors in each State shall have the qualifications requisite for electors of the most numerous branch of the State legislatures.

When vacancies happen in the representation of any State in the Senate, the executive authority of such State shall issue writs of election to fill such vacancies; *Provided,* That the legislature of any State may empower the executive thereof to make temporary appointments until the people fill the vacancies by election as the legislature may direct.

This amendment shall not be construed as to affect the election or term of any Senator chosen before it becomes valid as part of the Constitution.

AMENDMENT XVIII [1919]

Section 1.

After one year from the ratification of this article the manufacture, sale, or transportation of intoxicating liquors within, the importation thereof into, or the exportation thereof from the United States and all territory subject to the jurisdiction thereof for beverage purposes is hereby prohibited.
Section 2.

The Congress and the several States shall have concurrent power to enforce this article by appropriate legislation.
Section 3.

This article shall be inoperative unless it shall have been ratified as an amendment to the Constitution by the legislatures of the several States, as provided in the Constitution, within seven years from the date of the submission hereof to the States by the Congress.

AMENDMENT XIX [1920]

The right of citizens of the United States to vote shall not be denied or abridged by the United States or by any State on account of sex.

Congress shall have power to enforce this article by appropriate legislation.

AMENDMENT XX [1933]

Section 1.

The terms of the President and Vice President shall end at noon on the 20th day of January, and terms of Senators and Representatives at noon on the 3d day of January, of the years in which such terms would have ended if this article had not been ratified; and the terms of their successors shall then begin.

The Congress shall assemble at least once in every year, and such meeting shall begin at noon on the 3d day of January, unless they shall by law appoint a different day.
Section 3.

If, at the time fixed for the beginning of the term of the President, the President elect shall have died, the Vice PResident elect shall become President. If a President shall not have been chosen before the time fixed for the beginning of his term, or if the President elect shall have failed to qualify, then the Vice President elect shall act as President until a President shall have qualified; and the Congress may by law provide for the case wherein neither a President elect nor a Vice President elect shall have qualified, de-

claring who shall then act as President, or the manner in which one who is to act shall be selected, and such person shall act accordingly until a President or Vice President shall have qualified.
Section 4.

The Congress may by law provide for the case of the death of any of the persons from whom the House of Representatives may choose a President whenever the right of choice shall have devolved upon them, and for the case of the death of any of the persons from whom the Senate may choose a Vice President whenever the right of choice shall have devolved upon them.
Section 5.

Sections 1 and 2 shall take effect on the 15th day of October following the ratification of this article.
Section 6.

This article shall be inoperative unless it shall have been ratified as an amendment to the Constitution by the legislatures of three-fourths of the several States within seven years from the date of its submission.

AMENDMENT XXI [1933]

Section 1.

The eighteenth article of amendment to the Constitution of the United States is hereby repealed.
Section 2.

The transportation or importation into any States, Territory, or possession of the United States for delivery or use therein of intoxicating liquors, in violation of the laws thereof, is hereby prohibited.
Section 3.

This article shall be inoperative unless it shall have been ratified as an amendment to the Constitution by conventions in the several States, as provided in the Constitution, within seven years from the date of the submission hereof to the States by the Congress.

AMENDMENT XXII [1951]

Section 1.

No person shall be elected to the office of the President more than twice, and no person who has held the office of President, or acted as President, for more than two years of a term to which some other person was elected President shall be elected to the office of the President more than once. But this Article shall not apply to any person holding the office of President when the Article was proposed by the Congress, and shall not prevent any person who may be holding the office of President, or acting as President, during the term within which this Article becomes operative from holding the office of President or acting as President during the remainder of such term.

Section 2.

This article shall be inoperative unless it shall have been ratified as an amendment to the Constitution by the legislatures of three-fourths of the several States within seven years from the date of its submission to the States by the Congress.

AMENDMENT XXIII [1961]

Section 1.

The District constituting the seat of Government of the United States shall appoint in such manner as the Congress shall direct:

A number of electors of President and Vice President equal to the whole number of Senators and Representatives in Congress to which the District would be entitled if it were a State, but in no event more than the least populous State; they shall be in addition to those appointed by the States, but they shall be considered, for the purposes of the election of President and Vice President, to be electors appointed by a State; and they shall meet in the District and perform such duties as provided by the twelfth article of amendment.

Section 2.

The Congress shall have power to enforce this article by appropriate legislation.

AMENDMENT XXIV [1964]

Section 1.

The right of citizens of the United States to vote in any primary or other election for President or Vice President, for electors for President or Vice President, or for Senator or Representative in Congress, shall not be denied or abridged by the United States or any state by reason of failure to pay any poll tax or other tax.

Section 2.

The Congress shall have the power to enforce this article by appropriate legislation.

AMENDMENT XXV [1967]

Section 1.

In case of the removal of the President from office or his death or resignation, the Vice President shall become President.

Section 2.

Whenever there is a vacancy in the office of the Vice President, the President shall nominate a Vice President who shall take the office upon confirmation by a majority vote of both houses of Congress.

Section 3.

Whenever the President transmits to the President pro tempore of the Senate and the Speaker of the House of Representatives his written declaration that he is unable to discharge the powers and duties of his office, and until he transmits to them a written declaration to the contrary, such powers and duties shall be discharged by the Vice President as Acting President.

Section 4.

Whenever the Vice President and a majority of either the principal officers of the executive departments or of such other body as Congress may by law provide, transmit to the President pro tempore of the Senate and the Speaker of the House of Representatives their written declaration that the President is unable to discharge the powers and duties of his office, the Vice President shall immediately assume the powers and duties of the office as Acting President.

Thereafter, when the President transmits to the President pro tempore of the Senate and the Speaker of the House of Representatives has written declaration that no inability exists, he shall resume the powers and duties of his office unless the Vice President and a majority of either the principal officers of the executive department or of such other body as Congress may by law provide, transmit within four days to the President pro tempore of the Senate and the Speaker of the House of Representatives their written declaration that the President is unable to discharge the powers and duties of his office. Thereupon Congress shall decide the issue, assembling within 48 hours for that purpose if not in session. If the Congress, within 21 days after receipt of the latter written declaration, or, if Congress is not in session, within 21 days after Congress is required to assemble, determines by two-thirds vote of both houses that the President is unable to discharge the powers and duties of his office, the Vice President shall continue to discharge the same as Acting President; otherwise, the President shall resume the powers and duties of his office.

AMENDMENT XXVI [1971]

Section 1.

The right of citizens of the United States, who are 18 years of age or older, to vote shall not be denied or abridged by the United States or any state on account of age.

Section 2.

The Congress shall have the power to enforce this article by appropriate legislation.

Federalist 10
James Madison

Among the numerous advantages promised by a well constructed Union, none deserves to be more accurately developed than its tendency to break and control the violence of faction. The friend of popular governments never finds himself so much alarmed for their character and fate as when he contemplates their propensity to this dangerous vice. He will not fail, therefore, to set a due value on any plan which, without violating the principles to which he is attached, provides a proper cure for it. The instability, injustice, and confusion, introduced into the public councils, have, in truth been the mortal diseases under which popular governments have everywhere perished; as they continue to be the favorite and fruitful topics from which the adversaries to liberty derive their most specious declamations. The valuable improvements made by the American constitutions on the popular models, both ancient and modern, cannot certainly be too much admired; but it would be an unwarrantable partiality, to contend that they have as effectually obviated the danger on this side, as was wished and expected. Complaints are everywhere heard from our most considerate and virtuous citizens, equally the friends of public and private faith, and of public and personal liberty, that our governments are too unstable; that the public good is disregarded in the conflicts of rival parties; and that measures are too often decided, not according to the rules of justice, and the rights of the minor party, but by the superior force of an interested and overbearing majority. However anxiously we may wish that these complaints had no foundation, the evidence of known facts will not permit us to deny that they are in some degree true. It will be found, indeed, on a candid review of our situation, that some of the distresses under which we labor, have been erroneously charged on the operation of our governments; but it will be found, at the same time, that other causes will not alone account for many of our heaviest misfortunes; and, particularly, for the prevailing and increasing distrust of public engagements, and alarm for private rights, which are echoed from one end of the continent to the other. These must be chiefly, if not wholly, effects of the unsteadiness and injustice, with which a factious spirit has tainted our public administrations.

By a faction, I understand a number of citizens, whether amounting to a majority or minority of the whole, who are united and actuated by some common impulse of passion, or of interest, adverse to the rights of other citizens, or to the permanent and aggregate interest of the community.

There are two methods of curing the mischiefs of faction: The one, by removing its causes; the other, by controlling its effects.

There are again two methods of removing the causes of faction: the one, by destroying the liberty which is essential to its existence; the other, by giving to every citizen the same opinions, the same passions, and the same interests.

It could never be more truly said, than of the first remedy, that it was worse than the disease. Liberty is to faction what air is to fire, an aliment, without which it instantly expires. But it could not be a less folly to abolish liberty, which is essential to political life because it nourishes faction, than it would be to wish the annihilation of air, which is essential to animal life, because it imparts to fire its destructive agency.

The second expedient is as impracticable, as the first would be unwise. As long as the reason of man continues fallible, and he is at liberty to exercise it, different opinions will be formed. As long as the connection subsists between his reason and his self-love, his opinions and his passions will have a reciprocal influence on each other; and the former will be objects to which the latter will attach themselves. The diversity in the faculties of men, from which the rights of property originate, is not less an insuperable obstacle to a uniformity of interests. The protection of those faculties is the first object of government. From the protection of different and unequal faculties of acquiring property, the possession of different degrees and kinds of property immediately results; and from the influence of these on the sentiments and views of the respective proprietors, ensues a division of the society into different interests and parties.

The latent causes of faction are thus sown in the nature of man; and we see them everywhere brought into different degrees of activity, according to the different circumstances of civil society. A zeal for different opinions concerning religion, concerning government, and many other points, as well of speculation as of practice; an attachment to different leaders, ambitiously contending for preeminence and power; or to persons of other descriptions, whose fortunes have been interesting to the human passions, have, in turn, divided mankind into parties, inflamed them with mutual animosity, and rendered them much more disposed to vex and oppress each other, than to cooperate for their common good. So strong is this propensity of mankind, to fall into mutual animosities, that where no substantial occasion presents itself, the most frivolous and fanciful distinctions have been sufficient to kindle their unfriendly passions, and excite their most violent conflicts. But the most common and durable source of factions has been the various and unequal distribution of property. Those who hold, and those who are without property, have even formed distinct interests in society. Those who are creditors, and those who are debtors, fall under a like discrimination. A landed interest, a manufacturing interest, a mercantile interest, a moneyed interest, with many lesser interests, grow up of necessity in civilized nations, and divide them into different classes, actuated by different sentiments and views. The regulation of these various and interfering interests forms the principle task of modern legislation, and involves the spirit of party and faction in the necessary and ordinary operations of government.

No man is allowed to be a judge in his own cause; because his interest will certainly bias his judgment, and, not improbably, corrupt his integrity. With equal, nay, with greater reason, a body of men are unfit to be both judges and parties at the same time; yet what are many of the most important acts of legislation, but so many judicial determinations, not indeed concerning the rights of single perons, but concerning the rights of large bodies of citizens? And what are the different classes of legislators, but advocates and parties to the cause which they determine? Is a law proposed concerning private debts? It is a question to which the creditors are parties on one side, and the debtors on the other. Justice ought to hold the balance between them. Yet the parties are, and must be, themselves the judges; and the most numerous party, or, in other words, the most powerful faction, must be expected to prevail. Shall domestic manufactures be encouraged, and in what degree, by restrictions on foreign manufactures? are questions which would be differently decided by the landed and the manufacturing classes; and probably by neither with a sole regard to justice and the public good. . . .

It is in vain to say, that enlightened statesmen will be able to adjust these clashing interests, and render them all subservient to the public good. Enlightened statesmen will not always be at the helm; nor, in many cases, can such an adjustment be made at all, without taking into view indirect and remote considerations, which will rarely prevail over the immediate interest which one party may find in disregarding the rights of another, or the good of the whole.

The inference to which we are brought is, that the *causes* of faction cannot be removed; and that relief is only to be sought in the means of controlling its *effects.*.

If a faction consists of less than a majority, relief is supplied by the republican principle, which enables the majority to defeat its sinister views, by regular vote. It may clog the administration, it may convulse the society; but it will be unable to execute and mask its violence under the forms of the constitution. When a majority is included in a faction, the form of popular government, on the other hand, enables it to sacrifice to its ruling passion or interest, both the public good and the rights of other citizens. To secure the public good, and private rights, against the danger of such a faction, and at the same time to preserve the spirit and the form of popular government, is then the great object to which our inquiries are directed. Let me add, that it is the great desideratum, by which alone this form of government can be rescued from the opprobrium under which it has so long labored, and be recommended to the esteem and adoption of mankind.

By what means is this object attainable? Evidently by one of two only. Either the existence of the same passion of interest in a majority, at the same time must be prevented; or the majority, having such coexistent passion or interest, must be rendered, by their number and local situation, unable to concert and carry into effect schemes of oppression. If the impulse and the opportunity be suffered to coincide, we well know, that neither moral nor religious motives can be relied on as an adequate control. They are not found to be such on the injustice and violence of individuals, and lose their efficacy in proportion to the number combined together; that is, in proportion as their efficacy becomes needful.

From this view of the subject, it may be concluded, that a pure democracy, by which I mean a society consisting of a small number of citizens, who assemble and administer the government in person, can admit of no cure from the mischiefs of faction. A common passion or interest will, in almost every case, be felt by a majority of the whole; a communication and concert, results from the form of government itself; and there is nothing to check the inducements to sacrifice the weaker party, or an obnoxious individual. Hence it is, that such democracies have ever been spectacles of turbulence and contention; have ever been found incompatible with personal security, or the rights of property; and have, in general, been as short in their lives, as they have been violent in their deaths. Theoretic politicians, who have patronized this species of government, have erroneously supposed that by reducing mankind to a perfect equality in their political rights, they would, at the same time, be perfectly equalized and assimilated in their possessions, their opinions, and their passions.

A republic, by which I mean a government in which the scheme of representation takes place, opens a different prospect, and promises the cure for which we are seeking. Let us examine the points in which it varies from pure democracy, and we shall comprehend both the nature of the cure and the efficacy which it must derive from the union.

The two great points of difference, between a democracy and a republic, are, first, the delegation of the government, in the latter, to a small number of citizens elected by the rest; secondly, the greater number of citizens, and greater sphere of country, over which the latter may be extended.

The effect of the first difference is on the one hand, to refine and enlarge the public views, by passing them through the medium of a chosen body of citizens, whose wisdom may best discern the true interest in their country, and whose patriotism and love of justice, will be least likely to sacrifice it to temporary or partial considerations. Under such a regulation, it may well happen, that the public voice, pronounced by the representatives of the people, will be more consonant to the public good, than if pronounced by the people themselves, convened for the purpose. On the other hand, the effect may be inverted. Men of factious tempers, of local prejudices, or of sinister designs, may by intrigue, by corruption, or by other means, first obtain the suffrages, and then betray the interest of the people. The question resulting is, whether small or extensive republics are most favorable to the election of proper guardians of the public weal; and it is clearly decided in favor of the latter by two obvious considerations.

In the first place, it is to be remarked, that however small the republic may be, the representatives must be raised to a certain number, in order to guard against the cabals of a few; and that however large it may be, they must be limited to a certain number, in order to guard against the confusion of a multitude. Hence, the number of representatives in the two cases not being in proportion to that of the constituents, and being proportionally greatest in the small republic, it follows that if the proportion of fit characters be not less in the large than in the small republic, the former will present a greater option, and consequently a greater probability of a fit choice.

In the next place, as each representative will be chosen by a greater number of citizens in the large than in the small republic, it will be more difficult for unworthy candidates to practice with success the vicious arts, by which elections are too often carried; and the suffrages of the people being more free, will be more likely to center in men who possess the most attractive merit, and the most diffusive and established characters....

The other point of difference is, the greater number of citizens, and extent of territory, which may be brought within the compass of republican, than of democratic government; and it is this circumstance principally which renders factious combinations less to be dreaded in the former, than in the latter. The smaller the society, the fewer probably will be the distinct parties and interests composing it; the fewer the distinct parties and interests, the more frequently will a majority be found of the same party; and the smaller the number of individuals composing a majority, and the smaller the compass within which they are placed, the more easily they will concert and execute their plans of oppression. Extend the sphere, and you take in a greater variety of parties and interest; you make it less probable that a majority of the whole will have a common motive to invade the rights of other citizens; or if such a common motive exists, it will be more difficult for all who feel it to discover their own strength, and to act in unison with each other...

Hence, it clearly appears, that the same advantage, which a republic has over a democracy, in controlling the effects of faction, is enjoyed by a large over a small republic—is enjoyed by the union over the states composing it. Does this advantage consist in the substitution of representatives, whose enlightened views and virtuous sentiments render them superior to local prejudices, and to schemes of injustice? It will not be denied, that the representation of the union will be most likely to possess these requisite endowments. Does it consist in the greater security afforded by a greater variety of parties, against the event of any one party being able to outnumber and oppress the rest? In an equal degree does the increased variety of parties, comprised within the union, increase this security? Does it, in fine, consist in the greater obstacles opposed to the concert and accomplishment of the secret wishes of an unjust and interested majority? Here, again, the extent of the union gives it the most palpable advantage.

The influence of factious leaders may kindle a flame within their particular states, but will be unable to spread a general conflagration through the other states; a religious sect may degenerate into a political faction in part of the confederacy; but the variety of sects dispersed over the entire face of it, must secure the national councils against any danger from that source; a rage for paper money, for an abolition of debts, for an equal division of property, or for any other improper or wicked project, will be less apt to pervade the whole body of the union, than a particular member of it; in the same proportion as such a malady is more likely to taint a particular county or district, than an entire state.

In the extent and proper structure of the union, therefore, we behold a republican remedy for the diseases most incident to republican government. And according to the degree of pleasure and pride we feel in being republicans, ought to be our zeal in cherishing the spirit, and supporting the character of Federalists.

Here are a sampling of the many books that could be suggested for further reading. We have tried to vary the selections somewhat, including some texts, books of special readings, and original research on topics of wide interest. We have also included some accounts that challenge traditional perspectives as well as classic studies that have been widely influential. We offer brief descriptive comments about each book. Also note that the footnotes in each chapter provide a guide to the rich periodical and book-length literature in American politics and government.

Chapter One The Constitution

Beard, Charles A., *An Economic Interpretation of the Constitution* (New York: Macmillan, 1960 reprint). A classic and controversial account of the framing of the Constitution.

Becker, Carl, *The Declaration of Independence: A Study in the History of Political Ideas* (New York: Knopf, 1942). A classic study.

Epstein, David F., *The Political Theory of the Federalist* (Chicago: University of Chicago Press, 1984). Looks at the major theoretical themes that run through the Federalist papers.

Farrand, Max, *The Framing of the Constitution of the United States* (New Haven: Yale University Press, 1913). An authoritative account of the proceedings of the constitutional convention.

Fisher, Louis, *Constitutional Dialogues* (Princeton: Princeton University Press, 1988). Looks at the development of constitutional law as an interactive process among the three branches of government.

Kelly, Alfred H., Harbison, Winfred A., and Herman Belz, *The American Constitution: Its Origins and Development,* 6th edition (New York: Norton, 1983). A standard constitutional history text.

Levy, Leonard W. and Dennis J. Mahoney, eds., *The Framing and Ratification of the Constitution* (New York: Macmillan, 1987). A collection of essays representing recent perspectives on the framing and ratification.

McDonald, Forrest, *We the People: The Economic Origins of the Constitution* (Chicago: University of Chicago Press, 1958). A detailed examination of the framers and ratifiers of the Constitution.

Robinson, Donald L., *"To the Best of My Ability": The President and the Constitution* (New York: Norton, 1987). A bicentennial perspective on the exercise of presidential power.

Storing, Herbert J., *The Anti-Federalist: Writings by Opponents of the Constitution* (Chicago: University of Chicago Press, 1985). Presents important perspectives from those opposed to the Constitution.

Chapter Two Federalism and the States

Anton, Thomas J., *American Federalism and Public Policy* (New York: Random House, 1989). A major recent text on the subject.

Elazar, Daniel J., *Exploring Federalism* (Tuscaloosa: University of Alabama Press, 1987). Elazar is one of the leading experts on federalism and offers a broad view of the subject in this book.

Fino, Susan P., *The Role of State Supreme Courts in the New Judicial Federalism* (Westport, Conn.: Greenwood, 1987). A study of the implications of federalism for the protection of rights.

Gray, Virginia, Jacob, Herbert, and Kenneth N. Vines, eds., *Politics in the American States,* 4th ed. (Boston: Little, Brown, 1983). A collection of essays on various aspects of state government and politics.

Nathan, Richard P., Doolittle, Fred C., and Associates, *Reagan and the States* (Princeton: Princeton University Press, 1987). A study of the impact of Reagan's New Federalism on the states.

Nice, David C., *Federalism: The Politics of Intergovernmental Relations* (New York: St. Martins Press, 1987). Shows how institutions of state government play a role within the American system of federalism in affecting how public policy is made and implemented.

Peterson, Paul E., Barry G. Rabe, and Kenneth K. Wong, *When Federalism Works* (Washington: Brookings, 1986). An upbeat analysis that emphasizes the strengths of federalism.

Riker, William H., *The Development of American Federalism* (Boston: Kluwer Academic Publishers, 1987). Offers analyses of various aspects of federalism.

Wright, Deil S., *Understanding Intergovernmental Relations,* 3rd ed., (Pacific Grove, California; Brooks/Cole, 1988). A standard text.

Chapter Three Public Opinion, Socialization, and the Media

Abramson, Paul R., *Political Attitudes in America* (San Francisco: Freeman, 1983). A useful text.

Asher, Herbert, *Polling and the Public: What Every Citizen Should Know* (Washington, D.C.: CQ Press, 1988). A very readable and useful guide to modern polling.

Bennett, W. Lance, *Public Opinion in American Politics* (New York: Harcourt, 1980). A text that challenges many cherished notions of what public opinion is and how opinions are formed.

Graber, Doris A., *Mass Media and American Politics,* 3rd ed., (Washington: CQ Press, 1988). A comprehensive guide to the relationship of the m. s media to American politics.

Lichter, S. Robert, Stanley Rothman, and Linda S. Lichter, *The Media Elite* (Bethesda, MD: Adler and Adler, 1986). In-depth study of the most influential journalists—their characteristics, backgrounds, and attitudes.

Maddox, William S. and Stuart A. Lilie, *Beyond Liberal and Conservative* (Washington, D.C.: Cato Institute, 1984). A comprehensive and detailed study of attitudes on four basic dimensions.

McClosky, Herbert and John R. Zaller, *The American Ethos* (Cambridge: Harvard University Press, 1984). A study of Americans' core values, especially attitudes about democracy and capitalism. Includes a historical overview.

Ranney, Austin, *Channels of Power* (Washington, D.C.: American Enterprise Institute, 1983.) A look at the impact of television on American politics by a distinguished political scientist.

Yeric, Jerry L. and John R. Todd, *Public Opinion: The Visible Politics* (Itasca, IL: Peacock, 1983). A short and authoritative text.

Chapter Four   Interest Groups

Berry, Jeffery M., *The Interest Group Society,* 2nd ed. (Glenview, Il: Scott, Foresman, 1989). A useful text.

Cigler, Allan J. and Burdett A. Loomis, eds., *Interest Group Politics,* 2nd ed., (Washington, D.C.: CQ Press, 1986). A broadly focused selection of separate studies.

Domhoff, G. William, *Who Rules America Now?* (New York: Simon and Schuster, 1983). A view of the power elite in contemporary American society.

Hertzke, Allen D., *Representing God in Washington* (Knoxville: University of Tennessee Press, 1988). A study of the practices of religious lobbies.

Pertschuk, Michael, *Giant Killers* (New York: Norton, 1986). Cases of public interest groups which have succeeded in fighting established interests.

Truman, David B., *The Governmental Process,* 2nd ed. (New York: Knopf, 1971). A classic description of interest group politics from a pluralist perspective.

Wilson, Graham K., *Interest Groups in the United States,* (New York: Oxford University Press, 1981). Farm, labor, business, and voluntary groups.

Chapter Five   Political Parties and Nominations

Crouse, Timothy, *The Boys on the Bus* (New York: Ballantine, 1973). Valuable especially for descriptions of reporters covering nominating politics.

Epstein, Leon D., *Political Parties in the American Mold* (Madison: University of Wisconsin Press, 1986). Explains the distinctiveness of American parties as compared against a responsible-parties model.

Herrnson, Paul S., *Party Campaigning in the 1980s* (Cambridge: Harvard University Press, 1988). Presents new research showing how parties engage in fundraising and how PACs rely on them for advice.

Kessel, John H., *Presidential Campaign Politics,* 3rd ed. (Chicago: Dorsey, 1988). Analysis plus original research that shows how candidates build coalitions over time. Includes case descriptions of recent elections.

Key, V. O., Jr., *Politics, Parties, and Pressure Groups,* 5th ed., (New York: Crowell, 1964). The pioneering and classic work on political parties.

Sorauf, Frank J., and Paul A. Beck, *Party Politics in America,* 6th ed. (Glenview, IL: Scott, Foresman, 1988). A comprehensive text.

Wayne, Stephen J., *The Road to the White House,* 3rd ed. (New York: St. Martins, 1988). Nominations and elections with recent cases.

Chapter Six Voting and Elections

Asher, Herbert, *Presidential Elections and American Politics,* 4th ed. (Chicago: Dorsey, 1988). A comprehensive guide to the major patterns and issues in voting behavior and elections.

Campbell, Angus, Phillip E. Converse, Warren E. Miller, and Donald E. Stokes, *The American Voter* (New York: Wiley, 1964). A classic study of voting attitudes and choices, based on survey research.

Goldenberg, Edie N. and Michael W. Traugott, *Campaigning for Congress* (Washington, D.C.: CQ Press, 1984). Examines congressional campaigns and strategies from the standpoint of the candidates, the campaign managers, and the voters.

Hershey, Marjorie Randon, *Running for Office* (Chatham, New Jersey: Chatham House, 1984). An in-depth look at candidates when they first decide to run for office: what they face; how they learn; and what they do.

Jacobson, Gary C., *The Politics of Congressional Elections,* 2nd ed. (Boston: Little, Brown, 1987). A useful text.

Niemi, Richard G. and Herbert F. Weisberg, eds. *Controversies in Voting Behavior,* 2nd ed. (Washington, D.C.: CQ Press, 1984). A collection of studies that look at the major issues in analyzing voting behavior. For advanced students.

Piven, Frances Fox and Richard A. Cloward, *Why Americans Don't Vote* (New York: Pantheon, 1988). An analysis of who votes and who does not, showing how registration laws can bias the electoral process.

Sabato, Larry, *The Rise of Political Consultants* (New York: Basic Books, 1981). A detailed look at these new campaign experts.

Salmore, Stephen A. and Barbara G. Salmore, *Candidates, Parties, and Campaigns,* 2nd ed. (Washington, D.C.: CQ Press, 1989). A comprehensive look at campaigning for Congress.

Sorauf, Frank J., *Money in American Elections* (Glenview, Il: Scott, Foresman, 1988). A comprehensive and detailed study of the issues and consequences of campaign finance.

Wolfinger, Raymond E. and Steven J. Rosenstone, *Who Votes?* (New Haven: Yale University Press, 1980). Answers the title question and looks at the impact of socioeconomic factors, registration laws, and other influences.

Chapter Seven Congress

Congressional Quarterly, *Origins and Development of Congress,* 2nd ed. (Washington, D.C.: Congressional Quarterly, 1982). A brief history.

Dodd, Lawrence C. and Bruce I. Oppenheimer, eds., *Congress Reconsidered,* 4th ed. (Washington, D.C.: CQ Press, 1989). A collection of readings emphasizing topics of current interest.

Fenno, Richard F., *Congressmen in Committees* (Boston: Little, Brown, 1973). A comparative study of six committees looking at the goals of members, the committee environments, and the way decisions are made.

Fenno, Richard F., *Home Style* (Boston: Little, Brown, 1978). An in-depth look at how members present themselves in their districts.

Fisher, Louis, *Congressional Conflicts Between Congress and the President* (Princeton: Princeton University Press, 1985). Includes such basic topics as the power of the purse, vetoes, war power, treaties and agreements, and the appointment power.

Hinckley, Barbara, *Stability and Change in Congress,* 4th ed. (New York: Harper and Row, 1988). A comprehensive text.

Loomis, Burdett A., *The New American Politician* (New York: Basic Books, 1988). The new political entrepreneurs—running for election, dealing with the media, and more.

Oleszek, Walter J., *Congressional Procedures and the Policy Process,* 3rd ed. (Washington, D.C.: CQ Press, 1988). The only book of its kind with an up-to-date review of rules and procedures in the Senate and House. Includes a glossary of terms.

Ornstein, Norman J., et. al., *Vital Statistics on Congress, 1987–88* (Washington, D.C.: American Enterprise Institute, 1987). A fact-filled guide to committees, staff, ratings of members, turnover, and much more.

Parker, Glenn R., *Studies of Congress* (Washington, D.C.: CQ Press, 1985). A collection of major studies on Congress, previously published.

Sinclair, Barbara, *Congressional Realignment, 1925–1978* (Austin: University of Texas Press, 1982). Traces the development of issues and party voting over a 53 year period.

Smith, Steven S. and Christopher J. Deering, *Committees in Congress* (Washington, D.C.: CQ Press, 1984). Committees and subcommittees—their makeup, leadership, practices and outcomes.

Stern, Philip M., *The Best Congress Money Can Buy* (New York: Pantheon, 1988). A critical look at Congress, PACs, and the impact of money.

Wilson, Woodrow, *Congressional Government* (New York: Meridian reprint, 1956). A famous criticism of Congress by an advocate of a stronger presidential government. Wilson's critique has been followed by many modern critics.

Wright, Gerald, Leroy N. Rieselbach, and Lawrence C. Dodd, eds. *Congress and Policy Change* (New York: Agathon, 1986). Race in Congress, logrolling, blocking coalitions, and how elections and party leaders can effect change.

Chapter Eight The Presidency

Bailey, Harry A., Jr. and Jay M. Shaftritz, eds., *The American Presidency: Historical and Contemporary Perspectives* (Chicago: Dorsey, 1988). A collection of major studies, previously published.

Barber, James David, *Presidential Character,* 3rd ed. (Englewood Cliffs, New Jersey: Prentice-Hall, 1985). Barber uses presidential biographies to predict performance in the White House.

Cronin, Thomas E., *The State of the Presidency,* 2nd ed. (Boston: Little, Brown, 1980). A readable introduction to the powers, limits, and problems of the contemporary presidency.

Edwards, III George C., *The Public Presidency* (New York: St. Martins, 1983). Polls, press, and public opinion.

Heclo, Hugh and Lester M. Salamon, eds. *The Illusion of Presidential Government* (Boulder, CO: Westview, 1981). Contrasts the notion of presidential power with the real details of administration and policy making.

Janis, Irving L., *Groupthink,* 2nd ed. (New York: Houghton Mifflin, 1982). Looks at problems of decision-making in the White House, with examples from Vietnam, Watergate, and other cases.

Kernell, Samuel, *Going Public* (Washington, D.C.: CQ Press, 1986). Strategies of the public presidency: speeches, appearances, dealing with the press.

King, Gary and Lyn Ragsdale, *The Elusive Executive* (Washington, D.C.: CQ Press, 1988). An essential reference book with interpretive chapters: office, appearances, speeches, election and primary results, success in Congress, and much more.

Light, Paul C., *The President's Agenda* (Baltimore: Johns Hopkins, 1982). Original research from interviews and government documents that analyzes where the ideas come from and how the president's agenda is formed.

Lowi, Theodore J., *The Personal Presidency* (Ithaca: Cornell University Press, 1988). A critical look at the modern presidency, with suggestions for reform.

Neustadt, Richard E., *Presidential Power* (New York: Wiley, 1980). First published in 1960, this classic work looks at presidential power mainly as the power to persuade.

Reedy, George E., *The Twilight of the Presidency,* rev. ed. (New York: New American Library, 1987). An account of the pressures and problems from within the White House by one who was a presidential adviser.

Rossiter, Clinton, *The American Presidency,* 2nd ed. (New York: Harcourt, 1960). A classic account.

Tebbel, John and Sarah Watts, *The Press and the Presidency* (New York: Oxford University Press, 1985). A history of presidents' relations with the press from George Washington to Ronald Reagan.

Watson, Richard A. and Norman C. Thomas, *The Politics of the Presidency* (New York: Wiley, 1983). A comprehensive text.

Chapter Nine The Federal Bureaucracy

Foreman, Christopher H., Jr., *Signals From the Hill: Congressional Oversight and the Challenge of Social Regulation* (New Haven: Yale, 1988). A major study of agency-congressional relations.

Goodsell, Charles T., *The Case for Bureaucracy* (Chatham, New Jersey: Chatham House, 1983). A provocative essay, with examples.

Heclo, Hugh, *A Government of Strangers* (Washington, D.C.: Brookings, 1977). The bureaucracy, with Congress, are the "natives" who watch the presidents and their cabinet heads come and go.

Marks, John, *The Search for the 'Manchurian Candidate'* (New York: Quadrangle Books, 1979). A chilling account of illegal CIA activities within the country, based on actual government documents. Raises questions of how agencies should be subjected to democratic control.

Ripley, Randall B. and Grace A. Franklin, *Congress, the Bureaucracy, and Public Policy* (Homewood, IL: Dorsey, 1987). A useful and readable account of how the bureaucracy makes policy.

Rourke, Francis E., *Bureaucracy, Politics, and Public Policy,* 3rd ed. (Boston: Little, Brown, 1984). A very readable text.

Wildavsky, Aaron, *The New Politics of the Budgetary Process* (Glenview, IL: Scott, Foresman, 1988). A comprehensive and detailed look at the current practices and problems of the budget process.

Chapter Ten The Judiciary

Abraham, Henry J., *Justices and Presidents,* 2nd ed. (New York: Oxford University Press, 1985). A comprehensive historical account of the selection of Supreme Court justices.

Abraham, Henry J., *The Judicial Process,* 5th ed. (New York: Oxford University Press, 1986). A major text with a comparative perspective.

Baum, Lawrence, *The Supreme Court,* 3rd ed. (Washington: CQ Press, 1988). A major text.

Brigham, John, *The Cult of the Court* (Philadelphia: Temple University Press, 1987). An original analysis of the Supreme Court.

Carp, Robert A. and C. K. Rowland, *Policymaking and Politics in the Federal District Courts* (Knoxville: University of Tennessee Press, 1983). An empirical study of federal district judge decisionmaking.

Cooper, Phillip J., *Hard Judicial Choices: Federal District Court Judges and State and Local Officials* (New York: Oxford University Press, 1988). Case studies of federal district judges fashioning remedies to right constitutional wrongs.

Eisenstein, James, Flemming, Roy B., and Peter F. Nardulli, *The Contours of Justice* (Glenview, Ill.: Scott, Foresman, 1988). The workings of criminal courts are analyzed placing them within the context of the larger community.

Goldman, Sheldon and Austin Sarat, *American Court Systems,* 2nd ed. (New York: Longman, l989). A collection of classic and recent studies of various aspects of the judicial system.

Jacob, Herbert, *Law and Politics in the United States* (Boston, Mass: Little, Brown, 1986). A comprehensive text.

Marshall, Thomas R., *Public Opinion and the Supreme Court* (Boston: Unwin Hyman, 1989). A thorough exploration of the relationship of public opinion and Supreme Court policymaking.

Murphy, Walter F., *Elements of Judicial Strategy* (Chicago: University of Chicago Press, l964). A classic study.

O'Brien, David M., *Judicial Roulette: Report of the Twentieth Century Fund Task Force on Judicial Selection* (New York: Priority Press. l988). A useful overview of federal judicial selection.

Pritchett, C. Herman, *The Roosevelt Court: A Study in Judicial Politics and Values l937—l947 (New York: Macmillan, l948).* A classic study.

Schubert, Glendon, *Quantitative Analysis of Judicial Behavior* (New York: Free Press, 1959). Another classic.

Spaeth, Harold J. and David W. Rhode, *Supreme Court Decision Making* (San Francisco: Freeman, 1976). A major text.

Stumpf, Harry P., *The American Judicial Process* (San Diego: Harcourt Brace Jovanovich, 1988). A comprehensive new text.

Chapter Eleven Domestic Policy

Browning, Robert X., *Politics and Social Welfare Policy in the United States* (Knoxville: University of Tennessee Press, 1986). Explores in some depth the policy impact of social welfare programs.

Edwards, George C., III, *Implementing Public Policy* (Washington: CQ Press, 1980). A comprehensive analysis.

Freeman, J. Leiper, *The Political Process: Executive Bureau-Legislative Committee Relations,* revised edition (New York: Random House, 1965). A classic account of policymaking by subgovernments.

Jones, Charles O., *An Introduction to the Study of Public Policy* 3rd ed. (Monterey, Calif.: Brooks-Cole, 1984). A major text.

Pressman, Jeffrey L., and Aaron Wildavsky, *Implementation,* 3rd ed. (Berkeley: University of California Press, 1984). A classic study.

Robertson, David B. and Dennis R. Judd, *The Development of American Public Policy* (Glenview, Ill.: Scott, Foresman, 1989). An original analysis of public policy in its historical context emphasizing the institutional restraints that affect the substance of policy.

Van Horn, Carl E., Baumer, Donald C., and William Gormley, Jr., *Politics and Public Policy* (Washington: CQ Press, 1988). A text that offers a broad view of the making of public policy.

Wildavsky, Aaron, *The New Politics of the Budgetary Process* (Glenview, Ill.: Scott, Foresman, 1988). An informative account of how the budgetary process relates to the making of domestic policy.

Chapter Twelve Civil Liberties

Abraham, Henry J., *Freedom and the Court* 5th edition (New York: Oxford University Press, 1988). A comprehensive overview of civil liberties.

Adler, Renata, *Reckless Disregard* (New York: Knopf, 1986). The complex world of libel law as revealed in fascinating case studies.

Baker, Liva, *Miranda: Crime, Law and Politics* (New York: Atheneum, 1983). The famous *Miranda* decision and its impact.

Faux, Marian, *Roe v. Wade: The Untold Story of the Landmark Supreme Court Decision that Made Abortion Legal* (New York: Macmillan, 1988). A case study.

Friendly, Fred W., *Minnesota Rag* (New York: Random House, 1981). An account of the famous *Near* v. *Minnesota* case that became a landmark freedom of the press decision.

Irons, Peter, *Justice at War* (New York: Oxford, 1983). Focuses on the leading Supreme Court cases arising from the Japanese exclusion and detention program during World War II.

Keller, William W., *The Liberals and J. Edgar Hoover: Rise and Fall of a Domestic Intelligence State* (Princeton: Princeton University Press, 1989). Documents the impact of the FBI's activities on civil liberties.

Levy, Leonard W., *The Establishment Clause* (New York: Macmillan, 1985). A thorough historical analysis.

Lewis, Anthony, *Gideon's Trumpet* (New York: Random House, 1964). A classic case study.

Polenberg, Richard, *Fighting Faiths: The Abrams Case, the Supreme Court, and Free Speech* (New York: Viking, 1988). A study of a famous case raising issues of First Amendment freedoms.

Wiecek, William M., *Liberty Under Law: The Supreme Court in American Life* (Baltimore: The Johns Hopkins University Press, 1988). A short and useful history of the Supreme Court.

Chapter Thirteen Minorities, Women, and Equality

Amaker, Norman C., *Civil Rights and the Reagan Administration* (Latham, Md.: University Press of America, 1989). A critical examination of the Reagan record in civil rights.

Berry, Mary Frances, *Why ERA Failed: Politics, Women's Rights, and the Amending Process* (Bloomington: Indiana University Press, 1986). An informative account of the modern struggle for women's rights.

Bullock, Charles S. III, and Charles M. Lamb, eds., *Implementation of Civil Rights Policy* (Monterey, California: Brooks/Cole, 1984). A collection of original analyses of different aspects of civil rights policy.

Bumiller, Kristin, *The Civil Rights Society: The Social Construction of Victims* (Baltimore: The Johns Hopkins University Press, 1988). The limitations of law and the legal process in attacking continuing racial and sexual discrimination.

Kluger, Richard, *Simple Justice* (New York: Knopf, 1975). A classic account of the events leading to and including *Brown* v. *Board of Education*.

Litwack, Leon F., *North of Slavery* (Chicago: University of Chicago Press, 1961). A well-documented historical account of northern racism.

Morris, Aldon D., *The Origins of the Civil Rights Movement: Black Communities Organizing for Change* (New York: Free Press, 1984). A detailed study of events of historic importance.

Ross, Susan Deller, and Ann Barcher, *The Rights of Women* revised edition (New York: Bantam Books, 1983). Written for a popular audience, this book reviews the legal rights of women.

Chapter Fourteen Foreign Policy

Crabb, Cecil, Jr. and Pat Holt, *Invitation to Struggle,* 3rd ed. (Washington, D.C.: CQ Press, 1988). A useful supplementary text focusing on recent foreign policy cases.

Ford, Daniel, *The Button* (New York: Simon and Schuster, 1985). The nation's nuclear warning system and the various parts of the government responsible for it.

Hughes, Barry B., *The Domestic Context of American Foreign Policy* (San Francisco: Freeman, 1978). A carefully researched account of how public opinion affects foreign policy.

Kegley, Charles W., Jr. and Eugene R. Wittkopf, eds., *The Domestic Sources of American Foreign Policy* (New York: St. Martins, 1988). Twenty readings, wide-ranging in subject matter, including the effects of public opinion, interest groups, personalities, and institutions.

Nathan, James A. and James K. Oliver, *Foreign Policy Making and the American Political System,* 2nd ed. (Boston: Little, Brown, 1987). A short useful text.

Spanier, John, *American Foreign Policy Since World War* II, 11th ed. (Washington, D.C.: CQ Press, 1988). A standard text.

Sullivan, Michael, *The Vietnam War* (Lexington: University of Kentucky Press, 1985). Of the many books on Vietnam, this is distinctive for its close analysis of the decision-making process and the role of public opinion. Ideal for supplementary reading.

Abington School District v. Schempp
Landmark 1963 decision of the Supreme
Court that ruled that the reading of the
Lord's Prayer or passages from the Bible as
part of religious ceremonies in the public
schools violates the guarantee in the First
Amendment against the establishment of
religion.

adequate state ground doctrine Doctrine
that state court decisions based solely on
state law which does not conflict with federal law will not be struck down by the U.S.
Supreme Court.

admiralty law   Concerns the law of the high
seas.

advantage of incumbency The likelihood
that a person already holding an office will
be reelected over his or her opponent.

adversary system   The way cases are processed in American courts. Each side to a
dispute is represented by lawyers who are
adversaries at the bar who make their best
arguments, question witnesses, present evidence, and seek to establish facts favorable
to their clients.

affirmative action   The name given to education and hiring programs designed to redress past discrimination on the basis of
race and gender. Educational institutions
and public and private employers either
voluntarily or are required to expand their
recruitment nets to meet certain goals.

agents of socialization   The primary influences on social learning, such as family,
schools, peers.

Alien and Sedition Acts of 1798   Federal legislation that made it a crime to criticize the
president or Congress with the intent of
bringing either into disrepute.

**amateurs and professionals as party mem-
bers**   Amateurs are drawn to the party because of an issue or candidate, whereas
professionals work for the party regardless
of the issues or candidates.

amicus curiae brief   A friend of the court
brief, usually submitted by the Solicitor
General, other governmental officials, or
private groups all of whom are not an immediate party to the case.

anti-federalists   The name given to opponents of ratification of the U.S. Constitution
of 1787.

appellate jurisdiction (of a court)   The
higher court hears cases on appeal from a
lower court.

Articles of Confederation   America's first
constitution which provided the form of
government from 1781 when it legally took
effect until 1789 when the government provided for by the Constitution of 1787 began
to operate.

bandwagon effect   [In presidential nomina-
tions] the tendency of delegates to rush to
support the emerging nomination winner.
[The phrase is drawn from the actual use of
circus bandwagons in political campaigns
and from such phrases as "to get on the
wagon" meaning to join up. Political car-
toonists used the idea as early as 1848
showing a brass band on the way to a political rally.]

Baker v. Carr   Landmark 1962 ruling of the
Supreme Court that malapportioned state
legislative districts raised a constitutional
issue that could be litigated in the federal
courts.

bill of attainder   A statute that punishes or
penalizes a specific individual.

Bill of Rights The first ten amendments to the Constitution. Ratified in 1791, they contain guarantees of individual liberty.

bipolar [Having two poles or axes. In American foreign policy] a view of the world divided in two between the "Free World" and the communist nations.

block grants Grants to state and local governments for broad policy areas (for example, public health) rather than specific federal government programs. State and local officials construct a proposal of how the money will be spent. There is less paperwork than with categorical grants and states have more authority and discretion as to how the money is spent.

Brown v. Board of Education Historic ruling of the Supreme Court in 1954 ending enforced racial segregation in the public schools. By ruling that separate can never be equal and therefore violates the equal protection clause of the Constitution, the Court provided the legal basis for attacking all forms of racism.

Budget and Impoundment Control Act of 1974 Gave Congress more control of the budget process by creating the Congressional Budget Office and establishing Budget Committees that would set general guidelines for fiscal policy.

Budget and Accounting Act of 1921 The act increased the President's control over budget making in relation to Congress and the bureaucratic agencies. The act also created the Bureau of the Budget (now called the Office of Management and Budget).

bureaucracy A form of organization, found throughout modern society, characterized by specialization, hierarchy, detailed rules and procedures, and impersonality.

categorical grants Grants targeted for specific programs and must be spent according to agency specifications.

Caucus [for parties] A meeting of party officials.

challenger A person running for office against an incumbent.

checks and balances Each branch of government has powers that can check the actions of the other branches. Power is divided and each branch's power is balanced by the powers exercised by the other two branches.

civil law case Concerns law that applies to economic relationships (for example, contractual, property, employment), personal status (divorce, child custody, wills, probate), personal injury, or damage to property.

Civil Rights Act of 1964 Historic legislation that outlaws racial and sexual discrimination in employment and forbids racial discrimination in public accommodations and in federally assisted programs. Other provisions strengthened the Civil Rights Commission, created the Equal Employment Opportunity Commission to enforce the ban on discrimination by employers and labor unions, and strengthened the authority of the Justice Department to sue state and local governments to protect the rights of blacks.

civil service system A system of appointment, now used in the U.S. federal bureaucracy, based on a merit principle, ensuring that civil service employees cannot be hired or fired by elected officials.

clear and present danger test Government can invade fundamental First Amendment rights only when freedoms of speech and press pose an immediate danger of bringing about a substantive evil that government has a right to prevent. This test was devised by Justice Oliver Wendell Holmes.

clientele capture The tendency for bureaucrats to begin to identify with the clientele they are administering.

closed primary A nominating election open only to those voters who register as members of the party.

cloture A resolution bringing an end to debate, as during a filibuster. Under the current rule, it takes 60 Senators to invoke cloture.

coattails The extra votes the more popular candidate on a ballot is thought to give to the other candidates, usually of the same party, who run at the same time.

collegial courts Are courts in which groups of judges decide the same case. Usually they are appellate courts such as the U.S. Court of Appeals and the U.S. Supreme Court.

common law Traditionally defined as judge-made law that is long-standing and accepted as "law."

Common Sense The revolutionary pamphlet written by Thomas Paine and published in 1776 advocating American independence from Great Britain and the establishment of a republic.

conference committees Committees appointed for the occasion by the leadership to reconcile differences between House and Senate versions of a bill. [These are usually made up of members of the House and Senate standing committees that first considered the bill].

congressional party caucuses Four altogether, consisting of all Democrats and all Republicans in the House and Senate respectively.

consensus Widespread agreement.

Conservative Coalition: The joining together of Southern Democrats with Republicans to make congressional policy.

constitutional courts Are courts established under Article III of the Constitution that establishes the judicial branch of government and specifies that Article III judges are appointed for life and are guaranteed that their salaries will not be diminished while they hold office.

controllable expenditures Are discretionary expenditures for which no previous obligation exists. They can be cut back as may be necessary.

cult of the presidency [An exaggerated view of the president, fostered by some academics and journalists] which emphasizes the President's power and virtue while it focuses on the trivia of their personal lives.

dark horse [Originally a horse about whose racing powers little is known.] A little-known candidate who comes from behind to win the nomination.

Declaration of Independence Enacted by the Continental Congress on July 4, 1776, the Declaration announced independence from Great Britain, offered reasons for the break, a justification of the right of revolution, and a stirring vision of the purposes of government.

delegate role Delegates represent by following the opinions of their constituents, whether or not these opinions accord with their own.

democracy The form of government in which the people choose the government and the government is held accountable to the people.

descriptive representation The reflecting, or mirroring, of politically relevant characteristics of the citizens in the representative body.

direct veto Action taken by a president that automatically nullifies legislation unless it is overriden by a two-thirds vote in the House and Senate.

diversity of citizenship jurisdiction A citizen of one state can sue a citizen of another state in the federal district court situated in either state provided the amount at issue is at least $50,000.

doctrinaire party A minor party that is usually small in size, specific in program, and devoted in membership.

Dred Scott v. Sandford Notorious racist Supreme Court decision from 1857 in which the Court ruled that blacks are not United States citizens and that Congress could not prohibit slavery in the territories.

earmarking The practice by which congressional committees write into law specific portions of a budget, leaving the remainder open to the president's discretion.

electoral college The slate of electors drawn from each of the states who cast the official vote for president and vice-president, with each state allotted a number of electors according to its population.

Employment Act of 1946 Created the president's Council of Economic Advisers and provided for an annual national economic report.

entitlement programs Government programs in which all those who qualify and apply receive the benefits (cash, goods, or services) bestowed by the programs.

equity A special kind of law that historically was administered by courts in equity who render justice using remedies not used by the common law courts.

ERA The Equal Rights Amendment forbidding discrimination on the basis of gender was passed by Congress in 1972 but fell short of the 38 states needed to ratify the Amendment.

exclusionary rule Evidence seized in violation of the Fourth Amendment cannot be used as evidence in a trial.

executive agreement An agreement with other nations negotiated by the President or State Department officials that requires no Senate consent.

Executive Office Act of 1939 Empowered the president to form offices to implement the new demands of domestic and foreign policy making. This led to the Executive Office of the President.

Executive Office of the President The president's own bureaucracy which exists outside of the traditional departments and agencies of the federal bureaucracy. It includes such agencies as the Office of Management and Budget and the National Security Council. Also called the "institutionalized presidency."

ex post facto law A law that is applied retroactively. In American law applies only to criminal matters, for example, punishing someone for doing something that was not illegal at the time it was done.

extradite The legal duty to return a fugitive from another state to the state where the crime was committed.

federalism Is the concept of divided sovereignty over the same geographical area and its inhabitants. In the American system of federalism certain powers are reserved for the central government while others are exercised by the states.

Federalist Papers A series of 85 essays published in New York newspapers between October 1787 and July 1788 designed to win ratification of the Constitution in New York. Authored by James Madison, Alexander Hamilton, and John Jay but published under the name "Publius," they are an authoritative commentary on the Constitution and the intent of the framers.

federalists Supporters of the ratification of the U.S. Constitution.

filibuster The deliberate holding of the floor by a minority of senators to demonstrate opposition to a particular bill.

fiscal federalism Is the transfer of money from one governmental level to the next level and is marked by state dependency on the federal government to help finance a wide variety of programs.

fiscal year The financial year that for the federal government begins October 1 and extends through the following September 30. The fiscal year is known by the year in which it ends, thus, for example, fiscal year (FY) 1989 began on October 1, 1988 and ended September 30, 1989.

franking privilege In Congress, free mailing to constituents and local media.

free ride One who benefits from the actions of interest groups without expending effort or money for them.

general revenue-sharing A program for providing federal funds directly to local governments with no strings attached. It was discontinued in 1986.

Gibbons v. Ogden Landmark Supreme Court decision from 1824 in which the Court gave a broad interpretation of Congress's commerce power to include the regulation of navigation on interstate waterways.

Gideon v. Wainwright Important Supreme Court decision from 1963 that declared that the Constitution requires the states to provide poor criminal defendants with a free court-appointed lawyer.

government corporation A special kind of independent agency that is like a private corporation in its structure and services but like other government agencies in being subject to presidential and congressional control.

grand jury An investigative body consisting of specially selected members of the local community who hear testimony and receive other evidence presented by the prosecutor. The grand jury determines whether a crime has been committed and whether there is sufficient basis to bring one or more of the alleged perpetrators to trial.

Great Compromise The compromise agreed to by the constitutional convention of 1787 as to the makeup of Congress. One branch would be apportioned according to population, the other branch would have equal representation for each state.

Griswold v. Connecticut Major Supreme Court ruling from 1965 that the right to privacy is a constitutional guarantee and that in this case Connecticut cannot invade privacy by prohibiting married couples from using contraceptives.

groupthink A term coined by Irving Janis. The kind of faulty thinking often found in groups, where pressures for agreement override a look at alternatives and discourage criticism.

home style A term used by Richard Fenno to describe House members' symbolic activity of representation. They show they identify with the district, care about the people in it, and are good representatives.

House Majority Leader The elected leader who works with the Speaker, primarily in the role of chief lieutenant.

House Minority Leader The elected leader of the minority party and the losing candidate for Speaker.

ideology A belief system; a set of basic beliefs about politics and government that are related in a coherent fashion.

implied powers Powers that are implied by the nature of the Constitution and the purposes which it serves.

incorporated rights Rights the Supreme Court has determined are part of the Fourteenth Amendment guarantee that no state shall deny life, liberty, or property without due process of law.

incrementalism [In the budget process] The practice for decisions to be made by adding or subtracting a small amount to the existing budget. An increment means a small change to an existing base.

incumbent A person holding an office.

Independent Regulatory Commission An agency that is executive in its organization but performs rule-making activities and is not under the direction of the Office of the President or the cabinet heads.

indictment Grand jury names one or more individuals for whom there is sufficient evidence to bring to trial for allegedly having committed a specified criminal offense.

indirect veto [A device that nullifies legislation] whereby presidents simply do not sign a bill received in the last ten days of the session. Also called "pocket veto."

injunction A court order instructing the party being sued not to do or to continue to do some action that causes harm to the complaining party.

in-kind contributions Non-monetary campaign contributions, such as providing organizational or technical assistance to a campaign.

interdependent A relationship of nations whereby actions in one nation automatically produce effects in other nations.

interest aggregation Parties are said to aggregate interests when they combine many diverse and conflicting opinions in a broad party appeal.

interest groups Collections of people with shared attitudes who are conscious of their identity as a group and who form a concrete organization to influence government policy.

isolationist The position that American interests are best served by staying out of conflicts elsewhere around the world.

issue network A group of people who move in and out of policy areas, at times clustering around one issue and at other times connecting several issues.

joint committees Special committees made up of both House and Senate members.

judicial review Power of the federal courts to review the legality of the actions of the other branches of government and to uphold or strike down those actions. The U.S. Supreme Court has the final word as to the interpretation of the U.S. Constitution.

Judiciary Act of 1789 The statute that created the structure of the federal court system and specified the powers of the courts.

jurisdiction (of courts) The authority to hear and decide the subject matter of a case within the geographic boundaries serviced by the court.

landslide An extraordinarily large election victory in which the opposition is "buried."

law of anticipated reaction [In the budget process] The practice for decisions to be made by the various budget makers with an eye toward what all the other participants will do.

legislative courts Courts established under Article I of the Constitution as an exercise of Congress's power to govern the territories. These judges are appointed for a fixed term of office and not for life.

Legislative Reorganization Act of 1946 Consolidated the number of committees in Congress among other reforms. Title III of the act set the rules for who must register as lobbyists and what expenses should be reported.

legislative veto A provision inserted in federal laws that allowed either or both branches of Congress to invalidate a policy decision or action of the executive branch within a specified time. This practice was declared unconstitutional by the Supreme Court in 1983.

legitimate opposition A function performed by political parties offering a democratic and orderly way of criticizing the government in power and providing for government change.

line-item veto Veto of a particular item in spending legislation without striking down the rest of the legislation. Governors in 43 states have line-item veto. The president of the United States does not.

lobbying Broad definition: Communication aimed at a government decision maker in the hope of influencing a decision. Narrow definition: Communication by interest group representatives aimed at a government decision maker in the hope of influencing a decision. [Since lobbies were the rooms of public buildings where citizens could talk to officials, lobbying came to mean working in these areas to influence policy. The term dates from the middle of the nineteenth century.]

lobbyist An interest group representative who engages in the activity of lobbying.

long-term influences on the vote A term used to describe the effects of party identification in voting. It is independent of the candidates nominated, the campaign strategy, or the events in the world at the time of any one election.

Majority and Minority Party Leaders in the Senate The elected leaders of the two parties. [The party with the largest number of members is the majority party.]

Marbury v. Madison Famous 1803 Supreme Court decision in which Chief Justice John Marshall established the principle of judicial review and the Supreme Court's supremacy in interpreting the Constitution.

maritime law Concerns shipping law and the law of harbors, rivers, and waterways.

McCulloch v. Maryland Supreme Court decision from 1819 which gave a broad interpretation of the necessary and proper clause of the Constitution and ruled that Congress has implied powers to carry out its enumerated powers. Decision favored national sovereignty over state sovereignty.

Medicare A federal government sponsored medical insurance program for the elderly.

merit principle The principle that public employment and appointments would be based on merit. It provides for competitive examinations for prospective office holders and guarantees job security with adequate performance.

merit selection of judges A nominating commission submits a list of names of people qualified to fill a specific judicial position. The governor is legally required to choose the appointee from that list.

midterm election The election occurring two years after the presidential election when there is no presidential race. Also called off-year election.

minor party A political party that only rarely succeeds in electing candidates to government.

Miranda rules Derived from the Supreme Court decision in *Miranda v. Arizona* (1966) that spell out the conditions under which a confession or statement from the accused can be considered voluntary and thus introduced in a trial. Also called the Miranda

warnings and are the "rights" read to an individual when taken into custody by law enforcement authorities and before questioning begins.

multi-party system A country with more than two major parties.

Multiple Advocacy A term used by Alexander George. An advisory system designed to encourage advice for alternative, and even opposing, positions.

NAACP National Association for the Advancement of Colored People. Founded in 1910, this organization has been a major force in the struggle of black Americans to achieve racial equality.

narrowcasting A term coined to describe media targeting of specialized audiences in terms of age, education, and interests.

National Security Act of 1947 Established new offices within the Office of the President that would help the president make national security policy. These offices included the National Security Council and the Central Intelligence Agency. The act also consolidated the existing military services into one Cabinet department headed by a Secretary of Defense.

natural rights The concept that all people are born with and thus have certain fundamental rights.

New Federalism The name given the agenda of the Nixon and the Reagan administrations to change the balance of federalism by returning responsibility for certain problems to the states.

New Jersey Plan Introduced by the New Jersey delegation at the constitutional convention of 1787 and consisted of nine resolutions designed to amend the Articles of Confederation. It would have given Congress greater taxation and commerce powers, but would have preserved states' rights.

nonoccupational groups Interest groups that do not work primarily to secure material benefits for members. [These include single-issue groups and the so-called public interest groups.]

non-partisan election of judges Voters elect judges who, by law, do not have a party designation on the election ballot.

norm An unwritten rule of behavior in a social group.

normal vote A hypothetical vote based on the percentage of people identifying with each of the two parties, plus an estimate of the likelihood that they will vote. The normal vote is the hypothetical vote that would occur if there were no short-term influences.

occupational groups Interest groups that work primarily to secure improved material benefits for their members. Also called economic interest groups.

opinion leaders Those in a position to communicate with a large portion of the public, such as government officials and news media representatives.

original jurisdiction (of a court) The court is the first court to hear the case.

outside and inside strategies of interest groups Outside strategies seek to influence decision makers indirectly through appeals to public opinion. The inside strategies target decision makers directly.

oversight Congressional supervision of how executive agencies implement the laws it has passed and the programs it has funded.

palace politics mode A form of organization in which executives are linked to their subordinates in a fluid, personal, and nonhierarchical form. The executive is like a monarch with a court whose members are defined by and dependent on the royal pleasure.

parties Organizations that seek to influence government by nominating candidates and contesting their election. In so doing, they provide a label linking voters, workers, and candidates for office that can continue over time. (The word "can" simply recognizes that some parties may fail at continuing over time. They then cease to be parties.)

partisan election of judges Voters elect judges who run for office under a political party label that has been designated by the party primary or convention.

party identification A concept referring to people's psychological attachment to a political party, often measured by the question "Generally speaking, do you consider yourself a Democrat, a Republican, an Independent, or what?" This self-identification is what is meant by party identification.

party system A term used to describe the number and kind of parties in a country.

patronage Public employment and appointments which are available for distribution by public officials and political parties.

Pendleton Civil Service Act of 1883 Established the beginning of the U.S. Civil Service System and the use of a merit principle in appointments.

perks A slang term for prerequisites, or the material support that comes with a job.

petit jury The trial jury usually consisting of 12 people.

picket-fence federalism The label given when state or local agencies form a relationship with a federal agency that administers a categorical grant program. Together the state or local agency and the federal agency exercise power and responsibility in a particular policy area.

plausible denial A strategy that allows someone, such as the president, to deny knowledge of covert actions being carried out by the government.

pluralist interpretations of group influence Pluralists emphasize the multiplicity of groups and group interests. So many groups will form and compete with each other that no one will have a dominant influence. Interest group representation, then, is central to the American political process: it shows democracy at work.

political action committees (PACs) Organizations set up by interest groups to raise and contribute money to campaigns in the attempt to elect or defeat candidates for office.

political efficacy The feeling that one can have an impact or exert influence on political affairs.

popular sovereignty The idea or political principle that the people are the source of government power.

pork barrel The federal treasury is the barrel that members dip into for "pork"—the projects and spending for their own states and districts. The term, and the practice, dates from the nineteenth century.

power elitist interpretations of group influence Associated with C. Wright Mills and other writers, this argument emphasizes the lack of equality in the group representation process. Everyone is not equally able to develop and express interest, and groups with the most resources, such as power and money, will be more successful than other groups. Thus interest group representation gives us government not by the many but the few.

precedent In law, a precedent is a previous judicial ruling that is supposed to be followed by a court in deciding a similar case.

presidential popularity A term used for a president's public support often measured in the polls by a "job approval" question, as in "Do you approve of the way [president's name] is doing his job as President?"

preferred position doctrine The doctrine that First Amendment freedoms are worthy of special protection by the courts and were placed at the head of the Bill of Rights to signify their crucial importance for a free society.

presidential success in Congress A measure of congressional support for presidents. When Congress votes with the President's announced position, this is counted as a presidential success.

preventive detention Judges can refuse to set bail and hold suspects for whom certain objective criteria suggest that they pose a potential menace to the community.

primacy principle The principle that what is learned first is learned best.

primary An election to nominate candidates for office.

procedural rights The rights to fairness in the process used by government that can potentially deny an individual life, liberty, or property. Fair procedures, also known as due process, include rights to a public hearing or trial before an unbiased judge, to be represented by a lawyer, to confront adverse witnesses, to have evidence obtained illegally excluded from trials, and to appeal unfavorable trial court rulings.

proportional representation A method of allotting seats in the legislature according to the proportion of votes gained. A party receiving 49 percent of the vote would get 49 percent of the seats.

public interest groups Non-profit groups organized to educate the public about certain issues such as environmental or consumer protection and to lobby for legislation, bring pressure on regulatory agencies or commissions, and sponsor law suits.

public opinion The distribution of the public's views on politics and government. Although the term is used in the singular, there are many publics and many people with no opinion.

public policy The laws, executive orders, bureaucratic regulations, court decisions, and other actions taken by public officials that determine who gets what, when, and how.

rally 'round the flag effect The tendency for the public's support of presidents to increase in times of international crisis.

random sample A sample of the population drawn in some predetermined fashion so that everyone in the population has an equal chance of being selected for the sample.

reference group The particular group context one identifies with, such as an ethnic, occupation, or religious group.

republic A form of government in which the people, not a monarch, are considered to be the source of governmental power.

responsible parties A term describing relatively unified parties in which all party members campaign on the positions that the parties are able to take and attempt to carry out the policies once they are in office. Writers usually use the British parties as examples.

revolving door The tendency for ex-government officials to be hired at very high salaries to lobby their friends and former colleagues.

Reynolds v. Sims Landmark 1964 ruling of the Supreme Court that legislative districts of both houses of state legislatures must be apportioned on a one-person-one-vote basis.

Roe v. Wade Landmark Supreme Court decision from 1973 in which the Court ruled that the constitutional right to privacy includes the right of a woman in consultation with her physician to decide for herself whether or not to abort a non-viable fetus.

roll call vote A vote taken in Congress when members announce their position aye or nay when their name is called.

same-party and divided-party control Same-party control means that one party occupies the White House and has majorities in the Senate and House. Divided-party control means that one party controls the White House and the other controls the Congress.

sample error A statistical term that describes the limits within which the sample may deviate from the population.

sampling, statistical theory The theory states that a sample of individuals can be selected randomly from a population to be representative of the population, within a specified degree of accuracy.

selective incentives rewards given to dues-paying members of interest groups that are independent of the policy goal being sought.

selective perception Cognitive ways of dealing with information to fit in with one's own preconceptions.

senatorial courtesy Occurs when senators respect the wishes of a colleague not to confirm a presidential nominee because the colleague finds the nominee to be personally obnoxious.

seniority system The practice of ranking committee members by party according to years of consecutive service on the committee, thus designating the chair of the committee as the most senior member of the majority party.

separation of powers The idea that the legislative, executive, and judicial branches should be separate, each having distinct functions.

short-term influences on the vote A term used to describe people's perceptions of the candidates, the issues, and the parties in any one election.

single-member constituency The citizens of one designated geographical area are entitled to elect one member to a legislative body.

single member-winner-take-all system A method of allotting seats in the legislature in which the candidate winning the most votes in a state or district gets the seat; the losers, even if they win 49 percent of the vote, get nothing.

socialization Learning in a social context those rules and ways of thinking deemed most important for the success and survival of the individual and society. It is socially adaptive learning.

social security The major social welfare program financed by taxes on workers and business. Provides economic benefits to the aged, disabled, and their dependents.

Speaker of the House The elected leader of the majority party in the House.

special (or select) committees Committees created to consider special problems or new legislation. These may or may not stay in existence from one congress to the next and typically do not have power to report legislation to the floor.

special master An individual appointed by a court and given legal authority to conduct hearings, gather expert testimony, consider the claims of all parties, and make a report to the court with recommendations for the resolution of the dispute.

splinter party (or secessionist party) A minor party that is formed when a group within a major party splits off and forms a political party of its own.

spoils system A term for a system of appointment common in the nineteenth century that was based on patronage. With offices awarded to the friends and supporters of the elected officials, the appointments were the spoils, or rewards, of victory.

standing committees Chief power centers in Congress that stay in existence from one congress to the next and that alone have power to report legislation to the floor. When people say committees, they are usually referring to the standing committees.

standing to sue The legally recognizable basis for invoking a court's jurisdiction. There must be a genuine case or controversy, some concrete relationship between the litigant and the dispute brought to the court, and, if governmental action is challenged the government's internal appeals process must be exhausted.

stare decisis Is the rule of precedent, that is, a court is expected to follow previous court decisions that interpreted a particular statute or constitutional provision.

state party delegation The group of congressional members consisting of all representatives from the party in the state.

structuring principle The principle that what is learned first structures later learning.

subgovernment A mutually supporting relationship between an agency, a congressional committee or subcommittee, and a clientele, or interest group. [Also colloquially called a "cozy triangle" or an "iron triangle."]

substantive due process The concept that the phrase in the Constitution that life, liberty, and property shall not be denied without due process of law refers not only to procedural guarantees but actual rights themselves.

substantive representation According to Hanna Pitkin, acting in the interests of the represented, in a manner responsive to them.

supremacy clause The provision in Article 6, Section 2, that the Constitution and the laws made under it are the supreme law of the land. National law supersedes conflicting state law.

ticket splitting Voting for a candidate of one party while at the same time voting for a candidate of the opposite party. The ticket is the ballot.

treaty An agreement, legally binding in international law, that is formalized by two or more nations after negotiation.

trustee role Trustees represent by doing what they feel is in the best interests of their constituents, whether or not this accords with what the constituents want done.

turnout The percent of eligible voters who actually vote.

two-party system A country where only two major parties compete for office and win most of the elections.

two-presidencies thesis An argument made by Aaron Wildavsky that there are two presidencies, differing in power, one for domestic policy and one for foreign policy, with Congress more likely to support presidents on foreign policy compared to domestic policy issues.

two-step information flow   A theory of how information is spread from elites to the mass public.

uncontrollable expenditures   Are fixed costs or financial obligations that must be met.

unitary system   A form of government where the locus of power is in the central government and all other governmental units are subordinate to it.

veto override   A vote by two-thirds of the House and Senate cancelling the president's veto, thus making the bill become a law.

Virginia Plan   Introduced by the Virginia delegation at the constitutional convention of 1787 and consisted of 15 resolutions that provided for a strong central government with three separate branches. The legislative branch was supreme over the other branches and could also strike down state laws in conflict with the Constitution.

Voting Rights Act of 1965   Historic legislation that provides for federal supervision of elections in states violating the Fifteenth Amendment. The Act ensured that black Americans and other racial minorities would be able to vote.

War Powers Act of 1973   Passed over a presidential veto. An act by which Congress sought to check the President from committing military forces abroad for indefinite periods of time without congressional approval. The act specified that presidents must report to Congress within forty-eight hours following the commitment of forces; and Congress must decide within a sixty-day period (with a short extension possible) whether to validate or invalidate the presidential action.

whip organizations   Organizations charged with gathering information on members' positions on a vote of concern to the party and attempting to persuade them to the party's position. The term is derived from the British parliament, and was originally a fox-hunting term: the "whipper-in" was the person responsible for keeping the hounds from leaving the pack.

writ of ceriorari   An order to the court whose decision is being challenged to send the records of the case to the Supreme Court so that the decision can be reviewed. The granting of certiorari means that the Court has taken the case.

writ of habeas corpus   An order by a judge to the official confining someone to bring the person to court and justify the basis for detention. Is a guarantee against arbitrary and illegal imprisonment.

Acknowledgments

Chapter Two: 75 From *Politics in the American States*, 4th ed., by Virginia Gray, Herbert Jacob, and Kenneth N. Vines, eds. Copyright © 1983 by Little, Brown and Company. Reprinted by permission. **81** "Principal Methods of Judicial Selection in the States" as is in *American Court Systems: Reading in Judicial Process and Behavior* by Sheldon Goldman and Austin Sarat. Copyright © 1989 by Longman Inc. Reprinted with permission. **Chapter Three: 91** From *The Gallup Report*, December 1984. Copyright © 1984 by American Institute of Public Opinion. Reprinted by permission. **104** From *Beyond Liberal and Conservative: Reassessing the Political Spectrum* by William S. Maddox and Stuart A. Lilie. Copyright © 1984 by the Cato Institute. Reprinted by permission. **106–7** From *The American Ethos* by Herbert McClosky and John Zaller. Copyright © 1984 by Harvard University Press. Reprinted by permission. **118–19** From *"This is Judy Woodruff at the White House"* by Judy Woodruff with Kathleen Maxa. Copyright © 1982 by Judy Woodruff and Kathleen Maxa. Reprinted by permission of Judy Woodruff. **118–19** From *The Other Side of the Story* by Jody Powell. Copyright © 1984 by William Morrow and Company, Inc. Reprinted by permission. **Chapter Four: 141** From "PACs and Congressional Elections in the 1980s" in *Interest Group Politics*, 2nd ed., by Allan J. Cigler and Burdett Loomis, eds. Copyright © 1986 by CQ Press. Reprinted by permission. **142** From *Vital Statistics on American Politics* by Harold W. Stanley and Richard G. Niemi. Copyright © 1988 by Congressional Quarterly Inc. Reprinted by permission. **144** From *Congressional Quarterly Weekly Report*, November 17, 1984. Copyright © 1984 by Congressional Quarterly, Inc. Reprinted by permission. **146** From *Politics and Power: The United States Senate 1869–1901* by David J. Rothman. Copyright © 1966 by Harvard University Press. Reprinted by permission. **148** From "September Registrations" in *Congressional Quarterly*, December 24, 1988. Copyright © 1988 by Congressional Quarterly, Inc. Reprinted by permission. **151** From "Washington Lobbyists: A Collective Portrait" in *Interest Group Politics*, 2nd ed., by Allan J. Cigler and Burdett Loomis, eds. Copyright © 1986 by CQ Press. Reprinted by permission. **Chapter Five: 169** From "Parties in State Politics" in *Politics in the American States*, 4th ed., by Virginia Gray, Herbert Jacob, and Kenneth N. Vines, eds. Copyright © 1983 by Little, Brown and Company. Reprinted by permission. **181** From *Congressional Quarterly Weekly Report*, December 26, 1981. Copyright © 1981 by Congressional Quarterly, Inc. Reprinted by permission. **186–87** From *Marathon: The Pursuit of the Presidency 1972–1976* by Jules Witcover. Copyright © 1977 by Jules Witcover. All rights reserved. Reprinted by permission of Viking Penguin a division of Penguin Books USA, Inc. **Chapter Six: 201** From *Leadership and Change: The New Politics and the American Electorate* by Warren E. Miller and Teresa E. Levitin. Reprinted by permission of Warren E. Miller. **203** From *Vital Statistics on American Politics* by Harold W. Stanley and Richard G. Niemi. Copyright © 1988 by Congressional Quarterly, Inc. Reprinted by permission. **208–9** "Short-Term Effects in the 1988 Elections." Reprinted by permission of ABC News. **222, 230** From *Congressional Elections* by Barbara Hinckley. Copyright © 1981 by Congressional Quarterly, Inc. Reprinted by permission. **234** From *Campaigning for Congress* by Edie N. Goldenberg and Michael W. Traugott. Copyright © 1984 by Congressional Quarterly, Inc. Reprinted by permission. **Chapter Seven: 247** From *Congressional Quarterly Weekly Report*, November 12, 1988. Copyright © 1988 by Congressional Quarterly, Inc. Reprinted by permission. **Chapter Eight: 309** From *The Gallup Poll: Public Opinion 1935–1971*. Copyright © 1972 by American Institute of Public Opinion. Reprinted by permission. **317** From *The Elusive Executive: Discovering Statistical Patterns in the Presidency* by Gary King and Lyn Ragsdale. Copyright © 1988 by Congressional Quarterly, Inc. Reprinted by permission. **320** From *The President's Agenda* by Paul Charles Light. Copyright © 1982, 1983 by The Johns Hopkins University Press. Reprinted by permission. **322** From *Congressional Quarterly*, January 7, 1989. Copyright © 1989 by Congressional Quarterly, Inc. Reprinted by permission. **326** From *Vital Statistics on American Politics* by Harold W. Stanley and Richard G. Niemi. Copyright © 1988 by Congressional Quarterly, Inc. Reprinted by permission. **334** From *The Elusive Executive: Discovering Statistical Patterns in the Presidency* by Gary King and Lyn Ragsdale. Copyright © 1988 by Congressional Quarterly, Inc. Reprinted by permission. **Chapter Nine: 343** From *The State of the Presidency*, 2nd ed., by Thomas E. Cronin. Copyright © 1980 by Thomas E. Cronin. Scott, Foresman and Company. **Chapter Thirteen: 526** "Politics: Elected Officials" from *The New York Times*, February 29, 1988. Copyright © 1988 by The New York Times Company. Reprinted by permission. **530** "... and those who do" from *The New York Times*, February 29, 1988. Copyright © 1988 by The New York Times Company. Reprinted by permission. **Chapter Fourteen: 562–63** From *Congressional Quarterly Weekly Report*, March 29, 1986. Copyright © 1986 by Congressional Quarterly, Inc. Reprinted by permission. **566–67** From *Kennedy* by Theodore Sorensen. Copyright © 1965 by Harper & Row. **568** From *War, Presidents and Public Opinion* by John E. Mueller. Copyright © 1973 by John Wiley & Sons, Inc. Reprinted by permission. **573** From *The Elusive Executive: Discovering Statistical Patterns in the Presidency* by Gary King and Lyn Ragsdale. Copyright © 1988 by Congressional Quarterly, Inc. Reprinted by permission. **579** From *Vital Statistics on American Politics* by Harold W. Stanley and Richard G. Niemi. Copyright © 1988 by Congressional Quarterly, Inc. Reprinted by permission.